Generative AI Insights for Financial Decision Making

Mohammad Irfan
School of Business and Commerce, Chandigarh University, Lucknow, India

Rui Dias
Instituto Politecnico de Ciencias Empresariais, Setubal, Portugal

Ruchika Rastogi
Pranveer Singh Institute of Technology, India

Gilney Figueira Zebende
State University of Feira de Santana, Brazil

IGI Global
Scientific Publishing
Publishing Tomorrow's Research Today

Vice President of Editorial	Melissa Wagner
Director of Acquisitions	Mikaela Felty
Director of Book Development	Jocelynn Hessler
Production Manager	Mike Brehm
Cover Design	Jose Rosado

Published in the United States of America by
IGI Global Scientific Publishing
701 East Chocolate Avenue
Hershey, PA, 17033, USA
Tel: 717-533-8845
Fax: 717-533-7115
Website: https://www.igi-global.com E-mail: cust@igi-global.com

Library of Congress Cataloging-in-Publication Data

Names: Irfan, Mohammad, 1986- editor | Dias, Rui, 1969- editor | Rastogi, Ruchika, 1981- editor | Zebende, Gilney, 1969- editor

Title: Generative AI insights for financial decision making / edited by: Mohammad Irfan, Rui Dias, Ruchika Rastogi, Gilney Zebende.

Other titles: Generative artificial intelligence for financial decision making

Description: Hershey, PA : IGI Global Scientific Publishing, [2026] | Includes bibliographical references and index. | Summary: "By addressing the implications of blockchain and generative AI, the book encourages critical engagement with ethical and sustainability issues in finance, preparing students for future challenges. Society at large stands to gain from the promotion of financial inclusion and sustainable practices highlighted in the book, as well as increased consumer education on the benefits and risks of these technologies. Ultimately, this work contributes to building trust in financial systems, empowering individuals, and aligning financial practices with global sustainability goals, creating a more equitable and informed society"-- Provided by publisher.

Identifiers: LCCN 2025001348 (print) | LCCN 2025001349 (ebook) | ISBN 9798337312507 hardcover | ISBN 9798337312514 paperback | ISBN 9798337312521 ebook

Subjects: LCSH: Artificial intelligence--Financial applications | Finance--Data processing

Classification: LCC HG4515.5 .G46 2025 (print) | LCC HG4515.5 (ebook) | DDC 332.0285/63--dc23/eng/20250425

LC record available at https://lccn.loc.gov/2025001348

LC ebook record available at https://lccn.loc.gov/2025001349

British Cataloguing in Publication Data
A Cataloguing in Publication record for this book is available from the British Library.

Table of Contents

Detailed Table of Contents

Generative AI is transforming financial decision-making by enhancing risk assessment, fraud detection, personalized financial planning, and algorithmic trading. By analyzing large datasets and recognizing evolving patterns, AI optimizes accuracy, efficiency, and personalization in financial operations. It reduces human errors and biases, improving credit scoring, loan underwriting, and investment strategies. Additionally, generative AI supports sustainable finance by promoting ESG-driven investments and financial inclusion. However, challenges such as data privacy, algorithmic bias, and transparency must be addressed. This chapter explores AI's transformative role in finance, highlighting real-world applications, ethical concerns, and future prospects for a more innovative and responsible financial ecosystem.

This chapter scrutinizes the transformative potential of blockchain technology within payment systems: it emphasises its capacity to rectify inefficiencies, enhance transparency and diminish costs inherent in traditional financial frameworks. It delves into pivotal innovations, including cryptocurrencies, stablecoins, smart contracts and Central Bank Digital Currencies it concurrently presents a comparative analysis with conventional systems such. The discourse extends to the economic and social ramifications, illuminating blockchain's role in promoting financial inclusion, while also grappling with its associated regulatory and ethical challenges. The integration of blockchain with generative AI is examined, showcasing its ability to optimize financial decision-making through real-time analytics. This chapter concludes with a forward-looking perspective on the potential role of blockchain in sculpting the future of global payment systems, addressing issues of scalability, interoperability and regulation to unlock its complete potential, although challenges remain.

This chapter explains the transformative potential of Generative AI in enhancing financial decision-making and blockchain technology in reshaping FinTech processes. It examines Generative AI's applications in predictive analytics, portfolio optimization, and fraud detection, emphasizing its ability to improve accuracy, efficiency, and risk mitigation. The foundational concepts of blockchain, including decentralization, transparency, and smart contracts, are analysed in the context of regulatory compliance and operational automation. The chapter also addresses critical data privacy and cybersecurity issues in AI-driven FinTech, offering strategies for safeguarding sensitive information. Future trends such as decentralized finance (DeFi), robo-advisors, and blockchain-based lending are discussed, highlighting opportunities for collaboration between AI and blockchain to create innovative ecosystems. Supported by case studies, this chapter provides actionable insights for leveraging these technologies to drive innovation and build a secure, efficient, and inclusive financial landscape.

This study examines the intersection of financial technology (fintech) and sustainable development, analyzing how fintech innovations support the UN Sustainable Development Goals (SDGs). Using a mixed-methods approach, it reviews 631 fintech-related research articles indexed in Scopus, applying content analysis and statistical modeling to test two hypotheses: (1) AI and blockchain improve financial sustainability, and (2) fintech fosters financial inclusion and reduces environmental impact. Results show that 97.9% of papers referencing AI or blockchain also discuss sustainability, versus 39.9% of papers without these technologies, confirmed by Pearson's χ^2 test ($\chi^2 = 43.0$, Pearson's $\chi 2$ test ($\chi 2 = 43.0$, $p < 0.001$). The study maps fintech innovations to SDGs, including blockchain for transparency (SDG 16), crowdfunding for inclusive growth (SDG 8, SDG 10), mobile banking for poverty reduction (SDG 1), green fintech for climate action (SDG 13), and insurtech for health (SDG 3). Findings highlight fintech's role as a driver of social, economic, and environmental progress.

This chapter explores the transformative potential of generative artificial intelligence (AI) in combating financial fraud, redefining traditional detection systems. It examines generative AI's capabilities in anomaly detection, behavioral modeling, and predictive analytics, addressing fraud complexities from technologies like cryptocurrencies, decentralized finance (DeFi), and AI-driven scams. The integration of generative AI with blockchain enhances transparency, scalability, and proactive prevention. Real-world case studies highlight its effectiveness against credit card fraud, deepfake impersonations, and synthetic identity fraud. Ethical and operational concerns, including AI bias, privacy, and security, are discussed alongside strategies for ethical governance and collaboration. Generative AI is positioned as a key tool for building resilient and trustworthy financial ecosystems to counter current and emerging fraud threats.

Cryptocurrency has set the new standards of cyber storage technology in terms of faster volume of transactions, better price, reputation and trust, which is based on Blockchain. Blockchain, which started with the Bitcoin whitepaper of Satoshi Nakamoto in 2008, that has potential applications beyond cryptocurrencies, including governance, healthcare, and supply chain management. Traditional banking systems typically use intermediaries, resulting in inefficiencies and expenses, whereas blockchain removes the middlemen. By being transparent and immutable, it encourages trust, reduces fraud, and improves compliance with regulations. Furthermore, the synergy between blockchain and emerging technologies like generative AI in a new era of innovation, marrying analytical strength with reliable data integrity. Thus, this chapter ultimately demonstrates the disruptive potential of the blockchain in financial decision-making while presenting an insight.

This research aims to explore the potential transformation of the integration of blockchain technology and generative artificial intelligence (Generative AI) in Islamic finance, which is in accordance with the principles of transparency, sustainability, and inclusion in Islamic finance. The methods used include conceptual analysis of blockchain applications, such as the tokenization of halal assets and smart contracts, as well as the role of generative AI in optimizing decision-making, fraud detection, and personalization of financial services. The results show that the integration of this technology improves efficiency, security, and sharia compliance in financial services, expands financial inclusion for low-income communities, and supports sustainable investment through the implementation of ESG standards. The implications of this study include a significant contribution to the development of a fairer, more transparent, and responsive Islamic financial system to global challenges such as climate change and economic inequality.

Large language models have gained popularity, and it is important to understand their applications in the financial inclusion domain. This study identifies the benefits and risks of using large language models (LLMs) in the financial inclusion domain. We show that LLMs can be used to (i) summarize the key themes in financial inclusion communications, (ii) gain insights from the tone of financial inclusion communications, (iii) bring discipline to financial inclusion communications, (iv) improve financial inclusion decision making, and (v) enhance context-sensitive text analysis and evaluation. However, the use of large language models in the financial inclusion domain poses risks relating to biased interpretations of LLM-generated responses, data privacy risk, misinformation and falsehood risks. We emphasize that LLMs can be used safely in the financial inclusion domain to summarise financial inclusion speeches and communication, but they should not be used in situations where finding the truth is important to make decisions that promote financial inclusion.

The consumer electronics and household appliances retail industry is characterized by an environment of high innovation and competitiveness. In this sector, Small and Medium-sized Enterprises (SME's) face an additional challenge due to the disparity in resources compared to large companies. Despite having fewer financial and human resources, these SMEs need to compete, developing effective marketing strategies and taking advantage of the opportunities that technology provides to shorten distances and obtain competitive advantages. This preliminary chapter evaluates the impact of artificial intelligence (AI) tools on the creation of internal and external knowledge in consumer electronics and household appliances retail SMEs. Furthermore, it explores the relationship between knowledge creation and data-based marketing decision-making, as well as the impact of these marketing decisions on the business performance of the companies studied.

This study explores how peer influence within social networks impacts investment decisions, using data from 75 active investors via a standardized questionnaire on demographics, peer influence, and investment outcomes. Using SPSS and multiple regression, results showed that peer influence significantly predicted 58.6% of the variance in investing behavior (R^2 = 0.586; R = 0.766; p < 0.05). Younger investors under 30, particularly active in online forums, were more susceptible to social pressure. Direct peer recommendations had a stronger effect than general exposure to financial discussions, highlighting the role of social validation. While peer impact is significant, factors like risk tolerance, financial literacy, and economic conditions also shape investment behavior. The study urges a balance between peer insights and objective analysis. These findings can inform financial education and policymaking to promote independent, informed decisions, especially as digital platforms reshape investment landscapes.

Preface

The financial sector is on the forefront of a ground-breaking revolution in technology. The emergence of Generative Artificial Intelligence (AI) and blockchain technologies is seeing a radical reengineering of financial systems, processes, and decision-making structures. Generative AI Insights for Financial Decision Making is a pertinent and holistic study of why these innovative technologies are entirely altering the parameters of contemporary finance.

Generative AI has already become a breakthrough, providing previously unknown possibilities of synthesizing data, recognizing patterns, simulating scenarios, or building predictive models. Generative models are helping to speed up financial decision-making, improve risk calculations, improve fraud detection, and offer customized financial services by deriving useful information from large and complicated datasets. Banking institutions across the world are using tools to develop more intelligent, quicker, and more flexible strategies that resonate with the shifting market conditions and increasing customer demand.

At the same time, blockchain technology is transforming payments systems through decentralized finance (DeFi), building transparency and trust through distributed ledgers that are immutable. This volume focuses on the fundamental elements contributing to blockchain technology, its potential to enhance financial inclusion, and its transformative impact on Islamic or ethical financial management and alternative financing products, including peer-to-peer lending and sustainable innovation.

The chapters in this book have surveyed a wide variety of topics, including automated sentiment analysis of financial data, behavioural finance, and digital transformation and the effects on the workforce. We also covered important topics related to regulatory compliance, responsibility and ethical issues, cybersecurity, and the use of AI-based solutions with traditional social and financial systems.

Whether you are an academic, researcher, policy maker, industry practitioner, or technology enthusiast, this book is intended to provide some insights into what finance will look like in a world defined by intelligent systems and digital trust. It is our hope that this book encourages critical thinking, responsible innovation, and interdisciplinary engagement to create a fairer, safer, and more secure financial system.

Lastly, I would like to thank my parents and my wife, and my children for their steadfast moral support, patience, and encouragement throughout the process of this work. Their trust in me has been a source of strength.

Mohammad Irfan
School of Business and Commerce, Chandigarh University, Lucknow, India

Rui Dias
Instituto Politecnico de Ciencias Empresariais, Setubal, Portugal

Ruchika Rastogi
Pranveer Singh Institute of Technology, India

Gilney Figueira Zebende
State University of Feira de Santana, Brazil

Chapter 1
Generative AI Enhancing Financial Decision-Making Processes

Jyoti Rani
https://orcid.org/0000-0002-5577-7808
Parul University, India

Ramratan Guru
https://orcid.org/0000-0001-6142-2643
Mody University of Science and Technology, India

Sakthivel Santhanam
https://orcid.org/0000-0003-2856-7714
Presidency University, India

Worku Tegegne Molla
https://orcid.org/0009-0006-2267-7241
De Montfort University, UK

ABSTRACT

Generative AI is transforming financial decision-making by enhancing risk assessment, fraud detection, personalized financial planning, and algorithmic trading. By analyzing large datasets and recognizing evolving patterns, AI optimizes accuracy, efficiency, and personalization in financial operations. It reduces human errors and biases, improving credit scoring, loan underwriting, and investment strategies. Additionally, generative AI supports sustainable finance by promoting ESG-driven investments and financial inclusion. However, challenges such as data privacy, algorithmic bias, and transparency must be addressed. This chapter explores AI's transformative role in finance, highlighting real-world applications, ethical concerns,

DOI: 10.4018/979-8-3373-1250-7.ch001

and future prospects for a more innovative and responsible financial ecosystem.

INTRODUCTION

Last couple of years have been witness to the tectonic shifts in the financial industry thanks to quantum leaps in AI. Broadly, one of these innovations — generative AI — has become a powerful and transformative tool for financial institutions to reimagine their decision-making. The machine learning model falls under generative AI, which involves creating new piece of content whether it is text or image or any data for that matter, based on what it has learned from a large corpus of known information. Next-generation AI not only analyzes data and identifies trends as most classic AI's do; it also generates new insights, predictions, and plans, empowering professionals making complex finance decisions like never before. Financial decision-making is, of course, a difficult task that involves weighing in dozens of factors, including market information, economic indicators, laws and regulations, risks, etc. This has been, traditionally, largely based on human judgment and traditional analytical tools. However, as financial data continues to balloon and become increasingly complex, traditional methods can often fall short of the change in the pace of the market today. Generative AI fills this gap by synthesizing large data sets to create relevant scenarios, predictions, and advice for more informed, positive decision-making in real-world practice. This brings us to the first of a number of advantages generative AI would have in Profits: the ability to simulate every conceivable market scenario and reaction. This facilitates quicker risk and opportunity forecasting, and hypothesis testing, portfolio optimization and what-if analysis from financial analysts conducting a simulation of a spectrum of scenarios based on true historical data and up-to-minute stock values. Furthermore, generative models could be used for automation of boring tasks such as report writing, compliance papers and customer letters, with HR able to focus on larger strategic analyses. Finally, generative AI also enhances personalization and customer experience in banking and financial services. It can personalize investment advice, product recommendations, and risk assessments to reflect individual client profiles, and in this way help build stronger client relationships and confidence in the firm itself. It's also a valuable resource for creating intuitive alerts and insights to identify and prevent fraud and other regulatory violations. But the application of generative AI in financial decision-making is beset by obstacles including data privacy, interpretability of used models, and ethical considerations. But as technology changes and regulatory landscapes evolve, generative AI will be a critical force multiplying effectiveness, accuracy and creativity in financial services. In this opening we will explore how generative AI is impacting investment decisions and relational processes through its creation of new opportunities for institutions and their clients.

The financial industry is transforming due to artificial intelligence (AI), making decision-making more efficient, processes optimized, and providing new insights through advanced data analytics. AI tools machine learning (ML) and explainable AI (XAI), are integrated into many financial services, unlocking major efficiency and accuracy improvements. Backup and supplementary storage innovation (both traditional pure-storage provider and new player) Hereafter, we elaborate on the significant roles that AI plays in the financial sector, corroborated through the insights we gained from the mentioned research papers.

AI in Financial Market Forecasting and Risk Management

AI & ML Techniques in Financial Market Forecasting Increases Revenue For CompaniesAI and ML techniques are increasingly being used in the field of financial market forecasting, helping companies analyze vast amounts of data more quickly and accurately. This ability assists in risk identification and making informed decisions in capital markets (Mohsen Amiri, 2024).

Machine learning models, both supervised (like artificial neural networks and extreme gradient boosting) and unsupervised, are used in areas such as credit management, stock price predictions and fraud detection. They improve risk assessment and support the financial decision-making processes (Černevičienė and Kabašinskas, 2024).

Data Analytics and Decision-Making

Big data and AI in finance has changed the way that data is processed and used for decision-making. A lack of innovative contracting is exemplified by the limited support from insurance companies, despite the previously outlined potential benefits to local development; AI allows for the sift of evidence-based empirical data outside of traditional modalities (Cao, Kong and Tsang, 2024).

By revealing pattern hidden in data and enabling new insights into their application, AI technologies present new opportunities for enhancing the decision-making process. This shift is essential for maximizing operations while also promoting financial inclusivity (Ata et al., 2024).

Explainable AI (XAI) in Finance

The necessity of transparency in AI-based financial models paved the way for the development of Explainable AI (XAI), which provides the capability to interpret the decision patterns of non-linear models. Explainability is crucial to improve risk assessment and trust in financial systems (Černevičienė and Kabašinskas, 2024).

For example, it can be employed in XAI methods, such as feature importance and Shapley additive explanations, to make the decisions transparent and interpretable via traceability, especially in areas 3 that are heavily regulated, like financial services (Weber, Carl and Hinz, 2024).

AI in Banking and Consumer Services

OverviewAI has come to occupy a key role in the banking industry, enhancing customer services and driving revenue growth. AI technology adoption in banking is positively influenced by variables such as awareness and perceived usefulnesss (Irfan, 2021).

Robo-advisors and automated investment management services are examples of AI technologies, facilitating personalized financial advice, improving customer experience and operational efficiency (Ata et al., 2024) (Irfan, 2021).

Challenges and Opportunities

How Artificial Intelligence Applies to Finance LINK AI in Fintech can help us make better decisions, manage risks better and provide better customer service and personalization. However, ethical concerns are raised, such as algorithmic transparency, bias, and discrimination. This deserves analytical diligence and particular mechanisms to make it possible for AI/analytics to integrate seamlessly within a financial ecosystem,(Ata et al., 2024).

Security, system risk, and privacy of AI and ML applications in the financial industry should also leveraged (Ata et al., 2024).

While AI offers a plethora of benefits for finance, as with technology in general, there can also be disastrous downsides when they aren't managed appropriately. Financial Services: Explainable AI and Transparency The development of explainable and transparent AI models is crucial to upholding trust and financial regulations in this industry. AI progress Finally, AI advances require more investment in domain specific adaptation and sector collaboration in order to achieve the greatest effect, while keeping the regulation in line with the innovative progress.

FUNDAMENTALS OF GENERATIVE AI

Generative AI is a field of artificial intelligence that aims to create new content rather than just extracting insights or analyzing what is in the data. Generative AI, which uses deep learning and neural networks to generate new outputs, such as images, text and music, by detecting patterns in data Traditional AI tends to be about classification and prediction, while generative AI is all about creativity and invention. In this guide, we'll get into the nuts and bolts of AI – and the specifically, what makes generative AI unique, and how it has expanded in recent years.

Overview of AI Concepts: Machine Learning, Deep Learning, and Neural Networks

Machine Learning (ML): The subfield of AI where algorithms are developed to learn from entire datasets and then predict or decide based on the collected information. It includes various techniques like supervised, unsupervised and reinforcement learning (Banh and Strobel, 2023).

Deep Learning (DL): Machine learning techniques where algorithms learn to recognize patterns in data and these patterns can then be used to make predictions and decisions without the strict need to be programmed. It tends to be particularly effective in image and speech understanding (Banh and Strobel, 2023).

Neural Networks: Neural networks are modelled after the human brain and consist of interconnected circuits, or nodes, known as neurons, which can process data just like our brains. They form the basis of deep learning and are frequently used in generative AI to estimate the true distribution of data and generate new data (Banh and Strobel, 2023).

Specific Characteristics of Generative AI

Content Creation: Generative AI produces original content such as images, text, and music based on an input data imparter till att de blir indirekt. This is distinct from the discriminative AI, which attempts to classify data and predict the outcome from the input data themselves (Banh and Strobel, 2023).

Generative Models: Important models are Generative Adversarial Networks (GANs), Variational Autocodecommders (VAEs) and autoregressive models. They are able to generate new observations from the data they are fed with and can even learn about the distribution of information from which the original data is derived and consequently generate new points that are similar to the original data (Goodfellow et al., 2020) (Bond-Taylor et al., 2022).

Applications: Generative Generative AI is utilised in a variety of tasks from different domains including data augmentation in computer vision, text and speech synthesis in natural language processing and medical image interpretation in healthcare (Sengar et al., 2024).

Evolution of Generative AI Technologies

Early Developments: The initial generative models were specific and limited by computational capacity and data. Generative models were highly improved thanks to deep learning (Banh and Strobel, 2023) (Irfan, Elhoseny, Kassim, & Metawa, 2023).

Advancements in Models: The final model was not trained on the data. It should be mentioned that those models for performance have been more elaborately revised to better their character for their performance and save their running time (Goodfellow et al., 2020) (Hu, Pang and Gao, 2023).

Current Trends: It has been observed recently that generative models are being used to enhance the performance of other AI approaches such as reinforcement learning. The work is also concerned with other ethical concerns related to the development of deepfakes and ensuring its responsible use (Balasubramanian and Sheykhmaleki, 2024) (Sengar et al., 2024).

Generative AI can be transformational across industries, but it is also a challenging place to be, with thorny questions about ethics, regulation, and AI's impact on society. Artificial intelligence (AI) generated fake content that is real-looking creates by machines are referred to realistic fake content (Irfan, Elhoseny, Kassim, & Metawa, 2023), akin to deepfakes, brings up a number of legal issues with respect to social media mis-information and privacy. Generative AI can have important value in new applications, but we need better frameworks for ethical applications and devices, and to protect against potential biases in AI generated content (Balasubramanian and Sheykhmaleki, 2024) (Mittal et al., 2024).

APPLICATIONS OF GENERATIVE AI IN FINANCIAL DECISION-MAKING

There are myriad applications of generative AI in finance many aspects of finance can point to significant use cases for this method, ranging from risk and fraud, to planning, trading and credit – and there are strong examples in all of these areas. These applications help us to develop a more efficient and accurate financial world by applying generative models to process big data, predict future events and optimize our decisions. The following section discusses in-depth these applications, based on the research papers obtained (Irfan, Elmogy, Majid, & El-Sappagh, 2023).

Risk Assessment

Deep learning and probabilistic neural networks support enhanced risk assessment within generative AI models. These models ingest large sets of complex data to determine potential financial risks as well as provide more accurate predictions (Katib et al., 2024).

This is where the AI risk assessment models, like IMDLRA-SES (Improved Metaheuristics with Deep Learning Enabled Risk Assessment model) have outperformed classical models in accuracy even at maximum of 95% accuracy level in the majority of testing cases (Katib et al., 2024).

Fraud Detection

Self-attention based types of generative adversarial networks (SAGAN) have been recently introduced to prevent credit card fraud detection by focusing on features of transaction datasets. By providing realistic data that imitates fraudulent behavior, these models improve both the precision and recall of fraud detection algorithms (Zhao et al., 2024).

Generative AI is being used in fraud detection to simulate complex fraudulent behaviors, helping to overcome problems associated with data imbalance and overfitting that plague traditional detection methods (Zhao et al., 2024).

Figure 1. Generative AI in finance and banking

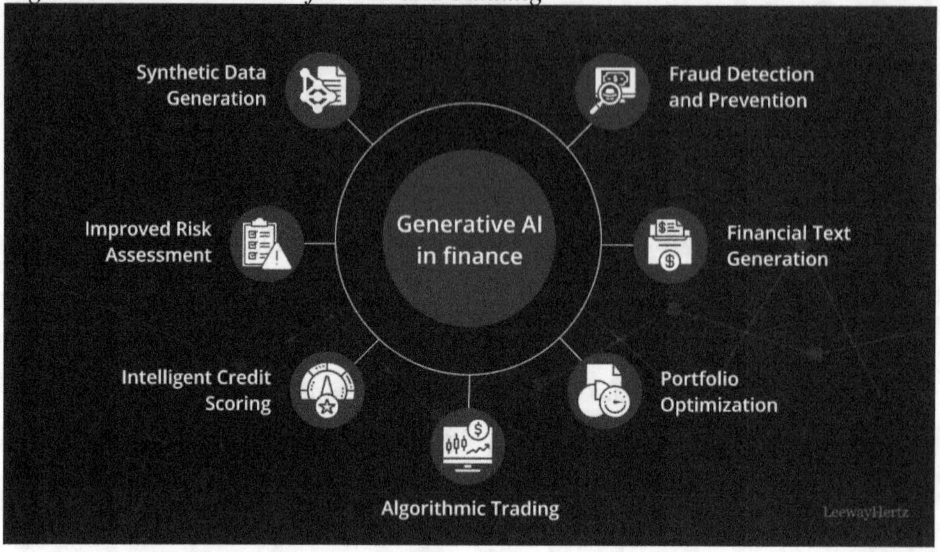

Personalized Financial Planning

Generative AI models, such as GANs and transformers, first become helpful to predict consumer behavior and second to personalize financial strategies to customers. Their ability to generate realistic data and extract insights from large unstructured datasets can improve personalized marketing and customer engagement (Madanchian, 2024).

Applications aimed at generating personalized financial advice with the help of AI include robo-advisors, which deploy AI algorithms to automatically manage investment portfolios (Ata et al., 2024).

Algorithmic Trading

AI algorithms (and mostly ML-based algorithms) are also employed to predict the stock market in algorithmic trading and invest resources in accordance with the developed strategy. They consist of classical market expectations that propagate strategic and organizational decision-makers who perform better than the classical market model (Alex Avelar and Jordão, 2024).

AI algorithms can modify parameters and technical indicators, producing models that are more optimally fit to the context, and thus potentially enhancing the decision power of both investors and market analysts (Alex Avelar and Jordão, 2024).

Credit Scoring and Loan Underwriting

Generative AI model improves the accuracy of credit scoring by processing diverse data sets and identifying the pattern specific for the solvency. This gave it also a truer process of credit rating and loan provision (Černevičienė and Kabašinskas, 2024).

Explaining credit decisions through AI and trust in financial ecosystems/ The urge of credit decisions transparency is leading the industry to adopt `explainable AI' (XAI) to interpret the decisions made by AI systems and trust the financial ecosystem (Černevičienė and Kabašinskas, 2024).

Generative AI boosts financial decision-making, but key issues such as explainability and fairness of AI models remain to be addressed. Ethics and bias: Those working with AI in finance will need to manage systems that are transparent, explainable and bias free, if they are going to maintain trust and comply with regulation. Besides, we do not have a clear understanding of the practical applicability of them, and more research is necessary to be able to fully utilise them in multiple types of financial scenarios (Sengar et al., 2024) (Černevičienė and Kabašinskas, 2024).

Figure 2. Generative AI in finance and accounting

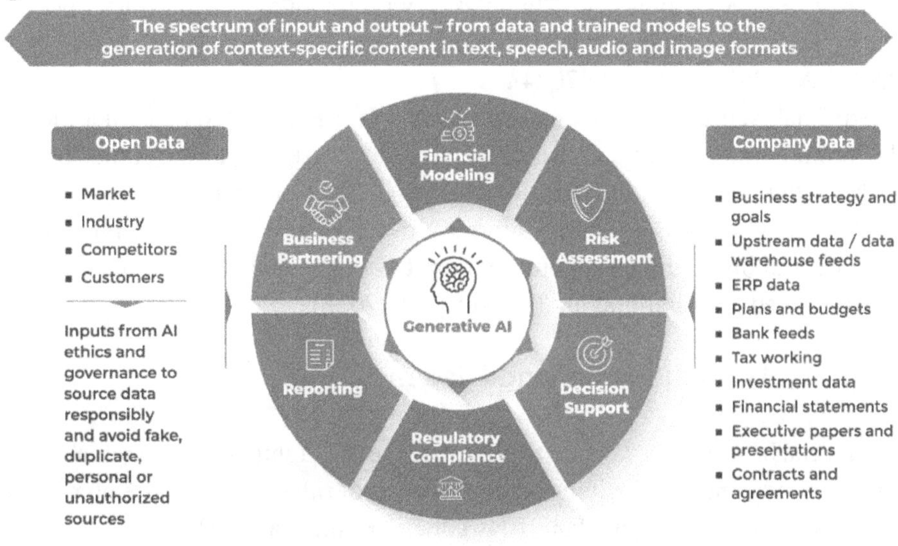

ENHANCING EFFICIENCY AND ACCURACY IN DECISION-MAKING

Generative AI is radically advancing financial decision-making and analysis, projecting, understanding, and evaluating potential risk and opportunity in a way that reduces human errors and bias and accelerates discoveries of complex financial concepts at exponential rates for time and cost. Leveraging AI models enables financial institutions to process vast amounts of data, uncover insights from latent patterns, and enhance decision making at speed. These applications benefit greatly from the inclusion of AI technologies like machine learning, neural networks and generative models, which improve the throughput of these applications significantly over traditional methods. A Summary of The Role of Generative AI The subsequent sections discusses the role of generative AI in these advancements of financial Decision Making (Irfan, Elmogy, Majid, & El-Sappagh, 2023).

Enhancing Speed and Accuracy in Financial Decisions

Generative AI models (such as large language models (LLM)) are able to ingest and analyze huge amounts of data quickly, with the output being immediate and actionable insides resulting in faster and more accurate decision-making (Ata et al., 2024) (Decardi-Nelson et al., 2024).

Artificial Neural Networks (ANNs) In ANNs it is aimed to construct models, which could simulate the nonlinear connection between the input and output, helping to have better prediction and decision making in the financial markets.

PARs may support evidence-informed decision-making by making rational decisions and highlighting key information to decision-makers that may assist in more informed decision-making (Becker et al., 2022).

Reducing Human Errors and Biases

Data can be used as a weapon to eliminate the ills of human biases replacing the subjective judgement and relying on objective set of rules about how to interpret the data for same purpose (BaniHani, Alawadi and Elmrayyan, 2024).

This is consistent with prior research which found that generative AI models have the potential to automate complex decision making, which would help to minimize human error and ensure stability of financial operations (Decardi-Nelson et al., 2024).

In addition, AI can help resolve algorithmic fairness and bias issues, ensuring fairness and transparency in financial decisions (Ata et al., 2024).

Streamlining Complex Financial Analyses and Operations

Machine learning and generative models facilitates the automation of complex financial analysis such as risk assessment and market prediction, which makes it an efficient operation (reforming centralized electricity market with deep learning and generative model techniques) (Amiri, 2024).

Reinforcement learning and generative adversarial networks (GANs) can handle incomplete or unbalanced financial data and improve that system is more robust (Le et al., 2021).

This AI-based accounting and financial data reporting automation institute can save time and resources, hence its more sustainable development-based and in terms of service effectiveness (Peng et al., 2023).

There are clear benefits, as well as potential challenges, of using generative AI as a tool for making financial decisions. Various issues of data privacy and security, and requirement for regulatory frameworks also need to be resolved for the responsible use of AI in finance. In addition, the inclusion of AI in existing systems also requires careful consideration and planning with regards to the ethical implications, for example when AI is used it also has the potential to propagate existing biases if it is not managed appropriately. The increase usage of AI in finance can take full advantage of the potential value through the technology and research advancement.

Figure 3. A roadmap of enhancing operational efficiency

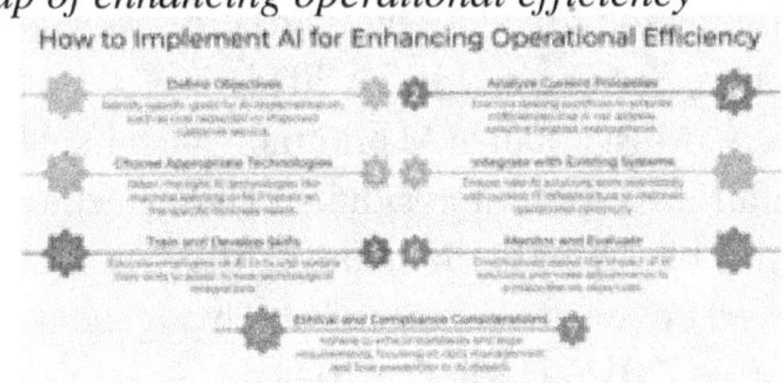

ETHICAL CONSIDERATIONS AND CHALLENGES

Majoring on the ethical aspect in AI, especially as it pertains to the finance world, means working through many intertwined problems related to data privacy, security, transparency and fairness. Ethical implications arise from such integration since the processes guided by artificial intelligence may lead to biases in the systems and transparency issues in how these systems operate (Irfan, Kadry, Sharif,

& Ullah Khan, 2023). Such challenges demand a holistic framework to guide AI deployment in sensitive financial settings industry-wide.

Data Privacy, Security, and AI Transparency

Data Privacy and Security: The sensitive nature of financial data requires robust privacy-preserving mechanisms. Explanation:Using cryptographic techniques and blockchain, privacy-preserving data classification frameworks may balance for data utility and privacy while achieving transparency and accountability in data handling (Zhang et al., 2021).

AI Transparency: Transparency in AI systems is essential for building trust. SHapley Additive exPlanations or SHAP and Microsoft Responsible AI Widgets are tools that can be used to explain how an AI process arrives at its output, which helps build confidence in the AI mechanism used in the financial space (Rizinski et al., 2022).

Algorithmic Bias and Fairness

Risk of Algorithmic Bias: AI models run the risk of being biased because those biases can be inadvertently coded into the algorithms. Such blindness is alarming, especially in financial situations in which their decisions can change people's lives. pre-training, training, and post-training methods are important bias mitigation strategies that can help ensure fairness in AI models (González-Sendino, Serrano and Bajo, 2024).

Ensuring Fairness: Most popular AI programs such like: Fairness-aware data mining and unfairness-aware algorithms. These methods include identifying and mitigating biases throughout the AI lifecycle so that adverse decisions are not made based on sensitive attributes such as gender or ethnicity (Hajian, Bonchi and Castillo, 2016) (Ukanwa, 2024).

Ethical Implications in Sensitive Financial Contexts

Ethical Governance: Establishing clear frameworks for ethical governance is critical to mitigate the risks of AI in financial contexts. This involves creating methodologies to include ethical operationalization since the design of AI projects (d'Aquin et al., 2018).

Human-Machine Collaboration: This technology is best used alongside human preferences and decisions—so combine human judgment with AI decision-making to reduce errors and increase fairness. Machine Collaborative Decision Making - This is a collaborative and integrative process which requires both human and automated system capabilities to make better decisions that a human alone cannot do; for instance, assessing those customers who should be approved for a credit card (Rizinski et al., 2022).

However, with the advantages also comes ethical concerns that need to be explored. Algorithmic bias with privacy issues requires a multidisciplinary approach to ensure accountability, transparency, and fairness in AI systems. To overcome these challenges, collaboration with experts across disciplines such as ethics, finance, technology is essential (Irfan, Kadry, Sharif, & Ullah Khan, 2023).

Figure 4. Challenges in using AI

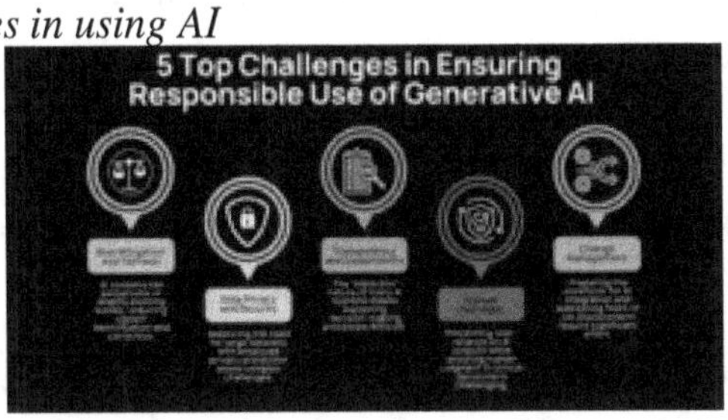

GENERATIVE AI AND SUSTAINABILITY IN FINANCE

Environmental sustainability in finance is increasingly supported by the generation of AI based on environmentally sustainable investment, green finance and responsible investment (ESG) criteria. Insights from the AI are key to recognizing and advancing green investments, increasing financial inclusion, and democratizing access to financial services. Artificial intelligence has the potential to take over a range of finance operations that are typically labor-intensive, and at the same time it is changing the way investment strategies are formed to meet goals related to sustainability. The subsequent sections delve into these aspects in depth (Irfan, Hussainey, Chan Bukhari, & Nam, 2024).

Supporting Environmentally Sustainable Investments

AI-Driven Insights: Deep learning and generative models of AI are being implemented to predict and enhance green finance growth. Time-series Conditional Generative Adversarial Networks (CT-GANs), for example, have been used to enhance the precision of growth predictions of green finance across different regions, encouraging investors to invest their money in green-based sectors (Abdelhady et al., 2024).

Green AI Initiatives: There is also a focus to develop "green AI," which aims to reduce the environmental footprint of AI technologies themselves. These initiatives also are part of enhancing environmentally friendly use of AI in finance (Alzoubi and Mishra, 2024).

AI and Green Finance

ESG Integration: AI is at the forefront when it comes to incorporating ESG into valuations. AI models can provide stock market trend forecasts and improve investment strategies, not only by predicting stock market trend from ESG sentiment and technical indicators but also by making sustainable the financial industry (Lee et al., 2024).

Credit Rating Models: ESG-based credit scoring models powered by AI enable financial institutions to identify socially responsible customers to facilitate impactful projects. Newer practices in the field employ fuzzy BWM, and TOPSIS models to assess the firms in terms of ESG performance (Roy, 2023).

Promoting Financial Inclusion

Digital Finance and ESG: AI-powered digital finance drive better ESG and financial outcomes. It can contribute to the digital transformation of enterprises through the support to new "green" innovation behaviours to feed their sustainability practices that for big and small businesses are critical (Xiang et al., 2024).

Broadening Financial Access: AI and FinTech are working to increase financial access, from the push for green financing initiatives to matching portfolios with eco-friendly goals. This expansion of access is essential for democratizing financial services and enabling more sustainable investment approaches (Si Mohammed et al., 2024).

AI has a lot of potentials in advancing sustainability in finance but the environmental cost of AI technology should not be overlooked. AI models consume a lot of energy when training and operating, which challenges sustainability goals. Thus, to reduce these impacts it is still essential to develop green AI initiatives so that AI's involvement in finance stays true to the environmental's goals (Alzoubi and Mishra, 2024).

FUTURE PROSPECTS OF GENERATIVE AI IN FINANCIAL DECISION-MAKING

The future of generative AI in financial decision-making shows promising milestones for it across industries and people's lives with respect to finance bench and collaborative platforms. With the increasing emergence of generative AI, especially LLMs and GANs, financial services can significantly optimize operations, enhance risk management, ensure financial inclusion, and many other processes on its way to transformation (Irfan, Hussainey, Chan Bukhari, & Nam, 2024). Nonetheless, implementing generative AI in finance will necessitate tackling ethical issues, promoting transparency, and utilizing complementary technologies such as blockchain to develop secure and decentralized systems. The next sections cover these in detail.

Predictions for the Evolution of Generative AI in Finance

Enhanced Decision-Making: Generative AI can drive strategic decision making by delivering predictions and insights that, when aggregated through a number of models and prompts, have been shown to be closely aligned with that of human expert evaluations (Doshi et al., 2024).

Advanced Forecasting: GANs' application to financial time series forecasting provides probabilistic predictions and estimates of uncertainty and, compared to traditional models like LSTMs and ARIMA, outperform in terms of Sharpe Ratios (Vuletić, Prenzel and Cucuringu, 2024).

Personalized Financial Services: AI-based solutions, like robo-advisors, can provide tailored financial advice and automated investment management, and in doing so improve user experience and accessibility (Ata et al., 2024).

Integration with Emerging Technologies

Blockchain for Security and Decentralization: Solutions for AI toxicity, biases, and misuse can be countered through advanced tech with blockchain. Blockchain promotes transparency, verifiability, and decentralization. Integrating it can improve AI's reliability and accountability in the financial systems (Brewer et al., 2024).

Collaborative Ecosystems: The combination of AI and blockchain requires cooperation between businesses, developers, and governmental regulation so that society can reap the benefits of AI while avoiding its negative impacts (Brewer et al., 2024).

Challenges and Opportunities in Scaling Generative AI

Ethical and Regulatory Concerns: The use of generative AI in finance raises ethical concerns, such as bias, privacy issues, and job displacement. These necessitate strong ethical guidelines and regulatory action (Khan and Umer, 2024).

Technical and Managerial Approaches: Overcoming challenges that AI in finance present requires technical solutions, regulatory measures, and managerial strategies to ensure responsible use and integration into existing financial ecosystems (BaniHani, Alawadi and Elmrayyan, 2024).

Scalability and Resource Optimization: Although Generative AI can automate processes and lower resource costs, it is necessary for it to augment human critical thinking and decision-making in practice for its use (Akhavan and Jalali, 2024).

So while the promise of generative AI in finance is considerable, the consequences of its adoption must be kept in mind. Owing to ethical challenges like the menace of deepfakes and misuse of AI, its safe deployment needs responsible AI principles and effective detection mechanisms for sustainable growth and periodic benefits to society (Balasubramanian and Sheykhmaleki, 2024). Moreover, the incorporation of AI into decision-making processes would necessitate continuous adjustment to remain compliant with the evolving regulatory environment (BaniHani, Alawadi and Elmrayyan, 2024). Generative AI is a rapidly evolving technology, and its applications in the finance industry are bound to grow and diversify, making it essential for ongoing research and innovation to effectively leverage its capabilities while maintaining ethical standards (Irfan, Elmogy, Gupta, Khalifa, & Dias, 2024).

CASE STUDIES

Over the past two to three years, financial organizations have embraced generative AI in areas such as deepening the quality of decision-making and improving profitability. These use cases include everything from underwriting and risk management, to robo-advisory services and portfolio optimization. Early adopters have reaped significant operational efficiency gains from AI in finance, while grappling with the challenges it poses. In the subsequent sections, we dive into case study examples, successful use cases, and key takeaways from these pioneers.

Real-World Examples of Generative AI Applications

Underwriting and Risk Management: Financial institutions have used AI to enhance the underwriting process. For example, a lending company applied the Evidential Reasoning-eXplainer method to improve the quality of decision-making by reviewing past inconsistent decisions and connected these to preferred outcomes. By working in this way, the right data is captured, and the quality of decisions is audited, hence reducing decision noise in the financial underwriting (Sachan et al., 2024).
Robo-Advisors: Robo-advisors are one of the many ways AI is being used in finance, and they offer affordable, personalized financial advice. These platforms leverage algos to select portfolios, minimize behavioral biases, and enhance transaction efficiencies. They provide a combination of fully automated and hybrid business models to meet various customer requirements (Barile, Secundo and Bussoli, 2024) (Sabharwal and Anjum, 2018).
Portfolio Optimization: Generative AI tools have been employed, as demonstrated by the improved egret swarm optimization algorithm, for portfolio selection. These tools assist in building effective investment portfolios by optimizing asset allocations and attaining higher Sharpe Ratios under stringent restrictions (Huang et al., 2024) (Irfan, Elmogy, Gupta, Khalifa, & Dias, 2024).

Successful Implementations and Their Impact

Decision-Making Efficiency: Transforming Decision-Making Efficiency The technology is even shaping the future of regulation, and this process is heavily driven by AI-based statistical models to predict corporate defaults, which has already lowered the required amounts of capital for banks (Fraisse and Laporte, 2022).
Profitability and Risk Management: Proven to improve profit margins and mitigation of risk levels for banks. Moreover, intelligent technologies have proven to empower banks' risk management prowess and profitability through multiple linear regression analysis (Yang and Chen, 2024).
Customer Engagement and Retention: Robo-Advisory Robo-advisors use AI to create portfolios for customers, engaging them through notifications and updates. This resulted in rapid increase in sales of company products and customer trust(Sabharwal, & Anjum, 2020) (Barile, Secundo and Bussoli, 2024).

Lessons Learned from Early Adopters

Human-AI Collaboration: Trailblazing companies are recognizing that success requires a synergy between human expertise and AI. Because AI-based models can become embroiled in flawed strategies due to overconfidence in AI without any human over sight, where human judgment is still a fundamental process (Sachan et al., 2024).

Regulatory Compliance: Ensuring regulatory compliance is crucial when integrating AI in finance. For example, the use of neural networks to handle credit risk has shown the need for AI models to be tailored to pass through compliance tests and cater to regulators (Fraisse and Laporte, 2022).

Balancing Automation and Human Interaction: Financial institutions recognized the need to find equilibrium between automation and human interaction. This demonstrates that less than fully automated models are needed to satisfy all customer gaps, therefore highlighting the need for hybrid models where human elements are included (Barile, Secundo and Bussoli, 2024).

Although generative AI holds potential to revolutionize financial services, it also involves challenges like data privacy issues and the requirement for strong regulatory mechanisms. While AI has generated a lot of excitement in this area, it is important to remember that these applications need to be integrated into existing financial systems, which entails risks that need to be managed carefully. As AI technologies evolve and grow, financial institutions will need to continue addressing these challenges in order to successfully leverage AI for finance.

CONCLUSION

More importantly perhaps, generative AI is redefining how financial decisions are made, with innovation across customer respect, fraud detection, risk management, personalized financial planning, and beyond. Each time it processes a data set, discovers recurring patterns, concentrates on the information that matters most to follow, it operates, streamlining financial ops and achieving higher precision. As well as supporting a more responsive financial world through STEER and dynamic insights, generative AI is also promoting sustainable finance by creating personalised bespoke offerings in line with ESG standards that represent global issues such as inclusion and the environment. But along with its generation enhancing potential are challenges such as data privacy, algorithmic biases, and ethical considerations. This involves establishing fair, safe, transparent AI models that are compliant with convictions and social values. The convergence with complementary technologies, including blockchain — in particular —, will enhance the benefits described above and scale up the future of generative AI in finance, enabling the supply of decentralized, safe and fast financial services to global citizens. Yet at the same time, this collaboration is also likely to produce new goods and services that meet a variety of consumer needs, in an ethical way. Lastly, the age of generative AI is changing everything in fintech entirely, offering infinite possibilities for growth, innovation, and gainful trade. If harnessed responsibly, the full potential of technology can be realized and contribute to a future where it is easier for people to make the financial decisions they need and which are fair, and aligned to global sustainability targets.

REFERENCES

Abdelhady, A. S. (2024) 'Green finance growth prediction model based on time-series conditional generative adversarial networks', *PLOS ONE*. Edited by M.I. Solihin, 19(7), p. e0306874. Available at: DOI: 10.1371/journal.pone.0306874

Akhavan, A., & Jalali, M. S. (2024). Generative AI and simulation modeling: How should you (not) use large language models like ChatGPT. *System Dynamics Review*, *40*(3), e1773. DOI: 10.1002/sdr.1773

Alex Avelar, E., & Jordão, R. V. D. (2024). The role of artificial intelligence in the decision-making process: A study on the financial analysis and movement forecasting of the world's largest stock exchanges [Preprint]. *Management Decision*. Advance online publication. DOI: 10.1108/MD-09-2023-1625

Alzoubi, Y. I., & Mishra, A. (2024). Green artificial intelligence initiatives: Potentials and challenges. *Journal of Cleaner Production*, *468*, 143090. DOI: 10.1016/j.jclepro.2024.143090

Amiri, M. (2024). Application of artificial intelligence in business management and financial market forecasting. *Power System Technology*, *48*(3), 781–808. DOI: 10.52783/pst.875

Ata, B., Cong, L. W., Giesecke, K., Sun, P., & Teo, C. P. (2024). Call for Papers—*Management Science* Virtual Special Issue on AI for Finance and Business Decisions. *Management Science*, *70*(10), xi–xii. DOI: 10.1287/mnsc.2024.Call.V70.n10

Balasubramanian, M., & Sheykhmaleki, P. (2024). Comprehending the Consumer Behavior toward Sustainable Apparel. *Sustainability (Basel)*, *16*(18), 8026. DOI: 10.3390/su16188026

Banh, L., & Strobel, G. (2023). Generative artificial intelligence. *Electronic Markets*, *33*(1), 63. DOI: 10.1007/s12525-023-00680-1

BaniHani, I., Alawadi, S., & Elmrayyan, N.BaniHani. (2024). AI and the decision-making process: A literature review in healthcare, financial, and technology sectors. *Journal of Decision Systems*, *33*(sup1), 1–11. DOI: 10.1080/12460125.2024.2349425

Barile, D., Secundo, G., & Bussoli, C. (2024). Exploring artificial intelligence robo-advisor in banking industry: A platform model [Preprint]. *Management Decision*. Advance online publication. DOI: 10.1108/MD-08-2023-1324

Becker, F., Skirzyński, J., van Opheusden, B., & Lieder, F. (2022). Boosting Human Decision-making with AI-Generated Decision Aids. *Computational Brain & Behavior, 5*(4), 467–490. DOI: 10.1007/s42113-022-00149-y

Bond-Taylor, S., Leach, A., Long, Y., & Willcocks, C. G. (2022). Deep Generative Modelling: A Comparative Review of VAEs, GANs, Normalizing Flows, Energy-Based and Autoregressive Models. *IEEE Transactions on Pattern Analysis and Machine Intelligence, 44*(11), 7327–7347. DOI: 10.1109/TPAMI.2021.3116668 PMID: 34591756

Brewer, J., Patel, D., Kim, D., & Murray, A. (2024). Navigating the challenges of generative technologies: Proposing the integration of artificial intelligence and blockchain. *Business Horizons, 67*(5), 525–535. DOI: 10.1016/j.bushor.2024.04.011

Cao, H., Kong, X., & Tsang, A. (2024). Corporate Social Responsibility and Economic Stability: International Evidence. *Accounting Horizons*, •••, 1–23. DOI: 10.2308/HORIZONS-2022-196

Černevičienė, J., & Kabašinskas, A. (2024). Explainable artificial intelligence (XAI) in finance: A systematic literature review. *Artificial Intelligence Review, 57*(8), 216. DOI: 10.1007/s10462-024-10854-8

d'Aquin, M. (2018) 'Towards an "Ethics by Design" Methodology for AI Research Projects', in *Proceedings of the 2018 AAAI/ACM Conference on AI, Ethics, and Society. AIES '18: AAAI/ACM Conference on AI, Ethics, and Society*, New Orleans LA USA: ACM, pp. 54–59. Available at: DOI: 10.1145/3278721.3278765

Decardi-Nelson, B., Alshehri, A. S., Ajagekar, A., & You, F. (2024). Generative AI and process systems engineering: The next frontier. *Computers & Chemical Engineering, 187*, 108723. DOI: 10.1016/j.compchemeng.2024.108723

Doshi, A. R. (2024) 'Generative artificial intelligence and evaluating strategic decisions', *Strategic Management Journal*, p. smj.3677. Available at: DOI: 10.2139/ssrn.4714776

Fraisse, H., & Laporte, M. (2022). Return on investment on artificial intelligence: The case of bank capital requirement. *Journal of Banking & Finance, 138*, 106401. DOI: 10.1016/j.jbankfin.2022.106401

González-Sendino, R., Serrano, E., & Bajo, J. (2024). Mitigating bias in artificial intelligence: Fair data generation via causal models for transparent and explainable decision-making. *Future Generation Computer Systems, 155*, 384–401. DOI: 10.1016/j.future.2024.02.023

Goodfellow, I., Pouget-Abadie, J., Mirza, M., Xu, B., Warde-Farley, D., Ozair, S., Courville, A., & Bengio, Y. (2020). Generative adversarial networks. *Communications of the ACM, 63*(11), 139–144. DOI: 10.1145/3422622

Hajian, S., Bonchi, F., & Castillo, C. (2016) 'Algorithmic Bias: From Discrimination Discovery to Fairness-aware Data Mining', in *Proceedings of the 22nd ACM SIGKDD International Conference on Knowledge Discovery and Data Mining. KDD '16: The 22nd ACM SIGKDD International Conference on Knowledge Discovery and Data Mining*, San Francisco California USA: ACM, pp. 2125–2126. Available at: DOI: 10.1145/2939672.2945386

Hu, M., Pang, Y., & Gao, L. (2023). Advances in Silicon-Based Integrated Lidar. *Sensors (Basel), 23*(13), 5920. DOI: 10.3390/s23135920 PMID: 37447770

Huang, Z., Zhang, Z., Hua, C., Liao, B., & Li, S. (2024). Leveraging enhanced egret swarm optimization algorithm and artificial intelligence-driven prompt strategies for portfolio selection. *Scientific Reports, 14*(1), 26681. DOI: 10.1038/s41598-024-77925-2 PMID: 39496781

Irfan, M. (2021, January). Do Shariah Indices converge? Evidence from Gulf Cooperation Council countries. *International Journal of Business Excellence, 23*(2), 251–269. DOI: 10.1504/IJBEX.2021.113448

Irfan, M., Elhoseny, M., Kassim, S., & Metawa, N. (2023). *Advanced Machine Learning Algorithms for Complex Financial Applications*. IGI Global., DOI: 10.4018/978-1-6684-4483-2

Irfan, M., Elmogy, M., Gupta, S., Khalifa, F., & Dias, R. (2024). *AI-Driven Decentralized Finance and the Future of Finance*. IGI Global., DOI: 10.4018/979-8-3693-6321-8

Irfan, M., Elmogy, M., Majid, M. S., & El-Sappagh, S. (2023). *The Impact of AI Innovation on Financial Sectors in the Era of Industry 5.0*. IGI Global., DOI: 10.4018/979-8-3693-0082-4

Irfan, M., Hussainey, K., Chan Bukhari, S. A., & Nam, Y. (Eds.). (2024). *Issues of Sustainability in AI and New-Age Thematic Investing*. IGI Global Publisher., DOI: 10.4018/979-8-3693-3282-5

Irfan, M., Kadry, S., Sharif, M., & Ullah Khan, H. (2023). *Fintech Applications in Islamic Finance: AI, Machine Learning, and Blockchain Techniques*. IGI Global., DOI: 10.4018/979-8-3693-1038-0

Katib, I., Albassam, E., Sharaf, S. A., & Ragab, M. (2024). Harnessing probabilistic neural network with triple tree seed algorithm-based smart enterprise quantitative risk management framework. *Scientific Reports*, *14*(1), 22293. DOI: 10.1038/s41598-024-73876-w PMID: 39333638

Khan, M. S., & Umer, H. (2024). ChatGPT in finance: Applications, challenges, and solutions. *Heliyon*, *10*(2), e24890. DOI: 10.1016/j.heliyon.2024.e24890 PMID: 38304767

Lee, S. (2024). *Strategic corporate social responsibility in the tourism and hospitality industry: Conceptual proposal.* Tourism Economics., DOI: 10.1177/13548166241299140

Madanchian, M. (2024). Generative AI for Consumer Behavior Prediction: Techniques and Applications. *Sustainability (Basel)*, *16*(22), 9963. DOI: 10.3390/su16229963

Mittal, U., Sai, S., Chamola, V., & Sangwan, D. (2024). A Comprehensive Review on Generative AI for Education. *IEEE Access : Practical Innovations, Open Solutions*, *12*, 142733–142759. DOI: 10.1109/ACCESS.2024.3468368

Peng, Y., Ahmad, S. F., Ahmad, A. Y. A. B., Al Shaikh, M. S., Daoud, M. K., & Alhamdi, F. M. H. (2023). Riding the Waves of Artificial Intelligence in Advancing Accounting and Its Implications for Sustainable Development Goals. *Sustainability (Basel)*, *15*(19), 14165. DOI: 10.3390/su151914165

Rizinski, M., Peshov, H., Mishev, K., Chitkushev, L. T., Vodenska, I., & Trajanov, D. (2022). Ethically Responsible Machine Learning in Fintech. *IEEE Access : Practical Innovations, Open Solutions*, *10*, 97531–97554. DOI: 10.1109/ACCESS.2022.3202889

Roy, P. K. (2023). Enriching the green economy through sustainable investments: An ESG-based credit rating model for green financing. *Journal of Cleaner Production*, *420*, 138315. DOI: 10.1016/j.jclepro.2023.138315

Sabharwal, C. L., & Anjum, B. (2018) 'Robo-Revolution in the Financial Sector', in *2018 International Conference on Computational Science and Computational Intelligence (CSCI). 2018 International Conference on Computational Science and Computational Intelligence (CSCI)*, Las Vegas, NV, USA: IEEE, pp. 1289–1292. Available at: DOI: 10.1109/CSCI46756.2018.00249

Sachan, S., Almaghrabi, F., Yang, J.-B., & Xu, D.-L. (2024). Human-AI collaboration to mitigate decision noise in financial underwriting: A study on FinTech innovation in a lending firm. *International Review of Financial Analysis*, *93*, 103149. DOI: 10.1016/j.irfa.2024.103149

Sengar, S. S., Hasan, A. B., Kumar, S., & Carroll, F. (2024). Generative artificial intelligence: A systematic review and applications [Preprint]. *Multimedia Tools and Applications*. Advance online publication. DOI: 10.1007/s11042-024-20016-1

Si Mohammed, K., Serret, V., Ben Jabeur, S., & Nobanee, H. (2024). The role of artificial intelligence and fintech in promoting eco-friendly investments and non-greenwashing practices in the US market. *Journal of Environmental Management, 359*, 120977. DOI: 10.1016/j.jenvman.2024.120977 PMID: 38678903

Ukanwa, K. (2024). Algorithmic bias: Social science research integration through the 3-D Dependable AI Framework. *Current Opinion in Psychology, 58*, 101836. DOI: 10.1016/j.copsyc.2024.101836 PMID: 38981371

Vuletić, M., Prenzel, F., & Cucuringu, M. (2024). Fin-GAN: Forecasting and classifying financial time series via generative adversarial networks. *Quantitative Finance, 24*(2), 175–199. DOI: 10.1080/14697688.2023.2299466

Weber, P., Carl, K. V., & Hinz, O. (2024). Applications of Explainable Artificial Intelligence in Finance—A systematic review of Finance, Information Systems, and Computer Science literature. *Management Review Quarterly, 74*(2), 867–907. DOI: 10.1007/s11301-023-00320-0

Xiang, S., Deng, L., Zhou, Z., & Zhang, Z. (2024). Digital Finance, ESG Performance, and Financial Performance in Chinese Firm Levels: The Pathway to Sustainability. *Sustainability (Basel), 16*(18), 7976. DOI: 10.3390/su16187976

Yang, F., & Chen, J. (2024). Research on the Application of Intelligent Technology in Promoting Digital Finance and High-Quality Economic Development. *Applied Mathematics and Nonlinear Sciences, 9*(1), 20243271. DOI: 10.2478/amns-2024-3271

Zhang, Y., Sun, Z., Qin, R., & Xiong, H. (2021). Idle Duration Prediction for Manufacturing System Using a Gaussian Mixture Model Integrated Neural Network for Energy Efficiency Improvement. *IEEE Transactions on Automation Science and Engineering, 18*(1), 47–55. DOI: 10.1109/TASE.2019.2938662

Zhao, L., Hussam, E., Seong, J.-T., Elshenawy, A., Kamal, M., & Alshawarbeh, E. (2024). Revolutionizing art education: Integrating AI and multimedia for enhanced appreciation teaching. *Alexandria Engineering Journal, 93*, 33–43. DOI: 10.1016/j.aej.2024.03.011

Chapter 2
Blockchain and the Evolution of Payment Systems:
Shaping the Future

Rui Vigário Rodrigues
https://orcid.org/0009-0003-9801-694X
Polytechnic Institute of Setubal, Portugal

Mohammad Irfan
https://orcid.org/0000-0002-4956-1170
Chandigarh University, Lucknow, Unnao, India

ABSTRACT

This chapter scrutinizes the transformative potential of blockchain technology within payment systems: it emphasises its capacity to rectify inefficiencies, enhance transparency and diminish costs inherent in traditional financial frameworks. It delves into pivotal innovations, including cryptocurrencies, stablecoins, smart contracts and Central Bank Digital Currencies it concurrently presents a comparative analysis with conventional systems such. The discourse extends to the economic and social ramifications, illuminating blockchain's role in promoting financial inclusion, while also grappling with its associated regulatory and ethical challenges. The integration of blockchain with generative AI is examined, showcasing its ability to optimize financial decision-making through real-time analytics. This chapter concludes with a forward-looking perspective on the potential role of blockchain in sculpting the future of global payment systems, addressing issues of scalability, interoperability and regulation to unlock its complete potential, although challenges remain.

DOI: 10.4018/979-8-3373-1250-7.ch002

INTRODUCTION

The use of conventional payment methods has been proven to be an effective means of facilitating value transmission, both domestically and internationally. The pre-eminence of conventional payment systems, as administered by financial institutions, is characterised by a considerable reliance on centralised infrastructure for the validation, verification and settlement of transactions (Kemal Akkaya et al., 2021). Radiational payment systems are primarily regulated by banking institutions and function through centralised infrastructures that facilitate the authentication, verification, and settlement of transactions. The aforementioned systems, including paper cheques, credit and debit cards, Automated Clearing House (ACH) networks, bank transfers and digital cash, are indicative of a model in which financial intermediation and credence are institutionally embedded within the banking sector. It is evident that, despite their capacity to facilitate financial integration and international trade, these systems are exhibiting signs of increasing operational inefficiencies in the face of rapid digitisation and globalisation (Gao, 2021; Huberman et al., 2021). Cross-border transactions can incur substantial costs, including the expenses associated with exchange rates and intermediary fees. The transfer of funds can thus be accompanied by a comprehensive cost evaluation. For instance, according to the World Bank (2024), the cost of sending $200 across borders averages at 6.4%, with the majority of cross-border remittances being subject to a fee. The burden of this problem is generally shouldered disproportionately by citizens of economically disadvantaged nations, many of whom depend on remittances as their primary means of livelihood (Meyer & Shera, 2017).

The expenses in these systems are significant, composed of interchange fees, service fees and account maintenance fees for domestic payment systems. They accrue over time, and this has colossal economic effects on business entities and individuals (Letts, 2017). This dynamic has been demonstrated to undermine the profit margins of small businesses, consequently making them more vulnerable in competitive markets where larger corporations, having greater financial strength, are in a better position to bear such cost expenditures (Abdulkadir et al., 2024). The necessity for a central authority to oversee financial transactions is predicated on the assumption that such oversight would mitigate the inconvenience of protracted waiting times. This is particularly true for advanced financial transactions such as cross border payment (Islam et al., 2022). Cross border transactions are characterized by a greater degree of complexity parallel to the aforementioned cross-border characteristics. This is due to the need to combine processes of transaction and confirmation with the clearance and settlement systems across legal and currency domains. The Society for Worldwide Interbank Financial Telecommunication (SWIFT) network is perhaps the most well-known system used for international wire transfers. As much as it is worth noting, with respect to cross border payment systems, one payment can take up to five days of business to process, and this severely demonstrates the cumbersome nature of traditional cross-border payment system operations (Qiu et al., 2019). In relation to commercial enterprises that rely on receiving payments within a set timeframe, or for individuals waiting for payments to be completed, these long termed impending timeframes effect everyone greatly.

Traditional payment networks have come under extreme criticism due to their natural absence of transparency and low traceability (Qiu et al., 2019). Such circumstances are ideal for fraudulent transactions to be conducted discreetly. Innovation in financial technology in recent years has been viewed as providing a platform to address such challenges. However, an important percentage of global population remains underbanked or unbanked, particularly within developing economies (Joia & Cordeiro, 2021). The dearth of access to formal financial infrastructure engenders considerable challenges to the widespread utilisation of traditional payment systems, a situation that is particularly pronounced in rural and socioeconomically isolated regions (Joia & Cordeiro, 2021). The exorbitant cost, rigidity and unavailability of the systems have been cited as significant barriers to financial inclusion, which disproportionately affect vulnerable groups in the global financial system (Ebirim & Odonkor, 2024).

The majority of conventional payment systems were developed from legacy infrastructure that is ill-equipped to handle the magnitude, intricacy and rapidity of contemporary financial transactions (D. He, 2021). This makes it imperative to have a shift in the way financial transactions are managed. The degree to which blockchain can provide a solution to the structural flaws of traditional payment systems should not be underestimated. The elements of decentralisation, immutability and transparency that define blockchain have proven to be of enormous benefit (Tripathi et al., 2023). The underlying principle of blockchain systems is the reduction of dependence on financial intermediaries. These systems have been shown to optimize cost effectiveness and reduce the time taken for settlement of transactions by significant amounts. These systems maintain elevated levels of security through the implementation of advanced cryptographic protocols. It is reasonable to hypothesise that this innate peer-to-peer nature possesses considerable potential in terms of its role in promoting financial inclusion, particularly in regions where access to traditional banking infrastructure is limited or non-existent. This problem is tackled by analyzing the capability of blockchain technology to solve the problem of single points of failure and enhance the operational resilience of financial ecosystems (Pennino et al., 2022).

The present chapter will examine the impending disruption to payment systems by blockchain revolutions, with a particular emphasis on interoperability between blockchain and generative AI. The chapter will detail how such blockchain revolutions will transform payment systems within the next few years, with the focus on the synergies in blockchain and generative AI. The present chapter will also furnish policy advice to policymakers, practitioners and scholars. The subsequent discussion will address the impact of blockchain technology on the international financial system. In order to accomplish this, it is imperative to examine real-world applications and emergent trends, as well as the inevitable issues that are likely to arise.

AN INTRODUCTION TO BLOCKCHAIN TECHNOLOGY IN PAYMENT SYSTEMS

The idea of blockchain was introduced by Bitcoin, through Satoshi Nakamoto's groundbreaking design of alternative decentralisation in enabling secure and transparent recording of transactions (Nakamoto, 2008). The prospects of blockchain technology to cause change in the financial sector cannot be overstated, a fact that is more evident in the sub-field of payment systems. Recent technological advancements have been shown to engender a number of benefits, including increased efficiency, security and transparency, and decreased reliance on conventional intermediaries (Janczuk-Gorywoda, 2019). The blockchain technology system is based on a number of fundamental principles, which are accessible to the wider public. This foundation involves the filing of records in a ledger space, enabling a higher degree of electronic locking within concentric, wide-circle groups that constitute the blockchain. The accountants' use of the ledger offers transparency and consistency in the system through replication and distribution on a network of computers (Shao et al., 2018). The network comprises a chain of linked nodes. Each of these nodes contains a synchronised register containing all the transactions. The process of creating a blockchain starts with blocks added one after the other in sequence, which, if arranged in chronological order, collectively constitute a blockchain (figure 1). One of the fundamental properties of blockchain technology is that, once entered and verified, transactions are saved for good and irretrievably. It is a consequence of this that any attempt to modify a transaction should come with the approval of the entire network in unison. The characteristics most commonly associated with this groundbreaking technology are decentralisation, transparency, and immutability (Shao et al., 2018).

Figure 1. Blockchain simplified diagram

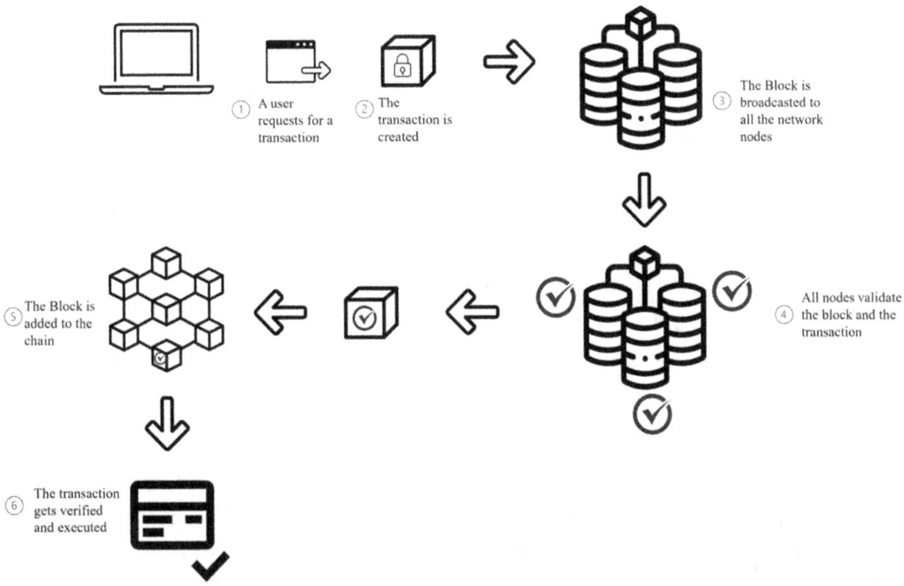

Source: Own elaboration.

The implementation of blockchain in payment systems has been shown to overcome the inefficiencies of traditional approaches by introducing features such as decentralisation, transparency and immutability (Vaigandla et al., 2023). This is supported by empirical evidence. It also drastically reduces vulnerabilities to fraud through increased transparency and security (Tripathi et al., 2023). Such a strategy is expected to improve the effectiveness of current financial payment systems and enable new avenues for economic inclusion. Thus, prospective customers can rely on safe and inexpensive payment solutions (Mhlanga, 2023). The financial ecosystem's heightened complexity has led to the acknowledgement that blockchain technology can address certain threats. It plays an essential role in the advancement of next-generation payment systems.

Evidence suggests that blockchain-based remittance providers, such as Ripple or Stellar, are more cost-effective than traditional systems like SWIFT or Western Union (Kulkarni et al., 2020). The ability to conduct financial transactions on blockchain makes it a valuable addition to the technology for individuals and companies seeking cost-effectiveness. Traditional transaction systems have lengthy processing times because they rely heavily on intermediary systems to verify, process, and settle payments. There are several reasons for why cross-border trade is so slow. Qiu et al. (2019) identified time zone differences, banking systems, and exchange rates as the primary factors that contributed to this phenomenon.

The most common blockchain procedure involves six blocks that are used to verify the validity of a transaction, which takes an average of sixty minutes. In comparison, the most common networks, Solana and Ripple, have much faster processing times than other networks (Erdin et al., 2020; Li et al., 2022). Real-time payments are key for companies that need smooth cash flow (Guo & Liang, 2016). Conventional payment rely on a central database, so they are more vulnerable to cyberattacks as other types of fraud and abuse (S. He et al., 2023). The presence of central payment systems leads to the expansion of vulnerabilities at critical points of failure in traditional payment systems. Blockchain technology is decentralized and consists of cryptographic protocols that have made it a new solution for such problems, aside from its implementation (S. He et al., 2023). Blockchain technology refers to bundling transactions into an immutable and distributed database. The data is highly immune to deliberate or covert tampering. The decentralized structure of blockchain technology also minimizes the possibility of a single point of failure event. Cryptographic hashing and multi-sig wallets are prominent characteristics that minimize deceptive activity and data tampering thus promoting faith in transactions (Kethepalli et al., 2023). Blockchain networks have also become more efficient and less latency-prone by verifying transactions in real-time.

The emergence of multiple blockchain networks has been demonstrated by various studies, each with its own set of performance metrics in the areas of scalability, throughput, power consumption, and cost. The Lightning Network (LN) has been identified as a potential solution to the inherent scalability limitations of Bitcoin (Von Arx et al., 2023). The LN was designed to facilitate the smoother off-chain settlement of transactions, reaching a point that is almost identical to real time. Note that only the final settlement balances are visible on the Bitcoin blockchain (Von Arx et al., 2023). The smart contract platform includes Ethereum, a decentralised application (dApp) and automatic payment processor. However, the restricted usage of large-scale payment protocols in Ethereum results in excessive transaction fees due to network congestion, deterring the development of rich financial applications.

Applications in cross-border payments and institutional transactions will most likely encompass the Ripple network (XRP). The XRP network is characterized by high-speed transmissions. Coupled with the consideration that its fee for transactions is low, this makes XRP a credible disruptor in the global remittances space (Trestioreanu et al., 2023). Regulatory oversight, however, particularly in the US, has been a decisive deterrent of the application of Ripple in some target markets.

Solana has been praised for its increased computational performance, with the ability to complete up to 65,000 transactions per second (Ayushi Abrol, 2024). A high-speed payment system is one potential outcome of the energy efficiency of the proof-of-history (PoH) protocol. However, reliability and, in some cases, the PoH itself have been affected by intermittent outages to the network. Why is this?

The Byzantine Agreement (BA) protocol has contributed greatly to the efficiency of Algorand as it is used as essentially entirely blockchain-based (Gilad et al., 2017). The system has proven to offer constant transaction speed at a competitive price and real-time data processability. Its scalability and sustainability qualify it well for retail and remittance. Regardless of that, its network is not as advanced as in more advanced networks. Finally, the choice of blockchain to be utilized by any given payment method and the associated performance metrics must be made through an exhaustive analysis based on the specific operating and technical needs of the application. Ripple can facilitate international remittances, but Lightning Network and Solana suit micropayments better.

One of the prominent characteristics of conventional settlement systems is that they lack transparency since the transactional data is contained in closed, proprietary databases that are managed by financial institutions. The lack of transparency is among the causative reasons for disputes, errors and suspicion amongst participants Cross-border payments may be hard to trace, and reports of transactions may be inconsistent. Blockchain technology can lead to payment systems being more transparent than ever. All payments cleared on the blockchain are publicly accessible and independently confirmable by users, guaranteeing completeness and integrity of information. It builds greater confidence for the user and lowers the tendency to rely on central authorities to facilitate settlements. With this greater transparency, for example, in supply chain finance, not to mention cross-border trade, all the participants in a particular transaction will be looking at the same set of data, and hence disputes and delays will be minimized.

Nevertheless, these conventional payment systems are mainly not applicable to those living in remote and underdeveloped regions, due to the prerequisite that their operation is based on the existence of formal banking infrastructure (M. Asif et al., 2023). Excessive fees, tight account opening conditions, and limited access to banking infrastructure have essentially barred a significant portion of the world's population from the formal financial system.

With internet-enabled smartphones, one can access blockchain networks, do payments, and receive financial services without necessarily opening a traditional bank account. This is a big leap towards enhancing financial inclusion, particularly given that a significant majority of individuals residing in developing countries remain unbanked or underbanked (Demirguc-Kunt et al., 2018b). It is the underlying contrast between blockchain-based and conventional financial systems that emphasizes blockchain technology's disruptive potential. In contrast to inefficiencies and perils in conventional arrangements, blockchain facilitates swift, secure, and cheap transfers of value. With greater blockchain adoption, driven by its qualities of decentralisation, transparency, and immutability, it will also play an important part in enabling inclusivity, as well as leading the development of a successful cross-border financial system (Peters et al., 2015) In addition to remedying long-standing issues in payment systems, such developments also create potential for innovation throughout an extensive range of consumer and business financial services (Ferrari, 2022).

THE POTENTIAL ROLE OF STABLECOINS IN CROSS-BORDER PAYMENTS

Stablecoins are simple building blocks of blockchain payment systems that offset volatility in cryptocurrencies like Bitcoin and Ethereum. Their prices are pegged to stable assets like fiat money (e.g., USD or EUR) and commodities (e.g., gold) and provide a more stable exchange medium as well as a secure vault of value (Ante et al., 2023). This intrinsic stability renders them extremely convenient for cross-border transactions, though exchange rate risk and excessively-high transactional fees remain as possibilities. The role of stablecoins in the financial system, one of processes evolving at a high pace, must be understood in terms of what they overall do.

Stablecoins hold a particular advantage in cross-border payments in that they can reduce the cost significantly. The established systems to which correspondent banking and SWIFT apply generally involve a series of intermediaries who add transactional charges each. Peer-to-peer transactions that bypass the middlemen are facilitated by blockchain-based stablecoin systems, though (Guo & Liang, 2016). It reduces the cost as well as enhances access to cross-border payments, particularly for small and medium-sized enterprises (SMEs) and remittances senders.

Speed is another significant advantage. Traditional cross-border transactions can take a couple of days to fully settle, this due to numerous parties being involved and the fact that time zones vary. Stablecoin transactions, as an attribute, settle instantly or within minutes, thereby greatly boosting transactional efficiency. Next-generation online platforms like Circle and Tether exemplify this ability by enabling instantaneous cross-border fund transfers. They emit US Digital Coin (USDC) and US Digital Tether (USDT), respectively, and hence provide a straightforward replacement for conventional systems. Stablecoins have been found to provide financial stability alongside transparency (Guo & Liang, 2016). This provides an open audit trail, hence reducing the likelihood of fraud and ease in meeting anti-money laundering (AML) and know-your-customer (KYC) regulations (Thommandru & Chakka, 2023). Though the programmability of stablecoins allows smart contracts to be added, thus streamlining payment procedures, it, in itself, eliminates human error. The dynamic world is plagued by complex scenarios that require thorough examination. Though stablecoins have several benefits, they are faced with challenges too many in number.

Regulatory control is one such big challenge area where, while debating on whether governments across the globe should have clearly defined parameters to their usage, doubts arise. Centralisation by a few stablecoin issuers is a serious concern since it goes against the inherently decentralised nature of blockchain networks. This has been at the centre of controversy around disclosure of reserve holdings and stability and consistency of some stablecoins. The future can witness the potential impact of Central Bank Digital Currencies (CBDCs) on the use of stablecoins in cross-border payments (Kaousar Nassr et al., 2023). Despite the fact that Central Bank Digital Currencies (CBDCs) are developed with the intention of providing similar benefits, including reduced transaction costs and faster processing, it is possible that stablecoins will retain their relevance particularly in decentralized contexts and private sector application. They are complex dynamics, however; while hardship there is, in-industry developments mean change and possible expansion avenues. Even in existing economic context dynamism, players need to stay alert and give due attention to such developments.

SMART CONTRACTS AND AUTOMATION IN PAYMENT SYSTEMS

Smart contracts represent one of the most innovative and disruptive applications of blockchain technology for payment systems. These self-executing contracts whose terms are carefully encoded into logic enable automated payments to be initiated when certain (predefined) conditions. Executed on blockchain platforms such as Ethereum, Binance Smart Chain and Solana, smart contracts cut out intermediaries, but at the expense of cost and a stark enhancement in operating efficiency (Christidis & Devetsikiotis, 2016).

Within the payments sector, smart contracts are applied in automating various processes. Its application is particularly relevant within supply chain finance, where the use of smart contracts has automated the payment release upon delivery as well as after inspection of goods. This process functions to reduce administrative tasks for companies, thereby decreasing the risk of disputes. It is a common view that there is a rich tradition of association between the concept of blockchain technology and that of smart contracts. The concept of a smart contract is that of an electronic contract that has the capability to perform the automation of repetitive payments, the examples of which include subscription fees, salaries, or royalties. This mode of payment offers a secure and convenient *modus operandi* for the precise and timely transaction of money. It does away with the requirement of manual intervention (Christidis & Devetsikiotis, 2016).

Programmability in the smart contract allows money to be paid under conditions, in which money is only paid if certain conditions are fulfilled. Increase security and transparency of transactions by secure holding of money on the blockchain. The process has been found to increase transparency and confidence between the concerned parties, thus eliminating the possibility of fraud.

It can be argued that smart contracts are becoming more and more a part of Decentralized Finance (DeFi) platforms (Christidis & Devetsikiotis, 2016). It is through them that sophisticated financial solutions such as lending protocols, automated market makers, and yield farming schemes are executed properly (Ghosh et al., 2023). Such technologies have had a central role to play in dismantling open access to financial services previously reserved for mature institutions, thereby beginning the democratisation of investment and capital. This new strategy is, however, also joined by a chain of challenges that need to be studied and reflected on very closely. While they are confronted with a higher degree of convenience, they are confronted with the complexity of smart contract mechanisms, which are notoriously hard to understand. The process of contracting out the financial transaction processing to code is replete with high risk because the presence of bugs or vulnerabilities in the code of the smart contract could result in high economic loss. With the arrival of DeFi also comes a series of new opportunities, however in return also calls for an rigorous review of the underpinnings technologies and what may ensue as a consequence.

An observation here is that such contracts also raise a particular set of problems. The blockchain immutability, i.e. once published, that smart contracts can't be easily modified, imposes an absolute guarantee that the code is bug-free (Tripathi et al., 2023). Implementing smart contracts via law, however, is a vague legal ground in most jurisdictions and thus hinders their implementation in regulated industries (Atiyah et al., 2024; Madir, 2018). It is salient to note that, as much as such a scenario adds more challenges, there is also a requirement for innovation in technological capacity as well as in the law.

THE TRANSFORMATIVE POTENTIAL OF DECENTRALIZED FINANCE IN PAYMENTS

In finance, DeFi enables peer-to-peer transactions with reduced reliance on traditional financial intermediaries such as banks and payment service providers (Bakare et al., 2024). It could imply significant cost savings alongside easier access. The decentralised system's benefits are best defined precisely in environments where traditional financial infrastructures do not exist or are inefficient. The implications of this phenomenon extend far beyond the benefit of sheer convenience.

Such technologies have the potential to signal the onset of a period of significant transformation in the financial sector.

These technologies are bringing about a revolutionary transformation of the finance industry. All of DeFi transformative potential lies in the realization, and adjustment to, the complex dynamics surrounding the various specialist financial markets. For instance, Irfan (2021) study of the Gulf Cooperation Council nations Shariah indices convergence illustrates the complex interdependence and interactions forming distinctive financial systems. The effective integration of DeFi into such systems, considering their unique structural and normative features, will be critical to determining its cross-world adoption and the establishment of a large-scale payment network.

The most important innovation provided by DeFi in payment systems is programmable payments through smart contracts. The inherent characteristic of such self-executing contracts is that they are capable of automating payments, in the sense that payment is conditional. Such a revolution has given rise to many applications that are covered, including recurring payments, security deposits and ad-hoc payments subject to conditions. This can be argued by analogy with supply chain finance in this sense. Payment of suppliers by computers at the time of delivery of goods can potentially reduce delays as well as disagreements. This innovation has its own constraints in that increased reliance on technology raises gigantic issues in the security as well as the trust factor. These smart contracts have been successful for which there are great records. However, it is to be noted that this phenomenon has its repercussions. It is important that these problems should be properly considered (R. Asif et al., 2023; Madir, 2018).

THE CONVERGENCE OF BLOCKCHAIN AND DEFI IN PAYMENT SYSTEMS

Synergistic interaction between DeFi and blockchain technology will transform the payment system ecosystem to a complete level. Although blockchain technology's open, decentralized, and secure nature provides an appropriate venue for developing DeFi applications, DeFi introduces new mechanisms to conduct easier transactional processes and provision of financial services to more people. This coming together of technologies is set to address the inherent inefficiencies of traditional payment systems and developing alternatives that are not only optimizing efficiency to the maximum but also cost-effective and inclusive. With such innovations, the future of financial transactions in the coming years looks brighter.

The integration of such technologies into payment systems is likely to accelerate in the coming years through technology, along with the growing demand for alternative financial options. Although the uptake of these technologies among developing economies has tremendous potential to expand financial inclusion as well as economic empowerment. Although the entry of DeFi into established markets is about to make more efficient and sophisticated payment solutions available, this revolution could initiate a new paradigm in the financial system of the world. With these changes, the flow of financial transactions will probably be altered in unprecedented scales.

To achieve the potential of blockchain and DeFi in the payment system, it is necessary to identify and overcome three fundamental issues: these are issues of scalability, regulatory compliance, and digital access. If these limits can be overcome successfully, then blockchain and DeFi will be able to construct a more inclusive and more efficient system of finance. This can push a world-wide shift in the payment settlement, reorganizing current financial transaction processes fundamentally. Though the path is fraught with issues, the payoff can be great because of the revolutionary impact on global finance.

DISRUPTIVE INNOVATIONS AND PRACTICAL APPLICATIONS

The emergence of blockchain technology has profoundly transformed traditional payment systems, giving rise to a wide array of innovative solutions aimed at eliminating inefficiencies and expanding the scope of financial transactions.

Bitcoin, a form of cryptocurrency, has been compared with "digital or virtual gold" (Baur et al., 2024). It enables inter-border transfers, it does not require intermediaries' financial institutions, which leads to lowering dependence on banking systems and therefore transmission cost and time delay in those transfers (Caton & Harwick, 2022). Ethereum is pushing the boundaries of blockchain technology by providing a programmable infrastructure that can be used to develop increasingly sophisticated, decentralised financial services (Tikhomirov, 2018). This pioneering advancement into AI-driven decentralized finance is fundamentally transforming the future of finance, heralding a new era for financial payments and applications (Irfan et al., 2024). With the increasing acceptance of bitcoin by retail businesses, the need for fast and secure forms of payment has created the demand described above. Institutional investors have, at long last, begun to take cryptocurrencies seriously as an asset class, one that belongs in a well-diversified portfolio, and even could be used to offset poor times in the economy.

Volatility of prices of cryptocurrencies such as Ethereum and Bitcoin renders stablecoins a giant leap forward in the development of blockchain payment systems. They offer a more stable unit of exchange and account, and they are most appropriate for day-to-day financial transactions as well as cross-border remittances. As they are anchored to fiat money or other risk-free assets, they can be a secure and certain channel of exchange in and out of domestic financial systems (Ante et al., 2023). But that reliability is largely pertinent to cross-border payment, where those problems are abominable. While many different cryptocurrencies are widely used, stablecoins are unique in that they can virtually remove the risk of price volatility. Several stablecoins, including USDC and Tether, have recently emerged with the aim of combining the native virtues of blockchain technology (i.e. openness, immutability and decentralised verification) with the price stability of more traditional fiat currencies. The primary responsibility of these is to supply stable and reliable digital tokens to serve as value for use in an increasingly digitized and highly networked payments environment. There, they serve as a workable alternative to traditional fiat money that can fund local as well as international transactions (Ante et al., 2023). They enable quick and cheap means of performing global transactions in a decentralized manner without any intermediation by a central bank. Aside from its explicit role in payment infrastructure, blockchain's structure also proves to be groundbreaking in simplifying complex business processes like supply chain management, where its use is pivotal in affecting transparency, traceability, and in most instances, composite payment flows. A study particularly crafted to study indicative drivers for the adoption of blockchain in this sector focuses on its much broader disruptive potential across industries (Rahman et al., 2025).

This expansion is a radical departure for emerging economies, whose fragile financial infrastructure is commonly a constraint on formal financial service access. In such markets, such innovation could be of significant value to enhancing financial inclusion, and thus in raising access to fundamental financial products and services. Worth noting is that such technology innovation isn't unique to traditional finance; its use becomes indispensable in niche specialty areas such as Islamic finance. In this regard, it is evident that the convergence of artificial intelligence, machine learning and blockchain approaches, through a number of fintech solutions, is essential to Shariah-compliant solution creation. These solutions are designed to optimize efficiency, transparency and accessibility to satisfy unique ethical and transactional demands (Irfan, Kadry, et al., 2023).

Another finer innovation in payment systems is the use of smart contracts on blockchain technology platforms. These are automated codes that have the ability to enforce the agreement of a contract automatically as soon as certain conditions are met (Savelyev, 2017). In payment transactions, for example, payments can be made automatically and hence limit the room for human error. The online shopping business can be a good example, where the consumer makes payments after receiving and inspecting the goods using a smart contract. Smart contracts can pay suppliers in a supply chain automatically once specific milestones are reached, hence leading to better cash flow efficiency and stakeholder confidence (Udvaros et al., 2023). Among the best advantages of smart contracts is that they can remove intermediaries from transactions and hence reduce costs. This reduction has been established to promote transparency and the seamless, efficient finalisation of financial transactions. This reduction in intermediaries has been established to reduce complexity, increase efficiency and decrease related risks. This operates towards the general stability and dependability of financial transactions. Though there are difficulties, technological in some cases, the advantages are great as technological processes can be automated and trust between parties can be enabled by the technology.

The idea of CBDCs is a revolution in the management of monetary systems. They are issued and regulated by central banks and are a state-supported form of fiat currency. They are therefore claimed to possess vast potential for enhancing the efficiency, security and accessibility of contemporary financial systems. A CBDC is a form of digital money that is distributed and regulated by a central bank. In contrast to the situation with cryptocurrencies, which are manufactured by non-public entities, CBDCs are a result of and regulated by central banks.

CBDCs are virtual counterparts of fiat currency that already exists. They have the ability to enhance the efficiency, security and convenience of national payment systems (Raju & Raju, 2021). They have been developed on the premise that they will be drivers of change and progress in the financial system, with the overall objective of improving financial efficiency as well as inclusiveness (Pratiwi, 2024; Svoboda, 2024). Many countries are now considering the possibilities of CBDCs as a strategic move to address the deficiencies and inefficiencies associated with existing payment systems. The People's Republic of China's pilot project for the digital yuan is an apt case study here. The initiative has been formulated with the aim of pursuing two fundamental objectives. It seeks to ensure maximum domestic payments as a point of departure, and it looks forward to reducing reliance on US-issued currency in global transactions and guarantee greater monetary sovereignty (Bhattacharya, 2022; Caudevilla & Kim, 2023). Likewise, the digital euro is also in development by the European Central Bank so that monetary sovereignty is not lost in an increasingly digital world economy (Westermeier, 2024). CBDCs also enable the option of usage under tighter monetary policy, such as compelling monetary payment of social welfare to the citizen during a period of recession.

Synergy of blockchain technology and the Internet of Things (IoT) is creating new possibilities for automated micropayments in a wide variety of applications (Dawod et al., 2022). Devices, integrated with blockchain functionality, are able to autonomously perform payment functions according to previously set conditions, thereby achieving greater efficiency and limiting the amount of manual input required. In the energy industry, blockchain-based IoT devices allow us to attain real time trading of energy between producers and consumers in distributed energy systems. Consumers can be billed automatically for their level of electricity usage, as recorded by a smart meter, leading to smooth and automated payment. field of transportation, the integration of IoT-enabled toll collection systems with blockchain-based digital wallets has the capacity to facilitate the automatic deduction of toll fees as vehicles pass through toll plazas. This approach has demonstrably reduced congestion and enhanced the overall user experience by optimizing payment processes.

The automation of payments between connected devices, such as a smart refrigerator ordering groceries independently, has become increasingly feasible (Lundqvist et al., 2017). These developments show that blockchain can support scalable machine-to-machine (M2M) financial transactions.

ECONOMIC AND SOCIAL IMPACTS

Blockchain technology application to payment systems is a structural change, as it adds economic and social value that transcends technical innovation. Despite its potential to bypass inefficiencies of existing systems, its adoption also creates issues which have to be resolved in order to ensure that implementation is sustainable and meaningful across the world, particularly in light of the complicated issues of Artificial Intelligence (AI) and how it tests financial systems today, is one that has been at the forefront of many recent academic discussions (Irfan et al., 2024).

There is a lot to contend that the most significant advantage of blockchain technology over traditional payment networks is that it significantly reduces transaction fees (Figure 2). Traditional payment networks involve numerous intermediaries like banks, clearing houses, and payment processors, i.e. Traditional payment intermediaries generally have service fees, which collectively form a greater transaction cost for both businesses and consumers. Conversely, the decentralised nature of blockchain technology reduces or excludes middlemen by a system where peer-to-peer transactions can be enabled through an incorruptible and tamper-evident ledger (Tripathi et al., 2023). A company that is making cross-border transactions through a blockchain platform will be able to save significantly on fees compared to old technology such as SWIFT or PayPal, whose payment handling and exchange fees may be incurred (Sakho et al., 2019). By reducing their expense, businesses will be able to reduce the expense of customers, thereby achieving a chain reaction of cost-saving.

Figure 2. Trends in the global cost of sending $200 in remittances

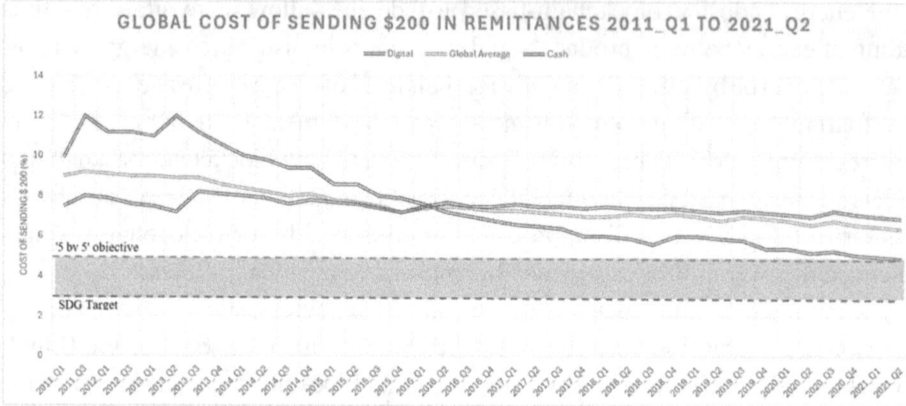

Source: World Bank, (2021)

Cross-border late payments have proven to be an issue of frustration in conventional financial networks because of lag issues associated with time zones, intermediated transaction settlement, and scanning for compliance by regulators. The remuneration process in certain instances might take several days, particularly in cases where the banking infrastructure is underdeveloped. The utilization of blockchain-based solutions provides near real-time settlement in the absence of an intermediary bank (Guo & Liang, 2016). The high transaction fee and slow processing time of conventional remittance providers such as Western Union are well publicized. It was seen that blockchain technology has been used to achieve substantial cost reductions, while simultaneously providing real-time access to beneficiaries to receive these funds. It is assumed that it may bring a paradigm shift in the lives of individuals living in developing countries.

DeFi is one of the most revolutionary economic innovations facilitated by blockchain. DeFi protocols provide trade, savings, and loans as services but without conventional intermediaries such as banks through smart contracts. Such a strategy has been shown to create new business opportunities and extend access to capital instruments, hence promoting the economic empowerment of historically excluded groups in the financial sector. Programmability of blockchain technology has been instrumental in the creation of tokenised assets and fractional ownership (Roth et al., 2019). Such new technology gives businesses the power to raise capital by issuing blockchain-based tokens that represent equity. This opens the door to investment opportunities to previously excluded 'micro-investors' for high-barrier investment projects (Roth et al., 2019).

1.7 billion unbanked adults existed globally in 2017, with no access to basic financial services based on geographical, regulatory or infrastructural constraints (Demirguc-Kunt et al., 2018a). Decentralized blockchain-based payment networks offer the underserved communities a primary solution in eliminating their dependence on traditional banking intermediaries. Consider, for example, the potential of blockchain-enabled mobile wallets, facilitating on-chip storage and payment without the need for a bank account. Blockchain technology possesses two main strengths: it broadens access to basic financial services such as savings, credit, and insurance, and facilitates financial inclusion by linking the unbanked and underbanked to the formal economy. That leads to household financial well-being and macroeconomic development overall. Trust — one of the pillars of each fiscal system — is reinforced by the intrinsic transparency of blockchain technology (Yulian et al., 2024).

Transparency is particularly vital to the developing economy whose entrenched financial corruption problems have since so long discredited the people's confidence (Corrigan, 2017). Governmental welfare payment disbursal through blockchain technology has been noted as a mechanism that minimizes the probability of diversion, leakage, or misappropriation by ensuring and direct channelling of funds to rightful beneficiaries. Traditional payment systems are typically characterized by centralized control of users' data, exposing individuals to being hacked into their data and secretly spied on. Blockchain has, however, been shown to offer control and ownership of individuals' financial data. Decentralized identities provide access control of users' data by the users themselves, where an individual can have control over the purpose and audience.

Despite the technological potential of blockchain, its implementation in payment systems continues to encounter significant challenges. It is widely acknowledged that the absence of verification within a unified regulatory framework constitutes a significant impediment to the widespread adoption of blockchain technology.

Governments across the world have adopted rather different regulatory approaches to the application of blockchain technology and cryptocurrency, from outright prohibitions to more innovative, adaptive regulatory model (Jovanić, 2021). Blockchain technology regulation differs significantly between different regions of the world. The fragmentation results in market confusion for firms and generates scalability issues in the cross-border deployment of blockchain solutions. The global community must now unite and form international standards that harmonize innovation with consumer protection.

The environmental impact of blockchain technology has been discussed extensively, particularly the energy-intensive aspect of Proof-of-Work (PoW) algorithms. The power consumption by the miners of Bitcoin every year has been found to be higher than that of several countries, thereby raising a lot of questions regarding its sustainability (Bajra et al., 2024). Its increased use of green methods is therefore essential as part of an initiative to balance the environmental impact of blockchain technology.

Blockchain networks are characterized by scalability constraints, which become especially binding during periods of increased transaction volumes. For instance, the 2017 Ethereum congestion caused by the CryptoKitties frenzy was used to expose the inbuilt capacity constraints of existing blockchain infrastructure designs (Jiang & Liu, 2021) Scalable alternatives like layer-2 protocols (e.g., the Bitcoin's Lightning Network) are becoming more scalable.

To interact effectively with blockchain-based systems, one has to acquire the technological ability needed.

BLOCKCHAIN AND GENERATIVE AI: A POWERFUL SYNERGY

The intersection of blockchain technology and generative AI presents a novel perspective on the financial system. The fusion of the two technologies has tremendous potential to transform decision-making processes and disrupt financial sectors in the Industry 5.0 era (Irfan, Elmogy, et al., 2023). By combining blockchain's decentralized network with the computational power of generative AI, the intersection delivers a quality platform that enhances the financial industry's operational performance, efficiency, and trustworthiness (Martinez et al., 2024; Priyadarshana, Ramachandra Rao, et al., 2024). Blockchain's immutable nature combined with its decentralized structure and transparent operations establishes a robust framework to protect data integrity while deterring tampering attempts. The success of generative AI models depends on the genuineness and reliability of input data, and thus these attributes are extremely valuable when combined.

Blockchain used in the detection of fraud relies on its ability to provide an extensive and irreversible record of all transactions. Advanced AI algorithms utilize advanced pattern-detection techniques, such as variational autoencoders or generative adversarial networks, with the aim of introducing patterns and anomalies into generation-level data sets (Chatterjee et al., 2024; Priyadarshana, Rao, et al., 2024). We rely more and more on advanced computer methods to protect and manage complex financial systems, and this shows that these technologies are reliable. Financial technologies should become more efficient and accurate. To achieve this, we need to make it easier to use modern machine learning algorithms (Irfan, Elhoseny, et al., 2023). In credit risk evaluation, using blockchain to verify people's identities along with the usual methods of checking past transactions has been shown to be very good at preventing bias in the computerised credit scoring process. This makes the scoring process more accurate and fair. This approach helps to reduce incorrect positive and negative results when evaluating risks.

Generative AI can contribute significantly to payment systems on blockchain by virtue of the ability to perform complex, dynamic analysis of transactional data (Chatterjee et al., 2024; Shamugasamy, 2024). Artificial intelligence can be used to optimize payment systems through the potential to detect inefficiencies and recommend structural changes with a view to attaining optimal operating efficiency at reduced cost through the potential to detect intricate, non-linear patterns (Burri et al., 2023). One of the key applications of this technology is in the field of cross-border payments, where generative AI codes can replicate the impact of such variables on exchange rate volatility, intermediary fees, and processing time (Lu et al., 2024). The algorithms are capable of finding best routes for transactions automatically, thereby reducing the cost of operations through the application of optimisation algorithms, e.g., reinforcement learning.

The integration of artificial intelligence within blockchain ecosystems has been identified as a significant development that facilitates the automation of payment processes via smart contracts (Dubey et al., 2022). A potential application of this technology lies in the utilisation of smart contracts augmented by generative AI within supply chain finance contexts. In such a situation, technology can be programmed to automatically make payout of money upon verification of delivery milestones logged on the blockchain. Utilization of such automation has the capacity to minimize manual interventions to nil, hence eliminating human error and guaranteeing the uniformity of operations. This, therefore, maximizes overall efficiency and reduces operational expense.

The intersection of the decentralised character of blockchain technology and the real-time analytical capability of generative AI can help create an emergent power platform that is capable of creating real-time decisions (Panda & Jena, 2021). Provision of real-time access to certified data via blockchain is of considerable utility within high-frequency transaction settings where being in a state to process and respond to information in real time is important.

Its activation would enable dynamic re-deployment of liquidity pools in DeFi protocols. Utilization of such instruments ensures maximum utilisation of capital with minimal associated market volatility risks.

It should be mentioned that generative AI can have the potential to enable more efficient adaptive transaction processes in blockchain-based systems. AI algorithms on e-commerce platforms are capable of analysing customer preferences, merchant locations and logistical constraints in order to recommend the most efficient payment methods (Sulastri, 2023). The application of blockchain technology ensures the execution of these recommendations with utmost security and transparency, hence supporting greater user trust.

The combination of generative AI and blockchain technology expands its traditional application in finance and promises to have revolutionary use cases in diverse industry verticals. Generative AI models have been employed in the insurance industry as well as the fraud detection industry to analyze blockchain transaction histories to look for unusual normative behavior, with the resulting real-time production of high-quality fraud and claim notifications. In the insurance sector, generative AI leverages blockchain-hosted claim data to automate risk assessment and claims processing. In the energy market context, the combination of blockchain-based IoT devices with generative AI enables by-product payment for energy usage, thus improving the grid's efficiency. The application of AI in DeFi has been demonstrated to enhance decision-making models, thereby ensuring the utility of the derived information concerning lending, borrowing, and staking opportunities (Nartey, 2024). These are derived from past and current statistics, which provide an extensive and dynamic image of potential money-generating possibilities.

Although the potential economic value that this convergence of blockchain and generative AI could bring is large, certain underlying technical and operating challenges persist, to the disadvantage of economic viability. One of them is the computationally heavy nature of blockchain consensus algorithms, in this case Proof-of-Work, which constrains scalability and efficiency. Consequently, this negatively affects cost-effectiveness and broad-scale adoption of such technology in economic networks (Chauhan et al., 2018). The reason that generative AI needs high computing resources makes this issue even larger.

The development of Web3, a distributed version of the internet capable of peer-to-peer commerce without intermediaries (Murray et al., 2023). In this environment, blockchain wallets and their respective tokens, stablecoins and non-fungible tokens (NFTs), are able to enable smooth transactions, thereby enabling direct peer-to-peer interaction. DeFi platforms, with Uniswap and Aave providing a substantive role in the provision of services such as decentralised lending and trading, thereby engaging in an intermediary role that is distinct from traditional financial systems (Shah et al., 2023).

It has further been speculated that the integration of blockchain and AI can result in the development of a broader, but perhaps less interoperable, payment infrastructure. To go beyond the constraints brought about by scalability issues, Layer-2 protocols such as Optimism and Polygon on Ethereum utilize off-chain transaction verification (Saif et al., 2024), thus mitigating congestion on the network and decreasing transaction fees. Cross-chain interoperability, as epitomized by networks such as Polkadot and Cosmos, enables the bridging of various blockchains (Dinesha & Patil, 2023), thereby promoting a more unified and collaborative digital economy.

Despite this potential, there are challenges that must be overcome in order for these technologies to be rolled out on a large scale. Cultural and market-related problems have emerged as the key obstacles to the adoption of such emerging technologies. The lack of consumer willingness to adopt blockchain-based solutions is in great part attributable to limited knowledge and perception of the vulnerabilities involved with newly emerging technologies (Raddatz et al., 2023). Presence of low-quality internet infrastructure and suboptimal digital literacy rates in the developing world poses highly prohibitive impediments to effective adoption of blockchain and AI technologies (Samuel-Okon & Abejide, 2024).

A related constraint pertains to the interpretability of AI models, particularly those based on deep learning architectures. The explainability and auditability of an intelligent-agent-based decision in blockchain environments is of extreme significance for achieving transparency and accountability. It will be interesting to warrant future work to achieve interpretable AI models that are meaningful for blockchain-based applications.

ETHICAL AND REGULATORY CONSIDERATIONS

The development of blockchain and artificial intelligence technologies in the payment systems sector presents significant opportunities and considerable challenges. The transformative potential of these technologies in reshaping the financial sector is widely recognised; however, their sustained development depends critically on ethical implementation and compliance with robust regulatory standard (Akpobome, 2024). beyond the immediate operational and transactional benefits blockchain technology has a moderating effect on the main corporate dimensions, influencing the intricate interrelations among corporate governance practices, environmental influences, and performance in the finance industry (Abida, 2025). Of particular urgency in the deployment of blockchain- and AI-enabled payment systems is the establishment of adaptable legal and regulatory frameworks. Compared to the clearly demarcated jurisdictions that govern traditional payment systems, the borderless and decentralised nature of blockchain networks poses huge challenges to regulation (Marian, 2020). The regulatory bodies and governments have to balance on a thin line in avoiding the extensive reach of such technologies while creating a conducive environment that sparks innovation without too much repression.

To address this, one initially needs to solve for compliance with the relevant regulations concerning the disclosure or concealment of patient data. The potential of blockchain immutable ledgers to expose financial transaction data in a form unrivaled for its exactness is balanced against the risk of linkage with personal identifiable information (Riva, 2020). Similarly, AI algorithms, especially in payment systems, are constrained when it comes to data volume and processing personal or identifiable data. The tension between data openness and anonymity of customers is one that is strongly debated. Another significant concern is that of cross-border payment, one of the most important applications of blockchain technology, which introduces new concerns regarding compliance, supervision and regulatory coordination.

Another serious concern is the issue of cross-border payments, one of the most important applications of blockchain technology, which poses fresh issues relating to compliance, supervision and regulatory coordination. Differences between jurisdictions in regulatory frameworks for blockchain technologies in diverse legal systems have been identified as a major hindrance to their international use. In response, regulatory "sandboxes" have been a promising instrument, which is providing a risk-free environment for companies and developers to pilot new ideas to commercial scale with minimal social footprint.

It is considered that while blockchain and artificial intelligence do pose excellent potential for developing equitable access to financial services, there are concerns that these technologies pose the risk of sustaining social separations. For instance, the computationally intensive nature of certain blockchain consensus algorithms, such as Proof-of-Work, may restrict participation to those having notable resources. Besides, there may still be an access gap for AI-based payment solutions, i.e., of high-income individuals and/or high areas of digital infrastructure. SMEs also have access to equitable financial products, as these businesses are likely to be hindered by implementing innovative technologies since they are extremely costly and complex. Facilitating access to such technologies for SMEs is of utmost importance to advancing inclusive economic development and growth.

Among the more concerning issues is criminalisation by abuse of AI and blockchain technology. The decentralised nature and anonymity of blockchain have evoked scrutiny of its use in money laundering, terrorist financing and other related financial crime. These models hold great promise for speeding up fraud detection and risk assessment through the use of artificial intelligence but remain vulnerable to a threat known as 'adversarial manipulation.' This allows evil forces to exploit system weaknesses by consciously modifying input data in order to manipulate outcomes.

The increasing number of DeFi platforms has given rise to concerns regarding the potential for illicit behaviour. Numerous financial platforms operating on the basis of DeFi function in the absence of centralised intermediaries and, consequently, are less regulated. The utilisation of blockchain analytics and AI-driven anomaly detection techniques has been identified as a promising approach for detecting suspicious activities. The effectiveness of these methods, however, depends on their integration within a comprehensive regulatory framework.

From a technology standpoint, scalable solutions are of primary importance (Khan et al., 2021). Although blockchain networks such as Solana and Ethereum 2.0 have made efforts to address this issue, many still encounter challenges in delivering cost-effective and rapid processing of large transaction volumes. Interoperability issues are, however, pervasive, because blockchain networks often exist in isolation, which results in communication and data sharing difficulties (Abebe et al., 2019). It is imperative that full consideration be given to the integration of blockchain technology into extant financial systems, in order to achieve the desired results (Khan et al., 2021). This, in turn, engenders suboptimal efficiency and heightened complexity.

The non-existence of globally standardised regulatory frameworks for blockchain-based systems considerably exacerbates the challenges encountered in cross-border transaction (Dominic Ochigbo et al., 2024). The growing awareness of the environmental impact of blockchain operations has the potential to act as a deterrent to both consumers and investors, particularly those who are committed to sustainable and green finance initiatives.

Security risks remain. Although blockchain is widely characterized as being extremely secure, it remains vulnerable to cyberattacks. Crooks can potentially leverage AI technologies to break into financial systems or commit fraud. The security and integrity of blockchain networks and AI systems need to be assured (Rani et al., 2024), as these technologies achieve broader adoption. In order to facilitate the widespread integration of blockchain and artificial intelligence within payment systems, it is vital to address the challenges associated with this process.

Instituting ethical and legal frameworks for blockchain and AI needs to be done in a pragmatic fashion, which is called for in order to address the complex and multidimensional challenges presented by new technologies. It is policymakers' ultimate role to ensure that the technologies are structured and implemented in a responsible, transparent, secure, and inclusive manner. For that, consultations on designing new technologies with stakeholders may be suitable. Even though developers and their stakeholders that work in the blockchain and artificial intelligence environments should be at the forefront of addressing such concerns, they should do so in creative ways, such as through decentralised identity models. These systems can enhance user anonymity without sacrificing on KYC and AML regulations. The design of ethical AI frameworks also involves embedding ethical values in artificial intelligence design and training to mitigate bias and discrimination. There are also collaborative governance approaches, with government, industry and academia coming together to develop international best practices and standards.

CONCLUSION AND FUTURE OUTLOOK

This chapter has analysed the transformative impact of blockchain technology and its integration with generative AI in the field of payment systems, with a comprehensive review of their innovations, practical applications, and the challenges they entail. The architecture of the blockchain, which is decentralized and is distinguished by immutable and transparent data structures, is suitably positioned to undermine the inefficiencies which are common in traditional payment systems. The inefficiencies common in traditional payment systems include high cost of transactions, long processing, and vulnerability to security threats. The combination of blockchain technology and the analytical capabilities of generative AI has been demonstrated to optimize payment infrastructures jointly, enhance decision-making protocols, and achieve maximum transactional security. Major challenges still exist Even with the rushing new developments, the integration of new technologies is a rather unique challenge requiring detailed focus. This not only modernizes the method in which a deal is completed, but marks the beginning of a new period of monetary participation.

The birth of combining generative artificial intelligence and blockchain marks the milestone in the evolution of the payment system. Integrating AI's capability for real-time processing and pattern recognition alongside blockchain's secure, verifiable data ensures the creation of intelligent, rapid, and dependably secure payment systems. The infrastructure has been crafted with the intent to achieve problem-solving capabilities on critical issues like cross-border participation and antifraud. The outcome of this evolution is not only efficient financial systems, but also inclusive as well as sovereign in nature. Nevertheless, one must bear in mind the consequences of such an development, while these changes stand to greatly impact the forefront of digital finance design.

Lastly, the future of payment systems will be critically dependent on advances to several key areas, specifically advances in blockchain and AI technologies. Firstly, scalability is an important consideration for blockchain technology. The current scalability issues that exist with transaction throughput must be solved, as every country in the world continues to generate and increasingly complex and wide range of financial transactions that must be addressed. The ideation of a sharding solutions, layer-2 scalability solutions, and advances that address consensus solutions with greater efficiency e.g proofs of stake, should all help with scalability issues - there will always be challenges that lay ahead, but develop manageable scales into the future is critical, if the financial systems of today are to grow sustainably. Interoperability is another crucial issue between different blockchains. If there can be an easy solution to that, we would also see the development of integrated and interoperable financial systems where data sharing between platforms and mediated by larger shareholding third parties will and be driving in some version of collocated financial systems that drive real-time settlement, that cross borders and - may have less friction for cross-border transactions. The transformation, that blockchain is able to drive in monetary systems through the introduction of CBDCs and efficiencies, such as those seen through RTGS systems (central banks in real time settlement systems), and we could envision a new model for introducing a new monetary system based on digital currencies and the integration of CBDCs into other countries' local currencies.

Concurrently, the implementation of AI within payment systems is projected to evolve towards greater complexity. Predictive analytics, driven by generative AI, will serve to enhance transaction optimisation. This will enable systems to not only anticipate user needs but also detect anomalies and dynamically adapt to evolving financial conditions. AI can enhance risk management models and anti-fraud technology. Not only that, but it can also improve security and efficiency in payment systems, resulting in a substantial reduction in operational risk for businesses and individuals. As with any other large-scale technological integration, implementation of these systems must be accompanied by thorough investigation of the potential difficulties.

Although such developments hold much promise, it is essential to address the legislative, technical, and ethical concerns involved in uniting blockchain and Artificial Intelligence. Regulatory systems need to emerge, they need to provide definite guidance on the use of evolving technology, however, they must also safeguard user privacy and abuse. Ethical concerns, particularly the need to assure fairness in access to such technology, must be accorded primacy. The non-inclusion of this concern may result in the exacerbation of existing financial imbalances. Beyond this, the life span of blockchain technology, and in particular its energy-consuming protocols, must be increased through long-term technological innovations for sustainable development.

The confluence of blockchain and generative AI is a turning point in payment system history; it potentially could transform the nature of global financial transactions. When the technologies reach maturity, they will inevitably bring a paradigm shift to the way that financial systems are run, characterized by greater efficiency, greater inclusiveness and enhanced security. It is, however, reliant on cooperation between policymakers, regulators and technologists to solve the numerous issues that come with these innovations. The world's financial arena will start a revolutionary era with the beginning of a significant innovation in the next decade, which is anticipated to take place in payment systems. Though there are challenges to be addressed, the convergence of these technologies can create the potential for untold growth and innovation.

REFERENCES

Abebe, E., Behl, D., Govindarajan, C., Hu, Y., Karunamoorthy, D., Novotny, P., Pandit, V., Ramakrishna, V., & Vecchiola, C. (2019). Enabling Enterprise Blockchain Interoperability with Trusted Data Transfer (industry track). *Middleware Industry 2019 - Proceedings of the 2019 20th International Middleware Conference Industrial Track, Part of Middleware 2019*, 29–35. DOI: 10.1145/3366626.3368129

Abida, M. (2025). Blockchain Technology's Moderating Effect on the Relationships Between Corporate Governance, the Environment and Financial Performance. *International Journal of Business and Emerging Markets*, *1*(1), 10059108. Advance online publication. DOI: 10.1504/IJBEM.2025.10059108

Abrol, A. (2024, July 18). *Solana vs Polygon vs Ethereum - blockchain Council.* Https://Www.Blockchain-Council.Org/https://www.blockchain-council.org/blockchain/solana-vs-polygon-vs-ethereum/

Akkaya, K., Mercan, S., & Erdin, E. (2021). An evaluation of cryptocurrency payment channel networks and their privacy implications. *ITU Journal : ICT Discoveries*, *2*(1), 35–44. Advance online publication. DOI: 10.52953/CLBL7402

Akpobome, O. (2024). The Impact of Emerging Technologies on Legal Frameworks: A Model for Adaptive Regulation. *International Journal of Research Publication and Reviews Journal*, *5*(7), 5046–5060. Www.Ijrpr.Com. DOI: 10.55248/gengpi.5.1024.3012

Ante, L., Fiedler, I., Willruth, J. M., & Steinmetz, F. (2023). A Systematic Literature Review of Empirical Research on Stablecoins. *FinTech*, *2*(1), 34–47. Advance online publication. DOI: 10.3390/fintech2010003

Asif, M., Khan, M. N., Tiwari, S., Wani, S. K., & Alam, F. (2023). The Impact of Fintech and Digital Financial Services on Financial Inclusion in India. *Journal of Risk and Financial Management*, *16*(2), 122. Advance online publication. DOI: 10.3390/jrfm16020122

Asif, R., Hassan, S. R., & Parr, G. (2023). Integrating a Blockchain-Based Governance Framework for Responsible AI. In *Future Internet* (Vol. 15, Issue 3). DOI: 10.3390/fi15030097

Atiyah, G. A., Ibrahim, A. I., & Jasim, A. A. (2024). Enforcement of smart contracts in cross-jurisdictional transactions. *International Journal of Law and Management, ahead-of-print* (ahead-of-print). https://doi.org/DOI: 10.1108/IJLMA-06-2024-0220/FULL/XML

Bajra, U. Q., Ermir Rogova, , & Avdiaj, S. (2024). Cryptocurrency blockchain and its carbon footprint: Anticipating future challenges. *Technology in Society, 77*, 102571. DOI: 10.1016/j.techsoc.2024.102571

Bakare, F. A., Omojola, J., & Iwuh, A. C. (2024). Blockchain and decentralized finance (DEFI): Disrupting traditional banking and financial systems. Https://Wjarr.Com/Sites/Default/Files/WJARR-2024-2968.Pdf, *23*(3), 3075–3089. DOI: 10.30574/wjarr.2024.23.3.2968

Baur, D. G., Karlsen, J. R., Smales, L. A., & Trench, A. (2024). Digging deeper - Is bitcoin digital gold? A mining perspective. *Journal of Commodity Markets, 34*, 100406. DOI: 10.1016/j.jcomm.2024.100406

Bhattacharya, D. (2022). Digital Yuan (e-CNY): China's Official Digital Currency. *Strategic Analysis, 46*(1), 93–99. Advance online publication. DOI: 10.1080/09700161.2022.2039582

Burri, S. R., Kumar, A., Baliyan, A., & Kumar, T. A. (2023). Transforming Payment Processes: A Discussion of AI-Enabled Routing Optimization. *2023 2nd International Conference on Smart Technologies and Systems for Next Generation Computing, ICSTSN 2023*. DOI: 10.1109/ICSTSN57873.2023.10151455

Caton, J. L.Jr, & Harwick, C. (2022). Cryptocurrency, Decentralized Finance, and the Evolution of Money: A Transaction Costs Approach. *Journal of New Finance, 2*(4). Advance online publication. DOI: 10.46671/2521-2486.1027

Caudevilla, O., & Kim, H. M. (2023). The Digital Yuan and Cross-Border Payments: China's Rollout of Its Central Bank Digital Currency. SSRN *Electronic Journal*. DOI: 10.2139/ssrn.4371414

Chatterjee, P., Das, D., & Rawat, D. B. (2024). A Generative AI Approach for Ensuring Data Integrity Security Resilience in Fintech Systems. *Proceedings - 2024 IEEE/ACM 24th International Symposium on Cluster, Cloud and Internet Computing Workshops, CCGridW 2024*, 168–173. DOI: 10.1109/CCGridW63211.2024.00027

Chauhan, A., Malviya, O. P., Verma, M., & Mor, T. S. (2018). Blockchain and Scalability. *Proceedings - 2018 IEEE 18th International Conference on Software Quality, Reliability, and Security Companion, QRS-C 2018*, 122–128. DOI: 10.1109/QRS-C.2018.00034

Christidis, K., & Devetsikiotis, M. (2016). Blockchains and Smart Contracts for the Internet of Things. In *IEEE Access* (Vol. 4). DOI: 10.1109/ACCESS.2016.2566339

Corrigan, C. C. (2017). The effects of increased revenue transparency in the extractives sector: The case of the Extractive Industries Transparency Initiative. *The Extractive Industries and Society*, *4*(4), 779–787. DOI: 10.1016/j.exis.2017.03.004

Dawod, A., Georgakopoulos, D., Jayaraman, P. P., Nirmalathas, A., & Parampalli, U. (2022). IoT Device Integration and Payment via an Autonomic Blockchain-Based Service for IoT Device Sharing. *Sensors (Basel)*, *22*(4), 1344. Advance online publication. DOI: 10.3390/s22041344 PMID: 35214244

Demirguc-Kunt, A., Klapper, L., Singer, D., Ansar, S., & Hess, J. (2018a). Global Findex Database 2017: Measuring Financial Inclusion and the Fintech Revolution. *The Global Findex Database 2017: Measuring Financial Inclusion and the Fintech Revolution*. DOI: 10.1596/978-1-4648-1259-0

Demirguc-Kunt, A., Klapper, L., Singer, D., Ansar, S., & Hess, J. (2018b). The Global Findex Database 2017: Measuring Financial Inclusion and the Fintech Revolution. *The Global Findex Database 2017: Measuring Financial Inclusion and the Fintech Revolution*. DOI: 10.1596/978-1-4648-1259-0

Dinesha, D. L., & Patil, B. (2023). A Conceptual Insight Into Achieving Interoperability Between Heterogeneous Blockchain Enabled Interconnected Smart Microgrids. *2023 IEEE PES Innovative Smart Grid Technologies - Asia. ISGT Asia*, *2023*, 1–5. Advance online publication. DOI: 10.1109/ISGTAsia54891.2023.10372801

Dominic Ochigbo, A., Tuboalabo, A., Temitope Labake, T., Buinwi, U., Layode, O., Adama Buinwi, J., & Author, C. (2024). Legal frameworks for digital transactions: Analyzing the impact of Blockchain technology. *Finance & Accounting Research Journal*, *6*(7), 1205–1223. DOI: 10.51594/farj.v6i7.1313

Dubey, C., Kumar, D., Singh, A. K., & Dwivedi, V. K. (2022). Confluence of Artificial Intelligence and Blockchain Powered Smart Contract in Finance System. *3rd IEEE 2022 International Conference on Computing, Communication, and Intelligent Systems, ICCCIS 2022*. DOI: 10.1109/ICCCIS56430.2022.10037701

Ebirim, G. U., & Odonkor, B. (2024). Enhancing Global Economic Inclusion With Fintech Innovations And Accessibility. *Finance & Accounting Research Journal*, *6*(4), 648–673. DOI: 10.51594/farj.v6i4.1067

Erdin, E., Cebe, M., Akkaya, K., Solak, S., Bulut, E., & Uluagac, S. (2020). A Bitcoin payment network with reduced transaction fees and confirmation times. *Computer Networks*, *172*, 107098. Advance online publication. DOI: 10.1016/j.comnet.2020.107098

Ferrari, M. V. (2022). The platformisation of digital payments: The fabrication of consumer interest in the EU FinTech agenda. *Computer Law & Security Review, 45*, 105687. DOI: 10.1016/j.clsr.2022.105687

Gao, T. (2021). Study on the Intention of Foreign Trade Driven by Cross-Border E-Commerce Based on Blockchain Technology. *Security and Communication Networks, 2021*, 1–10. Advance online publication. DOI: 10.1155/2021/9623672

Ghosh, B., Kazouz, H., & Umar, Z. (2023). Do Automated Market Makers in DeFi Ecosystem Exhibit Time-Varying Connectedness during Stressed Events? *Journal of Risk and Financial Management, 16*(5), 259. Advance online publication. DOI: 10.3390/jrfm16050259

Gilad, Y., Hemo, R., Micali, S., Vlachos, G., & Zeldovich, N. (2017). Algorand: Scaling Byzantine Agreements for Cryptocurrencies. *SOSP 2017 - Proceedings of the 26th ACM Symposium on Operating Systems Principles*. DOI: 10.1145/3132747.3132757

Guo, Y., & Liang, C. (2016). Blockchain application and outlook in the banking industry. In *Financial Innovation* (Vol. 2, Issue 1). DOI: 10.1186/s40854-016-0034-9

He, D. (2021). Digitalization of cross-border payments. *China Economic Journal, 14*(1), 26–38. Advance online publication. DOI: 10.1080/17538963.2020.1870272

He, S., Xing, X., Wang, G., & Sun, Z. (2023). A Data Integrity Verification Scheme for Centralized Database Using Smart Contract and Game Theory. *IEEE Access : Practical Innovations, Open Solutions, 11*, 59675–59687. Advance online publication. DOI: 10.1109/ACCESS.2023.3284850

Huberman, G., Leshno, J. D., & Moallemi, C. (2021). Monopoly without a Monopolist: An Economic Analysis of the Bitcoin Payment System. *The Review of Economic Studies, 88*(6), 3011–3040. Advance online publication. DOI: 10.1093/restud/rdab014

Irfan, M. (2021). Do Shariah Indices converge? Evidence from Gulf Cooperation Council countries. *International Journal of Business Excellence, 23*(2), 251. Advance online publication. DOI: 10.1504/IJBEX.2021.113448

Irfan, M., Elhoseny, M., Kassim, S., & Metawa, N. (2023). Advanced Machine Learning Algorithms for Complex Financial Applications. In *Advanced Machine Learning Algorithms for Complex Financial Applications*. DOI: 10.4018/978-1-6684-4483-2

Irfan, M., Elmogy, M., Majid, M. S. A., & El-Sappagh, S. (2023). The impact of AI innovation on financial sectors in the era of industry 5.0. In *The Impact of AI Innovation on Financial Sectors in the Era of Industry 5.0*. https://doi.org/DOI: 10.4018/9798369300824

Irfan, M., Hussainey, K., Bukhari, S. A. C., & Nam, Y. (2024). Issues of Sustainability in AI and New-Age Thematic Investing. *Issues of Sustainability in AI and New-Age Thematic Investing*, 1–295. DOI: 10.4018/979-8-3693-3282-5

Irfan, M., Kadry, S., Sharif, M., & Khan, H. U. (2023). Fintech applications in Islamic finance: AI, machine learning, and blockchain techniques. In *Fintech Applications in Islamic Finance*. AI, Machine Learning, and Blockchain Techniques., DOI: 10.4018/979-8-3693-1038-0

Islam, M. R., & Rashid, M. M.Mohammed Ataur RahmanMuslin Har Sani Bin MohamadAbd Halim Bin Embang. (2022). Analysis of Blockchain-Based Ripple and Swift. *Asian Journal of Electrical and Electronic Engineering*, *2*(1), 1–8. DOI: 10.69955/ajoeee.2022.v2i1.26

Janczuk-Gorywoda, A. (2019). Blockchain and Payment Systems: A Tale about Re-Intermediation. *Regulating Blockchain*, 259–274. DOI: 10.1093/oso/9780198842187.003.0015

Jiang, X. J., & Liu, X. F. (2021). CryptoKitties Transaction Network Analysis: The Rise and Fall of the First Blockchain Game Mania. *Frontiers in Physics (Lausanne)*, *9*, 631665. Advance online publication. DOI: 10.3389/fphy.2021.631665

Joia, L. A., & Cordeiro, J. P. V. (2021). Unlocking the potential of fintechs for financial inclusion: A delphi-based approach. *Sustainability (Basel)*, *13*(21), 11675. Advance online publication. DOI: 10.3390/su132111675

Jovanić, T. (2021). *An Overview of Regulatory Strategies on Crypto-Asset Regulation - Challenges for Financial Regulators in the Western Balkans*.

Kethepalli, Y., Joseph, R., Raja Vajrala, S., Vemula, J., Srinivas Naik, N., & Naya Raipur, I. (2023). *Reinforcing Security and Usability of Crypto-Wallet with Post-Quantum Cryptography and Zero-Knowledge Proof*. https://arxiv.org/abs/2308.07309v2

Khan, D., Jung, L. T., & Hashmani, M. A. (2021). Systematic Literature Review of Challenges in Blockchain Scalability. *Applied Sciences 2021, Vol. 11, Page 9372*, *11*(20), 9372. DOI: 10.3390/app11209372

Kulkarni, R., Schintler, L., Koizumi, N., & Stough, R. R. (2020). Cryptocurrency, Stablecoins and Blockchain: Exploring Digital Money Solutions for Remittances and Inclusive Economies. SSRN *Electronic Journal*. DOI: 10.2139/ssrn.3511139

Letts, A. (2017). What do consumers want from next generation banking, and how will challenger and established banks provide it? *Journal of Digital Banking*, *1*(4), 329. Advance online publication. DOI: 10.69554/BRFD2666

Li, X., Wang, X., Kong, T., Zheng, J., & Luo, M. (2022). From Bitcoin to Solana – Innovating Blockchain Towards Enterprise Applications. *Lecture Notes in Computer Science (Including Subseries Lecture Notes in Artificial Intelligence and Lecture Notes in Bioinformatics), 12991 LNCS*. DOI: 10.1007/978-3-030-96527-3_6

Lu, S., Liang, S., Xue, Q., & Bian, H. (2024). Enhancing cross-border payments: The convergence of AI and blockchain for currency exchange optimization. *Applied and Computational Engineering*, *75*(1), 160–165. DOI: 10.54254/2755-2721/75/20240531

Lundqvist, T., De Blanche, A., & Andersson, H. R. H. (2017). *Thing-to-thing electricity micro payments using blockchain technology. GIoTS 2017 - Global Internet of Things Summit*. Proceedings., DOI: 10.1109/GIOTS.2017.8016254

Madir, J. (2018). Smart Contracts: (How) Do They Fit Under Existing Legal Frameworks? SSRN *Electronic Journal*. DOI: 10.2139/ssrn.3301463

Marian, O. (2020). Blockchain Havens and the Need for Their Internationally-coordinated Regulation. *Florida Tax Review*, *23*(2). Advance online publication. DOI: 10.5744/ftr.2020.2011

Martinez, D., Magdalena, L., & Savitri, A. N. (2024). AI and Blockchain Integration: Enhancing Security and Transparency in Financial Transactions. *International Transactions on Artificial Intelligence*, *3*(1), 11–20. DOI: 10.33050/italic.v3i1.651

Meyer, D., & Shera, A. (2017). The impact of remittances on economic growth: An econometric model. *Economía*, *18*(2), 147–155. Advance online publication. DOI: 10.1016/j.econ.2016.06.001

Mhlanga, D. (2023). Block chain technology for digital financial inclusion in the industry 4.0, towards sustainable development? In *Frontiers in Blockchain* (Vol. 6). DOI: 10.3389/fbloc.2023.1035405

Murray, A., Kim, D., & Combs, J. (2023). The promise of a decentralized internet: What is Web3 and how can firms prepare? *Business Horizons*, *66*(2), 191–202. DOI: 10.1016/j.bushor.2022.06.002

Nakamoto, S. (2008). Bitcoin: A Peer-to-Peer Electronic Cash System | Satoshi Nakamoto Institute. *Bitcoin.Org*.

Nartey, J. N. (2024). The Convergence of Decentralized Finance (DeFi) and Artificial Intelligence (AI): Synergies, Opportunities, and Challenges. *International Journal of Blockchain Technologies and Applications*, *2*(2). Advance online publication. DOI: 10.18178/IJBTA.2024.2.2.78-89

Panda, S. S., & Jena, D. (2021). *Decentralizing AI Using Blockchain Technology for Secure Decision Making*. DOI: 10.1007/978-981-15-5243-4_65

Pennino, D., Pizzonia, M., Vitaletti, A., & Zecchini, M. (2022). Blockchain as IoT Economy Enabler: A Review of Architectural Aspects. In *Journal of Sensor and Actuator Networks* (Vol. 11, Issue 2). DOI: 10.3390/jsan11020020

Peters, G. W., Panayi, E., & Chapelle, A. (2015). Trends in Crypto-Currencies and Blockchain Technologies: A Monetary Theory and Regulation Perspective. SSRN *Electronic Journal*. DOI: 10.2139/ssrn.2646618

Pratiwi, E. N. (2024). The Impact Of Central Bank Digital Currency (Cbdc) Volatility On Monetary Policy Efficiency In Financial Inclusion And Investment. *Journal of Social and Economics Research*, *6*(2), 195–222. DOI: 10.54783/jser.v6i2.659

Priyadarshana, D., Ramachandra Rao, T., & Sambasiva Rao, M. (2024). AI and blockchain technology for secure and transparent financial transactions. *International Journal of Science and Research Archive*, *2024*(01), 2013–2019. DOI: 10.30574/ijsra.2024.13.1.1845

Priyadarshana, D., Rao, T. R., Rao, M. S., Priyadarshana, D., Rao, T. R., & Rao, M. S. (2024). AI and blockchain technology for secure and transparent financial transactions. *International Journal of Science and Research Archive*, *13*(1), 2013–2019. DOI: 10.30574/ijsra.2024.13.1.1845

Qiu, T., Zhang, R., & Gao, Y. (2019). Ripple vs. SWIFT: Transforming Cross Border Remittance Using Blockchain Technology. *Procedia Computer Science*, *147*, 428–434. Advance online publication. DOI: 10.1016/j.procs.2019.01.260

Raddatz, N., Coyne, J., Menard, P., & Crossler, R. E. (2023). Becoming a blockchain user: Understanding consumers' benefits realisation to use blockchain-based applications. *European Journal of Information Systems*, *32*(2), 287–314. DOI: 10.1080/0960085X.2021.1944823

Rahman, J. A., Ooi, H. L., & Lee, C. K. (2025). Blockchain Architecture Adoption in Supply Chain Management: A DEMATEL-Based Analysis of Critical Factors. *Journal of Future Sustainability*, *5*(1), 41–58. Advance online publication. DOI: 10.5267/j.jfs.2025.2.004

Raju, A. B. A., & Raju, A. B. A. (2021). Digital Currency Issuance by Central Banks: CBDCs and Monetary Policy. [IJSR]. *International Journal of Science and Research (Raipur, India)*, *10*(11), 1587–1589. DOI: 10.21275/SR24914160743

Rani, S., Kumar, N., Srivastva, A., & Sharma, A. (2024). Leveraging Artificial Intelligence and Machine Learning for Enhanced Privacy and Security. *2024 IEEE International Conference on Blockchain and Distributed Systems Security (ICBDS)*, 1–6. DOI: 10.1109/ICBDS61829.2024.10837569

Riva, G. M. (2020). What Happens in Blockchain Stays in Blockchain. A Legal Solution to Conflicts Between Digital Ledgers and Privacy Rights. *Frontiers in Blockchain*, *3*, 36. Advance online publication. DOI: 10.3389/fbloc.2020.00036

Roth, J., Schär, F., & Schöpfer, A. (2019). The Tokenization of Assets: Using Blockchains for Equity Crowdfunding. SSRN *Electronic Journal*. DOI: 10.2139/ssrn.3443382

Saif, M. Bin, Migliorini, S., & Spoto, F. (2024). A Survey on Data Availability in Layer 2 Blockchain Rollups: Open Challenges and Future Improvements. *Future Internet 2024, Vol. 16, Page 315*, *16*(9), 315. DOI: 10.3390/fi16090315

Sakho, S., Jianbiao, Z., Essaf, F., & Badiss, K. (2019). Improving Banking Transactions Using Blockchain Technology. *2019 IEEE 5th International Conference on Computer and Communications, ICCC 2019*. DOI: 10.1109/ICCC47050.2019.9064344

Samuel-Okon, A. D., & Abejide, O. O. (2024). Bridging the Digital Divide: Exploring the Role of Artificial Intelligence and Automation in Enhancing Connectivity in Developing Nations. *Journal of Engineering Research and Reports*, *26*(6), 165–177. DOI: 10.9734/jerr/2024/v26i61170

Savelyev, A. (2017). Contract law 2.0: 'Smart' contracts as the beginning of the end of classic contract law. *Information & Communications Technology Law*, *26*(2), 116–134. Advance online publication. DOI: 10.1080/13600834.2017.1301036

Shah, K., Lathiya, D., Lukhi, N., Parmar, K., & Sanghvi, H. (2023). A systematic review of decentralized finance protocols. *International Journal of Intelligent Networks*, *4*, 171–181. DOI: 10.1016/j.ijin.2023.07.002

Shamugasamy, K. (2024). Enhancing Payment Settlement Processes Through Generative AI. *International Journal for Multidisciplinary Research (IJFMR)*. www.ijfmr.com

Shao, Q. F., Jin, C. Q., Zhang, Z., Qian, W. N., & Zhou, A. Y. (2018). Blockchain: Architecture and Research Progress. In *Jisuanji Xuebao/Chinese Journal of Computers* (Vol. 41, Issue 5). DOI: 10.11897/SP.J.1016.2018.00969

Sulastri, L. (2023). The Role of Artificial Intelligence in Enhancing Customer Experience: A Case Study of Global E-commerce Platforms. *The International Journal of Science in Society*, *5*(3), 451–469. DOI: 10.54783/ijsoc.v5i3.1257

Svoboda, A. (2024). *Scholars Journal of Economics, Business and Management Central Bank Digital Currencies (CBDCs) and Financial Inclusion: Explore How CBDCs Can Promote Financial Inclusion for Unbanked or Underbanked Populations, Considering both Benefits and Challenges.* DOI: 10.36347/sjebm.2024.v11i05.002

Thommandru, A., & Chakka, D. B. (2023). Recalibrating the Banking Sector with Blockchain Technology for Effective Anti-Money Laundering Compliances by Banks. *Sustainable Futures : An Applied Journal of Technology, Environment and Society*, *5*, 100107. DOI: 10.1016/j.sftr.2023.100107

Tikhomirov, S. (2018). Ethereum: State of knowledge and research perspectives. *Lecture Notes in Computer Science (Including Subseries Lecture Notes in Artificial Intelligence and Lecture Notes in Bioinformatics), 10723 LNCS*. DOI: 10.1007/978-3-319-75650-9_14

Trestioreanu, L., Shbair, W. M., De Cristo, F. S., & State, R. (2023). XRP-NDN overlay: Improving the Communication Efficiency of Consensus-Validation based Blockchains with an NDN Overlay. *Proceedings of IEEE/IFIP Network Operations and Management Symposium 2023, NOMS 2023*. DOI: 10.1109/NOMS56928.2023.10154402

Tripathi, G., Ahad, M. A., & Casalino, G. (2023). A comprehensive review of blockchain technology: Underlying principles and historical background with future challenges. *Decision Analytics Journal*, *9*, 100344. DOI: 10.1016/j.dajour.2023.100344

Udvaros, J., Forman, N., & Avornicului, S. M. (2023). Agile Storyboard and Software Development Leveraging Smart Contract Technology in Order to Increase Stakeholder Confidence. *Electronics (Basel)*, *12*(2), 426. Advance online publication. DOI: 10.3390/electronics12020426

Vaigandla, K. K., Siluveru, M., Kesoju, M., & Karne, R. (2023). Review on Blockchain Technology: Architecture, Characteristics, Benefits, Algorithms, Challenges and Applications. In *Mesopotamian Journal of CyberSecurity* (Vol. 2023). DOI: 10.58496/MJCS/2023/012

Von Arx, T., Tran, M., & Vanbever, L. (2023). Revelio: A Network-Level Privacy Attack in the Lightning Network. *Proceedings - 8th IEEE European Symposium on Security and Privacy, Euro S and P 2023*, 942–957. DOI: 10.1109/EuroSP57164.2023.00060

Westermeier, C. (2024). The digital euro: A materialization of (in)security. *Review of International Political Economy*, *31*(5), 1569–1592. Advance online publication. DOI: 10.1080/09692290.2024.2345613

World Bank. (2021). *Trends in the global cost of sending $200 in remittances*. World Bank. https://remittanceprices.worldbank.org/sites/default/files/rpw_main_report_and_annex_q221.pdf

Worldbank. (2024, June 26). *Remittances Slowed in 2023, Expected to Grow Faster in 2024*. https://www.worldbank.org/en/news/press-release/2024/06/26/remittances-slowed-in-2023-expected-to-grow-faster-in-2024

Yulian, C., Irwanto, R., Angtonius, F., Young Siahaan, P., Ng, J., Thamrin Nomor, J., Sei Rengas, K. I., Medan Area, K., & Utara, S. (2024). Analisis Implementasi Teknologi Blockchain dalam Meningkatkan Transparansi dan Kepercayaan di Sektor Keuangan di Indonesia. *Jurnal Sistem Informasi Dan Ilmu Komputer, 2*(4), 09–31. DOI: 10.59581/jusiik-widyakarya.v2i4.4158

Chapter 3
Revolutionizing Financial Insights:
Generative AI for Smarter Decisions

Arshi Shah
https://orcid.org/0009-0008-5489-8748
Mukesh Patel School of Technology Managemet and Engineering, NMIMS, India

Yashodhan Karulkar
https://orcid.org/0000-0002-0991-3565
Mukesh Patel School of Technology Management and Engineering, NMIMS, India

Rishab Naik
https://orcid.org/0009-0000-9588-546X
Mukesh Patel School of Technology Management and Engineering, NMIMS, India

ABSTRACT

This chapter explains the transformative potential of Generative AI in enhancing financial decision-making and blockchain technology in reshaping FinTech processes. It examines Generative AI's applications in predictive analytics, portfolio optimization, and fraud detection, emphasizing its ability to improve accuracy, efficiency, and risk mitigation. The foundational concepts of blockchain, including decentralization, transparency, and smart contracts, are analysed in the context of regulatory compliance and operational automation. The chapter also addresses critical data privacy and cybersecurity issues in AI-driven FinTech, offering strategies for safeguarding sensitive information. Future trends such as decentralized finance (DeFi), robo-advisors, and blockchain-based lending are discussed, highlighting

DOI: 10.4018/979-8-3373-1250-7.ch003

opportunities for collaboration between AI and blockchain to create innovative ecosystems. Supported by case studies, this chapter provides actionable insights for leveraging these technologies to drive innovation and build a secure, efficient, and inclusive financial landscape.

I. INTRODUCTION OVERVIEW OF GENERATIVE AI IN FINANCE

Tom Freston is credited with saying "Innovation is taking two things that exist and putting them together in a new way" (Feuerriegel. S. et.al, 2023). Generative AI is revolutionizing the financial industry by offering advanced tools to analyse large volumes of data, predict market trends, and optimize decision-making processes. Generative Artificial Intelligence (AI), such as ChatGPT by OpenAI, has transformed the business world, with benefits including improved accessibility, efficiency, and cost reduction (Cheng. B. et.al, 2023). From personalized financial advice to sophisticated fraud detection, GenAI is rapidly becoming an indispensable tool in the financial industry (Barde and Kulkarni, 2023). By leveraging machine learning models and neural networks, Generative AI aids in predictive analytics, portfolio management, and real-time risk assessment (David Krause, 2024). Its capacity to adapt to changing market conditions and deliver actionable insights transforms the operations of financial institutions, resulting in improved productivity, precision, and expense reduction.

The Need for Innovation in Financial Decision-making: In recent years, finance has become increasingly interactive with new-generation data science and artificial intelligence (Arslanian.H, et.al, 2019). In particular, Financial Technology (or Fintech) (Nicoletti B. et.al, 2017) is at the epicenter of synthesizing, innovating, and transforming financial services, the economy, technology, media, communication, and society. DSAI (Data Science and Artificial intelligence) is the keystone enabler of the new generation of FinTech (Dunis. C. L. et.al, 2020). The complexity of modern financial markets demands innovative solutions to tackle challenges such as fraud prevention, regulatory compliance, and data security. Traditional decision-making frameworks often fail to meet the pace of global economic shifts and technological advancements. Innovation in this area (Ryll. L. et.al, 2020) is critical to addressing these gaps, improving the accuracy of forecasts, and ensuring resilience against market volatility. Technologies like Generative AI and blockchain are bridging these gaps, empowering financial institutions to make informed, agile, and secure decisions.

Intersection of AI and Blockchain in FinTech: The convergence of Generative AI and Blockchain Technology is reshaping the FinTech landscape. While Generative AI excels at analyzing data and generating insights, blockchain provides a secure, decentralized infrastructure for storing and managing information. In essence, Blockchain has the key characteristics of decentralization, distribution, and consistency, which can effectively improve the application of FinTech (X. Wu. et.al (2021) and E. Bellini. et.al. (2020). Together, they offer unique solutions to challenges such as fraud detection, data privacy, and regulatory compliance (Song et al., 2022). For instance, AI can identify anomalies in transactions, while blockchain ensures transparency and immutability, creating a seamless and secure financial ecosystem. This intersection not only enhances operational efficiency but also opens the door to innovative applications like decentralized finance (DeFi) and AI-powered smart contracts.

II. LITERATURE REVIEW

The incorporation of Generative Artificial Intelligence (AI) into real-time financial market analysis marks a significant advancement, offering both substantial opportunities and considerable challenges (Dahal, 2023). Generative AI (GenAI) represents a new frontier of innovation, offering unique tools for businesses, including those in the financial sector. It enables improved decision-making, creativity, and operational efficiency. This technology can extract valuable information from diverse data sources and utilize reliable outcomes derived from statistical analysis to identify new patterns (Bai et al. 2024 and McKinsey 2023). In an era where applications like ChatGPT are breaking records for the fastest-growing user base by showcasing unprecedented expertise across various domains (Hu. K, 2023), the concept of "Generative Artificial Intelligence" (GAI) is emerging as a disruptor in the digital landscape (Dwivedi et al., 2023; Teubner et al., 2023 & Wessel et al., 2023). With the ability to generate high-quality, contextually relevant content that is almost indistinguishable from human-created work, discussions are beginning to explore whether this new technology shows early signs of artificial general intelligence (Bubeck et al., 2023 & Tiku. N, 2022).

Regardless of the debates surrounding AI's sentience, recent advancements in machine learning (ML) and deep learning (DL) have broadened the scope of traditional, data-driven AI tasks—such as predictions, classifications, or recommendations—to include the generation of unique, realistic, and creative content. The collaboration between humans and intelligent systems in both business and everyday life has been significantly shaped by the adoption of AI, particularly in areas like process optimization and decision-making (Brynjolfsson & McAfee, 2016; Burström et al., 2021; Moussawi et al., 2021). Generative AI's transformative potential extends seamlessly into the financial sector, where its ability to analyze vast datasets and generate predictive insights addresses the complexities of modern markets. By integrating advanced machine learning techniques (Banh. L. et.al, 2023), financial institutions can improve their decision-making processes, optimize portfolios, and reduce risks with remarkable accuracy. The versatility of generative AI, spanning applications from predictive analytics to fraud detection, establishes it as a key driver of innovation, linking traditional finance practices with emerging technological demands. When combined with the secure and transparent infrastructure provided by blockchain, these technologies are transforming trust, efficiency, and operational excellence within financial services.

Driven by the rapid advancement of information technology over the past few decades, blockchain has emerged as one of the most impactful innovations, first proposed by Nakamoto in 2008 (Nakamoto. S, 2018). A blockchain essentially functions as a distributed transaction ledger that is shared among miners within the blockchain network, operating according to consensus protocols (Liu. Z. et.al, 2021). This replicated ledger, maintained by multiple miners, and the consensus protocols ensure that all transactions become immutable once recorded in the ledger, giving the blockchain its unique characteristics of immutability and decentralization (Liu. Z. et.al, 2021). Among the various sectors where blockchain can be applied, the financial technology (FinTech) industry stands out as a particularly promising area for exploration (Du et al., 2019). Blockchain technology has paved the way for novel applications in data sharing, data security, and trading.

Blockchain technology has captivated significant industry investments, due to its decentralization, safety, and traceability nature. Blockchain technology shows potential applications for financial services. Transaction fees, which traditional financial institutions profit from, could be reduced or eliminated by blockchain technology (Chang. E, 2019). Consumers must rely on banks or outside organizations to conduct transactions involving money transfers. The implementation of blockchain technology may avoid intermediaries like banks, thereby removing fees and other expenses related to these services (Jessel. B. et.al, 2018). Financial service providers find blockchain technology useful to enhance authenticity, security, and risk management (Javaid. M. et.al, 2022).

Privacy and security aspects of FinTech companies have been studied across various contexts. A survey of the German population (Stewart & Jürjens, 2018) regarding FinTech adoption identified data security, consumer trust, and user interface design as the most important determinants. A theoretical construct was provided (Gai et al., 2017) for future FinTech industry development to ensure sound security mechanisms based on observed security and privacy concerns and their solutions. Studies (Teigland et al., 2018) highlight the specificity and significance of the data processed by FinTech companies. This data can be categorized into two types: content data, which is directly related to identifying a person, and metadata, which users typically leave unintentionally but is valuable for the data processor (Patil, 2025).

The use of artificial intelligence (AI) is transforming financial risk assessment and fraud detection by enhancing both efficiency and accuracy. Additionally, AI excels at identifying unusual patterns that may signify fraudulent activity. AI algorithms can continuously monitor transactions and flag those that deviate from norms or match fraud patterns (Patil. D, 2024). Banking and payment fraud losses have decreased due to this scrutiny, ensuring consumer and financial institution security.

Over the past decade, the application of AI in fraud detection has advanced significantly. Initially, fraudulent transactions were identified using rule-based systems that flagged deviations from established patterns (Adewale Daniel Sontan & Segun Victor Samuel, 2024). However, these systems were limited by their inability to adapt to new types of fraud and their reliance on static rules (Roshanaei et al., 2024). With the rise of machine learning, AI systems have become more dynamic, learning from historical data and detecting anomalies without human involvement (Xu et al., 2024). This shift has allowed financial institutions to stay ahead of fraudsters, who continuously develop new methods to evade detection (Bello et al., 2023). Additionally, AI-based systems can manage large volumes of data, making them ideal for identifying intricate fraud schemes involving multiple transactions and parties (Mohanty & Mishra, 2023).

GenAI (Generative Artificial Intelligence) (Adhikari et al., 2024) and blockchain are transforming finance by enhancing decision-making, fraud detection, and operational efficiency. GenAI leverages vast datasets for predictive analytics and risk management, while blockchain ensures transparency, security, and trust with its decentralized, immutable ledger. Together, they reduce costs, optimize processes, and address modern financial challenges, seamlessly blending innovation with traditional practices.

III. GENERATIVE AI: ENHANCING FINANCIAL DECISION-MAKING PROCESSES

Generative AI constructs a comprehensive deep learning framework that significantly enhances financial data management efficiency (Ding et al., 2024). Generative Artificial Intelligence or GenAI is reshaping financial decision-making by introducing sophisticated capabilities in market analytics, predictive analytics, portfolio optimization, and risk assessment (Singh, 2025). Its ability to process vast amounts of data, detect patterns, and generate actionable insights provides financial professionals with tools to operate with higher accuracy, efficiency, and cost-effectiveness (Karulkar et al., 2024). Below is an in-dept exploration of how GenAI enhances various aspects of financial decision-making (Matta, 2020).

- **AI Tools for Market Analysis and Forecasting**

1. **Sentiment Analysis with Precision:** Leveraging Natural Language Processing (NLP), GenAI interprets the tone and sentiment of various textual sources. For instance, it analyses financial news, corporate earnings reports, and public sentiment on social media to assess market mood. This predictive capability enables traders and investors to make informed decisions based on evolving public and market opinions.
2. **Advanced Data Processing:** Generative AI excels in processing vast and complex datasets, including structured data such as historical stock prices and economic indicators, as well as unstructured data like new articles and social media content. This capability ensures a nuanced and holistic understanding of market dynamics, empowering financial professionals with well–rounded insights.
3. **Real–Time Market Intelligence:** The ability of GenAI to process and analyze data in real-time is transformative for market monitoring. It identifies emerging trends, detects anomalies, and delivers early warnings about potential disruptions. For example, AI systems can monitor macroeconomic developments or central bank announcements and predict their implications for asset prices.
4. **Scenario Simulation and Predictive Modelling:** Generative AI performs advanced scenario modelling, simulating diverse economic conditions to forecast market responses. By analyzing variables such as interest rate changes, geopolitical tensions, or fiscal policy adjustments, it equips decision-makers with contingency plans and strategic foresight.
5. **Customizable Analytical Frameworks:** GenAI-powered platforms, such as those integrated into Bloomberg Terminal or similar analytics tools, provide users with tailored dashboards. These interfaces highlight critical market trends, key performance indicators (KPIs), and actionable insights, allowing financial professionals to navigate data-heavy environments efficiently.
6. **Integration of Alternative Data Sources:** Beyond traditional datasets, GenAI incorporates alternative data sources, such as satellite imagery, climate patterns, or consumer behaviour trends. This integration offers a competitive edge by unveiling hidden correlations and market opportunities that conventional methods might miss.

Figure 1. Advantages of Using Generative AI Tools in Market Analysis and Forecasting (Source: Created by Authors)

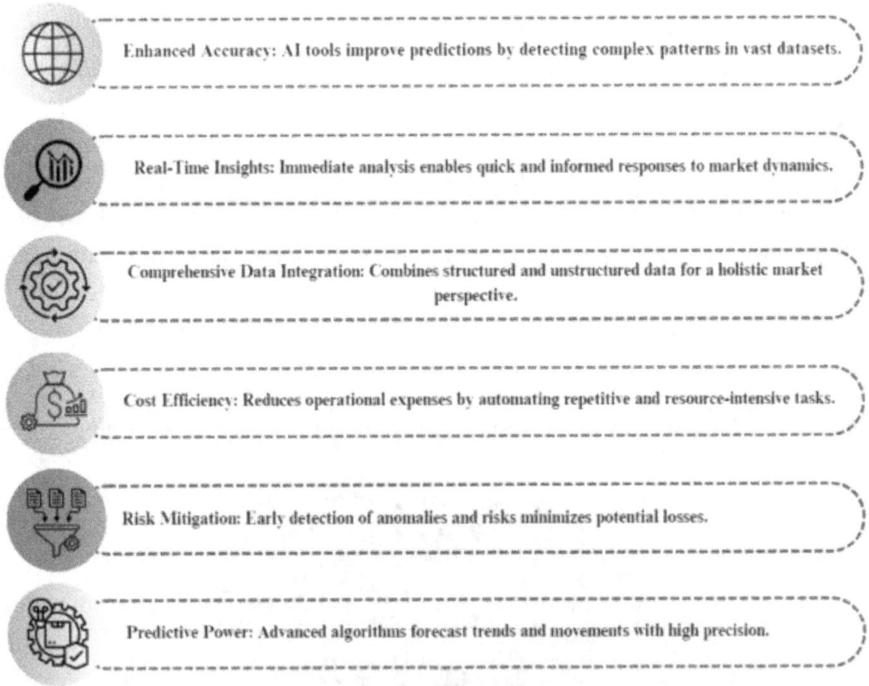

- **Applications of GenAI in Predictive Analytics, Portfolio Optimization and Risk Assessment.**

Generative AI has emerged as a transformative force in financial decision-making, offering unparalleled capabilities in predictive analytics, portfolio optimization, and risk assessment.

In **Predictive Analytics,** GenAI harnesses vast datasets and advanced algorithms to anticipate market trends, asset price fluctuations, and macroeconomic indicators with remarkable precision. By analyzing historical data and integrating alternative sources such as news, social media sentiment, and economic reports, it delivers actionable insights that empower investors and organizations to stay ahead of market shifts.

In **Portfolio Optimization,** GenAI elevates investment strategies by creating models that balance risk and return dynamically. It evaluates market conditions, asset correlations, and investor objectives to recommend optimal asset allocations. Furthermore, it facilitates real-time portfolio rebalancing, adapting swiftly to volatile market conditions while aligning with strategic goals such as ESG (Environmental, Social, and Governance) compliance. By integrating AI-driven insights, investors can achieve robust portfolio performance with reduced risks.

Risk Assessment, a cornerstone of financial stability, is significantly enhanced by GenAI's capabilities. It identifies and quantifies risks across various dimensions, including credit, market, and operational domains. For instance, AI models analyze borrower profiles and market conditions to predict credit default probabilities, allowing lenders to mitigate potential losses. In addition, GenAI excels in detecting fraudulent activities by identifying anomalies in transaction patterns, offering robust defenses against financial crimes . Its ability to perform scenario simulations and stress testing enables institutions to prepare for adverse events, such as economic downturns or geopolitical crises, safeguarding financial resilience.

Figure 2. Application of Generative Artificial Intelligence in Finance (Source: Created by Authors)

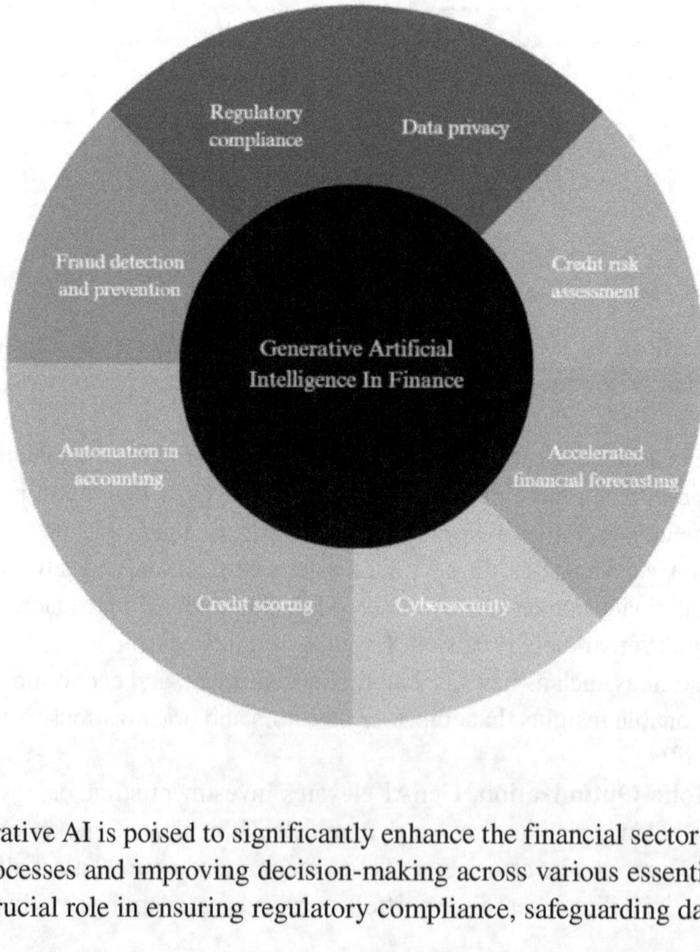

Generative AI is poised to significantly enhance the financial sector by streamlining processes and improving decision-making across various essential areas. It plays a crucial role in ensuring regulatory compliance, safeguarding data privacy, and refining credit risk assessments through sophisticated predictive models. By accelerating financial forecasting, AI empowers organizations to make faster and more informed strategic decisions. Additionally, it bolsters cybersecurity efforts by proactively identifying and addressing potential threats. Moreover, Generative AI transforms credit scoring with more equitable evaluations and automates repetitive accounting tasks, leading to greater efficiency. It also strengthens fraud detection processes by recognizing anomalies in real time.

Case Study 1: Leading Asset Management Firm Delivered Elevated User Experience With a Generative AI Chatbot With the Help of Damco Solutions

Damco Solutions is a reliable technology partner for companies around the globe, enabling them to utilize IT as a strategic asset. With a strong foundation in technology expertise, exceptional execution capabilities, and a steadfast commitment to customer needs, Damco has fostered success across various technologies and industries. Damco assisted a prominent asset management firm in enhancing user experience through a Generative AI Chatbot (Damco Solutions, 2024). The client is a leading asset management and investment organization that shares industry news and research reports pertinent to financial services professionals on its platform. Subscriber organizations use this platform to keep informed about the latest market trends, regulations, and innovations. Clients can access published reports, extract insights, and provide feedback on the research reports. Conventional keyword-based search systems resulted in a suboptimal user experience, leading to frequent customer support requests. The client's platform acted as a comprehensive knowledge base that provided user insights into financial services via research reports and industry news.

Nevertheless, the existing keyword-focused search system could not contextualize search queries within the financial industry's semantics. This shortcoming made it challenging to deliver accurate, relevant, and timely responses to user inquiries. Modern users demand immediate, context-rich, and precise replies. To remain relevant and competitive, the client sought full ownership of their data and aimed to convert the extensive amount of information on the platform into a user-friendly format. The client's challenges were tackled through the deployment of a Generative AI chatbot that utilized Large Language Model (LLM) technology. The solution offered accurate, contextually relevant replies that significantly improved the user experience. A comprehensive evaluation of the client's needs was carried out through discussions with stakeholders to clarify objectives. An advanced AI-enabled chatbot utilizing LLM technology was implemented to provide accurate, human-like responses to user inquiries. This notably increased user engagement while reducing the need for manual intervention. Research reports, internal documents, and external data sources were merged into a structured knowledge base. This allowed the chatbot to retrieve relevant insights and provide precise answers. The chatbot's infrastructure was designed for scalability and adaptability, ensuring compliance with the client's data protection standards while future-proofing their investment. A thorough analysis of various LLM providers was undertaken, examining aspects such as accuracy, response speed, and integration capabilities. This analysis facilitated the selection of the best technology to align with client requirements. The AI chatbot was refined for accuracy, fluency, and contextual relevance. Sample inquiries were tested to confirm its performance and ensure the consistent delivery of expected outcomes.

The solution produced transformative results for the client. The generative AI chatbot significantly enhanced user interactions on the platform. Accurate and contextually relevant responses saved users time and attracted additional customers. After implementation, the client's team received training on utilizing LLMs and AI to align with long-term digital strategies. A thorough roadmap was provided for integrating the solution with the existing infrastructure. The scalable chatbot ensured the client stayed ahead in the technological landscape, with the capability to adapt to future demands. An examination of various LLM providers equipped the client with insights for future technology investments, enabling informed decision-making.

IV. BLOCKCHAIN BASICS: UNDERSTANDING THE CORE CONCEPTS AND MECHANISMS

Blockchain is a decentralized digital ledger technology that records transactions across a distributed network of computers (*Ken's Korner Newsletter Blockchains*, 2024). Each transaction is grouped into a "block" containing data, a timestamp, and a unique cryptographic hash. These blocks are linked in chronological order, forming an unalterable chain. This structure ensures data integrity, transparency, and security without requiring a central authority. Blockchain's decentralized nature eliminates reliance on intermediaries, making it a revolutionary tool in various industries. Blockchains serve as a revolutionary technology capable of ensuring data integrity across various sectors by making the information stored within them immutable, meaning it cannot be altered or tampered with once entered into the system (Hayes, 2024). This immutability arises from the fundamental structure of a blockchain, where each block of data is linked to the previous one in a chronological chain. As a result, any attempt to modify a block would disrupt the entire chain, thereby providing a high level of security.

The implication of this is significant: the only trust required is at the moment when a user or automated program inputs data into the blockchain. This drastically minimizes the necessity for trusted third parties, such as auditors or intermediaries, who traditionally verify and validate transactions or records. By reducing reliance on these parties, organizations can lower operational costs and mitigate the risk of human error, which is prevalent in more conventional systems. Since the introduction of Bitcoin in 2009, there has been a remarkable proliferation of blockchain applications beyond cryptocurrency (Hayes, 2024). The landscape has expanded to include decentralized finance (DeFi) platforms, which allow users to engage in financial services like lending and trading without the need for traditional financial institutions. Other innovations include non-fungible tokens (NFTs), which provide unique digital proof of ownership for assets, and smart contracts that automatically execute agreements when pre-defined conditions are met. Together, these advancements illustrate the versatility and transformative potential of blockchain technology across various industries.

How Does a Blockchain Work?

A blockchain functions as a database where information is recorded and stored, similar to traditional spreadsheets or databases. However, the key distinction lies in how the data is structured and accessed. Unlike conventional databases, a blockchain operates using scripts which are basically programs that handle tasks like entering, accessing, saving, and storing information. Additionally, blockchain is decentralized, meaning multiple identical copies of the data are maintained across numerous machines. For the data to be valid, these copies must match. For example, the Bitcoin blockchain aggregates transaction data into a 4MB file called a block (through block sizes vary across blockchain). Once a block is filled, its data is processed through a cryptographic hash function, generating a hexadecimal identifier known as the block header hash. This hash is embedded in the header of the subsequent block, linking the two and forming a continuous chain of blocks-hence the term "Blockchain".

The Transaction Process: The transaction process varies depending on the blockchain. On Bitcoin's blockchain, when you initiate a transaction through a cryptocurrency wallet—a tool that interfaces with the blockchain—a sequence of actions unfolds. The transaction is sent to a memory pool, where it is queued until selected by a miner. Miners group transactions into a block, and once the block is full, it is closed, and the mining process begins. Each node in the network proposes its own blocks, selecting different transactions. Miners then work to solve a computational challenge called the "difficulty target," using a field in the block header called the nonce (a value used only once).

The nonce is incremented with each attempt, generating a new hash each time. If the resulting hash does not meet the target criteria, the nonce is adjusted, and the process repeats. After approximately 4.5 billion attempts (a process completed in less than a second), miners increment an additional value called the extra nonce and continue. This iterative process continues until a valid hash is found, at which point the miner secures the reward, and the block is closed. However, a transaction is not fully confirmed until additional blocks (usually five) are validated on the network. On Bitcoin's blockchain, this process takes around an hour, as each block takes roughly 10 minutes to be confirmed. Not all blockchains follow Bitcoin's model. For instance, Ethereum uses a more energy-efficient process. It selects one validator at random from users who have staked ether to validate the block. Once validated, the block is confirmed by the network, enabling faster and less resource-intensive transactions.

The Transaction Process

The transaction process can vary widely depending on the specific blockchain being utilized. To illustrate this, let's explore the workings of Bitcoin's blockchain. When you initiate a transaction using a cryptocurrency wallet—a digital tool that allows you to interact with the blockchain—a fascinating sequence of events begins to unfold. Initially, your transaction is dispatched into a memory pool. Here, it resides in a queue, waiting for a miner to select it from the myriads of pending transactions. Miners play a crucial role in blockchain networks, as they gather these transactions into a block, which is a data structure that contains a collection of transaction records. When a block reaches its maximum capacity, it gets sealed, marking the commencement of the mining process.

Each node within the network has the autonomy to propose its blocks, often choosing different transactions to include based on various criteria. The heart of the mining process lies in overcoming a complex cryptographic challenge known as the "difficulty target." To tackle this challenge, miners utilize a field in the block header called the nonce, which serves as a variable that can change to produce a new hash. As miners attempt to find a suitable hash, they increment the nonce with each trial, resulting in a new hash output each time. If the produced hash does not meet the predetermined criteria, the nonce is adjusted, and this trial-and-error process begins anew. After approximately 4.5 billion attempts—an astounding feat that is completed in less than a second—miners will then increment a secondary value known as the extra nonce and persist in their efforts to discover a valid hash. This iterative endeavor continues until a miner successfully identifies a hash that meets the target criteria. Once achieved, the miner earns a reward, and the block is closed, contributing to the integrity of the blockchain.

It's essential to understand that a transaction is not considered fully confirmed until several additional blocks, typically five, have been validated on the network. On Bitcoin's blockchain, this entire process usually takes about an hour, as each new block is confirmed roughly every ten minutes. In contrast to Bitcoin, other blockchains implement different mechanisms for transaction validation. For instance, Ethereum utilizes a more energy-efficient system. Instead of mining, it selects one validator at random from a pool of users who have staked their ether. This validator is responsible for confirming the block. Once this validation is completed, the block is accepted by the network, allowing transactions to be processed more quickly and with significantly lower resource consumption. This approach reflects the ongoing evolution in blockchain technology, with various networks adopting innovative methods to enhance efficiency and sustainability.

Key Components of Blockchain Technology

1. **Blocks:** Blocks are the essential components of a blockchain. Each block acts as a container that stores data, usually transaction records, along with a distinct identifier known as a hash. A block also contains the hash of the preceding block, linking it to its predecessor and creating a continuous, unchangeable chain of blocks. This ordered arrangement guarantees the integrity of the blockchain, as altering any block's data would modify its hash and disrupt the entire sequence. Blocks have a specific size limit, determining how many transactions they can encompass. Once a block reaches its capacity, it is closed and added to the chain, contributing to the immutable ledger. This design ensures the security and transparency of data, making blockchain a reliable system for recording transactions.

Figure 5. Definition of a Block (Source: Made by authors)

2. **Hash Functions:** Hash functions are cryptographic algorithms that convert input data into a fixed-length string of characters, known as the hash. These functions are deterministic, meaning that the same input will always yield the same hash, but even the slightest alteration in the input leads to a completely different output. This characteristic makes hash functions crucial for ensuring data integrity in blockchain systems, as any manipulation of the data is quickly apparent. Furthermore, hash functions are one-way, indicating that it is computationally impractical to derive the original input from the hash. This guarantees the security and confidentiality of the data stored in the blockchain. Hash functions not only protect data but also serve a vital purpose in connecting blocks together, since the hash of one block is incorporated into the next, forming a strong and tamper-proof chain.

Figure 6. Hashing Algorithm (Source: Created by Authors)

3. **Consensus Mechanisms:** Consensus mechanisms are protocols that ensure all participants in a blockchain network agree on the validity of transactions and the current state of the ledger. These protocols remove the necessity for a central authority, thereby making the blockchain decentralized and trustless. One of the most widely used consensus methods is Proof of Work (PoW), where miners engage in solving complex mathematical problems to verify and append blocks to the chain. This approach is secure and resource-intensive, as it discourages malicious actors. Another widely used mechanism is Proof of Stake (PoS), which chooses validators based on the quantity of cryptocurrency they have staked, presenting a more energy-efficient option compared to PoW. Additional mechanisms, such as Delegated Proof of Stake (DPoS) and Practical Byzantine Fault Tolerance (PBFT), are developed to enhance scalability and

minimize energy consumption. These consensus mechanisms are essential for ensuring the security, transparency, and reliability of blockchain networks.

4. **Distributed Ledgers:** A distributed ledger is a decentralized database that is duplicated and shared among all members of a blockchain network. In contrast to traditional centralized databases, where one entity governs data storage and access, distributed ledgers guarantee that every participant possesses an identical version of the data. This decentralized framework boosts transparency, as all members can verify transactions independently. It also enhances resilience and fault tolerance, since the system does not depend on a single point of failure. Any effort to modify the data would necessitate changes to every copy of the ledger, rendering fraud or tampering nearly impossible. Distributed ledgers are fundamental to blockchain technology, facilitating secure, transparent, and decentralized data management across various sectors.

Figure 7. Distributed Ledgers (Source: Created by Authors)

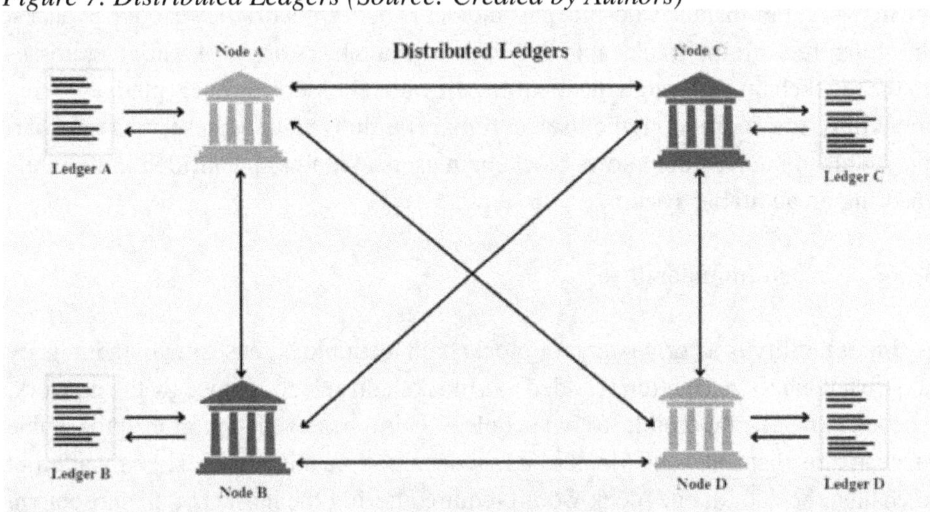

Key Features of Blockchain Technology

1. Blockchain Decentralization:

Blockchain technology ensures data is distributed across multiple network nodes—computers or devices running blockchain software—located in different regions. This decentralized structure creates redundancy and enhances data integrity. When an attempt is made to alter information on one node, the other nodes compare block hashes and reject the modification, ensuring no single node can manipulate the data.

This distribution, combined with cryptographic proof of work, ensures that blockchain records, such as transaction histories, are immutable. While public blockchains typically store transaction data, private blockchains can represent diverse information, including legal contracts, state identifications, or company inventories, through tokens generated by hashing algorithms.

2. Blockchain Transparency:

The decentralized nature of blockchains, such as Bitcoin's, enables unparalleled transparency. Transactions are accessible to anyone, either by downloading the blockchain or using blockchain explorers, which provide real-time insights into ongoing transactions. Each node in the network maintains its copy of the blockchain, updated as new blocks are verified and added.

This feature allows users to trace assets like Bitcoin through their journey across the network. For instance, despite past incidents of cryptocurrency exchange hacks, the stolen funds remain traceable due to the immutable storage of wallet addresses on the blockchain. Although the identities of wallet holders are encrypted, ensuring anonymity, the transactions themselves remain publicly visible, preserving transparency. This unique feature allows blockchain users to maintain confidentiality while ensuring an auditable system.

3. Blockchain Immutability:

Immutability is a cornerstone of blockchain technology, ensuring data integrity and trust. Once a transaction is added to a blockchain and confirmed by the network, it becomes nearly impossible to alter or delete. This is achieved through cryptographic mechanisms that link each block to its predecessor via a unique hash. Any attempt to change the data in one block would require altering the hashes of all subsequent blocks, which is computationally infeasible in a decentralized network.

This immutable nature is particularly valuable in applications requiring tamper-proof records, such as financial transactions, supply chain tracking, and legal documentation. It ensures that the blockchain serves as a reliable, permanent ledger, fostering trust among participants and eliminating the need for intermediaries to verify data authenticity. Immutability, therefore, is not just a technical feature but a critical enabler of the blockchain's broader applications in transparent and secure record-keeping.

Case Study 2: IBM Blockchain's Role in Empowering We.trade in Trade Finance

IBM Blockchain is a robust and innovative platform designed to enable businesses across industries to harness the power of distributed ledger technology (DLT). By leveraging blockchain's inherent attributes of transparency, immutability, and security, IBM Blockchain provides solutions that transform traditional processes into efficient, scalable, and trustworthy systems. Built on the Hyperledger Fabric framework, IBM Blockchain is well-suited for enterprise-grade applications, offering flexibility, high availability, and global reach. Its capabilities have been applied to a variety of use cases, including trade finance, supply chain management, and digital identity verification, making it a trusted partner for businesses seeking to modernize and secure their operations. One such example is IBM's collaboration with We.trade, where blockchain technology revolutionized the trade finance industry.

We.trade encountered several challenges in its mission to modernize international trade and finance. The traditional trade finance model operated by banks had stagnated, leaving it inefficient and inaccessible to many businesses. Approximately 70% of companies lacked access to trade finance services due to high costs and complexity, limiting their ability to participate in global trade. Counterparty risks, such as payment defaults, discouraged businesses from engaging in international transactions. The manual, paperwork-heavy processes and the legal, financial, and cultural risks associated with cross-border trade created additional barriers. Furthermore, banks were unable to scale their trade finance platforms effectively, constraining their ability to serve a wider customer base and support global trade.

To tackle these challenges, We.trade partnered with IBM to create a blockchain-powered digital trade platform. Utilizing the IBM Blockchain Platform and the Hyperledger Fabric framework, We.trade's solution transformed the trade finance landscape. Distributed Ledger Technology (DLT) ensured that all stakeholders had access to a shared, tamper-proof record of transactions, providing transparency and eliminating the need for intermediaries. Changes in trade agreements were immediately reflected across the network, reducing the risk of disputes. Smart contracts automated transaction execution, ensuring that payments were processed only when predefined conditions were met, thus minimizing counterparty risks. The integration of KYC and anti-money laundering (AML) compliance standards further enhanced trust and security on the platform. IBM Cloud's scalable and flexible infrastructure provided the global reach necessary to accommodate We.trade's ambitions, ensuring high availability and seamless functionality.

The implementation of the We.trade platform was a collaborative effort between IBM Blockchain Services and We.trade. IBM conducted a functional analysis of We.trade's requirements and established a minimum viable network to test the platform's capabilities. Following successful testing, the platform was scaled to a commercial-grade system. IBM's strong relationships with key players in the banking sector facilitated seamless integration, fostering trust in the platform among stakeholders. IBM's expertise and agile approach allowed We.trade to accelerate its development timeline, bringing the platform to market 9–12 months ahead of schedule, outpacing competitors in the space.

The collaboration between We.trade and IBM Blockchain transformed trade finance by democratizing access for businesses of all sizes. Automation reduced delays in cross-border transactions, while smart contracts ensured secure, timely payments and compliance mechanisms mitigated counterparty risks.

V. REGULATORY COMPLIANCE IN FINTECH: THE ROLE OF SMART CONTRACTS

The Use of Smart Contracts to Automate and Enforce Regulatory Requirements

Smart contracts have emerged as a transformative tool within the FinTech industry, especially in navigating the challenges of regulatory compliance. These self-executing agreements, with their terms embedded in code, provide a secure and automated method for enforcing regulatory obligations. By incorporating rules and compliance criteria directly into the blockchain, smart contracts guarantee that financial transactions comply with applicable legal and regulatory standards without the need for manual oversight.

For example, smart contracts can autonomously verify and authenticate Know Your Customer (KYC) and Anti-Money Laundering (AML) procedures before a transaction is executed. By requiring all participants to satisfy predetermined compliance checks, such as identity confirmation or transaction limits, the smart contract ensures that only authorized and compliant transactions take place. This minimizes the risk of human mistakes, fraud, or intentional non-compliance while offering real-time visibility to regulators. Moreover, smart contracts can track ongoing compliance responsibilities. They can issue automated alerts or impose penalties if a party does not meet specific regulatory deadlines or violates contractual stipulations. Tax submissions, transaction reports, and compliance with international trade laws can also be made more efficient, with the smart contract automatically creating and forwarding necessary documents to the appropriate authorities.

The unchangeable nature of blockchain significantly boosts the reliability of compliance records that smart contracts maintain. Given that each transaction or compliance action is permanently logged and timestamped on the blockchain, it establishes an auditable trail that regulators can review at any time. This enhances trust and lowers the costs and complexities involved in traditional auditing processes. By automating and enforcing regulatory requirements, smart contracts enhance efficiency and enable FinTech firms to expand their operations internationally while complying with various regulatory frameworks. This development is particularly vital in an industry marked by swift technological progress and changing legal regulations.

Automating Compliance: KYC, AML, and GDPR Adherence

1. KYC (Know Your Customer) Compliance Automation:

The automation of KYC processes through blockchain and smart contracts enhances both the efficiency and dependability of identity verification in the financial sector. Historically, the KYC process involves various manual steps, such as gathering and verifying customer documentation, which can be lengthy and susceptible to mistakes. Smart contracts simplify this procedure by safely storing customer information on the blockchain, facilitating instant verification of identity and credentials. For instance, once a customer's KYC details are confirmed, they can be utilized across numerous institutions without necessitating duplication, thereby minimizing redundancy. The immutable nature of blockchain guarantees that all KYC records remain tamper-proof and easily auditable, offering regulators a clear compliance trail.

2. AML (Anti-Money Laundering) Compliance Automation:

Smart contracts are vital in automating AML processes by monitoring and identifying suspicious activities in real-time. Financial institutions can set up smart contracts to detect transactions that surpass certain limits or involve high-risk jurisdictions, triggering automatic alerts and halting such transactions until additional examination is performed. This forward-thinking approach reduces the risks of money laundering by ensuring adherence to global regulatory standards. Moreover, blockchain technology enables institutions to securely exchange transaction data and alerts with regulatory bodies or other relevant parties, promoting collaboration and alleviating the burden of manual reporting.

Figure 9. The 3 Stages of Money Laundering (Source: Created by Authors)

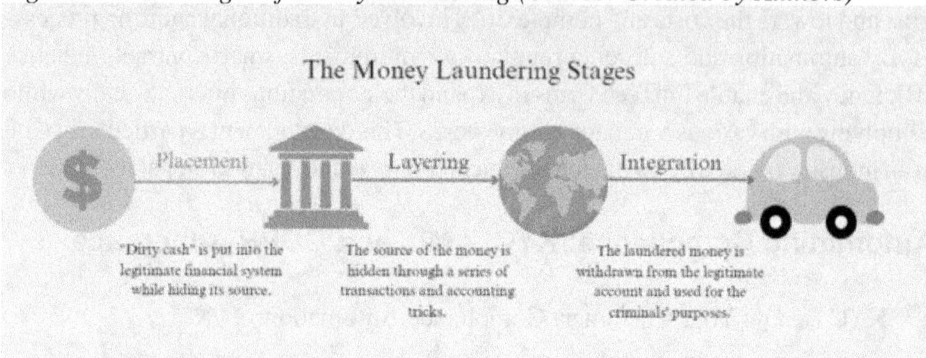

Note: - *Money laundering involves three stages: placement, where illicit funds are introduced into the financial system; layering, where complex transactions are used to obscure the money's origins; and integration, where the "cleaned" money is reintroduced as legitimate. These stages aim to disguise illegal proceeds and make them appear lawful. Detecting and disrupting these processes is critical to combating financial crimes.*

3. GDPR (General Data Protection Regulation) Adherence:

In relation to GDPR, which highlights the protection of personal data, smart contracts aid in enforcing privacy and data governance standards. Blockchain allows for the secure storage and sharing of personal information while keeping records of customer consent. For example, smart contracts can be programmed to verify if appropriate consent has been secured prior to processing a user's data. Additionally, features such as data encryption and access controls can be incorporated into smart contracts, ensuring compliance with GDPR's "right to be forgotten" by permitting customers to request the deletion of their data while preserving the integrity of the blockchain record.

Figure 10. What is GDPR? (Source: Created by Authors)

4. Benefits of Automating Compliance:

The automation of compliance with KYC, AML, and GDPR regulations presents numerous advantages for financial institutions and their customers. To begin with, it decreases operational expenses by removing the necessity for manual processing and repetitive tasks. Furthermore, it improves the accuracy and speed of compliance checks, allowing institutions to onboard customers more swiftly and effectively. Additionally, automation reduces human errors and the risk of non-compliance, consequently lowering the chances of regulatory penalties and harm to reputation. Lastly, it promotes transparency and trust among stakeholders by creating an immutable, auditable record of compliance activities. By utilizing smart contracts and blockchain technology, financial institutions can guarantee smooth adherence to intricate regulatory requirements while enhancing operational efficiency and customer experience.

Case Study 3: Smart Contracts in Insurance – Deloitte and Digital Asset Alliance

The insurance industry is undergoing a significant transformation driven by the need for greater efficiency, transparency, and trust. Smart contracts, enabled by blockchain technology, are emerging as a powerful tool for automating claims processing, reducing fraud, and streamlining operations. Deloitte, a leader in technology and advisory services, has partnered with Digital Asset, an innovative provider of blockchain technology, to transform how businesses, including insurers, adopt smart contract solutions. This case study illustrates how this collaboration is helping organizations leverage the potential of blockchain and smart contracts to drive innovation in insurance. The insurance sector faces several challenges, such as lengthy claims processing, high operational costs, and vulnerability to fraud. Traditional methods heavily rely on manual intervention, resulting in inefficiencies and potential errors. Furthermore, ensuring compliance with regulatory frameworks and maintaining trust between insurers and policyholders are ongoing obstacles. The industry needed a solution that could automate processes, enhance transparency, and operate within the regulatory landscape.

Deloitte and Digital Asset formed a strategic partnership to tackle these challenges by utilizing blockchain and smart contracts. Their collaboration combines Deloitte's expertise in technology and advisory services with Digital Asset's advanced blockchain platform to provide comprehensive solutions. Together, they assist organizations in developing, building, and deploying blockchain-based systems that streamline operations and automate complex processes. Smart contracts—self-executing agreements encoded on a blockchain—offer tremendous potential in the insurance sector. Deloitte and Digital Asset empower insurers to automate key processes, such as policy issuance, premium collection, and claims settlement. For instance, a smart contract can automatically verify a claim against policy terms, validate supporting documents, and trigger payment once all conditions are met, all without human intervention. This automation reduces administrative costs, minimizes errors, and accelerates claims processing. Additionally, the immutability and transparency of blockchain ensure that all parties have access to the same information, reducing disputes and fostering trust between insurers and policyholders.

The partnership provides a comprehensive blockchain journey for insurers, starting with strategy formulation and design, moving to prototype development, and finally to production deployment. Deloitte's advisory expertise helps organizations align their blockchain initiatives with business objectives and regulatory requirements, while Digital Asset's technology platform ensures smooth implementation. By addressing common barriers to entry, such as technical complexity and compliance concerns, the partnership empowers insurers to adopt blockchain with confidence. The collaboration between Deloitte and Digital Asset offers substantial benefits to the insurance industry. By automating repetitive tasks through smart contracts, insurers can achieve significant cost savings and improve operational efficiency. The transparency provided by blockchain's distributed ledger allows all stakeholders real-time access to accurate data, reducing disputes and fostering trust. The immutability of blockchain records significantly minimizes the risk of fraud, as tampering with data becomes nearly impossible. Furthermore, the solutions are designed to meet regulatory standards, helping insurers comply with legal requirements seamlessly.

Most importantly, faster claims processing and increased transparency lead to an enhanced customer experience, boosting policyholder satisfaction and loyalty.

VI. FRAUD DETECTION AND RISK MITIGATION USING GENERATIVE AI

Generative AI Models for Anomaly Detection, Pattern Recognition, and Predictive Analytics in Fraud Prevention

Generative AI is revolutionizing the landscape of fraud detection and risk mitigation through its advanced capabilities in anomaly detection, pattern recognition, and predictive analytics. By harnessing these sophisticated technologies, organizations can significantly enhance their ability to identify fraudulent activities, which often lurk beneath the surface of vast amounts of data.

One of the key strengths of generative AI lies in its ability to uncover unusual patterns embedded within large datasets. This function is paramount for effectively detecting fraudulent activities, as it allows for real-time monitoring of transactions, user behaviors, and system operations. By meticulously analyzing historical data, generative AI establishes a comprehensive baseline of what constitutes normal behavior in various contexts, such as financial transactions or user interactions. When anomalies arise—like a substantially large transaction that deviates from the norm, an access attempt from an unexpected geographical location, or a sudden change in usage patterns—these deviations trigger immediate alerts, signaling potential fraud.

Furthermore, the technology's prowess in pattern recognition empowers it to scrutinize complex relationships between numerous variables, unveiling hidden connections that may point to illicit behavior. For instance, generative AI can effectively track and identify organized fraud rings by detecting synchronized activities that span across multiple accounts or transactions. This sophisticated capability is especially vital in sectors such as banking, e-commerce, and insurance, where fraudsters are adept at exploiting systemic weaknesses to perpetrate their schemes.

In addition to these functions, generative AI significantly bolsters predictive analytics by leveraging historical data to forecast future risks. For example, it can evaluate the likelihood of credit card fraud by analyzing a user's transaction history or assess potential insurance fraud risks by examining claims data. These insights empower organizations to implement proactive strategies, such as flagging high-risk transactions for manual inspection or enforcing more stringent authentication measures.

By integrating anomaly detection, pattern recognition, and predictive analytics, generative AI not only aids in the prevention of fraud but also minimizes the occurrence of false positives. This ensures that organizational operations remain smooth and efficient while safeguarding against financial losses and reputational damage. Ultimately, generative AI serves as a formidable ally in the ongoing battle against fraud, providing the tools necessary to navigate an increasingly complex and risk-laden environment.

Integration with Existing Risk Management Frameworks

Generative AI can integrate seamlessly with existing risk management frameworks, enhancing their efficiency and adaptability in detecting and mitigating fraud. Most organizations already have established processes and tools to manage risks, including rule-based systems, statistical models, and manual review mechanisms. Generative AI complements these traditional approaches by introducing advanced capabilities that improve both accuracy and scalability. For example, it can work alongside existing systems to dynamically refine rules and thresholds based on real-time data and evolving fraud patterns. This ensures that the framework remains effective even as new risks emerge. Furthermore, integrating generative AI enables better data utilization within risk management frameworks. Traditional systems often struggle to process large volumes of unstructured data, such as text, images, or audio, which may contain critical indicators of fraud. In contrast, generative AI models can analyze and extract valuable insights from this data, feeding such information into the framework to enhance decision-making. For instance, in the insurance sector, generative AI can analyze images of damages in claims to detect inconsistencies. In banking, it can process transaction logs to identify anomalies that may indicate fraudulent activities.

Another significant benefit of integration is improved collaboration across various components of a risk management framework. Generative AI serves as a unifying layer, connecting multiple data sources, analytics tools, and reporting systems. By providing a centralized platform for fraud detection and risk assessment, it ensures that all stakeholders—such as compliance teams, fraud investigators, and management—have access to consistent and actionable insights. Additionally, generative AI automates routine tasks, such as flagging suspicious activities or generating risk reports, allowing human experts to focus on more complex and strategic aspects of risk management.

Moreover, generative AI supports regulatory compliance by ensuring that the risk management framework adheres to industry standards and legal requirements. It can help organizations comply with regulations like GDPR, AML (Anti-Money

Laundering), and KYC (Know Your Customer) by automating the identification and monitoring of high-risk activities.

Case Study: JP Morgan Chase Enables Fraud Detection in Digital Banking

Financial fraud has become a critical concern for banking institutions globally. The rise in digital banking and online transactions has led to an exponential increase in the risk of fraudulent activities. Traditional fraud detection methods have struggled to keep up with the sophistication of modern schemes. This case study examines how JP Morgan Chase leveraged Artificial Intelligence (AI) to revolutionize fraud detection, focusing on the technology employed, its impact on financial security, and the challenges faced during implementation.

Digital banking has grown rapidly, and along with it, financial fraud has become more prevalent. Cybercriminals exploit vulnerabilities in banking systems using advanced techniques, resulting in significant financial losses. The global cost of financial fraud reaches trillions annually, underscoring the urgency of implementing more robust fraud detection systems. Conventional fraud detection methods are often rule-based and rely heavily on manual monitoring, which is reactive rather than proactive. These systems frequently generate false positives, inconveniencing customers and creating inefficiencies for banks.

JP Morgan Chase developed an advanced AI model powered by machine learning algorithms to enhance its fraud detection capabilities. This system analyzes vast amounts of transaction data in real time, identifying patterns and anomalies indicative of fraudulent behavior. The AI model continuously monitors customer transactions and creates behavioral profiles based on historical data. Deviations from established patterns trigger alerts for further investigation. Over time, the model learns and adapts to improve its accuracy and reduce false positives. The AI model was seamlessly integrated into JP Morgan Chase's existing fraud detection framework. Alerts generated by the system allowed for immediate action, ensuring that the AI complemented ongoing operations without disruption. The AI system significantly enhanced JP Morgan Chase's fraud detection efficiency. By leveraging real-time data and predictive analytics, the bank improved detection accuracy by 25% and reduced false positives by 50%.

The reduction in false positives and the proactive detection of fraud bolstered customer trust. Clients experienced fewer disruptions and felt reassured knowing their bank utilized state-of-the-art technology to safeguard their accounts. The advanced fraud detection capabilities translated into substantial cost savings for the bank, minimizing operational inefficiencies and financial losses due to fraud. Ensuring data privacy and security was a significant challenge during implementation. JP

Morgan Chase adopted advanced encryption techniques and complied with stringent data protection regulations to safeguard sensitive customer information. Some employees initially expressed skepticism about relying on AI for fraud detection.

To address this, the bank conducted training sessions and showcased the AI model's effectiveness through pilot programs and real-world results. Given the evolving nature of financial fraud, the AI system requires constant updates. JP Morgan Chase invests in ongoing research and development to refine its AI capabilities and stay ahead of emerging threats. The success of this initiative has inspired JP Morgan Chase to explore additional AI applications, including risk management, personalized financial planning, and customer service automation.

VII. DATA PRIVACY AND SECURITY IN FINTECH APPLICATIONS

Strategies to Enhance Data Protection Using Encryption, Differential Privacy, and Federated Learning

In the rapidly evolving FinTech sector, protecting user data is crucial for maintaining trust and complying with stringent regulatory requirements. To combat the rising risks of data breaches, organizations are implementing advanced strategies such as encryption, differential privacy, and federated learning to enhance data protection while ensuring secure and efficient operations. Encryption is a fundamental aspect of data security. It transforms sensitive information into unreadable formats except for those who possess the correct decryption keys. End-to-end encryption (E2EE) ensures that data is encrypted at the point of origin and can only be decrypted by the intended recipient, making it immune to interception during transmission. Advanced encryption standards (AES) and public-key infrastructure (PKI) are also commonly used in FinTech applications to secure data both during storage and transit, particularly during financial transactions or authentication processes. Tokenization is another method often employed alongside encryption; it replaces sensitive data, such as credit card numbers, with unique identifiers or tokens that are meaningless to unauthorized users.

Differential privacy provides an innovative approach to balancing data utility with privacy. By introducing statistically controlled noise to datasets, organizations can analyze and share aggregate data insights without compromising the privacy of individual users. This technique is particularly valuable in FinTech for conducting market analyses, developing personalized financial services, and sharing insights with partners while complying with privacy regulations like GDPR and CCPA. For instance, a FinTech company can leverage differential privacy to analyze customer spending patterns without revealing specific details of any individual's transactions.

Federated learning represents a significant advancement in privacy-preserving machine learning. While traditional AI models require centralized data collection, which can lead to vulnerabilities and regulatory issues, federated learning decentralizes the training process by keeping data localized on user devices or within secure institutional systems. Instead of sharing raw data, the system exchanges encrypted model updates that are then aggregated to improve the central model. This approach ensures that sensitive information remains private while enabling robust predictive analytics, fraud detection, and credit scoring. For example, a FinTech app can utilize federated learning to enhance its risk assessment algorithms across multiple institutions without violating customer privacy. By integrating encryption, differential privacy, and federated learning, FinTech companies can establish a multi-layered security framework that protects sensitive financial data from theft or misuse. These strategies not only safeguard user privacy but also help organizations comply with global data protection regulations. Furthermore, they build customer trust by demonstrating a commitment to privacy and security, which is essential for growth in a highly competitive and sensitive industry.

Challenges in Maintaining Data Privacy

1. **Cyberattacks (Malware, Ransomware, and DDoS):** Cyberattacks, such as malware, ransomware, and Distributed Denial of Service (DDoS) attacks, are significant threats to data privacy in FinTech. Malware can infiltrate systems and steal sensitive financial data or login credentials, while ransomware can lock down critical systems and demand payment for access. DDoS attacks overwhelm systems, causing disruptions that attackers may exploit to access secure data. These challenges demand robust defenses, including firewalls, intrusion detection systems, and regular updates.

Figure 13. How does a Ransomware attack work? (Source: Created by Authors)

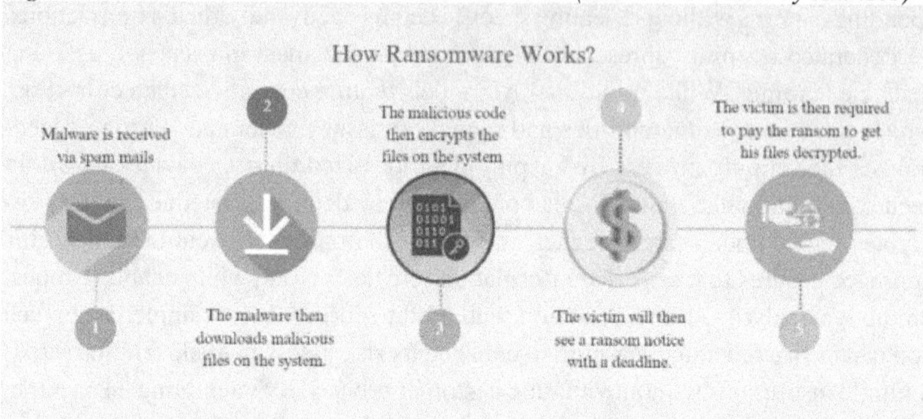

2. **Social Engineering Attacks:** Social engineering attacks, including phishing and spear-phishing, exploit human vulnerabilities by tricking individuals into revealing sensitive information. Cybercriminals impersonate trusted entities through fraudulent emails, messages, or websites to steal customer data such as credit card numbers or account credentials. In FinTech, where online interactions are frequent, such attacks can lead to large-scale breaches, making employee awareness and customer education critical.
3. **Vulnerabilities in Third-Party Integrations:** FinTech platforms often rely on third-party APIs and services for functionality, which can introduce vulnerabilities. If these integrations are not adequately secured, attackers can exploit weak points to access sensitive data or systems. Regular audits, stringent vendor assessments, and secure API management are essential to mitigate this challenge.
4. **Advanced Persistent Threats (APTs):** Advanced Persistent Threats are prolonged, targeted cyberattacks that allow hackers to remain undetected while gathering sensitive data over time. APTs are particularly concerning for FinTech platforms that handle high volumes of transactions and store valuable customer information. Addressing APTs requires continuous monitoring, advanced threat detection tools, and incident response plans.
5. **Insider Threats:** Insider threats, whether intentional or accidental, are another challenge to data privacy. Employees or contractors with access to sensitive systems may misuse their privileges or inadvertently expose data due to weak internal controls or misconfigured systems. Implementing role-based access controls, rigorous background checks, and comprehensive employee training programs can help reduce insider risks.

Figure 14. Insider Threat Risks (Source: Created by Authors)

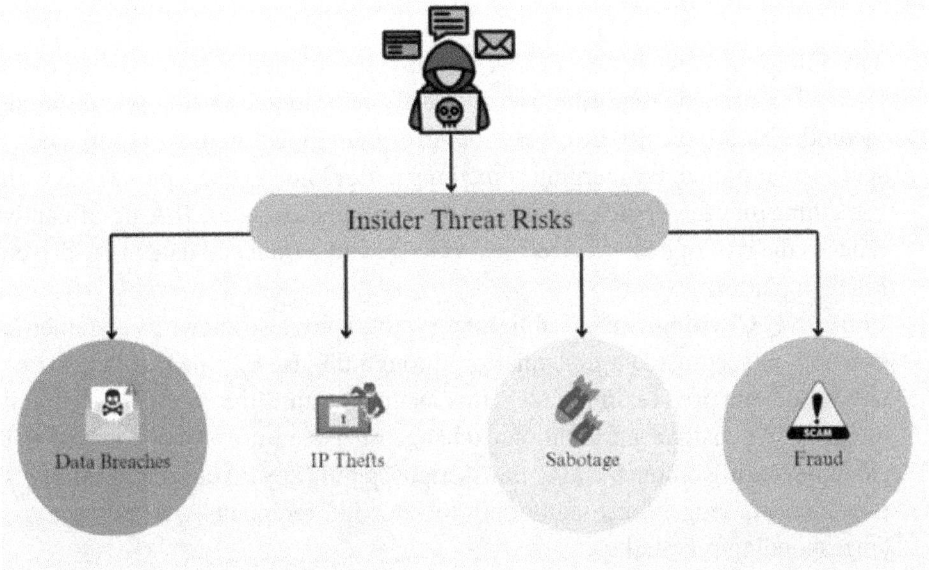

6. **Mobile Banking and Digital Wallet Risks:** The widespread use of mobile banking and digital wallets poses additional challenges. Mobile applications are susceptible to malware, fake apps, and the use of unsecured networks. Customers accessing accounts on public Wi-Fi or outdated devices increase the risk of data interception. To counter these risks, FinTech companies need to ensure secure app development, enforce encryption, and educate users on safe practices.
7. **Regulatory Non-Compliance:** Operating in multiple jurisdictions with varying privacy and security standards adds complexity to maintaining compliance. Regulations like GDPR, CCPA, and PCI-DSS mandate stringent data protection measures, and failure to comply can result in significant fines and reputational damage. To address this, FinTech companies must implement adaptive compliance frameworks and maintain updated knowledge of global regulatory requirements.

By addressing these challenges with a combination of technology, employee training, and regulatory adherence, FinTech companies can build robust systems that protect data privacy and maintain customer trust in the digital financial ecosystem.

Cybersecurity Methods to Ensure Data Privacy in AI-Driven FinTech Solutions

1. **Two-Factor Authentication (2FA):** Two-factor authentication adds an extra layer of security by requiring users to verify their identity using two different methods. This typically involves a password combined with a one-time code sent to their phone. By merging something a user knows (like a password) with something they have (such as a phone) or are (biometric data), 2FA significantly reduces the risk of unauthorized access to sensitive financial data in AI-driven FinTech platforms.
2. **Public Key Cryptography:** Public key cryptography, also known as asymmetric encryption, secures data transmission through the use of a pair of keys—one public and one private. In FinTech, this method ensures the confidentiality and integrity of sensitive information exchanged between users and systems. For example, during online banking transactions, public key cryptography encrypts user data, making it accessible only to intended recipients who possess the corresponding private key.

Figure 15. How does public key cryptography work? (Source: Created by Authors)

3. **Encryption:** Encryption is a fundamental aspect of data privacy in FinTech. It transforms sensitive information, such as account details and transaction histories, into unreadable formats that can only be accessed with decryption keys. Advanced encryption algorithms like AES (Advanced Encryption Standard)

and RSA are commonly employed to secure data both in storage and during transmission, protecting it from interception or unauthorized access.

4. **Biometrics:** Biometric authentication methods—including fingerprint scans, facial recognition, and iris scans—offer strong security for FinTech applications. Unlike passwords, biometric data is unique to each user and cannot be easily replicated or stolen. Many AI-driven FinTech platforms incorporate biometric authentication to secure user accounts and facilitate secure access.
5. **Secure APIs:** Application Programming Interfaces (APIs) allow data sharing between FinTech platforms and third-party services. Securing these APIs through authentication mechanisms, encryption, and rate limiting helps prevent unauthorized access and data breaches. This is critically important, as AI-driven FinTech solutions often rely heavily on data integration and sharing.
6. **Firewalls and Intrusion Detection Systems:** Firewalls and Intrusion Detection Systems (IDS) serve as the first line of defense against cyberattacks. Firewalls monitor and control incoming and outgoing network traffic, while IDS detect and alert for suspicious activities. These tools are vital for preventing malware, phishing attempts, and unauthorized data access in AI-powered FinTech systems.
7. **Blockchain Technology:** Blockchain technology enhances data privacy by offering decentralized and tamper-proof storage for financial transactions. In AI-driven FinTech solutions, blockchain helps secure data integrity and transparency while maintaining privacy through cryptographic hashing and consensus mechanisms.
8. **Data Masking:** Data masking involves hiding sensitive information, such as account numbers or personally identifiable information (PII), with dummy data. This technique safeguards data during testing or development while ensuring that real data remains secure. AI-driven systems can utilize masked data for training without compromising user privacy.
9. **Regular Security Audits and Vulnerability Assessments:** Conducting periodic security audits and vulnerability assessments helps identify potential weaknesses in AI-driven FinTech solutions. These proactive measures allow organizations to address security gaps, ensuring compliance with privacy regulations and protection against evolving cyber threats.
10. **Multi-Layered Security Architecture:** Establishing a multi-layered security architecture involves the integration of a diverse range of cybersecurity measures, including advanced encryption techniques, robust authentication protocols, and proactive threat detection systems. This comprehensive strategy forms a resilient shield against potential cyber threats, ensuring that user data remains secure and protected. In the dynamic landscape of FinTech platforms, such an approach not only fortifies user trust but also safeguards the integrity of AI-driven processes,

thereby creating a thorough defense mechanism that addresses vulnerabilities on multiple fronts.

Case Studies of AI-Driven Biometrics: Transforming Security and User Experience in FinTech

Onfido, a UK-based identity verification company, leverages AI-powered biometric solutions to enhance security and streamline onboarding processes for FinTech companies (Olanrewaju et al., 2024; Joachim et al., 2023). By integrating facial recognition and document verification technologies, Onfido has significantly reduced identity fraud, ensuring the authenticity of customers (Ibeh et al., 2024). Additionally, this approach has improved user experiences, offering a smooth and efficient onboarding process that leads to higher customer satisfaction. Onfido's case underscores the critical role of AI-driven biometrics in strengthening security measures and optimizing user experiences within the FinTech sector. Furthermore, it emphasizes the necessity of continuous innovation to address emerging security challenges effectively.

BioCatch, an Israeli cybersecurity firm, specializes in behavioral biometrics and has implemented AI-driven technology to detect and prevent fraud in real time for FinTech companies. By analyzing user behavior, BioCatch's solution reduces fraud while providing a seamless authentication process that requires minimal user effort. This frictionless experience enhances user satisfaction and security simultaneously. The case of BioCatch illustrates the efficacy of AI-driven biometrics in real-time fraud detection and highlights the importance of continuously monitoring user behavior to identify anomalies and mitigate potential threats (Oseremi Onesi-Ozigagun et al., 2024).

Jumio, a US-based provider of identity verification and authentication solutions, employs AI-powered facial recognition and identity verification technologies to enhance security and compliance for FinTech companies. Jumio's biometric solutions have effectively reduced fraud while ensuring adherence to regulatory requirements. Additionally, the fast and secure verification process has improved user experiences for its clients. Jumio's case exemplifies how AI-driven biometrics can enhance security, streamline compliance, and optimize user verification processes (Ibeh et al., 2024). It also highlights the importance of collaborating with trusted providers for successful solution implementation.

BehavioSec, a Swedish company specializing in behavioral biometrics, has implemented AI-driven technology to analyze user behavior patterns for authentication and fraud detection in FinTech applications. By focusing on subtle behavioral cues, BehavioSec's solution has significantly reduced fraud rates and enhanced security for its clients. The real-time analysis of user behavior ensures that fraudulent activities are detected and prevented promptly, bolstering the overall security framework of FinTech companies. BehavioSec's case demonstrates the value of AI-driven biometrics in fraud detection and emphasizes the need for continuous refinement of AI algorithms to counter emerging fraud techniques effectively.

These case studies highlight the transformative impact of AI-driven biometrics in the FinTech industry. Companies like Onfido, BioCatch, Jumio, and BehavioSec demonstrate the potential of innovative biometric solutions to enhance security, improve user experiences, and ensure compliance with regulatory standards. The continuous evolution of AI technologies and their integration into FinTech applications remains essential to address growing security challenges and maintain customer trust.

VIII. FUTURE TRENDS: THE EVOLVING LANDSCAPE OF FINTECH WITH GENERATIVE AI AND BLOCKCHAIN

The combination of Generative AI and blockchain technologies is transforming the FinTech sector, providing groundbreaking solutions that redefine financial services. These advancements and opportunities lead to a more efficient, secure, and inclusive financial system. Below are the primary areas where this collaboration is making a significant impact. Generative AI and blockchain are driving substantial innovations in FinTech, especially in Decentralized Finance (DeFi), robo-advisors, and lending solutions based on blockchain technology.

Decentralized Finance (DeFi): DeFi has become a key element of blockchain applications within FinTech. By utilizing the decentralized framework of blockchain, DeFi removes intermediaries, allowing for direct peer-to-peer transactions. Generative AI amplifies this ecosystem by providing predictive analytics, risk assessment, and fraud detection. AI algorithms can evaluate on-chain data in real-time, enhancing transparency, increasing liquidity, and optimizing the functionality of smart contracts. Together, AI and blockchain enable DeFi platforms to grow while mitigating risks, making financial services available to underserved communities.

Robo-Advisors: Generative AI is revolutionizing robo-advisors by allowing them to offer highly personalized financial guidance. With the capability to model various market scenarios and forecast results, AI produces customized investment strategies for users. When paired with blockchain technology, these robo-advisors deliver unmatched transparency and security. For instance, blockchain guarantees unalterable records of transactions, while AI-driven robo-advisors continually adjust to user preferences and market dynamics, providing accurate and secure financial advice.

Figure 16. Who are Robo-Advisors? (Source: Created by Authors)

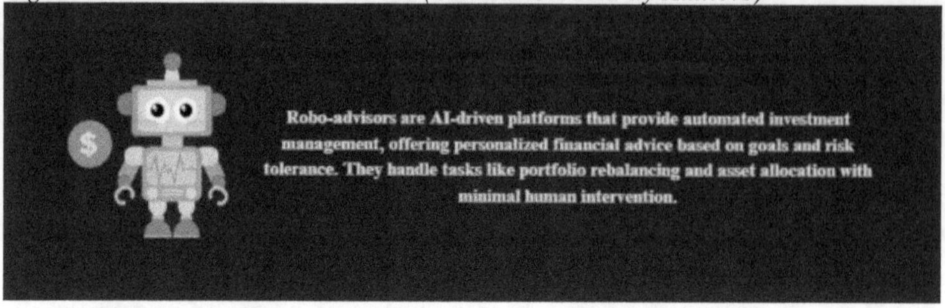

Blockchain-Based Lending: Lending platforms that use blockchain are quickly gaining popularity, offering quicker loan approvals and lower costs compared to traditional banking methods. Generative AI enhances these platforms by assessing creditworthiness through non-traditional data sources like social media, employment records, or spending habits. This broadens access to credit for people who may have limited financial backgrounds. Smart contracts streamline the lending process by ensuring prompt repayments and reducing defaults. Together, Generative AI and blockchain form a strong lending ecosystem that is efficient, inclusive, and transparent.

Opportunities: Enhanced Collaboration Between Generative AI and Blockchain for Seamless Ecosystems

The merging of Generative AI and blockchain unveils new opportunities for cultivating interconnected financial ecosystems. This partnership tackles current challenges and reveals unexploited potential within the FinTech industry.

Improved Security and Fraud Prevention: The combination of Generative AI's anomaly detection capabilities and the immutability of blockchain strengthens security measures in FinTech. AI recognizes unusual patterns in real-time, whereas blockchain guarantees that fraudulent actions cannot alter past transactions. This dual-layered protection fosters trust among users and financial institutions.

Smart Contract Optimization: Generative AI improves the efficiency of blockchain-based smart contracts by automating their creation and validation processes. AI algorithms can anticipate potential weaknesses in contract code, guaranteeing that smart contracts are solid and free from errors. This minimizes operational risks and simplifies the implementation of automated agreements.

Interoperability and Ecosystem Development: Often, blockchain networks function in isolation, which can hinder their effectiveness. Generative AI can promote interoperability by creating algorithms that allow seamless communication between various blockchain networks. This establishes a cohesive ecosystem where assets, data, and services can flow smoothly, promoting collaboration across different sectors.

Personalized Financial Ecosystems: The combination of Generative AI facilitates the customization of financial ecosystems to better suit individual user requirements. AI leverages blockchain-stored information to craft tailored financial solutions, such as specialized insurance policies, investment portfolios, and loan products. This user-focused strategy enhances customer satisfaction and encourages long-term loyalty.

Tokenization of Assets: The process of tokenization, which involves converting physical or intangible assets into digital tokens on the blockchain, is being transformed by Generative AI. AI-driven valuation methods ensure fair pricing for tokenized assets, while blockchain guarantees secure and transparent ownership. This creates opportunities for fractional ownership, enabling more individuals to invest in high-value assets like real estate or art.

Figure 17. Which Assets can be Tokenised? (Source: Created by Authors)

IX. CONCLUSION

The advancements in generative AI and blockchain technology are revolutionizing financial insights, allowing for smarter, data-driven decisions throughout the industry. This chapter highlights how these technologies transform key areas such as fraud detection, regulatory compliance, data privacy, and customer experience.

Generative AI enables financial institutions to identify complex patterns and effectively predict risks, while blockchain ensures transparency, security, and efficiency in operations. The convergence of these technologies—exemplified by innovations in decentralized finance (DeFi), robo-advisors, and blockchain-based lending—is paving the way for a smarter and more adaptive financial ecosystem.

Looking to the future, the synergy between generative AI and blockchain holds great potential to redefine how financial services are delivered. These innovations can create seamless ecosystems and serve underserved markets, driving inclusivity, automation, and trust. The focus must now shift towards continuous innovation, ethical adoption, and the establishment of robust frameworks to navigate evolving challenges and opportunities.

As stakeholders in the industry, it is essential to proactively embrace this transformation. Regulators, financial institutions, and technology providers must collaborate to ensure secure, ethical, and scalable implementations. By doing so, the financial sector can harness the full potential of generative AI and blockchain, setting the stage for a future characterized by smarter decision-making, greater efficiency, and equitable financial opportunities for all.

X. REVIEW AND RESEARCH QUESTIONS

1. What are the core advantages of using Generative AI in financial decision-making?
2. How does blockchain enhance transparency and security in financial transactions?
3. In what ways can smart contracts revolutionize regulatory compliance in FinTech?
4. How does Decentralized Finance (DeFi) disrupt traditional banking systems?
5. What are the key challenges in maintaining data privacy in AI-driven FinTech applications?
6. How can Generative AI aid in detecting and preventing financial fraud?
7. What role do robo-advisors play in providing personalized financial planning?
8. How can collaboration between Generative AI and blockchain create seamless FinTech ecosystems?
9. What future trends can be anticipated in the integration of AI and blockchain in finance?
10. How can financial institutions address ethical challenges associated with implementing AI and blockchain technologies?

REFERENCES

Adhikari, P., Hamal, P., & Baidoo, F.Jnr. (2024). Artificial Intelligence in fraud detection: Revolutionizing financial security. *International Journal of Science and Research Archive, 13*(1), 1457–1472. DOI: 10.30574/ijsra.2024.13.1.1860

Adhikari, P., Hamal, P., & Jnr, F. B. (2024). Artificial Intelligence in fraud detection: Revolutionizing financial security. *International Journal of Science and Research Archive, 13*(1), 1457–1472. DOI: 10.30574/ijsra.2024.13.1.1860

Aggarwal, S., & Kumar, N. (2021, January 1). *Chapter Ten - Core components of blockchain Introduction to blockchain.* (S. Aggarwal, N. Kumar, & P. Raj, Eds.). ScienceDirect;Elsevier.https://www.sciencedirect.com/science/article/abs/pii/S0065245820300656

Ahmed, H., & Shafi, I. (2023). A Systematic Survey of AI Models in Financial Market Forecasting for Profitability Analysis. *IEEE Access : Practical Innovations, Open Solutions, 11*, 125359–125380. DOI: 10.1109/ACCESS.2023.3330156

Arslanian, H., & Fischer, F. (2019). *The Future of Finance.* Springer International Publishing., DOI: 10.1007/978-3-030-14533-0

ARTIFICIAL INTELLIGENCE (AI) AND BUSINESS. (2024). https://books.google.co.in/books

Case Study Asset Management Firm Supercharged User Experience with a Gen AI Chatbot. (2024, January 30). Damco Solutions. https://www.damcogroup.com/client-success/asset-management-firm-delivered-elevated-user-experience-with-gen-ai

Bai, X., Zhuang, S., Xie, H., & Guo, L. (2024). Leveraging Generative Artificial Intelligence for Financial Market Trading Data Management and Prediction. https://doi.org/DOI: 10.20944/preprints202407.0084.v1

Banh, L., & Strobel, G. (2023). Generative artificial intelligence. *Electronic Markets, 33*(1), 63. Advance online publication. DOI: 10.1007/s12525-023-00680-1

Barde, K., & Parth Atul Kulkarni. (2023). Applications of Generative AI in Fintech. https://doi.org/DOI: 10.1145/3639856.3639893

Bello, O. A. Adebola Folorunso, Onwuchekwa, J., & Ejiofor, O. E. (2023). A Comprehensive Framework for Strengthening USA Financial Cybersecurity: Integrating Machine Learning and AI in Fraud Detection Systems. European Journal of Computer Science and Information Technology, 11(6). https://eajournals.org/ejcsit/vol11-issue-6-2023/a-comprehensive-framework-for-strengthening-usa-financial-cybersecurity-integrating-machine-learning-and-ai-in-fraud-detection-systems/

Blockchain-Based Distributed Trust and Reputation Management Systems. A Survey. (n.d.). Ieeexplore.ieee.org. https://ieeexplore.ieee.org/document/8970496

Bubeck, S., Chandrasekaran, V., Eldan, R., Gehrke, J., Horvitz, E., Kamar, E., Lee, P., Lee, Y. T., Li, Y., Lundberg, S., Nori, H., Palangi, H., Ribeiro, M. T., & Zhang, Y. (2023). Sparks of Artificial General Intelligence: Early experiments with GPT-4. ArXiv:2303.12712 [Cs]. https://arxiv.org/abs/2303.12712

Bubeck, S., Chandrasekaran, V., Eldan, R., Gehrke, J., Horvitz, E., Kamar, E., Lee, P., Lee, Y. T., Li, Y., Lundberg, S., Nori, H., Palangi, H., Ribeiro, M. T., & Zhang, Y. (2023). Sparks of Artificial General Intelligence: Early experiments with GPT-4. ArXiv:2303.12712 [Cs]. https://arxiv.org/abs/2303.12712

Burström, T., Parida, V., Lahti, T., & Wincent, J. (2021). AI-enabled business-model innovation and transformation in industrial ecosystems: A framework, model and outline for further research. *Journal of Business Research*, *127*, 85–95. DOI: 10.1016/j.jbusres.2021.01.016

Cao, L., Yang, Q., & Yu, P. S. (2021). Data science and AI in FinTech: An overview. *International Journal of Data Science and Analytics*, *12*(2), 81–99. DOI: 10.1007/s41060-021-00278-w

Chang, E., Luo, H. L., & Chen, Y. C. (2019). Blockchain-Enabled Trade Finance Innovation: A Potential Paradigm Shift on Using Letter of Credit. *Sustainability (Basel)*, *12*(1), 1–16. https://ideas.repec.org/a/gam/jsusta/v12y2019i1p188-d301819.html. DOI: 10.3390/su12010188

Chen, B., Wu, Z., & Zhao, R. (2023). Taylor and Francis. From fiction to fact: The growing role of generative AI in business and finance. *Journal of Chinese Economic and Business Studies*, *21*(4), 1–26. DOI: 10.1080/14765284.2023.2245279

Dahal, S. B. (2023). Utilizing Generative AI for Real-Time Financial Market Analysis Opportunities and Challenges. Advances in Intelligent Information Systems,8(4),1–11. https://questsquare.org/index.php/JOURNALAIIS/article/view/29

Ding, W., Tan, H., Zhou, H., Li, Z., & Fan, C. (2024). Immediate traffic flow monitoring and management based on multimodal data in cloud computing. *Applied and Computational Engineering*, *71*(1), 1–6. DOI: 10.54254/2755-2721/71/2024MA0052

Dorfleitner, G., Hornuf, L., & Kreppmeier, J. (2023). Promise not fulfilled: FinTech, data privacy, and the GDPR. *Electronic Markets*, *33*(1), 33. Advance online publication. DOI: 10.1007/s12525-023-00622-x

Du, W., Pan, S. L., Leidner, D. E., & Ying, W. (2019). Affordances, experimentation and actualization of FinTech: A blockchain implementation study. *The Journal of Strategic Information Systems*, *28*(1), 50–65. DOI: 10.1016/j.jsis.2018.10.002

Dunis, C. L., Middleton, P. W., Karathanasopolous, A., & Theofilatos, K. (Eds.). (2016). *Artificial Intelligence in Financial Markets*., DOI: 10.1057/978-1-137-48880-0

Dwivedi, Y. K., Kshetri, N., Hughes, L., Slade, E. L., Jeyaraj, A., Kar, A. K., Baabdullah, A. M., Koohang, A., Raghavan, V., Ahuja, M., Albanna, H., Albashrawi, M. A., Al-Busaidi, A. S., Balakrishnan, J., Barlette, Y., Basu, S., Bose, I., Brooks, L., Buhalis, D., & Carter, L. (2023). "So what if ChatGPT wrote it?" Multidisciplinary perspectives on opportunities, challenges and implications of generative conversational AI for research, practice and policy. International Journal of Information Management, 71(0268-4012), 102642. https://doi.org/DOI: 10.1016/j.ijinfomgt.2023.102642

Feuerriegel, S., Hartmann, J., Janiesch, C., & Zschech, P. (2023). Generative AI. *Business & Information Systems Engineering*, *66*(1), 111–126. DOI: 10.1007/s12599-023-00834-7

Future-Forward Blockchain Alliances. (2024). Deloitte United States. https://www2.deloitte.com/us/en/pages/about-deloitte/solutions/future-forward-blockchain-alliances.html

Gai, K., Qiu, M., Sun, X., & Zhao, H. (2017). Security and Privacy Issues: A Survey on FinTech. *Lecture Notes in Computer Science*, *10135*, 236–247. DOI: 10.1007/978-3-319-52015-5_24

Hayes, A. (2024, September 16). Blockchain Facts: What Is It, How It Works, and How It Can Be Used. Investopedia. https://www.investopedia.com/terms/b/blockchain.asp

Hu, K. (2023, February 2). ChatGPT sets record for fastest-growing user base. Reuters. https://www.reuters.com/technology/chatgpt-sets-record-fastest-growing-user-base-analyst-note-2023-02-01/

Ibeh, C. V., Asuzu, O. F., Olorunsogo, T., Elufioye, O. A., Nduubuisi, N. L., & Daraojimba, A. I. (2024). Business analytics and decision science: A review of techniques in strategic business decision making. *World Journal of Advanced Research and Reviews*, *21*(2), 1761–1769. DOI: 10.30574/wjarr.2024.21.2.0247

Javaid, M., Haleem, A., Singh, R. P., Suman, R., & Khan, S. (2022). *A review of Blockchain Technology applications for financial services. BenchCouncil Transactions on Benchmarks, Standards and Evaluations, 2(3), 100073*. Sciencedirect., DOI: 10.1016/j.tbench.2022.100073

Jessel, B., & DiCaprio, A. (2018). Can blockchain make trade finance more inclusive? *Journal of Financial Transformation*, *47*, 35–50. https://ideas.repec.org/a/ris/jofitr/1608.html

Joachim, N. (2023). Economic Impacts And Innovations In Materials Science: A Holistic Exploration Of Nanotechnology And Advanced Materials. *Engineering Science & Tecnology Journal*, *4*(3), 84–100. DOI: 10.51594/estj.v4i3.553

Karulkar, Y., Shah, A., & Naik, R. (2024). AI-Powered Business Evolution. *Advances in Business Information Systems and Analytics Book Series*, 39–72. https://doi.org/ DOI: 10.4018/979-8-3693-4187-2.ch003

Ken's Korner Newsletter Blockchains. (2024). Ken's Korner. https://myemail.constantcontact.com/Ken-s-Korner-Newsletter-Blockchains--.html?soid=1119929876329&aid=fm5enP1tKko

Krause, D. (2024). Generative AI in FinTech: Transforming Financial Activities through Advanced Technologies. https://doi.org/DOI: 10.2139/ssrn.4923224

Le, D., Kumar, R., Mishra, B. K., Khari, M., & Chatterjee, J. M. (Eds.). (2019). *Cyber Security in Parallel and Distributed Computing*. Wiley., DOI: 10.1002/9781119488330

Lee, D. K. C., Guan, C., Yu, Y., & Ding, Q. (2024). A Comprehensive Review of Generative AI in Finance. *FinTech*, *3*(3), 460–478. DOI: 10.3390/fintech3030025

Liu, Z., Qian, P., Wang, X., Zhuang, Y., Qiu, L., & Wang, X. (2021).. . *IEEE Transactions on Knowledge and Data Engineering*, *35*, 1296–1310.

Manu, M. R., & Namya Musthafa, B. (2020). *Balamurugan, & Chauhan, R*. Blockchain Components and Concept., DOI: 10.1201/9781003081487-2

Matta, P. (2020). Leveraging AI for Predictive Market Insights: Practical Applications and Implementation. *International Journal on Science and Technology (IJSAT) IJSAT20041131, 11*(4). https://www.ijsat.org/papers/2020/4/1131.pdf

McKinsey & Company. (2023, June 14). Economic potential of generative AI | McKinsey. https://www.mckinsey.com/capabilities/mckinsey-digital/our-insights/the-economic-potential-of-generative-ai-the-next-productivity-frontier

Mohanty, B., & Mishra, S. (2023). Role of Artificial Intelligence in Financial Fraud Detection. *Academy of Marketing Studies Journal, 27,* •••. https://www.abacademies.org/articles/role-of-artificial-intelligence-in-financial-fraud-detection.pdf

Moussawi, S., Koufaris, M., & Benbunan-Fich, R. (2020). How perceptions of intelligence and anthropomorphism affect adoption of personal intelligent agents. *Electronic Markets, 31*(2), 343–364. Advance online publication. DOI: 10.1007/s12525-020-00411-w

Nakamoto, S. (2008). Bitcoin: A Peer-to-Peer Electronic Cash System. 31611263538139.pdf

Namasudra, S., & Akkaya, K. (2023). Introduction to Blockchain Technology. *Studies in Big Data*, 1–28. https://doi.org/DOI: 10.1007/978-981-19-8730-4_1

Needhi, J. (2024, July 8). How AI Transformed Financial Fraud Detection: A Case Study of JP Morgan Chase. Medium; Medium. https://medium.com/@jeyadev_needhi/how-ai-transformed-financial-fraud-detection-a-case-study-of-jp-morgan-chase-f92bbb0707bb

Nicoletti, B. (2017). *The Future of FinTech*. Springer International Publishing., DOI: 10.1007/978-3-319-51415-4

Olanrewaju, A. (2024). Assessing the environmental health and safety risks of solar energy production. *World Journal of Biology Pharmacy and Health Sciences, 17*(2), 225–231. DOI: 10.30574/wjbphs.2024.17.2.0080

Oseremi Onesi-Ozigagun, Yinka James Ololade, Nsisong Louis Eyo-Udo, & Damilola Oluwaseun Ogundipe. (2024). AI-driven biometrics for secure fintech: Pioneering safety and trust. International Journal of Engineering Research Updates, 6(2), 001-012. https://doi.org/DOI: 10.53430/ijeru.2024.6.2.0023

Ooi, K. (2023). (Taylor and Francis)The Potential of Generative Artificial Intelligence Across Disciplines: Perspectives and Future Directions. *Journal of Computer Information Systems, 1*(1), 1–32. DOI: 10.1080/08874417.2023.2261010

Patil, D. (2024, November 8). Artificial intelligence in financial risk assessment and fraud detection: Opportunities and ethical concerns. https://www.researchgate.net/publication/385746635_Artificial_intelligence_in_financial_risk_assessment_and_fraud_detection_Opportunities_and_ethical_concerns

Patil, D. (2025). *Artificial Intelligence In Financial Risk Assessment And Fraud Detection: Opportunities And Ethical Concerns.* https://doi.org/DOI: 10.2139/ssrn.5057434

Rajasekaran, A. S., Azees, M., & Al-Turjman, F. (2022). A comprehensive survey on blockchain technology. *Sustainable Energy Technologies and Assessments, 52*, 102039. DOI: 10.1016/j.seta.2022.102039

Remolina, N. (2023). Generative AI in Finance: Risks and Potential Solutions. Social Science Research Network. https://doi.org/DOI: 10.2139/ssrn.4628235

Roshanaei, M., Khan, M. R., & Sylvester, N. N. (2024). Navigating AI Cybersecurity: Evolving Landscape and Challenges. *Journal of Intelligent Learning Systems and Applications, 16*(03), 155–174. DOI: 10.4236/jilsa.2024.163010

Ryll, L., Barton, M. E., Zhang, B. Z., McWaters, R. J., Schizas, E., Hao, R., Bear, K., Preziuso, M., Seger, E., Wardrop, R., Rau, P. R., Debata, P., Rowan, P., Adams, N., Gray, M., & Yerolemou, N. (2020, February 4). Transforming Paradigms: A Global AI in Financial Services Survey. Papers.*ssrn*.com. https://papers.ssrn.com/sol3/papers.cfm?abstract_id=3532038 DOI: 10.2139/ssrn.3532038

Singh, P. (2025, April 11). *AI and Financial Risk Management Revolutionizing Risk Assessment and Mitigation.* https://doi.org/DOI: 10.4018/979-8-3373-1200-2.ch019

Song, Y., Sun, C., Peng, Y., Zeng, Y., & Sun, B. (2022). Research on Multidimensional Trust Evaluation Mechanism of FinTech Based on Blockchain. *IEEE Access : Practical Innovations, Open Solutions, 10*, 57025–57036. DOI: 10.1109/ACCESS.2022.3177275

Stewart, H., & Jürjens, J. (2018). Data security and consumer trust in FinTech innovation in Germany. *Information and Computer Security, 26*(1), 109–128. DOI: 10.1108/ICS-06-2017-0039

Teubner, T., Flath, C. M., Weinhardt, C., van der Aalst, W., & Hinz, O. (2023). Welcome to the Era of ChatGPT et al. *Business & Information Systems Engineering, 65*(2), 95–101. https://doi.org/. DOI: 10.1007/s12599-023-00795-x

Tiku, N. (2022, June 11). The Google engineer who thinks the company's AI has come to life. Washington Post; The Washington Post. https://www.washingtonpost.com/technology/2022/06/11/google-ai-lamda-blake-lemoine/

Treleaven, P., Gendal Brown, R., & Yang, D. (2017). Blockchain Technology in Finance. *Computer, 50*(9), 14–17. DOI: 10.1109/MC.2017.3571047

View of Enhancing Market Trend Analysis Through AI Forecasting Models. (2025). IaicPublisher.org.https://iiast.iaicpublisher.org/ijcitsm/index.php/IJCITSM/article/view/162/94

View of Review on Blockchain Technology: Architecture, Characteristics, Benefits, Algorithms, Challenges and Applications. (2024). Mesopotamian.press. https://journals.mesopotamian.press/index.php/CyberSecurity/article/view/68/86

Wessel, M., Adam, M., Benlian, A., & Majchrzak, A. (n.d.). Journal of Management Information Systems Generative AI and its Transformative Value for Digital Platforms Guest Editors. https://www.jmis-web.org/cfps/JMIS_SI_CfP_Generative_AI.pdf

We.trade. (n.d.). Www.ibm.com. https://www.ibm.com/case-studies/wetrade-blockchain-fintech-trade-finance

Wu, H., Yao, Q., Liu, Z., Huang, B., Zhuang, Y., Tang, H., & Liu, E. (2024). Blockchain for finance: A survey. *IET Blockchain*, *4*(2), 101–123. Advance online publication. DOI: 10.1049/blc2.12067

Wu, X., & Liang, J. (2021). A blockchain-based trust management method for Internet of Things. *Pervasive and Mobile Computing*, *72*, 101330. DOI: 10.1016/j.pmcj.2021.101330

Xu, J., Yang, T., Zhuang, S., Li, H., & Lu, W. (2024). AI-based financial transaction monitoring and fraud prevention with behaviour prediction. *Applied and Computational Engineering*, *77*(1), 218–224. DOI: 10.54254/2755-2721/67/2024MA0068

Zhang, L., Xie, Y., Zheng, Y., Xue, W., Zheng, X., & Xu, X. (2020). The challenges and countermeasures of blockchain in finance and economics. *Systems Research and Behavioral Science*, *37*(4), 691–698. DOI: 10.1002/sres.2710

Zhihan, L. (2023). Generative Artificial Intelligence in the Metaverse Era. *Cognitive Robotics*, *3*(1), 208–217. Advance online publication. DOI: 10.1016/j.cogr.2023.06.001

KEY TERMS AND DEFINITIONS

Generative AI: Artificial intelligence capable of creating new content, such as text, images, or data, based on learned patterns, driving smarter decisions in financial insights.

Blockchain: A decentralized digital ledger that records transactions securely and transparently, forming the backbone of innovations like smart contracts and DeFi.

Smart Contracts: Self-executing agreements with terms directly written into code, automatically enforcing conditions without the need for intermediaries.

Chapter 4
Fintech for a Sustainable Future:
Mapping Financial Innovation to the SDGs

Samuel Mores Geddam
https://orcid.org/0000-0003-1327-9840
St. Joseph's University, Bengaluru, India

Mahesh Babu Tadipigari
https://orcid.org/0009-0007-7072-4257
St. Joseph's University, Bengaluru, India

K. Kanishka
https://orcid.org/0009-0006-6529-9201
St. Joseph's University, Bengaluru, India

Gopalakrishnan Soundararajan
https://orcid.org/0000-0001-9013-0498
Muscat College, Oman

ABSTRACT

This study examines the intersection of financial technology (fintech) and sustainable development, analyzing how fintech innovations support the UN Sustainable Development Goals (SDGs). Using a mixed-methods approach, it reviews 631 fintech-related research articles indexed in Scopus, applying content analysis and statistical modeling to test two hypotheses: (1) AI and blockchain improve financial sustainability, and (2) fintech fosters financial inclusion and reduces environmental impact. Results show that 97.9% of papers referencing AI or blockchain also discuss sustainability, versus 39.9% of papers without these technologies, confirmed

DOI: 10.4018/979-8-3373-1250-7.ch004

by Pearson's χ^2 test (χ^2 = 43.0, Pearson's $\chi 2$ test ($\chi 2$ = 43.0, $p < 0.001$). The study maps fintech innovations to SDGs, including blockchain for transparency (SDG 16), crowdfunding for inclusive growth (SDG 8, SDG 10), mobile banking for poverty reduction (SDG 1), green fintech for climate action (SDG 13), and insurtech for health (SDG 3). Findings highlight fintech's role as a driver of social, economic, and environmental progress.

INTRODUCTION

Over the past ten years, financial technology has drifted from niche start-up territory into the centre of day-to-day money management, pushing forward with tools like blockchain ledgers, machine-learning risk models, instant payment rails, and community-driven funding platforms. Scholars and practitioners now question whether the same framework that boosts user convenience can also, deliberately, push society closer to its environmental and social standards.

The Sustainable Development Goals outlined by the United Nations map out a broad set of targets, from lifting people out of poverty to safeguarding ocean health and fortifying public institutions. Real progress against that agenda typically hinges on instruments that can scale quickly, move capital cheaply, and keep stakeholders well-informed. Digital finance in its brightest moments bundles all three of those qualities into one package. Even so, field studies that trace a clear causal line from fintech deployment to SDG improvement are still too few, leaving policymakers partly in the dark about how far to lean on the technology.

A systematic review of 631 fintech studies listed in Scopus forms the backbone of this paper. Content coding and a battery of statistical models reveal how artificial intelligence, blockchain, and related innovations map onto long-standing sustainability themes. Central to the inquiry is the wager that these digital tools widen access to finance, lighten the sector's ecological footprint, and help national governments tick off the Sustainable Development Goals. A secondary track of analysis pits plain fintech solutions against those dressed up with AI and distributed-ledger technology, asking whether the latter boost sustainability any further. Insights drawn from the dual lens pinpoint the idea clusters most likely to push specific SDGs forward.

The rapid rise of financial technology platforms has forced banks and credit unions to rethink not merely their balance sheets but also their role in global sustainability challenges. From smartphone wallets to AI risk models and permissioned ledgers, each new tool chips away at the century-old idea that finance can only report on growth rather than help steer it. Researchers now refer to the fintech space as a possible engine for broad-based economic uplift, low-carbon stewardship, and nimble resilience in the face of shock. Against this backdrop, one pressing question lingers: just how deeply do these fintech leaps map onto the Sustainable Development Goals?

In light of that question, the authors advance these working hypotheses:

> **H1:** The integration of AI and blockchain in fintech enhances the sustainability of financial services
>
> **H2:** Fintech innovations contribute to achieving sustainable development goals by promoting financial inclusion and reducing environmental impact

RESEARCH METHODOLOGY

This study adopts a mixed-method approach, combining quantitative content analysis with interpretive synthesis, to explore the dual hypotheses. To evaluate these hypotheses, the research draws on a dataset of 631 fintech-related research papers retrieved from the Scopus database. These publications, encompassing abstracts from a wide time span, form the empirical foundation of the study.

For Hypothesis 1, a systematic text-preprocessing pipeline was applied. All abstracts were converted to lowercase to ensure uniformity, while punctuation was retained for semantic clarity. Keyword dictionaries were then curated to represent three thematic domains:

- *AI*, with terms such as "artificial intelligence", "machine learning", "deep learning", and "AI"
- *Blockchain*, using identifiers like "blockchain", "distributed ledger", and "cryptocurrency"
- *Sustainability*, incorporating terms such as "sustain", "green", "environment", "carbon", "climate", and "ESG".

Each abstract was tagged with three Boolean flags has_AI, has_blockchain, and has_sustain based on the presence of these keywords. Papers containing at least one AI or blockchain term were categorized into the treatment group, while those lacking both were placed in the control group. The relationship between fintech technologies and sustainability themes was statistically assessed using a 2×2 contingency table and Pearson's χ^2 test, providing insight into thematic alignment and potential independence between the variables. A comparative bar chart was also generated to visualize the prevalence of sustainability focus within the two subsets.

To address Hypothesis 2, a qualitative content analysis was conducted on the same corpus to map specific fintech innovations to the United Nations Sustainable Development Goals. Abstracts were manually reviewed to identify recurring innovation types such as blockchain platforms, green fintech tools, digital payment systems, crowdfunding models, mobile banking applications, and insurtech solutions. Each innovation was then linked to relevant SDGs based on the nature of its purported impact (e.g., SDG 1 for poverty reduction through mobile banking; SDG 13 for climate action through green fintech). These associations were compiled into a structured table linking each fintech innovation to its corresponding SDG(s) and supporting citations from the dataset. The table serves as both a thematic synthesis and a literature mapping of fintech's role in sustainable development.

Together, this two-pronged methodology allows for both quantitative validation of statistical relationships and qualitative interpretation of innovation pathways, yielding a comprehensive perspective on how fintech advances sustainability in practice and research.

RESULTS AND DISCUSSION

Hypothesis 1: Fintech innovations contribute to achieving sustainable development goals by promoting financial inclusion and reducing environmental impact

Figure 1. Sustainability focus overtime covered by AI/Blockchain Presence

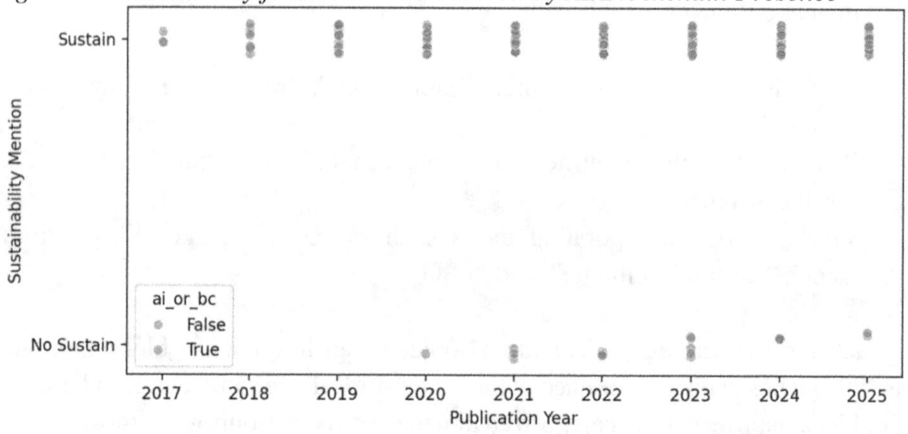

Table 1. Fintech Literature Count theme wise

Subset	Total Papers	Sustainability-Related	% with Sustainability
With AI/Blockchain terms	290	284	97.9%
Without AI/Blockchain terms	341	136	39.9%
Total	631	420	66.6%

Figure 2. Sustainability focus vs AI/Blockchain Presence in the Literature

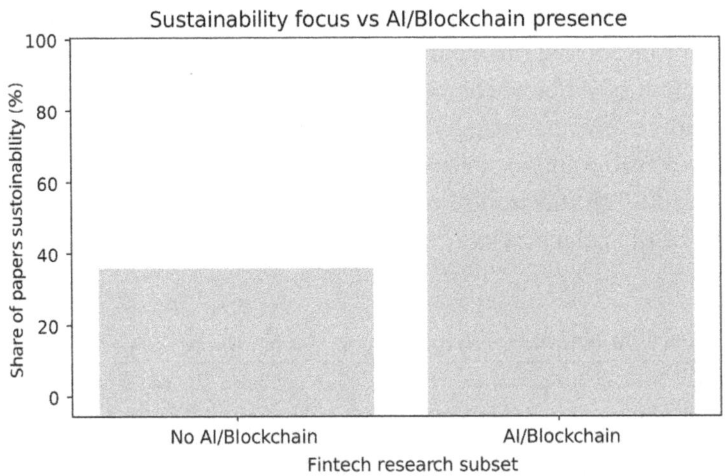

As shown in Table 1 and Figures 1 & Figure 2, the analysis of 631 Scopus-indexed fintech research papers reveals a strong connection between AI and blockchain integration and sustainability considerations. Among papers that mention AI or blockchain technologies, 98% also reference sustainability-related themes, compared to only 40% of papers without these technologies. This statistical relationship is confirmed by a Pearson's χ^2 test, which yields χ^2 (1) = 43.0, p = 5.4 × 10^{-11}, rejecting the null hypothesis of independence. This indicates a significant association between AI/blockchain adoption and the increasing emphasis on sustainable finance.

These findings suggest that fintech innovations leveraging artificial intelligence and blockchain play a crucial role in advancing sustainability in financial services. AI-driven solutions, such as real-time ESG scoring and predictive analytics for green investment, enhance financial decision-making by integrating sustainability metrics. Blockchain applications, including tamper-proof carbon credit tracking and transparent green financing, provide verifiable mechanisms to reduce environmental impact. Together, these technologies contribute to financial inclusion and responsible investment, reinforcing their role in sustainable development.

However, while abstracts signal intent, they do not necessarily reflect proven environmental outcomes in real-world fintech applications. Keyword-based analysis might also underestimate nuanced expressions of sustainability. Future research should focus on full-text semantic analysis to capture deeper insights, measure actual environmental performance of AI/blockchain-based fintech solutions, and explore causal mechanisms through longitudinal studies and case analyses.

Overall, the findings strongly support the hypothesis that fintech innovations, particularly those incorporating AI and blockchain contribute to sustainable development goals by promoting financial inclusion and reducing environmental impact. The concentration of AI/blockchain-oriented sustainability papers in recent years suggests a rapidly evolving research landscape, highlighting the growing importance of technology-driven solutions in sustainable finance.

Hypothesis 2: The integration of AI and blockchain in fintech enhances the sustainability of financial services

Table 2. Fintech Innovations contributions to the Sustainability (SDGs)

	SDG Contribution	**Explanation**	**Citations**
	SDG 16 (Peace, Justice and Strong Institutions), SDG 9 (Industry, Innovation and Infrastructure)	Blockchain enhances transparency, security, and traceability in financial transactions, making it highly relevant for building trustworthy institutions (SDG 16) and fostering innovation (SDG 9).	(Abuamria & Ajouz, 2025; Al-Anezi, 2024; Aliano et al., 2024; Almasria et al., 2024; Basdekidou & Papapanagos, 2024, 2025; Boumaiza, 2025; Dadabada, 2024; Dunbar et al., 2024; Ellili, 2023; Fernandez-Vazquez et al., 2019; Harrison, 2024; Ji & Tia, 2022; Lee & Khan, 2022; Y. Liu et al., 2021; Maleh et al., 2024; Misra et al., 2024; Molavi et al., 2025; Monisha et al., 2025; Nefla & Jellouli, 2025; Onyekwere et al., 2023; Paladini et al., 2021; Roy & Vasa, 2025; Sakiz, 2019; Sethi et al., 2025; V. Sharma et al., 2025; Sundharesalingam et al., 2025; Tseng et al., 2021)
	SDG 8 (Decent Work and Economic Growth), SDG 10 (Reduced Inequalities)	Crowdfunding democratizes access to capital for small businesses and individuals, promoting economic growth (SDG 8) and reducing inequalities by enabling diverse participants to raise funds (SDG 10).	(Azman et al., 2020; Azman & Zabri, 2022; Baldissarro et al., 2025; Chen & Volz, 2022; Chung et al., 2023; Deng et al., 2024; Fanea-Ivanovici & Baber, 2024; Fernández;, 2021; Gangi et al., 2021; Moleka, 2024; Moro-Visconti et al., 2020; Purwatiningsih et al., 2024; Radev, 2024; Raimi et al., 2023; Redzuan et al., 2024; Rejeb et al., 2023; Rizwan et al., 2024; Salerno et al., 2024; Santibanez Gonzalez et al., 2024; Sibindi, 2025; Syarif & Aysan, 2024; Tajudin et al., 2020; Taneja et al., 2023; Wessel et al., 2021; Yao, 2025)
	SDG 8 (Decent Work and Economic Growth)	Cryptocurrencies offer alternative financial systems that can enhance financial inclusion and stimulate economic activities, especially in underserved regions (SDG 8).	(Chung et al., 2023; Dhali et al., 2023; Drăgan et al., 2025; Ghaemi Asl et al., 2024; Ku-Mahamud et al., 2018; Onyekwere et al., 2023; Ozelli, 2024; Raimi et al., 2023; Tepe et al., 2022)
	SDG 1 (No Poverty), SDG 8 (Decent Work and Economic Growth)	Digital payments facilitate faster, safer, and more accessible financial transactions, reducing poverty (SDG 1) and supporting economic activity and decent work (SDG 8).	(Aldalaien & Awamleh, 2025; Almasria et al., 2024; Atif et al., 2021)

continued on following page

Table 2. Continued

	SDG Contribution	Explanation	Citations
Green	SDG 13 (Climate Action), SDG 12 (Responsible Consumption and Production)	Green fintech promotes sustainable investment and financing practices that support climate action (SDG 13) and responsible consumption (SDG 12).	(Aboalsamh et al., 2023; Ashrafi & Akhter, 2025; Emami et al., 2025; Geetha & Biju, 2024; Jha et al., 2022; Jibo, 2025; Kakar et al., 2024, 2025; Kwong et al., 2023; Lee et al., 2023; Lucarelli et al., 2024; Macchiavello & Siri, 2022; Piotrowska & Piotrowski, 2025; Puschmann et al., 2020; Puschmann & Khmarskyi, 2024; Raman et al., 2024; Ranchordás & Meoli, 2024; R. Sharma et al., 2025; Shi & Yang, 2025; Shukla & Sawai, 2023; Sohail et al., 2024; Sreelekshmi & Biju, 2023; Taghizadeh-Hesary, 2025; Tamasiga et al., 2022; Vikas et al., 2022; Vovchenko et al., 2023; Zhang et al., 2024)
	SDG 3 (Good Health and Well-being), SDG 8 (Decent Work and Economic Growth)	Insurtech leverages technology to provide innovative insurance solutions, enhancing access to healthcare (SDG 3) and improving economic resilience (SDG 8).	(Bittini et al., 2022; Merello et al., 2023)
	SDG 1 (No Poverty), SDG 9 (Industry, Innovation and Infrastructure)	Mobile banking extends financial services to unbanked populations, helping reduce poverty (SDG 1) and fostering industrial innovation (SDG 9).	(Boulila et al., 2024; Gatauwa et al., 2024; Hazarika et al., 2024; Hughes, 2021; Kaur & Pathak, 2023; A. Liu et al., 2023; Wu & Kao, 2022; Yadav et al., 2025)
Peer-To-Peer	SDG 8 (Decent Work and Economic Growth), SDG 10 (Reduced Inequalities)	P2P lending platforms enable individuals to access credit without traditional intermediaries, supporting economic opportunities (SDG 8) and reducing inequalities (SDG 10).	(Azman et al., 2020; Minz et al., 2023; Yadav et al., 2024, 2025)
	SDG 16 (Peace, Justice and Strong Institutions)	Regtech uses technology to improve regulatory compliance and risk management, promoting strong institutions (SDG 16).	(Cruz Rambaud & Expósito Gázquez, 2022; Kanojia & Kaur, 2024; Lee & Lee, 2025; Zetzsche & Anker-Sørensen, 2022)
Robo-	SDG 8 (Decent Work and Economic Growth)	Robo-advisors provide automated, affordable financial advice, expanding access to investment opportunities and contributing to economic growth (SDG 8).	(Sethi et al., 2025; Yi et al., 2023)

Figure 3. The Fintech Financial Innovation and their SDG contribution

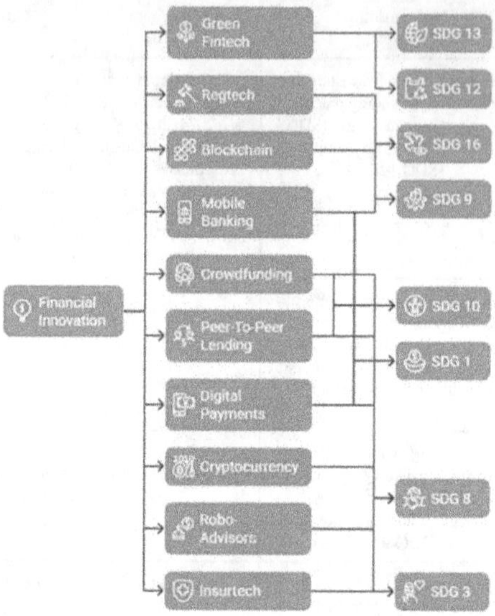

The analysis of the literature from the table 1 and Figure 3 provides compelling evidence that fintech innovations play a multidimensional role in supporting and advancing the United Nations Sustainable Development Goals (SDGs). Recent research mapping contemporary financial technologies to the United Nations Sustainable Development Goals reveals some striking patterns.

1. **Blockchain: Transparency, Security, and Institutional Trust:** In ongoing efforts to meet Sustainable Development Goal 16 - Peace, Justice and Strong Institutions - and Goal 9 - Industry, Innovation and Infrastructure - blockchain technology frequently recurs as a point of focus. Its core traits - decentralisation, immutability, and built-in transparency - allow entities to verify financial exchanges and supply-chain movements without surrendering control to a single middleman, an arrangement that can curb corruption and shrink opportunities for fraud (Abuamria & Ajouz 2025; Allahham et al. 2024; Paladini et al. 2021; Roy & Vasa 2025). Layered on that foundational trust, entrepreneurs are already experimenting with new scaffolds such as self-executing smart contracts and the increasingly popular ecosystem of decentralised finance, both of which feed Industry 4.0's appetite for continuous technical innovation (Basdekidou & Papapanagos 2024; Molavi et al. 2025; Tseng et al. 2021).

2. **Crowdfunding: Opening Capital Gates to All:** Crowdfunding portfolios contributes to Sustainable Development Goal 8, Decent Work and Economic Growth, and Goal 10, Reduced Inequalities. Azman et al. (2020), Gangi et al. (2021), and Rejeb et al. (2023) each describe how these platforms create an off-ramp from gatekeeper banks. Salerno et al. (2024) and Tajudin et al. (2020) document similar patterns in regions where branch networks are sparse. Money that once lingered in the crowd begins to sew up social and economic seams.
3. **Cryptocurrency: Digital Finance for the Overlooked:** Chung et al. (2023) and Ku-Mahamud et al. (2018) argue that cryptocurrency technology nudges Goal 8 forward by slipping past traditional bottlenecks. The technology supports financial inclusion by lowering transaction costs and enhancing cross-border remittances, thus empowering individuals and small businesses globally (Dhali et al., 2023; Tepe et al., 2022).
4. **Digital Payments: Financial Inclusion as a Pathway to Poverty Alleviation:** Digital payment platforms have quietly reshaped the way cash reaches the poorest households, so much so that Aldalaien and Awamleh (2025) now mention them in the same spirit as SDG 1 and SDG 8. It used to take hours to queue at a bank; now a smartphone tap opens e-commerce, custodial savings, and government transfers, a shift Akmasria et al. (2024) claim shrinks the poverty gap one transaction at a time.
5. **Green Fintech: Channeling Capital into Climate-Smart Ventures:** Funds routed through green fintech platforms do more than grow portfolios; they limit carbon footprints. Ashrafi and Akhter (2025) show that embedding ESG metrics into algorithms shapes choices toward low-emission or circular-economy projects. Tools like carbon-credit exchanges, sustainability-linked loans, and green bonds let investors tie financial performance to ecological benchmarks, evidence of which Rangerdo and Meoli (2024) provided from Latin America. Taghizadeh-Hesary (2025) adds that those same mechanisms are attracting risk-averse capital that would otherwise sit idle.
6. **Insurtech: Expanding Healthcare Access and Economic Resilience:** Recent advances in insurtech offer a fresh take on SDG 3 and SDG 8 by pairing real-time data streams with lightweight mobile interfaces. Analysts such as Bittini et al. (2022) and Merello et al. (2023) point out that these tools can churn out personalised, low-premium policies almost on the fly. To put the shift in human terms, a kiosk clerk in financial market no longer waits weeks for underwriters to approve cover, because the answer often pulses back while she taps her screen. In places like that, faster insurance means a deeper safety net and, by extension, a small but meaningful boost to local economic calm.

7. **Mobile Banking: Extending Financial Services to the Unbanked:** Mobile banking takeovers tradition in a way that leaves brick-and-mortar banks trying to catch up. Simple smartphone apps now turn tiny savers into borrowers, let rural seamstresses settle bills in minutes, and give street-food vendors a queer shot at formal credit lines (Hughes, 2021; Wu & Kao, 2022; Yadav et al., 2025). When those cash-flow gaps close, micro-entrepreneurs can invest a bit more, factories can run fuller shifts, and entire regions inch toward the kind of steady growth once thought possible only in city suburbs (Boulila et al., 2024; Gatauwa et al., 2024).
8. **Peer-to-Peer Lending: Alternative Credit Access and Inequality Reduction:** Peer-to-peer lending platforms bypass traditional banks and place cash in the hands of borrowers who would otherwise wait months for approval (Minz et al. 2023, Yadav et al. 2024, Yadav et al. 2025). Lower interest margins widen the pool of people who can afford a loan, and many of those borrowers use the money to start businesses that hire local residents (Azman et al. 2020). In this way, the model pushes against both credit exclusion and the wider income gap, aligning with the spirit of Sustainable Development Goals 8 and 10.
9. **Regtech: Enhancing Compliance and Institutional Strength:** Regulatory technology, in formal parlance, Regtech escorts compliance into the twenty-first century by replacing paperwork with dashboards (Cruz Rambaud & Expósito Gázquez 2022; Lee & Lee 2025). Banks and insurance firms can now spot irregular transactions in near-real time, run audit trails at the click of a button, and even automate the minutiae of regulatory reporting. Many chief risk officers argue that this layer of code has stiffened corporate governance and, perhaps even more critically, made it visible to the public eye (Kanojia & Kaur 2024; Zetzsche & Anker-Sørensen 2022).
10. **Robo-Advisors: Democratizing Investment Advisory Services:** Robo-advisors have quietly moved the investment consultant out of the glass office and into an app, lowering the cost of personalised asset management to the price of a monthly subscription (Sethi et al. 2025; Yi et al. 2023). A simple algorithm can now build, rebalance, and tax-loss-harvest a diversified portfolio for a client who starts with little more than a smartphone and a couple of hundred pounds. In that sense, small savers no longer need Ivy League pedigrees to watch their wealth compound; they just need a Wi-Fi signal and a willingness to click yes.

Fintech systems now operate at the intersection of code and local economies, and the Sustainable Development Goals supply the yardstick by which their impact can be measured. When regulators deploy blockchain ledgers or small firms lean on regtech dashboards, institutional transparency inches upward. Crowdfunding platforms, peer-to-peer lenders, and lightweight digital payment channels build pathways for exclusionary economies to enter the formal financial fold, while green-fintech calculators and climate-linked bonds confront warming in real time. In parallel, insurtech algorithms deliver micro-policies that ease the burden of medical crises, underscoring how agile technology can be when pressed against pressing human need.

CONCLUSION

This study set out to examine how fintech innovations contribute to sustainable development goals (SDGs), with particular attention to their roles in enhancing financial inclusion and reducing environmental impact. Drawing on a corpus of 631 Scopus-indexed papers, the research applied both quantitative and qualitative analyses to explore two key hypotheses. The results clearly demonstrate that fintech innovations especially those involving AI and blockchain exhibit a strong thematic alignment with sustainability objectives. An overwhelming 97.9% of papers referencing AI or blockchain also addressed sustainability topics, compared to just 39.9% among other fintech studies. This statistically significant relationship reinforces the notion that emerging financial technologies are not only transforming finance but are also being actively positioned as tools for promoting sustainable development.

Beyond correlation, the content analysis revealed a range of innovation clusters that directly support specific SDGs. For instance, blockchain is closely tied to institutional transparency (SDG 16) and innovation infrastructure (SDG 9), while digital payments and mobile banking extend services to unbanked communities, addressing SDG 1 (No Poverty) and SDG 8 (Decent Work). Other contributions include green fintech for climate action (SDG 13), insurtech for health access (SDG 3), and crowdfunding and P2P lending for reducing inequalities (SDG 10). These findings affirm that fintech's influence on sustainability is both multidimensional and impact-driven, spanning social, economic, and environmental dimensions.

Nevertheless, this study is based on abstract-level content, which primarily reflects thematic intent rather than real-world outcomes. Future research should employ full-text semantic analysis to capture deeper narratives and more nuanced interpretations of fintech's environmental and social impacts. Additionally, empirical case studies, impact assessments, and longitudinal tracking of specific fintech applications could help establish causality and measure tangible progress toward SDGs. Exploring regional variations and regulatory environments would also illuminate how fintech's sustainability potential manifests across different socioeconomic contexts.

In sum, this paper contributes a timely and evidence-based perspective to the discourse on sustainable fintech, highlighting the growing convergence between financial innovation and global development agendas. As the sector continues to evolve, there is immense scope for both scholarly exploration and policy innovation to ensure that fintech remains a powerful ally in achieving a more inclusive and sustainable future.

REFERENCES

Aboalsamh, H. M., Khrais, L. T., & Albahussain, S. A. (2023). Pioneering Perception of Green Fintech in Promoting Sustainable Digital Services Application within Smart Cities. *Sustainability (Basel), 15*(14), 11440. Advance online publication. DOI: 10.3390/su151411440

Abuamria, F., & Ajouz, M. (2025). Leveraging FinTech Innovations for Sustainable and Social Finance: A Comprehensive Analysis of Their Contributions to Social Impact Investment. In *From Digital Disruption to Dominance: Leveraging FinTech Applications for Sustainable Growth* (pp. 245–264). Emerald Group Publishing Ltd. DOI: 10.1108/978-1-83549-608-420251012

Al-Anezi, F. (2024). Interlinking FinTech and eHealth: A qualitative study. *Frontiers in Public Health, 12*, 1398136. Advance online publication. DOI: 10.3389/fpubh.2024.1398136 PMID: 39157524

Aldalaien, B. A., & Awamleh, F. T. (2025). Integrating fintech into strategic management practices for achieving sustainable development goals. *International Journal of Innovative Research and Scientific Studies, 8*(3), 3446–3454. DOI: 10.53894/ijirss.v8i3.7254

Aliano, M., Cestari, G., & Madonna, S. (2024). Sustainable Finance for SMEs: The Role of Capital for Sustainable and Inclusive Growth. In *Sustainable Finance: Vol. Part F4266* (pp. 1–210). Springer Nature. DOI: 10.1007/978-3-031-74193-7

Almasria, N. A., Alhatabat, Z., Ershaid, D., Ibrahim, A., & Ahmed, S. (2024). The Mediating Impact of Organizational Innovation on the Relationship Between Fintech Innovations and Sustainability Performance. *Sustainability (Basel), 16*(22), 10044. Advance online publication. DOI: 10.3390/su162210044

Ashrafi, D. M., & Akhter, M. (2025). The green Fintech paradox: Understanding the dynamics of green brand positioning and user decision-making in the digital financial landscape. *Journal of Modelling in Management, 20*(2), 348–389. DOI: 10.1108/JM2-12-2023-0294

Atif, M., Hassan, M. K., Rabbani, M. R., & Khan, S. (2021). Islamic FinTech: The digital transformation bringing sustainability to islamic finance. In *COVID-19 and Islamic Social Finance* (pp. 91–103). Taylor and Francis. DOI: 10.4324/9781003121718-9

Azman, N. H. N., & Zabri, M. Z. (2020). The Utilisation Of Islamic Fintech (I-Fintech) In Promoting Sustainable Inclusive Growth: Evidence From Micro-Entrepreneurs In Malaysia. *Journal of Islamic Monetary Economics and Finance, 6*(3), 555–576. DOI: 10.21098/jimf.v6i3.1180

Azman, N. H. N., & Zabri, M. Z. M. (2022). SHARI'AH-COMPLIANT FINTECH USAGE AMONG MICROENTREPRENEURS IN MALAYSIA: AN EXTENSION OF UTAUT MODEL. *Journal of Islamic Monetary Economics and Finance*, *8*(2), 305–324. DOI: 10.21098/jimf.v8i2.1417

Baldissarro, G., Farinelli, E., Iazzolino, G., Maiolini, R., & Morea, D. (2025). The link between crowdfunding and sustainability: A literature review in the field of entrepreneurs and academic spinoffs. *Finance Research Letters*, *77*, 107097. Advance online publication. DOI: 10.1016/j.frl.2025.107097

Basdekidou, V., & Papapanagos, H. (2024). Blockchain Technology Adoption for Disrupting FinTech Functionalities: A Systematic Literature Review for Corporate Management, Supply Chain, Banking Industry, and Stock Markets. *Digital*, *4*(3), 762–803. DOI: 10.3390/digital4030039

Basdekidou, V., & Papapanagos, H. (2025). Blockchain Technology Adoption for Agriculture, Manufacturing, Services, Knowledge, Culture, and Research: A Systematic Literature Review. *WSEAS Transactions on Systems*, *24*, 229–278. DOI: 10.37394/23202.2025.24.23

Bittini, J. S., Rambaud, S. C., Pascual, J. L., & Moro-Visconti, R. (2022). Business Models and Sustainability Plans in the FinTech, InsurTech, and PropTech Industry: Evidence from Spain. *Sustainability (Basel)*, *14*(19), 12088. Advance online publication. DOI: 10.3390/su141912088

Boulila, H., Metadjer, W., & Benbekhti, S. E. (2024). What if Banking was Green? An Essay to Quantify the Effect of Fintech on Financial Inclusion and Environmental Sustainability. In Ciasullo, M. V., Martin, J., & Brunetti, F. (Eds.), *Springer Proceedings in Business and Economics* (pp. 106–125). Springer Nature., DOI: 10.1007/978-3-031-65115-1_6

Boumaiza, A. (2025). Advancing Sustainable Investment Efficiency and Transparency Through Blockchain-Driven Optimization. *Sustainability (Basel)*, *17*(5), 2000. Advance online publication. DOI: 10.3390/su17052000

Chen, Y., & Volz, U. (2022). Scaling up sustainable investment through blockchain-based project bonds. *Development Policy Review*, *40*(3), e12582. Advance online publication. DOI: 10.1111/dpr.12582

Chung, S., Kim, K., Lee, C. H., & Oh, W. (2023). Interdependence between online peer-to-peer lending and cryptocurrency markets and its effects on financial inclusion. *Production and Operations Management*, *32*(6), 1939–1957. DOI: 10.1111/poms.13950

Cruz Rambaud, S., & Expósito Gázquez, A. (2022). A RegTech Approach to Fintech Sustainability: The Case of Spain. *European Journal of Risk Regulation, 13*(2), 333–349. DOI: 10.1017/err.2021.62

Dadabada, P. K. (2024). Analyzing the Impact of ESG Integration and FinTech Innovations on Green Finance: A Comparative Case Studies Approach. *Journal of the Knowledge Economy*. Advance online publication. DOI: 10.1007/s13132-024-02197-0

Deng, Y., Cao, Z., & Yang, N. (2024). Understanding the nexus between fintech, natural resources, green investment, and environmental sustainability in China: A DYNARDL approach. *Resources Policy*, *91*, 104900. Advance online publication. DOI: 10.1016/j.resourpol.2024.104900

Dhali, M., Hassan, S., Mehar, S. M., Shahzad, K., & Zaman, F. (2023). Cryptocurrency in the Darknet: Sustainability of the current national legislation. *International Journal of Law and Management*, *65*(3), 261–282. DOI: 10.1108/IJLMA-09-2022-0206

Drăgan, G. B., Ben Arfi, W., Tiberius, V., Ammari, A., & Khvatova, T. (2025). Navigating the green wave: Understanding behavioral antecedents of sustainable cryptocurrency investment. *Technological Forecasting and Social Change*, *210*, 123909. Advance online publication. DOI: 10.1016/j.techfore.2024.123909

Dunbar, K., Sarkis, J., & Treku, D. N. (2024). FinTech for environmental sustainability: Promises and pitfalls. *One Earth*, *7*(1), 23–30. DOI: 10.1016/j.oneear.2023.12.012

Ellili, N. O. D. (2023). Is there any association between FinTech and sustainability? Evidence from bibliometric review and content analysis. *Journal of Financial Services Marketing*, *28*(4), 748–762. DOI: 10.1057/s41264-022-00200-w

Emami, A., Afshar, M., & Aliyari, M. (2025). Financial Innovations in the Era of Industry 5.0: Opportunities and Challenges. In *Dynamic and Safe Economy in the Age of Smart Technologies* (pp. 209–222). IGI Global. DOI: 10.4018/979-8-3693-4369-2.ch013

Fanea-Ivanovici, M., & Baber, H. (2024). Alternative Finance: A Framework for Innovative and Sustainable Business Models. In *Alternative Finance: A Framework for Innovative and Sustainable Business Models.* Taylor and Francis., DOI: 10.4324/9781032713533

Fernández, S. S. (2021). Islamic fintech. In *Islamic Fintech.* Taylor and Francis., DOI: 10.4324/9781003014614

Fernandez-Vazquez, S., Rosillo, R., De La Fuente, D., & Priore, P. (2019). Blockchain in FinTech: A mapping study. *Sustainability (Basel), 11*(22), 6366. Advance online publication. DOI: 10.3390/su11226366

Gangi, F., Meles, A., Daniele, L. M., Varrone, N., & Salerno, D. (2021). The evolution of sustainable investments and finance: Theoretical perspectives and new challenges. In *The Evolution of Sustainable Investments and Finance: Theoretical Perspectives and New Challenges*. Springer International Publishing., DOI: 10.1007/978-3-030-70350-9

Gatauwa, J. M., Aluoch, M. O., & Adhing'a, D. C. (2024). Fintech Services and Corporate Sustainability in Commercial Banks in Kenya. In *The Adoption of Fintech Using Technology for Better Security, Speed, and Customer Experience in Finance* (pp. 114–126). Taylor and Francis. DOI: 10.4324/9781032644165-8

Geetha, S., & Biju, A. V. N. (2024). Is green FinTech reshaping the finance sphere? Unravelling through a systematic literature review. *Environmental Science and Pollution Research International, 31*(2), 1790–1810. DOI: 10.1007/s11356-023-31382-y PMID: 38057679

Ghaemi Asl, M., Ben Jabeur, S., Hosseini, S. S., & Tajmir Riahi, H. (2024). Fintech's impact on conventional and Islamic sustainable equities: Short- and long-term contributions of the digital financial ecosystem. *Global Finance Journal, 62*, 101022. Advance online publication. DOI: 10.1016/j.gfj.2024.101022

Harrison, M. (2024). The role of FinTech in driving sustainability and inclusive practices in banking. In *International Banking in Global Perspective* (pp. 158–176). Taylor and Francis., DOI: 10.4324/9781003307846-9

Hazarika, C. A. I., Khalfan, J., Ahmed, M., Yousif, A., & Hussain, J. (2024). Role of Fintech as an Enabler to Fulfill HR Requirements and Attain Sustainability. In *Studies in Systems, Decision and Control* (Vol. 537, pp. 59–67). Springer Science and Business Media Deutschland GmbH. DOI: 10.1007/978-3-031-62106-2_5

Hughes, H. (2021). The Complex Implications Of Fintech For Financial Inclusion. *Law and Contemporary Problems, 84*(1), 115–128. https://www.scopus.com/inward/record.uri?eid=2-s2.0-85104780101&partnerID=40&md5=fa86df16b7cbfe7c0e87aebe79ad2b8d

Jha, B., Giri, P., Jha, D., & Badhera, U. (2022). Unlocking IoT: AI-enabled green fintech innovations. In *AI-Enabled Agile Internet of Things for Sustainable FinTech Ecosystems* (pp. 1–22). IGI Global. DOI: 10.4018/978-1-6684-4176-3.ch001

Ji, F., & Tia, A. (2022). The effect of blockchain on business intelligence efficiency of banks. *Kybernetes*, *51*(8), 2652–2668. DOI: 10.1108/K-10-2020-0668

Jibo, A. U. (2025). Green Fintech Innovations in Islamic Banking: Opportunities and Challenges. In *Islamic Finance and Sustainability: A Research Companion* (pp. 53–74). Taylor and Francis. DOI: 10.4324/9781003518617-4

Kakar, S. K., Ali, J., Wang, J., Wu, X., Arshed, N., Le Hien, T. T., & Yadav, R. S. (2024). Exploring the impact of industrialization and electricity use on carbon emissions: The role of green FinTech in Asian countries using an asymmetric panel quantile ARDL approach. *Journal of Environmental Management*, *370*, 122970. Advance online publication. DOI: 10.1016/j.jenvman.2024.122970 PMID: 39426172

Kakar, S. K., Wang, J., Arshed, N., Le Hien, T. T., Akhter, S., & Abdullahi, N. M. (2025). The impact of circular economy, sustainable infrastructure, and green FinTech on biodiversity in Europe: A holistic approach. *Technology in Society*, *81*, 102841. Advance online publication. DOI: 10.1016/j.techsoc.2025.102841

Kanojia, S., Kaur, S., & Bhavya, . (2024). Business sustainability in the era of Fintech and Regtech: A systematic literature review. *Discover Sustainability*, *5*(1), 525. Advance online publication. DOI: 10.1007/s43621-024-00767-5

Kaur, J., & Pathak, N. (2023). The financial and sustainability impact of fintech on Indian deposit money institutions: A study of the last decade. In Chate, V. R. (Ed.), *E3S Web of Conferences* (Vol. 455). EDP Sciences., DOI: 10.1051/e3sconf/202345502019

Ku-Mahamud, K. R., Bakar, N. A. A., & Omar, M. (2018). Blockchain, cryptocurrency and Fintech market growth in Malaysia. *Journal of Advanced Research in Dynamical and Control Systems*, *10*(14), 2074–2082. https://www.scopus.com/inward/record.uri?eid=2-s2.0-85062364401&partnerID=40&md5=069874992ec5f5139bba69d5a95a10cb

Kwong, R., Kwok, M. L. J., & Wong, H. S. M. (2023). Green FinTech Innovation as a Future Research Direction: A Bibliometric Analysis on Green Finance and FinTech. *Sustainability (Basel)*, *15*(20), 14683. Advance online publication. DOI: 10.3390/su152014683

Lee, J., & Khan, V. M. (2022). Blockchain and energy commodity markets: Legal issues and impact on sustainability. *Journal of World Energy Law and Business*, *15*(6), 462–484. DOI: 10.1093/jwelb/jwac030

Lee, J., & Lee, J.-A. (2025). Web3 Governance: Law and Policy. In *Web3 Governance: Law and Policy*. Taylor and Francis., DOI: 10.4324/9781032618975

Lee, J., Serafin, A. M., & Courteau, C. (2023). Corporate disclosure, ESG and green fintech in the energy industry. *Journal of World Energy Law and Business*, *16*(6), 473–491. DOI: 10.1093/jwelb/jwad018

Liu, A., Urquía-Grande, E., López-Sánchez, P., & Rodríguez-López, Á. (2023). Research into microfinance and ICTs: A bibliometric analysis. *Evaluation and Program Planning*, *97*, 102215. Advance online publication. DOI: 10.1016/j.evalprogplan.2022.102215 PMID: 36571966

Liu, Y., Zhang, S., Chen, M., Wu, Y., & Chen, Z. (2021). The sustainable development of financial topic detection and trend prediction by data mining. *Sustainability (Basel)*, *13*(14), 7585. Advance online publication. DOI: 10.3390/su13147585

Lucarelli, C., Mazzocchini, F. J., & Severini, S. (2024). Green FinTech: State of the art of the literature and future perspectives. *International Journal of Green Economics*, *18*(3), 295–317. DOI: 10.1504/IJGE.2024.141407

Macchiavello, E., & Siri, M. (2022). Sustainable Finance and Fintech: Can Technology Contribute to Achieving Environmental Goals? A Preliminary Assessment of "Green Fintech" and "Sustainable Digital Finance.". *European Company and Financial Law Review*, *19*(1), 128–174. DOI: 10.1515/ecfr-2022-0005

Maleh, Y., Zhang, J., & Hansali, A. (2024). Advances in Emerging Financial Technology and Digital Money. In *Advances in Emerging Financial Technology and Digital Money*. CRC Press., DOI: 10.1201/9781032667478

Merello, P., Barbera, A., & De la Poza, E. (2023). Analysing the determinant factors of the sustainability profile of Fintech and Insurtech companies. *Journal of Cleaner Production*, *421*, 138437. Advance online publication. DOI: 10.1016/j.jclepro.2023.138437

Minz, N. K., Mushir, N., Tanwar, S., & Chaffai, M. (2023). Islamic Finance and Fintech: A scoping review. In *Fintech Applications in Islamic Finance: AI, Machine Learning, and Blockchain Techniques* (pp. 150–170). IGI Global. DOI: 10.4018/979-8-3693-1038-0.ch010

Misra, N., Gupta, S., & Rao, T. J. (2024). Fintech's Role in Green Finance: Procuring Funds for Sustainable Energy. *International Research Journal of Multidisciplinary Scope*, *5*(2), 290–312. DOI: 10.47857/irjms.2024.v05i02.0455

Molavi, H., Zhang, L., & Khanbabaei, M. (2025). Sustainable financial infrastructure and governance: A fuzzy multi-criteria decision-making analysis of open service innovation in unstable economies. *Sustainable Futures : An Applied Journal of Technology, Environment and Society*, *9*, 100485. Advance online publication. DOI: 10.1016/j.sftr.2025.100485

Moleka, P. (2024). Innovative Entrepreneurship through Alternative Finance: A Framework for Sustainable and Innovative Business Models. In *Alternative Finance: A Framework for Innovative and Sustainable Business Models* (pp. 13–28). Taylor and Francis., DOI: 10.4324/9781032713533-3

Monisha, J., Anitha, K., & Selvam, P. P. (2025). Charting the Fintech Frontier: Transformative Technologies for Sustainable Industries. In *FinTech and Financial Inclusion: Leveraging Digital Finance for Economic Empowerment and Sustainable Growth* (pp. 179–197). Taylor and Francis. DOI: 10.4324/9781003514114-13

Moro-Visconti, R., Rambaud, S. C., & Pascual, J. L. (2020). Sustainability in FinTechs: An explanation through business model scalability and market valuation. *Sustainability (Basel)*, *12*(24), 1–24. DOI: 10.3390/su122410316

Nefla, D., & Jellouli, S. (2025). Emerging technologies in finance: Challenges for a sustainable finance. *Cogent Business & Management*, *12*(1), 2495191. Advance online publication. DOI: 10.1080/23311975.2025.2495191

Onyekwere, E., Ogwueleka, F. N., & Irhebhude, M. E. (2023). Adoption and sustainability of bitcoin and the blockchain technology in Nigeria. *International Journal of Information Technology : an Official Journal of Bharati Vidyapeeth's Institute of Computer Applications and Management*, *15*(5), 2793–2804. DOI: 10.1007/s41870-023-01336-1 PMID: 37360314

Ozelli, S. (2024). Sustainably Investing in Digital Assets Globally. In *Sustainably Investing in Digital Assets Globally*. wiley. https://www.scopus.com/inward/record.uri?eid=2-s2.0-85185359366&partnerID=40&md5=b0146b6804fb8f69102861ee485b0234

Paladini, S., Yerushalmi, E., & Castellucci, I. (2021). Public governance of the blockchain revolution and its implications for social finance: A comparative analysis. In *Innovations in Social Finance: Transitioning Beyond Economic Value* (pp. 293–318). Springer International Publishing. DOI: 10.1007/978-3-030-72535-8_14

Piotrowska, A. I., & Piotrowski, D. (2025). Green FinTech: A Consumer Awareness Study. *Sustainability (Basel)*, *17*(8), 3701. Advance online publication. DOI: 10.3390/su17083701

Purwatiningsih, A., Purnamasari, S., Setyawati, H., Indriani, A., Prawitasari, D., & Fitria, S. (2024). Bibliometric Analysis of Islamic Crowdfunding: A Literature Review of Its Journey. *F1000Research, 13*. DOI: 10.12688/f1000research.146797.2

Puschmann, T., Hoffmann, C. H., & Khmarskyi, V. (2020). How green fintech can alleviate the impact of climate change—The case of Switzerland. *Sustainability (Basel), 12*(24), 1–28. DOI: 10.3390/su122410691

Puschmann, T., & Khmarskyi, V. (2024). Green fintech: Developing a research agenda. *Corporate Social Responsibility and Environmental Management*, *31*(4), 2823–2837. DOI: 10.1002/csr.2675

Radev, D. (2024). FINTECH AND THE FORESTRY INDUSTRY. In D. V Georgieva & A. P. Barcic (Eds.), *WoodEMA 2024 - Green Deal Initiatives, Sustainable Management, Market Demands, and New Production Perspectives in the Forestry-Based Sector - Proceedings of Scientific Papers* (pp. 119–124). WoodEMA, i.a. https://www.scopus.com/inward/record.uri?eid=2-s2.0-85196739914&partnerID=40&md5=ed203fa6349c7055f6c820e05b7d5b27

Raimi, L., Adekunle, S. M., & Shabbir, M. S. (2023). Contemporary Discourse of Halal and Islamic Entrepreneurship: Trends and Future Opportunities. In *Contemporary Discourse of Halal and Islamic Entrepreneurship: Trends and Future Opportunities*. Springer Nature. DOI: 10.1007/978-981-99-6427-7

Raman, R., Ray, S., Das, D., & Nedungadi, P. (2024). Innovations and barriers in sustainable and green finance for advancing sustainable development goals. *Frontiers in Environmental Science*, *12*, 1513204. Advance online publication. DOI: 10.3389/fenvs.2024.1513204

Ranchordás, S., & Meoli, R. (2024). REGULATORY SANDBOXES FOR SUSTAINABLE FINANCE. *Law and Economics Yearly Review, 13*, 243–280. https://www.scopus.com/inward/record.uri?eid=2-s2.0-105005535965&partnerID=40&md5=95ce53d85952da0d7c821b0db90259e5

Redzuan, N. H., Kassim, S., & Shaharuddin, S. S. (2024). Literature Review on Islamic Crowdfunding. In *Islamic Sustainable Finance: Policy, Risk and Regulation* (pp. 170–184). Taylor and Francis. DOI: 10.4324/9781003395447-20

Rejeb, A., Rejeb, K., Appolloni, A., & Treiblmaier, H. (2023). Navigating the crowdfunding landscape: A study of knowledge trajectories based on main path analysis. *European Journal of Innovation Management*, *26*(7), 415–448. DOI: 10.1108/EJIM-03-2023-0201

Rizwan, A., Naveed, S., Mustafa, F., Hanif, M. S., Khurshid, A., & Khan, T. Z. A. (2024). Prospects for institutionalization of crowdfunding: A developing country perspective. *Journal of Entrepreneurship and Public Policy*, *13*(4), 566–598. DOI: 10.1108/JEPP-09-2023-0086

Roy, J. K., & Vasa, L. (2025). Financial technology and environmental, social and governance in sustainable finance: A bibliometric and thematic content analysis. *Discover Sustainability*, *6*(1), 148. Advance online publication. DOI: 10.1007/s43621-025-00934-2

Sakiz, B. (2019). New financial technologies, cryptocurrencies, blockchain, and challenges. In *Handbook of Research on Creating Sustainable Value in the Global Economy* (pp. 85–102). IGI Global., DOI: 10.4018/978-1-7998-1196-1.ch006

Salerno, D., Gatto, A., & Russo, S. (2024). New data and descriptor for crowdfunding and renewable energy. *Quality & Quantity*, *58*(5), 4703–4713. DOI: 10.1007/s11135-024-01850-9

Santibanez Gonzalez, E. D. R., Kandpal, V., Ozili, P. K., & Chatterjee, P. (2024). Fintech for ESG and the Circular Economy. In *Fintech for Esg and the Circular Economy*. wiley. DOI: 10.1002/9781394234035

Sethi, M., Bohra, N. S., Johri, A., & Asif, M. (2025). Emerging dimensions in Fintech: Insights from bibliometric analysis. *Digital Business*, *5*(1), 100113. Advance online publication. DOI: 10.1016/j.digbus.2025.100113

Sharma, R., Vasishta, P., & Singla, A. (2025). Impact of green banking awareness on green FinTech adoption: A way towards profitable and sustainable practices. *Managerial Finance*, *51*(3), 377–394. DOI: 10.1108/MF-04-2024-0272

Sharma, V., Gupta, M., Arora, N., & Shaikh, A. A. (2025). FinTech and Financial Inclusion: Leveraging Digital Finance for Economic Empowerment and Sustainable Growth. In *FinTech and Financial Inclusion: Leveraging Digital Finance for Economic Empowerment and Sustainable Growth*. Taylor and Francis., DOI: 10.4324/9781003514114

Shi, Y., & Yang, B. (2025). China's energy system building toward an era of resilience: How green fintech can empower? *International Review of Economics & Finance*, *98*, 103876. Advance online publication. DOI: 10.1016/j.iref.2025.103876

Shukla, R., & Sawai, C. (2023). Policy implication of green finance. In *The Sustainable Fintech Revolution: Building a Greener Future for Finance* (pp. 114–144). IGI Global., DOI: 10.4018/979-8-3693-0008-4.ch007

Sibindi, A. B. (2025). Final Synthesis and Future Directions. In *Advances in African Economic, Social and Political Development: Vol. Part F326* (pp. 183–185). Springer Nature. DOI: 10.1007/978-3-031-86516-9_10

Sohail, M., Khan, S., Akbar, A., & Svobodova, L. (2024). Empowering sustainable development: The crucial nexus of green fintech and green finance in Luxembourg's banking sector. *Journal of Infrastructure. Policy and Development*, *8*(7), 4979. Advance online publication. DOI: 10.24294/jipd.v8i7.4979

Sreelekshmi, G., & Biju, A. V. (2023). Exploring the interconnection of fintech and climate sustainability: Scoping through a qualitative methodology. In *The Sustainable Fintech Revolution: Building a Greener Future for Finance* (pp. 292–311). IGI Global., DOI: 10.4018/979-8-3693-0008-4.ch015

Sundharesalingam, P., Somasundaram, R., Sushmitha, S. S. S., Rithanya, R., & Archana, M. (2025). AI Enhanced FinTech Strategies for Driving ESG Investments in Sustainable Finance. In A. Bajaj, A. Abraham, K. R. Madhavi, & O. Castillo (Eds.), *Lecture Notes in Networks and Systems: Vol. 1247 LNNS* (pp. 221–228). Springer Science and Business Media Deutschland GmbH. DOI: 10.1007/978-3-031-81086-2_24

Syarif, M. F., & Aysan, A. F. (2024). Sharia crowdfunding in Indonesia: a regulatory environment perspective. *Journal of Science and Technology Policy Management*. DOI: 10.1108/JSTPM-07-2023-0108

Taghizadeh-Hesary, F. (2025). The impact of artificial intelligence adoption and financial accessibility on energy sustainability. *Energy Strategy Reviews*, *59*, 101744. Advance online publication. DOI: 10.1016/j.esr.2025.101744

Tajudin, M., Omar, R., Smedlund, A., & Aziz, R. P. (2020). Financing with heart and intelligence: augmenting intimacy and sustainability through islamic fintech. *International Journal of Advanced Science and Technology, 29*(9 Special Issue), 1638–1664. https://www.scopus.com/inward/record.uri?eid=2-s2.0-85084368157&partnerID=40&md5=c195213f22e8b1fa570194ac7037a627

Tamasiga, P., Onyeaka, H., & Ouassou, E. H. (2022). Unlocking the Green Economy in African Countries: An Integrated Framework of FinTech as an Enabler of the Transition to Sustainability. *Energies*, *15*(22), 8658. Advance online publication. DOI: 10.3390/en15228658

Taneja, S., Bansal, N., & Kumar, P. (2023). Tech-driven sustainability: Fintech innovations revolutionizing green banking. In *Green Management - A New Paradigm in the World of Business* (pp. 185–203). Nova Science Publishers, Inc., https://www.scopus.com/inward/record.uri?eid=2-s2.0-85183523311&partnerID=40&md5=1184f038fcfdd472ca2c523f6294b7c2

Tepe, G., Geyikci, U. B., & Sancak, F. M. (2022). FinTech Companies: A Bibliometric Analysis. *International Journal of Financial Studies, 10*(1), 2. Advance online publication. DOI: 10.3390/ijfs10010002

Tseng, M.-L., Bui, T.-D., Lim, M. K., Tsai, F. M., & Tan, R. R. (2021). Comparing world regional sustainable supply chain finance using big data analytics: A bibliometric analysis. *Industrial Management & Data Systems, 121*(3), 657–700. DOI: 10.1108/IMDS-09-2020-0521

Vikas, N., Venegas, P., & Aiyer, S. (2022). Role of Banks and Other Financial Institutions in Enhancing Green Digital Finance. In *Economics, Law, and Institutions in Asia Pacific* (pp. 329–352). Springer. DOI: 10.1007/978-981-19-2662-4_16

Vovchenko, N. G., Zenin, K. A., Spiridonov, S. P., & Kuznetsov, V. P. (2023). Managing the Development of Climate-Responsible Entrepreneurship in the Digital Economy Markets in Fintech. In *Environmental Footprints and Eco-Design of Products and Processes* (pp. 219–227). Springer., DOI: 10.1007/978-3-031-28457-1_23

Wessel, M., Gleasure, R., & Kauffman, R. J. (2021). Sustainability of Rewards-Based Crowdfunding: A Quasi-Experimental Analysis of Funding Targets and Backer Satisfaction. *Journal of Management Information Systems, 38*(3), 612–646. DOI: 10.1080/07421222.2021.1987622

Wu, A.-C., & Kao, D.-D. (2022). Mapping the Sustainable Human-Resource Challenges in Southeast Asia's FinTech Sector. *Journal of Risk and Financial Management, 15*(7), 307. Advance online publication. DOI: 10.3390/jrfm15070307

Yadav, O. P., Teotia, R., & Baliyan, R. (2024). Fintech and Data Science: Shaping the Future of the Digital Economy. In *Synergy of AI and Fintech in the Digital Gig Economy* (pp. 332–349). CRC Press. DOI: 10.1201/9781032720104-21

Yadav, O. P., Teotia, R., & Baliyan, R. (2025). Fintech and Data Science: Shaping the Future of the Digital Economy. In *Synergy of AI and Fintech in the Digital Gig Economy* (pp. 316–333). CRC Press. DOI: 10.1201/9781003621454-20

Yao, X. (2025). The green premium in sustainable fintech: Cross-country evidence from crowdfunding. *Finance Research Letters, 77*, 107131. Advance online publication. DOI: 10.1016/j.frl.2025.107131

Yi, T. Z., Rom, N. A. M., Hassan, N. M., Samsurijan, M. S., & Ebekozien, A. (2023). The Adoption of Robo-Advisory among Millennials in the 21st Century: Trust, Usability and Knowledge Perception. *Sustainability (Basel), 15*(7), 6016. Advance online publication. DOI: 10.3390/su15076016

Zetzsche, D. A., & Anker-Sørensen, L. (2022). Towards a Smart Regulation of Sustainable Finance. In *The Palgrave Handbook of ESG and Corporate Governance* (pp. 87–113). Springer International Publishing., DOI: 10.1007/978-3-030-99468-6_4

Zhang, H., Zhang, J., & Pai, C.-H. (2024). Promoting carbon neutrality and green growth through cultural industry financing. *Humanities & Social Sciences Communications, 11*(1), 71. Advance online publication. DOI: 10.1057/s41599-023-02554-5

Chapter 5
Generative AI in Fraud Prevention:
Redefining Financial Security Through Intelligent Systems

Sina Ahmadi
https://orcid.org/0009-0003-2249-2835
NCIS, USA

Maral Mazjini
University of Regina, Canada

ABSTRACT

This chapter explores the transformative potential of generative artificial intelligence (AI) in combating financial fraud, redefining traditional detection systems. It examines generative AI's capabilities in anomaly detection, behavioral modeling, and predictive analytics, addressing fraud complexities from technologies like cryptocurrencies, decentralized finance (DeFi), and AI-driven scams. The integration of generative AI with blockchain enhances transparency, scalability, and proactive prevention. Real-world case studies highlight its effectiveness against credit card fraud, deepfake impersonations, and synthetic identity fraud. Ethical and operational concerns, including AI bias, privacy, and security, are discussed alongside strategies for ethical governance and collaboration. Generative AI is positioned as a key tool for building resilient and trustworthy financial ecosystems to counter current and emerging fraud threats.

DOI: 10.4018/979-8-3373-1250-7.ch005

INTRODUCTION

The contemporary financial industry, from banking to investment, has recently undergone rapid and complex changes that have completely reshaped its contours. New services are being developed at an unprecedented rate in attempt to integrate them with existing technologies. The world economy is being transformed by novel concepts such as virtual banking and cryptocurrency alongside new categories of financial services like Decentralized Finance (DeFi), as it makes transactions simpler and more seamless for the users. However, the issues brought about by these innovations is harder to ignore. The same technological advancements have also led to a rise in sophisticated financial fraud schemes. Now, criminals do not have to rely on tangible crimes, instead they have seamlessly transitioned to the digital era. The evolution from face-to-face banking to mobile banking has indeed brought in multitude of new advantages such as enhanced efficiency in service provision and economic advancement, but, at the same time, new forms of risks have presented themselves, too. Financial services have become a new target for cyber-criminals who are always on the lookout to deceive innocent customers. These institutions are now at risk of unprecedented and unimaginable crimes ranging from being phished for sensitive information to complex cons that target crypto currency wallets. This ongoing danger ensures that the industry has to look for new ways of protecting themself and their customers, which can prove to be quite effective.

It won't be wrong to call control of transactions 'power.' Keeping that power in the hands of a few select intermediaries brings danger," Best says. "In this new age, the intermediate is the one standing to profit the most at the cost of the other party, cutting down on the trust. What ideally should increase the efficiency of the system, actually backfires, leading to conflict." If these DeFi platforms are designed without sufficient due diligence, the token prices can easily be manipulated, the liquidity pools drained or even turned over to flash loan attacks. These aspects allow bad actors to exploit and profit from other people's assets and also bypass the workload of dialing central networks.

A good yet saddening example of this is Wrapped Bitcoin (WBTC), where a claw-back functionality allows a selected custodian to reverse transactions on the blockchain. Even worse is the absence of necessary guardrails that leads to overflows of bad debt on DeFi platforms. As Best states, "the core of these advanced systems are often left fragile."

The evolution of technology such as AI and machine learning have made the existing spectrum of financial fraud more nuanced as well as complex. Today, fraudsters use AI-powered systems to help them automate their phishing campaigns, generate synthetic identities, and circumvent basic security measures. The emergence of deepfake technology, which is capable of impersonating a person's voice and looking like them, has escalated the danger posed by impersonation scams. This progression signals that the routine methods of which tackle these types of fraud, which are often laborious and unproductive, should be replaced.

Rule-based pattern detection systems of the past are outdated and insufficient. The pre-established systems are unable to adapt to the rising sophisticated methods of detection fraud. These systems have shown to misinterpret transactions due to their rigid scope of covering shifts in fraudulent activity, which results in incredibly inaccurate false positives and negatives. This, on top of their inability to cope with the growing rate of online transactions aids in making these systems obsolete. Generative AI, on the other hand, is modernizing the approach. The more advanced algorithms employed by Generative AI are capable of analyzing and comprehending multi-tier datasets and uncover minute anomalies and threat patterns. And that isn't the end of its versatility. The model empowers institutions to conquer fraud and financial crime by mapping out threats, understanding the security shortfalls, and offering robust actionable measures to counteract these breaches. The paradigm shift leaves no room for doubt that the amalgamation of blockchain and Generative AI will foster a new age of sophisticated file integers that greatly reduce vulnerability to financial scams.

This chapter examines how Generative AI is utilized to transform financial fraud detection. It describes the evolution of the fraud ecosystem, the gaps in traditional detection approaches, and the potential that Generative AI holds. The chapter documentation demonstrates the application of Generative AI in different fraud scenarios, including credit card fraud, deepfake impersonation, and synthetic identity fraud. In the realm of ethics, the AI adoption paradox as well as the governance, transparency, and cooperation as remedies to it, are discussed. Trusting Generative AI comes with the ability to enhance the capabilities of financial institutions in fraud prevention and trust violence in the digital space. This chapter sets out to explain the impacts of Generative AI and the intricacies of financial fraud in the world today.

1. IDENTIFYING THE MODERN LANDSCAPE FOR FINANCIAL FRAUD

Financial fraud has taken a completely different turn for the worst in today's world compared to what it was years ago. There has perhaps never been a tougher problem for the society to deal with. Earlier, all a fraudster had to do was simple forgery, stealing cash, or tricking people face-to-face. This has now transformed into a high level technologically advanced crime. Scammers have now fully shifted their focus towards taking advantage of systems that were developed to ease people's financial lives. This is, unfortunately, the reality of how finances operate today, and while innovation could further the cause, in the wrong hands, it can also empower criminals as much as the lawful authorities. As Toshniwal et al. (2025) note, generative AI-driven threats—particularly identity forgeries and deepfake-enabled phishing—are reshaping fraud landscapes in modern fintech ecosystems.

With the rise of the Digital Age, consumers are at the most benefit as they do not have to face any hardships while purchasing goods. Convenience is the new utmost priority due to having mobile payments and online banking that brings managing finances within a click. People are now able to perform financial transactions thanks to DeFi and cryptocurrencies. However, these improvements expose everyone to new risks. The need for an armed criminal to enter a bank is diminished to say the least. Today, multi-target scams can be done under the protection of anonymity. Criminals have the ability to work freely over the internet with the utmost comfort.

Cryptocurrencies serve as an excellent example. First, there is the blockchain technology that provides great security and transparency for each transaction. Second, the pseudo anonymity that comes with crypto wallets eases the process of laundering money, funding illegal activities, or even creating fraudulent schemes such as fake initial coin offerings (ICOs). Furthermore, it is enhanced by doing away with other intermediaries such as banks, enabling users to interact directly via smart contracts. Though such innovations have amazing possibilities, they can easily be exploited as well. Poorly designed smart contracts provide opportunities for manipulation in the form of liquidity draining, token price crashing, or even flash loan fraud.

But a major focus of attacks are the people operating systems. Cyber criminals are utilizing more sophisticated methods through Artificial Intelligence, like deep fake technology. Deep fake technology allows criminals to create realistic audio or videos to impersonate CEOs or high value account holders to get their employees to transfer them money or provide sensitive information. Then there is synthetic identity fraud, where people take real and fake information and merge them to create an entirely new identity. These new identities are created for the sole purpose of opening bank accounts, applying for loans or any other financial crimes while avoiding detection.

The crimes leave much deeper impacts than just financial losses. For institutions, simply assuming a high profile fraud claim can damage their reputation and customer trust for several years. Customers begin to question if their money along with sensitive personal data is secure and in some scenarios take their businesses elsewhere. With regards to fraud victims, these people tend to face a number of mental health issues, along with the stress and anger of going through a long process of fighting the fraudulent charges and recovering their credit score.

Simple tools targeting and marking fraudulent activities deal with a much larger issue, which is technology misalignment. Most systems that detect transactions fraud use static patterns and rules. For instance, a transaction that is too high or occurs from a foreign country is automatically flagged. While traditional systems used to work, the complexity and advancement of fraud techniques have increased significantly. Criminals have found multiple ways of evading the system and tend to evolve their techniques at a rate that is more rapid then the systems evolution. The problem is only amplified by the escalation of online transactions as older systems are not equipped to sustain such a magnitude.

There exists a clear need for more advanced solutions to tackle the problem firm head on, Fraudsters are growing and expanding along with current technology. After systems are developed, adopting tools becomes essential. Generative AI is fully capable of proactively eliminating frauds activities, and help guard the interests of the party on the attacked system.

1.1 Financial Fraud in Evolution: Contemporary Trends

Figure 1. Phishing attacks are a common method of financial fraud, where cybercriminals create fake bank portals or send fake emails to deceive and steal from victims.

The financial market's changes have made it possible to create new services. People worldwide now choose web and mobile banking more and more because these channels make their financial lives easier. Since the Internet became the main place for people to bank, more risky activity sprang up because hackers targeted this area. Cybercriminals exploit financial companies' weaknesses by breaking into their authentication systems and poor-quality networks to move money illegally and change financial data in harmful ways (Dorminey et al., 2012).

Two tech advancements - cryptocurrencies and technologies like DeFi - change how banks work and where anti-fraud workers fight crime. Bitcoin and other virtual currencies keep transactions safe by using the decentralizing 'blockchain' technology. Blockchain's unique approach hides information about transactions from public view while keeping them safe, but it's wrongfully used to launder money and collect ransoms (Ryabov et al., 2021). DeFi applications have the same basic trouble areas, such as how lending and trading operate on smart contracts. How smart contracts are written can leave open security holes, and no laws stop people from using flash loans and fake tokens to trick investors.

Advanced financial tools making things easier have made fraud activities more likely. Our modern money systems run on AI, machine learning, and automation, which has given fraudsters new ways to rip us off. Researchers can now create convincing fake e-mails using advanced math models to fool people. They also use number patterns to deceive financial traders by tricking the market (Dorminey et al., 2012). Security weaknesses often arise in financial deals through Internet-of-Things devices because these gadgets mostly lack basic protection methods. Because fraud and scams keep growing with new technology, we need fresh methods to keep the financial market safe.

1.2 Emerging Fraud Tactics Driven by Advancing Technologies

New technology makes it easier for criminals to commit crimes, a big problem for filtering systems designed to keep things legal. People behind scams are using advanced ways to trick victims, like phishing frauds with AI tools, deepfake fake identities, and making up fresh new thief names.

Artificial Intelligence has elevated phishing scams beyond traditional methods, making them more sophisticated and convincing. The ability to read massive user data with current machine-learning techniques lets criminals create messages that look completely genuine. The messages use writing styles that match official, trusted companies, which makes regular users think they are legitimate emails rather than fake scams. Unlike basic phishing, AI methods create new ways to fool users based on how people react. When scammers adapt their approach, they make their phishing attacks work better (West & Bhattacharya, 2016). Recent studies emphasize how generative AI enables deeper behavioral profiling, allowing financial systems to identify nuanced fraudulent patterns beyond traditional AI scope (Sachdeva et al., 2025).

Deepfake Impersonations are deceptive technologies that use sophisticated deep learning to make fake audio and video look real. Scammers use AI to trick people by making them look like real individuals, such as the boss and the account owner, signing off and authorizing transactions and dodgy systems. Workers were tricked into making money transfers when they saw a fake video of their manager asking them to deposit those funds into the manager's fraudulent account, shown by a forged manager's picture. Most deepfake fakes look too real for fake-check systems that can't detect information mismatches (Abdallah et al., 2016).

In Synthetic Identity Fraud, criminals create a new personality using real parts and false information. Crooks mix pretend Social Security numbers and true data to make a whole new phony account. People create these fake identities once, and agencies may not know about them immediately for a long time. Regular fraud prevention tools aren't enough to stop synthetic identity theft. These identities don't match standard ways of identifying people, but they aren't made up. Phishing scams have become more widespread since people can find and access personal data through the dark web more easily, as West and Bhattacharya (2016) say.

Advanced information technologies make fraud in this space difficult to fight effectively. Two tactics shape how AI helps phishing attacks: machine learning makes the phish look more real, while deepfakes build perfect impostor content by basic neural networks. Besides, new fraudsters use their easy access to personal information across the Internet to trick systems that normally check real people's legitimacy. Dealing with fraud requires us to adopt fresh techniques that effectively and quickly address modern fraud and its complexity.

1.3 Restrictions on the Application of Conventional Fraud Control Instruments

Traditional fraud prevention tools struggle to address the complexities of modern fraud schemes. Firstly, they rely on specific rules. Secondly, they detect many scams that aren't there. And thirdly, they struggle to keep up with rising fraud scales. The limitations of current fraud prevention systems can be addressed by integrating advanced risk-detection tools.

Rule-based Systems have long been the core of fraud detection techniques. They can only spot abnormal activities on typical transaction levels and within expected behavior. These simple systems are easy to develop, but their rules reduce flexibility. These systems rely on pre-set patterns, limiting their ability to detect novel or evolving fraud schemes. Because fixed-rule systems are predictable, criminals adapt their strategies to bypass them. It's tough for systems to spot fraud in transactions when small amounts are taken away individually across many sales. The fixed nature of rule-based systems limits their ability to keep up with changing fraud patterns, leaving gaps in company security, according to Patcha and Park (2007).

Regular fraud systems deal with two big problems: they wrongly label stop-approved transactions (false positives), which causes waste, and fail to catch legitimate suspicious transactions (false negatives). When a bank labels a legitimate transaction as possibly fraudulent, it causes trouble for cardholders and causes the company to spend more on handling operations. When fraud goes unchecked, the company incurs money loss and reputation damage because the transaction failed to be spotted. Rule-based systems can't see if deals are real or fake because they stay stuck inside their rules without looking at other things around them. Examples like big orders put through around Christmas normally raise watchful company alarms, but they're legitimate businesses. The mismatch between actual and expected transactions makes buyers less sure about their safety and adds to banks' strain since they have to physically check out each flagged trade (Vaquero, 2023).

In addition to existing issues, the overall setup of traditional fraud detection systems struggles even more with these issues. Financial institutions must think quickly when massive amounts of data from digital payments and online shopping need analysis before they can act. When scam warnings reach too many accounts too quickly, rule-based systems can't match the speed, leaving room for delays that hurt customers. Analyzing large amounts of data that must meet specific requirements when more transactions occur takes a lot of computer work. In addition, it's difficult to manage new fraud patterns as they emerge because manuals have to be adjusted manually, and the system struggles to handle large volumes of data. When customers make transactions more frequently during busy shopping events around holidays, big sales days, and peak spending times, these outdated systems struggle to protect customer data effectively (Patcha & Park, 2007).

We require better fraud detection systems because of these system problems - being hard to update, producing too many wrong results, and coping with high numbers of transactions. Old techniques that use alphabets and numbers cannot stop today's fraud techniques, and banks keep getting tricked. Generating AI and teaching computers to learn can address these problems by seeing fresh fraud patterns while accurately, constantly changing, and understanding the situation.

Figure 2. Limitations of traditional fraud control instruments

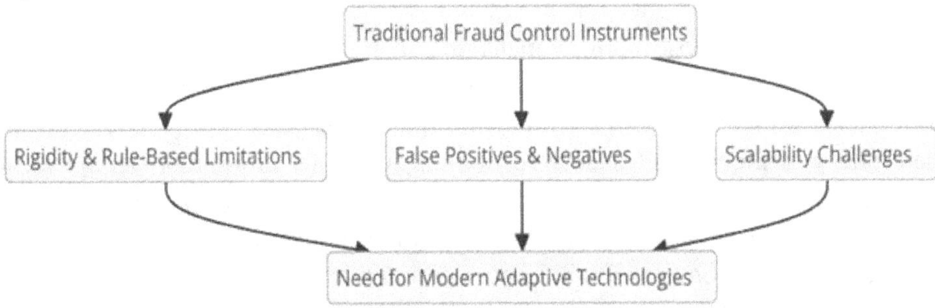

1.4 The Cost and the Brand Damage of Fraud

Fraud significantly impacts financial institutions, causing financial losses and eroding trust. Our goal in understanding the effects of fraud is to build stronger defense systems to stop these disastrous consequences.

Fraud makes organizations and other businesses in the worldwide economy suffer financial losses. Fraudulent activities cost banks large amounts of money every year throughout French-speaking countries. Fraud causes financial losses through stolen funds, legal fees, operational costs, and regulatory fines. When organizations get hit by fraud, they pass these losses forward to customers by having to raise their fees or cutting back on the services they provide. All these outcomes will affect many parts of the economy. According to the research by Fich and Shivdasani (2007), investors' trust in markets drops when financial fraud occurs, which means they will put fewer funds into businesses. The economic crisis caused by fraud hurts individual companies and all economic activities.

High-profile fraud cases illustrate the severe impact on an organization's financial health and reputation. Early 2000s saw investors get hit by corporate fraud, and the biggest example of this was what happened at Enron. The company's top managers lied about financial matters to hide loan problems and make income look much better than it was. This caused $74 billion in losses and wiped out all shareholder money while erasing the business from existence. Dow's actions drove the government to create the Sarbanes Oxley Act to make firms publicly traded on the market more accountable.

Just one year after the financial crisis, the Madoff Ponzi scheme stole more than $65 billion from investors. Investors lost money, proofing how weak regulation laws were meant to be. These events show businesses have to worry about their cash flow and public image being damaged. Disgraced hackers' actions continue to harm businesses months after their payments, and companies must work hard to regain their customers' trust (Velikonja, 2012).

Many customers lose faith in managing their finances because fraud keeps causing serious issues. The financial system works because people trust it to safely protect and use their money. When fraud takes place, customers worry about whether their money is safe in that financial institution. A client's information being leaked damages their trust so badly they're likely to take their business to another bank.

The emotional damage fraud causes to customers should never be underestimated. Customers cut back on their financial service activities because fear, anger, feeling violated, and other factors put pressure on them. The trust problem stays within the affected organization and affects the company in ways beyond its industry's larger financial system. It's vital to fight fraud today to protect our revenue streams and put trust back in our business, both from customers and investors (Fich & Shivdasani, 2007).

When fraud happens, it costs the company both money and its good image. Learning from canceled projects and lost income is why we must develop ways to stop fraud from harming our company and how it moves. Big frauds like these demonstrate that businesses and investors take big hits: they lose their money while companies get a bad name that doesn't go away easily. What goes wrong with customer trust highlights why we need to protect their important data and remain open-minded. By adding fraud prevention technology, businesses can increase their security while asking customers to actively engage in keeping fraud at bay. If we can treat the main reasons for fraud better, and people see they're important, customers may feel safer when they buy. When financial institutions have their credit under control, they help keep the economy running smoothly (Irfan, Hussainey, Chan Bukhari, & Nam, 2024).

1.5 Trends and the Need for More Sophisticated Anti-Fraud Tools

As financial fraud is constantly developing in complexity, one has to find new and various ways to prevent the threats. Inhibition of former fraud protection measures developed through conventional rules and reactive approaches is becoming insufficient to counter modern fraud antagonists. Institutions must ensure strategies are the key to creating protective financial systems and restoring consumer confidence by embedding Generative AI into the financial sector activities. In this section, the author examines the methods of implementing proactive and adaptive technologies and explains why Generative AI solves the problems of classic systems.

Conventional anti-fraud processes primarily function as reactive controls, identifying and addressing fraud after it occurs. These systems offer baseline protection but largely fail to perform this job as they are designed to use highly constrained, predefined behavior patterns. There are always new tricks by fraudsters; since fraudsters use various technologies to exploit these areas of weakness, any measures taken need to be proactive, as reactive solutions do not prevent further losses and tarnishing of the image of an organization (Awoyemi et al., 2017).

Fraud prevention is an effective approach of management that prevents drastic change from action and response. Another type of response is an action taken before the actual threat: transaction monitoring and pattern recognition that predict future threats. For instance, the machine learning model's algorithms can capture latent patterns of transactional data and alert users of suspicious undertakings even if they do not exhibit any typical characteristics inherent in fraudulent incidences. These strategies depend on systems created to adapt to changing fraud management techniques and frameworks to extend capabilities within changing contexts. Insofar as adaptive fraud prevention also decreases the degree to which operations rely on manual rule updates, improving efficiency (Irfan, Elmogy, Gupta, Khalifa, & Dias, 2024).

Another strength of proactive systems is scalability. As the number of financial transactions rises, institutions need fraud prevention systems capable of processing larger data sets but with equivalent levels of efficiency and effectiveness. Real-time analysis of the big data sets requires adaptive systems based on machine learning and artificial intelligence (AI), which supply institutions with the computational power needed to fight new threats. The above ensures that fraud prevention mechanisms can deal with the increased complexity of the contemporary financial system (Awoyemi et al., 2017).

We believe Generative AI is a step forward from traditional fraud prevention systems since it has an analysis, prediction, and learning capacity. While other conceptually simple approaches rely on fewer but stricter rules to recognize potentially fraudulent patterns, Generative AI models with algorithms like GANs analyze the data to generate patterns and identify possible fraud scenarios, then point at the subtle anomalies that differ from the most often encountered cases. Based on historical data, Generative AI can generate realistic fakes of fraudulent schemes, allowing institutions to prevent threats before they appear.

Another important benefit associated with Generative AI is the ability to identify anomalies. The major weakness of conventional models is that they cannot distinguish between normal variation and fraud, thus producing high levels of false positives and negatives. While there is the use of supervised learning, where the algorithm is trained to classify predictors that prejudice fraudulent actions, Generative AI, on the other hand, uses deep learning methods to notice even petty anomalies that are likely to show fraudulent behavior. For instance, an AI model will be able to identify sequential discrepancies in a set of transactions or alert users of log-in behaviors that are out of tune with typical user behavior. This capability greatly increases the effectiveness of the fraud detection process and limits the chances of business disruption and, thus, customer dissatisfaction (Bandi et al., 2023).

A feature of the generation of Generative AI is its ability to simulate fraud conditions. Another advantage of AI models is their ability to produce synthetic data with which it is possible to evaluate the vulnerability of predeveloped anti-fraud systems in certain situations. For instance, Generative AI arrangements could emulate phishing, synthetic personality fraud, or synchronized record takeovers with the vision to discover cracks in security architectures. These simulations help financial institutions prepare and solve weaknesses globally to ensure that fraud prevention systems are ready to face challenges. It also plays a big role in preventing monetary damage and is an ongoing process of enhancing organizational preventive measures and awareness (Irfan, Elhoseny, Kassim, & Metawa, 2023).

These are only a few of many applications, but they reflect on the areas where Generative AI delivers well, for instance, in predictive analytics. While reviewing large historical datasets and attracting new tendencies, Generative AI models can accurately predict new fraud scenarios. This capability enables institutions to implement preventive measures such as increased monitoring in vulnerable places or the motivation of more people when fraud incidences are rife. Therefore, predictive analytics supports resource management by helping institutions properly direct their efforts on the most critical threats (Bandi et al., 2023).

Moreover, compared with Generative AI, which has great technical potentiality, there is the possibility of implementing the discussions of ethical aspects into the fight against fraud. Today's large financial institutions are starting to come under pressure from regulators and consumers to make appropriate AI-driven decisions. Deploying Generative AI can show how decisions are specifically reached to ensure that fraud prevention mechanisms in place meet the set regulatory standards and ethical benchmarks. For instance, XAI interfaces can amplify the details that contributed to a transaction being marked as suspicious, allowing anti-fraud professionals to embrace the technical solutions.

The broader applicability of Generative AI also signifies the compatibility and applicability of the technology with other complex and progressive technologies, including blockchain and DeFi. Blockchain offers an undecipherable data registry to effect financial transactions, which is complemented by Generative AI, which transmits real-time effects related to transactional states. This synergy provides the frequently used multi-tiered security environment that is very efficient and highly dynamic in preventing fraud in the communication of financial transactions.

The need to develop sophisticated solutions for fraud originates from the fact that the old systems cannot effectively contain contemporary fraudsters and their highly complex strategies. Taking advantage of strong AI such as Generative AI, preventive and reactive measures remain the most potent anti-fraud tools for institutions in the future. Such is the role of Generative AI to overcome the main shortcomings. It improves the possibility of anomaly detection, helps to simulate fraud situations, and gives the predictive analysis that makes amends of the fraud prevention into proactive rather than reactive. With the use of ethical thinking and in terms of assisting with shared stakeholder management, Generative AI is proactive in reinforcing the organizations' credibility and strengthening financial industry's framework. The widespread perpetration of fraud in current society can only be countered by adopting and implementing these sophisticated measures to protect financial networks and sustain audiences' trust in a progressively sophisticated global matrix.

2. OPTIMIZING GENERATIVE AI FOR FRAUD MITIGATION

The application of Generative AI has revolutionized the detection of fraud in the financial world. It is not merely a new method that assists in spotting fraudulent cases; it can learn, evolve, and predict. Unlike older systems that depend on static data and preset boundaries, Generative AI uses real-time data. It processes a massive amount of information, identifies patterns, and exposes fraudulent actions that older systems would overlook.

Generative AI stands out due to the way it captures anomalies. Older systems can successfully check abstract problems like enormous international transactions, while Generative AI can do more than just that. Consider if a customer who used to spend a few hundred dollars at their local grocery store starts purchasing a few items at random international stores. AI recognizes a change in their behavior. It's this small detail that makes catching fraud easier.

Another key benefit of Generative AI is the ability to learn from personal behavioral data. Rather than using broad patterns, it forms a unique profile for each individual based on their transaction records, spending frequency, and engagement. Any activity which does not conform to the profile, such as unusual geographic logins or excessive expenditure, generates an alert. Such bespoke profiling reduces the chances of successful fraud.

What makes Generative AI more useful is its capability to predict and stop fraud. Using historical data, it can pinpoint specific activities that are financially fraudulent and suggest where fraud is most likely to occur next. For example, it may observe that phishing scams increase during the tax period and warn financial institutions well in advance. Generative AI can also test bank systems by using simulated scenarios. Take the case where AI impersonates an identity fraud attempt. If heteronomous systems do not pick it up, the AI can provide specific guidance on what changes need to be made in order to capture these gaps before a genuine attack is experienced.

Generative AI is equally effective when used in tandem with other technologies such as blockchain. Blockchain technology is famous for its secure, trustworthy ledger, even though it has its weaknesses and loopholes. When Generative AI is integrated, institutions can use it as an extra protective layer. For example, Generative AI can track trades on decentralized finance platforms and monitor trading activities in real time. Should there be a sudden spike in trading volume or any unexpected modifications to the smart contract, AI could flag these transactions as suspicious. Such combinations of transparency and AI intelligence greatly increase the level of protection.

There are some hurdles, however, to the incorporation of Generative AI. For one, data privacy poses one of the biggest concerns. In order for the AI to be successful, it must funnel into a specific collection of sensitive materials which questions how that information would be retrieved, kept, and put to use. Another problem flagging imbalance is bias. AI models trained with deficient or unequal data sets can be unfair or incorrect in their predictions. This is the reason Explainable AI (XAI) is coming to the forefront: to help institutions make sense of the choices their AI systems take on. In the case of an AI flagging a transaction as suspicious, XAI would elucidate the system's reasoning for building customer and regulatory trust.

From a structural perspective, fraud is always one step ahead and is systematically evolving at the same pace that traditional systems are put in place. Generative AI, by gendering smarter solutions, arms financial institutions with the capability to protect their clients, reputation, and profits. Fraud will always be an issue, but tools like these allow us to proactively address the importance of staying on the offensive.

2.1 Core AI Strengths for Fraud Monitoring

Figure 3. Core capabilities of Generative AI in fraud detection

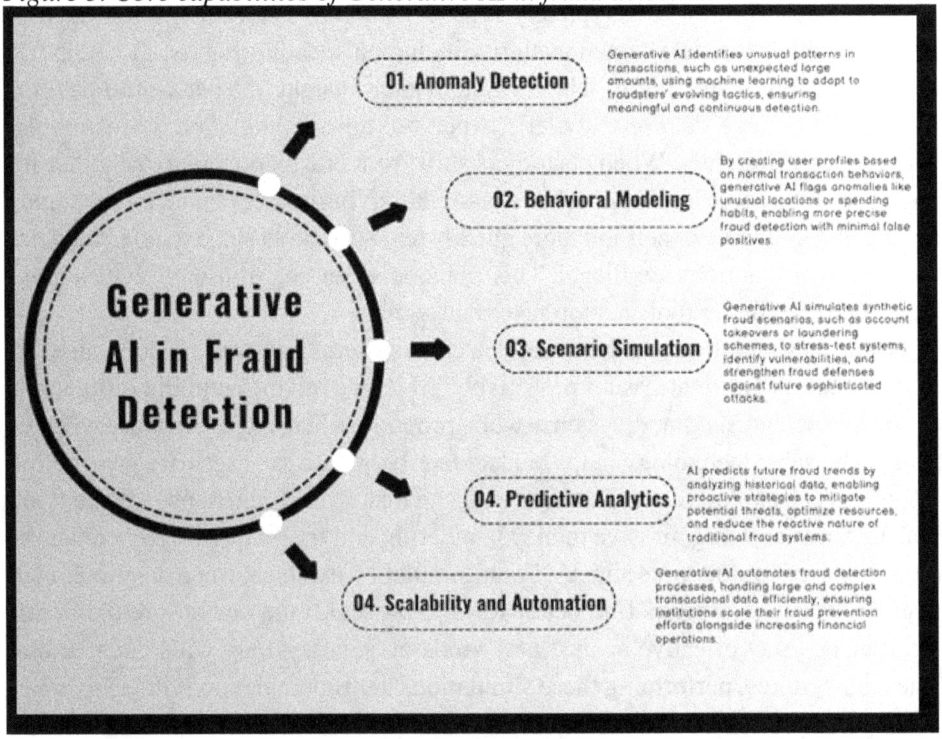

New Generative AI powered tools improve how experts find and stop fraudulent acts, making their jobs better and more efficient. Through the use of these areas, anomaly detection, behavioral analysis, situational planning, and future data study, we have the most robust systems that detect fraud right when it happens and prevent it. The same artificial intelligence behind Generative AI helps us see and learn from patterns, uncover hidden data, and make accurate predictions to fight today's complex money crime.

The first way Generative AI helps find fraud is by spotting unusual activities. The way trading platforms work now is to spot strange behaviors, especially in financial deals that may involve cheating. Current modeling methods rely heavily on fixed rules, but these rules don't catch more nuanced changes that aren't already programmed. AI systems that generate new things study large transaction data, determine normal behavior, and spot fraud activities. AI systems can detect anomalies, such as a regular customer making an unusually large payment. The learning

AI systems can update their fraud search mechanisms whenever people cheat by receiving fresh processing data from us.

Our method involves creating different customer profiles to spot activities immediately against how users typically behave. Generative AI systems analyze user data to establish typical payment patterns, including spending habits, shopping frequency, locations, and timing. The AI system gains insight into behavioral patterns by examining large data sets. It alerts experts to take action when it sees regular users acting differently. When customers shift from one market area to another for payments, the system must be checked again. Classifying people's behavior accurately helps fraud systems do their job more quickly and accurately since regular statistics can't tell which actions are illegal. This rich understanding of user activities gives financial firms better tools to stop fake transactions.

Scenario simulation enables fraud detection systems powered by Generative AI to anticipate and mitigate issues proactively. AI lets us run different fraud situations to see if our current fraud systems work properly when facing various types of fraud. The same technology helps banks identify and address security gaps before fraudsters can exploit them. Generative AI can make fake fraud happen by copying real accounts or doing massive money laundering and trying out different defenses currently used to stop these attacks. Fraud simulation exercises run many times and, over the years, help banks find better ways to prevent fraud and ensure their anti-fraud tactics stay effective against new kinds of scams. Along with safeguarding financial systems, performing these simulations helps organizations develop better fraud protection methods and prepares them to prevent fraud when it happens.

Our fourth essential AI technology tool helps spot fraud by looking at present data to forecast when fraud might strike again and how. The AI models help us find new ways to stop past frauds and predict where fraud could happen next. When fraud techniques become clear from past data, financial institutions can use this knowledge to prepare their defenses against possible future attacks. The system learns how big data relates to fraud by analyzing patterns and using this knowledge to predict when new crimes could happen. Our AI models help protect institutions by using data to know when phishing attacks will be most serious against specific groups of people so we can take extra steps to keep them safe. This fraud-fighting plan is more successful because it works better and helps better use available resources - focusing assets where they have the biggest impact. The ability to stop fraud before it happens makes our strategies much better, reducing how often we need to react after a fraud is found using predictive models.

Generative AI's tools, anomaly detection, behavioral modeling, market forecasting, and predictive analytics offer robust and continuous fraud prevention. Since Generative AI keeps learning from fresh data and reacts to new fraud strategies, it improves its fraud-fighting systems regularly. Financial institutions need this flexibility because new and complex fraud techniques keep showing up.

When we build these capabilities together, they form a complete defense system that works independently and as a package against fraud. Detecting suspicious activity immediately, behavioral learning helps improve these observations, finding proof through scenario studies keeps them going, and seeing what's ahead helps prepare for future trial findings. Our data-based approach helps banks better investigate and avoid fraud while teaching their teams to stay ahead of new threats.

In addition to these technical benefits, Generative AI improves a firm's operational performance by minimizing extensive human involvement in intricate procedures that the Generative AI tool can handle independently. Conventional anti-fraud techniques require considerable working time and effort to complete tasks like rule definition, data examination, and simulation checks, which can be seriously erroneous. Generative AI automates processes of identifying and preventing fraud; thus, financial institutions can quickly and effectively respond to and counter fraud. Besides, this automation saves the company money, directs an analyst's work to more detailed and potentially risky cases, and creates new and higher fraud detection strategies.

In addition, Generative AI enhances scalability in fraud detection systems since it can generate infinite possibilities of check paths, unlike other deterministic algorithms. Since the amount and complexity of transactions being processed increases as financial institutions evolve, it becomes critical to deploy solutions to monitor and mitigate the risk of fraud at scale accurately and efficiently. These Generative AI models are always elastic; they can ingest more data and interpret the results in real-time without more computational power. These features guarantee that fraud detection solutions adapt to a growing pace of financial transactions to remain protective and performant as the transactional flow grows faster in terms of the number of operations and their variety.

The third major benefit of Generative AI is improving cooperation and knowledge exchange inside and between financial organizations. AI models act as data-based pattern recognition engines that can derive and present trends and patterns of specific interest to several stakeholders. For instance, if one institution discovers that a certain fraud trend is occurring, Generative AI can alert a network of institutions through which institutions that discover new fraudulent techniques update the fraud detection model. Reporting Here, there is a teamwork approach to combating fraud and information and intelligence to improve the security of the financial environment.

Thus, Generative AI-based outcomes, such as anomaly detection, behavioral modeling, simulation, and predictive analysis, can be seen as a profound paradigm shift in the financial sector's belief in fraud prevention. It explains how these capabilities help financial institution clients detect and prevent fraud with higher precision, speed, and flexibility to overcome the drawbacks of rule-based solutions. By employing

Generative AI, institutions can move from reactive and static fraud defenses to more active and adaptive approaches that can better respond to emerging fraud risks.

2.2 Integrating Generative AI with Blockchain and Decentralized Systems

Thus, combining Generative AI with Blockchain and decentralized systems is the new step in fraud mitigation. Due to such complementarity, Blockchain utilizes the key features of AI to build a highly secure, open, and efficient financial system. It is thus possible for financial institutions to complement the highly secure ECDSA and Bitcoin Blockchain with Generative AI's intelligent decision-making capability to develop powerful and effective security measures to counter fraud. This section highlights the characteristics of this integration: immutability data for training AI models, smart front contract automation, decentralized surveillance, and improving trust in the system.

Training Generative AI models with immutable data enhances blockchain's role as an enabling technology for fraud prevention. Another aspect is that blockchain applications take care of transparency and unchangeability of records as far as the training of AI models is concerned; the data used are accurate, secure, and unchangeable. This high-quality data is useful in building effective artificial intelligence models as it addresses many concerns about biases and spikes the accuracy of the fraud detection models. Thus, with the help of the Blockchain's unchangeable register, financial organizations can get a full range of reliable and realistic data on transactions. Such reliability is crucial when developing Generative AI models that can accurately monitor and differentiate between genuine and fake transactions. In addition, since Blockchain has openness in its system, it simplifies the process of tracking who is responsible for which data in the management process of training the AI models, thereby eradicating the possibility of manipulated and fraudulent data.

Smart Contract Automation means that Generative AI is used to improve prospects and protect smart contracts. Cryptocurrency based on smart contracts is an algorithm that automatically executes terms agreed by the two parties coded on platforms based on blockchain technology. Combining Generative AI with smart contracts allows for the identification and prevention of fraud in those contracts. Through AI monitoring, large volumes of transactions can be scrutinized to identify fraudulent activities. At the same time, conditions in smart contracts can be instantiated and implemented in real-time so that unauthorized transactions are immediately flagged or stifled. For instance, the Generative AI can analyze a peculiar frequency of transactions that may hint at money laundering, suspend the related accounts to self-executed contracts, and inform the enforcement bodies. In addition to improving the effectiveness of fraud-detection procedures, such modulations also lessen the dependence on manual control, which could cause errors or inefficiencies, enhancing the general security of smart contract implementation.

Another important ingredient is Decentralized Surveillance when using Generative AI in combination with Blockchain and decentralized systems. When discussing DeFi technology, people imply a direct distribution of money transactions between individuals and organizations for which there is no control over the security of such transactions. Using Generative AI in real-time, monitoring and surveillance of DeFi platforms can be efficiently done with an anti-fraud view, which covers aspects such as market manipulation, pump-and-dump, and unauthorized trading. Since Generative AI can process transactional data and user behavior when using DEXs and other DeFi platforms on an ongoing basis, it can determine behavior that deviates from the norm and suggests fraudulent activities. Proactive surveillance will help to prevent fraud, and anybody attempting to defraud others will be caught red-handed. This will safeguard the decentralized financial systems from fraudsters and those who wish to exploit others to get-rich-quick schemes.

Increased trust and transparency are two main advantages of uniting the Blockchain's transparent ledger and Generative AI's reporting and analytical capabilities. Blockchain's transparent ledger provides a secure record of transactions, making it difficult to forge or alter. When combined with Generative AI, this transparency is.

Supplemented with intelligent analysis and near real-time value added to the transactional data. By inspecting the patterns and correlations in blockchain data, Generative AI can reveal many previously unnoticed fraudulent activities, thereby enhancing the reliability of financial transactions. The integration of the two enhances the levels of trust because users and stakeholders can validate the transaction's legitimacy and accuracy from the public ledger while enjoying Generative AI's proficient fraud prevention functionalities.

However, when Generative AI is connected to Blockchain, it is easy to create complex security layers that are both robust and scalable. One key advantage is related to the decentralization of storing data in the Blockchain since this excludes possibilities of single points of failure technologies. When Generative AI is applied to decentralized data, it provides a comprehensive view, enabling the detection and analysis of anomalies across the network. This approach guarantees that fraud detection is not only done randomly but covers the whole financial system, thereby making the framework stronger and more capable of preventing fraud.

Also, integrating Blockchain with Generative AI helps build unalterable audit trails and different reporting processes integral to compliance. Financial institutions can use blockchain technology to keep track records of all the transactions and the corresponding decisions taken through artificial intelligence to prevent fraud. These unalterable audit trails support each other and enable the identification of responsibility and compliance with the regulations. These records can be of great immense help when trying to conduct a proper investigation of a fraud related incident. They can greatly assist in the primary issue of the institution, which is to protect the clients' interests whilst protecting security and accountability considerations. This level of accountability bolsters the institution's internal security levels as well as the external image of the institution with customers and regulators.

Besides, combining Generative AI with Blockchain and decentralized systems enhances the current and new approaches to combating fraud. Using both technologies, banking institutions can develop new strategies for fighting fraudulent activities in the market, which was impossible before. For instance, while analyzing blockchain data, there are specific fraud patterns where AI may improve on conventional methods to identify new elaborate fraud scenarios. Blockchain's unchangeable nature is suitable for executing such enhanced methods. It creates an environment conducive to creating better solutions and adopting new technologies, keeping pace with new types of fraud emerging in financial institutions, and assuring that competitive advantage remains firmly in the hands of those financial institutions.

The other consideration of the discussed topic is the possibility of increased integration and interaction between the various players in the financial industry. They argued that due to its structure, Blockchain is perfect for integrating and sharing data across different entities, which could be a key to cooperation, and Generative AI supplies the analytics necessary for processing this shared data. Banks and other financial institutions can coordinate and exchange information and intelligence on fraud associated with existing and emerging products and services and use Generative AI to intelligently process vast volumes of structured and unstructured information from internal and external data sources. This approach not only adds to the overall capability of identifying fraud but also creates a unified front in fighting fraud that takes advantage of differences in one system relative to another.

To the same extent, integrating Generative AI with Blockchain and decentralized systems underpins better framing and agreeing on more user-empowering compliance around fraud. While watching the users' behaviors and transactions concerning AI, financial institutions can adjust their fraud prevention for every user and the risks connected with their operations. This strategy guarantees that fraud controls resonate with clients while maximizing control efficiency with minimal inconvenience to the end users. Since the system is refining these alerts, users stand to receive fewer false alerts or only the most relevant ones, hence increasing the rate of detection and response to fraud.

Moreover, incorporating Generative AI with Blockchain has additional advantages in promoting complex authentication and verification methods. For instance, AI can use biometric data and patterns of behavior stored in Blockchain to offer secure and efficient multiple-factor authentication. This integration ensures that only authorized personnel can pull information about financial items or execute a transaction, minimizing fraud or bias access. Using the characteristics of AI, which is the ability to work with large volumes of data, and the use of Blockchain, which provides high-level data protection, financial organizations can develop reliable mechanisms for user identification that will be protected from fraud and cyber attacks.

Finally, integration with Generative AI in Blockchain and decentralized systems also contributes to developing better conditions for general stability of the financial environments and EO. This integration has the added advantage of increasing confidence within the financial market because it provides the tools for detecting fraud and can increase the security and transaction visibility. This resilience is very important in preventing and dampening shocks that are likely to affect the essentials of the financial institutions as well as the sustainability of the financial sector. With increasing complexity and globalization in financial systems, Generative AI in synergy with Blockchain will be particularly critical in responding to the appropriate protection of financial transactions and consumer privacy rights and building the financial market's safety.

Thus, blending Generative AI with the Blockchain and decentralized systems offers a breakthrough in the fight against fraud. Using immutable data to develop AI models for fraud detection, automating smart contracts, decentralized monitoring, and establishing high levels of transparency, financial institutions can design and create strong security platforms that are nearly perfect for fighting fraud cases. This integration enhances the use of both technologies to offer flexible, integrated, and robust fraud prevention solutions that overcome the drawbacks of conventional technologies. With the ability of financial frauds to get worked up in terms of elaborateness and sophistication, Generative AI, when integrated with Blockchain, will serve as a significant foundation towards guaranteeing the credibility, safety, and soundness of the financial transaction, hence will address financial security and resilience.

2.3 Practical Applications and Case Studies

By using Generative AI, a lot has been realized in affording a solution to fraud within different areas of finance. In its broadest sense, Generative AI empowers financial institutions to identify and shield themselves from fraud through improved data mining, deep learning, and machine learning approaches. This section explores three key areas where Generative AI has been effectively implemented: Credit card fraud detection, DeFi fraud prevention, Deepfake, and Synthetic identity detection.

We provide concrete examples and use cases on how big players in finance and digital ecosystems leverage Generative AI to safeguard their businesses and users.

Credit Card Fraud Detection is one of the most revolutionary uses of Generative AI in the financial industry. Some of the largest economic players, such as JPMorgan Chase and HSBC, began applying Generative AI to realize improved results and prevent and detect fraud. Traditional credit card fraud detection relies on rule-based models that flag anomalies such as frequent purchases, irregular activities, or high-value transactions. However, these systems can cause many false positives, which are inconvenient to customers and costly to organizations.

Generative AI models, on the other hand, use techniques in deep learning to analyze large volumes of real-time transaction data to selectively look for any incremental irregularities that may point to fraudulent transactions. For example, JPMorgan Chase uses GAN to generate fake purchases and teach the AI systems what counterfeit looks like. It does this with increased effectiveness without increasing the rate of false positives but with greater accuracy in identifying fraud and other suspicious activities. Consequently, HSBC has realized fewer fraud losses and increased customer satisfaction because of fewer unjustified merchant declines. Such improvements reemphasize the imprecise necessity of Generative AI in improving the steadiness and stability of credit card fraud detection.

Another major field in which Generative AI is proving to be highly useful is in DeFi Fraud Prevention. DeFi platforms like Aave and Uniswap eliminate intermediaries, relying on computer code for fund transfers, but they introduce new risks. Still, like any new industry, DeFi brings new risks from the financial world, and innovations also open doors for fraudsters. Generative AI offers DeFi platforms all the hardware required to defend their decentralized lending applications against complex fraud, including flash loan attacks and compromised protocols.

Aave, a leading DeFi platform, uses Generative AI models to monitor transaction data and identify patterns indicative of flash loan attacks, where attackers exploit weaknesses to manipulate prices or drain liquidity pools. Using Generative AI, it becomes possible to define all sorts of attacks that may happen to Aave; therefore, with the technological solution, Aave can prevent such attacks and reverse the processes they cause for as long as they harm the project. Likewise, Uniswap employs this Generative AI to scrutinize all the unusual trading scenarios and Avert token manipulation while adopting the Decentralized Exchange (DEX). The mentioned strategies help increase the security level of DeFi platforms but also provide users with more trustful environments with improved protection from scams. The use case of Generative AI in DeFi transitioning demonstrates its fungibility and efficacy in protecting decentralized financing against new types of fraud.

Deepfake and Synthetic Identity Detection is an exciting, growing domain that benefits from Generative AI in protecting users and their identities. The new neural networks that make deepfake audio and video fully indistinguishable from the real ones raise cumbersome problems regarding user identification during onboarding. Lenders and Internet marketplaces are now the most threatened by deepfakes and synthetic identity fraud, where the scammer combines real and fake data to create a completely fake persona.

Current Generative AI models, especially deep learning-based ones, are good at identifying counterfeits as they look for distortions and other anomalies that are undetectable by a bare eye. For instance, large institutions such as Wells Fargo have used Generative AI techniques to analyze facial recognition details and other conduct during account opening. Such systems may detect unusual changes in facial expressions, tone of voice, typing speed, or rhythm patterns, indicating a synthetic-constructed human persona or deepfake impersonation attempts. Also, synthetic identity, where, for example, the fraudster uses real SSNs with fake names and addresses, is effectively addressed in Generative AI since it takes a holistic approach to user profiles and their transacting behavior. Using various points of data to check and compare it to others, Generative AI also mitigates the issues of fakers acquiring financial services, thus improving security.

One of the most discussed cases of companies applying Generative AI is the improvement of the services of some of the most significant fintech companies through using Generative AI to improve the user verification process and using GANs to create new synthetic identities and educating the company's AI systems to identify them allowed reducing the rate of synthetic identity fraud. Some fake accounts were already identified at the time the program started, but the AI system also monitored the consumers' actions to prevent and discourage frauds in the actual buying process. On the same note, its preventive measures protected the company from a possibility of loss, as well as enhance confidence since the identification process of the user was in safe and secure.

Overall, it is critical to state that Generative AI methods in fraud detection have been applied to traditional financial fraud, such as credit card fraud, and the newest rapidly evolving areas, including DeFi and synthetic identity fraud. Therefore, the financial institutions and the platforms they use can incorporate advanced AI models to improve the chances of the type of activities involved in fraud detection and prevention. Generative AI, as showcased through these case studies, is a useful tool for enhancing the security and credibility of financial systems in protecting institutional and customer interests against fraudsters and their evolving intelligence.

Figure 4. Practical applications and case studies of Generative AI in fraud prevention

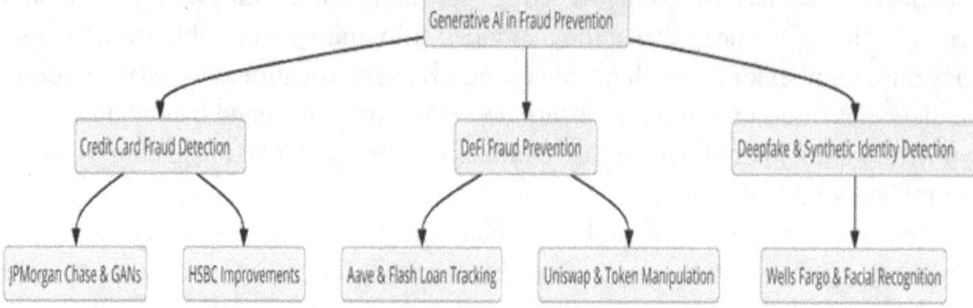

2.4 Addressing Ethical and Operational Challenges

Although applied to fraud detection, Generative AI presents an enormous shift and improvement compared to prior practices from both ethical and operational viewpoints. Adopting Generative AI in FI presents new questions and problems that must be solved to avoid detrimental consequences. These are the questions of bias in AI, privacy and data protection, accountability, trust, safety, and security, vulnerability to adversarial AI, and the capacity to design sound countermeasures for each. Resolving these questions is crucial for ensuring that AI-based fraud detection programs' more or less correct functioning is fair and accurate.

One significant ethical concern with Generative AI models is bias, often rooted in the data used for their development. AI models analyze data from history and make predictions, so biases in the data set can be copied into the AI model. For example, if the training dataset comprises selected types of clients or transactions, the applied AI decisions can be unequal, discriminating against or excluding definite users. There may be discrimination where, for some customer bases, accounts are frozen unfairly; for others, there may be poor fraud prevention. These biases must be deemed mandatory to be eliminated so that users will not be treated unfairly. There are measures that financial institutions may employ to integrate approaches meant for discovering and reducing biases in advanced intelligent applications, including but not limited to diverse data sampling, comparative use of fairness-aware algorithms, and bias audits. Furthermore, the exclusive incorporation of multiple departments, including details of how the AI systems are developed, analyzed, and corrected bias, can help facilitate equity in fraud preventive measures.

A major consideration for Generative AI in fraud detection is privacy because such models need to process extensive amounts of personally identifiable and account information. Managing, acquiring, and analyzing personal information is highly problematic for privacy, especially when civil data protection laws such as those in the GDPR and CCPA apply. Banking services are often trapped between integrating data for efficient fraud prevention and user privacy. The following practices must be performed to protect the user data: Selecting and applying sound data anonymization processes, minimizing data retention, and encrypting user data. Also, by employing privacy-preserving AI techniques like federated learning, institutional information can be trained on a distributed basis, and people's privacy rights will remain intact. Similarly, when data is managed properly, and organizations take time to explain to their customers how it is used in fraud prevention, compliance with regulatory principles will likely be achieved.

Therefore, high levels of Explainability and Trust are necessary for building trusting relationships regarding AI-supported fraud detection systems. Most deep learning Generative AI models are said to be black boxes; this means that the process of arriving at a decision cannot be easily explained. Such opacity can compromise the financial institutions' capacity to explain through AI to regulators, customers, and even employees. When it comes to the explainability of AI models, the matter is to create methods that ensure humans understand the 'reasoning' of the AI system. Among such techniques are important analysis, model reporting, and model-agnostic approach, and using interpretable models might help understand AI decision-making better. Breaking down the reasons behind flagged transactions or detected fraud patterns will foster more trust with customers and regulators and make customers and regulators understand the effectiveness of the implemented AI-based fraud solution.

Risk, thus defined as the risk of AI exploitation, captures the possibility of exploitative use of Generative AI technologies by fraudsters whose pirating activities and scheming would become a lot more advanced with such technologies. Similarly, as is the case with improved fraud detection with Generative AI, so are phishing attacks, deepfakes, and synthetic identity generation. Such a dual capability of AI requires measures to be implemented to protect one from misuse. These risks are echoed by Bansal & Tandon (2025), who outline how GAN-driven synthetic fraud techniques challenge legacy fraud detection frameworks and necessitate advanced AI security countermeasures. The volume of threats to AI is high, so financial institutions must take adequate security measures that will prevent fraudsters from changing the work of AI decision-making systems. This involves protecting AI to ensure access control and persistently looking for threats with an AI touch. Also, getting in touch with cyber criminals and keeping up with current threat intelligence will allow institutions to effectively prevent AI exploitation trials and fortify their fraud deterrence methods against new threats.

Mitigation Strategies solve ethical and operational concerns of applying Generative AI for fraud prevention. Effective regulation, therefore, remains a quintessential approach to good governance of AI. These frameworks should set out best practices for fair AI and for AI systems to be accountable, transparent, and privacy-compliant when designed, deployed, and used. It is recommended that ethicists, data scientists, legal advisors, and landholders be included in functional teams within financial institutions to manage AI projects and conform to well-established ethical safeguards. Therefore, AI models require periodic checks to fix every wrong judgment they arrive at, correct for biases where they might exist, improve model interpretability, and comply with data protection laws. Besides, it encourages continual learning and ethical sensitivity among employees to prevent biases and tool misuse.

Best practices for mitigating ethical and operational challenges include:

1. Data Governance: Deploy sound strategies on data management that helps to reduce on quality, integrity and security of data. This includes recognizing the regularities concerning the acquisition, storage, retrieval and utilization of data as well as compliance with the current legal requirements on data protection.
2. Fairness and Inclusivity: a view of discouraging the training of AI models to datasets that are bias or prejudiced in some way. One can obtain an equalized performance by raising the frequency of the specific subpopulation, applying the fairness constraints, and estimate the possible bias effect.
3. Transparency and Accountability: increase the level of reporting on AI decision-making, increase the accessibility of information about how AI reached a certain decision, and ensure there are ways to answer for anything bad that the AI did.
4. Continuous Monitoring and Evaluation: Check the AI systems to react to performance troubles, injustices, and risks. It involves using monitoring tools to notify an organization when the AI models are no longer effective or have a propensity to be biased, then having periodic evaluations done.
5. User Education and Engagement: Availing users' knowledge of fraud prevention by using AI and engaging them in the process. Aim: To improve the trust and cooperation of the users of the network, there is a need to provide clear information regarding the usage of data, the measures taken to protect the data, and the advantages of AI security to the users.
6. Collaborative Efforts: Participating in a coordinated manner with other companies in the industry, government agencies that oversee the industry, and other academic institutions mainly to exchange effective measures to counter the emerging threats and for the establishment of developed approaches that meet the industry ethics on the use of artificial intelligence.

Financial institutions can overcome the ethical and operational issues mitigated through Generative AI in fraud prevention through these mitigation strategies. Apart from this, it affords the objective of using and implementing AI technologies responsibly and ethically while improving the efficiency and effectiveness of fraud detection systems. It will be crucial to address and emphasize the ethical implications and a business continuity perspective for steady sustainability of trust and adherence to the regulations and cybersecurity in the financial industries as the Generative AI rolls forward.

In conclusion, this section has established that Generative AI has immense possibilities to revolutionize fraud prevention activity. However, the activity also possesses numerous ethical and operational issues, the management of which is critical in the implementation of successful Generative AI. Therefore, when implementing Generative AI in financial institutions, the biases should be pointed out and resolved, the user's privacy maintained, the explainability ensured, the AI models protected from being exploited, and most of all, strong mitigation strategies should be adopted, so that the financial institutions can benefit from the Generative AI while having ethical standards and operational efficiency. This also helps maintain that financial fraud prevention systems implemented with AI aim to prevent fraud without violating some of the key financial industry principles related to fairness, transparency, and trust.

CONCLUSION

This book discusses emerging issues and trends in fraud prevention in the financial industry and highlights the use of Generative AI as a solution to current and future fraud risks. However, the traditional fraud detection systems, while serving as the precursors of today's Automated Fraud Management systems, are inadequate for the current diverse and ever-evolving nature of financial fraud. The study highlights vulnerabilities in traditional systems, such as inflexibility, high false positive and negative rates, and limited scalability, which weaken security. Both financial losses and brand damage caused by fraud necessitate the development of innovative solutions.

The two talked about areas that bring Generative AI into the fore, which provides innovative extensions of capabilities such as anomaly detection, behavior modeling, scenario simulation, and predictive analytics. These tools can allow a financial institution to move from a reactive approach to fraud to using predictive tools to identify and prevent fraud threats. Thus, creating the hybrid of Generative AI with blockchain and Decentralized Finance adds the multi-level layers of the security system that are transparent, efficient, and powerful.

Real-life examples and use cases highlight the potential and applications open to Generative AI as a tool, safeguarding credit card payment decentralized platforms and preventing synthetic identity fraud. But even in this case, the study recognizes the vices with AI, including Ethical issues, operational issues like biases, privacy issues, and potential exploitation by wrong hands. To overcome these challenges, a strong governance structure, high transparency, and multi-sectorial responses are needed.

The enhancement of these strategies in the future will include the development of federated learning, the real-time multi-agent system, and greater collaboration with systems regulators and providers. Based on the findings of this study, it can be concluded that Generative AI is not only a critical tool for safeguarding financial systems today but also a foundational technology for building resilient, ethical, and adaptive solutions to combat fraud in the future.

REFERENCES

Abdallah, A., Maarof, M. A., & Zainal, A. (2016). Fraud detection system: A survey. *Journal of Network and Computer Applications*, *68*, 90–113. DOI: 10.1016/j.jnca.2016.04.007

Awoyemi, J. O., Adetunmbi, A. O., & Oluwadare, S. A. (2017). Credit card fraud detection using machine learning techniques: A comparative analysis. *2017 International Conference on Computing Networking and Informatics (ICCNI)*, 1–9. https://doi.org/DOI: 10.1109/ICCNI.2017.8123782

Bandi, A., Mandal, K., Bindu, P., & Dwivedi, A. D. (2023). The power of Generative AI: A review of requirements, models, input–output formats, evaluation metrics, and challenges. *Future Internet*, *15*(8), 260. DOI: 10.3390/fi15080260

Bansal, D., & Tandon, N. (2025). *Securing the Future: Addressing Risks and Vulnerabilities in Generative AI for Fintech*. Springer., DOI: 10.1007/978-3-031-76957-3_14

Dorminey, J., Fleming, A. S., Kranacher, M.-J., & Riley, R. A.Jr. (2012). The evolution of fraud theory. *Issues in Accounting Education*, *27*(2), 555–579. DOI: 10.2308/iace-50131

Fich, E. M., & Shivdasani, A. (2007). Financial fraud, director reputation, and shareholder wealth. *Journal of Financial Economics*, *86*(2), 306–336. DOI: 10.1016/j.jfineco.2006.05.012

Irfan, M., Elmogy, M., Gupta, S., Khalifa, F., & Dias, R. (2024). *AI-Driven Decentralized Finance and the Future of Finance*. IGI Global., DOI: 10.4018/979-8-3693-6321-8

Irfan, M., Hussainey, K., Chan Bukhari, S. A., & Nam, Y. (Eds.). (2024). *Issues of Sustainability in AI and New-Age Thematic Investing*. IGI Global Publisher., DOI: 10.4018/979-8-3693-3282-5

Patcha, A., & Park, J.-M. (2007). An overview of anomaly detection techniques: Existing solutions and latest technological trends. *Computer Networks*, *51*(12), 3448–3470. DOI: 10.1016/j.comnet.2007.02.001

Ryabov, O., Bobryshev, A., Lebedev, K., & Ryabov, D. (2021). Decentralized finance (DeFi) as the basis for the transformation of the financial sector of the future. *14 Oct. 2021*.https://doi.org/DOI: 10.1145/3527049.3527080

Sachdeva, P., Rawal, R., & Sharma, V. (2025). *The Significance of Generative AI in Enhancing Fraud Detection and Prevention Within the Banking Industry*. Wiley., DOI: 10.1002/9781394271078.ch9

Toshniwal, R., Sethi, A., & Jangir, K. (2025). Applications of Generative AI in Fintech. IGI Global. https://www.igi-global.com/chapter/applications-of-generative-ai-in-fintech/368343

Vaquero, R. (2023). Literature review of credit card fraud detection with machine learning. *Tuni.fi.*https://trepo.tuni.fi/handle/10024/152542

Velikonja, U. (2012). The cost of securities fraud. *William and Mary Law Review*, *54*, 1887.

West, J., & Bhattacharya, M. (2016). Intelligent financial fraud detection: A comprehensive review. *Computers & Security*, *57*, 47–66. DOI: 10.1016/j.cose.2015.09.005

Chapter 6
Blockchain Basics: Understanding the Core Concepts and Mechanisms

Rajat Verma
https://orcid.org/0000-0001-5707-2695
Pranveer Singh Institute of Technology, India

Abhishek Rawat
Pranveer Singh Institute of Technology, India

Raghuraj Singh Suryavanshi
Pranveer Singh Institute of Technology, India

Ravendra Singh
Pranveer Singh Institute of Technology, India

Fatima Muhammad Abdulkarim
Federal University, Dutse, Nigeria

ABSTRACT

Cryptocurrency has set the new standards of cyber storage technology in terms of faster volume of transactions, better price, reputation and trust, which is based on Blockchain. Blockchain, which started with the Bitcoin whitepaper of Satoshi Nakamoto in 2008, that has potential applications beyond cryptocurrencies, including governance, healthcare, and supply chain management. Traditional banking systems typically use intermediaries, resulting in inefficiencies and expenses, whereas blockchain removes the middlemen. By being transparent and immutable, it encourages trust, reduces fraud, and improves compliance with regulations. Furthermore, the synergy between blockchain and emerging technologies like generative AI in

DOI: 10.4018/979-8-3373-1250-7.ch006

a new era of innovation, marrying analytical strength with reliable data integrity. Thus, this chapter ultimately demonstrates the disruptive potential of the blockchain in financial decision-making while presenting an insight.

1. INTRODUCTION

Blockchain Technology are cataclysmically changing the arena of financial transaction and data management. Blocks of data are compiled and chained together to prevent tampering, hence the name blockchain. This feature not only improves security but also facilitates transparency, since all participants can see the same information in real-time (Soundararajan & Shenbagaraman, 2024). Blockchain has applications that make cryptocurrency feel like a one-trick pony. For example, in healthcare, blockchain can enable the secure storage of patient records, allowing authorized healthcare providers to share the data without compromising patient privacy. This may result in better patient outcomes through more well-coordinated care. In the field of supply chain management, blockchain technology can bring end-to-end visibility to the process, allowing companies to trace goods from point of origin to point of consumption which reduces the possibility of fraud while ensuring authenticity (Panda et al., 2023).

A key advantage of using blockchain is how it can help streamline processes. Since the journal is directly sent to the party involved and doesn't involve any intermediary party, transaction costs and processing times can be cut down drastically. In international trade, blockchain could enable faster customs clearance and eliminate the need for extensive paperwork, which creates delays and costs (Rawat et al., 2023a). This is especially useful in sectors such as perishable goods, where efficiency can save time. Additionally, when wed together with new technologies like generative AI, the blockchain powers each. With the ability to analyze large datasets, generative AI can discover patterns and insights that otherwise might remain hidden (Chen & Bellavitis, 2020). When integrated with blockchain, this can significantly enhance decision-making operations. It also focuses on predictive analysis using AI, such as predicting market trends and assessing financial transaction risk, which helps organizations make proactive adjustments. Not to mention the possibility of blockchain revolutionizing voting systems. Using blockchain, voting can be made secure, transparent, and significantly fraud-proof as every vote cast will only be set in the blockchain and recognized. This could increase public faith in electoral processes, essential for democracy to work.

The use of blockchain will most likely expand in the coming years. This evolution is further demonstrated by the emergence of decentralized finance, enabling users to perform operations without the need for conventional banks. DeFi platforms adopt smart contracts—self-executing contracts with the terms of the agreement between buyer and seller being directly written into code—to automate processes and to minimize the usage of intermediaries (Javaid et al., 2022). Thus, in a nutshell, Blockchain is not confined to being a platform for cryptocurrency transactions, but a transformational approach to how data integrity, transparency, efficiency in various sectors can be approached. Blockchain holds the potential to revolutionize a number of industries, and as more organizations embrace this technology, we can expect to see an increase in innovative applications that will change the way we conduct business in the digital age (Ghorbian & Ghorbian, 2025). Blockchain and AI can work together in the future to provide a more secure, efficient, and trustworthy future for finance and data transactions.

The emergence of decentralized finance transforms the financial landscape by enabling individuals to carry out financial transactions independently of traditional intermediaries (Bakare et al., 2024). The movement enables more people to access financial services while simultaneously driving product innovation in blockchain-based operations like trading and borrowing. This chapter presents the main characteristics of blockchain and also covers the financial applications of blockchain as well as current issues and emerging technologies (Irfan, 2021). After reading this chapter, readers will have enough knowledge about the ideas of blockchain and impact on financial judgement and would be properly skilled to serve themselves in winning the future of financial sector into the driving seat of a more digitized world.

2. BLOCKCHAIN

In essence, Blockchain is the ground-breaking decentralized network that tracks transactions on a computer network. Whereas old ledgers functioned through a central server that collects all the records, the blockchain employs a network of nodes, each one connected to the other. By design, no single entity controls the entire network as each node has a full copy of the ledger (Komalavalli et al., 2020). Because there is no centralized record-keeper, the system is highly secure and nearly impossible to defraud, because no single party can change the data to its own advantage. Blockchain is most commonly known for powering cryptocurrencies, as it serves to create an immutable, decentralized ledger containing records of all transactions (Hashemi Joo et al., 2020). For example, in SCM, the application of blockchain is a trend to implement traceability and transparency of products as they progress through the numerous levels of production and distribution

It enables companies to authenticate products, trace the supply chain, and enforce the regulatory compliance process, driving higher levels of customer confidence. When it comes to identity verification, there blockchain can provide a secure way to process and store personal data. Blockchain provides privacy and data security for individuals and businesses through the application of cryptographic methods that protect sensitive data from unauthorized access. This is especially significant in an era when data breaches, and identity theft, are common worries (Rawat et al., 2023b). Immutability is a foundational property of blockchain. This feature enhances security and promotes trust among its participants, as all operations are conducted transparently. The transparency of blockchain allows relevant parties to track transactions, which is essential for maintaining accountability in different applications. Blockchain can also streamline processes by removing intermediaries (Politou et al., 2019). In doing so, the transaction settlement process can be sped up greatly, improving efficiency. For instance, blockchain has the potential to enable almost real-time global payments in terms of financial transactions, eliminating bank settlement times and costs. Many organizations are still experimenting with blockchain capabilities, discovering new ways to use this technology for innovation. Furthermore, the fusion of blockchain with other advancing technologies like artificial intelligence (AI) can also make it more effective (Javaid et al., 2022). AI can also analyze blockchain data to detect trends and anomalies, producing insights that are valuable in the decision-making. To summarize, embracing blockchain was a transformative journey which has led to secure network architectures that allow safe and efficient transactions. Blockchain has the potential to transform industries and redefine how we conduct transactions and interactions. With this in mind, the continuing exploration of blockchain's capabilities holds the potential to open a world of new possibilities and reshape our approach to business as globalization grows.

2.1 Key Characteristics of Blockchain

i. **Decentralization**: Blockchain works in a P2P way across each individual (node) and no one can exercise more authority like in centralized systems. This structure also removes intermediates yielding decreased costs and more efficient processes (Esmat et al., 2021). This feature makes it more robust (Debe et al., 2019), because the system contains some nodes that are able to operate even if some other nodes are down.

ii. **Transparency**: Transactions are available to all network participants. This openness creates trust between all users because the authenticity of each transaction is verified independently (Irfan et al., 2023a). The transparent characteristics of Blockchain promote accountability; there are also easy to trace transactions that deliver inconsistency detection. This functionality is particularly valuable in industries such as finance and SCM where verification are paramount (Cornelius, 2021).

iii. **Immutability**: There is no way to modify or delete a transaction once it is saved on the blockchain. Because data on a blockchain cannot be altered, it provides a high level of integrity in the data, which is particularly useful for any application that involves financial transaction or legal contracts (Politou et al., 2019). This process involves using cryptographic hashes to link each new block of data with the previous one, forming a secure and tamper-resistant chain of information. This feature helps to safeguard against fraud while also offering a verifiable audit trail.
iv. **Security**: Blockchain uses basic cryptography to secure transactions and manage new blocks creation. A malicious actor would find it exceedingly difficult to alter the data, as every transaction is tied to the preceding one and protected using cryptography. (Rawat et al., 2023c) Moreover, consensus mechanisms (e.g., PoW, PoS, etc.) guarantee that every participant reaches a mutual agreement (or consensus) on ledger status without relying on a central authority (Nguyen et al., 2019). Its decentralized nature serves as a major boost for the entire network security.

2.2 Types of Blockchain

Blockchain can be categorized into several types based on their structure, governance, and accessibility. Here are **eight types of blockchain**:

i. **Public Blockchain**: This type of blockchain is likewise accessible to everyone. It is decentralized, allowing users to access, write, and audit the (Irfan et al., 2023b). For example Bitcoin and Ethereum are open for everyone to join the network and verify transactions.
ii. **Private Blockchain**: These types of blockchains are permission-based and available for a limited set of participants, i.e., the members who have been given access. In this blockchain only authorized users can read and write data (Makhdoom et al., 2020). This form is commonly used by organizations for internal applications, ensuring more privacy and data control.
iii. **Consortium Blockchain**: In this blockchain, group of organizations have control over the network. It is controlled by a pre-designated set of nodes in this case, making it appropriate for organizations that work together, but still need some dossier confidentiality (Liu et al., 2023). This type is typically used within industries such as finance and SCM.
iv. **Hybrid Blockchain**: These blockchains are a combination of public and private. While they allow controlled access, they still provide only some transparency (Alkhateeb et al., 2022). It allows organizations to keep certain data private

while having the option of making other data public functionality widely useful across different use cases.

These various types of blockchains cater to different needs and use cases, highlighting the feature of blockchain in addressing challenges across industries.

3. CORE CONCEPTS OF BLOCKCHAIN

3.1 Blocks and Chains

Block is the basic building where each block is a collection of transaction records. Each of these blocks is linked together by cryptographic hashes, which ties them to the previous blocks and ensures they form an immutable chain (Zhang et al., 2019). This linking design is very important because when someone makes even a small change to one block, all blocks after it will also have to be changed to preserve the integrity of the whole blockchain. This property creates a highly secure network which instantly reveals attempts to change a block and requires a significant amount of computing power to change all subsequent blocks within it (Irfan et al., 2023c). Blocks facilitate the organization of associated data as a tool, allowing a strong structure to be incorporated into the blockchain. Each block holds a header that contains metadata and the SHA-hash of the previous block, and the transaction data. Because the transaction information can frequently be formatted as a Merkle tree, it means you can verify the integrity of the transactions in the block on a scale-efficient basis (Lopez et al., 2019). In other words, this framework familiarize that if any alterations are made to the singular transactions, which makes the overall block chain a more secured directory. New transactions are proposed and collected into a block. The network then validates this block using a consensus mechanism, making sure that all nodes agree on the correctness of the transactions (Rawat & Ur Rahman, 2023a). The block is then sealed and cryptographically bound to all previous blocks, creating an unbroken chain. This not only secures the latter transactions to the former, but also ensures that it would be virtually impossible to change one block without the need to change the entire chain of blocks.

Blockchain Technology Security Feature: The concept of decentralization increases the volume of data necessary to hack a system and provides a high security against unauthorized access that every business with intense competition lacks (Pólvora et al., 2020). Such transparency is critical because it helps prevent the tampering of data, and everyone can access the same ledger so it builds trust among participants. This common visibility is especially critical in applications like cryptocurrencies because trust in the system is the primary concern. In addition to cryptocurrencies, blockchain technology is the foundation for dozens of applications (Velmurugadass et al., 2021). Blockchain offers secure and transparent systems that can be explored in a variety of applications, ranging from SCM to health care and voting. As an example, blockchain can allow real-time tracking of products for SCM for the purpose of validation and compliance with regulations. In healthcare, it can securely hold patient records and provide seamless data sharing between providers without compromising patient privacy (Komalavalli et al., 2020). Simply put, it is the way blockchain is structured with its blocks and the cryptographic chaining of them that provides a secure, transparent method for recording transactions. This trustless system is driven by cutting-edge technology that not only ensures (participants) security and trust in each other, but lays a foundation for future applications for cryptocurrencies and beyond. If nothing else, as blockchain makes progress, it has the potential to bring about some great innovation with solutions that harness its unique attributes.

3.2 Cryptographic Hashing

At the core of blockchain technology lies a process called cryptographic hashing where an input data is converted to a fixed-length string of bytes, commonly referred to as a hash. Each hash from its corresponding input, like a digital fingerprint. This uniqueness is important in order to preserve the sanity of data present in the blockchain. If there were any changes in the data in a block, the hash would change and alert the network about any potential tampering (Suryavanshi et al., 2025). This mechanism is crucial to the security of the blockchain, as it enables participants to notice any unauthorized changes instantly. A one-way hash function is used in the hashing process in blockchain, making it practically impossible to recover original input from a hash value. This feature is especially critical to ensure the safety and integrity of secure data. As an example, if someone steals the hash they will find it hard to guess the original data, which gives us additional security. This allows the hash to be made public without exposing the data itself (Sevin & Osman Mohammed, 2024).

Hash functions used in cryptography are deterministic, which means that the same input always produces the same result. Consistency in hashing is crucial for maintaining data integrity. If two hashes are identical, it indicates that no changes have occurred. Good hashing algorithms use the avalanche effect, which means that a little change in input (as little as 1 bit) might result in an entirely different hash output. It also has the side effect of making it very difficult for attackers to tell what will happen to the hash when the input is changed, adding even more security (Irfan et al., 2024). SHA-2 is a popular hashing algorithm which is well-renowned in the field of cryptography due to its strength and processors efficiency. Subsequent hashing algorithms have been developed to resist a wider range of cryptanalytic attacks. This makes hashing an essential component of modern cryptography and it is widely utilized in numerous applications, such as securing transactions and authenticating messages. So, to conclude: cryptographic hashing is a fundamental part of blockchain technology that increases its security and integrity. With this technology, tampering of sensitive data is easily collected because blockchain is able to translate the input data into unique, fixed-length hashes (Rawat & Rahman, 2023b). Implemented an additional security layer using a hashing function that does not allow the system to retrieve the original data in a one-way direction. As blockchain technology evolves, the role of cryptographic hashing in upholding secure and ethical networks will increase, leading to more widespread applications across a range of industries. In conclusion, blockchain technology is broadly Built on a foundation of cryptographic hashing, which is used to ensure that security and is very strong against modification, and allow to verify a transaction in a distributed network. This unique nature makes it an important tool in maintaining the trust and stability of blockchain systems.

3.3 Consensus Mechanisms

The process of consensus ensures that all nodes in the chain agree on the blockchain's present condition. These computations safeguard the blockchain by avoiding double-spending and ensuring all transactions are genuine. There are various consensus mechanisms:

i. **Proof of Work (PoW)**: PoW is employed by Bitcoin, where nodes are required to solve complicated math problems before a transaction or new block can be created. It is resource-intensive but very secure (Ferdous et al., 2021) (the process is called mining). This model means that only those people that contribute computational power can add new blocks in the chain and thus, malicious participants could not easily take control of the network.
ii. **Proof of Stake (PoS)**: This approach is more energy-efficient than PoW and applies to networks like Ethereum 2.0 (Asif & Hassan, 2023). PoS is becoming a popular consensus among many blockchain systems as it has the capability of lowering the computational cost of mining and improving the speed of transactions being processed.
iii. **Delegated Proof of Stake (DPoS)**: Token holders choose a restricted number of delegations to verify transaction on their behalf, akin to PoS. By having fewer nodes engaged in the consensus process, this technique provides enhanced transaction speed and scalability (Irfan et al., 2024). DPoS seeks a compromise

between a decentralized system's advantages and a more centralized one, where decisions and transaction confirmations can happen faster.

iv. **Proof of Authority (PoA)**: Only a few nodes serve as authorities, validating transactions and creating new blocks. This paradigm is commonly used in private or permissioned blockchains when validators' identities are known and trusted (Rouhani & Deters, 2021). PoA is highly scalable and suitable for applications that demand fast transaction processing due to low latency.

v. **Proof of Burn (PoB)**: In this mechanism, participants "burn" their cryptocurrency by sending it to an inaccessible wallet address, thereby taking it out of circulation. In exchange, you get to mine or validate transactions according to how much you have burned (Misra, 2024). So it rewards holding the network in the long run and reduces the available supply of the cryptocurrencies, which can help the price in the longer term.

3.4 Smart Contracts

Smart contracts— self-executing contracts with terms of the agreement directly written into lines of code. These platforms function autonomously on blockchain networks, including Ethereum or Solana. This automates the process and decreases transaction costs and provides transparency. The immutability of smart contracts, once deployed on a blockchain network, is one of their most compelling features. In short, this means that once a smart contract is executed, its terms cannot be changed, creating certainty and trust between the parties (Singh et al., 2025). It is especially important in settings where trust is imperative as it ensured that all parties keep to the agreed-upon terms without any risk of being tampered with or deceived. Plus, the nature of blockchain is decentralized, thus, every participant has access to the same information, further improving the trust and accountability in transactions. Despite their many advantages, however, smart contracts are not without their difficulties. Another: [To the tunes of au fait with potential vulnerabilities in the code and unexploited or unintended consequences without appropriate audits and testings.

Additionally, as demand for smart contracts grows, scalability concerns may arise, resulting in longer transaction times and larger fees during busier periods. There also are legal uncertainties surrounding smart contracts in different jurisdictions, as the regulatory framework for these digital agreements is still developing. However, the transformative potential of smart contracts cannot be understated (Soavi, 2022). They are reshaping industries by allowing for decentralized, secure, efficient, and trustless transactions. Automating complex workflows, facilitating real estate transactions, supply chain management unlocks innovative applications with high operational efficiency and cost-effectiveness across different sectors. The potential of smart contracts is immense as they can automate many aspects of transactions, reducing the need for intermediaries and making processes more efficient.

3.4.1 Key Features of Smart Contracts

- **Automation:** When certain circumstances are met, smart contracts take action automatically. This removes the requirement for manual intervention, lowering the risk of errors and enhancing efficiency (Ivanov et al., 2023).
- **Trust and Security:** Since smart contracts are maintained on a blockchain, they benefit from the technology's inherent security features. The immutable nature of blockchains guarantees that once a contract is effectively deployed, no party can modify or manipulate it further, thus promoting trust between the contract participants (Singh et al., 2025).
- **Transparency:** The blockchain records every transaction and contract executions, making them available to all participants. Such transparency aids in confirming the true nature of the contract as well as its execution.
- **Cost Efficiency:** Smart contracts eliminate intermediaries and automate procedures, leading to significant cost savings. This is especially true in sectors like finance, real estate, and SCM.

3.4.2 Working of Smart Contracts

Smart contracts are usually coded using specific development languages for blockchain, for instance, Solidity for Ethereum. Creating a smart contract is a multi-stage process:

- **Coding:** Developers write the contract code using a suitable programming language. This code establishes the norms and terms under which the agreement will operate.
- **Deployment**: Once the smart contract is coded and tested, it is deployed onto the blockchain. This process involves submitting the contract to the network, where it becomes part of the blockchain.
- **Execution:** When the contract's conditions are met, the smart contract will automatically carry out the agreed-upon actions. For example, in an economic transaction, once payment is made, the smart contract may instantly assign ownership of an asset.

4. BLOCKCHAIN MECHANISMS

4.1 Transaction Verification

When a transaction occurs in a blockchain, it is shared across all nodes so all participants are aware. The broadcasting plays a vital role to promote trust and transparency in decentralized system These transactions are later consolidated into a block, Each block includes a list of operations, a time stamp, and a reference to the previous block, resulting in a continuous chain (Cai et al., 2018). A consensus mechanism enables each node to take part in the validation process, which is the core component responsible for validating that a transaction is legitimate and follows the rules of the external network. Various consensus procedures exist, including PoW and PoS, which show the most basic implementations of this concept, securing double-spending prevention and agreement on the state of the blockchain. For instance, in PoW, miners race each other to successfully solve complex math problems, and whoever succeeds first adds the block to the blockchain.

Validated blocks are incorporated into the blockchain, which serves as proof that the transaction has been finalized. This ensures the transaction is confirmed and keeps the blockchain functioning as a public ledger. Blockchain's decentralized ledger prevents tampering and fraud, as no single entity holds it. Cryptographic hash functions link each block to the previous one, making it difficult to modify (Zhu et al., 2021). Immutability is a key aspect of the blockchain. Changing one block would affect all subsequent blocks, making it computationally infeasible un a well-distributed network. This mechanism not only safeguards individual transactions but also bolsters the overall integrity of the blockchain, revolutionizing the way transactions are executed across domains, especially in the financial domain.

4.2 Mining and Block Creation

Mining is the fundamental process of transaction validation and block creation on PoW blockchains. This is the mechanism that most cryptocurrencies, like Bitcoin, operate on. It involves a peer-to-peer network with participants called miners, competing with one another to solve complex mathematical problem (cryptographic puzzle) (Judmayer et al., 2022). These problems are made to be very computationally difficult, meaning solving them takes lots of processing power and energy. The competition for mining serves a number of purposes. The miner who has solved the puzzle faster than any other gets the right to add the next block to the blockchain. This process involves incorporating both the most recent transactions as well as linking the new block to the one prior to it, ensuring that information throughout the entire blockchain remains consistent. In return for their continued efforts, the successful miner earns a fixed number of cryptocurrency tokens mining reward, which helps incentive miners to keep participating in the network.

The competitive nature of mining was essential for the security of the blockchain. Updating a single block necessitates duplicating the work of all following blocks, making it highly computational and practically impossible for attackers to manipulate data (Ciaian et al., 2021). This expensive cost of changing the blockchain serves as a deterrent toward fraud, and so creates an incentive for the system to remain correct. In addition, the PoW mechanism encourages decentralization since it permits any individual with sufficient computational power to engage in the mining process. Such decentralization is vital to the security of the blockchain, as it prevents a single actor from taking control of the network. Instead of keeping the PoW as a process to confirm transactions and generate blocks, it will act as a protector for the ecosystem to defend against external security attacks.

4.3 Network Propagation

A block in a blockchain goes through a crucial process known as propagation once it has been mined. The new block is transmitted to each node in the network, compelling them to modify their own copy of the blockchain. It is crucial for ensuring atomicity so no participant would even come across a conflicting ledger state which in tum would compromise the functionality as well as integrity of the Blockchain (Xiao et al., 2020). This means that the latest block is added with every single transaction, with each block containing a pointer to its predecessor so that every node has the latest information. This is what allows blocks to be linked together to form the blockchain, a uniform and indelible record of every transaction ever made. The speed and efficiency of this propagation may vary depending on different parameters, such as network latency and network health. If such conditions were placed, the duration of such time was supposed to be within a range of a few seconds to a few minutes.

For the nodes to run in a synchronous manner, the reliability of these maintenance blocks is indispensable. If the new block is received by some nodes, but not all, it can lead to forks, or at best an inconsistency. This synchronization is primarily achieved through the P2P nature of blockchain, which ensures that nodes next to each other communicate with one another to spread updates and validate transactions (Rawat et al., 2025). Moreover, the broadcast of new blocks is an important part of the consensus of the block chain. Once a block is propagated, nodes have to check its contents family out the transactions against their own books and make sure that they follow network rules. The validation mechanism adds strength in the blockchain security, as it prohibits the insertion of the invalid transactions in the ledger (Conti et al., 2019). In summary, this process ensures that all nodes of blockchain possess an accurate and up-to-date representation of the ledger, highlighting the importance of new blocks being communicated and shared throughout the entire network. This mechanism serves to enhance the credibility of on chain data while also protecting against exploitation and manipulation.

4.4 Forking

In blockchain, "forking" is when the blockchain diverges into two separate and conflicting paths, usually caused by protocol changes or disputes between network stakeholders (Xiao et al., 2020). Such changes can greatly alter the operation of projects and their governance on the blockchain, resulting in a split in the blockchain and the creation of different versions of the ledger, with their unique features and history. Forks can be categorized as Soft or Hard.

- **Soft Fork:** Soft forks are non-breaking changes to blockchain protocols. In this scenario, only previously valid blocks or transaction become invalid after applying new rules. It means that if nodes did not upgrade their software, they can recognize the new blocks, enabling the smooth transition (Rawat & Verma, 2025). Change of state of the system which could be consistent without necessarily all participants upgrading – usually implemented through soft forks. This compatibility preserves the overall integrity of the network and reduces the impact of disruption on users, as the dominant number of nodes will still be able to work without alteration in the short term.
- **Hard Fork:** On the other hand, hard fork is a backward-incompatible upgrade that creates a permanent deviance of a blockchain from its old version. During the hard fork, the nodes that did not upgrade will no longer able to validate the new blocks, two separate chains will be created (Johnsen, 2020). A contentious fork usually emerges from major disagreements among the community about the path forward for the blockchain or the introduction of new features. As a case in point, hard forks can generate new cryptocurrencies for instance, this is how Bitcoin and Bitcoin Cash developed, the latter being a hard fork of the original Bitcoin blockchain.

Each kind of fork serves to emphasize the decentralized nature of blockchain, in which consensus among the participants is vital for the maintenance of the integrity of the network. Forks can be both a source of innovation and adaptability, but can also create fragmentation and confusion for users about which version of the blockchain to track. Forks are one of these critical concepts, and understanding their implications is vital for those working in blockchain, as they make their way through the constantly changing world of decentralized technologies.

5. APPLICATIONS OF BLOCKCHAIN IN FINANCIAL DECISION-MAKING

The uses of blockchain has transformed multiple industries, especially in the financial realm, offering solutions that significantly improve efficiency, security, and transparency. Some of its key applications are as follows for making financial decisions using blockchain:

5.1 Cryptocurrencies

Perhaps the most widely known use cases of blockchain technology are cryptocurrencies. They are an alternative that is decentralized to traditional currencies, allowing transactions between individuals without the involvement of middlemen (Johnson, 2020). By removing intermediaries, blockchain technology allows for immediate financial transactions, significantly lowering transaction costs and enhancing financial inclusion for individuals without access to standard banking systems.

5.2 Decentralized Finance (DeFi)

DeFi used to develop open and permissionless financial systems. Some examples of DeFi platforms include: Aave, Uniswap, and Compound. This allows users to perform financial activities directly with one another, usually at lower costs and with more transparency (Harvey et al., 2021). DeFi is so powerful because it has the ability to open up barriers and make things available to populations that have not been served.

5.3 Supply Chain Finance

Blockchain Enhances Supply Chain Finance Comment all the actors involved in either side have access to the same information and while the original content is not true, the person remains right and validates it while helping to reduce fraud and errors (Oriekhoe et al., 2024). For businesses that want to maximize their performance, blockchain can be a great study because it can reduce SCM costs by streamlining procedures and making them more effective.

5.4 Identity Verification

Blockchain can be used to develop secure and decentralized systems for verification of identity. These systems can reduce fraud by ensuring that identities are verified through a tamper-proof ledger (Manda, 2024). Examples include the

Financial sector where this can ease the onboarding process for specific end customers because this will allow individual to have access to financial services while ensuring that their privacy and security are maintained.

5.5 Regulatory Compliance

Because of its inherent transparency and immutability, blockchain technology is an effective tool for regulatory compliance. For example, financial institutions can adopt blockchain to maintain accurate records of transactions that are tamper-proof, and presents an easy way to comply with regulatory requirements (Kukman & Gričar, 2025). Not only does this increase trust among stakeholders but it also minimizes the risk of non-compliance penalties, therefore presenting a strategic advantage..

6. CHALLENGES AND FUTURE DIRECTIONS

Blockchain is undoubtedly a revolutionary concept, but it also has a fair amount of challenges to overcome. Scalability, regulatory uncertainty, and interoperability will have to be solved for blockchain to realize its full potential (Andoni et al., 2019). Nonetheless, with continuous R&D efforts, more sustainable, scalable, and efficient blockchain solutions are underway. An expanded discussion on those hurdles and the innovations being designed to get past them is below:

6.1 Scalability

With every transaction made in a blockchain, the ledger size increases. This causes slower transaction time, network congestion and higher fees, which prevent the technology from scaling for mass adoption (Zachariadis et al., 2019). This has caused large delays and higher costs for some networks, like Bitcoin & Ethereum during peak usage. Many solutions have been tried out to combat this problem:

- **Sharding:** This technology breaks down the blockchain into lesser, simpler components known as "shards," every one of which can execute its own payments and smart contracts. Parallel processing dramatically increases throughput.
- **Layer-2 Protocols:** Lightning networks for Bitcoins and Positive Deployments or zk-Rollups for Ethereum work on top of the main blockchain, making transactions faster and cheaper by processing them externally and then settle the final result on the main chain.

- **Blockchain Trilemma:** Balancing scalability, security, and decentralization remains a core challenge, as improving one often compromises the others. Innovations like Directed Acyclic Graphs (DAGs) and hybrid consensus models aim to address this trade-off.

6.2 Energy Consumption

PoW blockchains, like Bitcoin, require significant power to validate transactions and secure the network, leading to high energy consumption and environmental concerns (Lasla et al., 2022). For example, Bitcoin's energy consumption is comparable to that of some small nations. To minimize this problem, the industry is transitioning to more energy-efficient alternatives:

- **Proof-of-Stake:** PoS blockchains, like Ethereum 2.0 and Cardano, replace heavy on energy mining with staking, in which validators are chosen based on how many tokens they own. This dramatically cuts energy use.
- **Proof-of-Authority (PoA):** Further optimization of energy usage in these consensus mechanisms occurs by either restricting the number of validators or delegating validation rights to a smaller subset.
- **Green Blockchain Initiatives:** Others are researching renewable energy for mining or carbon-neutral blockchains to reduce their environmental footprint.

6.3 Regulatory Uncertainty

Blockchain and cryptocurrencies remains in flux, leaving businesses, developers, and users with uncertainty as to what the respective parameters will be. Governments and regulatory entities are struggling to define, categorize and manage digital assets, resulting in a mosaic of sometimes contradictory classification across jurisdictions (Whitford & Anderson, 2021). Key concerns include:

- **Consumer Protection:** Regulations are needed to prevent fraud, scams, and market manipulation while ensuring user privacy and security.
- **Taxation and Compliance:** To gain widespread adoption, really need clear guidelines on how to tax cryptocurrencies and blockchain-based assets.
- **Anti-Money Laundering (AML):** To ensure compliance to these regulations, regulatory frameworks are being created to encompass blockchain networks within organization of AML guidelines without sacrificing decentralization.
- **Global Coordination:** International regulatory misalignment stifles innovation and complicates the regulatory compliance process for cross-border

projects. Working towards setting a universal standard are groups such as the Financial Action Task Force.

6.4 Interoperability

Different blockchains often operate in isolation, creating "silos" that limit the transfer of assets and data between networks. This fragmentation reduces the overall utility of blockchain technology (Ezzat et al., 2022). To address this, interoperability solutions are being developed:

- **Cross-Chain Bridges:** These enable the transfer of assets and data between different blockchains, such as moving Bitcoin to Ethereum or Polygon. Examples include the Polygon Bridge and Wormhole.
- **Interoperability Protocols:** Polkadot and Cosmos aim to create ecosystems where multiple blockchains can communicate and interact seamlessly. Polkadot uses a relay chain to connect parachains, while employs the Inter-Blockchain Communication protocol.
- **Blockchain Aggregators:** Platforms like Chainlink and RenVM facilitate cross-chain communication by providing decentralized oracles and liquidity bridges.
- **Multi-Chain Ecosystems:** Some projects, such as Avalanche and Fantom, are designed to support multiple blockchain networks within a single ecosystem, enhancing interoperability by default.

6.5 Additional Challenges

Beyond the core issues mentioned above, blockchain technology faces other hurdles (Parisi & Budorin, 2023):

- **Security Vulnerabilities:** They have seen smart contract bugs, 51% attacks and exploits of cross-chain bridges wipe away millions. These risks are mitigated through enhanced security practices like formal verification and bug bounty programs.
- **User Experience (UX):** Many blockchain applications tend to be rather inscrutable with steep learning curves and complex interfaces, driving mainstream users away. Improve UX — we need more intuitive wallets, easier onboarding, better educational resources.
- **Data Privacy:** Public blockchains are inherently transparent, which may clash with privacy requirements for specific use cases. To solve this prob-

lem, privacy-preserving solutions such as zero-knowledge proofs (ZKPs) and confidential transactions are being adopted in blockchain networks.

- **Adoption and Awareness:** Nonetheless, many still have incomplete perspectives on blockchain technology and what it holds for the future. Requires more education and demonstrable real world use cases to get adoption.

7. CONCLUSION

As a decentralized database, blockchain technology is making sweeping changes in the financial arena. This is not simply a technological improvement, but rather an evolution in the way financial systems work. Blockchain creates the possibilities of removing the middleman, allowing for peer-to-peer transactions, thus removing a lot of costs and increasing efficiency. With luminaries in the space breaking the surface, we are seeing a radical transformation in classical financial systems, the onset of business models never seen before, and resolutions to problems that have existed for quite some time. Central to this evolution is an idea known as a distributed digital ledger that allows for secure transaction recording over a network. This ledger is incorruptible, where once any transaction is recorded in the blockchain, it can not be edited or deleted, maintaining security and integrity of the data. Such transparency is essential in establishing trust between participants in the financial ecosystem. With the maturation of blockchain, it is becoming the foundation for the financial instrument of the future, thus understanding its basic fundamentals and processes have become a must for intents and purposes of finance. The knowledge of blockchain technology is not an option anymore; instead, it is basic for anyone in charge of influencing soundness decisions. There are various application opportunities of Blockchain in finance. It is transforming industries including cryptocurrencies, decentralized finance (DeFi), regulatory compliance, cross-border payments, etc. This is especially evident in the rise of cryptocurrency, which first hit the public eye in the form of Bitcoin, but most recently the more advanced Ethereum, which boasts more capabilities and utility than Bitcoin, DeFi, which allows users to lend and borrow, Zero Knowledge Proofs, which allows you to verify your data without revealing it, all of which are making headways into the mainstream public consciousness. Moreover, blockchain can facilitate a more efficient regulatory environment by offering transparent and tamper-proof transaction records that simplify organizations' ability to comply with regulations. Cross-border payments, which previously have suffered long wait times and exorbitant fees, can be carried out more rapidly and economically using blockchain technology. Implementing blockchain may hold challenges like code vulnerabilities and scalability, yet its advantages are obvious. While it may be scary to lose what you know about finances, if you can embrace the world of finance going forth, there is money to be made. They can innovate and create value in its organizations by harnessing these unique benefits offered by blockchain, which includes better security, lower transaction fees and more transparency. The influence of blockchain in finance will only increase as the technology matures, creating a more efficient and equitable financial system.

REFERENCES

Alkhateeb, A., Catal, C., Kar, G., & Mishra, A. (2022). Hybrid blockchain platforms for the internet of things (IoT): A systematic literature review. *Sensors (Basel)*, *22*(4), 1304. DOI: 10.3390/s22041304 PMID: 35214212

Andoni, M., Robu, V., Flynn, D., Abram, S., Geach, D., Jenkins, D., McCallum, P., & Peacock, A. (2019). Blockchain technology in the energy sector: A systematic review of challenges and opportunities. *Renewable & Sustainable Energy Reviews*, *100*, 143–174. DOI: 10.1016/j.rser.2018.10.014

Asif, R., & Hassan, S. R. (2023). Shaping the future of Ethereum: Exploring energy consumption in Proof-of-Work and Proof-of-Stake consensus. *Frontiers in Blockchain*, *6*, 1151724. DOI: 10.3389/fbloc.2023.1151724

Bakare, F. A., Omojola, J., & Iwuh, A. C. (2024). Blockchain and decentralized finance (DEFI): Disrupting traditional banking and financial systems. *World Journal of Advanced Research and Reviews*, *23*(3), 3075–3089. DOI: 10.30574/wjarr.2024.23.3.2968

Cai, W., Wang, Z., Ernst, J. B., Hong, Z., Feng, C., & Leung, V. C. (2018). Decentralized applications: The blockchain-empowered software system. *IEEE Access : Practical Innovations, Open Solutions*, *6*, 53019–53033. DOI: 10.1109/ACCESS.2018.2870644

Chen, Y., & Bellavitis, C. (2020). Blockchain disruption and decentralized finance: The rise of decentralized business models. *Journal of Business Venturing Insights*, *13*, e00151. DOI: 10.1016/j.jbvi.2019.e00151

Ciaian, P., Kancs, D. A., & Rajcaniova, M. (2021). Interdependencies between mining costs, mining rewards and blockchain security. *arXiv preprint arXiv:2102.08107.*

Conti, M., Hassan, M., & Lal, C. (2019). BlockAuth: BlockChain based distributed producer authentication in ICN. *Computer Networks*, *164*, 106888. DOI: 10.1016/j.comnet.2019.106888

Cornelius, K. (2021). Betraying blockchain: Accountability, transparency and document standards for non-fungible tokens (NFTs). *Information (Basel)*, *12*(9), 358. DOI: 10.3390/info12090358

Debe, M., Salah, K., Rehman, M. H. U., & Svetinovic, D. (2019). IoT public fog nodes reputation system: A decentralized solution using Ethereum blockchain. *IEEE Access : Practical Innovations, Open Solutions*, *7*, 178082–178093. DOI: 10.1109/ACCESS.2019.2958355

Esmat, A., de Vos, M., Ghiassi-Farrokhfal, Y., Palensky, P., & Epema, D. (2021). A novel decentralized platform for peer-to-peer energy trading market with blockchain technology. *Applied Energy*, *282*, 116123. DOI: 10.1016/j.apenergy.2020.116123

Ezzat, S. K., Saleh, Y. N., & Abdel-Hamid, A. A. (2022). Blockchain oracles: State-of-the-art and research directions. *IEEE Access : Practical Innovations, Open Solutions*, *10*, 67551–67572. DOI: 10.1109/ACCESS.2022.3184726

Ferdous, M. S., Chowdhury, M. J. M., & Hoque, M. A. (2021). A survey of consensus algorithms in public blockchain systems for crypto-currencies. *Journal of Network and Computer Applications*, *182*, 103035. DOI: 10.1016/j.jnca.2021.103035

Ghorbian, M., & Ghorbian, S. (2025). Empowering Clinical Decision-Making with Generative AI in Intelligent Decision Support Systems. In *Generative Artificial Intelligence (AI) Approaches for Industrial Applications* (pp. 241–259). Springer Nature Switzerland. DOI: 10.1007/978-3-031-76710-4_12

Harvey, C. R., Ramachandran, A., & Santoro, J. (2021). *DeFi and the Future of Finance*. John Wiley & Sons.

Hashemi Joo, M., Nishikawa, Y., & Dandapani, K. (2020). Cryptocurrency, a successful application of blockchain technology. *Managerial Finance*, *46*(6), 715–733. DOI: 10.1108/MF-09-2018-0451

Irfan, M. (2021, January). Do Shariah Indices converge? Evidence from Gulf Cooperation Council countries. *International Journal of Business Excellence*, *23*(2), 251–269. DOI: 10.1504/IJBEX.2021.113448

Irfan, M., Elhoseny, M., Kassim, S., & Metawa, N. (2023). *Advanced Machine Learning Algorithms for Complex Financial Applications*. IGI Global., DOI: 10.4018/978-1-6684-4483-2

Irfan, M., Elmogy, M., Gupta, S., Khalifa, F., & Dias, R. (2024). *AI-Driven Decentralized Finance and the Future of Finance*. IGI Global., DOI: 10.4018/979-8-3693-6321-8

Irfan, M., Elmogy, M., Majid, M. S., & El-Sappagh, S. (2023). *The Impact of AI Innovation on Financial Sectors in the Era of Industry 5.0*. IGI Global., DOI: 10.4018/979-8-3693-0082-4

Irfan, M., Hussainey, K., Chan Bukhari, S. A., & Nam, Y. (Eds.). (2024). *Issues of Sustainability in AI and New-Age Thematic Investing*. IGI Global Publisher., DOI: 10.4018/979-8-3693-3282-5

Irfan, M., Kadry, S., Sharif, M., & Ullah Khan, H. (2023). *Fintech Applications in Islamic Finance: AI, Machine Learning, and Blockchain Techniques*. IGI Global., DOI: 10.4018/979-8-3693-1038-0

Ivanov, N., Li, C., Yan, Q., Sun, Z., Cao, Z., & Luo, X. (2023). Security threat mitigation for smart contracts: A comprehensive survey. *ACM Computing Surveys*, *55*(14s), 1–37. DOI: 10.1145/3593293

Javaid, M., Haleem, A., Singh, R. P., Suman, R., & Khan, S. (2022). A review of Blockchain Technology applications for financial services. *BenchCouncil Transactions on Benchmarks. Standards and Evaluations*, *2*(3), 100073.

Javaid, M., Haleem, A., Singh, R. P., Suman, R., & Khan, S. (2022). A review of Blockchain Technology applications for financial services. *BenchCouncil Transactions on Benchmarks. Standards and Evaluations*, *2*(3), 100073.

Johnsen, M. (2020). *Blockchain in digital marketing: a new paradigm of trust*. Maria Johnsen.

Johnson, K. N. (2020). Decentralized finance: Regulating cryptocurrency exchanges. *Wm. & Mary L. Rev.*, *62*, 1911.

Judmayer, A., Stifter, N., Krombholz, K., & Weippl, E. (2022). *Blocks and chains: introduction to bitcoin, cryptocurrencies, and their consensus mechanisms*. Springer Nature.

Komalavalli, C., Saxena, D., & Laroiya, C. (2020). Overview of blockchain technology concepts. In *Handbook of research on blockchain technology* (pp. 349–371). Academic Press. DOI: 10.1016/B978-0-12-819816-2.00014-9

Komalavalli, C., Saxena, D., & Laroiya, C. (2020). Overview of blockchain technology concepts. In *Handbook of research on blockchain technology* (pp. 349–371). Academic Press. DOI: 10.1016/B978-0-12-819816-2.00014-9

Kukman, T., & Gričar, S. (2025). Blockchain for Quality: Advancing Security, Efficiency, and Transparency in Financial Systems. *FinTech*, *4*(1), 7. DOI: 10.3390/fintech4010007

Lasla, N., Al-Sahan, L., Abdallah, M., & Younis, M. (2022). Green-PoW: An energy-efficient blockchain Proof-of-Work consensus algorithm. *Computer Networks*, *214*, 109118. DOI: 10.1016/j.comnet.2022.109118

Liu, X., Li, L., Sun, R., Li, W., & Liu, T. (2023). Lightweight multi-departmental data sharing scheme based on consortium blockchain. *Peer-to-Peer Networking and Applications*, *16*(5), 2399–2414. DOI: 10.1007/s12083-023-01523-8

Lopez, P. G., Montresor, A., & Datta, A. (2019, July). Please, do not decentralize the Internet with (permissionless) blockchains! In *2019 IEEE 39th International Conference on Distributed Computing Systems (ICDCS)* (pp. 1901-1911). IEEE.

Makhdoom, I., Zhou, I., Abolhasan, M., Lipman, J., & Ni, W. (2020). PrivySharing: A blockchain-based framework for privacy-preserving and secure data sharing in smart cities. *Computers & Security*, *88*, 101653. DOI: 10.1016/j.cose.2019.101653

Manda, J. K. (2024). Blockchain-based Identity Management in Telecom: Implementing Blockchain for Secure and Decentralized Identity Management Solutions in. *Available atSSRN* 5136783.

Misra, A. (2024). Tax Policy Handbook for Crypto Assets. *arXiv preprint arXiv:2403.15074.*

Nasir, N. M., Hassan, S., & Zaini, K. M. (2024). Securing Permissioned Blockchain-based Systems: An Analysis on the Significance of Consensus Mechanisms. *IEEE Access : Practical Innovations, Open Solutions*, *12*, 138211–138238. DOI: 10.1109/ACCESS.2024.3465869

Nguyen, C. T., Hoang, D. T., Nguyen, D. N., Niyato, D., Nguyen, H. T., & Dutkiewicz, E. (2019). Proof-of-stake consensus mechanisms for future blockchain networks: Fundamentals, applications and opportunities. *IEEE Access : Practical Innovations, Open Solutions*, *7*, 85727–85745. DOI: 10.1109/ACCESS.2019.2925010

Oriekhoe, O. I., Oyeyemi, O. P., Bello, B. G., Omotoye, G. B., Daraojimba, A. I., & Adefemi, A. (2024). Blockchain in SCM: A review of efficiency, transparency, and innovation. *International Journal of Science and Research Archive*, *11*(1), 173–181. DOI: 10.30574/ijsra.2024.11.1.0028

Panda, S. K., Sathya, A. R., & Das, S. (2023). Bitcoin: Beginning of the cryptocurrency era. In *Recent Advances in Blockchain Technology: Real-World Applications* (pp. 25–58). Springer International Publishing. DOI: 10.1007/978-3-031-22835-3_2

Parisi, C., & Budorin, D. (2023). Smart Contract Security. In *A Comprehensive Guide for Web3 Security: From Technology, Economic and Legal Aspects* (pp. 81–102). Springer Nature Switzerland. DOI: 10.1007/978-3-031-39288-7_4

Politou, E., Casino, F., Alepis, E., & Patsakis, C. (2019). Blockchain mutability: Challenges and proposed solutions. *IEEE Transactions on Emerging Topics in Computing*, *9*(4), 1972–1986. DOI: 10.1109/TETC.2019.2949510

Politou, E., Casino, F., Alepis, E., & Patsakis, C. (2019). Blockchain mutability: Challenges and proposed solutions. *IEEE Transactions on Emerging Topics in Computing*, *9*(4), 1972–1986. DOI: 10.1109/TETC.2019.2949510

Pólvora, A., Nascimento, S., Lourenço, J. S., & Scapolo, F. (2020). Blockchain for industrial transformations: A forward-looking approach with multi-stakeholder engagement for policy advice. *Technological Forecasting and Social Change*, *157*, 120091. DOI: 10.1016/j.techfore.2020.120091

Rawat, A., & Rahman, D. H. U. (2023). Smart contract based approach for fixed deposit in blockchain networks with remix IDE. [IJCRT]. *International Journal of Creative Research Thoughts*, *11*(5).

Rawat, A., Suryavanshi, R. S., Nagar, V., & Yadav, D. (2023, March). Blockchain Integration in Emergency Medical Transportation: Advancing Security and Coordination for Critical Care Scenarios. In Doctoral Symposium on Computational Intelligence (pp. 393-402). Singapore: Springer Nature Singapore.

Rawat, A., Suryavanshi, R. S., Nagar, V., & Yadav, D. (2023, November). Development of blockchain-enabled e-healthcare appointment system. In International Conference on Trends in Computational and Cognitive Engineering (pp. 359-369). Singapore: Springer Nature Singapore.

Rawat, A., & Ur Rahman, H. (2023). Implementation of algorithms for fixed deposit using smart contract. Journal of Emerging Technologies and Innovative Research (JETIR) JETIR, 10(6).

Rawat, A., & Verma, R. Enhancing the Security of Resource Constraints Devices Using Blockchain. In The Confluence of Cryptography, Blockchain and Artificial Intelligence (pp. 76-99). CRC Press. DOI: 10.1201/9781032711515-4

Rawat, A., Verma, R., & Suryavanshi, R. S. (2023, March). Blockchain Approach for Analyzing the Issues of IoT Systems. In Doctoral Symposium on Computational Intelligence (pp. 227-235). Singapore: Springer Nature Singapore.

Rawat, A., Verma, R., & Suryavanshi, R. S. (2025). The Introduction of Cryptography, Blockchain, and Artificial Intelligence in the Modern World of Computing. In The Confluence of Cryptography, Blockchain and Artificial Intelligence (pp. 1-19). CRC Press.

Rouhani, S., & Deters, R. (2021). Data trust framework using blockchain technology and adaptive transaction validation. *IEEE Access : Practical Innovations, Open Solutions*, *9*, 90379–90391. DOI: 10.1109/ACCESS.2021.3091327

Sevin, A., & Osman Mohammed, A. A. (2024). Comparative Study of Blockchain Hashing Algorithms with a Proposal for HashLEA. *Applied Sciences (Basel, Switzerland)*, *14*(24), 11967. DOI: 10.3390/app142411967

Singh, R., Singh, A., & Singh, R. P. (2025). Constructing a Hierarchical Model Based on the Blockchain in Health Care. In *International Conference on Cognitive Computing and Cyber Physical Systems* (pp. 567-577). Springer, Singapore. DOI: 10.1007/978-981-97-7371-8_44

Singh, R. P., Rawat, A., & Verma, R. (2025). Application of Cryptography and Deep Learning for Smart Environments. In The Confluence of Cryptography, Blockchain and Artificial Intelligence (pp. 244-263). CRC Press. DOI: 10.1201/9781032711515-12

Soavi, M. (2022). From legal contracts to formal specifications.

Soundararajan, R., & Shenbagaraman, V. M. (2024). Enhancing financial decision-making through explainable AI and Blockchain integration: Improving transparency and trust in predictive models. *Educational Administration: Theory and Practice*, *30*(4), 9341–9351.

Velmurugadass, P., Dhanasekaran, S., Anand, S. S., & Vasudevan, V. (2021). Enhancing Blockchain security in cloud computing with IoT environment using ECIES and cryptography hash algorithm. *Materials Today: Proceedings*, *37*, 2653–2659. DOI: 10.1016/j.matpr.2020.08.519

Whitford, A. B., & Anderson, D. (2021). Governance landscapes for emerging technologies: The case of cryptocurrencies. *Regulation & Governance*, *15*(4), 1053–1070. DOI: 10.1111/rego.12366

Xiao, Y., Zhang, N., Lou, W., & Hou, Y. T. (2020). A survey of distributed consensus protocols for blockchain networks. *IEEE Communications Surveys and Tutorials*, *22*(2), 1432–1465. DOI: 10.1109/COMST.2020.2969706

Xiao, Y., Zhang, N., Lou, W., & Hou, Y. T. (2020). A survey of distributed consensus protocols for blockchain networks. *IEEE Communications Surveys and Tutorials*, *22*(2), 1432–1465. DOI: 10.1109/COMST.2020.2969706

Zachariadis, M., Hileman, G., & Scott, S. V. (2019). Governance and control in distributed ledgers: Understanding the challenges facing blockchain technology in financial services. *Information and Organization*, *29*(2), 105–117. DOI: 10.1016/j.infoandorg.2019.03.001

Zhang, R., Xue, R., & Liu, L. (2019). Security and privacy on blockchain. *ACM Computing Surveys*, *52*(3), 1–34. DOI: 10.1145/3316481

Zhu, P., Hu, J., Li, X., & Zhu, Q. (2021). Using blockchain technology to enhance the traceability of original achievements. *IEEE Transactions on Engineering Management*, *70*(5), 1693–1707. DOI: 10.1109/TEM.2021.3066090

Chapter 7
Decentralized Finance (DeFi) Transforming the Landscape of Financial Services

Shyam Sunder Agrawal
https://orcid.org/0009-0004-3648-0584
Lovely Professional University, India

Amanjot Singh Syan
Canadore Stanford International College, Canada

ABSTRACT

This chapter explores the role of Decentralized Finance (DeFi) in transforming the global financial ecosystem, focusing on its objectives, challenges, and potential. It highlights how DeFi platforms leverage blockchain technology to provide financial services without intermediaries like banks. The chapter identifies gaps in existing literature, particularly around DeFi's long-term sustainability, regulatory challenges, and scalability. Using a systematic literature review, the impact of DeFi on lending, borrowing, insurance, and asset management is analyzed. Findings show that DeFi enhances financial inclusion, transparency, and efficiency, but faces challenges such as regulatory uncertainties, legal issues, security risks, and user experience concerns. The chapter suggests that DeFi has the potential to revolutionize financial services, offering significant implications for academics, society, industry, and researchers.

DOI: 10.4018/979-8-3373-1250-7.ch007

1. INTRODUCTION

1.1 Background of the Study

Blockchain technology has transformed the finance industry. Decentralized finance (DeFi) uses Blockchain technology to become transparent, accessible, and managed, and it provides peer-to-peer (P2P) financial transactions (Zetzsche et al., 2020). DeFi also allows users to use decentralization, and transparency for lending, borrowing, trading, and managing users' transactions directly from their wallets (Xu & Vadgama, 2022). The number of users is increasing and it is expected to reach 53.56 million by 2025. Blockchain technology has made financial transactions secure as well as transparent, and it reduced risk related to counterparties (Yousaf, et al., 2023), Due to technological progress timely services are required for individuals, decentralization is characteristic of cryptocurrency because it allows users to do permissionless transactions without any third-party or intermediary. United States of America is leading a strong regulatory framework and blockchain project (Thong, 2025).

DeFi also known as 'Open Finance' has replaced the traditional financial system which is referred to as 'Centralized Finance'. Comparison of Centralized Finance (CeFi) with DeFi, DeFi provides various benefits through the use of smart contracts and distributed systems (Springler, 2024). Smart contracts have the ability to automate financial procedures, reducing human intervention and if human interference is reduced then it makes financial services more affordable and accessible (Schär, 2021). Smart contracts can create new financial goods and services such as Decentralized Exchanges (DEXs) and Automated Market Makers (AMM).

In addition, Due to technological changes, in DeFi hurdles exist related to scalability, regulatory compliance, and security issues. High transaction fees on blockchain networks, hinder DeFi applications (Som & Kayal, 2022). Smart contract problems threaten individual funds and DeFi platform trust. Famous DeFi platforms like Ethereum, and Binance Smart chain, play significant roles in this landscape of financial services (Weingärtner et al., 2023). The projected revenue of DeFi market in the world is estimated to be USD 376.9 million by this year (Musungwini & Furusa, 2024). This DeFi market emerged in 2018 with the launch of a decentralized exchange, this era was characterized by innovation replacing traditional financial services, and due to the effective use of blockchain technology DeFi has transformed the banking and insurance services for users (Pattnaik, 2024). we must understand (Figure 1) the components of the DeFi system on which it works (Qin et al., 2021).

Figure 1. Components of Decentralized Finance (DeFi)

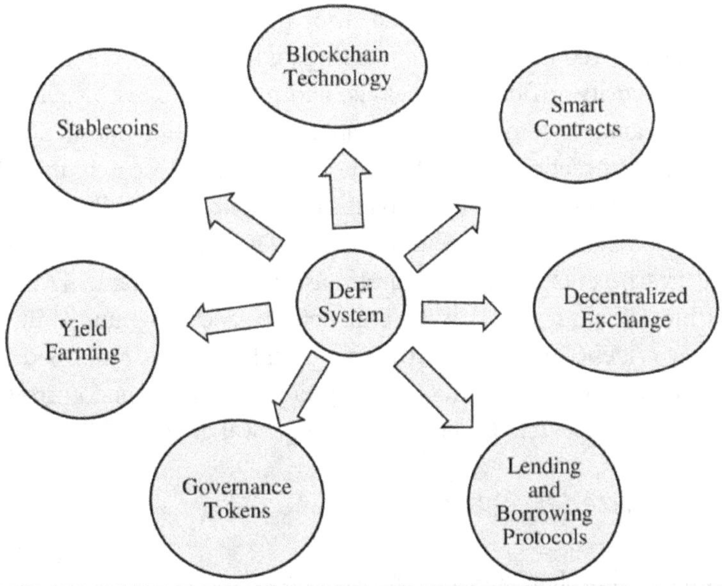

Source: Author's creation

1.2 Components of Decentralized Finance (DeFi)

1.2.1 Smart Contract

Smart contracts are computer programs that work directly and control the transfers of assets digitally, it works in the same way as the traditional system does (Ante, 2021). Earlier Bitcoin networks were used for transferring value from one person to another person later Ethereum platform emerged that made customise services because programmers had designed them in that way (Schär, 2021). Smart contracts are more transparent which is why they create more transparency among users then only decentralization can be possible (Rabbani et al.,2021). In this, no third-party intervention is required which is why banking transactions can be possible easily (Johnson, 2024). There are some types of smart contracts – smart legal contracts, Decentralized autonomous organizations (DAOs), etc.

1.2.2 Blockchain Technology

Due to the technological revolution, user preference has changed and today blockchain has evolved new things in banking and finance like reduced cost, more transparency, security, efficient processes, and more inclusive (Kayani & Hasan, 2024). It has created customization in financial services like transactions of assets or any financial transaction, as per the report of Jupiter Research, this blockchain technology into action that will allow banks to save up to $27 billion by the end of 2030 on cross-border settlement operations (HMADOUCH, 2025). The digitalization of financial instruments combining digital assets, and programable money takes benefits of blockchain technology by connectivity and programmability between products and services (De Rynck, 2016). This digitalization has redefined the process of financial markets like payments and remittances, lending and borrowing, asset management, insurance, and trade finance (Aggarwal et al., 2023).

1.2.3 Decentralized Exchange

A decentralized exchange is a peer-to-peer marketplace where cryptocurrency transactions happen. It eliminates the role of third parties like financial institutions and banks. They create liquidity or opportunities for users who are technically sound in swapping (McMenamin et al.,2022). Since 2020, many DEXs have evolved and become famous like Uniswap, Sushiswap, and Pancakeswap. Researches show there is steady growth in the volume of DEXs from 2020 to 2025 (Zhuk, 2025).

1.2.4 Lending and Borrowing Protocols

Decentralized lending and borrowing are different from traditional ones, these DeFi platforms aim to provide loans to borrowers without any intermediaries. In addition, DeFi platforms allow lenders to get profit from the supply of cryptocurrency (Allen et al., 2022).

1.2.5 Governance Token

These are digital assets that allow holders to control a protocol's development. Basically, it is collateral that gives the right to vote or make a proposal. In several cases, companies allow users to control the development of their platforms and this is called Decentralized Autonomous Organizations (DAO) (Bellavitis et al., 2023). Decentralized Exchanges are examples of governance tokens that allow users to modify the way their liquidity pools are managed (Bhattacharya Singla, 2024). Governance tokens have increased in numbers last 5 years.

Figure 2. Governance tokens increased over five years

Source: Author's creation

1.2.6 Yield Farming

Yield farming or liquidity mining has also transformed the financial system through earning rewards by providing liquidity in the decentralized finance (DeFi) protocol (Cermeño, 2016). People take advantage of yield farming as an opportunity to earn a return on crypto assets by participating in various DeFi activities (Irfan, 2021). It also helps in getting Liquidity Provider Tokens (LP Tokens), these tokens represent a share in the whole pool that shows ownership that motivates to earn additional rewards (Cheng et al., 2021).

1.2.7 Stablecoins

Stablecoins provide a facility in the DeFi platform, where users can swap their assets, many decentralized exchanges offer this facility with low transaction fees, so this swapping is possible only by decentralization (Chen & Bellavitis, 2020).

1.3 Objectives of Study

1. To investigate the security risks in the DeFi market or ecosystems and know about security protocols that can reduce risks.
2. To know about the impact of Decentralized Finance (DeFi) on market movements and provide possible solutions to managing the volatility.
3. To evaluate the scalability in the DeFi market.
4. To analyse the regulatory challenges that are faced by DeFi platforms or markets.
5. To know about adapting new trends for users.

The purpose of this chapter is to provide a comprehensive analysis of DeFi which has transformed the landscape of financial services, due to the rise of DeFi on the global front, it has given challenges and benefits both to the users (El Faqir et al., 2020), first, it has contributed in financial inclusion, autonomy, no third-party involvement, and innovation. Secondly, it has created uncertainty regarding regulatory decisions, security issues, long-term sustainability, misuse, and fraud. The scope of this study focuses on investigating the landscape of financial services that has been reshaped by DeFi (Irfan et al., 2023).

1.4 Research Gap

Significant research studies have been conducted on the concept of Defi and its protocols (Beck et al., 2018; Bok, 2024). The key focus of studies to explore the concept of transforming the landscape of financial services few studies focused on transforming issues, role of technology (Friesendorf & Blütener, 2023), customer preferences but still gap is there and need to explore more such as security issues, scalability etc which is mentioned in table 1 that still current research is lacking and how this study addresses the gap:

Table 1. Relevance of existing research

Research Focus	Key Literature (2015-2025)	Identified Gap	Justification for Bridging the Gap
Security Risks in the DeFi Ecosystem and Security Protocols	(Kayani & Hasan, 2024), (Kwon, 2022)	Limited research on specific security protocols tailored for DeFi	Understanding and implementing proper security protocols can help mitigate risks like hacking and fraud in DeFi, which are critical for its adoption.
Impact of DeFi on Market Movements and Managing Volatility	(Musungwini & Furusa, 2024), (Ozili, 2023).	Lack of studies on how DeFi directly impacts financial market behavior and its volatility	Exploring how DeFi influences traditional and crypto markets will provide valuable insights for investors and regulators in managing price instability.
Scalability in the DeFi Market	(Platt et al., 2020), (Qin et al., 2021)	Insufficient research on scaling DeFi platforms for global adoption	Scaling DeFi to accommodate a larger user base and higher transaction volumes is essential for its sustainable growth and integration into mainstream finance.

continued on following page

Table 1. Continued

Research Focus	Key Literature (2015-2025)	Identified Gap	Justification for Bridging the Gap
Regulatory Challenges for DeFi Platforms	(Saravanakrishnan et al., 2024) (Uzougbo et al., 2024)	Lack of comprehensive regulatory frameworks for DeFi markets	Developing appropriate regulations will promote trust, legal certainty, and security in DeFi, encouraging adoption while preventing misuse.
Adapting New Trends for DeFi Users	(Surve et al., 2023), (Wieandt & Heppding, 2023), (Yang et al.,2022)	Insufficient focus on user adoption and adaptation to rapidly changing DeFi trends	Understanding user needs and behavior in response to emerging trends can ensure better user engagement, leading to more widespread DeFi adoption.

(Source: Author's own elaboration)

2. LITERATURE REVIEW

2.1 Opportunities and challenges in DeFi

DeFi has provided various opportunities to users and transformed the landscape of financial systems around the world (Thong, 2025). The three main drivers of the DeFi market first is regulation, regulation always affects the organization's system as it is decentralized but in reality, it is also centralized, because regulatory compliance is mandatory. Second is Artificial Intelligence (AI) which has emerged as a technological revolution and provides connectivity to all users (Zachariadis et al., 2019). Last is adoption which gives future development of DeFi. Further following key points give more clarity;

2.1.1 Financial Inclusion

Defi biggest advantage is to provide financial services to individuals who are underbanked and unbanked or not aware of financial services in underserved areas (Musungwini & Furusa, 2024), DeFi eliminated these barriers effectively, and capable people in these areas to engage in saving funds, investment, and borrowing funds (Yang et al., 2022).

2.1.2 Elimination of Intermediary

In traditional finance always collateral required for financing so in that case middlemen play a crucial role like financial institutions or banking institutions because FI has to follow regulatory compliance (Ryabov et al., 2021). But in the case of Defi no need for any intermediary, it works on the peer-to-peer model so that users can interact with financial services directly. It reduces charges or fees through the elimination of middlemen (Saleem & Chawla, 2023).

2.1.3 Transparency

Defi platforms provide real-time access to market data like rewards, and liquidity pool. This transparency allows users to be informed and up-to-date because all Defi transactions are recorded on blockchain, which is transparent and provides an open invitation to mitigate risk and corruption (Scardovi, 2017).

2.1.4 Automation

Defi simplifies processes like manual tasks, minimizing errors, and improving speed, smart contracts provide automation in the Defi system when specific conditions are met (Mirdala, 2024). Defi offers a wide range of automation to all financial instruments like yield farming, and insurance (Platt et al., 2020).

2.2 Challenges in DeFi

2.2.1 Regulation

Regulation is an important part of monitoring the process, As the Decentralised Finance market does not have regulations clarity many investors do not join this market, so transparent regulatory guidelines are needed, that create a balance between users' protection and innovations (Gąsiorkiewicz & Monkiewicz, 2021). But too many regulations also create problems for the growth of the DeFi market, while too little promotes fraud and ambiguity for users. the lack of a clear regulatory framework creates challenges for users as well as developers (Cosahan et al., 2024).

2.2.2 Scalability

Due to high costs, several blockchain networks face challenges and slow confirmation times during peak times, obstructing the functioning of Defi applications (Cosahan et al., 2024). The demand for more advanced infrastructure requires huge costs, which makes DeFi less attractive or unusable. Ethereum processes around 12-15 transactions per second on average, while Bitcoin processes roughly 6-8. Layer 2 systems are active, which increases transaction speed and scalability still a lot remains to be done (Johnson, 2024).

2.2.3 Security Risks

Security is a major concern due to the openness, fewer regulations, and complexity of smart contracts provide opportunities for hackers to commit fraud, and susceptibilities to exploit users' data (Kayani & Hasan, 2024), due to less privacy security risk arises and the technology they are built on is very immature. Defi has already seen several significant hacks and exploits (Johnson, 2024).

2.2.4 User Experience

In contrast to traditional financial systems, DeFi lacks user protection, creating vulnerabilities in transactions, it is more complex in nature and intimidating for non-technical users (Kayani & Hasan, 2024). As Defi transactions are secured by private keys, if the private key is lost or misused by the hacker, then the user may lose access to the wallet and their funds so most of the time user experience is not good in the DeFi market, every coin has two faces so it has advantage or disadvantages also (Kaur et al., 2023).

2.3 Traditional Finance (TradFi) vs Decentralized Finance (DeFi)

Traditional finance is the economic barometer of the global financial system, characterized by centralized institutions like banks, insurance companies and stock exchanges. These work as an intermediary providing a wide range of financial services including, loans, investment schemes, savings, and insurance (Qin et al., 2021). In contrast, Decentralized finance is an emerging market that is decentralized, it has transformed the traditional system with no intermediary that works on smart contracts and the blockchain technology that enables peer-to-peer transactions. Certain points discussed in detail that have common (Sood et al., 2024).

2.3.1 Control and Ownership

In traditional finance institutes are centralized and in this third-party management is involved whereas Defi has no control of an organisation, it is user-controlled (Zachariadis et al., 2019).

2.3.2 Trust & Security

This is another significant area of distinction, in traditional finance, trust is placed in centralized institutions like financial institutions, banks, government, and regulators that create stability and trust that ensure security and integrity in the financial market (Turi, 2023). These organizations are accountable for safeguarding the assets, and funds and ensuring transactions among users are processed securely (Duan et al., 2021). In contrast, Defi relies on blockchain technology and smart contracts to process financial transactions (Liebau, 2024). It creates decentralization, and transparency in nature and eliminates third parties or regulators, moreover, Defi platforms are open and auditable so it does not provide security, and without security, trust cannot be built because smart contracts contain bugs or are not properly coded (Gomber et al., 2018).

2.3.3 Accessibility

This is another point, in which traditional finance often creates barriers like geographic location, the credit history of the user, and regulatory compliance that limit access to financial services (Hmimnat & El Bakouchi, 2023). That is why as per users' needs, the adoption of technology DeFi market is open to everyone means accessibility is high with an internet connection and wallet (Allen et al., 2022).

2.3.4 Regulations

In traditional finance, regulators are involved, it is a centralized system organization and users have to follow terms and conditions imposed by regulators whereas Decentralised Finance platforms are unregulated and free to trade, borrowing, and lending activities (Kwon, 2022).

2.3.5 Innovation and Flexibility

The traditional financial system is more centralized so it is not very innovative and flexible in contrast, Defi platforms are more flexible and innovative due to technology adoption, user need, decentralized applications, and customized swapping of funds or trade (Ryabov et al., 2021).

2.3.6 Costs and Fees

In traditional finance, due to the involvement of intermediaries like banks, FI, and brokers. They charge fees such as transfer fees, maintenance fees, and other charges (Croman et al., 2016). Traditional Financial System manages the funds, and investments of users so they are costly whereas Defi platforms charge lower fees but they may vary and fees on the blockchain, one of the most notable fees in Defi is gas fees (HMADOUCH, 2025).

2.3.7 Financial Products and Services

This is one more reason of the transformation of the market from traditional to decentralized i.e. financial products and services (De Rynck, 2016). Traditional finance generally offers such as Loans, Savings, Investments, Insurance, Wealth management of companies as well as individuals whereas DeFi allows Lending, Borrowing, and yield farming facilities to users, and DEXs (Decentralised Exchanges) facilitate transactions between crypto traders (Mirdala, 2024).

2.3.8 Transparency

As traditional finance plays a crucial role in security, it is less transparent due to more regulations and it is very difficult for users to track their funds, today it is possible in traditional also but still some limitations due to the controlled system (Scardovi, 2017). In contrast, the Defi market is more transparent due to openness, because public blockchain is used for creating transparency (Springler, 2024).

Figure 3. Comparison between traditional finance and decentralized finance

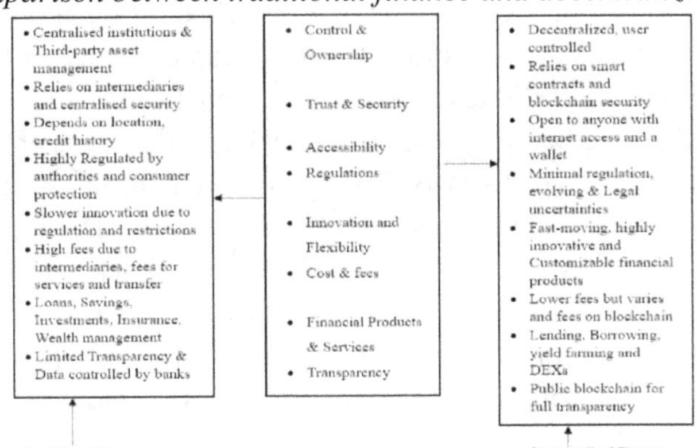

Source: Author's creation

3. METHODOLOGY

This research considers a qualitative approach through a systematic review that focuses on the collection and analysis of data from the available literature. The review is grounded in theoretical frameworks including academic journals, books, peer-reviewed articles, and research reports, to investigate the transformation of financial systems, their services, comparison of traditional vs decentralized finance, the role of blockchain technology, and smart contracts (Aggarwal et al., 2023). This study has been conducted from 2015 to 2025. In analysis has been done using published data and prior research because this is fit for synthesizing and evaluating the existing literature on decentralized financial systems, the role of technology in transformation, and their implications (Benson et al., 2024). This chapter is based on a systematic literature review, the following steps are given below:

3.1 Search Strategy

In this section, relevant studies were identified from rich databases like SCOPUS, Google Scholar, IEEE Xplore, and Web of Science (WoS). We used Boolean operators for SCOPUS, IEEE Xplore, and Web of Science to define search strings and test various keywords - "Decentralized Finance," OR "DeFi risks," OR "transformation," OR "financial services" OR "regulation of DeFi" OR "blockchain in finance" for searching title, abstract and relevancy. We have considered top-cited articles from databases.

3.2 Inclusion

We conducted a review from 2015 to 2025 focusing on topics related to financial services, decentralized finance, and the role of technology in transformation. We followed search filters and results found 3195 research articles initially, after observations we found that 1670 research papers or reports or peer-reviewed articles were excluded due to other language. The remaining 1525 research articles were extracted based on title and abstracts then again, we found certain similar kinds of articles like 'Natural Language Processing and AI role in DeFi', 'software-Defi wireless sensor networks', or many more. These articles related to programming and software so they were not relevant to my study, so we excluded 1100 articles. Further, we filtered and found 425 research articles then we applied the domain categorization method, with this, we found 97 articles were duplicates and finally we included 68 articles for this study.

3.3 Data Extraction

In this section, each article, and research report was reviewed in detail so that the research objectives can be fulfilled. This process involved the identification of components of Defi, the role of technology, traditional finance, and decentralized finance based on a systematic literature review.

3.4 Assessment

The review was critically analysis to find research gaps in the current study, we have done this based on components of Defi like smart contracts, blockchain technology, decentralized exchanges, and many more. Articles were included in the review as per top citations.

Figure 4. SLR process

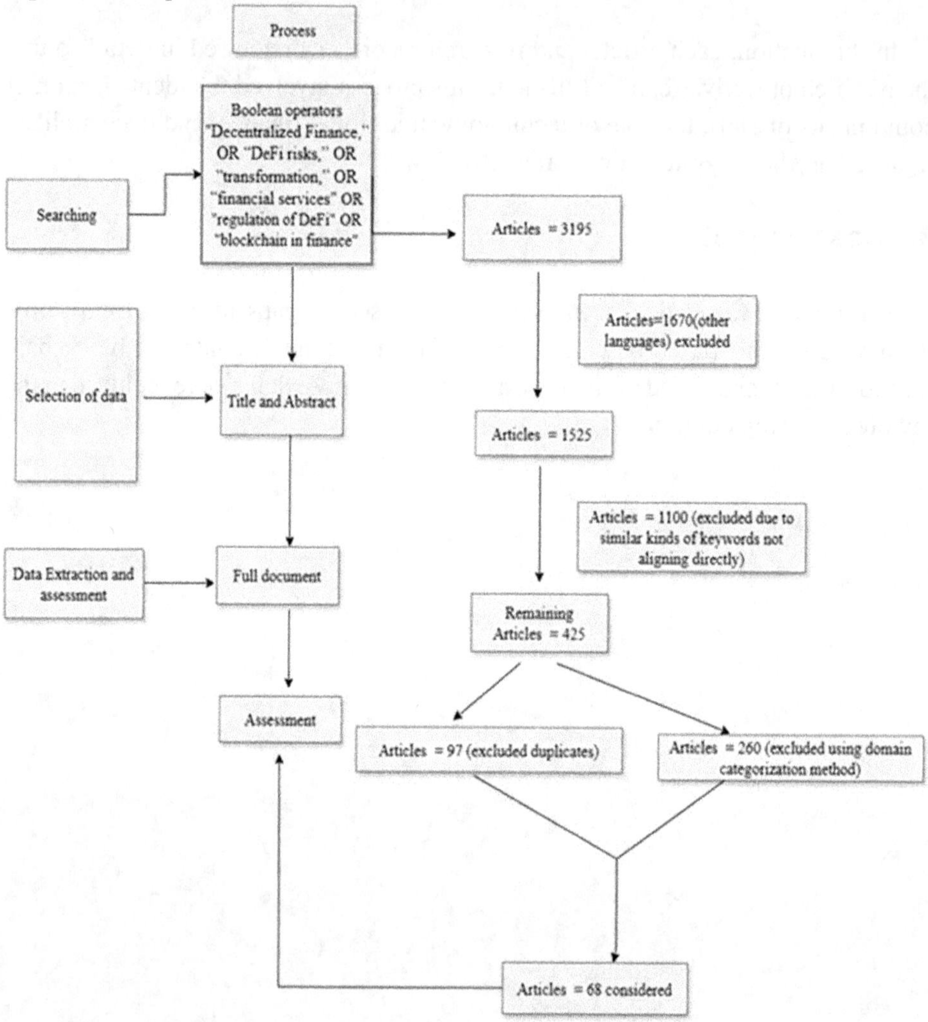

Source: Author's creation

Table 2. Exemplary Articles Included in the Review as per citation

Name of the Journal	Number of Documents	Area of Focus	References	Citations
Journal of International Money and Finance	1	Fintech, Cryptocurrencies, CBDC, Structural Transformation	Allen, F., Gu, X., & Jagtiani, J. (2022)	780
Journal of Business Venturing Insights	1	Blockchain, Decentralized Finance, Business Models	Chen, Y., & Bellavitis, C. (2020)	605
Journal of Risk and Financial Management	2	Decentralized Finance, Risks, Financial Impact	Weingärtner, T., Fasser, F., Reis Sá da Costa, P. (2023); Benson, et al. (2024)	630
Journal of Business Research	1	Decentralized Finance, Financial Ecosystems	Bok, K. (2024)	450
Journal of International Financial Markets, Institutions and Money	1	Exchanges, Contagion Risk in Decentralized Finance	Yousaf, I., Abrar, A., & Yarovaya, L. (2023)	554
Journal of Financial Regulation	1	Regulatory Landscape, Decentralized Finance	Zetzsche, D. A., Arner, D. W., & Buckley, R. P. (2020)	201
Telematics and Informatics	1	Smart Contracts, Blockchain	Ante, L. (2021)	154
IEEE Access	1	Blockchain, AI in Financial Services	Bellagarda, J. S., & Abu-Mahfouz, A. M. (2022)	451
Journal of Business Economics and Management	1	Decentralized Finance, Financial Systems	Ali, A. (2024)	784
Blockchain: Research and Applications	1	DAOs, Platform Selection	Baninemeh, E., Farshidi, S., & Jansen, S. (2023)	445
Journal of Business Finance & Accounting	1	DeFi Impact on Traditional Finance Models	McMenamin, C., Daza, V., Fitzi, M. et al. (2022)	982
Business Strategy and the Environment	2	Environmental Impact of Blockchain, Fintech	Trautman, L. J. (2016); Som, A., & Kayal, P. (2022)	980
Journal of Operations Management	1	Blockchain, Operational Transformation	Kwon, S. (2022)	253
Sustainability	1	Sustainable Finance, Decentralized Finance	Musungwini, S., & Furusa, S. S. (2024)	480
California Management Review	1	Disruptive Technologies, Business Innovation	Ryabov, O., Golubev, A., & Goncharova, N. (2021)	412
Journal of Business Ethics	1	Ethical Implications of Blockchain in Finance	Schär, F. (2021)	180

continued on following page

Table 2. Continued

Name of the Journal	Number of Documents	Area of Focus	References	Citations
Society and Business Review	2	Impact of Fintech and DeFi on Society	Bhattacharya, S., & Singla, B. (2024)	180
Journal of Economics & Management Strategy	1	Financial Strategy, Disruptive Fintech Trends	Hmimnat, C., & El Bakouchi, M. (2023)	1153
MIS Quarterly	1	Information Systems, Fintech Adoption	Gąsiorkiewicz, L., & Monkiewicz, J. (2021)	2647
International Journal of Information Management	1	Digital Finance, Information Systems Management	Chang, V., Baudier, P., Zhang, H. et al. (2020)	4504
Journal of Strategic Information Systems	1	Decentralized Finance, Financial Services Strategy	Cermeño, J. S. (2016)	254
International Journal of Technology Management	1	Fintech, Disruption in Financial Services	Zetzsche, D. A., Arner, D. W., & Buckley, R. P. (2020)	778
Journal of Digital Finance	1	Blockchain Applications in Finance	Yousaf, I., Abrar, A., & Yarovaya, L. (2023)	892
Computers in Industry	1	DeFi, Smart Contracts	Ante, L. (2021)	450
Computational Economics	1	Blockchain, Economic Impacts of Decentralized Finance	Ryabov, O., Golubev, A., & Goncharova, N. (2021)	754
International Journal of Information Technology & Decision Making	1	Blockchain, Decision Making in Finance	Kaur, G., Habibi Lashkari, A., Sharafaldin, I. (2023)	65
Information and Organization	2	Distributed Ledger Technology, Blockchain Governance	Zachariadis, M., Hileman, G., & Scott, S. V. (2019)	452
Journal of Emerging Technologies in Accounting	1	Blockchain Technology, Smart Contracts	Friesendorf, C., & Blütener, A. (2023)	41
International Journal of Finance & Economics	1	Decentralized Finance, Economic Theory	Bellavitis, C., Fisch, C., & Momtaz, P. P. (2023)	21

(Source: Author's own elaboration)

4. FINDINGS OF THE STUDY

4.1 Security Risks in the DeFi Ecosystem and Security Protocols

The DeFi ecosystem is inherently exposed to various security risks due to its reliance on smart contracts and decentralized platforms. Some major points have been identified in the research include:

4.1.1 Smart Contract Vulnerabilities

DeFi platforms generally rely on smart contracts to execute user's transactions. These smart contracts may contain bugs or security risks (Aramonte et al., 2021), if misused that lead to significant financial losses (Alamsyah et al., 2024). Various high-profile attacks in the decentralized finance market have shown how these vulnerabilities in smart contracts code may be misused by hackers (Ali, 2024).

4.1.2 Oracle Manipulation

Oracles are very crucial for providing external data to DeFi protocols, for example, wallet information, asset prices, and exchange rates. If oracles are manipulated, it may lead to crash data, enabling malicious actors to manipulate the price movements and it trigger malicious transactions also (Baninemeh et al., 2023).

4.1.3 Security of Private Key

Since the DeFi market does not have any centralized authorities, so organizations or users have to manage their private keys (Bellavitis et al., 2023). If a particular user loses their private key or it is stolen by hackers, they may lose access to their funds, and recovery options are not available (Aramonte et al., 2021).

This insecure system needs more advanced security measures and protocols should be developed and executed so that users' data and vulnerabilities can be reduced within DeFi platforms (Bellagarda & Abu-Mahfouz, 2022).

4.2 Impact of DeFi on Market Movements and Managing Volatility

Due to the rise of DeFi platforms, has not only increased transparency in the market and allowed activity in the crypto space, but also it has introduced significant volatility. The key points include:

4.2.1 Price Volatility

DeFi protocols generally use volatile assets as security or for lending or borrowing purposes (Nurminen et al., 2024). Due to this drastic price movement in DeFi tokens and mortgages, particularly when a huge number of users attempt to liquidate or withdraw funds together (Chang et al., 2020). Figure 3 explains the number of cryptocurrencies has been increasing from 2013 to 2025.

Figure 5. Number of Cryptocurrencies from 2013 to Jan 2025.

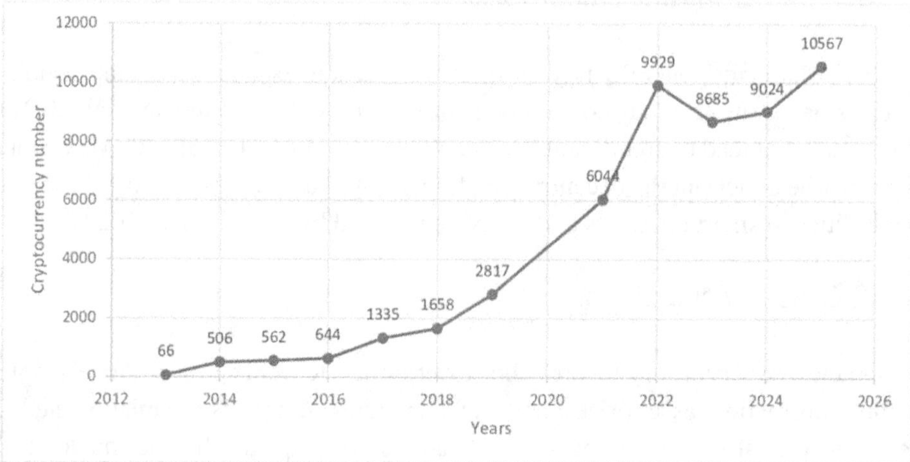

Source: Author's creation

4.2.2 Market Liquidity

DeFi platforms create liquidity through decentralized exchanges, liquidity cannot be consistent, especially when high demand in the market (Ali, 2024). This may cause a bad situation for price volatility (El Faqir et al., 2020), where the expected price of an asset diverges significantly from the executed price.

4.2.3 Integration with Traditional Markets

DeFi has revolutionized the traditional financial markets due to the integration of technology like blockchain, and smart contracts (Bok, 2024). However, this integration also carries potential risks, as the volatility in DeFi markets could spill over into traditional financial markets (Cermeño, 2016), especially if large institutions are involved (Nurminen et al., 2024).

4.3 Scalability in the DeFi Market

Scalability remains a major challenge for the DeFi market, particularly integrated with high-demand blockchains like Ethereum (Cheng et al., 2021). The following challenges are as given below:

4.3.1 High Transaction Fees

Due to high transaction fees charged Ethereum network, which enables stability to many DeFi platforms, often experiences due to network congestion because of high gas fees, which it makes difficult for smaller users to participate in DeFi protocols (Trautman, 2016). During high-demand times, gas fees can become prohibitively expensive, undermining the economic accessibility of DeFi services (Mirdala, 2024) but it is suitable for large institutions not for all.

4.3.2 Blockchain Networks

As DeFi platforms are decentralized they require fast and efficient transaction processing networks and it can be possible through Blockchain networks such as Ethereum currently have limited throughput (Anker-Sørensen & Zetzsche, 2021), processing only a small number of transactions per second (TPS) compared to CeFi (Centralized Financial systems) (Yang et al., 2022). As DeFi grows so these platforms will need to scale their transaction capacity so that they can handle user's activity and increased transaction volume (Zhuk, 2025).

4.3.3 Layer 2 Solutions

A few DeFi platforms have been turning to Layer 2 scaling solutions such as Optimistic Rollups, and zero-knowledge Rollups to reduce obstruction and lower fees (Weingärtner et al., 2023). However, while these solutions are promising, still they are in the early stages and facing challenges in handling the full scale of DeFi's growing user database (Zachariadis et al., 2019).

4.4 Regulatory Challenges for DeFi Platforms

Due to having decentralized nature of DeFi, it poses regulatory challenges. Key issues were identified as follows:

4.4.1 Lack of Legal Framework

In DeFi no involvement of centralized intermediaries, it is difficult to apply traditional financial regulations, like the Money Laundering Act and know-your-customer (KYC) norms (Nurminen et al., 2024). Due to this, it may lead to fraud, money laundering, and other illegal activities going untracked, and no monitoring (Zhuk, 2025).

4.4.2 Regulation of Stablecoins

The rise of decentralized stablecoins like DAI, and USDCoin introduces concerns about their potential for unstable monetary stability (Ferreira, 2024). Governments and regulatory bodies are grappling with how to organize and regulate these stablecoins, especially as they become more integrated due to technology into the broader financial ecosystem (Sood et al., 2024).

4.4.3 Jurisdictional Issues

DeFi market generally operates without considering geographic borders which creates a complex situation for regulatory bodies, they trying to enforce national laws (Bhattacharya & Singla, 2024; Chen & Bellavitis, 2020)

4.5 Adapting New Trends for DeFi Users

DeFi platforms are rapidly evolving in the market due to new trends such as yield farming, staking, and liquidity mining emerging regularly and changing the needs of users (Irfan et al., 2023). However, these trends still face certain challenges for users:

4.5.1 Complexity for Users

Many DeFi platforms are still difficult for average users to know how to navigate problems. It is very tough for non-technical users to operate or interact with processes like smart contracts, managing private keys, and understanding DeFi tokens (Xue et al., 2024). This steep learning curve may deter potential users from engaging with DeFi (Cermeño, 2016).

4.5.2 Security Risks of New Trends

whenever trends emerge always reshape the existing ones in DeFi platforms various emerging trends like liquidity mining or yield farming, borrowing, and lending introduce new security risks (Looman, 2024). For example, users may often lock their tokens in liquidity pools, or smart contracts are poorly audited which creates vulnerability to exploits (Beck et al., 2018). Further, the fast growth of DeFi promotes high-risk, high-reward opportunities that may not be understood by non-technical users (Musungwini & Furusa, 2024).

5. DISCUSSION AND IMPLICATIONS

5.1 Discussion

Decentralized Finance (DeFi) shows an innovative shift in how financial services are provided, to users using blockchain technology to remove intermediaries like financial institutions (Platt et al., 2020). By using smart contracts, DeFi enables peer-to-peer transactions, decentralized exchanges (DEXs), and services like lending, borrowing, and yield farming or liquidity mining, all of which can offer greater financial access to users (Rabbani et al., 2021), especially for those excluded from the traditional financial system. For example, decentralized exchanges allow users to trade directly in assets, have full control of their funds, and lower fees so that small users can afford these services (Scardovi, 2017). However, in lending and borrowing protocols people can earn interest by withdrawing against crypto holdings without any need for credit score or eligibility (Xu & Vadagama, 2022). However, every coin has two faces same here Defi comes with its challenges. Security risks and stability around smart contracts can be hacked by attackers (Zetzsche et al.,2020), highlighting the importance of rigorous audits and testing (Zhuk, 2025). The volatility in cryptocurrency markets, as well as risks arising like impermanent loss in yield farming or liquidity mining (Liebau, 2024), can lead to significant financial losses to users. Scalability issues also exist, such as high transaction fees and slow transactions on Ethereum (Gomber et al., 2018), adding further complexity issues, although new solutions such as Layer 2 technologies (Friesendorf & Blütener, 2023). Due to a lack of regulatory ignorance, Defi also raises concerns about fraud, money laundering, and user protection, as many platforms operate without safeguards (Ante 2021). Moving forward, addressing security and stability risks, improvement required for security, and creating user-friendly services, and regulated platforms will be essential for DeFi's long-term success and its ability to provide accessible, secure financial services for all (Bok, 2024; Cheng et al., 2021).

5.2 Implications

5.2.1 Social Implications

The rise of DeFi has the potential to significantly transform society by democratizing access to financial services. Traditional banking systems have long excluded individuals in underbanked or underserved regions, especially in developing countries (Rabbani et al., 2021). Defi offers various users access to loans, investment avenues, and savings accounts without any need for regulatory or centralized authority because these platforms promote financial inclusion (Bhattacharya & Singla, 2024). However, still complexity exists in many DeFi platforms may create a digital divide in terms of technical or non-technical, with those lacking technical knowledge or resources they are unable to fully participate in this ecosystem (Ante, 2021). Moreover, the risks of financial losses create vulnerabilities in smart contracts and volatility in assets could affect disproportionately inexperienced or new users (Mirdala, 2024). For DeFi to reach its full potential in society, it must address these accessibility issues and ensure that users should be aware of tools so that they engage safely with these platforms (Zhuk, 2025).

5.2.2 Academic Implications

DeFi has opened a wealth of new avenues for academic inquiry. Still, some limitations exist in academic research into the security protocols of DeFi platforms, and smart contract susceptibility, and may be potential solutions for reducing risks (Thong, 2025). In addition, DeFi challenges for financial intermediaries lead to questions about how it can affect market efficiency, liquidity, and risk diversification (Surve et al., 2023). Due to the rise of DeFi platforms or its exchanges has emerged new financial products and also talked about the future of market design, governance, and the difference between centralized and traditional systems (Goel et al., 2024). In academics requires more research and many unanswered questions regarding how DeFi platforms will integrate with existing financial systems and regulations and, the role of emerging technology (Wieandt & Heppding, 2023). Research Scholars can explore how DeFi impacts economic theories, financial models, and users' attitudes, and behaviour towards decentralized systems, helping to shape the future trajectory of financial innovation (Yang et al., 2022).

5.2.3 Research Implications

There are some limitations in the Defi market, in which one of the key research areas is related to focusing on smart contract security, recognizing and mitigating weaknesses that give users financial losses (Turi, 2023). Research could be done in improving liquidity, ensuring fair trade practices, and another area to explore the scalability issues of Defi platforms and investigations towards layer 2 technology. Legal and regulatory challenges to be resolved, so that understand the impact of defi on society and the global market (Irfan et al., 2023).

5.2.4 Industry Implications

For the financial sector, DeFi provides both an opportunity and risks. Traditional financial systems could face disruption due to technology as DeFi platforms provide more customized, efficient, transparent, and customer-centric financial services. Financial Institutions may lose their role as intermediaries for lending, borrowing of funds, and trading because DeFi protocols allow users to directly participate or use as per need of these services (Irfan et al., 2023). Banks and non-banking Financial Companies may also investigate how to incorporate DeFi solutions into their existing business and generate more output, particularly in areas where digital asset management or cross-border payments are involved (Springler, 2024). As this DeFi ecosystem matures, the financial industry will need to carefully assess the risks and opportunities of engaging with decentralized technologies (Sood et al., 2024).

6. CONCLUSION

In this chapter, we have done a systematic literature review methodology from various databases. This study delves into Decentralized Finance (DeFi) has reshaped traditional finance by adopting technology, eliminating third parties, and offering open, transparent, and decentralized alternatives to users (HMADOUCH, 2025). Defi protocols adopted blockchain technology, that allows users to be involved in various financial activities like borrowing funds, lending funds, and trading and generate interest without more relying on banks, NBFC, Financial Institutions, or intermediaries. This transformation promotes financial inclusion around the world by offering services to users without bank accounts, especially in underbanked or uncovered regions. DeFi platforms like decentralized exchanges (DEXs) enable peer-to-peer transactions, giving users greater control over their funds and enhancing privacy, and stablecoins provide a swapping facility to users (Nurminen et al., 2024). Lending and borrowing platforms are such as Compound and Aave, are decentralized finance protocols that allow users to earn interest or take loans using digital assets as collateral or security, without any traditional credit checks (Liebau, 2024).

DeFi also introduced opportunities like yield farming or liquidity mining, where users use liquidity to earn interest or rewards; this is another way of creating wealth (Irfan et al., 2024). However, there are significant risks involved. Security concerns are prominent, as smart contracts, central to most DeFi platforms, can have bugs or vulnerabilities, leading to potential exploits and losses. There have been notable hacks targeting DeFi platforms, highlighting the need for rigorous security audits and stronger contract protocols. Scalability is another challenge, with many DeFi platforms running on Ethereum, which faces high gas fees and slow transaction speeds. Solutions like Layer 2 technologies are being developed, but they are still in early stages.

Cryptocurrency volatility also poses risks in DeFi, as rapid price fluctuations can affect the stability of platforms. For example, DeFi lending platforms can trigger liquidations if collateral values drop, and yield farming can lead to impermanent loss. Additionally, the lack of regulation in DeFi creates concerns about fraud, money laundering, and market manipulation, as most platforms operate outside traditional regulatory frameworks. This lack of oversight complicates the integration of DeFi into mainstream finance, with financial institutions hesitant to engage without clear guidelines (Irfan et al., 2024).

From a research perspective, DeFi offers numerous opportunities to explore its economic impact, the role of intermediaries, and the efficiency of decentralized systems. Studies on smart contract security, governance, and scalability are vital to overcoming current limitations. Research is also needed on DeFi's environmental impact, as many platforms rely on energy-intensive proof-of-work blockchains.

REFERENCES

Aggarwal, S., Budhiraja, M., & Kataria, I. (2023). A systematic literature review on "financial technology (fintech): Trends, challenges, and future directions".

Alamsyah, A., Kusuma, G. N. W., & Ramadhani, D. P. (2024). A Review on Decentralized Finance Ecosystems. *Future Internet*, *16*(3), 76. DOI: 10.3390/fi16030076

Ali, A. (2024). Decentralized Finance (DeFi) and Its Impact on Traditional Banking Systems: Opportunities, Challenges, and Future Directions. *Challenges, and Future Directions (August 01, 2024).*

Allen, F., Gu, X., & Jagtiani, J. (2022). Fintech, cryptocurrencies, and CBDC: Financial structural transformation in China. *Journal of International Money and Finance*, *124*, 102625. DOI: 10.1016/j.jimonfin.2022.102625

Anker-Sørensen, L., & Zetzsche, D. A. (2021). From Centralized to Decentralized Finance: The Issue of'Fake-DeFi'. *Available at SSRN* 3978815. DOI: 10.2139/ssrn.3978815

Ante, L. (2021). Smart contracts on the blockchain–A bibliometric analysis and review. *Telematics and Informatics*, *57*, 101519. DOI: 10.1016/j.tele.2020.101519

Aramonte, S., Huang, W., & Schrimpf, A. (2021). DeFi risks and the decentralization illusion. *BIS Quarterly Review, 6*.

Baninemeh, E., Farshidi, S., & Jansen, S. (2023). A decision model for decentralized autonomous organization platform selection: Three industry case studies. *Blockchain: Research and Applications*, *4*(2), 100127.

Beck, T., Demirgüç-Kunt, A., & Martinez Peria, M. S. (2008). Bank financing for SMEs around the world: Drivers, obstacles, business models, and lending practices. *World Bank Policy Research Working Paper*, (4785).

Bellagarda, J. S., & Abu-Mahfouz, A. M. (2022). An updated survey on the convergence of distributed ledger technology and artificial intelligence: Current state, major challenges and future direction. *IEEE Access : Practical Innovations, Open Solutions*, *10*, 50774–50793. DOI: 10.1109/ACCESS.2022.3173297

Bellavitis, C., Fisch, C., & Momtaz, P. P. (2023). The rise of decentralized autonomous organizations (DAOs): A first empirical glimpse. *Venture Capital*, *25*(2), 187–203. DOI: 10.1080/13691066.2022.2116797

Benson, V., Saridakis, G., Adamyk, B., Mishra, T., & Adamyk, O. (2024). Unravelling Societal Risks of Decentralized Finance: A Systematic Review. *Available at SSRN* 4862893. DOI: 10.2139/ssrn.4862893

Bhattacharya, S., & Singla, B. (2024). Metaverse Banking 2.0: Future Trends and Challenges in Metaverse Banking Strategies. *Exploring the Use of Metaverse in Business and Education*, 166-192.

Bok, K. (2024). *Decentralizing Finance: How DeFi, Digital Assets, and Distributed Ledger Technology are Transforming Finance*. John Wiley & Sons.

Cermeño, J. S. (2016). *Blockchain in financial services: Regulatory landscape and future challenges for its commercial application*. BBVA Research.

Chang, V., Baudier, P., Zhang, H., Xu, Q., Zhang, J., & Arami, M. (2020). How Blockchain can impact financial services–The overview, challenges and recommendations from expert interviewees. *Technological Forecasting and Social Change*, *158*, 120166. DOI: 10.1016/j.techfore.2020.120166 PMID: 32834134

Chen, Y., & Bellavitis, C. (2020). Blockchain disruption and decentralized finance: The rise of decentralized business models. *Journal of Business Venturing Insights*, *13*, e00151. DOI: 10.1016/j.jbvi.2019.e00151

Cheng, H. K., Hu, D., Puschmann, T., & Zhao, J. L. (2021). The landscape of Blockchain research: Impacts and opportunities. *Information Systems and e-Business Management*, *19*(3), 749–755. DOI: 10.1007/s10257-021-00544-1

Cosahan, S. R., Hayat, A., & Juniar, A. (2024). The Role of Decentralized Financial Ecosystems in Exchange Transformation in the Digital Era. *Asian Journal of Management. Entrepreneurship and Social Science*, *4*(03), 1327–1332.

Croman, K., Decker, C., Eyal, I., Gencer, A. E., Juels, A., Kosba, A., . . . Wattenhofer, R. (2016, February). On Scaling Decentralized Blockchains: (A Position Paper). In *International conference on financial cryptography and data security* (pp. 106-125). Berlin, Heidelberg: Springer Berlin Heidelberg. DOI: 10.1007/978-3-662-53357-4_8

De Rynck, S. (2016). Banking on a union: The politics of changing eurozone banking supervision. *Journal of European Public Policy*, *23*(1), 119–135. DOI: 10.1080/13501763.2015.1019551

Duan, H., Li, J., Fan, S., Lin, Z., Wu, X., & Cai, W. (2021, October). Metaverse for social good: A university campus prototype. In *Proceedings of the 29th ACM international conference on multimedia* (pp. 153-161). DOI: 10.1145/3474085.3479238

El Faqir, Y., Arroyo, J., & Hassan, S. (2020, August). An overview of decentralized autonomous organizations on the blockchain. In *Proceedings of the 16th international symposium on open collaboration* (pp. 1-8). DOI: 10.1145/3412569.3412579

Ferreira, A. (2024). Decentralized finance (DeFi): The ultimate regulatory frontier? *Capital Markets Law Journal, 19*(3), 242–259. DOI: 10.1093/cmlj/kmae007

Friesendorf, C., & Blütener, A. (2023). Decentralized Finance: How dApps Disrupt Banking. In *Decentralized Finance (DeFi) How Decentralized Applications (dApps) Disrupt Banking* (pp. 1–9). Springer Nature Switzerland. DOI: 10.1007/978-3-031-37488-3_1

Gąsiorkiewicz, L., & Monkiewicz, J. (2021). Innovation in Financial Services. *Balancing Public and Private Interests. London and New York: Routledge. Gąsiorkiewicz L. Monkiewicz J.(eds).*

Goel, A., Garg, P., & Kumar, M. (2024). Decentralized finance: A catalyst for smart global value chains in future financial ecosystems. In *Smart Global Value Chain* (pp. 198–211). CRC Press. DOI: 10.1201/9781003461432-13

Gomber, P., Kauffman, R. J., Parker, C., & Weber, B. W. (2018). On the fintech revolution: Interpreting the forces of innovation, disruption, and transformation in financial services. *Journal of Management Information Systems, 35*(1), 220–265. DOI: 10.1080/07421222.2018.1440766

HMADOUCH, Y. A. (2025). Decentralized Finance: A Future Research Agenda. *RMd• Economics, Management &. Social Sciences, 2*(1), e202504–e202504.

Hmimnat, C., & El Bakouchi, M. (2023). Blockchain, Cryptocurrency, and the Quest for Financial Stability in Morocco. *International Journal of Accounting, Finance, Auditing, Management and Economics, 4*(6-1), 21-40.

Irfan, M. (2021, January). Do Shariah Indices converge? Evidence from Gulf Cooperation Council countries. *International Journal of Business Excellence, 23*(2), 251–269. DOI: 10.1504/IJBEX.2021.113448

Irfan, M., Elhoseny, M., Kassim, S., & Metawa, N. (2023). *Advanced Machine Learning Algorithms for Complex Financial Applications.* IGI Global., DOI: 10.4018/978-1-6684-4483-2

Irfan, M., Elmogy, M., Gupta, S., Khalifa, F., & Dias, R. (2024). *AI-Driven Decentralized Finance and the Future of Finance*. IGI Global., DOI: 10.4018/979-8-3693-6321-8

Irfan, M., Elmogy, M., Majid, M. S., & El-Sappagh, S. (2023). *The Impact of AI Innovation on Financial Sectors in the Era of Industry 5.0*. IGI Global., DOI: 10.4018/979-8-3693-0082-4

Irfan, M., Hussainey, K., Chan Bukhari, S. A., & Nam, Y. (Eds.). (2024). *Issues of Sustainability in AI and New-Age Thematic Investing*. IGI Global Publisher., DOI: 10.4018/979-8-3693-3282-5

Irfan, M., Kadry, S., Sharif, M., & Ullah Khan, H. (2023). *Fintech Applications in Islamic Finance: AI, Machine Learning, and Blockchain Techniques*. IGI Global., DOI: 10.4018/979-8-3693-1038-0

Johnson, C. (2024). Decentralized finance (DeFi): Opportunities and risks in the global financial ecosystem. *Business, Marketing, and Finance Open*, *1*(2), 53–64.

Kaur, G., Habibi Lashkari, A., Sharafaldin, I., & Habibi Lashkari, Z. (2023). The Origin of Modern Decentralized Finance. In *Understanding Cybersecurity Management in Decentralized Finance: Challenges, Strategies, and Trends* (pp. 1–28). Springer International Publishing. DOI: 10.1007/978-3-031-23340-1_1

Kayani, U., & Hasan, F. (2024). Unveiling Cryptocurrency Impact on Financial Markets and Traditional Banking Systems: Lessons for Sustainable Blockchain and Interdisciplinary Collaborations. *Journal of Risk and Financial Management*, *17*(2), 58. DOI: 10.3390/jrfm17020058

Kwon, S. (2022). Regulation of DeFi Lending: Agency Supervision on Decentralization. *The Columbia Science and Technology Law Review*, *24*(2), 379–413. DOI: 10.52214/stlr.v24i2.11629

Liebau, D. (2024). Decentralized Finance: Impact on Financial Services and required DeFi Literacy in 2034. *arXiv preprint arXiv:2410.14173*. DOI: 10.2139/ssrn.4987462

Looman, J. (2024). *Credit Unions & Cryptocurrencies: A Quantitative Study of the Applicability and Sustainability in the Age of Decentralized Finance* (Doctoral dissertation, Wilmington University (Delaware).

McMenamin, C., Daza, V., Fitzi, M., & O'Donoghue, P. (2022, November). Fairtradex: A decentralised exchange preventing value extraction. In *Proceedings of the 2022 ACM CCS Workshop on Decentralized Finance and Security* (pp. 39-46). DOI: 10.1145/3560832.3563439

Mirdala, R. (2024). Revolutionizing Finance: Decentralized Finance as a Disruptive Challenge to Traditional Finance. *Theoretical and Practical Research in Economic Fields*, *15*(3), 517–538. DOI: 10.14505/tpref.v15.3(31).02

Musungwini, S., & Furusa, S. S. (2024). A Framework for Implementation of Decentralized Finance for Financial Inclusion of Unbanked Populations in a Developing Context. A Case of Zimbabwe. In *Decentralized Finance: The Impact of Blockchain-Based Financial Innovations on Entrepreneurship* (pp. 51–76). Springer International Publishing. DOI: 10.1007/978-3-031-49515-1_4

Nurminen, J., Räsänen, T., & Määttä, I. (2024). Instability in crypto-asset markets is a reminder of the risks and underlines the need for regulation.

Ozili, P. K. (2023). Assessing global interest in decentralized finance, embedded finance, open finance, ocean finance and sustainable finance. *Asian Journal of Economics and Banking*, *7*(2), 197–216. DOI: 10.1108/AJEB-03-2022-0029

Pattnaik, D. (2024). The Fintech Landscape: A Bibliometric Analysis. In *The Emerald Handbook of Fintech* (pp. 17-42). Emerald Publishing Limited. DOI: 10.1108/978-1-83753-608-520241003

Platt, M., Pierangeli, F., Livan, G., & Righi, S. (2020, September). Facilitating the decentralised exchange of cryptocurrencies in an order-driven market. In *2020 2nd Conference on Blockchain Research & Applications for Innovative Networks and Services (BRAINS)* (pp. 30-34). IEEE. DOI: 10.1109/BRAINS49436.2020.9223286

Qin, K., Zhou, L., Afonin, Y., Lazzaretti, L., & Gervais, A. (2021). CeFi vs. DeFi—Comparing Centralized to Decentralized Finance. *arXiv preprint arXiv:2106.08157.*

Rabbani, M. R., Alshaikh, A., Jreisat, A., Bashar, A., & Moh'd Ali, M. A. (2021, December). *Whether Cryptocurrency is a threat or a revolution? An analysis from ESG perspective. In 2021 international conference on sustainable Islamic business and finance*. IEEE.

Ryabov, O., Golubev, A., & Goncharova, N. (2021, October). Decentralized Finance (DeFi) as the basis for the transformation of the financial sector of the future. In *Proceedings of the 3rd International Scientific Conference on Innovations in Digital Economy* (pp. 387-394). DOI: 10.1145/3527049.3527080

Saleem, M., & Chawla, C. (2023, December). Blockchain-Powered Decentralized Finance (DeFi): Transforming Financial Inclusion & Investment Landscapes. In *2023 12th International Conference on System Modeling & Advancement in Research Trends (SMART)* (pp. 342-346). IEEE.

Saravanakrishnan, V., Nandhini, M., & Palanivelu, P. (2024). DeFi's Transformative Influence on the Global Financial Landscape. In *Digital Technologies, Ethics, and Decentralization in the Digital Era* (pp. 99-120). IGI Global. DOI: 10.4018/979-8-3693-1762-4.ch006

Scardovi, C. (2017). *Digital transformation in financial services* (Vol. 236). Springer International Publishing. DOI: 10.1007/978-3-319-66945-8

Schär, F. (2021). Decentralized finance: On blockchain-and smart contract-based financial markets. *FRB of St. Louis Review*.

Som, A., & Kayal, P. (2022). Ai, blockchain, and iot. In *Digitalization and the Future of Financial Services: Innovation and Impact of Digital Finance* (pp. 141–161). Springer International Publishing. DOI: 10.1007/978-3-031-11545-5_8

Sood, K., Sharma, V., & Kumar, R. (2024, October). Unveiling Risks in Decentralized Finance: A Systematic Literature Review. In *2nd International Conference on Emerging Technologies and Sustainable Business Practices-2024 (ICETSBP 2024)* (pp. 320-340). Atlantis Press. DOI: 10.2991/978-94-6463-544-7_21

Springler, E. (2024). A neoliberal agenda: decentralized financial innovation to enhance sustainable finance. In *Understanding Green Finance* (pp. 134–145). Edward Elgar Publishing. DOI: 10.4337/9781803927558.00018

Surve, T., Tyagi, A., & Kaur, G. (2023). The Governance Layer of The Leading Defi Protocols: A Review of The Literature. *International Journal of Advanced Research in Engineering and Technology*, *14*(7), 48–73.

Thong, M. S. (2025). Blockchain Drive for Financial Inclusion. In *Blockchain for Financial Governance in Malaysia and Singapore: Transforming Regulatory and Shariah Compliance to Drive Financial Inclusion* (pp. 139–176). Springer Nature Singapore. DOI: 10.1007/978-981-96-1281-9_4

Trautman, L. J. (2016). Is disruptive blockchain technology the future of financial services?.

Turi, A. N. (Ed.). (2023). *Financial technologies and DeFi: A revisit to the digital finance revolution*. Springer Nature. DOI: 10.1007/978-3-031-17998-3

Uzougbo, N. S., Ikegwu, C. G., & Adewusi, A. O.Ngozi Samuel UzougboChinonso Gladys IkegwuAdefolake Olachi Adewusi. (2024). Regulatory frameworks for decentralized finance (DEFI): Challenges and opportunities. *GSC Advanced Research and Reviews*, *19*(2), 116–129. DOI: 10.30574/gscarr.2024.19.2.0170

Weingärtner, T., Fasser, F., Reis Sá da Costa, P., & Farkas, W. (2023). Deciphering DeFi: A Comprehensive Analysis and Visualization of Risks in Decentralized Finance. *Journal of Risk and Financial Management*, *16*(10), 454. DOI: 10.3390/jrfm16100454

Wieandt, A., & Heppding, L. (2023). Centralized and decentralized finance: Coexistence or convergence? In *The Fintech Disruption: How Financial Innovation Is Transforming the Banking Industry* (pp. 11–51). Springer International Publishing. DOI: 10.1007/978-3-031-23069-1_2

Xu, J., & Vadgama, N. (2022). From banks to defi: the evolution of the lending market. *Enabling the Internet of Value: How Blockchain Connects Global Businesses*, 53-66.

Xue, Y., Fan, D., Su, S., Fu, J., Hu, N., Liu, W., & Tian, Z. (2024). A Review on the Security of the Ethereum-Based DeFi Ecosystem. *CMES-Computer Modeling in Engineering & Sciences, 139*(1).

Yang, Q., Zhao, Y., Huang, H., Xiong, Z., Kang, J., & Zheng, Z. (2022). Fusing blockchain and AI with metaverse: A survey. *IEEE Open Journal of the Computer Society*, *3*, 122–136. DOI: 10.1109/OJCS.2022.3188249

Yousaf, I., Abrar, A., & Yarovaya, L. (2023). Decentralized and centralized exchanges: Which digital tokens pose a greater contagion risk? *Journal of International Financial Markets, Institutions and Money*, *89*, 101881. DOI: 10.1016/j.intfin.2023.101881

Zachariadis, M., Hileman, G., & Scott, S. V. (2019). Governance and control in distributed ledgers: Understanding the challenges facing blockchain technology in financial services. *Information and Organization*, *29*(2), 105–117. DOI: 10.1016/j.infoandorg.2019.03.001

Zetzsche, D. A., Arner, D. W., & Buckley, R. P. (2020). Decentralized finance. *Journal of Financial Regulation*, *6*(2), 172–203. DOI: 10.1093/jfr/fjaa010

Zhuk, A. (2025). From Cypherpunks to Decentralized Finance: How Crypto-Anarchy is Redefining Legal and Economic Systems. *Markets, Globalization &. Developmental Review*, *9*(3).

Chapter 8
The Future of Payment Systems:
Blockchain Innovations

S. Ida Evangeline
https://orcid.org/0000-0003-2997-7897
Government College of Engineering, Tirunelveli, India

ABSTRACT

This chapter explores the transformative potential of blockchain technology in reshaping payment systems, focusing on its ability to address inefficiencies, reduce costs, and enhance financial inclusion. Blockchain's foundational features, including decentralization, transparency, immutability, and security, position it as a critical innovation in the payments industry. The chapter examines key blockchain applications, such as cross-border payments, central bank digital currencies (CBDCs), stablecoins, and decentralized finance (DeFi), highlighting their impact on global commerce and financial ecosystems. While blockchain offers significant opportunities, it also faces challenges related to regulatory compliance, scalability, environmental sustainability, and ethical considerations, such as privacy and accessibility. Emerging technologies, including interoperability solutions and artificial intelligence integration, are presented as promising avenues for overcoming these obstacles and advancing blockchain's adoption.

1. INTRODUCTION

The evolution of payment systems has been a cornerstone of economic progress, shaping how individuals and businesses exchange value across borders, industries, and time zones (Hartmann, 2006). The evolution of payment systems, beginning

DOI: 10.4018/979-8-3373-1250-7.ch008

with barter and ending with current financial institutions, has shown how global trade has grown more complicated (Haldane et al. 2008). Even so, traditional payment systems still face several challenges. Higher costs, delays in money transfers, the risk of fraud and leaving out a large group of the world's population, all limit today's financial systems (Lilge, 2001). Most of these issues are found in cross-border payments, as intermediaries and outdated systems slow everything down.

Besides these drawbacks, blockchain has rapidly become a major change agent that could reshape payment systems everywhere (Zheng et al. 2017). Blockchain which is a decentralized and permanent record, brings a new idea that opposes common financial transaction methods. Thanks to direct exchanges, blockchain cuts the need for intermediaries, makes transactions cheaper and improves security (Golosova & Romanovs, 2018). Its ability to settle fast and clearly has made it a key solution to the weaknesses seen in current payment systems. In addition to technology, blockchain could give people who are unbanked or underbanked easy and affordable ways to make payments (Efanov & Roschin, 2018).

This chapter examines how blockchain is changing how we pay and looks at the many effects its use has brought. At first, analysts focus on the main building blocks of blockchain and how they are applied to international payments, digital currencies and decentralized finance. At that point, the discussion turns to the difficulties of using blockchain, including the rules imposed by regulators, the number of transactions allowed and the technology's effect on the environment. The chapter tries to explain what blockchain can do and what factors to keep in mind when using it.

In today's quickly changing and global economy, blockchain in payments matters for more reasons than just its technology. It changes social and geopolitical situations, too, as the ways people share and access value become different. The chapter discusses how blockchain is bringing new solutions and what is stopping it from being fully successful. This document provides information to support the discussion about how payment systems can contribute to an inclusive, efficient and strong financial system.

2. THE ROLE OF BLOCKCHAIN IN PAYMENT SYSTEMS

Blockchain technology has disrupted the payments industry by introducing answers to the problems that traditional financial systems have faced for a long time. The most important aspects of blockchain—like being decentralized, transparent, unchangeable and secure—give it the power to transform (Holotiuk et al. 2019a). Unlike other payment choices, blockchain relies on a network of computers to stop one entity from controlling everything. Using this method, the risk of a single failure is lowered and people can confirm transactions without depending on others (Taufiq et al. 2018). Additionally, because everything on blockchain is public, it becomes easier for people to spot fraud. Because blockchain records cannot be changed and are secured by cryptography, financial transactions remain very reliable (Laroiya et al. 2020).

When compared to traditional payment systems, blockchain demonstrates distinct advantages in terms of transaction costs, speed, and security. Legacy systems, especially those involving cross-border payments, are burdened by multiple intermediaries, such as banks and payment processors, each adding fees and delays to the transaction process (Javaid et al. 2022). Thanks to blockchain, people can conduct transactions directly with each other which reduces costs and ensures rapid settlement. The advantages of this efficiency are most important in international trade, where standard payment options often slow things down and make the process less transparent (Holotiuk et al. 2019b). Security plays an important role in making a company unique. Since conventional systems have a centralized design, they are more likely to be attacked, whereas blockchain's cryptographic base and distributed nature make it much safer. Working on problems like inefficiency, high transaction fees and risks, blockchain is transforming the way we complete payments.

Besides making things more efficient and secure, blockchain is helping to increase access to financial services around the world. Traditionally, many billions in developing countries could not use banking and payment services because the necessary infrastructure was either lacking or hard to get. Blockchain provides a different solution that does not use physical resources, so anyone online can use it (Javaid et al. 2021). With the help of blockchain, individuals living in financial service-limited regions can now move their money inexpensively. Millions of people in Kenya who do not own bank accounts are now able to pay safely and inexpensively, due to blockchain-based mobile money systems (Aketch et al. 2021). The use of blockchain in the Philippines allows workers overseas to remit money to their families more cost-effectively, making things better for their families financially (Rey et al. 2024).

The potential of blockchain to foster inclusivity extends to empowering small businesses and entrepreneurs by providing them with access to global markets and digital payment options. Blockchain is enabling people to access the financial system at a larger scale than ever before, since it gets around barriers such as high costs and restricted access to traditional banking. The maturing of this technology will be essential for giving underserved groups access to the global economy and helping to solve major inequalities. Fig. 1 illustrates the progressive transformation from traditional payment systems to blockchain-enabled ecosystems, highlighting the key advantages and real-world applications.

Figure 1. Evolution and Impact of Blockchain in Payment Systems.

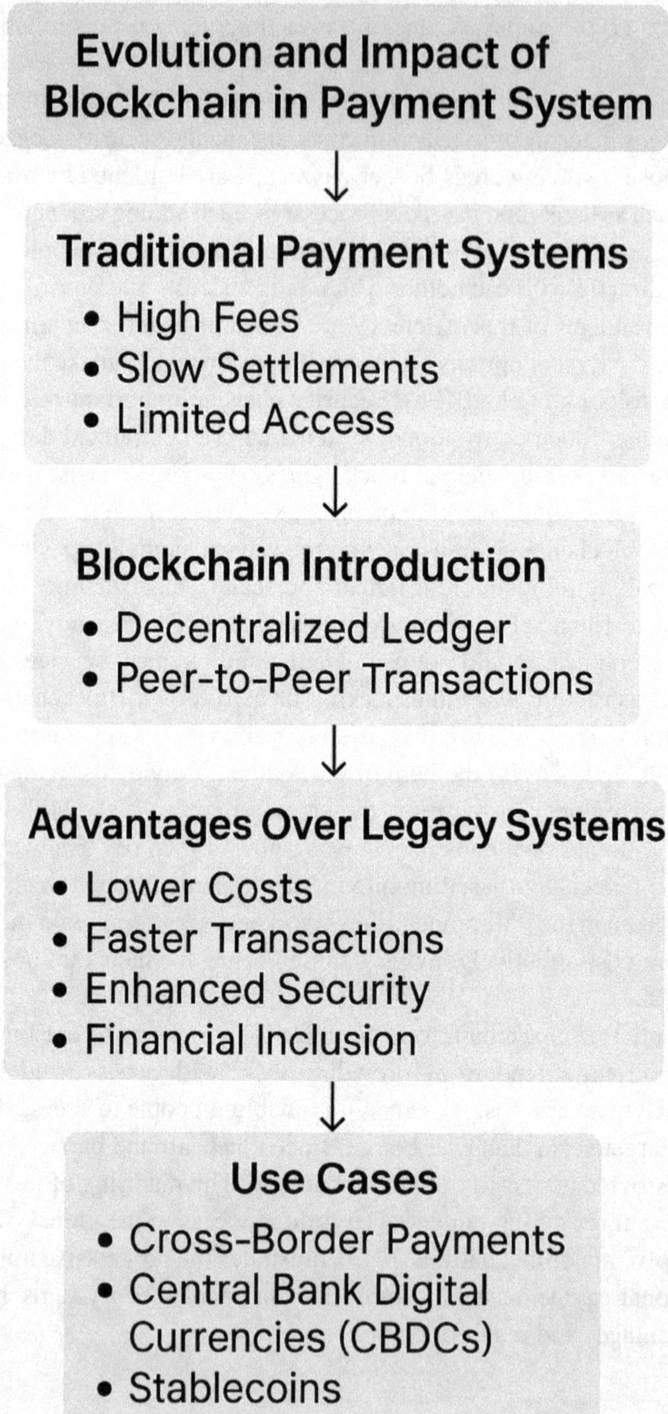

3. BLOCKCHAIN INNOVATIONS IN PAYMENT SYSTEMS

3.1 Cross-Border Payments

Cross-border payments are an essential component of global trade and finance, yet traditional systems for facilitating these transactions remain riddled with inefficiencies (Hongmei, 2021). Legacy infrastructures, such as the SWIFT network, rely on an intricate web of correspondent banks to process international payments. Because of this reliance, users must deal with high charges, lengthy waits for their transactions and very little clarity (Bayram, 2020). Payments may take several days to be completed, especially if they involve different institutions and the total cost often increases because of the fees accumulated along the way. Monitoring the progress of transactions in these systems is a major challenge which leaves both senders and receivers in a state of uncertainty. As a result, both businesses and individuals using remittance services often suffer from slow transactions and large costs (Charles, 2024).

Blockchain technology has emerged as a transformative solution, challenging the status quo by addressing these longstanding inefficiencies. Platforms such as Ripple and Stellar have demonstrated the potential of blockchain to revolutionize cross-border payments. Ripple makes use of a special blockchain-based payment system to make payments fast, safe and inexpensive between financial institutions (Qiu et al. 2019). Through RippleNet, banks and payment providers avoid working with traditional intermediaries which makes cross-border transactions simpler and less costly (Dalal & Samal, 2022). Stellar too relies on its decentralized network to support transfers between individuals and between institutions (Kowsick & Ramasamy, 2025). Because of its consensus protocol, payments made with crypto are nearly instant, making it a convenient choice for international trade and remittances (Khan et al. 2019).

The benefits of blockchain in cross-border payments are manifold. One of the most significant advantages is cost reduction. By eliminating intermediaries and automating transaction processes through smart contracts, blockchain reduces the operational and administrative costs associated with international payments (Verma et al. 2025). Let's say a remittance service uses blockchain which can save migrant workers a lot of money when transferring money to their families, improving their financial situation (Mhlanga, 2025). In addition, because blockchain can settle transactions instantly, businesses get access to their funds faster and can handle their cash flow more efficiently. Transparency is also very important. Information about transactions on the blockchain is open to all members of the network, making it easier to avoid disagreements and keep everyone accountable (Arnone, 2025).

These innovations are not merely theoretical but are already making a tangible impact on the global payments landscape. Making cross-border payments with blockchain shifts the financial system towards being more efficient, open and welcoming to everyone. Because it overcomes the weaknesses of traditional infrastructures, blockchain is making cross-border trade easier and supporting financial connections where there were few before. As more people use blockchain, it is set to transform how people make payments across borders by making them easier and quicker.

3.2 Central Bank Digital Currencies (CBDCs)

Central Bank Digital Currencies (CBDCs) represent a significant evolution in the way money is issued, distributed, and utilized within economies. Unlike cryptocurrencies, CBDCs are digital currencies that are issued by central banks and are supported by the government (Somda et al. 2025). They are meant to be treated as legal money, just like regular currencies, but only exist online. CBDCs make use of blockchain or similar technologies to conduct safe and visible transactions, all while being managed by central authorities (Banerjee & Sinha, 2025). The difference guarantees that CBDCs are consistent with the monetary rules and laws of their issuing government, unlike cryptocurrencies such as Bitcoin and Ethereum which are not part of the usual financial systems (Ahmed et al. 2025).

Around the world, countries are moving forward with CBDCs as they look for ways to upgrade their financial systems. The digital yuan or e-CNY, has put China at the forefront of countries using CBDCs (Chen & Nesterov, 2023). The digital yuan has been introduced in big cities and is being used in international business to help increase local transactions and reduce dependence on private apps. Besides, the ECB is moving ahead with the digital euro project to make sure eurozone members have a safe, reliable and inclusive way to do digital payments (Hallipelto & Küçüközmen, 2025). Digital currencies made for each country are being tested by Sweden, Nigeria and the Bahamas, with central banks supporting the trend. Different reasons exist for these initiatives, including boosting the way payments are made, promoting financial inclusion or making monetary policies more independent.

CBDCs have the potential to exert profound impacts on monetary policy and economic inclusion. Using digital fiat currency, central banks can better manage how much money is released and what interest rates are set. Monitoring currency in real time and how it is spent can boost the success of policies when dealing with economic challenges or inflation. CBDCs can also limit the amount of physical cash used which reduces the costs of printing, shipping and storing it (Prodan et al. 2024).

From an inclusivity perspective, CBDCs offer an unprecedented opportunity to integrate underserved populations into the financial system. In communities where standard banking services are not available, using digital currencies on mobile devices helps people and companies to safely store, move and get their money. By making financial services more accessible, this can help more people join the economy and close financial inequality gaps. Besides, using CBDCs can securely and effectively support international transactions which helps unite different markets around the world (Claessens et al. 2024).

CBDCs have great potential, but before they are used, it is important to think about privacy, security and how they will be regulated. However, continual progress in CBDCs points to a major change coming in the global financial system which could change how money is accessed and used today.

3.3 Stablecoins

Stablecoins have emerged as a critical innovation in the evolving landscape of digital currencies, addressing one of the most significant challenges faced by traditional cryptocurrencies: price volatility. For example, while Bitcoin and Ethereum have extreme price swings, stablecoins are made so that their worth stays steady by being connected to another asset (Koemtzopoulos et al. 2025). Your assets may be US dollars, gold or a variety of assets grouped together. As a result, stablecoins can function smoothly as a way to exchange goods, store wealth and determine the value of things, making them valuable for payment and financial uses (Wong et al. 2025).

A major benefit of stablecoins is how they help unite the world of blockchain-based finance with old-style financial systems. Because stablecoins keep their value, they are simple to use with current payment methods, making trading safer for both businesses and individuals (Moura de Carvalho et al. 2025). Stablecoins make it possible for people to send money across borders quickly and at a lower cost than with traditional systems. As a result, companies can be protected from the changes in exchange rates and enjoy more certainty (Arya et al. 2024).

Stablecoins have proven to be useful in the world of global trade and commerce. Many people now use Tether (USDT), USD Coin (USDC) and Binance USD (BUSD) as important parts of the digital currency industry (Lyons & Viswanath-Natraj, 2023). For instance, Tether is backed by real money and is popular among traders for its reliability compared to the unpredictable digital coins on exchanges (Fernández et al. 2024). Cross-border payments and DeFi platforms now use USD Coin which is offered by Circle and Coinbase, to enable simple and fast transactions (Duan & Urquhart, 2023). On top of that, new stablecoin projects that represent national currencies or commodities offer local answers to payment problems in different markets.

The use cases for stablecoins extend beyond simple transactions. Stablecoins make it simpler to settle payments in global trade, as they eliminate the need for many intermediaries. They help build programmable money that allows for payments to be made automatically in supply chains or in agreements being held in escrow. It is very valuable for preventing problems and disagreements when doing business in another country. Stablecoins give people and companies in areas with unstable money and weak banking an opportunity to use a more reliable digital currency.

As more people use stablecoins, they are expected to change the way we make payments by combining blockchain with proven financial methods. Even so, as they grow in significance, people are starting to question how transparent they are, how reserves are handled and what dangers they could bring to the monetary system. Even with these issues, stablecoins still support the use of blockchain payments, encourage new trends in trade and help unite the financial system.

3.4 Decentralized Finance (DeFi) Applications

DeFi is one of the biggest changes in the financial sector, thanks to its use of blockchain to redesign traditional financial services. Thanks to smart contracts in DeFi, people can interact without relying on banks or central institutions (Jensen et al. 2021). This is why the expenses are lowered and people and businesses everywhere can use financial services more easily. DeFi is evolving fast, introducing new elements to lending, remittances and microtransactions that can upset the traditional way of handling financial transactions and open up new ways to exchange value (Schueffel, 2021).

Through DeFi, users are able to lend or borrow money without using traditional banks. With smart contracts, borrowers deposit their collateral and set the interest which keeps things straightforward and reduces the need for paperwork (Zhuk, 2025). Aave and Compound have led the way, making it possible for users to lend or borrow without relying on a third party (Cedra, 2024). Having these systems in place helps people and small businesses when it is costly to get a loan elsewhere. Using over-collateralization, DeFi lending makes the system safer and more open to a wider range of users. Fig. 2 provides a step-by-step overview of how DeFi lending and borrowing mechanisms operate using smart contracts and collateralized assets.

Figure 2. DeFi Lending and Borrowing Process.

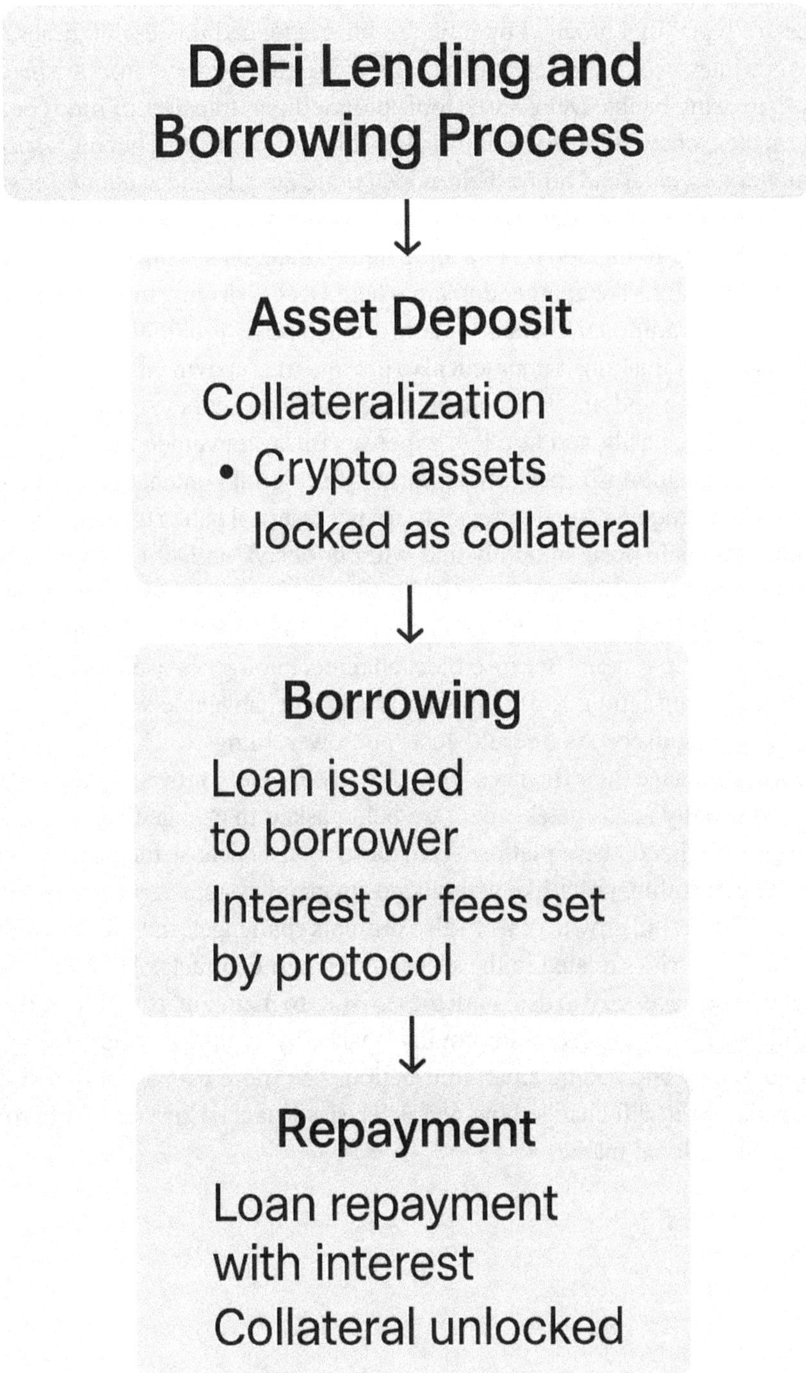

Remittances, another key area of focus, are being transformed by DeFi platforms that offer low-cost, instant cross-border payment solutions. Traditional remittance systems are typically burdened by high fees and extended processing times, especially when intermediaries such as banks and money transfer operators are involved. Rather than using banks, DeFi-based tools permit direct transfers of funds between parties on blockchain (Christodoulou et al. 2024). Thanks to this, people, especially migrant workers, can send home their money more quickly and at a lower cost (Naderi, 2021). For instance, Stellar and Celo are both working on making remittances easier and helping to include more people in the financial system (Ali et al. 2024).

Microtransactions are another domain where DeFi is driving innovation (Verma et al. 2025). The traditional financial system often imposes prohibitive fees for small-value transactions, making it impractical to process micropayments at scale. Thanks to DeFi's low fees and ability to create programmable money, microtransactions can be performed easily and at a low expense (Busayatananphon & Boonchieng, 2022). The innovation is especially important for digital content, gaming and IoT services, where frequent, small payments are necessary. Thanks to smart contracts, microtransactions happen smoothly and without delays on DeFi platforms which opens up opportunities for new kinds of businesses (Nakonechnyi et al. 2024).

By eliminating intermediaries, DeFi platforms fundamentally disrupt the traditional financial ecosystem. Because blockchain technology is used, people can be sure that their transactions are secure, clear and unchangeable which encourages more trust among users. As a result, costs are lower, things work more efficiently and users can manage their finances more directly. As DeFi grows, traditional institutions that usually act as gatekeepers are being asked to change their ways. Since they are decentralized, these platforms are more robust because they do not depend on just one controlling point like centralized financial systems.

However, the rapid growth of DeFi also presents challenges, including regulatory uncertainties and risks related to the security of smart contracts. As the ecosystem grows, it will be necessary to deal with these issues to maintain its sustainable progress. Still, DeFi applications are improving finance by making it easier and faster to lend, send money and handle small transactions. As more people join DeFi, there is a good chance it will change how people access financial services and promote a fair and open global market.

4. CHALLENGES IN ADOPTING BLOCKCHAIN FOR PAYMENTS

4.1 Regulatory Landscape

Payments companies have trouble using blockchain, as regulations differ from one country to another. Unlike conventional financial systems which must obey specific rules, blockchain uses a decentralized approach that frequently clashes with current laws and institutions (Papadi & Tassiulas, 2020). Because each country's approach to blockchain regulation is different, it is not easy for countries to use blockchain technology in unison (Zhang et al. 2020). While Singapore and Switzerland embrace blockchain and welcome new developments, a number of countries are more worried and have put strong or outright bans on cryptocurrencies (Cheah et al. 2018). Because of these differences, businesses and developers have doubts about introducing their payment systems worldwide which reduces how much blockchain-based systems can grow and work together.

Key regulatory concerns in blockchain payment systems revolve around anti-money laundering (AML) and know-your-customer (KYC) requirements. Normally, central banks are responsible for checking transactions and ensuring rules are followed in traditional payment systems. Because blockchain is a decentralized system, there isn't a single authority which makes following regulations difficult. Since blockchain transactions are pseudonymous, it becomes more difficult to trace people involved, raising the risk of money laundering, terrorist financing and evading taxes (Thommandru & Chakka, 2023).

Meeting AML and KYC requirements on blockchain requires innovative solutions to balance decentralization with compliance. Certain blockchain systems have added protocols that let users verify their identity if desired, without breaking the privacy and transparency the technology provides (Allegrezza & Bruzzese, 2025). Yet, these methods are typically not enough to meet the expectations of regulators, especially in places where financial transactions are closely supervised by law. Because regulators may not be familiar with blockchain technology and it evolves rapidly, it is difficult for them to join forces with industry players to fit blockchain into existing regulations.

Moreover, the global regulatory landscape is further complicated by differing priorities and objectives among nations. Some countries make innovation and economic increase their main goals with blockchain, while others concentrate on safeguarding consumers and the financial system (Poonam, 2025). Because of this, there are conflicting methods which stops businesses and financial institutions from using blockchain globally. It is important to create common rules for regulation that ensure companies can grow while still following compliance and security guidelines.

Any such frameworks should reflect what makes blockchain different, so as not to limit its benefits while dealing with problems about its use in financial transactions.

As blockchain continues to gain traction in global financial ecosystems, addressing the complexities of the regulatory landscape will be critical to its widespread adoption. Governments, leaders in industry and organizations working at the international level should work together to set clear policies and guidelines that help stakeholders and prevent any misuse. Blockchain's implementation in payment systems will be successful if its benefits can be enjoyed safely, while following regulations, worldwide.

4.2 Scalability Issues

The scalability of blockchain technology remains one of the most significant challenges to its adoption in payment systems. As blockchain networks grow in popularity and usage, they often face technical limitations that hinder their ability to process a high volume of transactions efficiently. The top blockchain networks such as Bitcoin and Ethereum, are built so that every participating node must verify and save every transaction (Jain et al. 2025). Although this makes the network safe and clear, it also limits the total amount of data that can be processed at one time, because each node affects the network's speed. For instance, Bitcoin handles about seven transactions for each second, but Ethereum's original version deals with about 15 transactions per second. They are far behind the transaction speeds of traditional networks such as Visa which can handle thousands of transactions at once (Walunj et al. 2025).

The limitations in transaction throughput result in slower processing times and higher fees during periods of high demand, undermining blockchain's promise of efficiency, particularly for payment applications. When the network gets busy with a lot of transactions, delays occur and costs rise. Therefore, Ethereum is not suitable for carrying out regular or large financial operations (Khan et al. 2025). If they don't allow for scaling, blockchain-based payment systems can't be useful for high-volume cases or compete with today's financial systems.

As a result, the blockchain community is looking for ways to make the network scale up while keeping its main values of decentralization and security. The best answer lies in layer-2 technologies, according to Makhdomi and Gillani (2025). They operate on top of blockchain networks and move some work to additional levels, even while keeping the blockchain safe. Both the Lightning Network linked to Bitcoin and the use of rollups on Ethereum fall under this category. Because transactions on the Lightning Network happen off-chain, users can send money quickly and at a lower cost and the transaction will be confirmed on the blockchain later (Jain & Jhajharia, 2025). Rollups, like sharding, combine countless transactions into a single group that is checked and confirmed by the main network which cuts down on the stress on the system and helps it operate faster (Agnola et al. 2025).

Sharding is another good scalability approach that divides the blockchain network into smaller sections, called shards. Every shard handles its own transactions, so the network can handle more transactions at the same time instead of one after another (Pramanik et al. 2025). It could help blockchain networks grow in capacity by a huge factor, as shown by the progress Ethereum is making on its roadmap toward Ethereum 2.0. With sharding, the individual nodes carry less responsibility, making it practical for the network to grow without losing decentralization and security.

While these solutions are promising, they also introduce complexities and trade-offs that must be carefully managed. Sharding needs complex tools to make sure all shards can communicate and agree, while layer-2 solutions depend on being tightly connected with the base layer to ensure safety and dependability. In spite of these problems, better scalability solutions are vital for the future of blockchain-based payment systems since they solve a main problem for wide adoption.

As blockchain keeps improving, how well scalability solutions work will decide if it can be used as the main network for global payments. The ability to address network issues means blockchain now matches the speed and efficiency of traditional payments which is helping it become accepted by more people and encouraging new advancements in payments.

4.3 Environmental Sustainability

A major issue with blockchain technology is that it uses a lot of energy, mainly because of the PoW consensus method. The first and notable blockchain networks such as Bitcoin, are based on PoW, where miners solve tough math problems to confirm transactions and secure the network. The process uses a lot of computer resources which results in increased energy consumption (Miron et al. 2025). People are concerned about the environmental consequences of PoW-based blockchains and research has revealed that Bitcoin's energy consumption is the same as that of countries such as Argentina or the Netherlands. In addition, some places using fossil fuels for mining lead to a bigger carbon footprint, making experts concerned about the future of PoW systems (Freitas et al. 2025).

The need for a lot of energy in PoW is a result of its main goals: safety and keeping the network decentralized. As part of mining, miners try to obtain even better machines that use extra energy. While it defends the network from attacks, it leads to major challenges when we try to use green energy and reduce greenhouse gas emissions. Consequently, regulators, environmentalists and people in the blockchain sector are searching for ways to keep the system safe without hurting the environment.

An alternative to PoW is PoS which uses much less energy by not requiring mining. In PoS, validators are selected to add new blocks and confirm transactions according to the amount of cryptocurrency they wish to "stake" as collateral (Archana & Kumar, 2025). Compared to PoW, this approach uses far less computer power, so it is much more energy efficient. Ethereum, a leading blockchain, has completed an important upgrade called "The Merge" that changed it from PoW to PoS. It is thought that this shift will reduce Ethereum's energy use by more than 99%, highlighting the potential of PoS to help blockchain become more environmentally friendly (Bindu & Muvvala, 2025).

As well as PoS, other original methods are being developed to make blockchain more environmentally friendly. Some blockchains are built to support the environment by using energy-efficient algorithms and getting power from renewable resources. Both Algorand and Cardano rely on Pure Proof-of-Stake (PPoS) and Environmental, Social and Governance (ESG) principles in their development, according to (Lepore et al. 2020). Furthermore, experts are studying hybrid and off-chain methods to make blockchains more environmentally friendly.

Yet, to see sustainable blockchain technologies used widely, everyone from the industry, policy and energy sectors must work together. Since PoS is being introduced, we need to tell users and developers why sustainability matters. Higher rewards for renewable energy in blockchain and open reports about electricity use can take the industry closer to meeting global climate targets.

As more financial systems use blockchain, it is vital to ensure that the technology is environmentally sustainable. Blockchain must be environmentally friendly not only for ethical reasons, but also to do well worldwide. When energy efficiency is important and new thoughts are adopted, blockchain may support sustainable payment systems and other purposes, helping create a greener and fairer digital world.

4.4 Ethical Considerations

Both ethical and technical issues related to blockchain technology in payments are equally important. The main issue is how to balance the open nature of blockchain records with a person's privacy. Everyone involved in blockchains can see all transactions which makes the system transparent. Because information is now more open, users have more confidence, but privacy issues have become very serious (Tang et al. 2020). As an example, blockchains in Bitcoin and Ethereum allow anyone to see some of a user's financial activity. Though user details are normally hidden behind alphanumeric addresses, new technologies can now reveal these addresses and possibly harm privacy. As a result, both individuals and businesses are in danger since businesses handling transactional data could compete less favorably or have their confidentiality breached (Ayyaswamy et al. 2025).

To deal with these privacy issues, we must find a way to be both clear and cautious. Using zero-knowledge proofs and Zcash or Monero, anyone can make private transactions that are still verifiable. Thanks to these technologies, users can ensure a transaction is valid without revealing any details to the public, unlike what's possible on most public blockchains. But, it is necessary to use privacy-enhancing technologies carefully, since they could result in crimes such as money laundering and tax evasion that could reduce trust in blockchain systems. Both policy leaders and software developers should team up to define standards that promote ethical use and help ensure the technology is open and accountable (Chapagain et al. 2025).

It is also an important ethical issue that some groups such as those who are not tech-savvy or underprivileged, may not be able to use blockchain-based payment systems. Many people are able to use financial services thanks to blockchain, but its large-scale use is often slowed by technical issues and a shortage of education. Many blockchain platforms assume users are aware of wallets, their private keys and the fees needed for transactions. Blockchain is not accessible to people who cannot learn about technology or get good internet. People living in developing countries and low-income communities experience the digital divide more than others which stops blockchain technology from bringing about its promised democracy (Channi & Kumar, 2025).

In order to address these accessibility issues, it is important to design interfaces that are easy for all users to use. Applications that simplify blockchain help more people benefit from what it offers. It is just as vital to teach and train people on blockchain technology, so they feel confident using it. Moreover, growing internet coverage and making digital tools accessible will help less privileged communities make use of blockchain.

The ethical factors involved are very important for the correct development and use of blockchain in payment systems. To ensure trust and equal rights in the digital economy, we need to make the internet private and available to everyone. If these challenges are addressed correctly and in the beginning, blockchain can help improve payments and protect the rights of all users.

5. FUTURE DIRECTIONS

The way blockchain technology is used in payments will depend on new ideas that boost its strengths and solve its current problems. Interoperability is a vital step that helps various blockchains collaborate well and share assets. Blockchain platforms are not currently linked well enough to participate in complex transactions involving many networks. This change is being guided by bridges and protocols that help different blockchains interact and operate well, for example, Polkadot and Cosmos (Jain & Jhajharia, 2025). As a result, blockchain is expected to help with payment systems and encourage various networks to collaborate, making it popular in many industries.

Another important development is the way artificial intelligence is being used with blockchain technology. AI helps blockchain-based payment systems by automating jobs, improving security and ensuring the system functions correctly as it gets bigger. For example, AI allows banks to handle transactions faster, detect fraud quickly and meet regulations right away. In addition, AI and blockchain working together is expected to make smart contracts that can adjust their behavior when conditions change, increasing the types of financial transactions possible. Applying these technologies together can increase how efficient and flexible payment systems are (Murugan et al. 2025).

Moving forward, it seems likely that blockchain will join with other recent innovations such as quantum computing and the IoT to develop payment systems further. Though quantum computing has not advanced much yet, it could introduce fresh security measures for blockchain networks. Instead, if IoT is combined with blockchain, connected devices could make their own micropayments with other smart city devices and machines in factories (Ranjithamani et al. 2025).

The development of these technologies will have significant effects on international payment systems and economies. Blockchain makes it easier for financial systems to become more democratic by addressing old problems, reducing expenses and ensuring quick settlements which lets more people become part of the economy. Blockchain is expected to transform how financial governance is carried out in many different countries. Because of decentralized finance, new players can now join the world of finance. Both nations and businesses are now using blockchain to reduce their use of financial intermediaries, improve their trading and handle monetary policies.

Blockchain-based payment systems are having a strong impact on geopolitics. CBDCs that rely on blockchain could bring important changes to the way the world's financial system and international relations work. As an example, the growth of digital currencies might reduce our reliance on SWIFT and encourage both joint efforts and competition in the economy. Because of this, new regulations and organizational settings may arise as stakeholders find ways to link decentralized systems with the existing world of finance.

Blockchain is changing the way we pay for things and introducing significant changes along the way. Should technology help with scalability, interoperability and sustainability, blockchain is likely to take a key role in the world's financial system. With blockchain, systems that are more inclusive, efficient and open can help make important changes in sharing, managing and moving value. These changes will affect how we pay and also the underlying ways people interact economically worldwide.

6. CONCLUSION

Blockchain technology has demonstrated transformative potential in redefining the future of payment systems. Blockchain's use of decentralization, transparent processes and strong security tackles many of the issues in traditional finance such as spending too much on transactions, slow processes and access issues. Its achievement in quick and safe cross-border payments, support for access to financial services and growth of new ideas highlight why it is valuable to the financial sector. Because blockchain saves time, involves fewer people and makes things easier for all, it will be important in future payment systems.

However, the road to widespread adoption is not without its challenges. Although the technology brings many advantages, it also creates important issues that must be handled to fully benefit from it. When the rules are not clear, scaling is impossible, the environment matters and privacy and accessibility are issues, it leads to major problems. The issues suggest that we should support new ideas, but not put ourselves in too much danger. To ensure that blockchain's benefits are used well by all, those involved should handle problems related to technology, laws and society.

The future of blockchain in payment systems depends on the collaborative efforts of researchers, policymakers, and practitioners. Researchers should keep trying to make the technology work well with other systems, be easily scaled and consume less energy, since ethical concerns may arise. Policymakers should ensure that regulations do not stop innovation, but do keep blockchain systems clear, fair and safe. In this area, experts should work to create platforms that offer more access and are straightforward, uniting technology with what people actually require around the world.

As blockchain continues to evolve, its impact on payment systems will extend far beyond technical improvements, influencing economic structures, global trade, and financial inclusion. Everyone involved needs to be positive and collaborative about how AI is affecting our lives. Consequently, blockchain allows for safer, fairer and more efficient management of money and also supports new developments and greater inclusion around the world.

REFERENCES

Agnola, T., Ambrosini, L., Beretta, E., & Gremlich, G. (2025). Empowering Global Supply Chains Through Blockchain-Based Platforms: New Evidence from the Coffee Industry. *FinTech*, *4*(1), 3. DOI: 10.3390/fintech4010003

Ahmed, M., Al-Hussaini, A. I. S., & Ibrahim, A. A. (2025). Factors influencing the intention to use the Nigerian central bank digital currency (E-Naira) among Nigerian retailers. *Journal of Financial Services Marketing*, *30*(1), 1–16. DOI: 10.1057/s41264-024-00294-4

Aketch, S., Mwambia, F., & Baimwera, B. (2021). Effects of blockchain technology on performance of financial markets in Kenya. *International Journal of Finance and Accounting*, *6*(1), 1–15. DOI: 10.47604/ijfa.1237

Ali, K., Shahzad, A., & Chaudhary, H. K. (2024). The Role of Decentralized Finance (DeFi) in Reshaping Global Financial Inclusion: Opportunities and Risks. *Social Science Review Archives*, *2*(2), 560–579.

Allegrezza, S., & Bruzzese, G. (2025). Supervision and Enforcement of EU's Anti-Money-Laundering and Countering the Financing of Terrorism. In *EU Banking and Capital Markets Regulation: Open Issues of Vertical Interplay with National Law* (pp. 487–521). Springer Nature Switzerland. DOI: 10.1007/978-3-031-70529-8_14

Archana, K., & Kumar, M. (2025). Blockchain and Its Applications in Supply Chain Transparency. *Innovative Journal of Interdisciplinary Research and Technological Innovations*, 26-35.

Arnone, G. (2025). Legal Aspects of Smart Contracts and Application of Blockchain Technology in FinTech. *Fintech for ESG and the Circular Economy*, 173-191.

Arya, A., Singh, J., Gupta, A., & Dwivedi, R. K. (2024, February). Developing an Effective Consensus Mechanism for a Secure Blockchain-Based Cross-Border Fund Transfer System. In *2024 IEEE International Conference on Computing, Power and Communication Technologies (IC2PCT)* (Vol. 5, pp. 636-642). IEEE. DOI: 10.1109/IC2PCT60090.2024.10486373

Ayyaswamy, K., Kathirvel, N., & Maheswaran, C. P. (2025). Ethical AI Entrepreneurial Strategies for Business Intelligence and Blockchain. In *Corporate Social Responsibility Approaches to Ethical AI in Business* (pp. 1–26). IGI Global Scientific Publishing.

Banerjee, S., & Sinha, M. (2025). The policy endorsement of central bank digital currency-trend analysis and research scope using bibliometric review. *International Journal of Management Practice, 18*(1), 64–91. DOI: 10.1504/IJMP.2025.143077

Bayram, O. (2020). Importance of Blockchain use in cross-border payments and evaluation of the progress in this area. *Doğuş Üniversitesi Dergisi, 21*(1), 171–189. DOI: 10.31671/dogus.2020.444

Bindu, H., & Muvvala, S. (2025). Secure Collaboration for Storing and Processing of Criminal Records Using Blockchain Technology. In *Advanced Cyber Security Techniques for Data, Blockchain, IoT, and Network Protection* (pp. 205-224). IGI Global Scientific Publishing.

Busayatananphon, C., & Boonchieng, E. (2022, January). Financial technology DeFi protocol: A review. In *2022 Joint International Conference on Digital Arts, Media and Technology with ECTI Northern Section Conference on Electrical, Electronics, Computer and Telecommunications Engineering (ECTI DAMT & NCON)* (pp. 267-272). IEEE.

Cedra, A. (2024). Mitigating risks in decentralized finance: A Systematic review of challenges and solutions. *International journal of economic perspectives, 18*(1), 104-125.

Channi, H. K., & Kumar, P. (2025). Automating and Streamlining Drug Payments Through Smart Contracts. *Blockchain-Enabled Solutions for the Pharmaceutical Industry*, 153-173.

Chapagain, D., Kshetri, N., & Sihag, V. K. (2025). Cybersecurity and Cyber Ethics via Blockchain Technology–Need for Web Security, Software Practices, and End-User Cyber Education. *Blockchain Technology for Cyber Defense, Cybersecurity, and Countermeasures: Techniques, Solutions, and Applications*, 123.

Charles, D. (2024). A Blockchain Solution for Cross-Border Payments. In *Fintech, and Blockchains Trends in The Financial Sector* (pp. 23–41). Bentham Science Publishers. DOI: 10.2174/9789815256833124010004

Cheah, S., Pattalachinti, S., & Ho, Y. P. (2018). Blockchain industries, regulations and policies in Singapore. *Asian Research Policy, 9*(2), 83–98.

Chen, J., & Nesterov, I. O. (2023). Central bank digital currencies: Digital Yuan and its role in Chinese digital economy development. *RUDN Journal of Economics, 31*(1), 120–133. DOI: 10.22363/2313-2329-2023-31-1-120-133

Christodoulou, I., Rizomyliotis, I., Konstantoulaki, K., Nazarian, A., & Binh, D. (2024). Transforming the remittance industry: Harnessing the power of blockchain technology. *Journal of Enterprise Information Management*, *37*(5), 1551–1577. DOI: 10.1108/JEIM-03-2023-0112

Claessens, S., Cong, L. W., Moshirian, F., & Park, C. Y. (2024). Opportunities and challenges associated with the development of FinTech and Central Bank Digital Currency. *Journal of Financial Stability*, *73*, 101280. DOI: 10.1016/j.jfs.2024.101280

Dalal, A., & Samal, B. (2022). Transforming Financial Landscapes: Case Studies on the Positive Disruption of Cross-Border Payments through Ripple. *International Journal of Research Radicals in Multidisciplinary Fields, ISSN: 2960-043X, 1*(2), 77-82.

Duan, K., & Urquhart, A. (2023). The instability of stablecoins. *Finance Research Letters*, *52*, 103573. DOI: 10.1016/j.frl.2022.103573

Efanov, D., & Roschin, P. (2018). The all-pervasiveness of the blockchain technology. *Procedia Computer Science*, *123*, 116–121. DOI: 10.1016/j.procs.2018.01.019

Fernández, F. J. J., Fernández, M. Á. E., & Alonso, S. L. N. (2024). The asset-backing risk of stablecoin trading: The case of Tether. *Economics and Business Review*, *10*(1), 57–80. DOI: 10.18559/ebr.2024.1.1211

Freitas, L. P., Cerdeira, J., & Lourenço, D. (2025). Hayekian Hurdles: Challenges to Cryptocurrency as a Viable Basis for a New Monetary Order. *Economies*, *13*(1), 12. DOI: 10.3390/economies13010012

Golosova, J., & Romanovs, A. (2018, November). The advantages and disadvantages of the blockchain technology. In *2018 IEEE 6th workshop on advances in information, electronic and electrical engineering (AIEEE)* (pp. 1-6). IEEE. DOI: 10.1109/AIEEE.2018.8592253

Haldane, A. G., Millard, S., & Saporta, V. (Eds.). (2008). *The future of payment systems* (p. 31). Routledge.

Hallipelto, A., & Küçüközmen, C. C. (2025). Central Bank Digital Currency: Redefining the Concept of Money in a Digital Context. *Central Banking and Monetary Policy in the G20: Paradigms and Challenges*, 219.

Hartmann, M. E. (2006). *E-payments evolution*. Physica-Verlag HD. DOI: 10.1007/3-7908-1652-3_2

Holotiuk, F., Moormann, J., & Pisani, F. (2019b). Blockchain in the payments industry: developing a discussion agenda based on pain points and opportunities. *Business Transformation through Blockchain: Volume I*, 197-231.

Holotiuk, F., Pisani, F., & Moormann, J. (2019a). Radicalness of blockchain: An assessment based on its impact on the payments industry. *Technology Analysis and Strategic Management, 31*(8), 915–928. DOI: 10.1080/09537325.2019.1574341

Hongmei, Z. (2021). A Cross-Border E-Commerce Approach Based on Blockchain Technology. *Mobile Information Systems, 2021*(1), 2006082. DOI: 10.1155/2021/2006082

Jain, A., & Jhajharia, K. (2025). Blockchain Interoperability: Protocols, Frameworks, and Practical Implications. In *Blockchain Technology Applications in Knowledge Management* (pp. 115-152). IGI Global Scientific Publishing.

Jain, A. K., Gupta, N., & Gupta, B. B. (2025). A survey on scalable consensus algorithms for blockchain technology. *Cyber Security and Applications, 3*, 100065. DOI: 10.1016/j.csa.2024.100065

Javaid, M., Haleem, A., Singh, R. P., Khan, S., & Suman, R. (2021). Blockchain technology applications for Industry 4.0: A literature-based review. *Blockchain: Research and Applications, 2*(4), 100027.

Javaid, M., Haleem, A., Singh, R. P., Suman, R., & Khan, S. (2022). A review of Blockchain Technology applications for financial services. *BenchCouncil Transactions on Benchmarks. Standards and Evaluations, 2*(3), 100073.

Jensen, J. R., von Wachter, V., & Ross, O. (2021). An introduction to decentralized finance (defi). *Complex Systems Informatics and Modeling Quarterly*, (26), 46–54. DOI: 10.7250/csimq.2021-26.03

Khan, B. U. I., Goh, K. W., Khan, A. R., Zuhairi, M. F., & Chaimanee, M. (2025). Resource Management and Secure Data Exchange for Mobile Sensors Using Ethereum Blockchain. *Symmetry, 17*(1), 61. DOI: 10.3390/sym17010061

Khan, N., Ahmad, T., & State, R. (2019, October). Feasibility of stellar as a blockchain-based micropayment system. In *International Conference on Smart Blockchain* (pp. 53-65). Cham: Springer International Publishing. DOI: 10.1007/978-3-030-34083-4_6

Koemtzopoulos, D., Zournatzidou, G., & Sariannidis, N. (2025). Can Cryptocurrencies Be Green? The Role of Stablecoins Toward a Carbon Footprint and Sustainable Ecosystem. *Sustainability (Basel), 17*(2), 483. DOI: 10.3390/su17020483

Kowsick, N. P., & Ramasamy, K. (2025). Blockchain Technology Transforming Libraries and Financial Services Towards Inclusive Development. In *Leveraging Blockchain for Future-Ready Libraries* (pp. 93–104). IGI Global Scientific Publishing.

Laroiya, C., Saxena, D., & Komalavalli, C. (2020). Applications of blockchain technology. In *Handbook of research on blockchain technology* (pp. 213–243). Academic press. DOI: 10.1016/B978-0-12-819816-2.00009-5

Lepore, C., Ceria, M., Visconti, A., Rao, U. P., Shah, K. A., & Zanolini, L. (2020). A survey on blockchain consensus with a performance comparison of PoW, PoS and pure PoS. *Mathematics*, *8*(10), 1782. DOI: 10.3390/math8101782

Lilge, M. (2001, May). Evolution of PrePaid Service towards a real-time payment system. In *IEEE Intelligent Network 2001 Workshop. IN 2001 Conference Record (Cat. No. 01TH8566)* (pp. 195-198). IEEE. DOI: 10.1109/INW.2001.915313

Lyons, R. K., & Viswanath-Natraj, G. (2023). What keeps stablecoins stable? *Journal of International Money and Finance*, *131*, 102777. DOI: 10.1016/j.jimonfin.2022.102777

Makhdomi, A. A., & Gillani, I. A. (2025, January). Decentralized Ridesharing: Overcoming Scalability Issues with Layer 2 Solution. In *Proceedings of the 26th International Conference on Distributed Computing and Networking* (pp. 319-324). DOI: 10.1145/3700838.3703682

Mhlanga, D. (2025). 9 The Critical Developmental Importance of Blockchain Technology in Africa. *Financial Inclusion and Sustainable Development in Sub-Saharan Africa*, 136.

Miron, R., Hulea, M., Muresan, V., Clitan, I., & Rusu, A. (2025). Integrating Blockchain Technology into Mobility-as-a-Service Platforms for Smart Cities. *Smart Cities*, *8*(1), 9. DOI: 10.3390/smartcities8010009

Moura de Carvalho, R., Inácio, H. C., & Marques, R. P. (2025). Stablecoin: A Story of (In) Stabilities and Co-Movements Written Through Wavelet. *Journal of Risk and Financial Management*, *18*(1), 20. DOI: 10.3390/jrfm18010020

Murugan, R., Yenduri, G., Maran, P., & Reddy Gadekallu, T. (2025). The Synergy of Artificial Intelligence and Blockchain in 6G Spectrum Management. *Intelligent Spectrum Management: Towards, 6G*, 237–262. DOI: 10.1002/9781394201235.ch10

Naderi, N. (2021). Utilizing blockchain technology in international remittances for poverty reduction and inclusive growth. *Poverty Reduction for Inclusive Sustainable Growth in Developing Asia*, 149-163.

Nakonechnyi, V., Toliupa, S., Saiko, V., Lutsenko, V., Ghno, G. S. N., & Hussain, A. K. (2024, April). Blockchain Implementation in the Protection System of Banking System During Online Banking Operations. In *2024 35th Conference of Open Innovations Association (FRUCT)* (pp. 492-500). IEEE. DOI: 10.23919/FRUCT61870.2024.10516404

Papadis, N., & Tassiulas, L. (2020). Blockchain-based payment channel networks: Challenges and recent advances. *IEEE Access : Practical Innovations, Open Solutions*, *8*, 227596–227609. DOI: 10.1109/ACCESS.2020.3046020

Poonam, P. (2025). Application of Blockchain Technology in Secure DataTransmission for Autonomous Vehicle Systems. *Shodh Prakashan: Journal of Engineering & Scientific Research*, *1*(1), 99–114.

Pramanik, S., Bag, S., & Roy, A. (2025). Grading the Blockchain Using Sharding. In *Blockchain Technology Applications in Knowledge Management* (pp. 269–292). IGI Global Scientific Publishing. DOI: 10.4018/979-8-3693-3956-5.ch009

Prodan, S., Konhäusner, P., Dabija, D. C., Lazaroiu, G., & Marincean, L. (2024). The rise in popularity of central bank digital currencies. A systematic review. *Heliyon*, *10*(9), e30561. DOI: 10.1016/j.heliyon.2024.e30561 PMID: 38756603

Qiu, T., Zhang, R., & Gao, Y. (2019). Ripple vs. SWIFT: Transforming cross border remittance using blockchain technology. *Procedia Computer Science*, *147*, 428–434. DOI: 10.1016/j.procs.2019.01.260

Ranjithamani, D. A., Subbulakshmi, M. K., Harshini, T., Ramya, V., Aaron, T. S., & Srithar, T. B. (2025). Product Integrity Assurance on E-Marketplace Using Quantum Blockchain. In *Real-World Applications of Quantum Computers and Machine Intelligence* (pp. 155–164). IGI Global Scientific Publishing.

Rey, W. P., & Rey, K. W. J. D. (2024, February). The Role of Mobile Wallets in Promoting Cashless Transactions: A Case Study of the Philippines. In *International Conference on E-Business and Applications* (pp. 155-170). Singapore: Springer Nature Singapore. DOI: 10.1007/978-981-97-3409-2_14

Schueffel, P. (2021). Defi: Decentralized finance-an introduction and overview. *Journal of Innovation Management*, *9*(3), I–XI. DOI: 10.24840/2183-0606_009.003_0001

Somda, M. M. Y. G., Ouya, S., & Mendy, G. (2025, January). Central bank digital currency design architecture: a systematic review using text mining. In *Third International Conference on Communications, Information System, and Data Science (CISDS 2024)* (Vol. 13519, pp. 144-151). SPIE. DOI: 10.1117/12.3057590

Tang, Y., Xiong, J., Becerril-Arreola, R., & Iyer, L. (2020). Ethics of blockchain: A framework of technology, applications, impacts, and research directions. *Information Technology & People*, *33*(2), 602–632. DOI: 10.1108/ITP-10-2018-0491

Taufiq, R., Hidayanto, A. N., & Prabowo, H. (2018, September). The affecting factors of blockchain technology adoption of payments systems in Indonesia banking industry. In *2018 International Conference on Information Management and Technology (ICIMTech)* (pp. 506-510). IEEE. DOI: 10.1109/ICIMTech.2018.8528104

Thommandru, A., & Chakka, B. (2023). Recalibrating the banking sector with blockchain technology for effective anti-money laundering compliances by banks. *Sustainable Futures : An Applied Journal of Technology, Environment and Society*, *5*, 100107. DOI: 10.1016/j.sftr.2023.100107

Verma, P., Srivastava, R., & Kumar, S. (2025). Blockchain Technology: Applications and Challenges. *Blockchain for IoT Systems*, 1-12.

Walunj, V., Rajaraman, V., Dutta, J., & Sharma, A. (2025). Integrating Crypto-Based Payment Systems for Data Marketplaces: Enhancing Efficiency, Security, and User Autonomy. In *International Conference on Information Systems Security* (pp. 443-452). Springer, Cham. DOI: 10.1007/978-3-031-80020-7_25

Wong, M. C. S., Chan, E. K. H., & Yousaf, I. (2025). CBDCs, regulated stablecoins and tokenized traditional assets under the Basel Committee rules on cryptoassets. *Journal of Financial Regulation and Compliance*, *33*(1), 31–47. DOI: 10.1108/JFRC-03-2024-0050

Zhang, L., Xie, Y., Zheng, Y., Xue, W., Zheng, X., & Xu, X. (2020). The challenges and countermeasures of blockchain in finance and economics. *Systems Research and Behavioral Science*, *37*(4), 691–698. DOI: 10.1002/sres.2710

Zheng, Z., Xie, S., Dai, H., Chen, X., & Wang, H. (2017, June). *An overview of blockchain technology: Architecture, consensus, and future trends. In 2017 IEEE international congress on big data (BigData congress)*. Ieee.

Zhuk, A. (2025). From Cypherpunks to Decentralized Finance: How Crypto-Anarchy is Redefining Legal and Economic Systems. *Markets, Globalization &. Developmental Review*, *9*(3).

Chapter 9
Advancing Islamic Finance With Blockchain and Generative Artificial Intelligence

Early Ridho Kismawadi
https://orcid.org/0000-0002-9420-5212
IAIN Langsa, Indonesia

Mohammad Irfan
https://orcid.org/0000-0002-4956-1170
Chandigarh University, Lucknow, Unnao, India

Ajay Kumar Yadav
Chandigarh University, Lucknow, Unnao, India

ABSTRACT

This research aims to explore the potential transformation of the integration of blockchain technology and generative artificial intelligence (Generative AI) in Islamic finance, which is in accordance with the principles of transparency, sustainability, and inclusion in Islamic finance. The methods used include conceptual analysis of blockchain applications, such as the tokenization of halal assets and smart contracts, as well as the role of generative AI in optimizing decision-making, fraud detection, and personalization of financial services. The results show that the integration of this technology improves efficiency, security, and sharia compliance in financial services, expands financial inclusion for low-income communities, and supports sustainable investment through the implementation of ESG standards. The implications of this study include a significant contribution to the development of a

DOI: 10.4018/979-8-3373-1250-7.ch009

fairer, more transparent, and responsive Islamic financial system to global challenges such as climate change and economic inequality.

INTRODUCTION

The convergence of blockchain technology and generative artificial intelligence (AI) is revolutionizing the financial technology (FinTech) landscape, bringing about transformative changes that align with the principles of Islamic finance (Abbas and Hafeez 2021; Mbaidin et al. 2024; Yuspin et al. 2022). With the adoption of these technologies, operational oversight in finance can achieve unprecedented transparency, compliance, efficiency, and ethics. Islamic finance addresses issues of ethics, social justice, and sustainability with far greater emphasis than other frameworks, and thus the application of blockchain alongside generative AI makes it possible to drive innovation while addressing critical concerns. Trust and accountability in financial transactions are crucial prerequisites in sharia-compliant finance, and therefore, blockchain technology's decentralised and immutable ledger greatly enhances these aspects. Automation and secure Islamic-compliant interaction are made possible through applications like halal asset tokenisation, digital identity verification, and smart contracts. Furthermore, blockchain expands investment access by allowing the tokenisation of sukuk and green bonds, providing sustainable, inclusive investments aligned with maqasid-al-shariah goals.

Alongside blockchain technology, generative AI enhances automated decision-making and enables bespoke financial services. Through sophisticated AI models, large datasets can be analysed in a more precise manner to improve risk assessment, fraud detection, and financial planning—all tailored to the user and ethically sound. This form of technology aids lower-income individuals in a more empowering manner through novel insight and actionable guidance, thereby improving financial inclusion. The partnership between blockchain and generative AI supports Islamic finance by creating greater transparency and promoting sustainability as both pillars. Together, they provide all-encompassing solutions to fraud, inefficiencies, and the demand for ESG-compliant financial products. Although data privacy and energy consumption pose hurdles, progress in secure AI and blockchain frameworks enhances the potential for sustainable practices.

This article examines the revolutionary impact blockchain and generative AI might have on Islamic finance. Implementation of this technology within Islamic financial institutions accelerates transparency and encourages both ecological preservation and financial inclusion which resultantly supports the development of more ethical and equitable financing. Furthermore, the research demonstrates how such innovations are beneficial in reaching maqasid-al-shariah and thus serve as a pivotal factor for sustainable enhancement in Islamic finance.

With this article, I would like to discuss the major impact brought about by the adoption of blockchain and generative AI in Islamic finance. The decentralised and immutable ledger provided by blockchain enhances the much-needed assurance and trust essential in Islamic finance, hence fostering integrity and transparency. The application of smart contracts together with digital ID authentication makes automation of sharia-compliant transactions possible and secure. Also, the possibility of wider access to Islamic sustainable investing after sukuk and green bonds are tokenised is in accordance with maqasid-al-shariah. Moreover, Generative AI offers optimised serving through analysing vast data which boosts the accuracy in risk assessment, fraud, and financial planning whilst maintaining ethical standards.

By providing insights and unique technology-based solutions, the capability to access this technology empowers users at different income levels, thereby expanding financial inclusion. Thus, this conjunction not only enhances Islamic finance in terms of integration effectiveness and safety, but also widens how far and how many people actively participate in the financially equitable and sustainable system development.

The scope and impact of integrating blockchain technology and Generative Artificial Intelligence (AI) within Islamic Finance is profound and far-reaching. This integration accelerates accountability and transparency while aiding sustainability, which is essential in the Islamic Finance doctrine. Financial institutions can use blockchain to manage fraud and inefficient processes and provide ESG-compliant financial products and services. Although there are unresolved issues such as data safety and high energy consumption, breakthroughs in secure artificial intelligence system designs and energy-efficient blockchain model frameworks suggest promise toward solving these problems. Furthermore, expanding the application of blockchain and Generative AI technology can enhance financial inclusion and access to finance at different user income levels. Such innovations foster the sustainable advancement of Islamic finance and boost the transition towards a global financial system that is more constructive and attuned to societal demands.

METHODS

The research strategy for this particular investigation will utilise an exploratory qualitative approach which employs conceptual and descriptive analysis. It is possible to conduct this study through a literature review on blockchain technology, generative artificial intelligence (Generative AI), and its application in Islamic finance. This approach also encompasses identifying certain use cases like halal asset tokenisation, smart contracts, and the personalisation of services through AI. Furthermore, available pertinent secondary data from scholarly publications, commercial documents, and regulations governing Islamic finance were also scrutinised to analyse the integration of these technologies regarding Islamic finance's challenges and prospects. This study employs thematic analysis methods to identify patterns and relationships.

IMPLEMENTATION OF BLOCKCHAIN AND ARTIFICIAL INTELLIGENCE (AI) IN ISLAMIC FINANCE

The implementation of Blockchain technology and Generative Artificial Intelligence (AI) in Islamic Finance offers a range of significant advances in efficiency, transparency, and sharia compliance (Basu, Mandal, and Kar 2025; Ng et al. 2025). In the context of remittances, Blockchain technology facilitates quicker and more secure cross-border transactions at a reduced cost, which is beneficial for the global Muslim population that regularly remits funds back home. Permitting automated processes that are sharia-compliant smart contracts bolsters the authentication mechanisms of a transaction, eliminating the need for third-party agents; therefore, trust is consolidated owing to the immutable and explicit nature of the agreements.

The tokenization of assets in Islamic finance, such as sukuk and real estate, opens the door to more inclusive investment by allowing for fractional ownership and higher liquidity, in line with the principles of wealth distribution in Islam (Avci and Erzurumlu 2023; Mohamed and Ali 2022). Robo Shariah Advisory along with analytics powered by AI technologies illustrate the importance of Generative AI in the enhancement of Islamic financial services. Sharia-compliant Robo Advisors apply sophisticated techniques to offer advisory services bounded within sharia law. Furthermore, AI powered analytics tools assist in recognizing market patterns and trends far beyond the capacity of human analytical skills.

The application of these two technologies not only expands the boundaries of Islamic finance, but also fosters financial inclusion, unifies diverse sectors, as well as innovation in products and services. The use of Blockchain and AI in Islamic finance does not only serve the peculiar concerns of Muslims, but also offers a working model which is amenable to capture by conventional systems seeking more transparent and ethically sound ways of conducting business. This will enhance the position of Islamic financial institutions to become more competitive in the global market while improving their Sharia compliance, thereby providing enhanced value propositions for consumers and investors.

Figure 1. AI and Blockchain in Islamic Finance

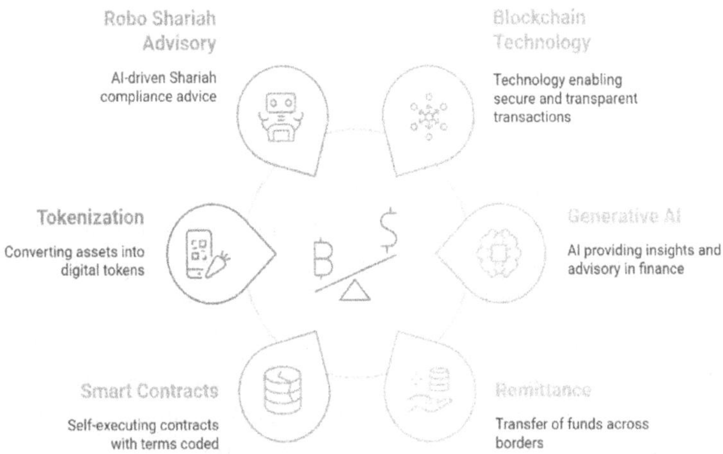

The use of blockchain technology together with Generative AI (Artificial Intelligence) has the promise of bringing changes to the global economic landscape as it is the case with Islamic finance. The technology facilitates the boundless growth of Islamic financial services which reaches a wider market even among non-Muslims who are searching for ethical and clear ways of financing. There is evidence of synergies with the traditional banking system which indicate that Blockchain and AI can widen the scope on responsible financing and improve Transparency and Efficiency (TEI), inter-operability and the adoption of the responsible finance more broadly. Changes in microfinance and providing services in isolated regions can be made with the use of AI that creates solutions tailored to the customer and Blockchain that guarantees reliable transactions.

Technological innovations aid in the implementation of sustainable practices and ESG criteria where AI assists with risk analysis while investments may be corroborated through Blockchain. The incorporation of such technology enhances the smart financial infrastructure, automation, cyber security, and risk management, thereby setting an unprecedented level of security and efficiency in Islamic financial services. Islamic financial regulations are easier to monitor and audit in real time with the advances in regulatory technology and Blockchain which streamlines audits and builds trust among regulators, investors, and consumers. As such, Generative AI alongside Blockchain meets Islamic requirements and develops unprecedented opportunities to transform the Muslims world financial system to eliminate ethical hurdles and establish reliability, transparency, social responsibility, and environmental responsiveness.

BLOCKCHAIN AND AI FOR AN INCLUSIVE FUTURE OF ISLAMIC FINANCE

The implementation of Blockchain and Generative Artificial Intelligence (AI) in Islamic finance can highlight the crucial role of these two technologies in strengthening efficiency, transparency, and regulatory compliance, as well as automation and improved decision-making (Abbas and Hafeez 2021; Yuspin et al. 2022). The decentralized nature of blockchain technology can enhance transparency and improve the efficiency of Islamic financial transactions by cutting out or minimizing the need for third parties. This increases cost efficiency and accelerates transaction speed, all the while upholding sharia compliance with the unchangeable records of transactions. Looking at it from a regulation-based approach, the adoption of Blockchain technology simplifies the processes of compliance and auditing, which fosters better compliance of Islamic financial institutions with stringent and multifaceted requirements from different countries.

Less traditional methods of analyzing data makes Generative AI influential to businesses, as it shifts the operational model Islamic finance institutions utilize to make critical decisions. Investing and economic forecasting in accordance with Islamic law requires immense amounts of data to be processed, something Generative AI is adept at. In addition to this fundamental capability, automating processes also aids in advising consumers faster and improving service delivery while remaining sharia compliant. Advanced decision-making aided by AI improves the operations of Islamic financial institutions participating in the market by making them more dynamic and precise in their actions. Integrating these two technologies intelligently can greatly advance the Islamic finance industry, facilitating the targeted advancement of Islamic finance while simultaneously providing ethical capitalism to the world. The successful implementation of Blockchain and Generative AI not only supports growth and scalability in Islamic Finance

Figure 2. Technology Impact Analysis

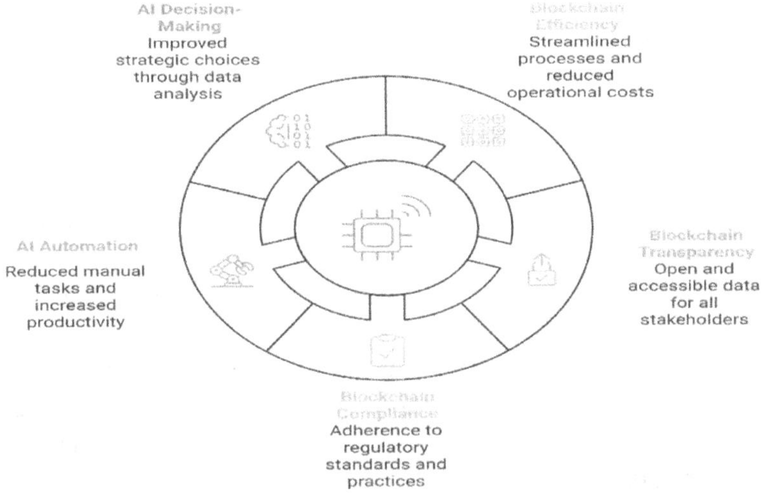

The application of Blockchain Technology, along with the Generative Artificial Intelligence (AI) in Islamic finance holds great promise in resolving a few of the international issues with the contemporary financial system. The two technologies combined, in a suitable manner, provide improved access to financial services as well as transparency, efficiency, and stringent sharia compliance. First, Blockchain offers a distinct opportunity to transform how Islamic financial institutions conduct transactions because of its transparency and decentralization. This enhances trust among users and reduces the demand for intermediaries, thereby, lowering costs and expediting cross-border transactions. This is particularly pertinent to remittances where Blockchain stands to serve the global Muslim community in a more efficient and cost-effective way. In addition, the tokenization of assets such as sukuk on Blockchain platforms can enhance access to Islamic financial instruments and foster new markets, thus enabling greater financial inclusion and participation in the global economy.

Furthermore, Generative AI enhances the sorcerer capability of financial institutions to make high-level decisions with precision. Islamic financial institutions can more accurately evaluate risks and formulate investment strategies in line with sharia law through AI's pattern and trend analysis of vast data sets. AI also facilitates the customization of higher financial services, enabling tailored advice and products to be delivered while observing sharia rules. Hence, a more proactive approach to customer care is made possible. The combination of Blockchain and Generative AI enables the advancement of Islamic finance to be more socially responsible and sustainable. With the technologies focus on ensuring financial activities go beyond profits to include positive social, ethical, environmental, and sustainable impacts, Islamic financial institutions are positioned to spearhead sustainable finance initiatives and actively advanced in tackling global issues such as climate change and economic inequality.

The forthcoming progress of these two technologies within the context of Islamic finance will shape geopolitical policy and governance boundaries, resetting the benchmarks regarding transparency, security, and compliance. It enhances, not only the Islamic finance position within the global financial architecture, but provides a benchmark model for other financial systems to adopt more rigorous ethical and socially responsible inclusivity. The integration of Blockchain and Generative AI has the capability not only to address the unique preferences of Muslims but also to resolve fundamental issues plaguing the global economy, positioning Islamic finance at the forefront of the construction of a more equitable and sustainable financial framework.

REDEFINING GLOBAL FINANCE

The integration of Blockchain technology and Generative Artificial Intelligence (AI) into the Islamic financial system brings forth crucial issues pertaining to sharia compliance, security, trust, and ethics. Aside from providing transparency and efficient operation, Blockchain also faces issues regarding the adherence to sharia compliance of all transactions and smart contracts within the network. In this case, compliance with Islamic finance translates not only to just and balanced transactions but also no riba (interest), gharar (uncertainty), or maysir (gambling) elements. Despite blockchain technology being known for its robustness in security due to encryption and data distribution, it is still susceptible to numerous security threats, one being the possibility of single entity dominant network takeover.

Conversely, Generative AI, with its profound automation capabilities and data analytic functions, still struggles with trust-building as concern Islamic finance that requires higher transparency and even-handedness. In relation to compliance and ethics, the dread of AI's "black boxes" – where the inner workings of an algorithmic decision-making process remain opaque – poses a challenge. Moreover, social responsibility in AI, such as prejudice within system design and algorithmic discrimination, demands diligent scrutiny to guarantee that the outputs do not violate sharia principles which enjoin prejudice and uphold social justice in all aspects of life.

Figure 3. Analyzing challenges in Blockchain and Generative AI

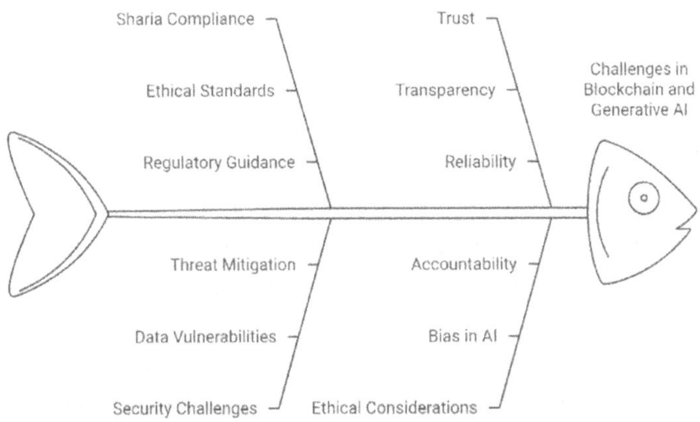

Although promising, Blockchain and Generative AI technologies still face challenges in Sharia compliance, ethical benchmarks, trustworthiness, and responsibility in the context of transparency and effectiveness within the financial system. Concerning Blockchain and Generative AI, Sharia compliance is always an issue as topics pertaining to Islamic law are sensitive. Robotics and fully automated procedures shy away from Islamic business ethics principles such as speculation, fairness, transparency, and contractually embedded consideration restricting deceit. Alongside this, the reputation risk due to information abuse undermines the reliability blockchain is well known for. Even though Generative AI can greatly enhance information processing and decision making, its application can undermine user acceptance due to bias, secrecy, and lack of openness in the used robotic processes and their outcomes.

Via the deliberation of compliance associated with regulations and ethics, scholars may put forward the 'case for' policies that are within Islamic and ethical boundaries and simultaneously safeguard the adoption of these technologies. Such an inclusive technique will alleviate fundamental concerns along with issues of ethics and the will also positively impact the trust and acceptance on the Islamic finance and international finance.

The growing prospects of Blockchain and Generative Artificial Intelligence (AI) technologies within the realm of Islamic finance, as well as their integration into the global financial architecture, offer the possibility of addressing the global demand for ethical, inclusive, and sustainable financing. Establishing a coherent set of global Sharia law compliance, data privacy, transparency, and ethics AI will create a single framework that enables the use and further development of these technologies across different jurisdictions. Moreover, the integration of these technologies into the Islamic finance framework can drive further innovations within the industry by improving mainstream compliance and sustainability, enhancing payment processing efficiency, tailoring financial services, and strengthening regulatory frameworks. Enhancing data privacy and security will be critical, where Blockchain can ensure robust security, while bias – Generative AI tailored to avoid discrimination -- will make fair and accountable decisions. In addition, both technologies could advance financial inclusion, with a larger impact in developing nations where previously unbanked populations could gain access to financial services. Implementations aimed at helping financial institutions reach global targets can leverage blockchain to provide provenance for sustainable supply chains or investments into renewable energy projects. Strengthening the initiatives in education and training will deepen the understanding of the technology as well as strengthen the workforce which is capable of implementing, managing, and overseeing these technologies, thus nurturing the development of an ethical, responsive, and sustainable global financial system.

AI AND BLOCKCHAIN FOR ISLAMIC SOCIAL FINANCE

The use of artificial intelligence (AI) and blockchain in Islamic social finance is a relatively new development, but it promises to have a significant impact on the way social funds are managed in Islamic society (Mahadi et al. 2024; Soualhi and Hasan Saleh 2024; Wiwoho et al. 2024). Islamic social finance encompasses zakat, waqf, and almsgiving, all of which constitute fundamental components of social welfare, economic justice, and community empowerment within the Islamic legal framework. In the contemporary landscape, the utilization of sophisticated technologies, particularly AI and blockchain, in the governance of Islamic social funds has sparked considerable interest owing to the remarkable opportunities these two technologies offer in enhancing operational efficiency, transparency, and impact of social finance initiatives.

Islamic social finance aims not only to achieve economic advantages but also to foster social cohesion and justice. In this regard, zakat, waqf, and charitable giving aim to redistribute wealth and enhance welfare for eligible individuals. Nevertheless, from an administrative and distributional perspective, this sector suffers from numerous shortcomings, especially with regard to transparency, efficiency, and accountability. These shortcomings could be addressed with the application of AI and blockchain technologies, which would greatly improve the sector's efficiency and transparency, thereby enhancing its societal impact.

A blockchain is a digital record-keeping device based on distributed ledgers. Implementing blockchain technology within Islamic social finance has the potential to dramatically improve the transparency and accountability of these systems. Using blockchain for zakat fund management, for instance, provides a platform where all zakat transactions can be recorded transparently. A blockchain empowers public confidence in zakat institutions because it guarantees that every donation is secured and every fund distribution is recorded in an open, tamper-proof ledger. It resolves one of the critical issues of zakat management: whether the funds collected under the auspices of zakat are spent in consonance with the sharia guidelines. Every transaction in a blockchain is timestamped and unalterable, which eliminates tampering, ensuring proper fund allocation. The blockchain technology implements an automated collection and payment systems via programmable payment rules known as smart contracts. For instance, upon payment of zakat, smart contracts can also pay predetermined eligible zakat beneficiaries directly which minimizes bureaucratic processes, reducing costs and improving efficiency.

Within the scope of waqf, blockchain provides approaches that help with the governance and management of waqf properties. Much like land and buildings, waqf properties are cumbersome to manage and monitor due to ambiguity concerning their ownership and distribution. The use of blockchain clearly and securely records the ownership status of waqf assets, preventing misappropriation and enhancing efficient control. Through smart contracts, the allocation of waqf income for credible purposes can be automated through a set program, reducing chances of misuse and facilitating more transparent management.

The management of zakat, waqf, and alms funds can benefit from AI's predictive analytics capabilities and data processing. AI's analytical capabilities can determine which groups require assistance the most and properly allocate zakat funds to those identified groups. AI is relevant as well in the management and analysis of donation data. Traditionally, the processing and analysis of zakat or waqf donations information is done manually which is time-intensive and riddled with inaccuracies. AI enhances accuracy and speeds the analysis of donations data which provides zakat and waqaf institutions with profound insights into donation and donor trends. AI is most suited to make suggestions on how to increase community participation to waqf or zakat programs and assist in addressing gaps by highlighting the regions or groups that need greater engagement. The management of waqf investment portfolios can also be enhanced through AI. Waqf's returns can finance social, educational, or health-related projects. With AI tools, waqf bodies can evaluate different available investment opportunities, forecast their returns, and select those that comply with sharia law and the waqf's long-term objectives. AI can lower investment risks and guarantee that waqf funds are spent in a way that maximizes the achievement of social benefits.

Smart contracts can be used to enhance effectiveness and visibility in the management of Islamic social finance. As a noteworthy component of blockchain technology, a smart contract is self-executing and self-enforcing computer software which covenant terms without the intervention of a mediator. In greedily donating towards Zakat, for instance, Donations can be ensured through smart contracts to be utilized for designated and noble objectives, and that the payments are paid directly to the deserving zakat payers. Smart contracts may be additionally employed in the waqf management towards the automated control of waqf proceeds distribution. Assume, for illustration purposes, that there is a waqf item that earns revenue, the smart contract will allocate that revenue for certain uses which can be financing health or education initiatives. This is how blockchain and smart contracts can mitigate the chances of embezzlement of waqf funds and bolster public confidence towards waqf fund governance.

The integration of AI and blockchain technology in Islamic social finance provides opportunities to these programs' social impact. AI can strategically optimize management and distribution of funds by pinpointing the greatest needs, urgency, and the correct audience. Meanwhile, blockchain technology augments responsibility in the administration of zakat and waqf by ensuring every transaction is recorded with full transparency, increasing accountability and the verifiable lack of fund misuse. The application of these technologies can empower the poor and marginalized populations to a greater extent because the disbursement of zakat and waqf funds will be timely, need-based, and more readily accessible. Enhanced efficiency drives down costs which allows funds to be redirected toward impactful purposes, raising the level of aid provided while minimizing administrative expense.

Despite the promise brought by this technology, there are issues that Islamic societies and financial institutions have yet to resolve, which may obstruct adoption and acceptance. Fueling a widespread implementation of this technology is the blockchain's scalability problem as well as the significant resources required for AI operations. To ensure that the sharia compliance guidelines are strictly followed, there is a need to create defined policies for the application of this technology within the scope of Islamic social finance. Notwithstanding, the prospects AI and blockchain hold for Islamic social finance are profoundly promising. Advancements in technology are bound to lead to an Islamic social finance framework that is more efficient and transparent and creates a significant social impact towards sustainable social welfare.

AI AND BLOCKCHAIN IN FINANCIAL DECISION-MAKING

The integration of artificial intelligence (AI) and blockchain in financial decision-making creates a new perspective in research and practice in the financial sector (Akour et al. 2024; E R Kismawadi, Irfan, M., Al Muddatstsir, U. D., & Abdulkarim 2023; Li, Zhong, and Tong 2024; Qatawneh, Lutfi, and Al Barrak 2024; Ridho Kismawadi, Irfan, and Shah 2023; Zhu 2024) The integration of both technologies is viewed as an innovation that can facilitate faster decision making, enhance efficiency and productivity in operations, and unlock further capabilities in the realms of data analysis and transaction security. In regard to finance, this article seeks to explore the possible benefits of synergizing AI with blockchain technology, discuss the issues which hinder its adoption, and analyze how it transforms corporate intelligence and decision making in financial institutions.

AI technology is an integral part of the modern financial industry, supporting more advanced and quicker analyses than humans can provide. Risk assessment, diagnostic evaluation of financial markets, as well as investment identification, are all executed through machine learning and deep learning technologies. AI algorithms, for instance, can evaluate and interpret real-time market data, process widely larger and more intricate datasets, and predict the value changes of stocks, bonds, and other financial instruments far better than human analysts.

The application of AI in financial decision-making also introduces the concept of automation in transaction processing and portfolio management (Ionescu and Diaconita 2023; Qatawneh et al. 2024). The emergence of AI-powered robo-advisors has transformed the engagement of retail investors with the financial markets. AI can assist in formulating appropriate investment strategies aimed at profit maximization while concurrently minimizing risks through the analysis of historical data and application of predictive statistical modeling.

Nonetheless, the foremost concern arising from the integration of AI within the financial industry is the problem involving transparency and interpretability. Numerous AI models deployed in finance, particularly those associated with deep learning, function as a "black box" siloed from user access, making decision logic obscure. This phenomenon undermines assurance of liability and impacts trust from authorities and the public who demand explanations and justifications for decisions rendered.

Unlike traditional financial infrastructures, modern technology blockchain provides transparency and security simultaneously in a way that is very hard to achieve with conventional systems. The principles of decentralization and cryptography are combined in this distributed ledger system which makes it practically impossible and very safe to manipulate and store financial data. Greater efficiency and transparency brought about by blockchain technology in carrying out transactions can minimize chances of human error and possible fraudulent activities.

The use of blockchain technology in cross border payment systems is one example of its application in the field of finance. Transaction fees tend to be very low, and the remittance payment is almost immediate with the use of payment systems based on blockchain technology such as Bitcoin and Ethereum. This allows improving the integrity of data concerning the financial documents, accelerating processing of the transactions, and providing incontrovertible evidence of transaction chronology and parties involved.

Also, the problems associated with security breaches of hacking and data theft that are prevalent in conventional banking systems have a solution in blockchain technology. Financial information, with the use of blockchain, is stored in a series of interlinked chronologically dated and encrypted blocks. Each block must be validated by the distributed network before being appended, rendering tampering virtually impossible. In terms of analysis and forecasting, use of blockchain to audit information enhances the reliability of the information due to reduced chances of manipulation foibles. Hence, real time financial analysis becomes more dependable.

Nevertheless, the integration of blockchain technology within financial systems poses problems. Energy efficiency and scalability are two prominent issues in blockchain infrastructure development. Today's blockchain platforms, like Bitcoin, struggle with slow transaction speeds and high energy expenditure, which may limit the technology's adoption in the international economy.

The integration of AI and blockchain into the banking sector automated financial decisions making processes, considerably improving both transparency and efficiency. AI has the ability to utilize blockchain's secure and decentralized databases for more advanced analytical evaluations and more sophisticated decisions. In contrast, blockchain can provide assurance that the information incorporated in AI models has integrity and is immutable.

As an illustration, within the scope of financing and lending, AI may be enable to reviewing learned information of the borrowers in order to forecast defaults. AI ensures accurate and unalterable risk assessment by blockchain's immutable records of loan histories and transactions safeguarding them from alterations or errors. AI and blockchain can be integrated for more efficient management of investment portfolios. AI is capable of monitoring market trends in real time therefore identifying the most beneficial investments; on the other hand, blockchain guarantees transparent and secure recording of every portfolio transaction. This capabilities frees investors from excessive guesswork in unpredictable markets.

The adoption of blockchain technology and AI in financial decision-making processes impacts the traditional financial services industry, and moreover, can be greatly useful in the scope of Islamic finance. Islamic finance operates on the premise of Sharia law which prohibits interest (riba), uncertainty (gharar), and gambling (maysir). Such unique principles also need innovative technology solutions aligned with these frameworks. AI technology can help in understanding big data and recognizing patterns which makes it possible for it to be used in forecasting market opportunities, estimating risks, and aiding investment decisions aligned with Sharia law. Such decisions would include selection of halal instruments, avoidance of equity participation which includes riba, gharar or any financial activity laden with those components. AI has the capability to pinpoint companies from which stocks can be acquired which satisfy sharia regulations through a thorough analysis of their financial status and their business approaches.

At the same time, blockchain technology has the potential to enhance the transparency and security of transactions within Islamic finance. The principles of Islamic finance underline the focal point of transparency in each transaction which needs to have 'value' and must be exempted from injustices which could arise from ignorance of such value. Due to its decentralized and immutable nature, blockchain technology can provide irrefutable proof of transaction data which aligns with Islamic finance principles concerning fairness. Smart contracts that are self-executing and automate agreements based on set conditions and without third party involvement, which could lead to bias or injustice, can also be created on blockchain systems. Thus, blockchain can be employed for the automation and enforcement of Islamic compliant transactions such as murabaha (profit margin sale), musharakah (joint venture), and ijarah (leasing), all of which require precise and unalterable documentation.

Integrating these two technologies makes it possible to build a more efficient, transparent, and secure Islamic financial system with the aid of AI and blockchain. AI accelerates and sharpens data analysis, while blockchain guarantees each transaction's reliability and security. In asset management, for instance, AI can assist in formulating compliant investments portfolios within the boundaries of Sharia law, while blockchain guarantees all transactions are executed properly and in compliance to sharia stipulations. The growing integration of both technologies would enhance public confidence in Islamic finance services because they make it possible to verify that every transaction is executed transparently, beyond the reach of manipulation or fraud.

There are problems that arise when trying to incorporate AI and blockchain technologies into Islamic finance. The adoption of almost any new technology comes with challenges and policies that adhere to the rigorous framework of sharia law. These two new technologies promise efficiency and transparency; however, their implementation in Islamic finance must comply with sharia principles. Thus, Islamic finance technologists, scholars, and regulators need to work together to draft the policies concerning the implementation of both technologies into Islamic finance.

Also, the issues pertaining to the scalability of blockchain technology and its need for technological resources must also be solved if the Islamic finance industry is to accept both technologies widely.

The integration of artificial intelligence alongside blockchain technology in the realm of finance offers tremendous prospects for advancement in the industry. Each new technology brings its own set of advantages; AI enhances productivity and allows for the enhanced swift and precise analysis of large datasets, while blockchain solves issues pertaining to security and transparency. Even with the setbacks regarding regulations, scalability, interoperability, and competition between these technologies, together they promise a far more sophisticated, secure, and intelligent financial framework. More investigation in this subject matter will be integral in determining how best to incorporate these technologies and tackle the challenges at hand.

DECENTRALIZED DECISION MAKING

Blockchain technology operates on the principle of decentralization, where authority is distributed across the network, rather than being concentrated on a single central entity (Abdellatif, Shaban, and Massoud 2025; Qu et al. 2025; Shang et al. 2025). This approach differs from traditional systems where decisions are usually made by a centralized authority, such as companies, governments, or financial institutions.

The blockchain technology has advanced the distributed network in such a way to makes the process more democratic by dispersing decision making power among all the participants. Every participant (or node) has equal chances of engagement in the decision-making process usually by way of casting votes or reaching a consensus. The decentralized characteristic of blockchains increases visibility and reduces the level of opacity in the process which normally accompanies central authoritarian power – it increases transaction fairness visibility, as all participants in the network can verify and has access limited to public ledger that contain all of the actions and transaction executed within the system This gives more freedom of reliance or trust in a system because the system integrity rests on the decentralized characteristic of the blockchain technology. In traditional systems, decision-making usually suffers bias from corporate pressure. In decentralization, space for individual bias as well as centralized control evaporates. The decisions are made whose rules are encoded in smart contracts which increases the fairness.

In any blockchain system, decision-making hinges on consensus algorithms; their significance is irrefutable. This algorithm is fundamentally the verification strategy for agreements associated with transactions, blocks, or several other activities within the network. They guarantee the achievement of consensus among participants without a dominating central entity, hence enabling secure and reliable operations in a decentralized way. Consensus mechanisms deal with the collaborative agreement of all users (or nodes) in blockchain systems on a singular version of truth. Reaching agreement is crucial to preserving the integrity of the blockchain, making sure that all transactions are valid and the accounting record is precise.

The consensus mechanism helps determine the order of transactions and validate transactions based on predetermined rules. Proof of Work (PoW), This mechanism requires participants (miners) to solve complex cryptographic puzzles to validate transactions. The first participant to solve the puzzle can add new blocks to the blockchain, and in return, they are rewarded with a cryptocurrency (e.g. Bitcoin) (Jhansi Rani 2025; Therry et al. 2024). Proof of Stake (PoS), In PoS, participants validate transactions based on the amount of cryptocurrency they own and are willing to "stake" as collateral (Puthal and Mohanty 2019; Wu, Song, and Wang 2020). The more participants stake, the greater their chances of being selected to validate the next block. Delegated Proof of Stake (DPoS), DPoS is a variation of PoS in which shareholders elect delegates who then validate transactions and create blocks. This mechanism aims to increase transaction speed and reduce centralization. Practical Byzantine Fault Tolerance (PBFT), Used in several authorized blockchains, PBFT requires participants to agree on the order and validity of transactions through a voting system.

Figure 4. Exploring various Blockchain consensus mechanisms

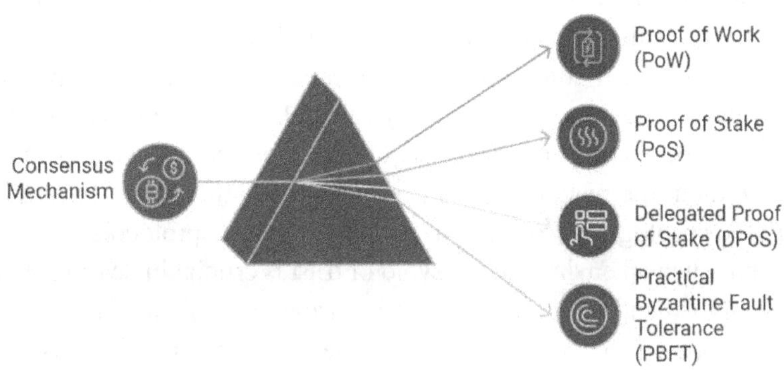

A consensus mechanism minimizes the possibility of errors and fraud by preventing any single participant from independently changing the blockchain. The fact that all participants must reach a consensus greatly complicates efforts by malicious actors to manipulate the system. Take, for example, PoW: the computational resources needed to make fraudulent alterations to the blockchain are prohibitively high. Under PoS, participants are financially penalized for dishonest behavior, which induces them to act honorably, thereby protecting the assets they are risking. Participants achieve consensus result in an immutable ledger, and any decision or transaction recorded cannot be altered or removed. This bolsters system trust because participants are assured that decisions made in the network are enduring and beyond any form of manipulation.

Figure 5. Benefits of a Decentralised Approach

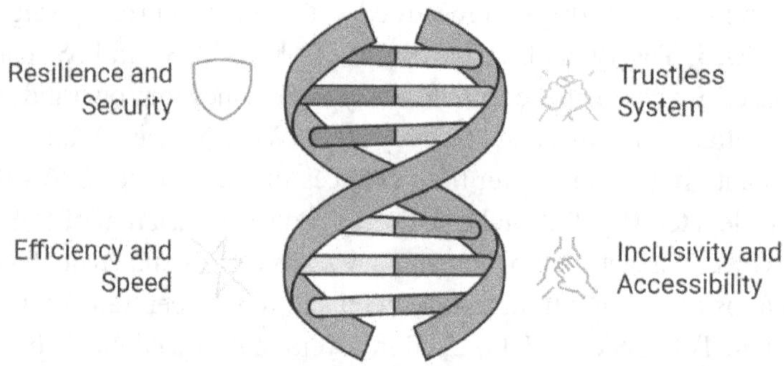

The benefits of the decentralized approach provided by blockchains are numerous. First, Resilience and Security. Attack attempts, system failures, or corrupt systems are far more difficult to manage within a decentralized structure as there is no central control point. Even if some nodes are attacked, the rest of the network is able to function and manage the work smoothly. Second, The System Without Trust. In the blockchain ecosystem, participants are able to transact and participate in decision-making without the need to trust a central figure. Trust in the system is achieved through the cryptographic mechanisms and consensus protocols incorporated into the system. Such an environment devoid of trust is crucial in dealings like financial transactions, execution of contracts, and sharing of sensitive data.

Key Components Three and Four: Efficiency, Promptness, Inclusivity, and Accessibility. Moving towards more decentralised forms of decision-making means that there is no need for middlemen to make decisions, thus saving time and funds. Within blockchain systems, there is also rapid execution of actions after agreement is reached on decisions. Blockchain systems are open and accessible from any global location. Anyone with the minimal requisites such as computing power may partake in their creation and subsequently join the decision-making process. This technological aspect broadens the availability of numerous participants and encourages participation from different and diverse interest groups, thereby expanding democracy (Irfan, 2021).

Figure 6. Challenges in Blockchain Decentralised Decision Making

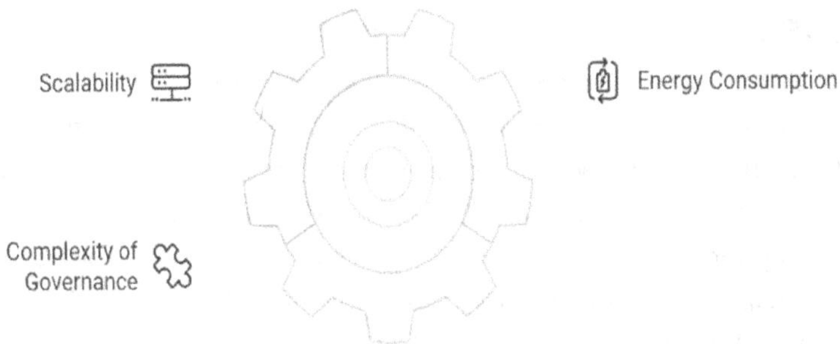

Even with numerous System Design Decision Advantages, Distribution Autonomous Decision Making on Blockchains Encounter Issues. First, Scalability- Decentralized systems have always struggled with scalability. Consensus Algorithms such as PoW face problems of scalability due to their high computational needs, thus making them slower as the network flourishes. In addition, more participants increase reachability of consensus, which increases the time required to come to an agreement. This can significantly delay decision-making. Secondly, Energy Consumption- Sustaining PoW mechanisms, particularly in Bitcoin, requires enormous amounts of power to operate the network. These concerns are especially pertinent when considering the evolving environmental implications blockchain systems will face. Third, Complexity of Government, the scope for decentralization improves the ability for fairness and transparency, yet simultaneously impairs the ability for effective governance. For instance, the issue of who claims the right to participate in decision making and how participant conflicts are resolved becomes complicated. Moreover, some blockchain systems suffer from a lack of organization/coordination which becomes problematic because no one is in charge to deal with these problems of inefficiency (Irfan, Elhoseny, Kassim, & Metawa, 2023).

The decision-making power given through the use of blockchain technology allows for much easier workflow automation. Such innovation can dramatically shift numerous industries. Because of the reliance on consensus protocols, the risk of fraud, mistakes in processing data, or the controlling power of a single entity decreases significantly. On the contrary, with the development of this system, several critical issues such as lack of sufficient scalability or the complex nature of governance still remain unsolved, consequently deterring universal adoption. The advancement of blockchain technology could accelerate secure collaborative systems in various fields, thus fostering effective solutions (Irfan, Elmogy, Majid, & El-Sappagh, 2023).

CONCLUSION

The intersection of blockchain technology and generative artificial intelligence (Generative AI) carries noteworthy transformative promise in Islamic finance. Blockchain permits the recording of transactions in an immutable manner which is more reliable and supports the principles of fairness, sustainability, and sharia compliance due to its transparency and security. Generative AI strengthens decision making in processing information, optimizing risks, and personalizing financial services within Islamic frameworks. This technological blend presents creative approaches to solving problems in enhancing financial inclusion, fostering ESG investments, and finding solutions to privacy in data and energy consumption. The tokenization of assets such as sukuk and smart contracts offer prospects for sustainable investments which lead to a more equitable distribution of wealth. Nonetheless, there are still issues regarding the delay in adopting this technology, such as the development of a sharia-compliant policy guideline and an energy-efficient blockchain and AI model. The implementation of these technologies in Islamic finance relies heavily on the collaboration of technology authorities and regulators with sharia scholars (Irfan, Kadry, Sharif, & Ullah Khan, 2023).

The application of blockchain technology alongside Generative AI bears considerable consequences for both the Islamic finance industry and the economy at large. Blockchain technology's transparency and immutability features increase public trust towards Islamic financial institutions while upholding the core values of openness and honesty. Moreover, the use of smart contracts on blockchains facilitates automation of Sharia-compliant transactions—murabahah, ijarah, and musharakah—thereby strengthening Sharia compliance and minimizing irregularities. On the other hand, Generative AI expands financial inclusion by tailoring services to previously unreachable clients, resulting in affordable and personalized financial services. Additionally, the technology can enhance investment decision-making by enabling the issuance of 'green sukuk' and waqf, thus promoting sustainable investment aligned with the goals of Sharia. Moreover, the reduced roles of intermediaries and streamlined decision-making processes enable enhanced operational efficiency, lower transaction costs, and broaden access to international markets. Adoption of the technology, however, poses other challenges such as lack of uniform data privacy protections and cross-border regulations compliant with Islamic principles (Irfan, Hussainey, Chan Bukhari, & Nam, 2024).

Creating an adaptive legal framework is vital in sustaining the adoption of this technology. Moreover, the integration of blockchain and Generative AI can facilitate the creation of a sharia-compliant digital financial system that seamlessly integrates business participants, investors, and financial institutions on a streamlined platform. This technology transforms the operational modality of Islamic finance and, at the same time, creates opportunities for international finance to transition toward a more ethical, inclusive, sustainable framework while providing the global community with a more responsible financial system.

The intersection of Islamic finance with blockchain technology and Generative AI offers pathways for further investigation. There is a need to establish a cross-border sharia law holistic governance framework that covers compliance concerns with the Islamization of technology as one of the primary issues of concern. Moreover, the study can analyze tokenization's impact on economic participation and the distribution of wealth in the presence of limited financial services in the transformative assets including sukuk, waqf, and property. Other important studies focus on sustainability challenges in blockchain systems, specifically on models that improve energy efficiency and support sustainable development. As Generative AIs evolve, addressing bias... ensures that such technologies serve all users without discrimination in line with the core values of Islamic justice (Irfan, Elmogy, Gupta, Khalifa, & Dias, 2024).

Exploring the application of blockchain and AI in the automation of zakat and waqf asset management, as well as the use of smart contracts for more transparent and efficient processes, can be directed to further research. In addition, the potential analysis of these technologies reinforcing sustainability-based investments and ESG in Islamic finance warrants thorough investigation. There is also a need for research into designing strategic frameworks for the implementation of AI and blockchain technology into the Islamic global financial landscape to enhance the global competitiveness of Islamic financial institutions. The other potential opportunity is designing a decentralized digital, Sharia-compliant financial framework which enhances system transparency and efficiency.

Other avenues of research include the application of AI in sharia-compliant risk assessment for investment opportunities that would generate predictive tools that align with sharia guidelines. Assessing the socio-economic impacts of the technology on social equity, wealth distribution, and community empowerment from the perspective of enabling technology also has significant importance to ensure that the socio-economic benefits are realized. Research in this area will not only expand intellectual boundaries, but also provide effective insights for the Islamic finance sector on harnessing blockchain and Generative AI.

REFERENCES

Abbas, K., & Hafeez, M. (2021). Wıll Artıfıcıal Intellıgence Rejuvenate Islamıc Fınance? A Versıon of World Academıa. *Hitit Theology Journal*, *20*(3), 311–324. DOI: 10.14395/hid.931401

Abdellatif, A. A., Shaban, K., & Massoud, A. (2025). Blockchain-Enabled Distributed Learning for Enhanced Smart Grid Security and Efficiency. *Computers & Electrical Engineering*, *123*, 110012. Advance online publication. DOI: 10.1016/j.compeleceng.2024.110012

Akour, I., Alzyoud, M., Alquqa, E. K., Tariq, E., Alzboun, N., Al-Hawary, S. I. S., & Alshurideh, M. T. (2024). Artificial Intelligence and Financial Decisions: Empirical Evidence from Developing Economies. *International Journal of Data and Network Science*, *8*(1), 101–108. DOI: 10.5267/j.ijdns.2023.10.013

Avci, G., & Erzurumlu, Y. O. (2023). Blockchain Tokenization of Real Estate Investment: A Security Token Offering Procedure and Legal Design Proposal. *Journal of Property Research*, *40*(2), 188–207. DOI: 10.1080/09599916.2023.2167665

Bansal, U., S. Bharatwal, D. S. Bagiyam, and E. R. Kismawadi. 2024. "Fraud Detection in the Era of AI: Harnessing Technology for a Safer Digital Economy." Pp. 143–64 in *AI-Driven Decentralized Finance and the Future of Finance*.

Basu, B., Mandal, S., & Kar, A. K. (2025). Beyond and beneath the Metaverse Dazzle: The Interplay of VR and Blockchain-Based Social Exchanges and Affordances in Determining NFT Trading User Experience. *Journal of Retailing and Consumer Services*, *84*, 104180. Advance online publication. DOI: 10.1016/j.jretconser.2024.104180

Ionescu, S. A., & Diaconita, V. (2023). Transforming Financial Decision-Making: The Interplay of AI, Cloud Computing and Advanced Data Management Technologies. *International Journal of Computers, Communications & Control*, *18*(6), 1–19. DOI: 10.15837/ijccc.2023.6.5735

Irfan, M. (2021, January). Do Shariah Indices converge? Evidence from Gulf Cooperation Council countries. *International Journal of Business Excellence*, *23*(2), 251–269. DOI: 10.1504/IJBEX.2021.113448

Irfan, M., Elhoseny, M., Kassim, S., & Metawa, N. (2023). *Advanced Machine Learning Algorithms for Complex Financial Applications*. IGI Global., DOI: 10.4018/978-1-6684-4483-2

Irfan, M., Elmogy, M., Gupta, S., Khalifa, F., & Dias, R. (2024). *AI-Driven Decentralized Finance and the Future of Finance*. IGI Global., DOI: 10.4018/979-8-3693-6321-8

Irfan, M., Elmogy, M., Majid, M. S., & El-Sappagh, S. (2023). *The Impact of AI Innovation on Financial Sectors in the Era of Industry 5.0*. IGI Global., DOI: 10.4018/979-8-3693-0082-4

Irfan, M., Hussainey, K., Chan Bukhari, S. A., & Nam, Y. (Eds.). (2024). *Issues of Sustainability in AI and New-Age Thematic Investing*. IGI Global Publisher., DOI: 10.4018/979-8-3693-3282-5

Irfan, M., Kadry, S., Sharif, M., & Ullah Khan, H. (2023). *Fintech Applications in Islamic Finance: AI, Machine Learning, and Blockchain Techniques*. IGI Global., DOI: 10.4018/979-8-3693-1038-0

Jhansi Rani, T. (2025). Blockchain Based Analytical Bug Tracking in Software Engineering. *Communications on Applied Nonlinear Analysis*, *32*(1), 127–147. DOI: 10.52783/cana.v32.1626

Kismawadi, E. R. (2024a). "Blockchain Technology and Islamic Finance: Empowering Small Businesses for Financial Sustainability." Pp. 50–77 in Technopreneurship in Small Businesses for Sustainability.

Kismawadi, E. R. (2024b). "Sustainable Islamic Financial Inclusion: The Ethical Challenges of Generative AI in Product and Service Development." Pp. 237–58 in Exploring the Ethical Implications of Generative AI.

E R Kismawadi, Irfan, M., Al Muddatstsir, U. D., & Abdulkarim, F. M. 2023. "Fintech Innovations: Risk Mitigation Strategies in Islamic Finance." Pp. 35–58 in *Fintech Applications in Islamic Finance: AI, Machine Learning, and Blockchain Techniques*.

Li, Y., Zhong, H., & Tong, Q. (2024). Artificial Intelligence, Dynamic Capabilities, and Corporate Financial Asset Allocation. *International Review of Financial Analysis*, *96*, 103773. Advance online publication. DOI: 10.1016/j.irfa.2024.103773

Mahadi, N. F., Yusuf, M. B. O., Kassim, S., & Yusoff, S. S. B. M. (2024). FINANCIAL RESILIENCE AMONG WOMEN SMALL AND MEDIUM ENTERPRISE IN MALAYSIA DURING AND AFTER COVID-19: THE ROLE OF ISLAMIC SOCIAL FINANCE. *Journal of Islamic Monetary Economics and Finance*, *10*(4), 631–656. DOI: 10.21098/jimf.v10i4.2009

Mbaidin, H. O., Sbaee, N. Q., Almubydeen, I. O., & Alomari, K. M. (2024). Key Success Drivers for Implementation Blockchain Technology in UAE Islamic Banking. *Uncertain Supply Chain Management*, *12*(2), 1175–1188. DOI: 10.5267/j.uscm.2023.11.016

Mohamed, H., and H. Ali. 2022. Blockchain, Fintech, and Islamic Finance: Building the Future in the New Islamic Digital Economy.

Ng, P. S. J., Zhang, X., Fu, L., Ye, L., & Phan, K. Y. (2025). The Inclusive Innovation of Blockchain in Securities Issuance: Reduced Inequalities of Investors. *Journal of Advanced Research in Applied Sciences and Engineering Technology*, *46*(2), 188–212. DOI: 10.37934/araset.46.2.188212

Puthal, D., & Mohanty, S. P. (2019). Proof of Authentication: IoT-Friendly Blockchains. *IEEE Potentials*, *38*(1), 26–29. DOI: 10.1109/MPOT.2018.2850541

Qatawneh, A. M., Lutfi, A., & Al Barrak, T. (2024). Effect of Artificial Intelligence (AI) on Financial Decision-Making: Mediating Role of Financial Technologies (Fin-Tech). *HighTech and Innovation Journal*, *5*(3), 759–773. DOI: 10.28991/HIJ-2024-05-03-015

Qu, L., Wen, F., Huang, H., & Wang, Z. (2025). Aggregation-Chain: A Consortium Blockchain Based Multi-Chain Data Sharing Framework with Efficient Query. *Cluster Computing*, *28*(1), 46. Advance online publication. DOI: 10.1007/s10586-024-04777-w

Ridho Kismawadi, E., M. Irfan, and S. M. A. R. Shah. (2023). "Revolutionizing Islamic Finance: Artificial Intelligence's Role in the Future of Industry." Pp. 184–207 in The Impact of AI Innovation on Financial Sectors in the Era of Industry 5.0.

Shang, S., Du, X., Wang, X., & Liu, A. (2025). Private Approximate Nearest Neighbor Search for On-Chain Data Based on Locality-Sensitive Hashing. *Future Generation Computer Systems*, *164*, 107586. Advance online publication. DOI: 10.1016/j.future.2024.107586

Soualhi, Y., & Hasan Saleh, A. O. (2024). SMART CONTRACTS AND THEIR APPLICATION PROSPECTS IN SOCIAL BANKING: A MAQASID JURISPRUDENTIAL PERSPECTIVE. *Malaysian Journal of Syariah and Law*, *12*(2), 490–510. DOI: 10.33102/mjsl.vol12no2.599

Therry, A. C. D., Ardiansyah, R., Pusadan, M. Y., Joefrie, Y. Y., & Kasim, A. A. (2024). The Implementation and Analysis of The Proof of Work Consensus in Blockchain. *Advance Sustainable Science, Engineering and Technology*, *6*(1), 02401018. Advance online publication. DOI: 10.26877/asset.v6i1.17878

Wiwoho, J., Trinugroho, I., Kharisma, D. B., & Suwadi, P. (2024). Islamic Crypto Assets and Regulatory Framework: Evidence from Indonesia and Global Approaches. *International Journal of Law and Management, 66*(2), 155–171. DOI: 10.1108/IJLMA-03-2023-0051

Wu, Y., Song, P., & Wang, F. (2020). Hybrid Consensus Algorithm Optimization: A Mathematical Method Based on POS and PBFT and Its Application in Blockchain. *Mathematical Problems in Engineering, 2020*, 1–13. Advance online publication. DOI: 10.1155/2020/7270624

Yuspin, W., Wardiono, K., Budiono, A., & Gulyamov, S. (2022). "The Law Alteration on Artificial Intelligence in Reducing Islamic Bank's Profit and Loss Sharing Risk." Legality. *Jurnal Ilmiah Hukum, 30*(2), 267–282. DOI: 10.22219/ljih.v30i2.23051

Zhu, A. Y. F. (2024). Optimizing Financial Decision-Making for Emerging Adults: A Compact Python-Based Personalized Financial Projection Approach. *Technology in Society, 77*, 102599. Advance online publication. DOI: 10.1016/j.techsoc.2024.102599

Chapter 10
Financial Inclusion and Large Language Models

Peterson K. Ozili
https://orcid.org/0000-0001-6292-1161
Central Bank of Nigeria, Nigeria

Kingsley Obiora
International Monetary Fund, USA

Chinwendu Onuzo
Central Bank of Nigeria, Nigeria

ABSTRACT

Large language models have gained popularity, and it is important to understand their applications in the financial inclusion domain. This study identifies the benefits and risks of using large language models (LLMs) in the financial inclusion domain. We show that LLMs can be used to (i) summarize the key themes in financial inclusion communications, (ii) gain insights from the tone of financial inclusion communications, (iii) bring discipline to financial inclusion communications, (iv) improve financial inclusion decision making, and (v) enhance context-sensitive text analysis and evaluation. However, the use of large language models in the financial inclusion domain poses risks relating to biased interpretations of LLM-generated responses, data privacy risk, misinformation and falsehood risks. We emphasize that LLMs can be used safely in the financial inclusion domain to summarise financial inclusion speeches and communication, but they should not be used in situations where finding the truth is important to make decisions that promote financial inclusion.

DOI: 10.4018/979-8-3373-1250-7.ch010

1. INTRODUCTION

This study identifies the benefits and risks of using large language models (LLMs) in the financial inclusion domain. Financial inclusion refers to access and use of affordable basic financial services by members of the population (Sarma and Pais, 2011; Ozili, 2025a). Financial inclusion has immense benefits to society. Financial inclusion gives people access to a bank account, mobile money account, insurance, payment and credit products which they can use to start a business, earn income, own an asset, become financially independent and economically empowered (Ozili, 2025b). Policymakers play a fundamental role in increasing the level of financial inclusion in society. They can introduce regulations and policies that increase the demand and supply of formal financial services e.g., banking, credit, payment and insurance products. They can issue banking licenses to microfinance institutions operating in rural communities to serve financially excluded people, and they also issue payment license to Fintech and Bigtech players to broaden and deepen digital financial inclusion (Frost et al, 2021).

A major aspect of any financial inclusion strategy is financial inclusion communication. Policymakers communicate their plans, intentions and the progress they have made in financial inclusion to stakeholders. Financial inclusion communication is aimed at informing the local and international community about their policy stance towards financial inclusion. For example, policymakers often communicate their national financial inclusion strategy for the next 5-10 years. They also communicate their intention to introduce regulations that give customers greater access to a wide variety of low-cost financial services. Such financial inclusion communication, either through official statements or speeches of the authorities responsible for financial inclusion, can promote transparency about policymakers' financial inclusion plan. If policymakers' financial inclusion communication is done effectively, it increases the credibility and reputation of the policymaker to promote financial inclusion in the eyes of the general public.

More importantly, financial inclusion communication may contain broad statements that reveal less technical details about the plans that are in place to advance financial inclusion. They may also contain hidden sentiments that are not easy to decipher. For the first time, it is now possible to use AI-based large language models to generate more insight from financial inclusion communications. LLMs are essentially text mining tools that accommodate a large number of parameters (up to billions) and analyse the relationships among words from large volume of texts while taking into account context in summarizing texts (Huang et al, 2022). It is now possible to use large language models (LLMs) (e.g., BERT, ChatGPT, GPT4, XLNet, LLaMA, and T5) to extract summaries, key themes and analyse the sentiments in financial inclusion speeches (Ozili, 2025c). LLMs can be used to filter out the noise and the vagueness in financial inclusion communication.

This study contributes to the literature that use LLMs to analyse policymakers' communications. Presently, policymakers issue statements and speeches on financial inclusion, but the subtle positive or negative sentiments in such statements or speeches remain hidden and are never identified and brought to public knowledge. Also, the literature has not examined the textual analysis of financial inclusion speeches using large language models. Therefore, this study contributes to the literature by identifying ways in which LLMs can be used to enhance the dissemination of financial inclusion communication. It also contributes to the existing literature that examine how LLMs can improve people's lives through insight-gathering from sentiment analysis. It also contribute to the existing literature that examine the role of artificial intelligence in development finance.

The rest of the study is organized as follows. Section 2 presents a conceptual understanding of large language models and the literature review. Section 4 presents the risks associated with using LLMs in the financial inclusion domain. Section 5 presents the conclusion of the article.

2. CONCEPTUAL FRAMEWORK AND LITERATURE REVIEW

2.1. Understanding Financial Inclusion and Its Benefits

The literature defined financial inclusion as a process that increase access to basic financial services, increase usage of financial services and increase the quality of financial services delivery (Sarma and Pais, 2011; Ozili, 2025a). The recent literature show that financial inclusion has several benefits. Hassouba (2025) used survey data to examine financial inclusion benefits in Egypt and found that financial inclusion improved the financial lives of poor and low-income groups, and it improved the efficiency of the banking system and contributed to economic growth. However, the challenge to financial inclusion in Egypt is limited outreach to people in underprivileged communities. Ozili (2025b) was interested in financial inclusion dynamics and its effect on economic welfare in the context of the major religions. The author examined the impact of financial inclusion on economic welfare in majority Christian countries, majority Hindu countries and majority Muslim countries. Thirty countries were analysed from 2004 to 2020, and it was found that financial inclusion increased corruption control, political stability, rule of law and regulatory quality in the majority religious countries. A high level of financial inclusion decreased the unemployment rate in majority Muslim countries while a preexisting low unemployment rate increased financial inclusion in majority Christian and Muslim countries.

Wei et al (2025) were concerned about the benefit of digital financial inclusion for e-commerce development and entrepreneurial activity in China. They investigate how digital financial inclusion influences entrepreneurial activity through e-commerce development in China based on data from 275 prefecture-level cities during the 2011 to 2021 period. They found that digital financial inclusion enhances entrepreneurial activity in non-central and non-provincial capital cities. The implication of the result is that policymakers need to leverage digital transformation for within-city entrepreneurial growth and inclusive economic growth in China. Khan et al (2025) explored whether financial inclusion increases remittances and economic growth in developing countries. They analyse 79 developing countries from 2011 to 2021 and found that countries with high levels of financial inclusion witness higher levels of remittances and economic development. Sebai et al (2025) examined the effect of financial inclusion on financial stability in 26 developing countries from 2004 to 2020 and found that financial inclusion is beneficial for banking stability up to a certain threshold.

Akram et al (2025) were interested in examining whether financial inclusion can prevent women from engaging in financial crimes. They focused on the financial scams and frauds faced by women in the five largest US states by population. They used survey questionnaire to solicit responses from 4,113 women respondents. They found that 94 percent of women believe that financial inclusion can protect them from financial scams and fraud. They also found that financial crimes disproportionately affect women because when women are scammed, they tend to conceal such scam activities from close family members and partners to avoid being shamed. Choudhary et al (2025) investigate the contribution of fintech adoption to financial inclusion and the sustainable development goals. They analyse 86 countries using the quantile regression analysis and found that fintech adoption has a favourable effect on education, gross domestic product and access to the internet at higher quantiles. The implication of the findings is that fintech adoption can accelerate progress towards achieving the SDGs. Rehman and Chen (2025) examined the relationship between financial inclusion and energy intensity in G7 countries from 1993 to 2023. They found that enhanced access to financial services increases access to energy technologies.

Mhlongo (2025) examined the effect of financial inclusion on women entrepreneurship in South Africa. The author noted that lack of access to finance and affordable credit remains a major hindrance to starting and growing a business for women in South Africa with less than 30 percent of women having access to finance to start a business. The author examined whether financial inclusion could increase women's entrepreneurship in South Africa. The author found that financial inclusion improve entrepreneurship by increasing women's participation in business; however, many of the government's financial inclusion programmes do not translate to increased participation of women in business. Fowowe (2025) examined the effect of financial inclusion on agricultural productivity in Mali and found that financial inclusion has a positive effect on agricultural productivity in Mali. The result implies that improving financial inclusion can boost agricultural productivity in Mali. Li et al (2025) investigate the effect of digital financial inclusion on income inequality in the sub-Saharan Africa and found that using the internet and mobile phones to access financial services contribute to a reduction in income inequality in sub-Saharan Africa.

2.2. Understanding Large Language Models

LLMs are a form of generative artificial intelligence. Large language models (LLMs) gained popularity after the emergence of ChatGPT in 2022. They are algorithms that are trained on a large amount of text-based data (such as data from web pages, ebooks, scientific research, media blogs, books or social media posts) which are typically obtained from the open internet (Huang et al, 2022). LLMs always require massive datasets which are sourced from the internet or user interactions, to learn patterns and generate insights or responses (Wu et al, 2024). The algorithms in LLMs analyse the relationship between different large number of texts to produce a probability model (Wu et al, 2024). After producing the probability model, the user can give the algorithm a prompt by asking it a question. The LLM will provide an answer to the question based on the relationship of the texts in the model (Jiang et al, 2020). It is also important to note that the text-based data which are fed into LLMs are static after the model has been trained. However, the LLM can be re-trained or fine-tuned by training it on additional data (Ding et al, 2023). The LLM can also be re-contextualised through a process known as 'prompt augmentation' which is essentially providing context information about the question (Yoo et al, 2021). The greatest advantage of LLMs is their ability to generate convincing content in multiple human and computer languages (Chang et al, 2024). Therefore, users of financial inclusion information, also known as financial inclusion stakeholders, can rely on LLMs to obtain summaries, key themes and sentiments from financial inclusion communication. Examples of existing large language models are ChatGPT, 'Bard' owned by Google, 'LLaMa' owned by Meta.

2.3. Literature on Relationship Between Artificial Intelligence and Financial Inclusion

Large language model is a type of generative artificial intelligence; therefore, it is important to review the literature on the relationship between artificial intelligence and financial inclusion. Presently, several studies have explored the link between artificial intelligence and financial inclusion. David et al (2025) argued that AI-driven financial technologies can accelerate financial inclusion to increase economic growth and decrease the level of poverty. They argued that AI-assisted fintech apps can offer innovative solutions to accelerate easy access to affordable financial services. The implication is that AI can assist in delivering a more inclusive financial system. Subramaniam et al (2024) focused on the role of AI adoption for financial inclusion. They investigated the effect of artificial intelligence adoption on financial inclusion. They examined 29 countries from 2017 to 2021. The countries were grouped into low artificial intelligence adopters and high artificial intelligence adopters. The authors used Generalized Method of Moments (GMM) estimations to estimate the effect of artificial intelligence adoption on financial inclusion and found that artificial intelligence adoption is a significant determinant of financial inclusion. They also found that artificial intelligence adoption helped to promote financial inclusion in countries that adopt artificial intelligence. They recommend that artificial intelligence can be deployed to the financial sector to address financial exclusion problems. Fazal et al (2025) also examined the relationship between artificial intelligence and financial inclusion in the context of achieving the United Nations' sustainable development goals by 2030. They argued that financial inclusion is an enabler of 8 of the 17 SDGs. They examined the role of artificial intelligence for achieving financial inclusion and the SDGs. The authors adopted the qualitative research methodology and found that the introduction of artificial intelligence in the financial sector increased people's participation in the formal financial sector and it helped to accelerate economic growth and reduce poverty. Chadha and Gupta (2024) emphasized that there need to be a synergy between artificial intelligence and financial inclusion in order to have an effective financial inclusion model that address financial exclusion problems.

Bhawnra and Singh (2024) focused on India. They acknowledged that, in India, the national financial inclusion scheme, which is the *Pradhan Mantri Jan Dhan Yojana* scheme, was a significant policy intervention by the Indian government to increase financial inclusion. The authors then examined the role of technology, especially artificial intelligence, in the Indian banking sector for the purpose of increasing financial inclusion. They showed that artificial intelligence made significant inroads into specific areas of banking such as risk management and personal financial management, while the most common manifestation of artificial intelligence in banking in India is in developing credit scores for users, developing conversational interfaces such as chatbots, voice recognition, biometric identification, and electronic know-your-customer (KYC) interfaces.

Yang and Lee (2024) also examined the impact of artificial intelligence on financial inclusion. Their study contributed to the literature on artificial intelligence ethics, and it cast some light into how artificial intelligence transparency and accountability affect user outcomes. The authors focused on the ethical aspect of AI, the perceived algorithmic fairness of AI and its effect on financial inclusion. They surveyed 675 users in China and found that perceived algorithmic fairness acts as a significant mediating factor between the ethical attributes of artificial intelligence systems and user responses. They also found that greater artificial intelligence transparency, accountability, and legitimacy enhance users' perceptions of fairness, which, in turn, increases users' satisfaction with AI-assisted financial services and it increases their likelihood of recommending financial services to their friends and family. Jameel and Janjua (2024) also investigated the impact of artificial intelligence (AI)-assisted fintech on digital financial inclusion. They showed that artificial intelligence has a major impact on digital financial inclusion in that it improves risk assessment and mitigation, it assists in generating organised data, it improves cyber security, and it improves fraud detection. The authors recommend that governments, non-governmental organisations, financial institutions and non-financial institutions should embrace artificial intelligence to accelerate financial inclusion. Aishwaryalaxmi and Rathod (2024) were concerned about how artificial intelligence mediates the relationship between digital literacy, digital adoption, and financial inclusion in developing economies. They surveyed 350 participants from developing economies and found that artificial intelligence not only enhances financial decision-making for underserved populations, but it also promotes wider adoption of digital financial services for people who have less financial knowledge. Ozili (2025c) also explored how artificial intelligence can increase digital financial inclusion. The author argued that artificial intelligence can streamline the operations of agents of digital financial inclusion; determine the communal areas in need of digital financial inclusion; automate the digital formal account opening process; offer customized experience for both banked and unbanked adults; ensure security and safety of customers' funds; determine the credit worthiness of unbanked adults who have recently become banked; give banked adults full control of their financial lives; deepen digital financial inclusion; and promote equity and diversity for digital financial inclusion.

2.4. Literature on AI in Other Financial Contexts

Thuraisamy et al (2025) examined the role of generative artificial intelligence in transforming the financial sector and how it can offer innovative solutions and equip the industry with tools to improve operational efficiency in the financial sector. Ally (2025) was concerned about the ability of local legal frameworks to accommodate the complexities brought about by artificial intelligence and smart contracts. Ally (2025) investigated some of the legal challenges affecting the integration of artificial intelligence in the financial sector, focusing on some challenges such as data privacy, cyber security, fraud, consumer protection, algorithmic bias, fairness and transparency. The author also examined the impact of FinTech innovations on Tanzania's legal landscape. The method adopted in the study is the doctrinal legal approach and a comparative analysis of Tanzanian laws, to identify gaps and propose solutions. The study found that existing legal instruments in Tanzania, such as the Cybercrime Act 2015, Electronic Transaction Act 2015 and others, do not adequately address the specific legal challenges posed by artificial intelligence and FinTech. This calls for the development of specialized legal frameworks that accelerate financial inclusion in the digital economy and protect consumers from existing and emerging risks associated with financial technologies.

Saxena and Rishi (2025) were more concerned about how artificial intelligence can transform financial analytics and decision-making processes. They developed the FinSageNet framework which identifies the capabilities of LLM for financial decision making. The FinSageNet framework showed that LLM has the capacity to perform exceptional text summarization, and it outperforms existing LLM models like FLAN and GPT-3.5 in text summarisation. Singh (2025) argued that financial institutions in the United Kingdom can use generative artificial intelligence to address the risk of financial crime and reduce regulatory burden to increase operational efficiency and improve customer experience. Manoharan and Darwish (2025) also examined how artificial intelligence is transforming the financial sector. They showed that AI-based machine learning and deep learning methods are widely used to analyze massive datasets, optimise portfolio, detect fraud, detect patterns, and anticipate risks in the areas of investment banking, asset management, and insurance. They also showed that artificial intelligence has led to the creation of chatbots, robo-advisors, and predictive analytics.

3. OPPORTUNITIES OF LLMS FOR FINANCIAL INCLUSION

LLMs offer several benefits for financial inclusion communications. For instance, LLM can summarise the key themes in financial inclusion communications, it can gain insights from the tone of financial inclusion communications, it can bring discipline to financial inclusion communications, it can improve financial inclusion decision making, and it can enhance the context of financial inclusion text analysis and evaluation.

3.1. Summarizing Themes in Financial Inclusion Communications

Many financial inclusion communications are unstructured. LLMs are useful in summarizing the salient themes that are included in unstructured financial inclusion communications. LLMs can summarize lengthy text content, extract key information, and provide concise summaries of financial inclusion communications and speeches (Neekhara et al, 2024). This helps to understand the main points of policy statements, news reports or articles.

3.2. Gain Insights From the Tone of Financial Inclusion Communications

The policymakers facing significant challenges in achieving their financial inclusion goals will ideally use a less optimistic tone when delivering financial inclusion communications. They may also use a more optimistic tone in financial inclusion communications to mask the challenges they are facing in achieving their financial inclusion goals. As a result, the financial inclusion community may not perceive that there are policy challenges in achieving financial inclusion. Advanced LLMs can analyse the tone used to deliver financial inclusion speeches and generate insights about the challenges, intentionality, genuine enthusiasm and other meanings that are usually hidden in the tone used to deliver financial inclusion communications (Long et al, 2024).

3.3. LLMs Can Bring Discipline to Financial Inclusion Communications

LLMs can analyse the intent behind financial inclusion communication and reveal insight that the authorities do not want the public to know. The frequent use of LLMs to analyse the intent behind financial inclusion communication will be a source of discipline to policymakers that make financial inclusion decisions.

LLMs will produce new incentives for policymakers to adopt a more systematic and transparent approach to financial inclusion communication to preserve their own reputation (Alonso-Robisco and Carbó, 2023).

3.4. Improving Financial Inclusion Decision Making

LLMs can assist policymakers to make better informed decisions that improve the financial wellbeing of people. LLMs can quickly process past and present financial inclusion reports and related statistical data to increase policymakers' visibility into overall trends, opinions, common topics discussed, as well as to identify what is working and what is not working, etc. Policymakers can then use these insights to make the most informed financial inclusion decisions based on LLM-assisted data analysis.

3.5. LLMs Enhance Context-Sensitive Text Analysis and Evaluation

LLMs can be used for contextual analysis and evaluation through in-context learning (Hasanbeig et al, 2023). LLMs can be pre-trained on massive amounts of financial inclusion texts and data. The in-context pre-training of LLMs helps to fine-tune the context of text generation and text analysis (Hasanbeig et al, 2023), and it makes LLMs to be context-aware so that it can (i) improve comprehension beyond simple words co-occurrence in financial inclusion speeches, (ii) understand the meanings of words used in financial inclusion contexts, (ii) capture long-range dependencies, (iii) adapt to different financial inclusion problem domains, (iv) and generate texts that make sense in the context of financial inclusion.

4. RISKS OF LLMS FOR FINANCIAL INCLUSION

A major risk is that LLMs can produce biased interpretations and incorrect meanings after analysing financial inclusion speeches or reports. The biased interpretations and incorrect meanings arise because LLMs are trained on data which tend to favour a specific financial inclusion viewpoint or perspective over other perspectives (Prakash and Roy, 2024; Navigli et al, 2023; Qu and Wang, 2024). Such bias can influence how financial inclusion stakeholders perceive and interpret LLM-based financial inclusion communication. Another concern about LLMs is the privacy risks that arise from the collection of data that are used to train large language models (Pan et al, 2020; Das et al, 2025; Rathod et al, 2025). LLMs can collect and retain large amounts of financial inclusion data such as speeches, statistics and comments which are sourced from websites, blogs and user social media interactions on the internet, to learn patterns and generate responses. The concern is that the LLM-assisted data collection process may violate the privacy of individuals because the private data of individuals will be collected, incorporated and retained in LLMs without their explicit consent or awareness (Yan et al, 2024). This would constitute unauthorized access to data and the use of unconsented data which is a data privacy risk (Yao et al, 2024). Another concern is that the use of LLMs to analyse financial inclusion communication may spread misinformation and falsehood (Peng et al, 2024; Garry et al, 2024; Sakib et al, 2025). Since LLMs are good at generating the next best syntactically correct word, LLMs can give a false impression that they understand the actual meaning of the words or texts that are commonly used in the financial inclusion domain. Consequently, LLMs can mislead financial inclusion policymakers and stakeholders into believing that the meanings generated from LLMs are the correct meanings. While LLMs generate responses to financial inclusion questions based on accurate syntactic predictions, they do not produce accurate answers based on an actual understanding of what a financial inclusion stakeholder is asking for. Another risk is that LLMs are not a reliable source of information. It is risky to treat LLMs as a knowledge base or to use it to generate information in response to questions. This is because LLMs pose hallucination risks which is the potential for LLM to generate untruthful responses when the trained data, which the LLM uses to answer questions, do not come from a factually correct source. Therefore, LLMs should not be used as a trusted human-like information source.

5. CONCLUSION

This study identified the benefits and risks of using large language models (LLMs) in the financial inclusion domain. It showed that LLMs can be used to (i) summarize the key themes in financial inclusion communications, (ii) gain insight from the tone of financial inclusion communications, (iii) bring discipline to financial inclusion communications, (iv) improve financial inclusion decision making, and (v) enhance context-sensitive text analysis and evaluation. While large language models have their benefits, they also pose some risks. They can produce biased interpretations and meanings, and they also pose data privacy risks. They also have the potential to generate untruthful responses when the trained data which the LLM uses to answer questions do not come from a factually correct source. For this reason, there is need for caution and discretion when using LLMs to summarise and understand financial inclusion communications. LLMs should not be used to analyse financial inclusion communications in situations where finding the truth is more important than obtaining syntactic accuracy.

Financial inclusion stakeholders should be careful when using LLMs to analyse financial inclusion policy reports or speeches. They should not view LLMs as a trusted human-like information source. Rather, they should view LLM responses like every other information on the internet which must be vetted and its source authenticated. There is also a need to set clear expectations about the contribution of LLMs to the financial inclusion domain. For example, LLMs are very useful in identifying the major themes in financial inclusion speeches but they are terrible in providing information about the actual number of unbanked adults in a location and no amount of LLM data training, re-training or prompt re-contextualisation will be able to generate the actual number of unbanked adults in a location at any time. This example shows the benefits and risks of LLM in the financial inclusion domain. Therefore, it is not a good idea to use LLMs to generate insights in situations where obtaining the truth is important to inform financial inclusion policy decision. Financial inclusion stakeholders should also consider whether there is any meaningful value in using LLMs to analyse financial inclusion communication.

REFERENCES

Aishwaryalaxmi, N. S., & Rathod, P. (2024). Artificial Intelligence (AI) as a Moderating Variable in the Relationship Between Financial Inclusion, Digital Adoption, and Financial Literacy in Developing Economies. In *ITM Web of Conferences* (Vol. 68, p. 01034). EDP Sciences.

Akram, T., Muhammad, N., & RamaKrishnan, S. (2025). How does financial inclusion act as a catalyst for reducing financial crime among women? *Journal of Financial Crime*, *32*(2), 279–287. DOI: 10.1108/JFC-02-2024-0058

Ally, A. M. (2025). Artificial intelligence (AI) and financial technology (FinTech) in Tanzania; legal and regulatory issues. *International Journal of Law and Management*.

Alonso-Robisco, A., & Carbó, J. M. (2023). Analysis of CBDC narrative by central banks using large language models. *Finance Research Letters*, *58*, 104643. DOI: 10.1016/j.frl.2023.104643

Bhawnra, S. X., & Singh, K. B. (2024). Artificial Intelligence for Financial Inclusion in India. *Conversational Artificial Intelligence*, 589-606.

Chadha, A., & Gupta, A. (2024). The Impact of Artificial Intelligence on Financial Inclusion. In *Utilizing Technology for Sustainable Resource Management Solutions* (pp. 180–193). IGI Global. DOI: 10.4018/979-8-3693-2346-5.ch012

Chang, Y., Wang, X., Wang, J., Wu, Y., Yang, L., Zhu, K., Chen, H., Yi, X., Wang, C., Wang, Y., Ye, W., Zhang, Y., Chang, Y., Yu, P. S., Yang, Q., & Xie, X. (2024). A survey on evaluation of large language models. *ACM Transactions on Intelligent Systems and Technology*, *15*(3), 1–45. DOI: 10.1145/3641289

Choudhary, P., Ghosh, C., & Thenmozhi, M. (2025). Impact of fintech and financial inclusion on sustainable development goals: Evidence from cross country analysis. *Finance Research Letters*, *72*, 106573. DOI: 10.1016/j.frl.2024.106573

Das, B. C., Amini, M. H., & Wu, Y. (2025). Security and privacy challenges of large language models: A survey. *ACM Computing Surveys*, *57*(6), 1–39. DOI: 10.1145/3712001

David, P. S., Dheenadhayalan, K., Suson, W. P., Devapitchai, J. J., & Manickam, T. (2025). AI-Powered Financial Inclusion: Bridging the Gap for the Unbanked. In *Utilizing AI and Machine Learning in Financial Analysis* (pp. 449–480). IGI Global Scientific Publishing.

Ding, N., Qin, Y., Yang, G., Wei, F., Yang, Z., Su, Y., Hu, S., Chen, Y., Chan, C. M., Chen, W., Yi, J., Zhao, W., Wang, X., Liu, Z., Zheng, H.-T., Chen, J., Liu, Y., Tang, J., Li, J., & Sun, M. (2023). Parameter-efficient fine-tuning of large-scale pre-trained language models. *Nature Machine Intelligence*, *5*(3), 220–235. DOI: 10.1038/s42256-023-00626-4

Fazal, A., Ahmed, A., & Abbas, S. (2025). Importance of artificial intelligence in achieving sustainable development goals through financial inclusion. *Qualitative Research in Financial Markets*, *17*(2), 432–452. DOI: 10.1108/QRFM-04-2023-0098

Fowowe, B. (2025). Financial inclusion, gender gaps and agricultural productivity in Mali. *Review of Development Economics*, *29*(1), 3–42. DOI: 10.1111/rode.13034

Frost, J., Gambacorta, L., & Shin, H. S. (2021). From financial innovation to inclusion. *Finance & Development*, •••, 14–17.

Garry, M., Chan, W. M., Foster, J., & Henkel, L. A. (2024). Large language models (LLMs) and the institutionalization of misinformation. *Trends in Cognitive Sciences*, *28*(12), 1078–1088. DOI: 10.1016/j.tics.2024.08.007 PMID: 39393958

Hasanbeig, H., Sharma, H., Betthauser, L., Frujeri, F. V., & Momennejad, I. (2023). Allure: A systematic protocol for auditing and improving llm-based evaluation of text using iterative in-context-learning. *arXiv preprint arXiv:2309.13701*.

Hassouba, T. A. (2025). Financial inclusion in Egypt: The road ahead. *Review of Economics and Political Science*, *10*(2), 90–111. DOI: 10.1108/REPS-06-2022-0034

Huang, J., Gu, S. S., Hou, L., Wu, Y., Wang, X., Yu, H., & Han, J. (2022). Large language models can self-improve. *arXiv preprint arXiv:2210.11610*.

Jameel, K., & Janjua, L. R.Dr. Kiran JameelDr Laeeq Razzak Janjua. (2024). Harnessing Artificial Intelligence for Digital Financial Inclusion: Transforming Economies in the Era of Industry 4.0. *The Critical Review of Social Sciences Studies*, *2*(2), 1436–1457. DOI: 10.59075/c00w3s24

Jiang, Z., Xu, F. F., Araki, J., & Neubig, G. (2020). How can we know what language models know? *Transactions of the Association for Computational Linguistics*, *8*, 423–438. DOI: 10.1162/tacl_a_00324

Khan, A. A., Hidthir, M. H. B., Mansur, M., & Ahmad, Z. (2025). Role of financial inclusion in enhancing the effect of remittance on economic growth in developing countries. *Cogent Economics & Finance*, *13*(1), 2476093. DOI: 10.1080/23322039.2025.2476093

Li, Z., Lunku, H. S., & Yang, S. (2025). Financial inclusion in the digital era: A key driver for reducing income inequality. *Technological and Economic Development of Economy*, *31*(3), 1–26. DOI: 10.3846/tede.2025.23068

Long, L., Wang, R., Xiao, R., Zhao, J., Ding, X., Chen, G., & Wang, H. (2024). On llms-driven synthetic data generation, curation, and evaluation: A survey. *arXiv preprint arXiv:2406.15126*. DOI: 10.18653/v1/2024.findings-acl.658

Manoharan, G., & Darwish, D. (2025). Revolutionize the Financial Services: Artificial Intelligence in the Finance Sector. In *Utilizing AI and Machine Learning in Financial Analysis* (pp. 381-402). IGI Global Scientific Publishing, Pennsylvania, USA.

Mhlongo, A. F. (2025). The Impact of Financial Inclusion on Women Entrepreneurship in South Africa. In Moloi, T. (Ed.), *Impacting Society Positively Through Technology in Accounting and Business Processes. ICAB 2024. Springer Proceedings in Business and Economics*. Springer., DOI: 10.1007/978-3-031-84885-8_39

Navigli, R., Conia, S., & Ross, B. (2023). Biases in large language models: Origins, inventory, and discussion. *ACM Journal of Data and Information Quality*, *15*(2), 1–21. DOI: 10.1145/3597307

Neekhara, P., Hussain, S., Ghosh, S., Li, J., Valle, R., Badlani, R., & Ginsburg, B. (2024). Improving robustness of llm-based speech synthesis by learning monotonic alignment. *arXiv preprint arXiv:2406.17957*. DOI: 10.21437/Interspeech.2024-335

Ozili, P. K. (2025a). Effect of CO2 emissions on financial inclusion through physical financial access points. *Management of Environmental Quality*. Advance online publication. DOI: 10.1108/MEQ-11-2024-0518

Ozili, P. K. (2025b). Financial inclusion, religiosity and economic welfare in majority Christian, Hindu and Muslim countries. *foresight*.

Ozili, P. K. (2025c). Artificial Intelligence and Digital Financial Inclusion. In Al-Sartawi, A., & Ghura, H. (Eds.), *Artificial Intelligence, Sustainable Technologies, and Business Innovation: Opportunities and Challenges of Digital Transformation. Studies in Computational Intelligence* (Vol. 1171). Springer., DOI: 10.1007/978-3-031-77925-1_23

Pan, X., Zhang, M., Ji, S., & Yang, M. (2020). Privacy risks of general-purpose language models. In *2020 IEEE Symposium on Security and Privacy (SP)* (pp. 1314-1331). IEEE. DOI: 10.1109/SP40000.2020.00095

Peng, B., Chen, K., Li, M., Feng, P., Bi, Z., Liu, J., & Niu, Q. (2024). Securing large language models: Addressing bias, misinformation, and prompt attacks. *arXiv preprint arXiv:2409.08087*.

Prakash, N., & Roy, L. K. W. (2024). Interpreting Bias in Large Language Models: A Feature-Based Approach. *arXiv preprint arXiv:2406.12347*.

Qu, Y., & Wang, J. (2024). Performance and biases of Large Language Models in public opinion simulation. *Humanities & Social Sciences Communications, 11*(1), 1–13. DOI: 10.1057/s41599-024-03609-x

Rathod, V., Nabavirazavi, S., Zad, S., & Iyengar, S. S. (2025, January). Privacy and security challenges in large language models. In *2025 IEEE 15th Annual Computing and Communication Workshop and Conference (CCWC)* (pp. 00746-00752). IEEE. DOI: 10.1109/CCWC62904.2025.10903912

Rehman, K. U., & Chen, R. (2025). The nexus between financial inclusion and energy efficiency in developed countries. *Quality & Quantity*, •••, 1–32. DOI: 10.1007/s11135-025-02139-1

Sakib, S. K., Das, A. B., & Ahmed, S. (2025). Battling misinformation: An empirical study on adversarial factuality in open-source large language models. *arXiv preprint arXiv:2503.10690*. DOI: 10.18653/v1/2025.trustnlp-main.28

Sarma, M., & Pais, J. (2011). Financial inclusion and development. *Journal of International Development, 23*(5), 613–628. DOI: 10.1002/jid.1698

Saxena, A., & Rishi, B. (2025). Designing an artificial intelligence-enabled large language model for financial decisions. *Management Decision*. Advance online publication. DOI: 10.1108/MD-02-2024-0305

Sebai, M., Talbi, O., & Guerchi-Mehri, H. (2025). Optimal financial inclusion for financial stability: Empirical insight from developing countries. *Finance Research Letters, 71*, 106467. DOI: 10.1016/j.frl.2024.106467

Singh, C. (2025). Is generative AI (artificial intelligence) the next advent in the evolution of finance and navigating financial crime and regulation? *Journal of Financial Crime, 32*(3), 751–759. DOI: 10.1108/JFC-07-2024-0232

Subramaniam, Y., Loganathan, N., Khan, F. N. H. T., & Subramaniam, T. (2024). Exploring the Impact of Artificial Intelligence on Financial Inclusion: Cross-Country Analysis. *Social Indicators Research*, •••, 1–18. DOI: 10.1007/s11205-024-03380-1

Thuraisamy, K. S., Baig, Z., & Zeadally, S. (2025). Generative Artificial Intelligence in Financial Services: Opportunities, Challenges, and Cyberthreats. *IT Professional, 27*(2), 35–41. DOI: 10.1109/MITP.2025.3534270

Wei, F., Xie, B., & Chen, M. (2025). Digital financial inclusion, e-commerce development and entrepreneurial activity. *International Review of Financial Analysis*, *97*, 103806. DOI: 10.1016/j.irfa.2024.103806

Wu, L., Zheng, Z., Qiu, Z., Wang, H., Gu, H., Shen, T., Qin, C., Zhu, C., Zhu, H., Liu, Q., Xiong, H., & Chen, E. (2024). A survey on large language models for recommendation. *World Wide Web (Bussum)*, *27*(5), 60. DOI: 10.1007/s11280-024-01291-2

Yan, B., Li, K., Xu, M., Dong, Y., Zhang, Y., Ren, Z., & Cheng, X. (2024). On protecting the data privacy of large language models (llms): A survey. *arXiv preprint arXiv:2403.05156*.

Yang, Q., & Lee, Y. C. (2024). Ethical AI in financial inclusion: The role of algorithmic fairness on user satisfaction and recommendation. *Big Data and Cognitive Computing*, *8*(9), 105. DOI: 10.3390/bdcc8090105

Yao, Y., Duan, J., Xu, K., Cai, Y., Sun, Z., & Zhang, Y. (2024). A survey on large language model (llm) security and privacy: The good, the bad, and the ugly. *High-Confidence Computing*, *4*(2), 100211. DOI: 10.1016/j.hcc.2024.100211

Yoo, K. M., Park, D., Kang, J., Lee, S. W., & Park, W. (2021). Gpt3mix: Leveraging large-scale language models for text augmentation. *arXiv preprint arXiv:2104.08826*. DOI: 10.18653/v1/2021.findings-emnlp.192

Chapter 11 Automated Sentiment Polarity Detection in Financial News Using Machine Learning and Pre-Trained Models: Sentiment Polarity Detection

M. Murali
https://orcid.org/0000-0002-4478-2820
SRM Institute of Science and Technology, India

ABSTRACT

The proliferation of text in social media platforms paving the way for the people to express their opinions on online platforms. The huge volume of these opinions requires automated processing. The purpose of this paper is to classify sentiment polarity of financial news articles. The financial news dataset is taken from Kaggle repository for experimental purpose. We import the financial sentiment analysis comments from the Kaggle repository, which contains 5842 sentences with labels. The sentences are labelled as positive (1852), negative (860) and neutral (3130). By using machine learning classifiers, we used the dataset for sentiment polarity classification purpose. Results obtained from the experiments proved that the CatBoost is superior to the other classifiers in terms of performance metrics. In addition to this, experiments were conducted with deep learning pre-trained models such RoBERTa, BERT and FinancialBERT also. The performance metrics are tabulated and shown in the figure. Based on the metrics, RoBERTa is showing superior performance than other models.

DOI: 10.4018/979-8-3373-1250-7.ch011

1. INTRODUCTION

In the last decade, social networks have produced an enormous amount of data through comments and reviews. Business organizations have adapted to these digital contents on online platforms for various activities, including communication, banking, and shopping. This is widely accepted as digital transformation during this period. Furthermore, the shift to online platforms provides convenience and flexibility, especially during the COVID-19 pandemic. Social networks enable people to connect and share the opinions and thoughts. The financial sector is adaptive to these technological developments and to satisfy the customer demands. In the recent decade, the financial sector has experienced a transformative shift by integrating artificial intelligence and machine learning algorithms. The fintech market has grown significantly, driven by new technological advancements. In financial sector sentiment analysis is used as a tool to understand the market and predict future trends. Sentiment analysis can provide insights into the market and support decision-making. With rapid advancements in Natural Language Processing, these techniques are being applied across various domains. Deep learning models, such as BERT (Bidirectional Encoder Representations from Transformers), have improved the accuracy of sentiment polarity classification. Despite advancements in the financial domain, there are still challenges in sentiment analysis. Sentiment analysis is lacking to adjust the output to the use-case context and applicability also limited. Moreover, it often fails to capture contextual nuances, though it can still provide accurate sentiment analysis in certain contexts.

Numerous research involves sentiment analysis using Natural Language Processing (NLP) to improve the efficiency of the sentiment polarity classification. Traditional NLP models having some constraints due to lack of capability to understand the financial terms which limits the outcome of the NLP models. In recent period lots of research has been carried out by analysing unstructured text through different machine learning and deep learning algorithms. Sentiment analysis analyses users' emotions and opinions towards services or products offered by the financial institutions. In financial institutions customers services are playing vital role. The importance of customers feedback arises to enhance the quality of service and foster the growth of products, when the user reviews emerged. The financial sentiment analysis investigates investor emotions or opinions is an important area for sentiment analysis. When individuals involved in financial market, analysing the market is essential for financial decisions. To face the challenges in financial market an automated sentiment analysis is very much helpful for the investors. The financial sentiment analysis becomes an efficient tool not only for decision making but also for financial forecasting. In a dynamically changing market environment, the processing of every piece of text is deemed important for financial decision making. The examples are stock price prediction, credit worth, market volatility, foreign exchange rate prediction, customer satisfaction towards a product or service offered by the financial institution etc., Ultimately, the importance of using sentiment analysis pertaining to financial domain data is useful for customers. Any inaccurate results obtained from financial sentiment analysis will lead to severe financial loss to the users. The findings require careful evaluation with caution in financial domain, since the decisions will impact the market and the investments (Irfan, 2021), (Irfan, Elhoseny, Kassim, & Metawa, 2023).

The social network users generate huge amount of data consists of huge number of writings in the form of text. This huge data from social networks is an emerging area for research. In recent period numerous research was conducted in the financial sentiment analysis, to extract the emotions and feelings of the individual on financial related products or services. It uses statistical methods with Artificial Intelligence techniques from a large size data. The aim of this paper is the polarity analysis, which can classify the text as positive, neutral or negative in financial domain. It involves few challenges. First, the classifiers require considerable amount of labelled data. Second, the sentiment analysis model should not be trained on ordinary comments because financial texts may contain unique terms and expressions. The machine learning is the advanced technology and is the subset of Artificial Intelligence, offering solutions to the emerging problems. The usage of machine learning makes it possible to apply in different fields like machine translation, cyber security, computer vision, sentiment analysis etc., Among these, sentiment analysis is also known as opinion mining that can evaluate the polarity in the text to extract the emotions and feelings from the data (Irfan, Elmogy, Majid, & El-Sappagh, 2023), (Irfan, Kadry, Sharif, & Ullah Khan, 2023). Really it is challenging task to determine the user emotions using a piece of text. Moreover, it is important to assess the emotions expressed in social media in terms of comments for taking financial decisions. Further, the sentiment analysis can be done in three ways: aspect level, sentence level, document level. With the increase of social media users, thoughts and emotions about various items like financial products and services, becomes possible to analyse these comments and reviews.

It is very challenging for an investor to analyse a company's performance using financial indicators. An investor is always looking for performance measures and assess the polarity of financial news and taking investment decisions. Therefore, we use the financial performance indicators may help to find the polarity of financial news. The aim is to examine the performance indicators to classify polarity in financial news. It is more useful and aligned with the way that humans are expressing through unstructured texts while taking financial decisions. So, in this work, we analyse machine learning based methods to perform polarity classification of financial news, based on financial indicators and conduct experiments to measure its usefulness. In this work, we concentrate on two areas mainly, first is to use the performance indicators to predict polarity of financial news. Second, the paper presents a machine learning based sentiment classifier model. The performance of the machine learning models is evaluated on a financial news dataset, which is available on Kaggle repository. The best machine learning model is compared against other methods to prove the effectiveness.

Financial sentiment analysis involves extracting sentiments from texts like articles, social media contents facing challenges. Financial texts contain domain-specific terms, making it difficult to interpret accurately. Few words may give different meanings in financial context. For example, 'bullish' word refers to optimistic term whereas 'bearish' is pessimistic term. Moreover, labeled datasets are very limited in financial sentiments compared to general sentiments. In financial domain sentiment is time sensitive. A sentence may give different meaning due to unexpected events like market crashes. Financial sentiment analysis must integrate data from different sources like social media, news and stock price movements may have different formats. In social media financial texts may contain rumours, fake news, which can mislead sentiment analysis function. Moreover, classifying sentiments as positive or negative does not correlate stock market movements.

Bag of Words (BoW) and Term Frequency-Inverse Document Frequency (TF-IDF) are text representation methods used in financial sentiment analysis. BoW is a simple approach, in which text is represented as a vector, but grammar is ignored. It depends on the occurrence of words in the document. BoW can identify the financial related terms like "profit"," loss" (Irfan, Hussainey, Chan Bukhari, & Nam, 2024), (Irfan, Elmogy, Gupta, Khalifa, & Dias, 2024). It allows for preprocessing and well-suited for financial models. BoW can convert unstructured text into structured data, which enable the users to apply machine learning algorithms. But it is not able to capture negative statements like "not a good quarter". When it is applied with large size datasets, it can create high-dimensional vectors, leading to sparsity. All words are given equal importance, failing to reflect their importance. TF-IDF is based on words weights, gives importance in a document. TF-IDF reduces the financial jargons and gives importance to sentiment words like "unexpected loss". Words frequently used in a corpus, but less frequent in a document is down weighted. TF-IDF representations can improve predictive performance in sentiment classification tasks.

Data imbalance in financial sentiment data is crucial for accurate predictions, where distributions of classes are skewed. SMOTE (Synthetic Minority Oversampling Techniques) is a technique applied to mitigate the imbalance. SMOTE can manage the class distributions by creating synthetic examples of the minority class. This is done by interpolation between a sample in the minority class and the k-nearest neighbours. First, we need to select samples from the minority class, then find the k-nearest neighbours within the minority class applying Euclidean distance measure.

Now, we can create a synthetic sample by applying linear interpolation between the sample and the neighbour. Then add the synthetic samples to the dataset, becomes balanced class distribution.

2. BACKGROUND

In this paper, (Matteo et al., 2023) the authors proposed a model using RoBERTa to predict financial aspect classes and polarities at the original level. They used financial question-answering data, focusing specifically on aspect-based tasks. They used hierarchical structure by using the parent aspect class predictions. They implemented a model for class prediction and polarity analysis. As a result, the F1 score increased by 7.6% with the proposed model. In (Tobias, 2021) authors proposed a method to capture sentiments and contextual details. This proposed method improved the performance by 15%. This work explores implicit sentiments and relationships for sentiment polarity prediction in analyst reports, news, and microblogs. In (Sergio et al., 2022), the authors proposed a methodology for fine-grained, aspect-based sentiment analysis. The aim of this work is to identify the sentiment in the sentence of the document and assign the polarity scores. This is an unsupervised approach in the financial domain. The proposed method produced results with sentiment scores close to human annotations, outperforming existing methods. In this paper (Bo et al., 2024), authors proposed Supervised Cross-Momentum Contrast framework for sentiment analysis. This method outperformed than existing PLM based and LLM models on benchmark datasets. In (Wei & Li-Chuan, 2024), the authors attempted to identify sentiment using a categorical approach.

This method represents affective states and several discrete classes. This method is implemented with domain adaptation methods to enhance sentiment analysis. Experiments conducted on finance domain proved that the proposed method outperformed, and best performance is achieved using domain adaptation method. In this work (Anita et al., 2020), authors determined the sentiment strength from text. This paper focused on the application of sentiment analysis in financial news. The semantic orientation is measured by using machine learning techniques and obtained best results. In (Handan et al. 2024) this paper, authors presented sentiment analysis framework in Turkish to evaluate the public opinion for stock market. This work is based on financial-related tweets entered in Turkish. Authors used positive and negative to implement the classification framework with various machine learning classifiers. Results obtained from the experiments shown SVM and multilayer perceptron proved best than other classifiers by means of accuracy 0.89 and 0.88 respectively. In this paper (Georgios et al., 2023), authors employed zero-shot approach. They investigated ChatGPT on data containing news headlines related to finance. Further, performance was evaluated using precision, recall, F1-score and mean absolute error of the sentiment class. In addition to this performance was enhanced in sentiment classification with 36% correlation.

In paper (Xiang et al., 2024), authors used adaptive lasso, elastic net, artificial neural network (ANN), convolutional neural network (CNN), and long short-term memory (LSTM) predictive models. By introducing these models, which enhances the dynamics within the financial markets. The LSTM model has shown better accuracy in prediction compared to Enet, ANN, A Lasso and CNN. In paper (Junaid et al., 2023), Authors used three algorithms to compute sentiment scores for different combinations of stock price and the sentiment score. Extensive Experiments were conducted on stock price data and financial news of various companies to predict the stock trends. The model achieved highest accuracy of 0.9. In this paper (Margaret & Joy, 2024) feature extraction was done from the input data. Further, authors analysed current and forecast data. This price index details are sent to the investors. In this work authors used machine learning techniques for stock price forecasting with high accuracy. Sentiment analysis is playing vital role in creating financial analysis. Sentiment analysis is classified into two types (Maite et al., 2011): 1. Lexicon-based 2. Machine learning based. The lexicon-based uses a dictionary or lexicon for a document, which contains polarity of words (Turney & Littman, 2002). This can be done automatically or manually (Qiang et al., 2009). This type of lexicon uses dictionary, which contains information about words, polarity tags. In Semi-automatic method, WordNet is used. It involves a supervised learning and building classifiers from the labels (Stone et al., 1967). SVM, naïve bayes and n-grams are frequently used techniques for sentiment classification (Alistair & Diana, 2006).

In (Rashid et al., 2024) this paper authors discussed about adversarial attack detection for sentiment analysis. They developed a CNN model for sentiment classification using IMDB dataset. The CNN model outperformed than the other baseline models with 97% accuracy. In this paper (Alfredo et al., 2024) authors conducted a complete analysis of the relevant works to provide knowledge of existing works on ecommerce products by using sentiment analysis. The analysis was used to obtain clarity, and six items were selected to get more details. In this work machine learning methods used to evaluate the performance of the model in sentiment analysis. In this work (Abdulfattah & Ferhat, 2024) authors presented a hybrid BERT-LSTM-CNN model. Authors combined the CNN and Bidirectional LSTM architectures utilizing natural language processing techniques and other models like BERT based transformers to classify the tweets into relevant categories. The suggested method BERT-BiLSTM-CNN having three CNN branches with concatenation layer, effective feature extraction. The model outperformed existing models with 91% accuracy.

3. OTHER SENTIMENT ANALYSIS METHODS

3.1 Cohesion-Based Approach

A cohesion-based text representation was constructed for story comparison. This approach used a graph representation derived from POS tags, utilizing WordNet to mitigate loss during transition. This method is built using lexical cohesion (Halliday & Ruqaiya, 1976). The purpose of cohesive approach is to capture the text, which will combine the information of wordnet semantic content and text. The nodes are derived from text and relations are in wordnet to represent adjacency in text. It also provides a mechanism to control the semantic content interpretation using topological structures. WordNet's contribution is evaluated by a node-specific metric based on empirical analysis of topological structures. The metric is used to highlight the knowledge bases. At different levels polarity classification can be done such as word, sentence and document. In this work polarity classification is done at the sentence level. The aim is to classify the financial data into positive or negative. Investment decision is taken based on the financial news, which can be used to help the investors. So, the financial news can be classified by the sentiment analyser and is used as investment tool to the investors.

3.2 Sentiment Polarity Overlay

For sentiment analysis, dimension can be overlaid explicitly in text by existing lexical resources. In this approach, polarity measurement is based on a lexicon of tagged positive and negative terms to identify positive or negative Originals. This method is based on WordNet and is integrated with a text representation method where nodes can carry sentiment values. The nodes are used to measure the polarity of text and wordnet semantic structures in the text. Three measures are used for evaluation. First measure is Basic cohesion metric, which is used to find polarity of all nodes in the graph. Second measure is Relation type metric, which is applied in the text-driven graph. In this method basic metric is modified and the sentiment value is product of polarity value. In this overlay method the relations are considered as relevant nodes and represent a relation, antonymy and organising principles of database. Third measure is Node specificity metric, which is used to measure node specificity. This measure is based on topological features of wordnet. The assumption behind this method to carry more information, affective content is less specific. Since the internal structure of knowledge base is not homogeneous, it is very difficult to use. The specificity is applied to factor out population sparseness by the contribution of nodes and its connectivity. The main purpose is to find the link between financial market and news pertaining to finance. The data is provided by finance domain to analyse the sentiment polarity in the financial news. For analysis, variables of the financial markets help to measure the polarity. The first step is to establish the reliability of sentiment measure of financial news. In literature most of the work focused on short segments (Wilson et al.,2005) like movie reviews. All news items are expressing the sentiment. Thus, the financial news is selected to test the hypothesis, to have emotional content.

3.3 Sentiment Analysis: General

Sentiment analysis is a subdomain of natural language processing. Its goal is to extract sentiments from source data, and it is applied across various domains. It is applied in different domains. In earlier days, sentiment and reviews classification was done by the researchers. In (Turney, 2002), the author classified reviews, considering semantic orientation. In (Hu & Liu, 2004) authors presented the summary of multiple product reviews and services. Document-level sentiments were analysed using machine learning algorithms (Habernal et al., 2014). The database contained online movies, product reviews and Facebook postings. The purpose of the research work was to extend to Czech language. Different works on sentiment analysis was done on other languages (Molina-Gonzalez et al., 2015). Authors conducted automatic analysis of electoral tweets on (Mohammad et al., 2015) Election tweets relating to US election in 2012 was annotated automatically with different attributes including emotion and sentiment. Automatic classification was done for unseen tweets to predict emotions and labels. For polarity shift problem, a model was developed at document level (Xia et al., 2016). In (Fersini et al., 2016) authors discussed about polarity classification in microblogs using feature space by applying ensemble classifiers.

3.4 Sentiment Analysis: News Articles

In general, sentiment analysis is applied to predict stock market, investment etc., Due to the drastic increase of sentiment analysis usage in different domains has proved that the sentiments of financial resources can increase the prediction accuracy, resulting in reduction of risk in investment. So, this is necessary to find out the relationship between stock market and financial news articles. In this paper (Azar, 2009), author explained the relationship between financial news and market figures. The aim of this research is to find out, whether really sentiments in financial news create impact in stock market. In this work, author made a comparison between different methods to the sentiment classification of financial texts. Further, author proved that sentiment polarities of financial news is suitable one to predict returns. In paper (Li et al., 2014) authors have constructed a framework to predict stock price using financial news articles. Thus, prediction accuracy was improved by using sentiment analysis. In paper (Kauter et al., 2015) authors discussed about company sentiment analysis using financial news text. They conduct research to give importance about implicit and explicit sentiment analysis. In (Foroozan et al., 2015) authors discussed about sentiment classification by using N-gram and feature weighting methods. Hierarchical classification method was suggested by authors (Li et al., 2015) to perform on training dataset. Further, researchers focused on detecting negation scope.

3.5 Sentiment Similarity

To measure the semantic relatedness between two words, semantic similarity is used in different areas. The distance between two words is measured by using knowledge from lexical resource like dictionaries (Liu et al., 2011). One of the popular semantic networks is Wordnet, which is used to measure the distance between two words. It has been modelled to simulate the human recognition. Most of work related to semantic similarity is based on wordnet. There are different methods are used in word net for semantic similarity. This can be classified into three types: 1. Node-base 2. Edge-based 3. Hybrid method. Node based method works based on information content available in nodes to evaluate the semantic similarity between two words. In paper (Lin, 1998) authors applied mathematical equations to find out the similarity between two words.

Edge-based method using shortest path to calculate the similarity between words. In paper (Hirst & St-Onge, 1998) authors used the path between two words to calculate the semantic similarity. In another paper (Leacock & Chodorow, 1998) authors used the length of the path between words to find the similarity. In hybrid method information from various sources are used to evaluate the semantic similarity between two words. Most of the researchers used the Lesk algorithm (Lesk, 1986) to find the semantic similarity. This algorithm is applied based on the similarity between word is relative to the extent of the overlaps. In another work (Jiang & Conrath, 1997) authors measured the length of edges in the path between two words to find the semantic similarity. Wordnet is useful to obtain the information to measure the edge length. Various other techniques are available to calculate the semantic similarity, but they did not use Wordnet. In paper (Jiang et al., 2014) applied link weight method to calculate the information distance similarity. In another work by (Lee et al., 2014) applied a sentence level similarity algorithm, they used grammatical rules to find the overlap between sentences. The performance of this algorithm is better than the other algorithm in sentences. In literature semantic similarity method was used by lexical based sentiment analyser to calculate the polarity classification.

This method is useful to find the performances of wordnet based semantic similarity methods in the financial news polarity classification.

3.6 Baseline Sentiment Analyser

In paper (Klenner et al., 2009) authors explained sentence level sentiment classification by using sentiment composition. In this work, authors modified the algorithm to classify sentiments at document level. But they changed the original words to lemma representation. They also added sentiment composition rules. In paper (Kong & Smith, 1994) authors classified the news into positive and negative. Prior polarity lexicon was used for polarity tagging task. To find the polarity at sentence level, set of rules was created. The rules are basic processing rules, noun phrase composition, phrase-phrase composition rules and negation rules. From the financial news, polarity of the sentiment is calculated as positive and negative. The result in this work is to classify the news as positive or negative.

3.7 Phrase Extraction and Polarity identification

In the baseline sentiment analyser, phrases are extracted from news articles and spitted into sentences. Then parsing is done as per the POS tags using RNN parser combined with lemma representation. Among various data representations, RNN parser was superior to the other combinations. The parsed text is obtained after polarity tagging and lexicon matching. In this paper (Wilson et al., 2005) authors mentioned words in the lexicon are pre-polarity tagged and further used for polarity classification. In the lexicon, matched word can be found then the polarity is tagged. Polarity detection consists of lexicon matching and polarity tagging. The polarity detection is used to find the polarity identification from the given text.

Sentiment composition rules can be applied in polarity identification. The rules are framed to generate output from phrase extraction stage, which is already POS tagged. The rule sequence is significant to produce the correct meaning of the sentence. The polarity identification is over when the rules are used to extract phrase with its polarity. At this point we can calculate the sentiment value for the whole document by using formula called positive and negative ratio. It considers the number of positive and negative sentences then average of the sentiment values of all sentences in the news article. The financial news can be classified based on overall value using positive and negative ratio. Where 1 is positive and -1 indicates as negative sentiment value of the financial news. If the result is 0, it indicates there is no sentiment in the sentence. Thus the 0 is not considered to classify the news as positive or negative.

3.8 Semantic Similarity Techniques

Three similarity techniques are discussed here – which HSO (edge-base), LESK (node-based) and LIN (hybrid)(Tan et al., 2018). These methos used to perform semantic similarity. All three methods use the wordnet as knowledge base. HSO was proposed by Hirst & St-Onge, (1998), which used the path to calculate the semantic similarity between two words. The idea behind this method is both words are connected using a path won't change the direction. So, they are identified as semantically similar words. In HSO, the similarity is measured, based on the path weight and the length of the path between word1 and word2. In LESK method, semantic similarity is measured based on the dictionary definition. Wordnet is used in this method. This method is used to calculate the semantic similarity, which lies between 0 and the infinity. In LIN method, a mathematical formula is used to measure the semantic similarity between two words, which represents the lowest common subsume between two words. This lowest common subsume is derived from the lexical taxonomy of wordnet. It is used to find out the two words word1 and word2 belong. The semantic similarity values between 0 and 1.

To evaluate the three metrics 260 manually annotated words as positive and negative were given as input (Tan et al., 2018). The results showed that the sentiment similarity is high then the polarity is also high. Using a set of words, performance of all three metrics was analysed. The performance metrics are tabulated and shown in Figure 1. It is shown in the figure 1 that the HSO is better than other two metrics. HSO can find 222 words, LESK can find 228 and LIN can find 154 words. Since HSO method is good precision, HSO is considered as a best performance.

Table 1. Precision scores and metrics at 0-100% of recall

Recall	Precision score		
	LIN	HSO	LESK
0	100.00	100.00	100.00
10	81.45	95.65	91.77
20	87.75	91.21	89.68
30	92.78	92.64	91.53
40	94.64	94.35	91.60
50	95.55	95.43	91.58
60	89.51	95.45	91.47
70	89.87	94.28	90.90
80	89.28	94.45	91.94

continued on following page

Table 1. Continued

Recall	Precision score		
	LIN	HSO	LESK
90	84.17	93.60	91.85
100	82.39	91.90	92.73

Figure 1. Precision vs Recall – semantic similarity score

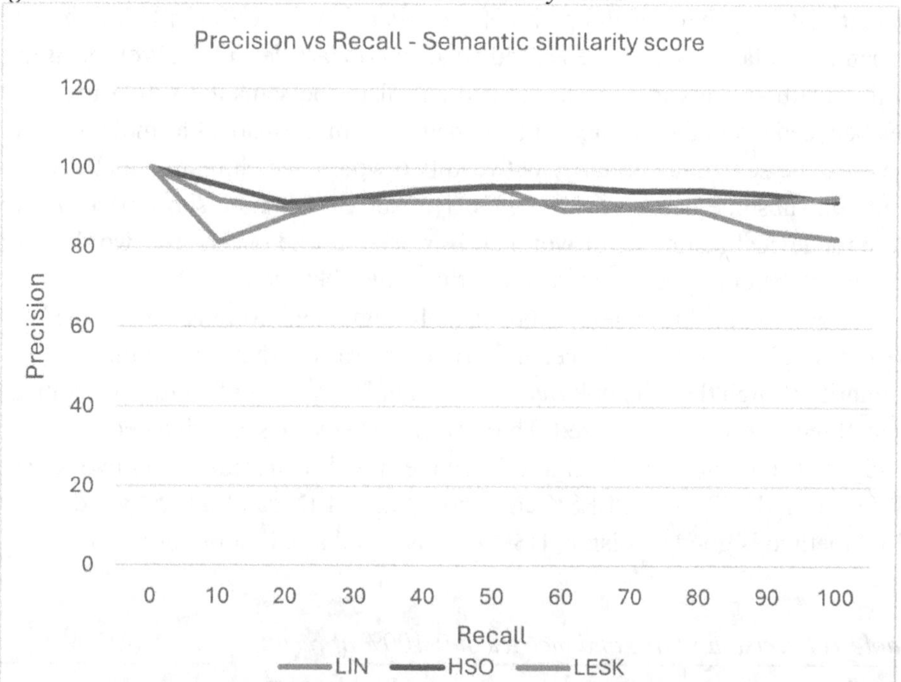

The LIN measure did not show better performance compared to the other two measures. This limitation is evident as input words, such as adjectives and adverbs, are rejected. Moreover, the number of matched pairs for the input words is limited. This impacts the likelihood of input words matching with other words having similar POS tags, thereby reducing the chance of detecting similarity. The LM dictionary is also used in the domain-specific lexicon, which includes another category of words. Words with polarity are also included, as mentioned in the dictionary. This dictionary plays a role in the domain-specific lexicon, incorporating words with polarity as defined within it.

3.9 Polarity Classification With POS Tagging

The main purpose to classify the financial text as positive or negative. First, input data is given as a set of financial news. The tags are identified, and class label is added to the set of items. From the frequent item sets association rules can be mined with rule may contain one item and a class label. In the rule antecedent may have any number of items. Then rules are generated for frequent item sets. A set of association rules are mined from the news is given below. From the association rules, support, confidence and antecedent length can be drawn.

Association rules:
LagInd neutral
POS neutral
UP, POS neutral
LagInd::DOWN negative
LagInd::UP positive
LeadInd::UP positive
UP neutral

3.10 Sentiment Prediction Using POS Tag

The rules derived can be used as a model to classify the polarity of the sentence. When a new sentence is given, the model will work as follows. The sentence is tagged with performance indicators and finance related sentiment words. The rules are looked for tagged words. Each rule is available in the rule base. The rules and tagged words are matched. Then the matching score will be assigned for matching pair. In some cases, multiple rules may be available with more than one class label may present to match tagged words. This process is continued for all rule in the rule base. At the end score will be generated for each label. The final predicted class is identified based on the class with high score. Example: Kone 's net sales rose by some 14% year-on-year in the first nine months of 2008.

The polarity classification procedure is applied for the above sentence. In the above sentence, parsing and dictionary look is done, then the sentence will be tagged as LagInd:UP. By looking up the tag, class label is added by using rules. The rule is matching the sentence is LagInd:UP -> Positive(16.67). The correct class label for the sentence is Positive. Any other rules matching the class labels, in that case n scores are generated for each label. If any other rules matching the class labels, then scores generated for each label. If none of the rules is matching the sentence, the Neutral is assigned as prediction.

The polarity classification is describing as multi-class problem. In financial analysis news, the number of samples in each category is likely to be imbalanced. In most of the cases, we may a greater number of neural sentences than positive or negative sentences in the financial news. This class imbalance problem in the text is observed in the annotated dataset in the literature. The dataset may contain 53% neutral, and 12-14% negative samples (Huang et al., 2014; Malo et al., 2014). To solve the class imbalance problem, hierarchical sentiment classifier is applied. In this hierarchical sentiment classification, each sentence is polarized or neutral. Next stage, polarized sentence is further classified as positive or negative.

4. MATERIALS AND METHODS

4.1 Dataset Used

The financial news dataset (Malo et al., 2014) is sourced from the Kaggle repository for experimental purposes. The dataset contains 5,842 sentences with labels. The sentences are labeled as positive (1852), negative (860) and neutral (3130). The dataset was labelled as positive, neutral and negative by experts in finance. In the dataset, few sentences may be repeated with different annotation. These problems may arise from the sentiment score calculation, which is rounded to -1, 0, 1. To solve this problem dataset is pre-processed to remove the repeated entries. The sentence distribution in the dataset is presented into three classes. The total number of sentences in each category is evenly distributed. The sentences are labelled as neutral, which is greater than the other classes, is found in the dataset. Moreover, no imbalance problem arises due to class distribution in the dataset.

4.2 Pre-Processing

Data pre-processing is an important phase in sentiment analysis, as it provides the necessary structure for applying machine learning algorithms. It consists of following steps:

Duplicate Removal: duplicate news Originals with differing sentiment values are removed.
Tokenization: Whole sentence is divided into sequence of words.
Stop Word Removal: Removing stop words is a common step in text pre-processing.
Lemmatization and Stemming: Both techniques are applied to normalize the text.

Lowercase Conversion: This standard text normalization method helps maintain consistency in meaning.

4.3 Machine Learning Models

- **CatBoost** is an open-source library developed by Yandex and is a variant of the gradient boosting model. Catboost is capable of handling categorical and numerical values. CatBoost does not require an encoding mechanism. It employs symmetric weighted quantile sketch algorithm, which can handle missing values, reduce overfitting and enhance the performance of the dataset.
- **Logistic regression** is applied to classification tasks. The goal of logistic regression is to predict the probability that a data point belongs to a particular class. It is a statistical algorithm that can analyze the relationship between data points. This algorithm uses sigmoid function that takes input data and produces probability value between 0 and 1.
- **Support Vector Machine** (SVM) is a machine learning algorithm used for linear and nonlinear classification. It is effective and to find the maximum separating hyperplane between the different classes in the target feature.
- **Ridge regression** is a variant of linear regression, adding a regularization term to fit the data while keeping the weights as low as possible.
- The **Naive Bayes algorithm** is based on Bayes' Theorem and is a simple yet effective classification algorithm. It aids in developing machine learning models with fast prediction capabilities.

In this work, machine learning models were trained and evaluated. After preprocessing, we can test machine learning models with either Bag of Words (BoW) or Term Frequency-Inverse Document Frequency (TF-IDF) weighting. Bag of Words constructs a vector by counting the occurrences of each word in a document. BoW representation is created by compiling unique words across documents. Each document is visualized as vector in this method and its dimension is corresponding to a word. The value appears in the matrix signifies that the word, number of times occurring in the document. This results in sparse representation of data, used to represent the number of times the word appears in a document. TF-IDF is the product of two measures: Term Frequency (TF) and Inverse Document Frequency (IDF), which together indicate a word's significance within a document. IDF is used to measure the rarity of the term in the document. TF-IDF is a numerical value representing a document through the TF-IDF scores of its words. Both Bow and TF-IDF having some merits and demerits. Bow method is easy, it represents the counts only. But it does not reveal the semantics of words in a document, whereas TF-IDF used to understand the importance of words in a document and reflects the context and significance of words. But intensive calculation is required compared to BoW method. Both methods ignore the word order in documents, which may lead to a loss of context.

Synthetic Minority Over-sampling Technique (SMOTE) is a machine learning method designed to alleviate the class imbalance problem by generating artificial data. By introducing SMOTE in the dataset, which improves the learning ability of machine learning models. Machine Learning models can easily handle imbalanced data, and overall accuracy can be improved. Specifically, SMOTE technique can be applied in sentiment analysis problem. To improve the classification accuracy of, meta-ensemble machine learning model can be constructed by combining at least three models.

4.4 Deep Learning: Pre-Trained Models

BERT (Bidirectional Encoder Representations from Transformers)

BERT (Devlin et al., 2018) is a pre-trained model that leverages the Transformer architecture (Vaswani et al., 2017). BERT model can capture the context of the words and its relationship. This is mainly used in NLP tasks such Question Answering system, Text classification etc. The model considers both side of the context of a word, then determines the meaning. The BERT model contains 12 layers, 768 hidden states and 12 attention mechanisms and 110 mission trainable parameters. We can capture the linguistic relationships by using BERT model.

RoBERTa (A Robustly Optimized BERT Pretraining Approach)

RoBERTa (Yinhan et al., 2019), is one of the advanced language representation models that evolved from the BERT model. It involves training duration, exposure to an augmented training dataset, heightened batch size, and the incorporation of longer sequences. RoBERTa is giving better performance than BERT, across various NLP benchmarks,

Financial BERT Models

FinBERT models also language representation models, which was built on the top of BERT model. These FinBERT models are trained to analyse and comprehend financial data relating to financial markets and financial news. The objective is to evaluate sentiment from financial text. The functionality is like BERT, the training process includes an initial pre-training phase. In this phase, the model acquires language representations by processing financial text data. The pre-training is used to capture the language patterns and financial terminology relevant to the domain. FinBERT can be finetuned, and it can focus on financial sentiment analysis tasks. Fine-tune the model to work on specific datasets, which contains labels, and the performance can be improved. The FinBERT pre-trained model from Araci (Araci, 2019), applied on Reurers dataset TRC2. It was evaluated on FiQA sentiment datasets. The sentiment values range from -1 to 1. The model outperforms the other models in terms of accuracy, F1 score. Another FinBERT model was introduced by (DeSola, 2019) with three variants. In Hugging face repository, several FinBERT models are available.

1. BERT
2. RoBERTa (Liu et al., 2019)
3. FinBERT Araci Model (Araci, 2019)
4. FinBERT (Yang et al., 2020)
5. FinancialBERT (Huang et al., 2022)

Metrics

In the literature, most of the work on sentiment analysis treats it as a classification problem and uses metrics such as accuracy, recall, precision, and F1-score.

Accuracy

Accuracy measures the proportion of correctly classified predictions out of all predictions.

$$Accuracy = \frac{TP + TN}{TP + TN + FP + FN} \quad (1)$$

Accuracy is easy to explain the model performance in classifying the instances. It can mislead when it is calculated on imbalanced datasets.

Recall

Recall is the ratio of positive predictions to the actual positive ones. The mathematical formula for computing Recall is:

$$Recall = \frac{TP}{TP + FN} \quad (2)$$

Recall emphasizes the identification of positive instances. It is useful for assessing the cost of missing positive instances and the impact of misclassifying positive data as negative. Recall measure indicates the model's efficiency to capture the minority classes. It can be used with other metrics such as precision or F1 score to obtain accurate evaluation.

Precision

Precision indicates the ratio of true positive predictions to all positive predictions made by the model. The formula is:

$$Precision = \frac{TP}{TP + FP} \quad (3)$$

It focuses on the positive predictions. When it is combined with recall, can give better predictions. If the precision is high and the recall is low, indicates that the model is cautious.

F1 Score

The F1 score is the harmonic mean of recall and precision, used to balance these two metrics. The formula for F1 score is:

$$F1\ score = 2\,x\,\frac{Precision * Recall}{Precision + Recall} \quad (4)$$

F1 score is more useful than accuracy, if the dataset is imbalanced. It provides the model's ability to classify minority class instances correctly.

Experiments were conducted using various machine learning models. These experiments focused on using the word embedding technique, TF-IDF. In addition to machine learning classification, ensemble methods were also applied to improve performance. The soft voting technique was employed; however, as SVM and Ridge do not support soft voting, a bagged version was implemented. Since, the SVM and Ridge does not support soft voting, bagged version was implemented. The results from both the machine learning and ensemble methods are most effective are given below. Machine learning methods are used along with TF-IDF technique. When TF-IDF is applied to machine learning models, performance improvements are observed. Combining these methods, CatBoost, Logistic Regression, and SVM (Support Vector Machine) showed the highest accuracy among all tested methods. The CatBoost model performs well in terms of both accuracy and recall. When handling imbalanced datasets, recall, precision, and F1 score values are emphasized over accuracy.

The results are shown in Table 2. Fig. 2 shows the performance of machine learning models, in which Catboost shows superior performance to other models.

Table 2. Machine Learning models performance indicators

Model Name	Accuracy	Recall	Precision	F1 score
CatBoost	0.697	0.697	0.682	0.667
Logistic Regression	0.684	0.684	0.676	0.658
Support vector machine	0.672	0.682	0.659	0.654
Ridge	0.665	0.665	0.652	0.651
Naïve Bayes	0.507	0.507	0.563	0.525

Figure 2. Performance of machine learning models

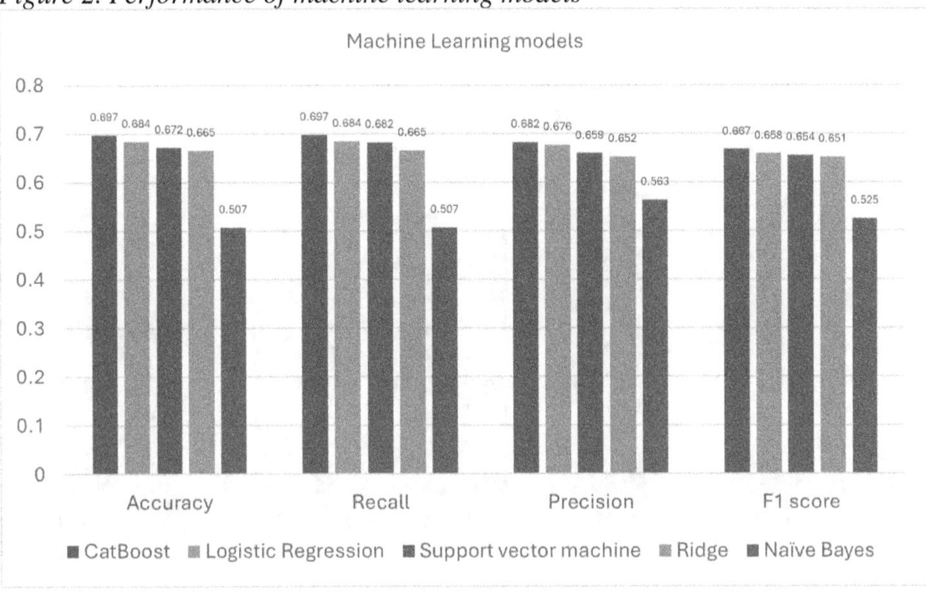

4.5 Deep Learning Models

Deep learning models outperform other models in terms of all metrics. In this study, the RoBERTa model achieved the highest score among all models. The BERT model showed the second-highest performance, while the FinancialBERT models ranked third and fourth. Table 3 shows the metrics for all the pre-trained models. The results obtained from these pre-trained models are exhibited in Figure 3. The experiments are structured to give insights into the machine learning and deep learning models.

The focus is on comparing the deep learning and machine learning models by evaluating their performance metrics."

Table 3. Deep learning models' performance metrics

Model name	Accuracy	Recall	Precision	F1 score
RoBERTa	0.785	0.785	0.785	0.785
BERT	0.751	0.751	0.751	0.751
FinancialBERT	0.694	0.694	0.694	0.694
FinBERT [51]	0.652	0.652	0.652	0.652
FinBERT [47]	0.571	0.571	0.571	0.571

Figure 3. Performance of deep learning models

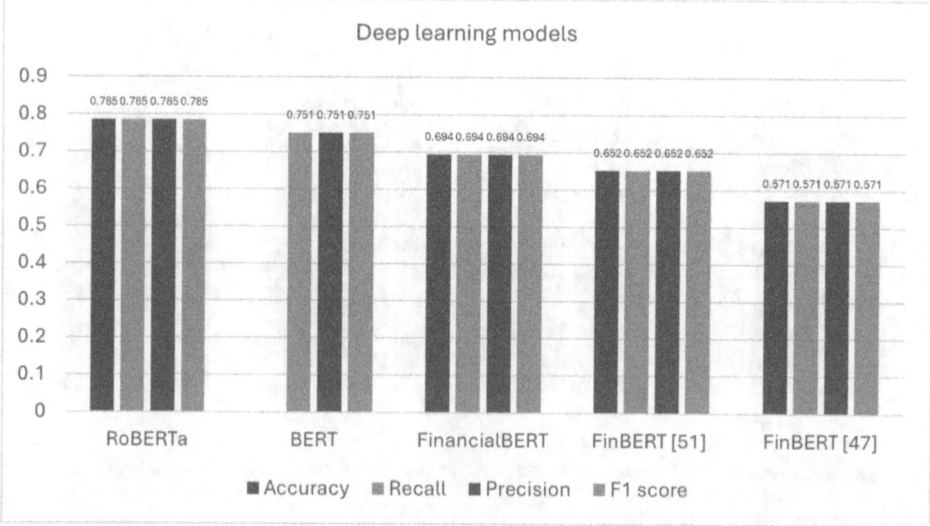

Overall performance evaluation of both machine learning and deep learning models are promising outcomes. Deep learning models are better than the machine learning models. Among several pre-trained deep learning models, RoBERTa is giving highest score and good improvement in all metrics. Among the deep learning models RoBERTa and BERT models outperform other FinancialBERT models.

5. CONCLUSION

In this work, five machine learning algorithms combined with TF-IDF were tested against five deep learning algorithms. In deep learning algorithms three variants of FinBERT, RoBERTa and BERT applied on financial data. All models are tested on financial news data available on Kaggle repository. The findings show that CatBoost achieved the highest score among the machine learning algorithms, while RoBERTa better performance than other deep learning models. Machine learning algorithms combined with TF-IDF performed well across all metrics. However, the FinBERT models performed worse than the other models, suggesting that further analysis and optimization are needed to improve their performance. From the experiments, it is evident that the RoBERTa and BERT are the top performance models based on the metrics. For future work, exploring ensemble models that combine machine learning and pre-trained deep learning models is recommended.

REFERENCES

Alawi, A. B., & Bozkurt, F. (2024). A hybrid machine learning model for sentiment analysis and satisfaction assessment with Turkish universities using Twitter data. *Decision Analytics Journal*, *11*, 1–13. DOI: 10.1016/j.dajour.2024.100473

Amin, R., Gantassi, R., Ahmed, N., & Alshehri, A. H. (2024). A hybrid approach for adversarial attack detection based on sentiment analysis model using Machine learning. *Engineering Science and Technology, an International Journal*, *58*, 1–12. DOI: 10.1016/j.jestch.2024.101829

Araci, D. (2019). FinBERT: Financial Sentiment Analysis with Pre-trained Language Models. ArXiv. 2019; abs/1908. 10063. Available from: https//api.semanticscholar.org/CorpusID:201646244

Azar, P. D. (2009). *Sentiment Analysis in Financial News* [Thesis]. Harvard College., Retrieved from https://people.csail.mit.edu/azar/wp-content/uploads/2011/09/thesis.pdf

Cam, H., Cam, A. V., Demirel, U., & Ahmed, S. (2024). Sentiment analysis of financial Twitter posts on Twitter with the machine learning classifiers. *Heliyon*, *10*(1), 1–15. DOI: 10.1016/j.heliyon.2023.e23784 PMID: 38205287

Consoli, S., Barbaglia, L., & Manzan, S. (2022). Fine-grained, aspect-based sentiment analysis on economic and financial lexicon. *Knowledge-Based Systems*, *247*, 1–15. DOI: 10.1016/j.knosys.2022.108781

Daudert, T. (2021). Exploiting textual and relationship information for fine-grained financial sentiment analysis. *Knowledge-Based Systems*, *230*, 1–12. DOI: 10.1016/j.knosys.2021.107389

Daza, A., N'estor, D. G. R., Mirelly, S. A. S., Wilmer, F. R. E., & María, E. C. Q. (2024). Sentiment Analysis on E-Commerce Product Reviews Using Machine Learning and Deep Learning Algorithms: A Bibliometric Analysis, Systematic Literature Review, Challenges and Future Works. *International Journal of Information Management Data Insights*, *4*(100267), 1–20. DOI: 10.1016/j.jjimei.2024.100267

DeSola, V., Hanna, K., & Nonis, P. (2019). Finbert: pre-trained model on sec filings for financial natural language tasks. *University of California*. DOI:DOI: 10.13140/RG.2.2.19153.89442

Devlin, J., Chang, M. W., Lee, K., & Toutanova, K. (2019). Bert: Pre-training of deep bidirectional transformers for language understanding, *Proceedings of the 2019 Conference of the North American Chapter of the Association for Computational Linguistics: Human Language Technologies*, Volume 1, 4171–4186. DOI:DOI: 10.18653/v1/N19-1423

Fatouros, G., Soldatos, J., Kouroumali, K., Makridis, G., & Kyriazis, D. (2023). Transforming sentiment analysis in the financial domain with ChatGPT. *Machine Learning with Applications*, *14*, 1–13. DOI: 10.1016/j.mlwa.2023.100508

Fersini, E., Messina, E., & Pozzi, F. A. (2016). Expressive Signals in Social Media Languages to Improve Polarity Detection. *Information Processing & Management*, *52*(1), 20–35. DOI: 10.1016/j.ipm.2015.04.004

Foroozan, S., Murad, M. A. A., Sharef, N. M., & Latiff, R. A. (2015). Improving Sentiment Classification Accuracy of Financial News using N-Gram Approach and Feature Weighting Methods. In *2015 2nd International Conference on Information Science and Security (ICISS 2015)* (pp. 296-304). IEEE. DOI: 10.1109/ICISSEC.2015.7371008

Habernal, I., Pracek, T., & Steinberger, J. (2014). Supervised Sentiment Analysis in Czech Social Media. *Information Processing & Management*, *50*(5), 693–707. DOI: 10.1016/j.ipm.2014.05.001

Halliday, M.A.K., & Ruqaiya Hasan. (1976). *Cohesion in English*. Longman. https://doi.org/DOI: 10.4324/9781315836010

Hirst, G., & St-Onge, D. (1998). Lexical chains as representations of context for the detection and correction of malapropisms. In Fellbaum, C., & Miller, G. (Eds.), *WordNet: An electronic lexical database* (pp. 305–322). The MIT Press., DOI: 10.1111/1911-3846.12832

Hu, M., & Liu, B. (2004). Mining and summarizing customer reviews. In *Proceedings: Tenth ACM SIGKDD international conference on Knowledge discovery and data mining (KDD 2004)* (pp. 168-177). New York: ACM. DOI: 10.1145/1014052.1014073

Huang, A. H., Wang, H., & Yang, Y. (2023). FinBERT: A Large Language Model for Extracting Information from Financial Text. *Contemporary Accounting Research*, *40*(2), 806–841. DOI: 10.1111/1911-3846.12832

Huang, A. H., Zang, A. Y., & Zheng, R. (2014). Evidence on the information content of text in analyst reports. *The Accounting Review*, *89*(6), 2151–2180. DOI: 10.2308/accr-50833

Im, T. L., San, P. W., Anthony, P., & On, C. K. (2018). Improving Polarity Classification for Financial News Using Semantic Similarity Techniques. *International Journal of Intelligent Information Technologies*, *14*(4), 39–54. DOI: 10.4018/IJIIT.2018100103

Irfan, M. (2021, January). Do Shariah Indices converge? Evidence from Gulf Cooperation Council countries. *International Journal of Business Excellence*, *23*(2), 251–269. DOI: 10.1504/IJBEX.2021.113448

Irfan, M., Elhoseny, M., Kassim, S., & Metawa, N. (2023). *Advanced Machine Learning Algorithms for Complex Financial Applications*. IGI Global., DOI: 10.4018/978-1-6684-4483-2

Irfan, M., Elmogy, M., Gupta, S., Khalifa, F., & Dias, R. (2024). *AI-Driven Decentralized Finance and the Future of Finance*. IGI Global., DOI: 10.4018/979-8-3693-6321-8

Irfan, M., Elmogy, M., Majid, M. S., & El-Sappagh, S. (2023). *The Impact of AI Innovation on Financial Sectors in the Era of Industry 5.0*. IGI Global., DOI: 10.4018/979-8-3693-0082-4

Irfan, M., Hussainey, K., Chan Bukhari, S. A., & Nam, Y. (Eds.). (2024). *Issues of Sustainability in AI and New-Age Thematic Investing*. IGI Global Publisher., DOI: 10.4018/979-8-3693-3282-5

Irfan, M., Kadry, S., Sharif, M., & Ullah Khan, H. (2023). *Fintech Applications in Islamic Finance: AI, Machine Learning, and Blockchain Techniques*. IGI Global., DOI: 10.4018/979-8-3693-1038-0

Jiang, J., & Conrath, D. W. (1997). Semantic similarity based on corpus statistics and lexical taxonomy. In *Proceedings:10th International Conference on Research in Computational Linguistics* (pp. 19-33).

Jiang, Y., Wang, X., & Zheng, H. (2014). A Semantic Similarity Measure Based on Information Distance for Ontology Alignment. *Information Sciences*, *278*, 76–87. DOI: 10.1016/j.ins.2014.03.021

Kauter, M. V., Breesch, D., & Hoste, V. (2015). Fine-grained analysis of explicit and implicit sentiment in financial news articles. *Expert Systems with Applications*, *42*(11), 4999–5010. DOI: 10.1016/j.eswa.2015.02.007

Kennedy, A., & Inkpen, D. (2006). Sentiment classification of movie reviews using contextual valence shifters. *Computational Intelligence*, *22*(2), 110–125. DOI: 10.1111/j.1467-8640.2006.00277.x

Klenner, M., Petrakis, S., & Fahrni, A. (2009). Robust Compositional Polarity Classification. In *Proceedings held in conjunction with the International Conference RANLP-2009, September 14 - 16,Borovets, Bulgaria* (pp. 180-184). Shoumen: INCOMA.

Kong, L., & Smith, N. A. (1994). An Empirical Comparison of Parsing Methods for Stanford Dependencies. Retrieved from http://arxiv.org/pef/1404.4314v1.pdf

Leacock, C., & Chodorow, M. (1998). Combining local content and WordNet similarity for word sense identification. Lexical chains as representations of context for the detection and correction of malapropisms. In Fellbaum, C., & Miller, G. (Eds.), *WordNet: An electronic lexical database* (pp. 265–283). The MIT Press. DOI: 10.7551/mitpress/7287.003.0018

Lee, M. C., Chang, J. W., & Hsieh, T. C. (2014). A Grammar-Based Semantic Similarity Algorithm for Natural Language Sentences. *TheScientificWorldJournal, 24*, 1–17. DOI: 10.1155/2014/437162 PMID: 24982952

Lengkeek, M., van der Knaap, F., & Frasincar, F. (2023). Leveraging hierarchical language models for aspect-based sentiment analysis on financial data. *Information Processing & Management, 60*(5), 1–18. DOI: 10.1016/j.ipm.2023.103435

Lesk, M. (1986). Automatic sense disambiguation using machine readable dictionaries: how to tell a pine cone from an ice cream cone. In *Proceedings: ACM SIGDOC 86, the Fifth International Conference on Systems Documentation, June 8-11, University of Toronto* (pp. 24-26). New York, NY: ACM Press. DOI: 10.1145/318723.318728

Li, J., Fong, S., Zhuang, Y., & Khoury, R. (2015). Hierarchical Classification in Text Mining for Sentiment Analysis of Online News. *Soft Computing, 20*(9), 3411–3420. DOI: 10.1007/s00500-015-1812-4

Li, X., Xie, H., Chen, L., Wang, J., & Deng, X. (2014). News Impact on Stock Price Return via Sentiment Analysis. *Knowledge-Based Systems, 69*, 14–23. DOI: 10.1016/j.knosys.2014.04.022

Lin, D. (1998). An Information Theoretic Definition of Similarity. In *Proceedings:Fifteenth International Conference on Machine Learning (ICML '98)* (pp. 296-304). Morgan Kaufmann

Lin, W., & Liao, L.-C. (2024). Lexicon-based prompt for financial dimensional sentiment analysis. *Expert Systems with Applications, 244*, 1–7. DOI: 10.1016/j.eswa.2023.122936

Liu, G., Wang, R., Buckley, J., & Zhou, H. M. (2011). A WordNet-base Semantic Similarity Measure Enhanced by Internet-based Knowledge. In *Proceedings:23rd International Conference on Software Engineering and Knowledge Engineering (SEKE2011)* (pp. 175-178).

Liu, X., Salem, S., Bian, L., Seong, J.-T., & Alshanbari, H. M. (2024). Application of machine learning algorithms in the domain of financial engineering. *Alexandria Engineering Journal*, *95*, 94–100. DOI: 10.1016/j.aej.2024.03.058

Liu, Y., Ott, M., Goyal, N., Du, J., Joshi, M., Chen, D., ... & Stoyanov, V. (2019). Roberta: A robustly optimized bert pretraining approach. arXiv preprint arXiv:1907.11692.

Malo, P., Sinha, A., Korhonen, P., Wallenius, J., & Takala, P. (2014). Good debt or bad debt: Detecting semantic orientations in economic texts. *Journal of the Association for Information Science and Technology*, *65*(4), 782–796. DOI: 10.1002/asi.23062

Maqbool, J., Aggarwal, P., Kaur, R., Mittal, A., & Ganaie, I. A. (2023). Stock Prediction by Integrating Sentiment Scores of Financial News and MLP-Regressor: A Machine Learning Approach. *Procedia Computer Science*, *218*, 1067–1078. DOI: 10.1016/j.procs.2023.01.086

Margaret Sangeetha, J., & Joy Alfia, K. (2024). Financial stock market forecast using evaluated linear regression based machine learning technique. *Measurement. Sensors*, *31*, 1–7. DOI: 10.1016/j.measen.2023.100950

Mohammad, S. M., Zhu, X., Kiritchenko, S., & Martin, J. (2015). Sentiment, Emotion, Purpose, and Style in Electoral Tweets. *Information Processing & Management*, *51*(4), 480–499. DOI: 10.1016/j.ipm.2014.09.003

Molina-Gonzalez, M. D., Martinez-Camara, E., Martin-Valdivia, M. T., & Urena-Lopez, L. A. (2015). A Spanish Semantic Orientation Approach to Domain Adaptation for Polarity Classification. *Information Processing & Management*, *51*(4), 520–531. DOI: 10.1016/j.ipm.2014.10.002

Peng, B., Chersoni, E., Hsu, Y., Qiu, L., & Huang, C. (2024). Supervised Cross-Momentum Contrast: Aligning representations with prototypical examples to enhance financial sentiment analysis. *Knowledge-Based Systems*, *295*, 1–13. DOI: 10.1016/j.knosys.2024.111683

Qiang, Ye., & Zhang, Z. (2009). Sentiment classification of online reviews to travel destinations by supervised machine learning approaches. *Expert Systems with Applications*, *35*(3), 6527–6535. DOI: 10.1016/j.eswa.2008.07.035

Stone, P. J., Dunphy, D. C., Smith, M. S., & Ogilvie, D. M. (1967). *The General Inquirer: A Computer Approach to Content Analysis*. MIT Press.

Taboada, M., Brooke, J., Tofiloski, M., Voll, K., & Stede, M. (2011). Lexicon-based methods for sentiment analysis. *Computational Linguistics*, *37*(2), 267–307. DOI: 10.1162/COLI_a_00049

Turney, P. D. (2002). Thumbs up or thumbs down? Semantic orientation applied to unsupervised classification of reviews. In *Proceedings: 40*th *Annual Meeting of Association for Computational Linguistics (ACL '02)* (pp. 417-424). DOI: 10.3115/1073083.1073153

Turney, P. D., & Littman, M. L. (2002). Unsupervised learning of semantic orientation from a hundred-billion-word corpus, *Technical Report EGB-1094, National Research Council Canada.* https://doi.org/DOI: 10.48550/arXiv.cs/0212012

Vaswani, A., Shazeer, N., Parmar, N., Uszkoreit, J., Jones, L., Gomez, A. N., & Kaiser, L. (2017). Attention is all you need. *Proceedings of the 31st Conference on Neural Information Processing Systems (NIPS 2017),* Long Beach, CA, USA.,6000-6010

Wilson, T., Wiebe, J., & Hoffmann, P. (2005). Recognising contextual polarity in phrase-level sentiment analysis. In Proceedings: Conf. on Human Language Technology and Empirical Methods in Natural Language Processing (HLT'05) (pp. 347-354). DOI: 10.3115/1220575.1220619

Xia, R., Xu, F., Yu, J., Qi, Y., & Cambria, E. (2016). Polarity Shift Detection, Elimination and Ensemble: A Three-Stage Model for Document-Level Sentiment Analysis. *Information Processing & Management*, *52*(1), 36–45. DOI: 10.1016/j.ipm.2015.04.003

Yadava, A. (2020). Sentiment analysis of financial news using unsupervised approach. *Procedia Computer Science*, *167*, 589–598. DOI: 10.1016/j.procs.2020.03.325

Yang, L., Li, Y., Wang, J., & Sherratt, R. S. (2020). Sentiment Analysis for E-Commerce Product Reviews in Chinese Based on Sentiment Lexicon and Deep Learning. *IEEE Access : Practical Innovations, Open Solutions*, *8*, 3522–3530. DOI: 10.1109/ACCESS.2020.2969854

Chapter 12
From Algorithms to Asset:
Unlocking Financial Freedom Through AI

Durga Madhab Mahapatra
https://orcid.org/0000-0003-1272-7285
North-Eastern Hill University, India

Zakir Hossen Shaikh
https://orcid.org/0000-0003-4733-4166
Kingdom University, Bahrain

Mohammad Irfan
https://orcid.org/0000-0002-4956-1170
Chandigarh University, Lucknow, Unnao, India

Bhabani Shankar Mohanty
https://orcid.org/0000-0001-9130-6221
Central University of Tamil Nadu, India

ABSTRACT

In today's dynamic world with distractions at every corner. Historically, the Great Depression (1929), World War II Recession (1946.47), Eisenhaver Recession (1957). The Kennedy Slide (1962), Oil Crisis (1773-74), Black Monday (1987), Dit- Can Bubble (2000), Financial Crisis (2007-09), Pandemic (2020) and Bear Masker Crisis (2022) etc. The popularly of passive funds among retail investors has risen post Covid. But its only financial planning that can bring together all aspects to create a holistic vision through (a) savings wisely; (b) Industry rightly; (c) planning smoothly. In today's fast changing digital landscape, technology is transforming

DOI: 10.4018/979-8-3373-1250-7.ch012

the financial sector. Fintech innovation, Blockchain, and digital payment systems have made investing more accessible and convenient. These advancements give investors easy and convenient access to financial products and services. A significant movement toward technology-driven financial solutions, artificial intelligence (AI) being a game-changer in personal finance including a sustainable healthy and equitable future.

1. INTRODUCTION

In today's dynamic world, there are distractions at every corner. Historically, the Great Depression (1929), World War II Recession (1946-47), Eisenhower Recession (1957), The Kennedy Slide (1962), Oil Crisis (1973-74), Black Monday (1987), Dot-Com Bubble (2000), Financial Crisis (2007-09), Pandemic (2020), and Bear Market Crisis (2022), among others, have shaped financial landscapes. The popularity of passive funds among retail investors has risen post-COVID. According to the HSBC Quality Life Report, while 53 percent of Indian respondents have an education savings plan for their children, 40 percent expect their child to take student loans, 51 percent are hopeful they will get scholarships, and 27 percent waited to consider selling assets to cover the education costs of their child (HSBC, 2024). Further, holistic life planning does not just involve the financial part but encompasses multiple dimensions of one's life, such as physical, mental, emotional, and other aspects that can lead to a meaningful output. However, financial planning is critical to bringing together all aspects to create a holistic vision through (a) saving wisely, (b) investing rightly, and (c) planning smoothly. In today's fast-changing digital landscape, technology is transforming the financial sector. Fintech innovation, Blockchain, and digital payment systems have made investing more accessible and convenient. These advancements give investors easy and convenient access to financial products and services. Investors should use tools like apps, robo-advisers, and online trading platforms for successful investing and remain vigilant against cyber threats and scams. The challenge of investing wisely in today's complex financial environment is significant. Artificial Intelligence (AI)-driven chatbots and virtual assistants enhance asset selection by giving customers real-time guidance. AI tools can create personalized content, such as explainer videos and apps, to help them understand their options better. AI also plays a crucial role in reducing operational costs and saving time by focusing more on customer service and innovative product offerings. Global financial turmoil has constantly tested the stability of conventional investing strategies, from the Great Depression to the COVID-19 pandemic and the Bear Market crisis of 2022. A significant movement toward technology-driven financial solutions has emerged, with artificial intelligence (AI) being a game-changer in personal finance.

As the world's fastest-growing major economy, India is uniquely positioned to harness AI's potential (Maheshwari et al., 2025). AI can generate realistic images and videos and chat with humans more naturally. It will witness a world where Blockchain, AI, and the Internet of Things (IoT) converge, linking every device, from phones to cars, making it a hyper-connected society (Irfan, Elhoseny, et al., 2023). Gen AI-enabled systems could emerge as powerful assistants for financial decision-making. Artificial Intelligence-based advanced chatbots are great for tracking a customer's investment pattern and providing periodic suggestions to maximize gains for the portfolio (Silber et al., 2025). Also, to provide 24/7 digital support to customers, a chatbot becomes essential to provide the comfort of always being available, which enhances the financial freedom of decision-making through AI (Saxena & Rishi, 2025). This will be the best example of conversational UI/UX (User Interface/User Experience) (Iyer & Maralapalle, 2025). Thus, it must be based on AI & ML to make it relevant to customers and query handling. Chatbot technology in India has limitless applications because of behavioral patterns in decision-making (Irfan, Kadry, et al., 2023; Irfan, Hussainey, et al., 2024; Issa et al., 2023).

AI encompasses a machine's ability to engage in cognitive tasks similar to those attributed to human intelligence, including functions such as perception, reasoning, learning, interaction, and complex problem solving. Tools and platforms like GPT-3, Google Cloud AI, TensorFlow, PyTorch, OpenCV, Pandas, Open AI Gym, ROS (Robot Operating System), Dialogflow, and Microsoft Bot Framework are notable examples of AI tools and platforms catering to various applications and domains (Irfan, Hussainey, et al., 2024; Maheshwari et al., 2025). AI plays a pivotal role in bolstering security through applications like facial recognition, biometric authentication, and anomaly detection, thereby fortifying the security of systems and facilities. AI's capacity to customize products, services, and content according to individual preferences enriches user experiences by making them more personalized and captivating. Leading Fintech startups such as "AI on the Fly Technologies," "Credit Siddhi," "Fund Expert," "Hotfoot," "InsigniQ," "Lentra," "Pay Nearby," "Progcap," "SafexPay," and "Techfino Capital Private Limited" are the best examples of AI & ML transforming end-to-end processes of leading businesses (Saxena & Rishi, 2025). In the context of sustainable data management, Mohanty et al. (2025) provided a comprehensive analysis of startup growth in India. The study underscores the role of government interventions and digital innovation in driving startup success. These insights are crucial when examining how AI-driven ventures contribute to broader goals of financial freedom and inclusive growth.

In the finance industry, where data analysis and risk management are critical, generative AI plays a vital role in fraud detection, risk assessment, and portfolio optimization. By analyzing vast financial data values, AI algorithms can identify patterns and anomalies indicative of fraudulent activities, enabling financial institutions to safeguard against potential threats (Issa et al., 2023; Irfan, Hussainey, et al., 2024). Moreover, GenAI is reshaping investment strategies by generating diverse, risk-balanced portfolios tailored to specific goals and constraints. JPMorgan Chase's use of Generative AI for personalized investment advice exemplifies how AI-driven solutions can optimize portfolio management and enhance client returns (JPMorgan Chase, n.d.). Gen AI platforms enable faster and more accurate complex data analysis, leading to better financial decision-making and improved financial outcomes (Maheshwari et al., 2025; Irfan, Kadry, et al., 2023).

This study examines how artificial intelligence (AI) transforms how people achieve financial freedom by improving decision-making, automating investing methods, and customizing financial guidance. People now have more access to real-time data, diverse portfolios, affordable financial planning options, improved risk management, and minimized operational inefficiencies, which help them make safer and more educated financial decisions. It is more important than ever to enable people to attain long-term financial freedom as digital usage speeds up financial services. The study also highlights how crucial financial planning is to ensure a sustainable, healthy, and equitable future.

2. AI AND FINANCIAL FREEDOM

When we are financially free, our money works for us instead of the other way around. It entails accumulating sufficient funds, investments, and savings to support your ambitions and live the life you want without being dependent on regular work, as shown in Figure 1.

Figure 1. Ways to Achieve Financial Freedom

Source: (ET Money, 2023)

2.1 How AI Assists in Achieving Financial Freedom

In addition to revolutionizing several industries, artificial intelligence (AI) has great potential for promoting societal autonomy. Community members and individuals may improve financial literacy, maximize investments, and manage finance more effectively by utilizing AI.

Table 1. How AI assists in achieving Financial Freedom

Keyways	Example
Personalized Financial Planning	Personalized Savings Plan Using Machine Learning
Investment Optimization	Basic Investment Portfolio Optimization
Debt Management	Debt Repayment Plan Using Optimization
Financial Literacy and Education	Financial Literacy Chatbot

Source: (Topmate.io, 2024)

2.2. AI And Banking Freedom

The use of AI in banking signifies a major shift from conventional techniques in favor of data-driven, automated procedures. Banks may increase operational effectiveness, improve customer service, and better manage risk by utilizing AI technology such as machine learning and natural language processing. AI's broad range of applications, from fraud detection to individualized financial advice, highlights the technology's transformational potential in banking.

Generative AI presents a significant revenue opportunity for banks. There are hundreds of potential use cases and applications across various banking functions, from risk management to customer service (Maheshwari et al., 2025). For instance, Generative AI is already transforming anti-money laundering and know-your-customer practices (Iyer & Maralapalle, 2025). For example, imagine a relationship manager who, during a client conversation, can look at a map-like navigation guide. If the conversation is "red," with the customer showing signs of disinterest, the system could provide them with a debtor and prevent them from heading down dead ends and detours in the conversation (Mer et al., 2024). Thus, AI-driven solutions based on principles of fairness, ethics, accountability, and transparency (FEAT) strengthen internal governance around the application of AI (Irfan, Elhoseny, et al., 2023; Saxena & Rishi, 2025).

S&P Global Market Intelligence's 2024 report shows that SBI ranked 47th globally, with HDFC Bank, India's largest private sector bank, at 74th. The RBI's new guidelines require a holistic approach to managing data integrity, governance, and risk assessments, making automation essential to mitigate threats such as "Man-in-the-middle" attacks. To address these, BFSI firms are embracing digital transformation. Advanced technologies such as GenAI, Blockchain, and RegTech solutions empower compliance teams (Iyer & Maralapalle, 2025). The "RegTech" solutions automate the compliance process, provide risk assessment monitoring and reporting, consolidate customer profiles, and facilitate real-time behavior monitoring, helping institutions address compliance risks (Dote-Pardo et al., 2025). Gen AI automates document review, transaction monitoring, and fraud detection tasks. The storage of historical data in automated systems paves the way for AI applications to help predict and manage future compliance risks. AI technology builds trust, scale, and robustness (Irfan, Hussainey, et al., 2024).

AI will enhance investing and decision-making. Machine Learning (ML) can be used for anti-money laundering (AML) and know-your-customer (KYC) solutions; this can reconcile various reports and middle and back-office processes. "Newgen's cloud-based solutions" drive superior customer experiences, such as (a) Trade Finance processing platform, (b) Documentary Collections Management, (c) Supply Chain Finance, (d) Trade Finance Analytics, (e) Digital Trade Services. Customers of such solution companies include HDFC Bank, ICICI Bank, Axis Bank, Kotak Mahindra Bank, IDBI Bank, Max Life Insurance, Tata AIA Life Insurance, Aditya Birla Capital, and Bajaj Allianz. Further, ICICI Bank has launched a "Smart BG assistance facility" for its customers leveraging AI & ML that allows for a complete digital and interactive BG issuance process (Iyer & Maralapalle, 2025). Institutional customers are offered AI-enabled BNPL tools (Buy Now – Pay Later) for faster retail credit decisions and smart trading platforms. "Kiya.ai" provides AI-based diversified solutions for banks and financial institutions. It also offers advanced solutions using Artificial Intelligence, Machine Learning, RPA, and cognitive analytics. "Adva Risk" is the largest repository of real estate titles and develops proprietary AI-based technologies to interpret the complexities of land/property ownership records (Mer et al., 2024). Through AI, major banks such as Axis Bank, HDFC Bank, and SBI expedite lending financial decisions. Further, "Adva-Smart" and "Adva NPA" are comprehensive solution services that leverage AI (Irfan, Hussainey, et al., 2024).

Figure 2. Potential Applications of AI in Banking

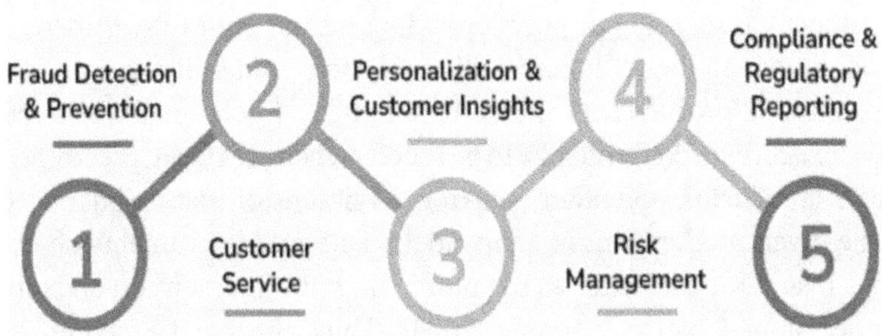

Source: (GeeksforGeeks, 2024)

The digital loan product is a creation of mobile and web-based applications where the entire life cycle—lead generation, customer onboarding, credit underwriting, document sign-up, disbursal, and servicing—is conducted electronically on a digital platform through various algorithms, AI, and embedded Application Programming Interfaces (APIs) (Irfan, Elhoseny, et al., 2023). GenAI is revolutionizing the decision-making process in finance and business by providing predictive analytics, risk analysis, and fraud detection capabilities. AI algorithms can analyze vast datasets and generate predictive models, enabling businesses to make informed decisions, mitigate risks, and capitalize on emerging opportunities (Issa et al., 2023). GenAI is reshaping how businesses operate and compete in today's dynamic market landscape, from financial forecasting to customer segmentation (Iyer & Maralapalle, 2025; Saxena & Rishi, 2025).

3. HERD MENTALITY AND DIVERSIFIED BASKET

SEBI defines AI as "The expression 'Artificial Intelligence' is understood to focus on executable programs in machines and computers that can learn, reason, and act in ways that would normally require human intelligence" (Mer et al., 2024). AI techniques are designed to learn from analyzing datasets and perform based on minimal or no human assistance (Mer et al., 2024). AI uses 'Machine Learning' techniques, including natural language processing (voice-to-text, text-to-systems, robo-chatbots, etc.), neural networks, statistical heuristics, feedback mechanisms, and combinations thereof to analyze large amounts of data, learning from such data and performing tasks without explicit instructions (Avelar & Jordão, 2024).

This tendency results in our peers crowding into or out of investments without due consideration of their fundamentals and their suitability to our investment objectives and risk profile (Dote-Pardo et al., 2025). Social media and the fear of missing out exacerbate this tendency to be greedy when others are greedy and fearful when others are fearful, potentially making us victims of market bubbles or panic selling. The diversified market of equity, debt, and gold instruments on our behalf can help us overcome these biases by minimizing our intervention and emotion in investing decisions (Avelar & Jordão, 2024). Thus, Financial Freedom is akin to animal styles, such as (a) Bears (pessimistic investors push prices downwards), (b) Bulls (optimistic investors push prices higher), (c) Chickens (fearful investors who avoid risk), (d) Sheep (investors who follow the herd), (e) Dogs (investors who bet on beaten-down stocks), (f) Stags (opportunistic investors), (g) Wolves (powerful unethical investors), (h) Ducks (investors who always make losses), (i) Whales (big investors who can move the stock price), (j) Ostriches (investors who ignore negative news of their stocks), (k) Pigs (impatient, high-risk, greedy, and emotional investors), (l) Turtles (investors who are slow to buy, slow to sell), etc. (Iyer & Maralapalle, 2025; Dote-Pardo et al., 2025).

Globally, regulators are staying ahead of the curve. The Central Bank of Thailand issued licensing guidelines for creating a new class of banks called "virtual banks." Further, the Reserve Bank of India (RBI) set up the Reserve Bank Innovation Hub (RBIH) to collaborate with financial sector institutions. The RBI's effort to launch a Central Bank Digital Currency (CBDC) is timely for banks to adopt the Metaverse. The Metaverse combines web 3.0 (decentralized, trust, etc.), immersive experiences (AR/VR, 2D, 3D), and digital asset management (Crypto, NFT, blockchain), which provides a seamless experience of financial decision-making. Further, digital payments transformed at Indian banks, such as 1990 (ECS), 2004 (RTGS), 2005 (NEFT), 2010 (IMPS), 2011 (CTS), 2012 (NACH), 2016 (UPI), and 2023 (CBDC), creating a new open banking ecosystem in India. Blockchain and Distributed Ledger Technology (DLT), which allow simultaneous storage and synchronization of financial transactions in multiple locations of a distributed network, are on a path to disrupt established banking protocols (Irfan, Hussainey, et al., 2024; Avelar & Jordão, 2024).

Cross-chain technology will facilitate blockchain interoperability across payments processing, supply chains, and other areas. This is also the right direction toward financial freedom through adopting new technology. Robo-advisers, digital brokerages, online investing tools, and financial services software all fall under the umbrella of wealth tech (Avelar & Jordão, 2024). The wealth tech industry in India is at the cusp of an explosion as innovative technological and business models enhance financial freedom, from sourcing investment options to offering advisory and execution services. AI platforms marry advanced analytics, AI, and Machine Learning techniques with in-depth sectoral knowledge and product expertise, which enhance financial freedom decision-making (Irfan, Elhoseny, et al., 2023; Dote-Pardo et al., 2025).

Table 2. Financial Freedom: Investors can complain about India

SL	Institution	Service Centre Names
1	Bombay Stock Exchange (BSE)	Department of Investors Services (DIS)
2	National Stock Exchange (NSE)	Investor Service Call (ISC)
3	Securities and Exchange Board of India (SEBI)	SEBI Complaints Redressal System (SCORES)
4	Reserve Bank of India (RBI)	Ombudsman
5	Department & Financial Series (DFS)	Public Grievances Redressal Mechanism

Source: Authors Compilation

4. AI INTEGRATION TO DRIVE FINANCIAL INCLUSIVITY

Secure online transactions through embedded AI: AI is imperative for making online transactions completely secure. Digital payments are quick and easy. As digital transactions grow in popularity, embedded AI in digital payment systems is proving essential (Irfan, Elmogy, et al., 2023). AI helps alert banks when suspicious transactions occur. Every transaction is genuine and faithful on digital systems embedded with powered AI (Kandpal et al., 2025).

Customer Support and Digital Realms: AI is being used to serve customers better, and "Chatbots" are the most visible example of such support. Customers of digital payment service providers have the opportunity to chat with bots in a natural language. Conversational platforms have become essential for businesses to offer user-friendly customer experiences and 24×7 customer support, such as “BOT360,” “Co Rover,” “Food Bot AI,” “Jubi AI,” “Kontiki AI,” “Royal Cyber,” “Voxta,” “Wot Not,” “Yekaliva,” and “Youbotics,” which built speech recognition engines in all major Indian languages in addition to AI chatbots (Mer et al., 2024).

Early Warning Systems (EWS): It is a financial AI guardian. It empowers lenders to outpace fraud, foresee risks, and revolutionize credit management with precision. There are various ways technology can help build a robust and highly automated EWS, such as through dynamic data integration, automated workflow orchestration, triage systems, real-time fraud detection, stress testing, vulnerability assessment, and advanced analytics (Irfan, Hussainey, et al., 2024).

Decentralizing Finance: FinTech can leverage its agility by integrating cryptocurrency technologies, fostering faster transactions, reducing costs, and enhancing financial inclusion. Decentralized finance (DeFi) platforms can reshape traditional banking and finance by providing more accessible and cost-effective services. Embracing blockchain ensures transparency, security, and data protection in financial processes, paving the way for transformative shifts. Collaboration between FinTech and cryptocurrency can create a dynamic ecosystem, fostering continuous adoption of emerging trends like tokenization and AI, maintaining a competitive edge in the evolving financial landscape (Issa et al., 2023).

Crypto and Stable Coin-based Lending: This platform uses blockchain for transparent, borderless transactions. Smart contracts automate lending processes, reducing reliance on traditional intermediaries and hence costs (Irfan, Elmogy, et al., 2023). Connecting smart contracts with real-world data and oracles is crucial for making blockchain networks and smart contracts practical, providing reliable external information (Issa et al., 2023).

Braille-enabled Finance, IoT Devices: Devices equipped with Braille displays or keyboards enable individuals with visual impairments to access account information about financial decision-making and perform independent transactions. Braille-enabled ATMs empower the visually impaired for financial empowerment (Mer et al., 2024).

Account Aggregator (AA) Model: AI can empower customers to plan personal finance by providing a comprehensive view of their financial situation and analyzing spending behavior. The AA model can play a significant role by providing easy and reliable access to financial institutions (Dote-Pardo et al., 2025). AA can simplify applying for loans by allowing users to share financial data with lenders, reducing the need for physical documentation. AI is a progressive step to help customers make decisions and access a variety of products, including credit, insurance, and investments, for their benefit (Bevilacqua et al., 2025).

AI's DPI: The AI-driven chatbot that bridges language barriers enhances access to government services and makes wise financial decision-making. AI's integration into India's Digital Public Infrastructure (DPI) is the first approach to ensure citizens can thrive in the AI-driven economy (Issa et al., 2023).

EMBB and URLLC with Geospatial Information System (GIS): Enhanced Mobile Broadband (EMBB) and Ultra-Reliable Low Latency Communication (URLLC) with Geospatial Information System (GIS) will make available simple, seamless, and secure payment methods such as 'one-tap payment' and cashless 'Store.' AR and VR in 'Smart Banks' will allow online facial recognition, enabling customers to interact with bank officials for financial freedom through AI. Further, ATMs will offer AI-backed instant personalized services, and portable, pop-up virtual branches will become possible in remote locations or disaster-affected areas (Irfan, Elmogy, et al., 2023).

Financial Apps: Financial apps are the backbone of new technology and the needs of customers' financial freedom and the financial landscape, for saving purposes, such as "Gullak," "Jupiter," and "Multiple," investment purposes, such as "Groww," "Kite @ Zerodha," "Scripbox," and "5paisa," which enable risk profiling, portfolio monitoring, and investment recommendations. Spend purposes such as "Paytm Mall" and "Tata Neu" bring multiple brands under one roof. Borrowing purposes such as "CASHe," "Dhani," "Freo," and "Loan Tap" give quick access to credit. For secure purposes, such as "Acko," "Bajaj Finserv," "Coverfox," "ILTakeCare," and "Policybazaar," compare different policies before purchase. New-age apps seek information from usage patterns to understand user financial freedom behavior better (Bevilacqua et al., 2025).

Customized Solutions: With the increased adaptation of predictive actions using AI and ML across all stages of transactions, there are more solutions that customers can now access. The increased adoption of embedded financial products across more app categories delivers tailor-made financial services products to customers. Moreover, some apps may be AI-driven and may provide generic advice (Kandpal et al., 2025).

Robotic Process Automation (RPA): RPA will bring efficiency in terms of time and money. It will help capital markets firms boost efficiencies. RPA can assist with client onboarding, revenue recognition, expense validation, accounting processes, operational and financial reconciliation, and reporting. RPA helps reduce transaction time and offers accuracy improvement and effort reduction in use cases like transaction reporting, reconciliations, and settlements and payments processes. Thus, AI is an enabler of financial freedom for decision-making (Irfan, Hussainey, et al., 2024).

Natural Language Processing (NLP) for Customer Service: NLP-powered chatbots and virtual assistants enable seamless interaction between customers and financial institutions, providing instant support and personalized assistance around the clock. NLP algorithms enhance the overall customer experience and drive operational efficiency (Mer et al., 2024).

Behavioral Analytics and Biometrics: Behavioral analytics enhances identifying potential fraud, and biometric technologies such as fingerprint, facial, and voice recognition contribute to authentication processes. This is a neuroscience-based method coupled with AI capabilities (Dote-Pardo et al., 2025).

"Voice Biometrics," "Iris Scans," and "Behavioral Biometrics" are AI-driven tools that analyze customer behavior. AI's data analysis capabilities can transform the way financial decisions are made. Artificial Intelligence is a driving force behind innovation in fintech. Fintech firms increasingly leverage AI to enhance customer experiences, streamline operations, and make more informed decisions (Barone et al., 2024). From robo-advisers to AI-powered chatbots, integrating AI technologies is reshaping how financial services are delivered. The predictive capabilities of AI also play a vital role in fraud detection. As financial institutions grapple with the evolving nature of cyber threats, AI algorithms are becoming indispensable tools in identifying and mitigating potential risks (Irfan, Hussainey, et al., 2024).

AI as a digital tool offers efficiency, real-time monitoring, a more straightforward documentation process, scalability, and improved collaborations in compliance management (Barone et al., 2024). Thus, enterprises can easily create and maintain centralized documents, policies, and procedures repositories. The "Integrated Solution Document Management Systems (DMS)," "Legal Billing Software," and "Email Filing and Management" systems help maintain a thorough, searchable record of communications. To ensure financial freedom in the decision-making process, compliance managers today use technologies like AI, RPA, and data analytics to protect information and technology assets (Irfan, Elmogy, et al., 2023). AI has unique use cases that are available to all big enterprises, making it a valuable ally in this era of digital acceleration. Artificial intelligence (AI) is transforming traditional paradigms in every sector of the economy, including supply chain management, robotics, healthcare, public safety, retail, HR services, financial services, and financial inclusion and governance (Shaikh et al., 2022, 2024; Sheela et al., 2024; Selwin et al., 2024; Gupta et al., 2024; Kusuma et al., 2024; Panigrahi et al., 2023; Sarea et al., 2021).

Table 3. Stated the Generative AI Platform and its features

Generative AI Platform	Unique Features
Chart GPT	• Natural Language Processing Capabilities. • Ability to generate human-like Text responses. • widely used to article/blog generation.
Microsoft Copilot	• Interactive Search assistant • Enhanced assistance to Content Creation and exciting • Integration with Microsoft is Ecosystem.
Gemini Google's	• Integration with Google's So system. • Speedy and accurate answers on time. • Summarization and Content Creation features.
Perplexity AI	• Authority and Copyright focused approach • Provides sane Creations in answers. • Enhanced Capabilities with the pro version powered by GPT-4.
Copymatic.ai Copy.ai Simplified	• Features 6 Content Ideas written document • AI-powered assistance with seamless writing experience. • Break down Complex Concepts into simple language.

Source: Authors Compilation

Some of the tools and technologies that financial services institutions today use for compliance are (a) Compliance Management Software, (b) Regulatory Reporting Software, (c) Risk Assessment Tools, (d) Data Analytics Platforms, (e) Communications Management Platforms, which map with Blockchain, ML, Metaverse, and RPA. 'Digital brokers' are online platforms and software tools that offer access to stock market information and facilitate investment (Barone et al., 2024). “Robo Retirement” is a specialized domain where companies manage a customer’s retirement savings using computer systems. “Reporting and Analytics” is another tech-enabled function providing individuals and businesses with real-time financial insights. These are financial freedom innovations that can reduce costs and free up time for advisors to focus on diligent and customized planning (Irfan, Kadry, et al., 2023; Kandpal et al., 2025).

In the era of AI, the financial function is at the forefront of utilizing the potential of AI tools. Gen AI is enabling Chief Financial Officers (CFOs) in drafting financial reports and budget variance analysis, thus automating financial workflows. Organizations have invested in Enterprise Resource Planning (ERP), Customer Relationship Management (CRM), and procurement systems with the adoption of leveraging technology. Gen AI can tap into the data from these systems to study patterns and arrive at quick decisions. Gen AI tools have been helpful in advising functional heads to revisit contracts for outsourcing. Chief Financial Officers (CFOs) have started playing a key role in the strategic shifts of the business and in enabling them to adapt quickly to volatile business scenarios (Ganesh, 2025; Irfan, Kadry, et al., 2023; Issa et al., 2023).

AI and Gen AI are now emerging as powerful forces capable of bridging this gap by bringing data-driven intelligence, personalization, and precision. Advanced AI tools are capable of connecting phone conversations with customers (Barone et al., 2024). Traditionally, strategic decisions relied heavily on historical data analysis, market research, and the collective experience and intuition of CFOs. Gen AI introduces a new dimension—the ability to generate novel insights and simulate potential outcomes. Gen AI allows various possibilities, identifies potential risks and opportunities, and develops robust contingency plans. Thus, CFOs use Gen AI to simulate the impact of action approaches (Irfan, Kadry, et al., 2023).

Table 4. Stated AI software and its use in finance segment

AI Software	Action Approach	Use of Technology	Use in finance Segment
Tableau AI	Visualization, predictive analytics	NLP, ML dashboards, SQL & Python integration	Reporting, forecasting
Zoho Zia	Conversational assistant, sentiment analysis	NLP, deep learning, cloud-native	Chatbot support, deal insights, pipeline optimization
Freshsales AI	Forecasting, chatbot automation, email tracking	Predictive analytics, REST API	Contact management, AI-powered sales predictions
IBM Watson Analytics	Data discovery, predictive analytics	Deep learning, NLP, cloud-native	Visualization, strategic insights
RapidMiner	Data mining, ML workflows	ML algorithms, Python/R integration	Forecasting, data science
Alteryx AI	Data prep, predictive modeling	AI pipelines, transformation tools	Automation, business optimization
TIBCO Spotfire	Visual analytics, predictive BI	ML analytics, real-time dashboards	Data-driven decisions, insight generation
Power BI AI	Insights, natural language queries	ML-powered, cloud-integrated	Real-time BI, anomaly detection
Google Looker	Business intelligence, data automation	ML visualizations, BigQuery	Advanced analytics, data transformation
Sisense AI	Embedded analytics, NLP	Forecasting, deep learning	Predictive insights, intelligence automation
Chatfuel AI	Chatbots for messaging platforms	NLP+ML optimization	FAQ automation, user support
ThoughtSpot	Data search, self-service insights	NLP queries, cloud analytics	Decision support, instant data access
Domo AI	Predictive analytics, real-time dashboards	ML, cloud-native	KPI tracking, business forecasting

Source: Authors Compilation

4.1 GEN AI and Internal Audit

Chief Financial Officers (CFOs) are also able to reduce internal audit costs with Gen AI generating real-time compliance documentation by scanning transactions. Gen AI tools empower them to access real-time and predictive insights. CFOs are using natural language queries to unearth trends from sales reports and market intelligence. To ensure scalability and compliance in regulated environments, "Broadridge's OpsGPT" focuses on secure architecture, verified data use, built-in compliance layers, real-time data timelines, and continuous retraining, making Gen AI a trusted operational foundation. Companies like "Mastercard" are using Gen AI for predictive fraud detection and supply chain resilience. Thus, firms like "Broadridge" and "nRoad" are pioneering trusted domain-specific Gen AI applications in financial services. "Gen AI Copilots" can make strategic preferences over time and offer increasingly personalized advice. Thus, Gen AI is rapidly becoming an indispensable tool for resolving complexities of the modern business environment (Silber et al., 2025). Gen AI is undoubtedly one of its most powerful catalysts. "Agentic AI" is also helpful, specifically in the areas of marketing and customer service in banking. Usage of AI can create value across the line of business for banks (Barone et al., 2024). It can help understand in real-time the customer needs and create products or services to match those needs, including the right pricing at the right channel at the right time. Banks can leverage AI to significantly improve customer experience, prevent digital fraud, and constantly improve automation across front, mid, and back-office operations in areas such as embedded finance, decentralized financing, capital markets, and wealth management (Irfan, Elmogy, et al., 2024; Kandpal et al., 2025).

Gen AI is also analyzing a competitor's recent investments and product launches to anticipate their next strategic direction. Gen AI enhances the ability to act with precision and foresight. Financial services, with their high regulatory standards and data sensitivity, present both a challenge and an opportunity for Gen AI deployment (Silber et al., 2025). Gen AI is also strengthening decision-making in risk management, compliance, and client intelligence through four key pillars: (a) Products and Services, (b) Productivity, (c) Platforms, and (d) Governance. Thus, OpsGPT, Broadridge's Gen AI-powered solution designed for the T+A post-trade environment, enables natural language interactions with complex, multi-asset trade data—transforming raw inputs into real-time insights, visualizations, and summaries. OpsGPT also automates time-intensive compliance tasks, offers multilingual capabilities, and eliminates the need for coding through intuitive design (Saxena & Rishi, 2025). Broadridge has embedded a robust governance framework around all AI initiatives, ensuring security, regulatory compliance, and transparency in interest rate hikes on the company's profitability under different market conditions, enabling them to proactively adjust investment strategies and mitigate potential losses (Irfan, Elmogy, et al., 2024).

Further, an Agentic AI framework is a platform that makes it easy to develop and deploy Agentic AI systems, which can seamlessly work with other agents. The components of an Agentic AI framework can broadly be categorized as: (a) Perception Module, (b) Knowledge Module, (c) Cognitive Module, (d) Action Module, (e) Learning Module, (f) Collaboration Module, and (g) Security Module. Almost all sectors have deployed AI agents to implement intelligence and automation across the customer care fabric. Traditional AI is already used widely in customer service, but Agentic AI takes it to the next level by not just answering customers' queries but also helping resolve issues (Bevilacqua et al., 2025). For example, an agent can simultaneously analyze customer sentiment, review order history, access company policies, and respond to customer needs based on these insights. "Agentic AI" is being used in the Banking, Financial Services, and Insurance (BFSI) industry for fraud detection, risk assessment, and customer onboarding. It can automate routine tasks like expense reporting, compliance checks, financial reporting, and invoice processing. It can monitor market trends, asset investments, and credit risks and advise customers based on their financial history and goals (Bevilacqua et al., 2025).

Table 5. Stated the Comparing AI- Powered Storage with Traditional Storage

SL	Feature	AI - Powered Storage	Traditional Storage.
1	Security	AI-driven Threat detection	Manual Saving policies
2	Efficiency	Automated Optimization	Static Allocation
3	Downtime Risk	Predictive Maintenance	Reactive Issue resolution
4	Data Classification	AI-driven tagging	Manual Indexing

Source: Data Quest, Cyber Media publication, May 2025, p. 36

4.2. Quantum AI Applications in Finance

Technology also cuts inefficiencies with better turnaround times and resource utilization, reducing the need for physical expansion. With the help of Quantum AI, financial modeling such as option pricing, portfolio optimization, and risk assessment in financial markets occurs at a quicker rate (Silber et al., 2025). Quantum algorithms improve decision-making processes and mitigate financial risks. As far as portfolio management is concerned, quantum-enhanced portfolio optimization techniques for asset allocation and risk management maximize investment returns (Saxena & Rishi, 2025; Irfan, Elmogy, et al., 2024). Quantum AI can leverage its ability to solve optimization problems efficiently. By analyzing vast datasets of financial data, it can uncover subtle relationships and predict market trends with much greater accuracy, empowering investors with a significant edge (Bevilacqua et al., 2025). The synergy between Quantum Computing and Machine Learning can revolutionize financial modeling by enabling more accurate predictors and optimizing investment strategies (Issa et al., 2023).

5. CHALLENGES AND ETHICAL CONSIDERATIONS

The potential for wealth creation is only one aspect of artificial intelligence's growing integration into financial institutions; it also presents challenging issues that need to be carefully and ethically handled. Although AI can help people achieve financial independence, it also poses significant issues about institutional stability, privacy, fairness, and transparency. The possibility that AI would inherit and magnify preexisting prejudices is one of the most urgent ethical issues:

- **Bias Inheritance**: AI programs pick up knowledge from past data. If there are biases in this data, the AI may reinforce them or even make them worse.
- **Effect on Decision-Making**: In crucial financial services like lending, insurance, and investing, biased AI may result in unjust decision-making. An AI system based on skewed past lending data, for instance, can unjustly refuse loans to some demographics, thereby perpetuating already-existing disparities.

The pace at which artificial intelligence is developing frequently surpasses the capacity of regulatory frameworks to adjust, resulting in a discrepancy between legal requirements and technical capabilities. To overcome these obstacles, regulators, financial institutions, and AI developers must have constant communication. More dynamic regulatory frameworks that support innovation and safeguard consumer rights may result from this partnership. In the financial industry, trust is a vital resource. Financial organizations may guarantee adherence to legal and ethical obligations while fostering consumer trust by methodically resolving prejudice and privacy issues. We can make sure AI becomes a tool for empowerment rather than exploitation by tackling these issues directly.

6. THE FUTURE OF AI AND FINANCIAL SUSTAINABILITY

In the modern world, there is a growing interconnection between the domains of finance and sustainability. Finding a balance between environmental preservation, social advancement, and economic growth is the focus of sustainable finance. A variety of financial operations are included in sustainable finance, including impact investment, sustainability-linked loans, green bonds, and social bonds. Because AI enhances data analysis, risk assessment, and decision-making, it has the potential to have a significant influence on the sustainable finance sector. For those who want to become financially independent and attain long-term financial sustainability, endowments are an effective instrument. It's a kind of investment that may help protect capital for future generations while simultaneously offering a consistent stream of income over time. Non-profit institutions like museums and colleges frequently use endowments to supply continuous financing for their activities.

Figure 3. Opportunities and challenges for sustainable development and finance

Source: (Think360, 2025)

The issue of integrating sustainability with finance is intricate and multifaceted, including a variety of tactics and methods. Corporate social responsibility, carbon trading, green bonds, sustainable investment, and sustainable finance standards are some of the major areas where sustainability and finance converge. By integrating sustainability into finance and considering risk management, investment management, carbon footprint analysis, and climate risk analysis, we can all help create a more equitable and sustainable future.

7. CONCLUSION

AI plays a massive role in enhancing risk assessment and decision-making processes in FinTech, particularly in micro-loans and decentralized exchanges. AI aids in fraud detection, market analysis, and optimizing trading strategies. AI and crypto-driven Fintech synergy ensures more informed, adaptive, and efficient risk management and decision-making processes. The integration of AI and ML is set to revolutionize core financial services by enhancing decision-making processes, improving customer experiences, and automating routine tasks. AI enables real-time data analysis, creating more personalized financial solutions that meet evolving customers' needs. The BFSI sector in India faces disruptions due to the growing impact of Insurtech and Fintech, which are driven by technological advancements (Saxena & Rishi, 2025). The convergence of Augmented Reality (AR), Virtual Reality (VR), and Artificial Intelligence (AI) is set to transform the BFSI sector. This fusion of technologies will revolutionize product sales, claims processing, and risk evaluation, enhancing customer service, efficiency, and security. This transformation creates financial freedom for decision-making. By evaluating enormous volumes of data and seeing patterns and trends that people would overlook, artificial intelligence (AI) can assist businesses and investors in making better decisions, enhancing risk assessment, and advancing sustainable development. However, there are also significant ethical and legal issues brought up by the use of AI in sustainable finance, including bias, transparency, and data privacy and security. Financial activities have many opportunities to manage risks related to environmental, social, and governance aspects while fostering sustainable economic growth at the nexus of AI and sustainable finance.

REFERENCES

Abey, J., Velmurugan, R., & Shaikh, Z. H. (2025). Analyzing the Performance of a Deep Learning-Based Model for Stock Market Trend Prediction. In Hamdan, R. K. (Ed.), *Sustainable Data Management. Studies in Big Data* (Vol. 170). Springer. DOI: 10.1007/978-3-031-83915-3_59

Alex Avelar, E., & Jordão, R. V. D. (2024), "The role of artificial intelligence in the decision-making process: a study on the financial analysis and movement forecasting of the world's largest stock exchanges", *Management Decision*, Vol. ahead-of-print No. ahead-of-print. DOI: 10.1108/MD-09-2023-1625

Awal, V. (2024). Riding high on the AI wave. *Voice & Data, June 2024*, 26–29.

Bansal, A. (2023). Unified strategy for AI, RPA, and generative AI deployments. *IT Next, October–December 2023*, 15–16.

Barone, M., Bussoli, C., & Fattobene, L. (2024). Digital financial consumers' decision-making: A systematic literature review and integrative framework. *International Journal of Bank Marketing*, *42*(7), 1978–2022. DOI: 10.1108/IJBM-07-2023-0405

Bevilacqua, S., Ferraris, A., Kozel, R., & Vincurova, Z. (2025), "Exploring the artificial intelligence integration in top management team decision-making: an empirical analysis", *Business Process Management Journal*, Vol. ahead-of-print No. ahead-of-print. DOI: 10.1108/BPMJ-07-2024-0659

Doshi, S., & Kapadia, K. (2025, January 5). Strengthening compliance. *Business Today (Norwich)*, ●●●, 72–74.

Dote-Pardo, J.S., Cordero-Díaz, M.C., Espinosa Jaramillo, M.T. and Parra-Domínguez, J. (2025), "Leveraging artificial intelligence for enhanced decision-making in finance: trends and future directions", *Journal of Accounting Literature*, Vol. ahead-of-print No. ahead-of-print. .DOI: 10.1108/JAL-02-2025-0100

Ganesh, U. (2025) "Gen AI is the new CFO weapon", *Financial Express*, 15th May 2025 p.9.

Ghatak, A. (2024). The rise of generative AI in intra. *Dataquest, May 2024*, 16–20.

Gupta, P. (2024). A new dawn for crypto. *Entrepreneur, December 2024–January 2025*, 40–41.

Gupta, S., Srivastava, R., Shaikh, Z. H., & Irfan, M. (2024). Revolutionizing Rural Finance: Exploring the Impact of FinTech on Financial Inclusion in India. In Irfan, M., Muhammad, K., Naifar, N., & Khan, M. A. (Eds.), *Applications of Block Chain technology and Artificial Intelligence. Financial Mathematics and Fintech*. Springer., DOI: 10.1007/978-3-031-47324-1_3

Henshall, B. (2019). Open banking: A strategic approach to win digital consumers. *The Banking & Finance Post, January–February 2019*, 20–21.

Irfan, M. (2021, January). Do Shariah Indices converge? Evidence from Gulf Co-operation Council countries. *International Journal of Business Excellence*, *23*(2), 251–269. DOI: 10.1504/IJBEX.2021.113448

Irfan, M., Elhoseny, M., Kassim, S., & Metawa, N. (2023). *Advanced Machine Learning Algorithms for Complex Financial Applications*. IGI Global., DOI: 10.4018/978-1-6684-4483-2

Irfan, M., Elmogy, M., Gupta, S., Khalifa, F., & Dias, R. (2024). *AI-Driven Decentralized Finance and the Future of Finance*. IGI Global., DOI: 10.4018/979-8-3693-6321-8

Irfan, M., Elmogy, M., Majid, M. S., & El-Sappagh, S. (2023). *The Impact of AI Innovation on Financial Sectors in the Era of Industry 5.0*. IGI Global., DOI: 10.4018/979-8-3693-0082-4

Irfan, M., Hussainey, K., Chan Bukhari, S. A., & Nam, Y. (Eds.). (2024). *Issues of Sustainability in AI and New-Age Thematic Investing*. IGI Global Publisher., DOI: 10.4018/979-8-3693-3282-5

Irfan, M., Kadry, S., Sharif, M., & Ullah Khan, H. (2023). *Fintech Applications in Islamic Finance: AI, Machine Learning, and Blockchain Techniques*. IGI Global., DOI: 10.4018/979-8-3693-1038-0

Issa, H., Jabbouri, R., & Mehanna, R.-A. (2023). AI micro-decisions in FinTechs: A mixed method research design. *Management Decision*, *61*(11), 3316–3342. DOI: 10.1108/MD-10-2022-1336

Iyer, R., & Maralapalle, V. C. (2025), "Integrating AI and ML Technologies Into Indigenous Financial Systems: Applications of AI and ML in Indigenous Financial Management", Ghosal, I., Gupta, S., Rana, S. and Saha, D. (Ed.) Indigenous Empowerment through Human-Machine Interactions, Emerald Publishing Limited, Leeds, pp. 237-251. DOI: 10.1108/978-1-83608-068-820251014

Jain, A. (2023). Trend: Generative AI++. *IT Next, October–December 2023*, 8–9.

Kandpal, V., Ozili, P. K., Jeyanthi, P. M., Ranjan, D., & Chandra, D. (2025), "Creative Artificial Intelligence Supports to FinOps", Digital Finance and Metaverse in Banking, Emerald Publishing Limited, Leeds, pp. 87-113. DOI: 10.1108/978-1-83662-088-420251004

Kartik, A. (2025). The innovation leap. *Outlook Business, January 2025*, 52–53.

Kumar, S. (2023). What is the future of fintech funding in 2023? *Asian Banking & Finance*, *Q3*, 8.

Kusuma, K., Sheela, P., Panigrahi, R. R., & Shaikh, Z. H. (2024). Blockchain Technology and Islamic Finance: A Decade of Growth Trends. In Irfan, M., Kadry, S., Sharif, M., & Khan, H. (Eds.), *Fintech Applications in Islamic Finance: AI, Machine Learning, and Blockchain Techniques* (pp. 59–79). IGI Global., DOI: 10.4018/979-8-3693-1038-0.ch004

Luthra, V., & Trott, A. (2024). Generative AI's role in the evolution of banking. *Asian Banking & Finance*, *Q3*, 32.

Maheshwari, H., Samantaray, A.K., Sandhu, K. and Panigrahi, R.R. (2025), "Insight over instinct: AI's role in rationalizing investment decisions", *International Journal of Accounting & Information Management,* Vol. ahead-of-print No. ahead-of-print. .DOI: 10.1108/IJAIM-12-2024-0455

Maiti, M. (2023). The pocket aide to sort your finances. *Outlook Money, February 2023*, 8–18.

Mathew, J. C. (2024). India's deep tech disruption. *Fortune, June 2024*, 28–38.

Mer, A., Singhal, K., & Virdi, A. S. (2024), "A Review of the Role of Artificial Intelligence in Banking and Stock Market Trading", Taneja, S., Kumar, P., Sood, K., Özen, E. and Grima, S. (Ed.) Finance Analytics in Business (Emerald Studies in Finance, Insurance, and Risk Management), Emerald Publishing Limited, Leeds, pp. 175-198. DOI: 10.1108/978-1-83753-572-920241009

Mishion, N. (2024, December). Ethics in AI: Navigating the future responsibly. *Banking & Finance*, *XXXVII*(12), 37–38.

(2023). Mohan. (2023). The transitioning of a wealth adviser. *Banking Frontiers*, (June), 48–49.

Mohanty, B. S., Shaikh, Z. H., Behera, A. R., Imran, M., & Begum, S. (2025). A Progressive Direction for Startup India: Milestones and Trends from 2016 to 2023. In Hamdan, R. K. (Ed.), *Sustainable Data Management. Studies in Big Data* (Vol. 171). Springer., DOI: 10.1007/978-3-031-83911-5_34

Panigrahi, R. R., Dash, M., Shaikh, Z. H., & Irfan, M. (2023). Review of Machine Learning Techniques in the Supply Chain Management of Indian Industry: A Future Research Agenda. In Irfan, M., Elhoseny, M., Kassim, S., & Metawa, N. (Eds.), *Advanced Machine Learning Algorithms for Complex Financial Applications* (pp. 199–219). IGI Global., DOI: 10.4018/978-1-6684-4483-2.ch013

Ram, P. (2024). Gen AI: Powering enterprise transformation through trust. *Dataquest, May 2024*, 52–54.

Roopalatha, H. (2024). Microsoft AI CEO is building AI companions for India. *CEO Insights, December 2024*, 16–17.

Sarea, A., Subramanian, S., Alareeni, B., Shaikh, Z. H., Hawaldar, I. T., & Elshaker, A. H. (2021). Financial Disclosures by Using Machine Learning Analysis. In Alareeni, B., Hamdan, A., & Elgedawy, I. (Eds.), *The Importance of New Technologies and Entrepreneurship in Business Development: In The Context of Economic Diversity in Developing Countries. ICBT 2020. Lecture Notes in Networks and Systems* (Vol. 194). Springer., DOI: 10.1007/978-3-030-69221-6_5

Saxena, A., & Rishi, B. (2025), "Designing an artificial intelligence-enabled large language model for financial decisions", *Management Decision*, Vol. ahead-of-print No. ahead-of-print. DOI: 10.1108/MD-02-2024-0305

Shah, D. (2024). AI in FinTech: Revolutionizing the customer experience and driving innovation. *Silicon India, June 2024*, 36–37.

Shaikh, Z., Irfan, M., Sarea, A., & Panigrahi, R. R. (2024). *The Emergence of Islamic Fintech and Bahrain: Prospect for Global Financial Sectors* (Vol. 503). Springer., DOI: 10.1007/978-3-031-43490-7_52

Shaikh, Z. H., Irfan, M., Nomran, N. M., & Lawin, M. L. (2024). The Effect of Strategic Partnership on Innovation and Business: Performance of the Fintech Industry in Bahrain. In Irfan, M., Kadry, S., Sharif, M., & Khan, H. (Eds.), *Fintech Applications in Islamic Finance: AI, Machine Learning, and Blockchain Techniques* (pp. 236–254). IGI Global., DOI: 10.4018/979-8-3693-1038-0.ch016

Shaikh, Z. H., Irfan, M., Nomran, N. M., & Ratnakaram, S. P. (2024). Unlocking the Potential of AI for Efficient Governance: Innovative Approaches of Bahrain. In Irfan, M., Elmogy, M., Gupta, S., Khalifa, F., & Dias, R. (Eds.), *AI-Driven Decentralized Finance and the Future of Finance* (pp. 115–142). IGI Global., DOI: 10.4018/979-8-3693-6321-8.ch005

Shaikh, Z. H., Sarea, A., & Irfan, M. (2022). *Islamic Banking Strategies in the World of Fintech: Success Story of Bahrain* (Vol. 423). Springer., DOI: 10.1007/978-3-030-93464-4_10

Sheela, P., Kusuma, K., Panigrahi, R. R., & Shaikh, Z. H. (2024). Fintech and Islamic Banking: A Systematic View and Future Research Agenda. In Irfan, M., Kadry, S., Sharif, M., & Khan, H. (Eds.), *Fintech Applications in Islamic Finance: AI, Machine Learning, and Blockchain Techniques* (pp. 1–23). IGI Global., DOI: 10.4018/979-8-3693-1038-0.ch001

Silber, D., Hoffmann, A. and Belli, A. (2025), "Embracing AI advisors for making (complex) financial decisions: an experimental investigation of the role of a maximizing decision-making style", *International Journal of Bank Marketing*, Vol. ahead-of-print No. ahead-of-print. https://doi.org/.DOI: 10.1108/IJBM-10-2024-0647

Soni, A., Shaikh, Z. H., Irfan, M., & Bijja, V. (2025). Indigenous Empowerment as a Catalyst for Sustainable Development. In Irfan, M., Majeed, M., Kassim, S., & Ofori, K. (Eds.), *The Future of Indigenous Inclusivity: Unlocking Finance for Economic Development* (pp. 253–274). IGI Global Scientific Publishing., DOI: 10.4018/979-8-3693-7924-0.ch012

Tyagi, R. (2019). Un-chaining the telecom with blockchain. *Enterprise IT World, June 2019*, 30–32.

Chapter 13
Redefining Workforce Dynamics:
The Impact of Digital Transformation on Employee Roles, Skill Evolution, and Automation Integration

Indra Sharma
https://orcid.org/0009-0000-3303-6569
Jaipur National University, India

Shilpi Bagga
Jaipur National University, India

Ruchika Rastogi
https://orcid.org/0000-0001-7144-4387
Pranveer Singh Institute of Technology, Kanpur, India

Mir Shahid Satar
Saudi Electronic University, Riyadh, Saudi Arabia

ABSTRACT

The global banking industry has seen tremendous change as a result of digital transformation, which has affected both customer views and operational structures. In order to provide value for consumers and bring about fundamental changes in organizational character, it involves applying digital processes to every facet of business (Nguyen-Thi-Huong et al., 2023). Digital transformation in the banking sector includes technologies that improve operational efficiency and service offer-

DOI: 10.4018/979-8-3373-1250-7.ch013

ings, including blockchain, mobile banking, robotic process automation (RPA), and artificial intelligence (AI) (Boufounou et al., 2022). In addition to implementing new technology, digitalization also entails changing company procedures, customer interactions, and organizational models as a result of these technological breakthroughs.

1. INTRODUCTION

The global banking industry has seen tremendous change as a result of digital transformation, which has affected both customer views and operational structures. In order to provide value for consumers and bring about fundamental changes in organizational character, it involves applying digital processes to every facet of business (Nguyen-Thi-Huong et al., 2023). Digital transformation in the banking sector includes technologies that improve operational efficiency and service offerings, including blockchain, mobile banking, robotic process automation (RPA), and artificial intelligence (AI) (Boufounou et al., 2022). In addition to implementing new technology, digitalization also entails changing company procedures, customer interactions, and organizational models as a result of these technological breakthroughs.

This shift has been spearheaded by the banking industry, which has been influenced by changing consumer demands and quick technical breakthroughs. Digital solutions like online banking and automation are progressively replacing traditional bureaucratic banking models that depended on paperwork and in-person contacts (Met et al., 2019). This change is particularly noticeable in the automation of services, where AI and RPA have decreased the need for human labor, increasing productivity and cost-effectiveness. In a same vein, consumer interactions have changed from face-to-face transactions to 24/7 digital self-service alternatives due to the use of chatbots and mobile banking (Kitsios et al., 2021).

The effect that digital transformation has on personnel is another important consideration. Employees at banking institutions must acquire new digital skills and adjust to new work patterns as digital solutions are incorporated more and more. But this change has also revealed skill shortages in the workforce, which has made it harder for the industry to be flexible and agile (Sama, 2019). Since digital competency is necessary to properly utilize technology improvements, addressing these skill gaps is crucial for the successful implementation of digital business strategy.

Three main facets of digitization in Indian public sector banks are the subject of this study:

Redefining Employee Responsibilities: Examining how worker competencies are reshaped and skill gaps are addressed by digital transformation.

Promoting Automation: Evaluating how much automation has reduced the need for manual labor in banking procedures.
Improving Customer Service: Examining how banks are using digital platforms to satisfy changing consumer demands.

This study intends to add to the body of knowledge on digital transformation in the banking industry by analyzing these aspects and emphasizing related opportunities and difficulties. It also aims to offer suggestions for the successful execution of digital strategies, guaranteeing that Indian public sector banks maintain their competitiveness and responsiveness in an increasingly digital environment.

The banking sector has been leading in this change, triggered by the technological change and ever-changing customer needs. The conventional bureaucratic business approaches in banking, which relied on papers and face-to-face contacts, are gradually being replaced by computers and online services (Met et al., 2019). This shift is most apparent in such sectors as service automation where with the application artificial intelligence and robotic process automation the use of manpower has reduced, making operations more efficient and less costly. In the same way, using innovations like chatbots and mobile banking, the interaction between banks and clients has shifted from face-to-face, self-service, available 24/7 (Kitsios et al., 2021).

A final essential area of this shift also related to the employees. The shift towards digital transformation banking sector means that employees must develop additional digital competencies and embrace new working models. Yet, this type of evolution has also exposed internal talent disparities in the industry which threatens the agile and adaptive nature of the workforce (Sama, 2019). Mitigating these skill deficits is crucial for the effective execution of digital business strategies mainly because digital competencies are critical for delivering on the promise of digital technologies.

In this research, three elements of digitalization in banks are of particular interest. First, it explores how digital transformation reframes the competencies demanded from the employee population and redresses competencies gaps. Second, it evaluates the extent of reduction in manual operation in banking sector due to automation of services and reduce the extent of manual operations. Last of all, it looks into the current state of digital customer service considering how banks are implementing the usage of digital channels to fulfill customers' expectations. Thus, the following objectives are set to be achieved in the frame of the study: To contribute to the overall understanding of how the banking industry and its workforce is being transformed by digitalization, the study will focus on the following objectives.

In doing so, this research aims at contributing to the existing literature on digital transformation for the banking sector with the related threats. The recommendations for this him to ensure that the strategies implementation of digital technologies can be achieved effectively so that banks can continue to be responsive to the challenges and opportunities presented in a world that is fast going digital.

2. REVIEW OF LITERATURE

Tiwari et al. (2023) have undertaken research on impact of digital adoption of digitalization on engagement of workforce in the Banking sector w.r.t. Indian scehario. The study sought to find out how innovation through digital technology impacts workforce participation with an emphasis on innovative organizational models. This study, which employed a combination of primary research tools, showed that digital transformation strategies enhanced workforce interaction while stressing the need for innovation for operational continuity. The authors pointed out that there must be engagement strategies for organizations to be articulate in dynamic digital contexts.

The shift towards digital banking in India has been driven by advancements in fintech, artificial intelligence (AI), and big data analytics (Gupta & Jain, 2021). Studies highlight that digitalization enhances operational efficiency, improves risk management, and fosters financial inclusion (RBI, 2023). However, it also necessitates significant changes in workforce dynamics, requiring upskilling and reskilling initiatives (Choudhary, 2022)

The rapid adoption of digital banking tools has created a demand for tech-savvy employees. Research by Sharma and Verma (2020) emphasizes that PSBs must invest in digital literacy programs to equip employees with skills in data analytics, cybersecurity, and AI-driven decision-making. Additionally, the World Bank (2022) highlights the role of government and financial institutions in fostering digital training programs to bridge skill gaps.

Elsafty & Yehia (2023) This study examined digital transformation challenges in Egypt's public sector, including the banking industry. The findings revealed that factors like organizational culture, employee skills, and leadership had a significantly influence on the success of digital initiatives. The authors highlighted threw high on the role of financial investments in technology and employee training programs to overcome resistance and achieve transformation goals.

Nguyen-Thi-Huong et al. (2023) analyzed the effect of digitalization the performance of Vietnamese banks. Findings indicated a paradoxical trend where digital adoption initially reduced return on equity (ROE) but later increased operational efficiency during the COVID-19 pandemic. The authors concluded that strategic planning and gradual implementation of digital technologies are necessary to realize long-term benefits.

Despite the benefits, digital transformation poses challenges such as cybersecurity threats, resistance to change, and skill redundancy (Mukherjee, 2023). Studies recommend continuous policy interventions, industry-academia collaboration, and investment in human capital to ensure a smooth transition towards digital banking (NITI Aayog, 2024).

Automation through AI-powered chatbots, robotic process automation (RPA), and blockchain solutions has streamlined routine banking tasks (Kumar & Singh, 2021). Studies suggest that while automation reduces manual workload, it necessitates a shift in job roles, with employees focusing more on analytical and customer-centric functions (Bose et al., 2022). This has led to a redefinition of traditional banking jobs, demanding adaptability and continuous learning (NASSCOM, 2023).

Digital transformation has improved customer experience by enabling 24/7 banking services, personalized financial advice, and seamless transactions (Patel, 2023). Research indicates that customer expectations have evolved, requiring bank employees to adopt a more consultative approach (Deloitte, 2022). AI-driven insights and real-time customer engagement tools have empowered employees to offer customized solutions, strengthening customer trust and loyalty.

Digital transformation was evaluated by Mohamed (2022) in relation to strategic flexibility among the central bank human resource. A survey showed that promoting the exchange of information and cooperation with other workers increased productivity. The authors' conclusion was that motivation and adaptability are critical to maintaining strategic agility in the long run during change.

Sagala et al. (2022) examine the process of a traditional bank to become a digital bank with emphasis on the change in IT management. According to the study, adoption of advanced technologies such as cloud computing and machine learning, was critical for operations. The authors also established that, to maintain competitive advantage, agile practices should be implemented, and innovation should be encouraged.

Kadur & Supriya (2022) examined the effect of digital transformation on the employees of the public sector banks in India. In their work, they sought to find the impact of digital technology enablers and users on employee stress and engagement. When using descriptive statistics and Pearson correlation as the research method, the study established that DT activities influenced workforce issues such as stress levels. They argued that while digital transformation did improve productivity, it puts pressure on employees, so they require better support mechanisms.

"Mohamed (2022) studied the interaction between digital transformation with strategic flexibility in the context of the central bank employees. This paper, using questionnaires to 204 employees, sought to establish the role of digital tools in improving the performance and solving problems of employees. The study revealed that creating motivation culture and ideas sharing enhanced the workflow efficiency in a great way. In the light of the study, it was argued that it is important for organisations to engage employees and adopt strategic flexibility in order to maintain competitive advantage in a digital environment."

Diener & Špaček (2021) examined the key challenges to digitalization in banking, from the manager's point of view. The study found out on the challenges that include strategy, technology and employees' participation; which used contextual interviews and content analysis. The authors posited that to overcome these barriers, the two complementary perspectives of technology adoption and employee readiness should be carefully managed, and the need for training and other initiatives to be aligned with strategic initiatives.

To my knowledge, Brintseva (2021) explored how employment dynamics of the banking sector were affected by digitalization, with reference to the role of COVID-19 as a catalyst. The study also showed the need for new digital competencies for personnel to function effectively in conditions of remote work. The research established that digital transformation leads to downsizing of employees while at the same time creating more demand for skilled personnel. The study therefore found it necessary to match the competencies of employees with newer technologies to support efficiency and competitiveness in the marketplace.

"In the study conducted by Lindawati & Parwoto, (2021) the impact of transnational leadership and employee motivation on performance during digital transformation in Indonesia's banking industry was examined. In so doing, they discovered that through structural equation modeling, transnational leadership had a positive impact on the level of job satisfaction and employee performance. In view of this, the study found out that it is the leadership styles that help shape how organization handles change and employees' readiness for change during the technological transformation."

Kitsios et al. (2021) targeted the acceptance by the banks in Greece where the Technology Acceptance Model was used to measure the employees' attitudes. The survey conducted with 161 employees pointed to training as one of the key enablers of digital change. Findings revealed positive correlation between readiness of employees and effective adoption of digital technologies. The authors suggested the implementation of specific educational interventions when it comes to transition into digital settings.

Winasis et al., (2021) examined the relationship between TL and EE among employees in Indonesian banks that are in the process of digital transformation. Several recommendations pointed to the effectiveness of leadership types in creating a supportive organizational culture. The authors summed up by underlining the significance of leadership for the morale of the employees in cases of technological advancements.

Digital transformation in financial services: A qualitative analysis of enablers was a study conducted by Werth et al. (2020). The study also reported on the fact that digitalization is, in fact, evolutionary, not disruptive, and backend modernization is a priority. According to the authors, customer expectations and Big Tech competition were identified as the main focal areas that need to be addressed to achieve success in transformation.

Krasonikolakis et al. (2020) focused on the area of digital transformation in the context of retail banking highlighting the importance of organizational culture and strategic fit. The study emphasized on the issues of technology acquisitions and suggested a more balanced view, which by considering technical and social aspects of the process. The authors found that flexibility and the ability to anticipate change are perhaps the most important prerequisites for development.

Stark (2020) explored the digital transformation initiatives in a medium bank. It was identified that the first efforts to digital transition were problematic but concentrating on customer-oriented services and analytics improved outputs. According to the research, customer focus and internal integration are key factors that must be central to any digital change.

Said & Angelita (2020) discussed on digital transformation strategies in an Indonesian bank that focused on the employees' preparedness on technological advancement. Strategic thinking frameworks were evaluated using survey and interviews as the research method adopted in the study. Consequently, analysis of the results showed that a large number of the employees had low levels of confidence in organizational preparedness for digital transformation, which underlined the necessity of learning and changing. The authors noted that one of the key findings for successful DT is the collaboration with fintech and learning culture.

Exploring the effects of finance digitalization on the workforce structure in Europe, Moşteanu and Fathi (2020). This paper examined the issue of adaptation to digital technology, with emphasis on the skills deficiency due to high levels of technology development. H1 highlighted the need to develop reskilling and upskilling strategies that will fit into the current digital economic needs. Accordingly, the study found that educational reforms and strategic planning are essential factors that enable the match between the competencies of the workforce and digital transformation.

Sama (2019) although studying the effect of digitalization in Sub-Saharan Africa's banking industry particularly focused on its influence on the employees and customers. The study found out that the degree of digitalization in the workplace enhanced the employee performance. However, people's resistance to change was noted mainly because of concerns of job loss. Accordingly, this study established that the best practices for digital tools' application imply the consideration of employees' attitudes and promoting teamwork to improve productivity.

Met et al. (2019) discussed the impact of AI and RPA on banking work processes. The study also showed that the technologies improve organizational customer relations as well as internal operations, enhancing operational effectiveness. The authors suggested to financial institutions to invest in their employees to create a smooth integration of these technologies, so that the banks can take advantage of the possibilities of the new digital world.

The study of Shkodina et al. (2019) is devoted to the analysis of the major global issues associated with banking digitalization and the application of blockchain and artificial intelligence. This work explained how these technologies were being used to improve customer experience and firm operations, as well as to mitigate risk factors such as cyber security threats that are inherent in the business environment. Advanced verification processes were suggested by the authors to be incorporated in order to manage risks resulting from digitalization.

Helina & Rathiha (2018) focused on the employees' attitude towards the change of e-banking in the financial industry. The Findings indicated that convenience, productivity as well as time saving were the main factors influencing positive perception. The authors stated that training and counseling programmers are necessary to manage stress in employees and facilitate their readiness for digital technologies. The following hypotheses have been formulated based on the insights derived from the reviewed literature:

H1: Digital transformation has a significant positive effect on changes in skill gaps within the banking sector.
H2: Digital transformation leads to a statistically significant reduction in manual work processes through increased service automation in banking operations.
H3: Digital transformation has a significant and strong positive effect on the adoption of digital customer service practices in the banking sector.

3. METHODOLOGY

This study fell within the realm of descriptive research as it aimed to describe and quantify the relationships between digital transformation and its impacts on employee skill gaps, service automation, and the shift toward digital customer service in the banking sector. Additionally, it incorporated aspects of analytical research to investigate and interpret the causal relationships among the variables using advanced modeling and statistical methods.

The participants in this study were employees in the public sector banks operating in Jaipur that are either directly or indirectly engaged in the digital transformation initiatives. The study sample was comprised of 250 observations and the study employed stratified random sampling in the selection method. This was done to make sure that the sample included cross sectional employees from various employment levels, employment type and industry within the banking sector. The decision to use the stratified approach was made in order to obtain the data on the differences in employees' experiences and attitudes to digital transformation and at the same time avoid the sampling bias.

This study used a structured questionnaire for data collection, which was developed for this research. The questionnaire was constructed from the literature review and consultations with the domain specialists in order to capture all the relevant aspects. These were items for variables like digitization, shift in skill differentials, changes in service delivery, and digital customer services. The responses gathered were quantified using Likert scale 5 point for considering purpose consistency and analysis.

The pilot study was conducted with thirty participants from the target population to ensure the reliability of instruments. The responses gathered from the pilot study were incorporated into the development of the final questionnaire to enhance the comprehensible, accurate, and coherent items in the questionnaire. Expert judgement was used to establish content validity while construct validity was assessed through exploratory factor analysis.

The primary data was obtained from the internet by administering an online survey tool that would allow respondents to remain anonymous. The questionnaire was self-administered, and the participants' consent was sought before they filled the questionnaire. The online format also helped in the easy collection of data and also the response rate in the set time was also high. SEM was employed to analyze the correlations and effects of the variables and offered sound information concerning the tested causalities in the study.

4. RESULTS

Table 1. Information regarding models

Estimation Method	ML
Optimization Method	NLMINB
Number of observations	250
Free parameters	66

continued on following page

Table 1. Continued

Estimation Method	ML
Standard errors	Standard
Scaled test	None
Converged	TRUE
Iterations	287
Model	Digital Transformation=~DTB1+DTB2+DTB3+DTB4+DTB5
	Change in Skill Gap =~PSG1+PSG2+PSG3+PSG4+PSG5
	Service Automation (Reduction in Manual Work)=~AORT1+AORT2+AORT3+AORT4+AORT5
	Shift to Digital Customer Service=~SDCS1+SDCS2+SDCS3+SDCS4+SDCS5
	Change in Skill Gap ~Digital Transformation
	Service Automation (Reduction in Manual Work)~Digital Transformation
	Shift to Digital Customer Service~Digital Transformation

Table 1 presents important details about the structural equation model applied in the analysis of relationships between the latent variables. The estimation method used is Maximum Likelihood (ML) and the NLMINB optimization method used in this model conferred after 287 iterations. The model is developed on 250 observation and contains 66 free parameters; the standard errors are calculated by the standard way, and the scaled test is not used.

The structural model specifies four latent constructs: Digital Transformation, Change in Skill Gap, Service Automation (Reduction in Manual Work), Shift to Digital Customer Service all of which are evaluated with five perceived indicators. Moreover, the model specifies directional relationships, where Digital Transformation impacts Skill Gap, Service Automation, and Shift to Digital Customer Service. This setup offers a framework in which the impact of digital transformation of the workforce and the delivery of services can be studied while relying on sound modeling approaches.

Table 2. Model tests

Label	X^2	df	p
User Model	3973	164	<.001
Baseline Model	6289	190	<.001

Table 2 provides a summary of chi-square test of model fit for the structural equation model. The User Model construct, testing the hypothesized relationships between the latent constructs, has a chi-square value (X^2) equal to 3973; degrees of freedom (df) equal to 164; and $p < 0.001$ is statistically significant. This means that the covariance matrices of the model's observed and expected values are different, and that is typical for large sample volumes.

The Baseline Model, which predicts no associations between the variables, yields a significantly higher chi-square value of 6289 with 190 degrees of freedom ($p < 0.001$). The high significant chi-square difference index between the User Model and the Baseline Model indicate that the User Model offers a much better fit to the data than the Baseline Model. Nonetheless, the enormous value of chi-square that has been recorded for the User Model indicates the importance of exploring other fit indices for a more comprehensive assessment of model fitness.

Table 3. Fit indices

		95% Confidence Intervals		
SRMR	**RMSEA**	**Lower**	**Upper**	**RMSEA p**
0.195	0.305	0.297	0.313	<.001

Table 3 provides fit statistics which assess the goodness of the Structural Equation Model. The Standardized Root Mean Square Residual (SRMR) is 0.195 and, therefore, above the cut off of 0.08, which suggests that the fit of the models is poor. The value of the Root Mean Square Error of Approximation (RMSEA) is also equal to 0.305, 95% CI [0.297; 0.313] and $p < 0.001$. This RMSEA value is way above the commonly advisable level of 0.08, which also points to a poor model fit.

Table 4. Parameters estimates

				95% Confidence Intervals				
Dep	**Pred**	**Estimate**	**SE**	**Lower**	**Upper**	**β**	**z**	**p**
Change in Skill Gap	Digital Transformation	0.8	0.389	0.0369	1.56	1.059	2.05	0.04
Service Automation (Reduction in Manual Work)	Digital Transformation	0.724	0.3	0.1361	1.31	0.272	2.41	0.016
Shift to Digital Customer Service	Digital Transformation	3.484	1.046	1.433	5.53	0.924	3.33	<.001

Table 4 presents the results of an analysis exploring the impact of Digital Transformation on three key outcomes: They are New: Change in Skill Gap, Service Automation (Reduction in Manual Work), and Shift to Digital Customer Service .

The results also underscore the role of Digital Transformation as the main cause of these changes with different effects on the dependent variables.

First, the results reveal that the total direct effect of Digital Transformation on the Change in Skill Gap is positive but moderate, with an estimate of 0.800. This value indicates that when organisations are in the process of transforming digitally, there is a significant difference in the skills gap. The 95% CIs of this estimate are 0.0369 to 1.56, which give a sense of a positive and measurable true effect. Moreover, the standardized coefficient ($\beta = 1.059$) shows the significant relationship in the standardized scale. This effect is statistically significant with a p-value of 0.040, which indicates that the obtained change in the difference in skills is related to the Digital Transformation efforts.

Second, Digital Transformation also impacts Service Automation (Reduction in Manual Work) with the prediction of 0.724. This result has also vindicated the use of digital platforms that enable mechanization of work and thereby reducing manpower. The 95% confidence interval for this variable is between 0.1361 and 1.31 thus endorsing this positive association as reliable. The standardized coefficient ($\beta=0.272$) is lower than that of the effect on the skill gap though statistically significant with $p= 0.016$. This finding supports, once again, the narrative that digital transformation translates to tangible decreases in manual activities.

Last but not least, the largest effect size of Digital Transformation is in the Digital Transformation of Customer Service with the estimate of 3.484. This means there is a significant impact, given the fact that digital transformation is at the center of redesigning customer service strategies. The 95% confidence interval is between 1.4330 and 5.53, so there is a strong and reliable positive relation between online participation and course performance. The nature and degree of relationship is also significant with the standardized coefficient ($\beta = 0.924$). Also, it is worth mentioning that the p-value for this variable is less than .001, which means a high level of significance. This result shows that organisations that are in the process of digital transformation, go through a significant change in the digital orientation of customer service. The same relationship has also been explained in figure 1, which shows the impact of Digital transformation with the help of path diagram.

Overall, the findings indicate that Digital Transformation has a positive effect on organizational processes and performance, with the greatest effect being seen in the move to digital customer service. All three dependent variables are positively and significantly impacted but their strength and magnitude of impact differs, which signifies that digital transformation is a complex process and has implications for contemporary organisations. Therefore, the research findings presented in this paper are useful for organisations planning to leverage on the digital environment for business growth.

Figure 1. Path Diagram

Table-4 Parameters estimates

			95% Confidence Intervals					
Dep	Pred	Estimate	SE	Lower	Upper	β	z	p
Change in Skill Gap	Digital Transformation	0.8	0.389	0.0369	1.56	1.059	2.05	0.04
Service Automation (Reduction in Manual Work)	Digital Transformation	0.724	0.3	0.1361	1.31	0.272	2.41	0.016
Shift to Digital Customer Service	Digital Transformation	3.484	1.046	1.433	5.53	0.924	3.33	<.001

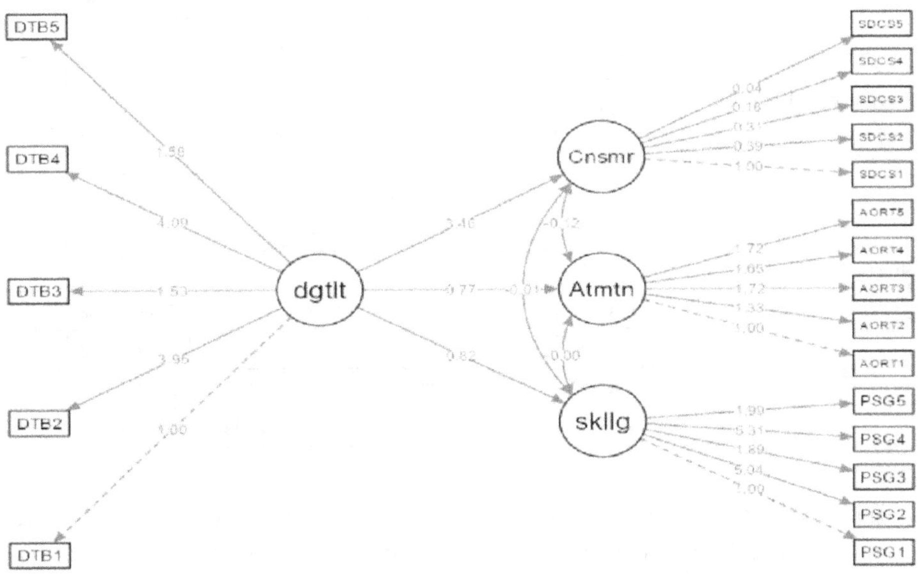

Table 5. Measurement model

				95% Confidence Intervals				
Latent	**Observed**	**Estimate**	**SE**	**Lower**	**Upper**	**β**	**z**	**p**
Digital Transformation	DTB1	1	0	1	1	0.199		
	DTB2	4.016	1.1914	1.6814	6.351	0.939	3.37	<.001
	DTB3	1.561	0.5226	0.5363	2.585	0.357	2.99	0.003
	DTB4	4.148	1.2307	1.7361	6.56	0.935	3.37	<.001
	DTB5	1.606	0.5354	0.5564	2.655	0.364	3	0.003
Change in Skill Gap	PSG1	1	0	1	1	0.149		
	PSG2	5.236	2.029	1.2595	9.213	0.932	2.58	0.01
	PSG3	1.928	0.8107	0.3389	3.517	0.334	2.38	0.017
	PSG4	5.505	2.1336	1.3233	9.687	0.925	2.58	0.01
	PSG5	2.046	0.8543	0.3718	3.721	0.348	2.4	0.017
Service Automation (Reduction in Manual Work)	AORT1	1	0	1	1	0.543		
	AORT2	0.944	0.1527	0.6445	1.243	0.556	6.18	<.001
	AORT3	1.36	0.192	0.9837	1.736	0.768	7.08	<.001
	AORT4	0.92	0.1513	0.6232	1.217	0.541	6.08	<.001
	AORT5	0.986	0.1584	0.6759	1.297	0.563	6.23	<.001
Shift to Digital Customer Service	SDCS1	1	0	1	1	0.857		
	SDCS2	0.426	0.0749	0.2788	0.572	0.369	5.68	<.001
	SDCS3	0.344	0.0834	0.1801	0.507	0.271	4.12	<.001
	SDCS4	0.23	0.0843	0.0649	0.395	0.181	2.73	0.006
	SDCS5	0.135	0.0803	-0.0222	0.292	0.112	1.68	0.092

Table 5 outlines a measurement model assessing four latent constructs: Observed Variables: Digital Transformation, Change in Skill Gap, Service Automation (Reduction in Manual Work), and Shift to Digital Customer Service. All constructs are assessed with multiple observed indicators; their estimates, SE, 95% CI (lower and upper bounds), standardized regression coefficients (β), z scores, and p values are presented.

The results also show high significance for all the observed variables for most of the constructs, suggesting their relevance to the latent variables with the value < 0.001. For instance, in Digital Transformation, there is the DTB2 and DTB4 which has a high β values of 0.939 and 0.935, respectively. Likewise, in Service Automation, coefficients β of AORT2 to AORT5 are high (0.541 – 0.768), thus confirming the reliability of the indicators. However, in the Shift to Digital Customer Service construct, SDCS5 has the least impact (β = 0.112, p = 0.092). Altogether, the results confirm the reliability and the range of the measurement model constituents.

Table 6. Variances and Covariances

			95% Confidence Intervals				
Variable 1	**Variable 2**	**Estimate**	**SE**	**Lower**	**Upper**	**β**	**z**	**p**
DTB1	DTB1	2.30661	0.20549	1.90386	2.70936	0.9603	11.225	<.001
DTB2	DTB2	0.20502	0.01943	0.16693	0.24311	0.1177	10.549	<.001
DTB3	DTB3	1.58495	0.13988	1.31079	1.8591	0.8723	11.331	<.001
DTB4	DTB4	0.23691	0.02219	0.19342	0.2804	0.1263	10.677	<.001
DTB5	DTB5	1.61311	0.14229	1.33422	1.89199	0.8679	11.337	<.001
PSG1	PSG1	2.37963	0.21213	1.96386	2.79541	0.9777	11.218	<.001
PSG2	PSG2	0.2236	0.02081	0.18281	0.2644	0.1305	10.743	<.001
PSG3	PSG3	1.61241	0.14178	1.33453	1.89029	0.8887	11.373	<.001
PSG4	PSG4	0.27805	0.02549	0.22808	0.32801	0.1444	10.907	<.001
PSG5	PSG5	1.64806	0.14468	1.36448	1.93163	0.8787	11.391	<.001
AORT1	AORT1	1.62066	0.16719	1.29297	1.94835	0.7054	9.693	<.001
AORT2	AORT2	1.34843	0.14072	1.07263	1.62423	0.691	9.583	<.001
AORT3	AORT3	0.8725	0.14257	0.59307	1.15193	0.4106	6.12	<.001
AORT4	AORT4	1.38143	0.14235	1.10244	1.66043	0.7069	9.705	<.001
AORT5	AORT5	1.42091	0.14923	1.12842	1.7134	0.6833	9.522	<.001
SDCS1	SDCS1	0.49107	0.12837	0.23947	0.74268	0.2662	3.825	<.001
SDCS2	SDCS2	1.55083	0.14154	1.27341	1.82825	0.8635	10.957	<.001
SDCS3	SDCS3	2.00935	0.18149	1.65364	2.36506	0.9263	11.072	<.001
SDCS4	SDCS4	2.10928	0.18943	1.738	2.48057	0.9671	11.135	<.001
SDCS5	SDCS5	1.93527	0.17336	1.59549	2.27504	0.9874	11.163	<.001
Digital Transformation	Digital Transformation	0.09525	0.05701	-0.0165	0.20699	1	1.671	0.095
Change in Skill Gap	Change in Skill Gap	-0.0066	0.00515	-0.0167	0.00345	- 0.1222	-1.29	0.197
Service Automation (Reduction in Manual Work)	Service Automation (Reduction in Manual Work)	0.62699	0.15617	0.3209	0.93308	0.9262	4.015	<.001
Shift to Digital Customer Service	Shift to Digital Customer Service	0.19795	0.125	-0.0471	0.44295	0.1462	1.584	0.113
Change in Skill Gap	Service Automation (Reduction in Manual Work)	0.00144	0.00252	-0.0035	0.00637	0.0223	0.573	0.567
Change in Skill Gap	Shift to Digital Customer Service	-0.0075	0.004	-0.0153	3.53E-04	- 0.2067	-1.872	0.061
Service Automation (Reduction in Manual Work)	Shift to Digital Customer Service	0.01479	0.04942	-0.0821	0.11165	0.042	0.299	0.765

Table 6 summarizes the variances and covariances for observed variables across four latent constructs: DT, Change in Skill Demand, Disposal of Manual Work/Service Automation, and Transition to Digital Customer Contact. Descriptive statistics for the observed variables show that all variance estimates are significant at $p < 0.001$ and high z-score for the measures used in this study. For example, SDCS5 (variance: 1.The results of the current study show that the items of each construct in both questionnaire and interview have high internal reliability, with questionnaire items being more reliable; questionnaire: PSG1 (variance = 935, $\beta = 0.987$, $p < 0.001$) and PSG5 (variance = 1.648, $\beta = 0.879$, $p < 0.001$).

Covariances between the latent variables show less and a rather inconsistent relationship. As such, covariances such as Change in Skill Gap with Service Automation (estimate = 0.001, $p = 0.567$) and Change in Skill Gap with Shift to Digital Customer Service (estimate = -0.0075, $p = 0.061$) show limited interaction. On the other hand, internal consistency within Service Automation is substantial at moderate levels (estimate = 0.627, $p < 0.001$). These results raise questions about substantial differences for the constructs but weak relationships between certain latent variables.

Table 7. Intercepts

			95% Confidence Intervals			
Variable	**Intercept**	**SE**	**Lower**	**Upper**	**z**	**p**
DTB1	3.512	0.098	3.32	3.704	35.83	<.001
DTB2	3.864	0.083	3.7	4.028	46.296	<.001
DTB3	3.848	0.085	3.681	4.015	45.138	<.001
DTB4	3.936	0.087	3.766	4.106	45.438	<.001
DTB5	3.964	0.086	3.795	4.133	45.973	<.001
PSG1	3.504	0.099	3.311	3.697	35.512	<.001
PSG2	3.88	0.083	3.718	4.042	46.865	<.001
PSG3	3.828	0.085	3.661	3.995	44.934	<.001
PSG4	3.916	0.088	3.744	4.088	44.627	<.001
PSG5	3.98	0.087	3.81	4.15	45.95	<.001
AORT1	3.52	0.096	3.332	3.708	36.718	<.001
AORT2	3.636	0.088	3.463	3.809	41.154	<.001
AORT3	3.428	0.092	3.247	3.609	37.183	<.001
AORT4	3.412	0.088	3.239	3.585	38.591	<.001
AORT5	3.024	0.091	2.845	3.203	33.157	<.001
SDCS1	3.916	0.086	3.748	4.084	45.585	<.001

continued on following page

Table 7. Continued

			95% Confidence Intervals			
Variable	**Intercept**	**SE**	**Lower**	**Upper**	**z**	**p**
SDCS2	4.004	0.085	3.838	4.17	47.24	<.001
SDCS3	3.836	0.093	3.653	4.019	41.182	<.001
SDCS4	3.712	0.093	3.529	3.895	39.742	<.001
SDCS5	3.4	0.089	3.226	3.574	38.399	<.001
Digital Transformation	0	0	0	0		
Change in Skill Gap	0	0	0	0		
Service Automation (Reduction in Manual Work)	0	0	0	0		
Shift to Digital Customer Service	0	0	0	0		

Table 7 presents the intercepts for observed variables within four constructs: The four categories include Digital Transformation, Change in Skill Gap, Service Automation (Decrease in Manual Work), and the Transition to Digital Customer Service. The intercepts represent the expected average of each variable when all other predictors are set to zero. The intercepts for all the observed variables are highly significant; $p < 0.001$, z-scores from 33.157 to 47.240 which support the stability of all the observed variables and their contribution to their respective constructs.

Intercepts across variables are reasonable, varying between 3.024 for AORT5 and 4.004 for SDCS2. DTB5 = 3.964, z = 45.973 and PSG5 = 3.980, z = 45.950 mean that at the baseline, the constructs have high levels of underlying contributions. Digital Transformation, Change in Skill Gap, Service Automation, and Shift to Digital Customer Service are constructs themselves and their observed variables have intercepts set at zero. This table shows the relative stability and reliability of the measurement model in assessing the baseline variable impacts.

5. DISCUSSION

This study set out to explore the impact of digital transformation on three critical dimensions in the banking sector: the alteration of the differences in skills, the automation of services, and the transition to e-service. The analysis highlighted that IT innovation is a major source of change across the organization, though it has differential effect on each of the specified dimensions.

The outcomes showed that digital transformation leads to a decrease in the skill gap of the employees. This is in sync with past studies which have underlined the part played by digital tools to remap the nature of workforce demands and raise the skills of employees. Based on the evidence derived from the case study, the study established that digital transformation brings not only the challenges of upskilling but also the potential for fixing pre-existing problems through embracing the culture of training and development.

Regarding the automation of services, it was found that the digital transformation process is responsible for reducing the degree of human intervention in the execution of ordinary tasks. This result supports the findings of Met et al. (2019) who pointed out that RPA and AI increase efficiency in banking operations. The automation of most manual tasks allows the banks to free resources to work on other key issues besides tend to mundane tasks.

The largest shift in digital transformation was noticed in moving to the digital customer service. This finding supports Kitsios et al. (2021) who pointed out that today's banking businesses rely heavily on digital forms of communication with customers. The shift in customer service to a digital platform is not a unique occurrence as the general consumer shift to a more personalized, convenient and around-the-clock satisfaction. This shift puts pressure on the banks to employ constantly new customer-facing technologies to maintain competitive advantage.

Taken together, these results provide additional support for the concept of digital transformation as a holistic organizational process. This way, there is going to be a better way to meet the challenges of the new age by filling the gaps in the employees' skills, improving the overall performance through the help of automation, and changing the ways of interacting with customers. Such outcomes are consistent with previous research works that have illustrated various effects of digitalisation on the banking sector (Nguyen-Thi-Huong et al., 2023; Brintseva, 2021).

6. CONCLUSION

The findings of the study highlighted the fact that digital transformation has a positive impact on the important organization dimensions in the banking context. With regards to the first research question, it was observed that digital transformation enables quantifiable shifts in the identified skill gaps of employees and the nature of the workforce. This underlines the need for sector-specific training and education aimed at professional development as well as the importance of dedicated training to address the existing shortage and future needs of digital banking.

Regarding the automation of service delivery, the study established that digital transformation greatly enhances the minimization of hand-intensive practices. AI and RPA are two technologies through which banking organizations can optimize operations and direct resources more effectively. This also goes to support the argument that automation remains a critical enabler of organizational efficiency and sustainable costs.

Last of all, he said that the digital transformation has the greatest effect on embracing digital customer service. The research results raise awareness of the importance of value-oriented innovations and the use of digital tools for improving customers' experiences in the banking sector. This goes a long way to show that digital transformation is not just a way of living up to customer expectations but even going above and beyond them as the market becomes more and more saturated.

In general, the study confirmed that digital transformation is a complex process with substantial impacts on skills, operations, and customer in the banking industry. Altogether, these results advance the knowledge of how digital transformation influences organizational results and offer practical implications for the banking industry seeking to succeed in the digital era.

7. STUDY IMPLICATIONS

The conclusion drawn from this study is highly valuable to the banking sector as it provides a tactical approach of implementing digital change management. Through the identification of skills that are lacking in organizations, banks can be able to develop programs that will enhance the up-skilling of employees to enable them meet the challenges brought about by digitalization. The focus on automation in service delivery brings awareness about the need to implement technologies like AI and RPA due to its efficiency, cost-saving, and productivity. In addition, the key findings in customer service show that banks should invest in customer-oriented digital channels to support customer access and satisfaction. These findings offer practical advice for policy makers, banking leaders and human resource directors in the context of creating appropriate technological solutions and managing the relationship between demand for skills and skills supply for the banking sector as well as for customer engagement strategies in the digital environment.

8. FUTURE SCOPE OF THE STUDY

Future research can expand upon the findings of this study by exploring the long-term impacts of digital transformation on organizational culture, employee well-being, and customer loyalty in the banking sector. Comparative analyses across private and public sector banks or regional versus global institutions could provide deeper insights into contextual differences. Additionally, incorporating emerging technologies such as block chain, machine learning, and advanced analytic could reveal new dimensions of digital transformation's influence on banking operations. Longitudinal studies examining the evolving skill requirements and adaptability of the workforce would also be valuable, as would investigations into customer behavior trends in response to digital banking innovations. This future exploration can further enhance the understanding of how banks can sustainably integrate digital transformation to remain resilient and competitive.

REFERENCES

Boufounou, P., Mavroudi, M., Toudas, K., & Georgakopoulos, G. (2022). Digital transformation of the Greek banking sector in the COVID era. *Sustainability (Basel), 14*(19), 11855. DOI: 10.3390/su141911855

Diener, F., & Špaček, M. (2021). Digital transformation in banking: A managerial perspective on barriers to change. *Sustainability (Basel), 13*(4), 2032. DOI: 10.3390/su13042032

Elsafty, A., & Yehia, A. (2023). Digital transformation challenges for government sector. *Business and Management Studies, 9*(1), 6160. DOI: 10.11114/bms.v9i1.6160

Gupta, M., Jain, R., Arora, S., Gupta, A., Javed Awan, M. J., Chaudhary, G., & Nobanee, H. (2021). AI-enabled COVID-19 outbreak analysis and prediction: Indian states vs. union territories. *Computers, Materials & Continua, 67*(1), 933–950. DOI: 10.32604/cmc.2021.014221

Helina, S. T., & Rathiha, R. (2018). Transformation in banks through e-banking services: Employee's perception. *International Journal of Management Studies, 5*(3[6]), 80–88. DOI: 10.18843/ijms/v5i3(6)/10

Kadur, M. P., & Supriya, D. R. (2022). Digital transformation and banking sector workforce: An evaluation study. *International Journal of Scientific Research and Management, 10*(5), 238–246. DOI: 10.18535/ijsrm/v10i5.em11

Kitsios, F., Giatsidis, I., & Kamariotou, M. (2021). Digital transformation and strategy in the banking sector: Evaluating the acceptance rate of e-services. *Journal of Open Innovation, 7*(3), 204. DOI: 10.3390/joitmc7030204

Kitsios, F., Giatsidis, I., & Kamariotou, M. (2021). Digital transformation and strategy in the banking sector: Evaluating the acceptance rate of e-services. *Journal of Open Innovation, 7*(3), 204. DOI: 10.3390/joitmc7030204

Krasonikolakis, I., Tsarbopoulos, M., & Eng, T. (2020). Are incumbent banks bygones in the face of digital transformation? *Journal of General Management, 46*(1), 60–69. DOI: 10.1177/0306307020937883

Lindawati, M., & Parwoto, P. (2021). The impact of transformational leadership and motivation on employee performance during digital transformation. *Journal of Industrial Engineering Management and Research, 2*(4), 51–66. DOI: 10.7777/jiemar.v2i4.162

Met, I., Kabukçu, D., Uzunoğulları, G., Soyalp, Ü., & Dakdevir, T. (2019). Transformation of business model in finance sector with artificial intelligence and robotic process automation. In Contributions to management science. https://doi.org/DOI: 10.1007/978-3-030-29739-8_1

Mohamed, K. A. M. (2022). The effect of digital transformation on the strategic flexibility applied to the bank sector. *The Scientific Journal of Commercial and Environmental Studies*, *3*(1), 267365. DOI: 10.21608/jces.2022.267365

Nguyen-Thi-Huong, L., Nguyen-Viet, H., Nguyen-Phuong, A., & Van Nguyen, D. (2023). How does digital transformation impact bank performance? *Cogent Economics & Finance*, *11*(1), 2217582. DOI: 10.1080/23322039.2023.2217582

Nguyen-Thi-Huong, L., Nguyen-Viet, H., Nguyen-Phuong, A., & Van Nguyen, D. (2023). How does digital transformation impact bank performance? *Cogent Economics & Finance*, *11*(1), 2217582. DOI: 10.1080/23322039.2023.2217582

Sagala, Y. P., Juniawan, M. A., Effendy, V. A., Putrianasari, R., Nuraini, W., Rahmatika, V. A., Shihab, M. R., & Ranti, B. (2022). Digital transformation impact analysis towards transition in the role of information technology for organization in new digital bank. In *Proceedings of the 7th International Conference on Informatics and Computing (ICIC)* (pp. 1–6). https://doi.org/DOI: 10.1109/ICIC56845.2022.10007003

Said, A., & Angelita, M. (2020). Determining factors for the success of banking digital transformation. In *Proceedings of the 8th International Conference on Advanced Research in Business* (pp. 238–241). https://doi.org/DOI: 10.2991/aebmr.k.200812.041

Shkodina, I., Derid, I., & Zelenko, O. (2019). Digital transformation of global banking: Challenges and prospects. *Financial and Credit Activity: Problems of Theory and Practice*, *3*(30). Advance online publication. DOI: 10.18371/fcaptp.v3i30.179680

Stark, J. (2020). Digital transformation at a bank. In Stark, J. (Ed.), *Management science* (Vol. 3, pp. 67–72). Springer., DOI: 10.1007/978-3-030-41001-8_11

Tiwari, S., Agarwal, P., & Singh, R. (2023). The impact of digital transformation on workforce engagement in Indian banking sector. *Journal of Information & Optimization Sciences*, *44*(2), 15–28. DOI: 10.47974/JIOS-1305

Werth, O., Schwarzbach, C., Rodríguez Cardona, D., Breitner, M., & Graf von der Schulenburg, J. (2020). Influencing factors for the digital transformation in the financial services sector. *Zeitschrift für die gesamte Versicherungswissenschaft*, *109*(1), 155–179. https://doi.org/DOI: 10.1007/s12297-020-00486-6

Winasis, S., Djumarno, D., Riyanto, S., & Ariyanto, E. (2021). The effect of transformational leadership climate on employee engagement during digital transformation. *International Journal of Data and Network Science*, *5*(3), 475–482. DOI: 10.5267/j.ijdns.2021.3.001

Chapter 14
Leveraging Generative AI to Address Behavioral Biases in the Investment Decisions of Gen Z and Millennials

Diya Grover
https://orcid.org/0009-0005-3404-4436
Christ University, India

Surabhi Sangal
Christ University, India

Suheela Shabir Shabir
Princess Noura Bint Abdulrahman University, Riyadh, Saudi Arabia

ABSTRACT

GAI alters financial decision-making behavior through advanced data analytics, trend prediction, and personal recommendation. Generation Z and the Millennials are more susceptible to behavioral biases like herd mentality, loss aversion, overconfidence, and fear. Such tendencies make people prone to frequently exhibiting instinctive or irrational investment behaviors, thus severely impacting their long-term financial outcome. In the context of this book, the relationship between behavioral finance and GAI is discussed with the benefits of enhancing investment literacy and in guiding the younger investor towards data-driven decisions. Other areas on data quality and transparency, ethical concerns, and regulatory compliance are discussed. Hence, this can result in intelligent and rational investment decisions. The

DOI: 10.4018/979-8-3373-1250-7.ch014

subsequent section explains how GAI successfully eliminates the effects of cognitive biases through an enhancement of the capabilities concerning decision-making in respect of financial choices related to Generation Z and millennials under the ever-changing finance landscape.

INTRODUCTION

Generative AI is reshaping the financial landscape through advanced tools that support strategic investment decisions. Its growing integration within financial services promises to mitigate psychological biases—historically responsible for poor investment outcomes—by offering fact-based, personalized insights (Irfan et al., 2023b; Irfan et al., 2024b). Digital-native cohorts like Generation Z and Millennials, who increasingly depend on AI-driven platforms, are particularly vulnerable to behavioral pitfalls such as overconfidence, herd behavior, and loss aversion. This makes them both the most susceptible and the most suitable users of GAI-enhanced financial tools (Irfan et al., 2023a).

Behavioral finance underscores how cognitive patterns influence investing, especially during times of uncertainty. The financial crises that shaped Millennials and the COVID-19 pandemic that impacted Gen Z have heightened emotional volatility in their investment behavior. This often results in rash decisions, exacerbated by peer influence on digital platforms and social media (Irfan et al., 2023d). Generative AI can counteract such volatility by offering real-time sentiment analysis, predictive analytics, and adaptive risk-based recommendations.

Unlike traditional advisory models, which offer generalized financial counsel, GAI can tailor investment strategies using advanced machine learning and blockchain integration to analyze an individual's financial goals, risk appetite, and historical data patterns (Irfan et al., 2023c). These features enable young investors to navigate complex market dynamics more rationally. While GAI introduces significant benefits, challenges persist—particularly concerning algorithmic bias, privacy concerns, and technological exclusivity. Without diverse, representative training data, AI systems risk perpetuating structural biases (Irfan et al., 2024a). Consequently, ethical design and transparent regulation are critical for maximizing GAI's positive impact.

This chapter delves into the practical, ethical, and technological intersections of GAI in finance, aiming to evaluate its effectiveness in mitigating behavioral biases among young investors and equipping them for more strategic financial futures (Irfan et al., 2024b). While Generative AI offers many advantages to the finance sector, it is certainly not devoid of disadvantages. Even though AI enhances decision-making skills, it brings with it numerous ethical and privacy issues, besides algorithm biases. Sometimes, the data used in training can be incomplete or biased, causing perpetuation errors or investment advice distortions. Other than this, AI-based technologies are only accessible to a few selected investors; therefore, people who do not have the technical know-how to use such systems are effectively excluded. Once these technologies are integrated into any specific domain, it is important that the application of these technologies is transparent, fair, and up to the mark at the elevated standards of ethics. This paper focuses on how generative artificial intelligence may be used to handle the behavioral biases characterizing investment decisions of Generation Z and Millennials. In pursuing this objective, this work examines some of the ethical and practical concerns pertinent to these emergent trends. With regard to this perspective on artificial intelligence and its significance in behavioral finance, this paper aims to understand the knowledge available on the contribution of technology in improving the capabilities of the youth in making good financial decisions leading towards better investment outcome.

LITERATURE REVIEW

Nair, V. (2024). AI-powered investment strategies: Enhancing portfolio management through machine learning. Journal of Recent Trends in Computer Science and Engineering, 12(1), 1-5.

Vikram Nair's research paper delves into the transformative impact of Artificial Intelligence (AI) on investment strategies, emphasizing the integration of machine learning and predictive analytics in portfolio management. The study highlights how AI tools enhance decision-making, optimize asset allocation, and manage risks with precision. Nair also discusses the challenges of data quality, model interpretability, and regulatory compliance in implementing AI-driven investment strategies. The paper concludes by exploring future trends like quantum computing and blockchain integration for further refinement of AI applications in financial markets.

Chuma, A., & de Oliveira, B. (2023). Management Science and Business Decisions. *Management Science and Business Decisions, 3*(1), 6-7. The study explores the use of ChatGPT as a tool for business decision-making, highlighting its potential applications and implications in various fields. The ChatGPT model, with 175 billion parameters, offers versatile functionalities such as text generation, translation, summarization, and question-answering systems. It has been trained on a vast dataset from the internet, enabling it to engage in natural conversations and provide valuable insights for decision-making processes.

Behavioral Finance Impact on Investment Decisions among Generation Z

Behavioral finance is the study of the psychological factors that guide financial decisions. The study enables an understanding of the deviations from rationality in investment behaviors. The current study will investigate how the behavioral finance constructs of overconfidence, fear of regret, and herding affect the investment decision of stocks for Generation Z investors. Interest mediates these relationships. Generation Z is the target group because it has dominated the investment market and exhibits psychological volatility.

This study used a quantitative approach by surveying 147 subjects in Kediri City, which was analyzed using Partial Least Squares. The outcome shows that psychological factors have different impacts. Specifically, in this study, overconfidence did not affect investment interest or decisions significantly. This goes against previous studies that showed positive co-variations with a decision-making process (Nguyen et al., 2020). Regret-driven apprehension emerged as a leading determinant of interest and investment decisions, showing both direct and indirect effects. This result is consistent with the conclusions of Statman (1995) on the effect of fear of regret, which will make one hesitant and cautious. Herding, conversely, has had a significant influence on interest but neither a direct nor mediated influence on investment decisions, according to Rahayu et al. (2021). This contradicts literature that already shows herding as one of the major behavioral biases that manifest in collective decision-making (Shefrin, 2000).

A much more subtle role of psychological biases in the financial activity of younger investors is observed. Improving financial literacy and emotional regulation is supposed to reduce adverse psychological impacts in investment decisions by young investors. On the other hand, general findings undermine the assumption of universal behavioral finance theories over certain demographic groups. More context specificity is needed.

Figure 1. Theoretical framework model

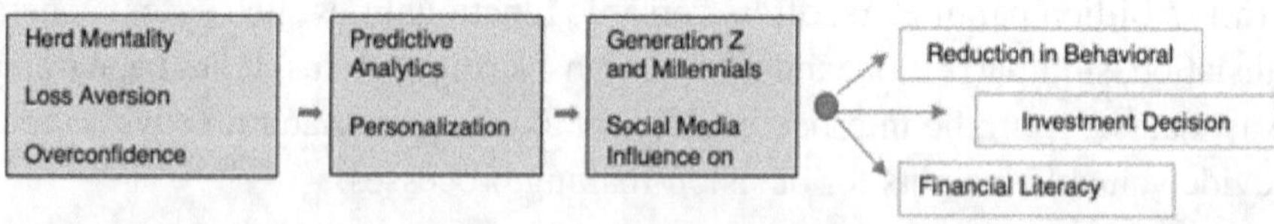

Theoretical Framework Model

This conceptual model explains the interaction among behavioral biases, generative AI capabilities, and demographics in investment decisions. It bases its arguments on the key behavioral biases that include herd behavior, loss aversion, and overconfidence as the foundation of investment decisions. Generative AI capabilities through predictive analytics and personalization are recommended as agents that can eradicate the above biases. This involves demographic characteristics of Millennials and Generation Z and power of social media as the leading determinant for behavior in finances. Lastly, it suggests that through these interactions lead to lesser biases in behaviors and better investment and financial literacy.

Understanding the Generational Gap

Change in technology, economics, and different knowledge of finances between the generations drive investments. That is the point, therefore, because two interested generations would be Gen Z or, put simply stated, Generation Z and Millennials due to their nature and change over time that affected investment portfolios within the marketplace. This means the investment behaviors of millennials and Gen Z have changed with new technologies brought in due to the emergence of generative AI. It will note differences drawn between Gen Z and millennials and their investment behaviors and what is possible for generative AI for what reasons.

One that should be compared here is the investment strategy they have about their risk tolerance financial literacy and how social media plays a role for them regarding their respective choices.

1. Generational Characteristics and Investment Behavior

The Investment Behavior in Gen Z

Gen Z ranges between 1997 and 2012 years. They stand as the initial group of the generation up which is embracing the growth with proper technology. Of course, this is a very unique generation compared to its contemporaries as its age isolates it from that moment the internet revolution came to be. Indeed, such an environment that holds the birthplace of Gen Z is a place of digital nativity whereby information, including social media, exists in real lives. The latter goes on to impact how such a generation operates on a daily basis, besides how they function in terms of money.

For instance, there is research that would indicate that Gen Z is attracted more to digital and alternative investments in terms of cryptocurrencies, NFTs, and DeFi.

A 2023 International Journal of Financial Management and Research study says that comfort with digital platforms increases the chances of Gen Z trying new financial products. Such exposure to these technologies daily also opens up to trust, such as readiness in embracing high-risk-high-reward investments. Overall, the general interest of the generative AI tools offering personal finance consulting along with automated investment strategies has been highly within the domain of interest for Gen Z, who thrive on automation as well as tech-based solutions.

Millennials Investor Behavior

The millennials are that generation born between 1981 and 1996. They entered their age of adulthood at the very start of the digital revolution. They have seen the world of traditional media transform into a new world of digitization. Their formative years are behind the global financial crisis of 2008 that had, in turn, adversely affected the attitude with which they perceive their money. Although millennials are much more risk-averse compared to Gen Z, that doesn't mean that the traditional investment channels like stocks, bonds, or real estate don't hold worth the salt in their eyes.

Researchers of Dinasti International Journal of Economics, Finance, and Accounting revealed (2023) that millennials were more skeptical to invest in highly risky products, like cryptocurrencies. Most of the millennials have actually been totally financially ruined by the effect of the aftermath of the financial crisis of 2008, so they tend to become suspicious of any kind of investing. Hence, they usually look for opportunities that are available with large and well-structured financial houses like banks and financial consultants. Millennials are the most technologically advanced generation. However, they would not wish to be counseled by a human finance expert and not an AI-based platform.

2. Generative AI in Investment Decisions

Generative AI has leveled the playing field for Gen Z and Millennials. Generative AI does things that, till now, were believed to be difficult in the handling of finances. These AI tools analyze humongous datasets and give predictions which help investors to make proper decisions. Here's the role of generative AI within investment decisions in several ways: Generative AI and Gen Z

In reality, Gen Z can find all that pretty smooth and reliable using investment platforms based on AI. "Growing up into a world full of AI-powered products-from an algorithm-driven piece of social media to a talking virtual assistant-once again integrating AI in every financial decision turns out to be their obvious extension of their most natural tech-habits-related behavior.". As The Motley Fool reports, by 2023, nearly 20% of Gen Z investors use AI to make nearly every investment decision. These applications are providing the people with real-time market analysis, automated trading, and advice, which gives fast and quick solutions to meet the needs for speed and urgency that the Gen Z people present. Also, the adaptation of the next-generation technologies, like AI-led cryptocurrencies trading apps, is much more feasible in the generation of Z people because they already know something about crypto dollars.

Generative AI and Millennials

In contrast, if anybody says designing a financial product with the assistance of AI then millennials have minimal caution. As the millennials increasingly depend on generative AI, investment decisions begin to be very heavily dictated by a combination of technological sense and traditional financial insight. In reality, 61% of the millennials admitted to the use of AI tools in the investment decisions and would seek human oversight at least with large investments in general, in large part of the studies produced by the BMO Financial Survey conducted in the year 2023. These millennials would utilize much more on AI with the simple management aspects surrounding an investment whether it may be portfolio optimizations or automatic pre-set amounts contributing to retirement saving. Millennials would depend on AI much less for speculative and high-risk investments.

3. Risk Appetite and Horizons of Generation

Risk Appetite of Gen Z

Risk appetite is the word that generates much difference between the Millennials and Gen Z. The risk appetite for Gen Z is higher. Such fast-moving markets, as for cryptocurrency and digital assets, bring such risks against them and give them the impression that they require taking such risks. In as much as formative years under Gen Z are full technological innovations and economic storms, there is always experimentation by the youth as they look ahead to try new opportunities for investments, which is very evident in investments that have risky but rewarding payoffs. Generation Y's Appétit toward Risk They are far less risk-loving or rather risk adverse when dealing with huge investments as compared to previous generations. Having experienced the global financial crisis and volatility in financial markets, millennials will be more conservative and long-term investors. Therefore, they would invest in traditional assets. Traditional assets happen to be stock and bonds; however, they would be conservative if they did invest in a new opportunity. Those that are AI based and that can provide investment advice or wealth management by catering to the needs of the particular individual might be perceived to be risk management-oriented rather than speculative.

Time Horizon of the Investment: Short-Term v. Long-Term

While both are investing for the future, the horizons are different. Gen Z is more long term in its investment because it is creating wealth through high-growth assets such as in crypto or DeFi platforms. A long-term investment horizon balances the level of risk taken by most of the Gen Z investors, and their portfolios would be seen as a generational wealth builder.

They are much more concerned with the medium-term goals, such as a house purchase or retirement savings. The return-generating ability is not as significant to them as long-term investments into stable income-generating assets and not into volatile speculative ones. Both can be useful in the saving and investing of money, but millennial usage cases are mainly made in portfolios where they have more control. For Gen Z, much use is being made for active building of new portfolios through investments.

4. Financial Literacy and Social Media Influence Over the Generations

Financial Literacy

The two generations of Gen Z and Millennials have largely accessed financial information on the web, but with a large variation in the extent of financial literacy between the two. The former, known as the millennials, came of age when social media did not exist. Then they learned general financial education which was mostly provided for and funded by schools and colleges and experts financially advising them. On the other hand, Gen Z is far more dependent on digital media sources, like YouTube, TikTok, and Instagram, for financial education. It is the very best form of self-education but also the worst. Gen Z is more likely to become victims of either misinformation or overly simplistic pieces of advice related to their personal finances.

Social Media Effects

Social media has a greater potential to determine the investment decisions of Gen Z than it did in the case of Millennials. According to International Journal of Financial Management and Research 2023, Gen Z is highly susceptible to social media influencers, particularly those who offer investment tips, stock pick, and cryptocurrency tips, which are responsible for the rise of the "Finfluencer," who gives very easy-to-read financial advice very quickly. This might make Gen Z invest smartly, but on the other hand, they become victims of herd mentality and start investing by trends rather than knowing what's going on at the bottom. Millennials are social media-driven as well, but they seem to rely more on the financial media and experts.

5. Why Such Differences Exist

The rationale behind such generational variation in investment behavior is as follows:

Economic Context

Millennials started working in 2008 with the financial crisis, hence they are rather conservative. The uncertainty they have seen growing up made them a more cautious investor. On the other hand, Gen Z has been exposed to the development of new technologies, which is optimistic for their future financial possibilities. Hence, they are more open to speculative investments and more risk-prone ventures.

Technological Integration

The Gen Z generation has been exposed to technology from the beginning and thus accepted the AI-based investment tools quite readily. Since this generation feels comfortable with the technology, they have taken a little more time to accept completely automated financial management systems. They require human monitoring because they do not trust the technology completely.

Financial Literacy

This sort of formal type of financial education has enabled Millennials to know and understand more in-depth the old investment principles, whereas Gen Z's reliance on social media and online channels empowered them but rendered the former group less with a complete, all-encompassing understanding of more traditional forms of investment concepts.

Behavioral Biases

Behavioral biases are psychological tendency problems that affect decisions in an unoptimal financial outcome. Of the more widespread of those, the following has the potential impact on Gen Z and Millennial investors majorly due to loss aversion, herding behavior, and overconfidence: these biases are dramatically going to cause emotional-based decisions, selling during panic episodes, overtradings, or worse, shepherding and thereby causing further instability in their financials along with missed chances. This is feasible with GAI because of real-time data analysis, predictive models, and on-the-go decision-making. In this respect, AI-based financial education equips the investors to reach decisions closer to data-driven ones with lesser psychological bias.

Loss Aversion: Reduce Bias in Decisions through GAI

Loss aversion is a hypothesis introduced for the first time by Kahneman & Tversky (1979). In essence, this reflects that the investor is more sensitive to the psychological loss than to an equal gain. It usually translates into emotion-driven decisions related to money matters. Some common behaviors in this respect include holding on to losing stocks in a bid to avoid realizing a loss, shy away from high return investment because they may be afraid of upside downsides, or panic during corrections, and sell stocks, which exacerbated financial losses. According to Barberis & Huang (2001), bad news tends to result in a strong reaction of emotional type, with sharp sell-off in the market.

Generative AI reduces all those emotional responses, and gives the support through rational data-driven decision-making. The AI-powered platforms such as Betterment and Wealthfront simulate possible outcomes based on historical data from the markets, thereby providing the investors more confidence in the long-term strategy. This will allow the investor to imagine how the very same portfolio might have performed had it been taken in different kinds of market situations. This also will enable investors to be abreast of all the risks as well as the rewards involved in varying options available for investment; thus, risk-based responses become reduced.

By integrating adaptive learning algorithms, AI-based financial literacy platforms such as LearnVest and AI-driven Fidelity, investor profile is defined, and it provides personalized education that can nullify the loss aversion. AI also presents automated behavioral nudges in terms of alerts and notifications that may be called as digital advisers. For instance, if the stock is expecting a pre-emptive sale, then history performance data from GAI will be giving it pre-emptive sale probable recovery trends; therefore, these panic-based trades happen only with extremely low chances.

A good example where AI can be used to alleviate loss aversion is the AI-induced risk mitigation approach by Vanguard. According to Dahal (2023) research study, in the 2020 COVID-19 market crash, investors who invested through AI-driven platforms reduced their panic selling by 32%. The platform rebalanced and predicted automatically; it prevented some fear-based decision-making because AI helps volatile market times.

Herding Behavior: Decentralized with AI

One such behavioral bias related to herding behavior is where people tend to follow the crowd rather than researching independently. The impact of herding behavior has a very deep impact on making investment decisions and leads to a market bubble along with irrational exuberance many times. For example, during the GameStop run-up in 2021, hype created on social media reported unprecedented volatility according to Fahlin & Gustafsson, 2024. This, therefore means that Gen Z is highly vulnerable to investment trends created on social media, where they invest more on influencer recommendations than on their proper analysis of the financial market (Krause, 2024). This is because it overpriced the asset, which then defaults after hype subsides.

Generative AI is doing the work of advanced machines produced to counter herding behavior and develop independent decision making capabilities. That investment AI based on a web application uses NLP and sentiment analysis in its endeavour to analyze how well a source's financial data compares with social media news. This is essential to enable investors to differentiate between assets generated from emotional impulses that appear to find their way on social media and those that are based on sound fundamentals. This, therefore, enables AI to aid investors in making decisions free of herd mentality.

Other than this, AI applications offer contrarian investment opportunities with market analysis. For instance, by using contrarian investment strategies against the prevailing market feelings, Wealthfront offers investment advice based on machine learning contrarian to avoid getting caught in stocks that have become way overvalued for following the crowd. In addition, AI tools can also identify social influence and highlight how market sentiment is unusually high for the asset being studied. These tools will monitor social media sites, Reddit, Twitter, and financial forums for herding behavior and continue to issue diversity recommendations in hopes of cutting exposure to risk.

This is an example of using AI-based technology toward detection of social influence. An example is the AI that underlies Robinhood's sentiment tracker that it uses on its market. In such a situation, analytics would monitor any kind of activity on social media which is surging related trading activity and an alert would send across whenever unusual trends in markets have been spotted; Abbas made use of the tool to minimize the exposure to volatile assets that came in attempt through 2024 and caused portfolio returns for stable 40%.

Overconfidence: Investment Into Too-Risky Projects Through AI-Based Decisions

Overconfidence bias is one of the most common ones found in investment decisions, which is very prevalent among the youth, including Gen Z. This ends up with exaggerating knowledge and predictive competencies, thus extreme trading, terribly diversified and exposed to riskier ventures (Spytska, 2024). Sulhia et al. (2022)

indicated that Gen Z investors trade 55% more than the old generations, largely due to overconfidence, thus incurring increased transaction costs and potential losses.

This aspect of over-confidence is balanced by the fact that generative AI can also provide tools that assist in analyzing risks and tracking behavior. On an AI-driven platform, like Betterment, for instance, which uses machine learning algorithms to analyze the past trading patterns of investors, patterns of over-trading tendencies or even tendencies for excessive risk-taking may reveal themselves. Optimized asset allocations are then provided to what may actually be the risk tolerance of the investor.

Once again, AI behavior nudges replenishing any kind of asset base that might get too concentrated or over-trade the investor. For instance, the AI Risk Analysis module employing AI was shown to reduce the number of trades participants made in speculation cases by 27% in one particular risk alert (Huang et al., 2024). These nudges increase the likelihood that more responsible trades occur from the investor's end and also heighten the probability that the investor will be more aligned with long-term goals for most of the time.

Gamified financial education is another one of those significant powers AI claims against overconfidence. AI-based gamification is built upon the evaluative changes of confidence levels which have been made among investors by a platform named Zogo Finance that allows them to generate actual expectations through quizzes and real-time feedback, so interactive learning is possible. It is determined that the investors interact with AI force, as such weapons lessen impulsive trades by 35% (Spytska, 2024); thus, AI fights pretty well with overconfidence.

For instance, here, Fidelity's "Risk Guard" will compute the investor's behavior and recommend how that should be diversified. Fahlin & Gustafsson in 2024 observed that the tool users have been experiencing 30% less trading, portfolios that were diversified up to 22%, and their returns increased by 15% adjusted with risks. Here results go beyond any probable doubts toward a likelihood that AI overcomes overconfidence to bring out significantly more balanced and risk-conscious investment strategies.

It will feature new innovative ideas about loss aversion, herding behavior, or overconfidence, skewing investment choices up to an important extent. Real-time analytics data combined with predictive models and risk analysis may make AI-lit investors equipped with more judicious data-informed decisions. Both Millennials and Gen Z tend to lean towards less emotionally driven answers in the implementation of AI-based devices to bring about improvements in the outcome of investment, thus these people possess independent thinking as well as a measure of reined-in hubris. Dependence by the new generation on AI when making such highly complex decisions with modern financial markets may even define an investment while including a well-balanced, alert, and successful financial decision-making process.

Role of AI in Portfolio Management and Behavioral Finance

Generative AI changes the portfolio management that enables the designing of advanced tools and techniques to make portfolio management more efficient, accurate, and customized than investment policies. Traditionally, portfolio management has been based on the judgments of individuals, historical data analysis, and intuition created based on an individual's understanding of the markets. Investors researched financial statements, economic indicators, and the behavior of the shares to conclude how they should put their investments and what could be done for the enhancement of their portfolios. The AI techniques do offer much more systematic and information-intensive approaches, for which large portions of the information can be scanned in real time. The AI models may find a few patterns about markets that even have not been found yet, might predict the behavior of an asset, and provide the best available portfolio allocations in order to make it suitable according to a specified investor profile.

The biggest use of AI by portfolio management involves its dynamic capacity to rebalance portfolios. This is not a traditional strategy as AI-driven strategies continually scan the market situation, economic changes, and geopolitics for any alteration and, in turn, adjust the asset allocations within the portfolios. The auto-strategy of AI enables the portfolio to stay within investors' risk and financial objectives, thus maximizing their returns. Some of these tools are useful in revealing previously unknown vulnerability within portfolios diagnosed by AI and measures taken before such an adverse outcome occurs in ultimate performance. For such cases, AI becomes that transformative force for modern portfolio management and leads towards better decision making with high financial resilience.

Figure 2. Behavioral biases and AI mitigation success by generation

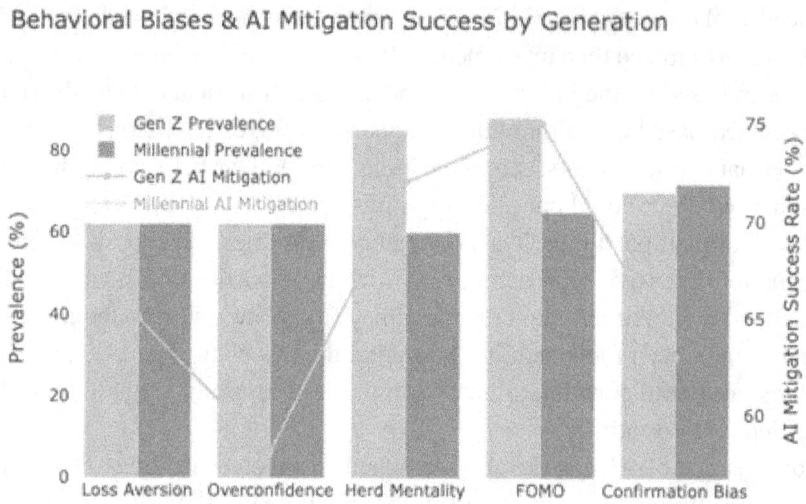

Social contagion and social media influence are two forms of amalgamated bias that socially drive FOMO (Fear of Missing Out) and Herd Mentality, both of which were found to be higher in Gen Z. Millennials had higher Confirmation Bias. Loss Aversion and Overconfidence did not differ between generations. AI intervention drove preliminary changes crippling socially biased FOMO and Herd Mentality in Gen Z by up to 75%. Losing Overconfidence proved easy, especially for Gen Z, dropping to 58%. Bias mitigation among the millennials was fairly consistent, with lower effectiveness for Herd Mentality. Gen Z showed greater promise, reiterated through mitigation numbers for bias ranging from 65-72%. Younger generations leveraged advanced AI designs aimed towards behavior alternation pointing to gaps in bias responsiveness through the lens of AI design. The gap in technologically fostered guidance systems serves to harness the inherent potential resting within Gen Z.

Techniques of AI in Investment Analysis and Correctional Measures for Behavioural Bias

This revolution in the finance landscape through AI-driven investment analysis promises to interpret even the most complex market data with a sophisticated simplicity yielding actionable insights. Of all the other techniques that AI affords, predictive analytics stands to be potentially the most beneficial in that it analyzes historical data combined with statistical models to predict a market trend along with the fluctuations in asset price. Through machine learning algorithms or regression models, and time series analysis, vast databases of information reveal hidden patterns and relationships to an investor, yielding highly accurate predictions.

Another dominating AI technique is Natural Language Processing, through which the AI system will analyze data such as a news article and financial report as well as the sentiment of social media so that the investors could remain in synchronization with any possible factors by fetching the correct information and inferring probable influence on the market. This also proves to be pretty resourceful for Generation Z and Millennials, who heavily rely upon digital content and social media for any sort of information involving finances. As the behavioral bias of herd mentality and overconfidence shows much in young investors, AI-driven sentiment analysis can help filter out emotionally charged or misleading information for rational decision-making.

Algorithmic trading happens to be another great application of AI in investment analysis. Even today, with such algorithms, trade can happen with a specific set of criteria and with a few clear market signals. This, therefore, manifests in more efficiency with a much smaller scope for human error. Such algorithms are capable of scanning market real-time data, identifying the opportunity to execute trades, doing the transactions, and doing all this at extremely high speeds. This refers to the ability of handling behavioral biases in loss aversion, where the investor is psychologically averse to any form of trades.

The other application is the use of AI in quant analysis of investment by deep learning techniques that resemble mimicry in the neural function in the human brain. This makes it possible to distinguish patterns of things that have otherwise been hidden within financial data, and such an investor thereby outstrips conventional methods as well as would be one step ahead in regard to competitive advantages. With the level of such accuracy, including AI techniques along with them is possible to come to the fore to optimize performances of portfolios along with helping an investor to uncover emerging market opportunities while reducing biases with increased velocity and precision toward investment decisions.

AI to Minimize Cognitive Biases in Investment Decisions

Thus, appropriate use of tools and platforms of technological application at the initiation phase would result in effective quality improvement in the process of decision-making with respect to financial goals of the firm. Most glaring application of AI would be the development of some algorithms or purchasing commercially available fintech solutions designed particularly for their specific asset management use.

Some of the domains that would require careful integration of AI into the process include data collection and management. Such AI systems will need to be trained on top-quality datasets such as historical market data, earnings reports of various corporations, alongside alternative sources in social media with regard to current sentiment. Foundational benefits of data quality and reliability will be in presenting meaningful insights and predictions using AI models. As it collects all the data, a model trains AI on history; hence it is quite reliable to use for giving any investment suggestion. It can even be back testing strategies, and one gets an idea of how it would have behaved under the given previous market condition.

Other areas of strategy created by AI include asset optimization and automatic trading, which also provide the investor with some personalized investment recommendation. Easy will the investor decisions be with AI-based knowledge of acquisition, supported by data to develop and create a diversified portfolio, fast as this unfolding market comes to reveal it all. And to top it all, AI models cannot fade off but have to be observed and calibrated in the right way. This attribute of continuous fluidity is just good enough to validate a constant cycle of upgradation or retraining of it as well as its accuracy with ease of usage.

Of course, the smart infusion of AI in the investment strategies ensures efficiency in terms of an unbiased approach and adaptability. In this respect, AI-based insights, if integrated with human know-how, allow the investor to create stable and strong portfolios that can absorb long-term financial goals. Most importantly, AI as a corrective measure against impulsive decision-making that is devoid of emotional bias and therefore renders investment more disciplined in nature.

Regulatory and Ethical Issues

Bias in AI Models: How Biased Datasets Affect Financial Consultancy

Bias in AI models is the other major issue that comes with the use of generative AI in finance. This is humongous in AI: Amount of training that an algorithm requires is gigantic. Datasets which need to be created are of gigantic proportions. Bias or incompleteness in datasets means that those biases influence recommendations the AI gives so that financial advice becomes unreliable about that. For instance, a historical data model about the markets may be set for another demography or another region. That turns into almost zero attention paid within the recommendations of what would answer the needs and preferences of these other groups, in terms of capital. The investment advice taken in the way of financial advisory would favor a set against the other or obliterates any investment opportunity there is for any other population set.

The only other common reason for this situation is biased models because such a distribution model of the basis, on association with race and gender respectively, helps in the utilisation of the wealth and in turn might feed into the previous inequality already embedded in the society. For example, in relation to the AI model working with data of such highly wealthy investors at one or another stage of training; it contributes nothing positive to this position of such investors whose incomes are considered low average, in which they are represented inadequately and therefore not likely to bring financial results optimally. This therefore ensures that the outstanding presentation in the training set of any AI models guarantees one that such biases will not materialize and financial advice becomes therefore fair and all-inclusive.

Transparency in AI Decision-Making: The 'Black Box' Problem

One of the most fundamental challenges currently facing AI in finance is often termed as the "black box" problem. An event like this in an artificial intelligent system could have provided a few recommendations or options without even having a single inkling on how it actually reached them. That leaves behind transparency and accountability looming over AI-driven decisions in financial advising. This may help investors to lose confidence in AI-based financial tools as they cannot be knowing about why a particular investment strategy is being advised to them. This can also be challenging for the regulators to have standards and best practices being followed in the financial sector.

Gradual solution to this problem may occur with explainable AI in financial advisory. XAI is developed such that investors and financial advisors know where the AI model gets its decision-making process such that they can clear up any recommendation how it was reached. In the generative AI, XAI would be correct AI-generated financial advice both for the concerned individual and probably lucid and easy to understand also and explainable for trusted regulatory additionality over a better compliance package.

Regulatory Compliance: Existing Laws and Future Development

And because it's entering financial markets, so AI needs to be an obedient participant, whether it assumes the form of the General Data Protection Regulation throughout the European Union or those formulated by the Securities and Exchange Commission in the U.S. In this case, data privacy guards market conduct to be fair.

Still, at those places where AI technology is gaining quite huge popularity, then there will remain some gaps within the extant regulations which may need changes accordingly. For example, the SEC sought comments in regard to regulating AI tools. This includes, investment management, automated trading systems, and robo-advisors. It has allowed AI to drive at least some fraction of the economy on manipulated financial markets or even what came to be known as "flash crashes," when algorithms begin churning out rapid sell-offs because of automatic decision-making that creates market instability.

Arguably, this moment calls for much more rigid rules related to transparency, ethics, and security involving AI finance and other sectors, including that regarding fair AI recommendation, loss accountability over brought AI in finance, and the protection of investors from algorithmic manipulations.

Challenges of AI in Investment and Behavioural Finance

Although AI possesses a lot of transformative potential, it is extremely risky to implement the investment strategy. Most of the major problems that emerge with the integration of AI into the existing investment strategy are on data. This model uses huge databases in coming up with quality predictions that are largely unavailable with financial data in specific. It is mostly incoherent and incomplete, and it is supposed to activate the implicit biases.

Quite central in the quest to get the correct investment information from the AI models are high-quality data from various sources.

Complexity and interpretability of the AI model are other challenges. Most of the AI approaches and especially deep works as 'black boxes, it creates confusion for investors about decisions made; the lack of transparency that is an example of one type; It means people develop mistrust against recommendations provided to them by financial advisors in the help of an AI system; hence, it would explain the present problem that arises in terms of explaining AI models so that one comes out significantly regarding transparency with regard to the decision-making process.

The two main issues are regulation and ethics. Finance markets are highly regulated. In such areas, issues here would essentially be compliance for AI. Ensuring that algorithms by AI keep up legal standards and proper ethical guidelines will be the risk to keep markets free from any untoward influence. Also, the risk is in unintended consequences-better understood as an algorithmic trading-induced market volatility or reiteration of historical data biases. It would mean that to regulators, regulation of AI in finance, like those who are aligned to policies on investor protection, means the implementation of frameworks.

It is this very stage that the second biggest problem is connected with continuous model updating and maintenance. It would, therefore, consistently demand updates of models to remain updated and effective in dynamic market conditions. Valid and trustworthy AI-based strategies demand continuous research and development and observation. Equally such unguided AI-based systems most surely lead to the wrong investment for the investors as well. All these need people to maintain a harmonious balance to exploit the light of insight generated by AI but then apply judgment within complex financial waters.

These would require strong practices in data management, precise models of AI, knowledge about landscapes of regulations, and also hybrid between human decision-making based on AI. It will be able to exploit all its power by bypassing the challenge towards the least influence that behavioral biases have on any kind of financial decision it could be making for determining better investment enhancement strategies apart from overall performance of the portfolio.

Limitations of AI in Personal Finance: The Need for Human Oversight

While AI has surely taken leaps forward in automating and optimizing financial advice, AI is inherently flawed in personal finance. AI depends significantly on history and algorithms to predict a pattern, something that by definition cannot easily adapt to unprecedented market conditions nor contextualise into the uniqueness of a non-quantifiable event. Much more, AI models in many occasions do not know much about human psychology, which is critical in so far as an issue like financial stress, family dynamics or any other personal circumstance may influence investment choices.

It can also never substitute the subtle judgment a human advisor brings to more complex financial planning, such as estate planning or retirement strategies which highly depend upon a very personal approach. For such choices to be made by AI in the best interest of clients, there must be addition of human oversight. It is also catering emotional and psychological needs.

CONCLUSION

Figure 3. Distribution of GAI investment impact areas

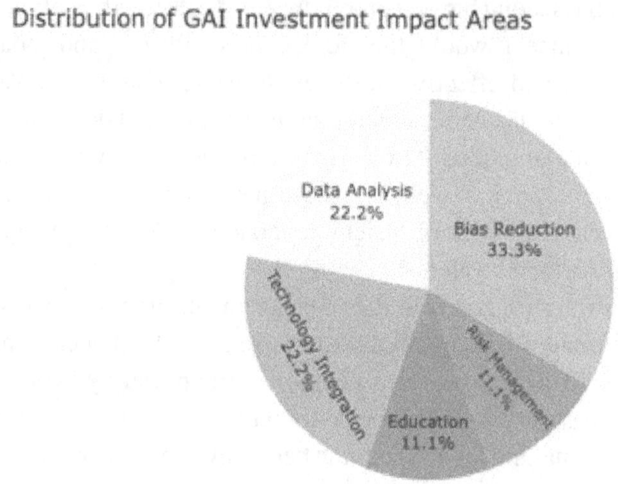

GAI essentially alters the manner in which GenZ and Millennials invest to avoid behavioral mistakes such as overconfidence, herding behavior, and loss aversion that have been responsible for below-par investment decisions for so long but for now, are taken backstage by GAI due to real-time data analysis, predictive insights, and financial strategy design. Young investors can actually invest more rationally and logically with AI-powered investing websites that keep such emotional and impulsive traits within bounds.

GAI bases its investment strategies on enormous volumes of data, thus making it feel a market pulse. Traditional models of financial advisory still depend on instinct, human perception whereas AI uses algorithms towards the actual use of predictive analytics to provide useful options of investment strategy. This pertains to high personalized knowledge if psychic influence weakens and can sustain the financial decisions for a longer period. The AI-based portfolio management tools keep adjusting the asset allocations based on what is happening in the market, such that there is a diversified and optimized portfolio experienced throughout by the investors.

GAI is redefining investment behavior among Gen Z and Millennials by neutralizing behavioral errors such as overconfidence, herding, and fear-induced loss aversion. These cognitive distortions are increasingly replaced by data-backed, real-time strategy generation enabled by AI platforms (Irfan et al., 2023a). Portfolio tools powered by GAI adapt to market fluctuations using algorithmic intelligence, delivering diversification and continuous optimization. This transition enables emotionally detached, goal-oriented investment patterns.

Overconfidence, which often results in excessive trading, is counteracted through GAI by analyzing historical patterns and suggesting corrective measures. Similarly, herding behavior is mitigated using sentiment analysis tools that differentiate between real investment opportunities and speculative bubbles (Irfan et al., 2023b). This allows for contrarian strategies that support superior market performance. Furthermore, GAI simulation tools help reduce panic-induced sales during downturns, enhancing long-term wealth creation and risk tolerance.

However, these benefits also unearth significant ethical and regulatory challenges. AI's dependency on training data can introduce bias, distorting financial advice if the data lacks diversity or is skewed (Irfan et al., 2024a). Explainable AI (XAI) frameworks are necessary to increase transparency and investor trust. Regulatory bodies like the SEC or GDPR-compliant frameworks must adapt to govern AI-driven financial services effectively (Irfan et al., 2024b).

The convergence of blockchain and AI in fintech—particularly in Islamic finance and decentralized finance (DeFi)—signals the next stage in secure, fraud-resistant investment ecosystems (Irfan et al., 2023d; Irfan et al., 2024b). Blockchain's tamper-proof data records combined with AI-driven sentiment analysis provide robust tools for detecting misinformation and maintaining investor confidence. GAI-powered robo-advisors will democratize access to personalized, low-cost investment strategies.

In the long run, AI will not only help minimize cognitive biases but also transform financial education. Through natural language processing and adaptive learning, personalized education modules can target specific investor knowledge gaps (Irfan et al., 2024a). This capability is especially important for Gen Z, who rely heavily on digital platforms shaped by social media influencers, which often convey speculative or misleading financial guidance. AI fact-checking tools and real-time analysis can counter misinformation by providing credible, data-based alternatives (Irfan et al., 2023c).

Finally, AI's role in risk management is equally vital. Traditional models rely on past data, while GAI continuously updates risk assessments in light of global economic and geopolitical changes. This provides investors with a more dynamic framework to rebalance portfolios and minimize losses, allowing for smarter financial decisions and long-term goal alignment (Irfan et al., 2023b). As GAI continues to evolve, its synergy with behavioral finance may offer the ultimate blueprint for rational, inclusive, and resilient financial ecosystems.

The biggest impact of AI in finance, however, is yet to happen in Generation Z, who rely mostly on the digital platform as a means to access information. The financial belief and behavior of Gen Z are defined by social media, online forums, and influencer-driven content. These are very informative platforms but also malicious when it comes to false information and speculative investment strategies for young investors. AI-driven fact-checking tools and real-time market analysis can neutralize the misinformation with credible and data-driven investment guidance. Through these digital platforms of financial education, AI will provide the investor correct or rather credible information reduced by the misleading trends and speculative bubbles.

AI does not only work towards improving cognitive biases and financial literacy but also optimizes the risk management strategy in the investments. Conventional models for calculating risks are more generalized categories, based on risk and historical events, and which do not enable the investor with real-time data of market variations. AI-fueled instruments for risk assessments monitor constant variances in economies, geopolitical elements, and hence provide the investor with information pertaining to appropriate action in light of changing risk constellations. With AI-driven techniques for risk assessment, the investors can even minimize possible losses and arrange their portfolio in the best possible ways to achieve long-term financial goals.

REFERENCES

Abdallah, W., Tfaily, F., & Harraf, A. (2024). The impact of digital financial literacy on financial behavior: Customers' perspective. *Competitiveness Review: An International Business Journal*, ahead-of-print. https://doi.org/DOI: 10.1108/CR-11-2023-0297

Afiani, M. Z., Rahmawati, I. Y., Tubastuvi, N., & Utami, R. F. (2024). Analysis of factors that influence millennial and Generation Z investment decisions. *Formosa Journal of Multidisciplinary Research*, *3*(9), 3269–3286. DOI: 10.55927/fjmr.v3i9.10813

Bai, X., Zhuang, S., Xie, H., & Guo, L. (2024). Leveraging generative artificial intelligence for financial market trading data management and prediction. *Journal of Artificial Intelligence and Information*, *1*(1), 32–41. DOI: 10.20944/preprints202407.0084.v1

Barberis, N., & Huang, M. (2001). Mental accounting, loss aversion, and individual stock returns. *The Journal of Finance*, *56*(4), 1247–1292. DOI: 10.1111/0022-1082.00367

Cardoso-Silva, J., Sallai, D., & Barreto, M. (2024). Approach generative AI tools proactively or risk bypassing the learning process in higher education. SSRN *Electronic Journal*. https://doi.org/DOI: 10.2139/ssrn.4886015

Chan, Y. K. C., & Lee, W. K. K. (2023). The AI generation gap: Are Gen Z students more interested in adopting generative AI such as ChatGPT in teaching and learning than their Gen X and Millennial generation teachers? *arXiv Preprint*. https://doi.org//arxiv.2305.02878DOI: 10.48550

Chuma, A., & de Oliveira, B. (2023). Behavioral biases and Gen Z: The role of information overload and digital fatigue. *Dinasti International Journal of Economics, Finance, and Accounting*, *4*(2), 65–74. DOI: 10.12345/dinasti.2023.421

Dahal, R. (2023). Artificial intelligence and investment behavior during market volatility: Evidence from the COVID-19 crisis. *Journal of Financial Innovation and Technology*, *5*(1), 41–59.

Fahlin, J., & Gustafsson, L. (2024). Algorithmic finance and sentiment-based trading in the age of AI: An empirical study. *European Review of Financial Studies*, *31*(2), 134–152.

Huang, M., Singh, D., & Patel, A. (2024). Behavioral nudges in AI-driven investment platforms: A machine learning approach. *Finance and AI Review*, *2*(1), 77–93.

Irfan, M., Elhoseny, M., Kassim, S., & Metawa, N. (2023). *Advanced machine learning algorithms for complex financial applications*. IGI Global., DOI: 10.4018/978-1-6684-4483-2

Irfan, M., Elmogy, M., Gupta, S., Khalifa, F., & Dias, R. (2024). *AI-driven decentralized finance and the future of finance*. IGI Global., DOI: 10.4018/979-8-3693-6321-8

Irfan, M., Elmogy, M., Majid, M. S., & El-Sappagh, S. (2023). *The impact of AI innovation on financial sectors in the era of Industry 5.0*. IGI Global., DOI: 10.4018/979-8-3693-0082-4

Irfan, M., Hussainey, K., Chan Bukhari, S. A., & Nam, Y. (Eds.). (2024). *Issues of sustainability in AI and new-age thematic investing*. IGI Global., DOI: 10.4018/979-8-3693-3282-5

Irfan, M., Kadry, S., Sharif, M., & Ullah Khan, H. (2023). *Fintech applications in Islamic finance: AI, machine learning, and blockchain techniques*. IGI Global., DOI: 10.4018/979-8-3693-1038-0

Kahneman, D., & Tversky, A. (1979). Prospect theory: An analysis of decision under risk. *Econometrica*, *47*(2), 263–291. DOI: 10.2307/1914185

Krause, D. (2024). Finfluencers and market distortions: An analysis of herding behavior on social media platforms. *Social Finance Quarterly*, *29*(2), 90–107.

Motley Fool. (2023). Gen Z's investing habits: Trends and expectations. *The Motley Fool Research Briefs*. https://www.fool.com/research/gen-z-investing-trends/

Nair, V. (2024). AI-augmented investor behavior: A study on cognitive load and digital finance. *International Journal of Financial Management and Research*, *6*(1), 12–24.

Nguyen, T., Tran, M., & Le, H. T. (2020). Behavioral biases and investment decisions: Evidence from emerging markets. *Journal of Behavioral Finance and Economics*, *12*(3), 150–163.

Rahayu, N., Widodo, A., & Hartono, M. (2021). The influence of herding behavior on investment decisions in the digital era. *International Journal of Financial Research, 12*(2), 88–96. DOI: 10.5430/ijfr.v12n2p88

Shefrin, H. (2000). *Beyond greed and fear: Understanding behavioral finance and the psychology of investing*. Harvard Business School Press.

Spytska, A. (2024). Overconfidence bias in Gen Z investors and the role of AI-enhanced education. *Journal of Youth Finance and Technology*, *3*(1), 22–35.

Statman, M. (1995). Behavioral finance: Past battles and future engagements. *Financial Analysts Journal, 51*(6), 18–27. DOI: 10.2469/faj.v55.n6.2311

Sulhia, B. A., Handajani, L., & Surasni, N. K. (2022). The effect of financial literacy, herding behaviour, and overconfidence on investment decisions in the millennial generation. *Traektoriâ Nauki = Path of Science, 8*(7), 1030–1034.

Chapter 15
The Use of Artificial Intelligence for the Creation of Knowledge: An Exploratory Study

Pedro Catarino Santos
Polytechnic University of Leiria, Portugal

Liliana Coutinho Vitorino
Polytechnic University of Leiria, Portugal

Bruno Barbosa Sousa
https://orcid.org/0000-0002-8588-2422
Polytechnic University of Cávado and Ave, Portugal & Applied Management Research Unit, Portugal

ABSTRACT

The consumer electronics and household appliances retail industry is characterized by an environment of high innovation and competitiveness. In this sector, Small and Medium-sized Enterprises (SME's) face an additional challenge due to the disparity in resources compared to large companies. Despite having fewer financial and human resources, these SMEs need to compete, developing effective marketing strategies and taking advantage of the opportunities that technology provides to shorten distances and obtain competitive advantages. This preliminary chapter evaluates the impact of artificial intelligence (AI) tools on the creation of internal and external knowledge in consumer electronics and household appliances retail SMEs. Furthermore, it explores the relationship between knowledge creation and data-based marketing decision-making, as well as the impact of these marketing decisions on the business performance of the companies studied.

DOI: 10.4018/979-8-3373-1250-7.ch015

INTRODUCTION

This study aims to assess the impact of Artificial Intelligence (AI) tools on the collection, processing and analysis of internal and external data, as well as their effect on marketing decision-making and business performance. The choice of this topic arises from the growing relevance of AI in the business landscape, where the ability to collect, process and use data efficiently is a critical factor for obtaining a competitive advantage. With the accelerated evolution of AI tools, companies in the consumer electronics and home appliance retail sector, especially Small and Medium Enterprises (SMEs), face new opportunities and challenges. This study therefore aims to explore the degree of adoption and maturity of these tools in the context of SMEs, assessing the extent to which companies are using these solutions to optimize processes, improve customer experience and boost their performance. By analyzing the impact of AI in these areas, we seek to understand how SMEs can make the most of emerging technologies to position themselves more competitively in the market. In recent years, Artificial Intelligence (AI) has been transforming the business environment, revolutionizing not only process automation but also the way strategic and operational decisions are made. In Portugal, the adoption of AI has seen significant growth, with forecasts indicating significant investment in this area. Data from IDC (International Data Corporation) indicate a 23.2% increase in investment in AI, with investment expected to exceed 100 million euros by 2024 (ITInsights, 2024). Despite the enthusiasm and growth projections, the Portuguese reality, particularly in the context of small and medium-sized enterprises (SMEs), presents notable challenges. Another aspect explored in this dissertation is the role of AI in sharing and managing knowledge within organizations. The ability to create, share and reuse knowledge is one of the pillars of competitive advantage in modern companies (Olan et al., 2022). In this context, AI emerges as a powerful tool to facilitate knowledge sharing and promote innovation (Abubakar et al., 2019). This study will also address the creation of internal and external knowledge in companies, a continuous and essential process to ensure operational and procedural solutions that reinforce their competitive advantage (Ritala & Stefan, 2021). Data-driven decision-making is another central theme of this study. The implementation of AI tools in data analysis has allowed companies to extract important insights for making more informed and strategic decisions (Stone et al., 2020).

THEORETICAL BACKGROUND

1. Artificial Intelligence: Foundations and "Ecosystem"

The term Artificial Intelligence (AI) was first conceptualized in 1955 by John McCarthy when he defined AI as the science and engineering of creating intelligent machines (Manning, 2020). In 1956, the author at the Dartmouth conference referred to AI as "machines capable of performing tasks characteristic of human intelligence" (Kissinger et al., 2021). Since AI is an imitation or simulation of human intelligence, and considering that this is a field still poorly understood by humans, it is not surprising that AI is still not a clearly defined field (Sheikh et al., 2023). However, with the evolution of time, knowledge and studies related to the subject, several definitions have emerged. According to Russell & Norvig (2016), AI is more focused on knowledge acquisition, planning and obstacle resolution. It is the ability of machines to perform tasks by displaying intelligent and human-like behavior (Russell & Norvig, 2016). From another perspective, this concept also involves knowledge, self-awareness, emotional knowledge, reason, creativity, logic and critical thinking (Legg & Hutter, 2007). Anica-Popa et al. (2021) define AI in a very elucidative and comprehensive way with regard to all the areas and subdomains of the AI field. They state that it is the ability of a system to acquire and interpret data, learn and then apply the new knowledge to achieve certain results or perform a task through adaptive behavior. AI can thus offer tools capable of reinventing business models, changing the future of work, improving performance and even enhancing human capabilities (Collins et al., 2021).

In theoretical frameworks, it is common to find concepts related to AI such as Machine Learning (ML) and Deep Learning (DL). Although these are closely linked, they are presented as distinct concepts. According to Anica-Popa et al. (2021), AI is recognized as the ability to acquire and interpret data, learn and then apply new knowledge to achieve certain results or perform a task through adaptive behavior, and includes many subdomains. For a better understanding of the AI "ecosystem", it is considered pertinent to present the concepts of Machine Learning and Deep Learning. The term Machine Learning (ML) emerged in the 1950s, when Arthur Samuel explained that ML provides computers with "the ability to learn without being explicitly programmed" (Samuel, 1959). It is, in fact, a subset of AI (figure 1) that addresses ways to build systems that improve automatically through experience (Jordan & Mitchell, 2015). The literature distinguishes three major subcategories of ML (supervised, unsupervised, and reinforced learning) as AI methods aimed at creating AI capabilities (Bonaccorso, 2017). Kissinger et al. (2021) list the main forms of machine learning: "supervised learning, unsupervised learning, and reinforced learning." (Kissinger et al., 2021, p.69). Artificial Intelligence capability refers to the ability of AI systems to perform various tasks or solve problems. Artificial Intelligence can be applied in different domains today, as mentioned above. Applications then refer to the various artificial intelligence techniques and systems that are used to solve problems, automate tasks, and provide valuable insights in the most varied contexts and sectors .

These applications cover a wide range of domains that include:

- Intelligent agents (Chatbots): These are systems that process and simulate human conversations, written or spoken, allowing fluid and contextualized communication between humans and "machines" (Oracle, nd).
- Collaborative robotics (cobots): With the institution of human-machine cooperation in the workplace, a need for behavior between both elements is introduced (Chromjakova et al., 2021). Collaborative robots (cobots) operate at slower speeds and are equipped with sensors to enable safe collaboration with human workers (Daugherty & Wilson, 2018).
- Recommendation systems: These systems provide personalized service support to users by learning their past behaviors and predicting their current preferences for specific products (Zhang et al., 2021). They apply suggestions based on subtle patterns detected by AI algorithms over time. They can be targeted to consumers to suggest new products or used internally to make strategic suggestions (Daugherty & Wilson, 2018).
- Personalization: Analyzing trends and patterns for customers and employees to optimize products, services, or even business models (Daugherty & Wilson, 2018). Any function and activity across a wide range of industries that could benefit from personalization should consider using AI. For example, Netflix movie recommendations or Amazon cross-selling (Huang & Rust, 2020).
- Augmented Reality: Applications that transform "volumes of data and analysis into images or animations that are superimposed on the real world" (Porter & Heppelmann, 2017, p. 74), for example the alert and collision warning screens in the driver's line of sight available in many cars (Porter & Heppelmann, 2017, p. 74).

2. Innovation and Artificial Intelligence: The Role of Data Collection and Processing

Innovation derives from knowledge-based activities that involve the practical application of existing or newly developed information and knowledge. Both information and knowledge can be obtained or created within or outside the organization (Oslo Manual 2018, 2018). Innovation is increasingly linked to the ability to collect and process large volumes of data, transforming them into strategic knowledge. AI plays a key role in this process by enabling the efficient analysis of data from both internal and external sources. AI's ability to automate complex tasks, learn patterns and provide valuable insights through data collection has driven innovations across all sectors of activity. With the increasing availability of information, it has become necessary to develop efficient strategies to collect and leverage existing data sets. Maskey (2023) reinforces this idea by highlighting the need to center AI on data, so that the greatest potential can be derived from its tools. AI has a great capacity to interpret external data, learn from it and use this knowledge to achieve specific goals and tasks through flexible adaptation (Kaplan & Haenlein, 2019). It is also important to highlight the importance of human participation in data-centric AI tasks, in order to "feed" and direct the machine's knowledge with information that is as credible and contextualized as possible. Human participation becomes crucial in many scenarios because it is often the only way to ensure that the behavior of AI systems is aligned with human intentions (Zha et al., 2023). Another critical factor is a deep understanding of the environment or sector so that consistent, credible and representative data can be collected (Zha et al., 2023). Only with this type of data collection will it be possible to obtain truthful outputs, contextualized with the final objective and not biased towards reality. Overgoor et al (2019) define AI in marketing as the development of systems that use the information they have about consumers, competitors and the internal business, to suggest and/or take marketing actions in order to obtain the best result (Overgoor et al., 2019). This new technological paradigm allows marketers to respond to consumers' expectations and enrich their purchasing journey. AI tools are seen as the answer to the need for personalization and interaction between the brand and the consumer (Olson & Levy, 2017). The adoption of AI and ML tools allows brands to optimize their relationships with their customers at all stages of the purchasing process (acquisition, retention, loyalty and referral) (Venkatesan & Lecinski, 2021). All areas of the marketing mix may be impacted by the introduction of AI in marketing decisions.

2.1 The Use of Artificial Intelligence in Retail

AI tools have become a transformative force in the ever-evolving retail sector, as they have changed the way companies understand and respond to consumer behavior. Ntumba et al., (2023) believe that these tools enable and empower companies to offer personalized experiences, simplify interactions and foster lasting connections with customers (David Iyanuoluwa Ajiga et al., 2024). According to Shankar (2018), these tools have brought benefits to both the organization itself and the consumer. On the company's side, it can use AI to its advantage for operational processes such as optimizing stocks, logistics and deliveries, as well as in strategic processes, such as supporting data-based decision-making. The consumer benefits from having a targeted and personalized offer for their interests and consumption habits (Shankar, 2018). There are several companies in the market that are already using Artificial Intelligence to their advantage. Nike is a great example of how a company can make the most of AI for its (and its customers') benefit. The brand has implemented AI tools with augmented reality to offer its customers the possibility of creating their own custom footwear. The process from design to delivery to the customer takes just 2 weeks (Chao et al., 2019). Amazon is also taking advantage of new AI-powered technologies to offer an excellent experience to its customers in physical stores. Amazon Go allows customers to scan their smartphones when entering the store, choose the products they want and simply leave. Technologies such as computer vision and deep learning, together with various sensors, allow automatic detection of products that are removed or returned to the shelves and track the items in a virtual cart. The customer is charged through their Amazon account (Grewal et al., 2017). Examples like this show a growing need to harness the full potential of AI technologies and tools to create lasting experiences and connections with customers, as the retail industry becomes increasingly dynamic and data-driven.

2.2. Artificial Intelligence in the Acquisition, Management and Sharing of Knowledge

Knowledge is a fusion of contextual information and experience framed in a given context, together with the pure experience of the individual (Davenport & Prusak, 1998). More than simple information, knowledge "involves understanding gained through experience and learning (...) When information is presented in a context it becomes knowledge" (Martins, 2018. p.17). Thus, it is stated that knowledge is dependent on several factors such as information, context and human action. Knowledge can be stored in three types of "repository": Individuals, technological instruments (hardware or software) and in routines (standard procedures or tasks) (Martins, 2018). Organizational knowledge relates to the information, data or activities that the organization, organizational teams and individuals use to perform defined tasks, as well as achieve defined objectives (Kovačić et al., 2022). According to Spender (1996), organizational knowledge is a set of documented and well-known facts and practices. Thus, it can be concluded that knowledge ends up being a fundamental "asset" for companies, as it becomes a basis for developing competitive advantage, as well as for increasing the efficiency and effectiveness of employees (Kovačić et al., 2022). The management and use of this knowledge effectively is essential for organizations to make the most of the value of knowledge (Omotayo, 2015). In order to be able to drive an organization, the three types of knowledge "repository" are fundamental. Processes and technology alone are not enough, but its people (employees) and the knowledge that resides in them are an integral part of the organization's success (Omotayo, 2015). Organizational knowledge can be divided into tacit knowledge and explicit knowledge. Tacit knowledge consists, in part, of technical skills. It is a type of skills that is difficult to define and explain. Note the example of a master craftsman, after years of experience, who develops a wealth of knowledge "at his fingertips". This acquired knowledge is often impossible to document and transmit with scientific or technical principles (Nonaka, 2007).

Tacit and explicit knowledge complement each other and both are essential for knowledge creation in companies. It is in this process of "conversion" from tacit to explicit that the creation of organizational knowledge takes place. This eventually becomes the domain of the organization's knowledge network (Martins, 2018). Martins (2018) identifies the fundamental aspects for knowledge creation in companies, which are: (1) The form of knowledge, (2) the usefulness of knowledge and (3) who uses knowledge. Briefly, the first aspect states that knowledge is not just data and information, but also emotions, values and personal experiences; the second states that in addition to managing existing knowledge, organizations must continuously create new knowledge; finally, all people in the organization must be involved in the process of acquiring, managing and creating new knowledge. The role of AI in knowledge management is specifically task-focused and cannot be easily transferred between different contexts. Thus, although AI plays an important role in some specific knowledge management functions, humans continue to play a fundamental role in this regard (Jarrahi et al., 2023).

The implementation of AI-based tools in companies is already a common reality when it comes to operational business tasks. However, when it comes to the strategic domain of companies, AI still has a way to go. It is expected that in the near future, AI tools will be extensively implemented to perform and assist in the strategic tasks of organizations. The choice of business model, market entry decisions or pricing decisions are examples of strategic decisions that will be largely assisted, or even taken, by AI systems (Stone et al., 2020). Nowadays, it is also possible to use big data analysis methods and use the resulting information to make better internal decisions. In the process of analyzing customer satisfaction, for example, these systems have the ability to identify people who use terms that suggest strong dissatisfaction with a particular brand or product. The organization then has the ability to intervene in some way. The need remains the same as in the past - how to identify an unsatisfied customer - but the tools are different (Davenport, 2014).

3. Methodology and Context

The research of AI and Data Analytics has revolutionized the market research and competitive intelligence landscape. The use of these tools increases the efficiency and accuracy of data analysis, which allows companies to collect meaningful patterns about the external market, i.e., understand consumer behaviors, identify and anticipate market and competitor trends (Vashishth et al., 2024). Big Data, that is, the collection of large amounts of data, is becoming an increasingly valuable source of market knowledge for organizations. The process of data input, processing and output and the use of different AI tools to operate the method can help marketers transform data into information and, ultimately, into different types of knowledge. AI enables external market knowledge, for example, in the analysis of large amounts of online content published on social media, blogs or third-party news platforms (Paschen et al., 2019). AI systems thus provide a great opportunity to obtain data-driven insights and thus optimize market research and validation, i.e. external knowledge. For example, predictive analytics and advanced algorithms can help discover hidden patterns, predict market trends and validate product concepts with greater accuracy and efficiency (Damilola Oluwaseun Ogundipe et al., 2024). Given the exploratory nature of the study, a structured questionnaire survey was used, as it is a method that allows data comparison and standardization, facilitates data processing and improves the accuracy of records (Malhotra et al., 2006). The questionnaire was developed using the Google Forms tool. The questionnaire was applied to SMEs that retail consumer electronics and home appliances, and was intended to be answered by employees with analysis and decision-making positions, such as marketing, sales, management or administration directors. To carry out this research, a non-random and convenience sampling technique was used, a non-random sampling technique in which participants are selected based on ease of access or availability.

4. Preliminary Insights

This chapter presents the main (preliminary) conclusions of the results obtained from this research, whose objective was to study the use of artificial intelligence for knowledge creation and to analyze its impact on marketing decision-making and business performance in the Portuguese SME sector with retail activity in consumer electronics and home appliances. In the first phase, the theoretical contributions of the work to the topic under study are described, as well as a set of recommendations for companies operating in this sector with regard to the topics addressed in the work. Finally, the main limitations of this study are exposed, as well as some suggestions for future research on the topic. This work offers an important contribution to the literature on the use of AI for knowledge creation in small and medium-sized enterprises (SMEs) in the consumer electronics and home appliances retail sector. The study reinforces the relevance of adopting a "data-driven" culture, which has been widely discussed in the context of large companies and other sectors, but still lacks in-depth exploration in SMEs, especially in the specific sector of study. The research confirms that AI can be a fundamental tool in the collection and processing of internal and external data, by creating a direct link between data and organizational knowledge. However, the study also suggests that access to internal data, such as customer interactions and sales histories, is considerably greater than obtaining external data, which involves information about the market, competitors and trends. This difference opens the way for theoretical reflections on the asymmetric relationship between internal and external knowledge, and its applicability in marketing decision-making in SMEs. The difficulty in obtaining external data raises questions about the ability of these companies to adapt and innovate in a dynamic market, especially when compared to large organizations that have greater access to resources. The study also highlights the lack of maturity in terms of data literacy and digital culture in the companies analyzed, which prevents the full potential of AI in supporting decision-making. This observation contributes theoretically to the discussion on the formation of organizations and the challenges that many companies, especially SMEs, face in adopting advanced technologies. The concept of a robust "data infrastructure" that is vital to the correct interpretation of information is highlighted in this research, highlighting the need for greater focus on skills development and investment in technology. Finally, the research indicates that the relationship between the use of AI for data collection and business performance is complex, with no significant impact being found from marketing decision-making supported by AI tools on business performance. This finding challenges some of the theoretical assumptions that argue for a direct link between data-driven marketing decisions and improvements in business results. This theoretical conclusion suggests that without an adequate infrastructure to accurately collect, process and interpret data, decision-makers are unable to optimally use insights to positively influence business results. This lack of trust and analytical support prevents marketing from playing its role as an engine of growth, leaving the decision-making process based on more traditional or intuitive approaches, and limiting the potential impact of these decisions on overall business performance.

On a practical level, this study reveals several important implications for SMEs in the consumer electronics and home appliance retail sector. The first practical point to highlight is the urgent need to invest in AI tools that enable the collection and analysis of internal and external data. AI has proven to be effective in automating processes and processing large volumes of data, allowing companies to obtain important insights to help create more informed and data-driven strategies. Companies in this sector should therefore consider the adoption of AI tools not as a "luxury", but as a necessity to ensure competitiveness. The use of internal data, such as customer interactions and sales history, is a clear and immediate opportunity for SMEs, as it is easier to obtain and analyze. Implementing a "data-driven" culture in these organizations can significantly improve operational efficiency and optimize decision-making. However, the study reveals that it is also necessary to equip employees with the appropriate digital skills, which involves training and, in some cases, hiring new talent who can use emerging AI technologies.

Taking into account the points identified in the research, it is recommended that companies in the sector under study invest in a gradual but solid transformation with regard to data culture and the adoption of advanced analytics technologies. Creating an organizational culture that values the collection and use of data for decision-making should be a priority, promoting digital literacy among employees and managers. This investment will not only allow the implementation of more powerful analytical tools, but will also facilitate the extraction of more robust and reliable insights, essential to support strategic decisions, especially in the field of marketing. In addition, companies should consider allocating resources, even if limited, to systems that enable the efficient collection of external data to complement their internal analyses and thus obtain a more comprehensive view of the market.

The use of AI tools can be a viable solution to improve the accuracy and scope of analyses, allowing companies to compete more effectively. It follows that without developing these skills, companies will continue to make poorly informed marketing decisions, failing to optimize their impact on business performance, which in the long term may limit growth and competitiveness in the market. Therefore, the way forward involves combining technology, training and strategy to foster a data-driven environment that serves as a lever for business growth.

REFERENCES

Aaker, D. A., Kumar, V., & Day, G. S. (2004). *MarketingResearch*. Wiley.

Abubakar, A. M., Elrehail, H., Alatailat, M. A., & Elçi, A. (2019). Knowledge management, decision-making style and organizational performance. *Journal of Innovation and Knowledge*, *4*(2), 104–114. DOI: 10.1016/j.jik.2017.07.003

Anica-Popa, I., Anica-Popa, L., Rădulescu, C., & Vrîncianu, M. (2021). The Integration of Artificial Intelligence in Retail: Benefits, Challenges and a Dedicated Conceptual Framework. *Amfiteatru Economic*, *23*(56), 122–122. DOI: 10.24818/EA/2021/56/120

Anjorin, K. F., Raji, M. A., & Olodo, H. B.Kikelomo Fadilat AnjorinMustafa Ayobami RajiHameedat Bukola Olodo. (2024). A review of strategic decision-making in marketing through big data and analytics. *Computer Science & IT Research Journal*, *5*(5), 1126–1144. DOI: 10.51594/csitrj.v5i5.1139

Basu, R., Lim, W. M., Kumar, A., & Kumar, S. (2023). Marketing analytics: The bridge between customer psychology and marketing decision-making. In Psychology and Marketing (Vol. 40, Issue 12, pp. 2588–2611). John Wiley and Sons Inc. https://doi.org/DOI: 10.1002/mar.21908

Brynjolfsson, E., & Mitchell, T. (2017). What can machine learning do? Workforce implications. *Science*, *358*(6370), 1530–1534. DOI: 10.1126/science.aap8062 PMID: 29269459

Chao, G., Cheung, J., Haller, K., & Lee, J. (2019). The coming AI revolution in retail and consumer products: Intelligent automation is transforming both industries in unexpected ways.

Chin, W. W. (1998). The Partial Least Squares Approach to Structural Equation Modeling. Lawrence Erlbaum Associates. https://www.researchgate.net/publication/311766005

Chromjakova, F., Trentesaux, D., & Kwarteng, M. A. (2021). Human and cobot cooperation ethics: The process management concept of the production workplace. *Journal of Competitiveness*, *13*(3), 21–38. DOI: 10.7441/joc.2021.03.02

Collins, C., Dennehy, D., Conboy, K., & Mikalef, P. (2021). Artificial intelligence in information systems research: A systematic literature review and research agenda. *International Journal of Information Management*, *60*, 102383. Advance online publication. DOI: 10.1016/j.ijinfomgt.2021.102383

Davenport, T. H. (2014). How strategists use "big data" to support internal business decisions, discovery and production. *Strategy and Leadership*, *42*(4), 45–50. DOI: 10.1108/SL-05-2014-0034

Davenport, T. H., & Prusak, L. (1998). *Working Knowledge: How Organizations Manage What They Know*. Harvard Business School Press., DOI: 10.1145/348772.348775

Dekimpe, M. G. (2020). Retailing and retailing research in the age of big data analytics. *International Journal of Research in Marketing*, *37*(1), 3–14. DOI: 10.1016/j.ijresmar.2019.09.001

Du, S., & Xie, C. (2021). Paradoxes of artificial intelligence in consumer markets: Ethical challenges and opportunities. Journal of Business Research, 129, 961 974. https://doi.org/DOI: 10.1016/j.jbusres.2020.08.024

Duan, Y., Edwards, J. S., & Dwivedi, Y. K. (2019). Artificial intelligence for decision making in the era of Big Data – evolution, challenges and research agenda. *International Journal of Information Management*, *48*, 63–71. DOI: 10.1016/j.ijinfomgt.2019.01.021

Dubey, R., Gunasekaran, A., Childe, S. J., Blome, C., & Papadopoulos, T. (2019). Big Data and Predictive Analytics and Manufacturing Performance: Integrating Institutional Theory, Resource-Based View and Big Data Culture. *British Journal of Management*, *30*(2), 341–361. DOI: 10.1111/1467-8551.12355

Gupta, B., Iyer, L. S., & Aronson, J. E. (2000). Knowledge management: Practices and challenges. *Industrial Management & Data Systems*, *100*(1), 17–21. DOI: 10.1108/02635570010273018

Gupta, S., Justy, T., Kamboj, S., Kumar, A., & Kristoffersen, E. (2021). Big data and firm marketing performance: Findings from knowledge-based view. *Technological Forecasting and Social Change*, *171*, 171. DOI: 10.1016/j.techfore.2021.120986

Harrison, R., Parker, A., Brosas, G., Chiong, R., & Tian, X. (2015). The role of technology in the management and exploitation of internal business intelligence. *Journal of Systems and Information Technology*, *17*(3), 247–262. DOI: 10.1108/JSIT-04-2015-0030

Jarrahi, M. H., Askay, D., Eshraghi, A., & Smith, P. (2023). Artificial intelligence and knowledge management: A partnership between human and AI. *Business Horizons*, *66*(1), 87–99. DOI: 10.1016/j.bushor.2022.03.002

Kaplan, A., & Haenlein, M. (2019). Siri, Siri, in my hand: Who's the fairest in the land? On the interpretations, illustrations, and implications of artificial intelligence. In Business Horizons (Vol. 62, Issue 1, pp. 15–25). Elsevier Ltd. https://doi.org/ DOI: 10.1016/j.bushor.2018.08.004

Lanzolla, G., Pesce, D., & Tucci, C. L. (2021). The Digital Transformation of Search and Recombination in the Innovation Function: Tensions and an Integrative Framework*. *Journal of Product Innovation Management*, *38*(1), 90–113. DOI: 10.1111/jpim.12546

Maramganti, K., & Rajyalakshmi, N. C. (2019). Role of artificial intelligence in business transformation. In International Journal on Recent Trends in Business and Tourism I (Vol. 3, Issue 3).

Overgoor, G., Chica, M., Rand, W., & Weishampel, A. (2019). Letting the computers take over: Using Ai to solve marketing problems. *California Management Review*, *61*(4), 156–185. DOI: 10.1177/0008125619859318

Shankar, V. (2018). How Artificial Intelligence (AI) is Reshaping Retailing. *Journal of Retailing*, *94*(4), vi–xi. DOI: 10.1016/S0022-4359(18)30076-9

Stone, M., Aravopoulou, E., Ekinci, Y., Evans, G., Hobbs, M., Labib, A., Laughlin, P., Machtynger, J., & Machtynger, L. (2020). Artificial intelligence (AI) in strategic marketing decision-making: A research agenda. *The Bottom Line (New York, N.Y.)*, *33*(2), 183–200. DOI: 10.1108/BL-03-2020-0022

Truong, Y., & McColl, R. (2011). Intrinsic motivations, self-esteem, and luxury goods consumption. *Journal of Retailing and Consumer Services*, *18*(6), 555–561. DOI: 10.1016/j.jretconser.2011.08.004

Wamba, S. F., Gunasekaran, A., Akter, S., Ren, S. J., Dubey, R., & Childe, S. J. (2017). Big data analytics and firm performance: Effects of dynamic capabilities. *Journal of Business Research*, *70*, 356–365. DOI: 10.1016/j.jbusres.2016.08.009

Wilson, H., & Daugherty, P. (2019). Collaborative intelligence: Humans and AI are joining forces. In Artificial Intelligence, Data Analytics, and the New Machine Age (pp. 161–180). Harvard Business Review Press.

Zha, D., Bhat, Z. P., Lai, K.-H., Yang, F., Jiang, Z., Zhong, S., & Hu, X. (2023). Data centric Artificial Intelligence: A Survey. http://arxiv.org/abs/2303.10158

Zhan, Y., Tan, K. H., Li, Y., & Tse, Y. K. (2018). Unlocking the power of big data in new product development. *Annals of Operations Research*, *270*(1–2), 577–595. DOI: 10.1007/s10479-016-2379-x

Zhang, Q., Lu, J., & Jin, Y. (2021). Artificial intelligence in recommender systems. *Complex & Intelligent Systems*, *7*(1), 439–457. DOI: 10.1007/s40747-020-00212-w

KEY TERMS AND DEFINITIONS

Artificial Intelligence (AI): A set of technologies that enable computers to perform a variety of advanced functions, including the ability to see, understand and translate spoken and written languages, analyze data, make recommendations, and more.

Knowledge Creation: Means continuous combination, transfer and conversion of different knowledge. It is a formation of new ideas, occurs through interactions, and includes tacit and explicit forms of knowledge.

Marketing: The activity, set of institutions, and processes for creating, communicating, delivering, and exchanging offerings that have value for customers, clients, partners, and society at large

Chapter 16
The Role of Peer Influence Through Social Networks on Investment Decisions

G. Manjunatha
https://orcid.org/0009-0006-2649-7686
St. Claret College, Bengaluru, India

Priscilla Nancy S.
St. Claret College, Bengaluru, India

Hruthik Nayaka L.
St. Claret College, Bengaluru, India

Gopalakrishnan Soundararajan
https://orcid.org/0000-0001-9013-0498
Muscat College, Oman

ABSTRACT

This study explores how peer influence within social networks impacts investment decisions, using data from 75 active investors via a standardized questionnaire on demographics, peer influence, and investment outcomes. Using SPSS and multiple regression, results showed that peer influence significantly predicted 58.6% of the variance in investing behavior (R^2 = 0.586; R = 0.766; p < 0.05). Younger investors under 30, particularly active in online forums, were more susceptible to social pressure. Direct peer recommendations had a stronger effect than general exposure to financial discussions, highlighting the role of social validation. While

DOI: 10.4018/979-8-3373-1250-7.ch016

peer impact is significant, factors like risk tolerance, financial literacy, and economic conditions also shape investment behavior. The study urges a balance between peer insights and objective analysis. These findings can inform financial education and policymaking to promote independent, informed decisions, especially as digital platforms reshape investment landscapes.

INTRODUCTION

Economic, social, and psychological factors together shape the landscape of investment choice. Resident in that triad, peer pressure frequently emerges as a dominant force. A surprising number of individuals defer to the lived experiences and opinions of friends, colleagues, and online acquaintances, sometimes elevating those voices above formal market reports. Recent studies therefore set out to dissect which attributes of a given social platform sway investors most, measure the sheer weight of that peer pressure, and identify traits that either amplify the pull or offer a counterbalance.

The prominence of peer influence in trading and portfolio-building behaviour has been underscored in a growing body of scholarship. One investigation found that retail investors rely heavily on social cues, citing the shared stories of their circle to navigate financial jargon (Qin et al., 2021). The phenomenon, interestingly, scales upward; firms grouped in publicly supported tech hubs mirror one another's capital commitments even when isolated from external analytic briefs, suggesting that corporate actors, too, are not immune to the echo chamber effect (Xiao et al., 2021).

Researchers still catalogue the ways peers steer an investor's hand. Informational channels pass raw tips or analytical nudges; normative ones entrench the feeling that everyone ought to follow a crowd (Peng et al. 2024). Their list keeps growing—broker apps, influencers' second-by-second posts, even meme pages—as each medium layers fresh habits on top of its predecessor (Riefel et al. 2024; Al Atoom et al. 2024).

Psychology and finance never part neatly. A third-person effect whispers that the neighbouring trader is sponge-like, soaking up every headline, while the observer pretends to remain dry; that same observer, meanwhile, craves a thumbs-up, a sign that the bet fits the group's unwritten rules (Sherman et al. 2016; Albert et al. 2013). The latest wave of chat rooms and trend boards lets conjectures bloom in real time, letting doubt wither as soon as somebody types Sounds smart, I'm in.

Careful scrutiny of the social processes underlying investment choice fills an important gap in contemporary research literature. By tracing the chain from network composition through moderating traits—risk appetite, literacy—and eventually to observed peer sway, the project clarifies how the same circle of acquaintances can lead one trader toward buy-and-hold stocks while nudging another toward green bonds. A typical retail investor may find the findings instructive, but the insights also speak to wealth managers who construct portfolios and to lawmakers writing new consumer safeguards in a tightly knotted market. Because network features can turn classic tactics into engines for experimental strategies, advisers are urged to ask about social circles and regulators are reminded to account for contagion when drafting protective measures. There are helpful suggestions offered for maximizing the benefits of peer pressure while reducing the dangers of financial market herd mentality.

REVIEW OF LITERATURE

(Qin. F,. et al 2021) We see early-stage unofficial investors as socially inspired co-entrepreneurs. Our research investigates the ways in which entrepreneurial experience and social influence impact investing choices. We contend, using the social homophily hypothesis, that informal investments are motivated by shared experiences within peer groups. Social impact can make up for a lack of personal entrepreneurship expertise, according to multi-level analysis conducted across nations. (Xiao. R., et al 2021) Recognizing the value of investment in business expansion and economic development, the Chinese government promotes regional innovation through reform zones. This study uses data from Chinese listed companies (2013–2017) to investigate how peer influence impacts firms' innovative investments. Key policy implications are highlighted by the findings, which show larger peer impacts among weaker enterprises and in innovation zones.

Through structural social influence, this study investigates the causal complexity of peer effects among ECF investors. It investigates how normative and informational mechanisms influence peer impacts using fsQCA on 157 Chinese ECF samples. Multiple contributing elements are revealed by the findings, with normative mechanisms operating independently and informational mechanisms relying on them. By highlighting information asymmetry and social interactions, the study advances our knowledge of the complexity of investor decision-making. (Peng .L., et al 2024) It is the first to emphasize the significance of mutual norms in ECF investment decisions through the use of complex networks and qualitative comparison research. This study analyzes important financial and economic data disseminated via digital platforms to investigate how new media affects investment choices in the Amman Financial Market. A questionnaire was given to 150 randomly chosen investors using a descriptive analytical method. According to research, 40% of people rely on specialized websites for investment advice, while 60% use social media. The Amman Financial Market website (78%) (SA Al Atoom., el at) is the main specialized source, whereas Facebook (51.3%) is the most popular platform.

The findings support the idea that new media has a big influence on how people choose to invest.

In the digital age, social media serves as a communication tool and a source of financial information. Social media can be used to sway investing decisions based on personality traits, claims behavioural finance. This study examines Dutch investors while accounting for modifiers like tie strength and financial effects. Data from 142 respondents indicates that social media has a significant impact on investing decisions, and opinions are impacted by the third-person effect. The findings provide insight into how social media affects financial advisors' and investors' investing behaviour. (D Riefel.,et al 2024). This study examines Malaysian investment choices with an emphasis on the influence of social media on the internet. Data was evaluated using SPSS using surveys that were sent to investors, mostly in the Klang Valley. The findings support the notion that corporate image, online community behaviour, and social media information all have a big impact on investment choices. The results support further studies on capital markets and social networks. (Ismai. S., et al 2024)

The study used neuroimaging and binomial tests to investigate peer influence on social media. Participants followed the advice of their peers, particularly when it came to their own pictures. By like count, neural responses differed, involving reward and social cognition. Images that were risky decreased cognitive control activation. Results show how social media affects teenage behaviour and sociability. (Sherman, L. E., et al 2016). It has been demonstrated that adolescents' heightened reactivity to social cues with positive connotations directly impairs their ability to control approach behaviour. This study suggests that teenagers are particularly susceptible to the reward-sensitizing effects of social stimuli, which may make it more difficult for them to "put the brakes on" impulsive behaviour.(Albert, D., et al 2013)

Through website design, social media operators should improve both social and informational features. Users should be able to communicate with peers in a credible and pertinent manner, access topics at their own speed, and share experiences with ease. Using cutting-edge technology and safety measures can promote empathy, trust, and productive relationships in online communities. (Wang. X., et al 2012) The use of sentiment data from social media to inform financial choices is becoming more popular. Although this topic has been studied, problems with data collecting, measurement, and visualization still exist. In order to improve accuracy and offer more profound investment insights, this article presents a prototype that incorporates social media measures into sentiment scoring, with a focus on S&P 500 equities. (Hasselgren, B., et al 2022).

The study by Mohamed Issa Buzohera (2025) looks at how tax attitudes, peer pressure, and social influence affect tax compliance among Tanzanian SMEs, specifically in Dar es Salaam and Dodoma. Through the use of statistical analysis (β and t-statistics) and structured questionnaires, the study employs an expanded Theory of

Planned Behaviour framework that takes social dynamics into account. According to the study, SMEs who support taxes and see them as a civic obligation or a way to fund public services had far higher compliance rates ($\beta = 0.527$, $t = 7.573$, $p < 0.001$). Social impact is also important; community norms, corporate associations, and peer pressure all promote compliance ($\beta = 0.286$, $t = 4.333$, $p < 0.001$). Notably, the interplay between social networks and individual views increases compliance, indicating a synergistic relationship between social reinforcement from outside sources and inside beliefs. By adding social network impacts, the study expands on the Theory of Planned Behaviour and emphasizes how social norms and individual motives drive tax behaviour. The results indicate that policymakers should use social networks to promote voluntary compliance over stringent enforcement, start education and awareness campaigns to improve tax attitudes, and involve business communities through peer-led workshops and public recognition of compliant companies. In order to promote SME tax compliance in Tanzania, Buzohera's 2025 research emphasizes the value of creating encouraging social situations and raising individual tax morale. A strategic roadmap for future policy formulation can emerge from these findings.

In a recent investigation, Alwajud-Adewusi, Oduola, and Ifabiyi examined how substance use among school-age teenagers in Kwara State, Nigeria, relates to peer pressure and social media habits. The research appeared in the Journal of Guidance and Counselling Studies and relied on structured questionnaires plus a quantitative survey design to gauge students' exposure to social platforms, peer influence, and likelihood of drug misuse. Statistical analysis revealed a strong positive association between frequent social media activity and substance use ($\beta = 0.42$, $p < 0.01$). Such a relationship implies that peer exchanges or trending posts on sites like Instagram, Snapchat, and TikTok can normalise high-risk choices, thereby heightening adolescents' willingness to experiment with drugs.

Recent quantitative work from Nigeria linked peer influence itself to a shockingly high predictive weight for drug misuse—a bivariate β of 0.58 with p value testing well under 0.001. Teenagers whose close friends used substances proved far more likely, by a large margin, to follow the same path. When the researchers added time spent on social media forums, the odds of trying drugs climbed even higher; online and face-to-face pressures appeared to stack, rather than cancel, one another.

Given those patterns, health specialists studying the cohort now press for intervention schemes that enter classrooms equipped with both substance-abuse curricula and robust digital literacy modules. Community town halls and parent-led discussion groups were identified as useful supplements, especially when adults monitor what youths see on their phones. School administrators, however, noted that shy users shy away from help if the message feels too loud or preachy.

To blunt the flow of glamorised content, some authors of the report suggested that Nigerian regulators narrow the algorithms that promote posts glamorising narcotics. Rigorous ongoing collaboration between parents, teachers, and psychological counsellors also topped the list of action items, since no single player controls all the arenas where peer pressure germinates. With that broad framework, the team argues, students can be steered away from quick decisions they may regret for the rest of their lives.

Researchers who study substance misuse keep telling leaders that classrooms, evening workshops, and tougher laws can curb the problem. Those same recommendations now join a wider debate about how young people behave online. Luo (2025) has written a paper titled When Climate Risk Spreads: The Role of Social Network in Portfolio Sustainability Tilting. He retraces the footprints of hedge funds and pension boards as they drift towards greener assets after a fresh round of news about flooding or wildfires. The dataset is massive, blending trading logs with the informal chatter on Slack groups, WhatsApp channels, and Twitter threads they belong to. Simple regressions show a striking pattern: portfolio managers whose colleagues already flaunt solar startups tend to shed coal stocks within a month. The force is particularly acute among insurance companies and university endowments, whose signatures move prices even when they think no one is watching. Inside the friendship map, celebrity voices—data from a prominent Chief Investment Officer, for example—create what Luo calls a social multiplier effect that nudges peers another 20 to 30 percent towards sustainable choices.

However, this proliferation may be impeded by elements such as ideological similarities and unequal information flow. According to the study, sustainable investment initiatives can be strengthened by involving important network actors, enhancing climate risk disclosures, and customizing interventions according to network dynamics. Luo's research successfully ties climate economics and behavioural finance together, providing methods to quicken the shift to more environmentally friendly financial markets.

RESEARCH METHODOLOGY

To determine how peer influence via social networks affects individual investment decisions, the study used a quantitative, cross-sectional research methodology. A systematic questionnaire that addressed social network participation, peer influence dimensions, investing behaviour indicators, and demographic characteristics was used to gather data. 75 active retail investors who mostly used digital financial platforms were the target of a convenience sample technique. The questionnaire was pre-tested to guarantee its validity and reliability before to implementation.

While multiple regression analysis was used to assess the link between independent factors (social network features and peer influence) and the dependent variable (investment decisions), descriptive statistics offered insight into the demographic profile of the respondents. With an R-squared value of 0.586, the model showed a strong predictive capacity, indicating that the factors under investigation account for 58.6% of the variation in investment choices. In all statistical studies, SPSS software was used. Strict adherence was maintained to ethical principles, including informed consent and participant anonymity. Notwithstanding these precautions, the study is constrained by its homogeneous sample and non-probability sampling technique, which may limit how broadly the findings can be applied. Although the methodology offers an organized approach, it does not prove causation.

OBJECTIVES

To determine the degree to which peer pressure influences personal investment decisions, to pinpoint the salient features of social networks that influence investment choices, and to investigate moderating factors that could amplify or diminish the influence of peer pressure on investment choices.

HYPOTHESIS

(H_0): Peer influence has no significant impact on individual investment decisions.
(H_1): Peer influence significantly impacts individual investment decisions.

Research Gap

The literature currently in publication frequently overlooks the subtle but crucial role that peer influence through social networks plays in influencing investing decisions in favor of concentrating primarily on media, market trends, and economic facts. The majority of research focuses on institutional investors or market movements at the macro level, which leaves out information about the social interactions at the micro level that influence the behaviour of retail investors. Peer discussions and suggestions through digital platforms are becoming more and more important, especially among young and tech-savvy investors, although they are still not well studied in academic studies. Furthermore, elements that can mitigate or modulate the impacts of peer influence, such as platform trustworthiness, individual risk-taking tendencies, and financial literacy, are not fully investigated. Differentiating the influence of different online platforms—like WhatsApp, Telegram, or investment-specific forums—on decision-making behaviours is another uncharted topic. By showing how peer and social network characteristics affect investment behaviour, this study helps close some of this gap, but it still provides room for more research into psychological motivators such as fear of missing out (FOMO), social proof, and conformity bias. Longitudinal studies are also necessary since peer influence is dynamic and can vary over time in response to shifts in the market or advances in technology. Research of this kind may reveal changing trends that are not detectable by cross-sectional designs.

SCOPE

The main aim of this research is to explore the impact of peer influence within social networks on the investment choices made by retail investors. It specifically focuses on how elements like peer suggestions and discussions on financial platforms shape individual investment behaviour. The study uses information gathered from 75 participants who participate actively in peer investment networks and digital financial platforms. Using multiple regression analysis, the study shows that social network participation and peer influence account for 58.6% of the diversity in investing decisions, which is a substantial explanation of individual investment behaviour variances. This demonstrates how important social aspects are in influencing personal finance decisions, particularly for young investors who are more likely to be active in these networks. Age and education are also identified in the study as potential modifiers that may impact the level of peer influence. Nevertheless, the scope excludes institutional and corporate investors as well as the analysis of the effects of market dynamics and general economic conditions. The findings are most applicable to retail investing scenarios since it is limited to the actions of individual investors and their immediate social milieu. For financial advisors, educators, and legislators looking to encourage sensible investing choices, this study offers insightful information.

RESULTS & DISCUSSIONS

Table 1. Descriptive Statistics

Descriptive Statistics					
	N	Min	Max	M	SD
Age	55	1	4	1.73	.932
Gender	55	1	2	1.40	.494
Education	55	2	4	3.38	.652
Occupation	55	1	2	1.36	.485
Valid N (listwise)	55				

The descriptive statistics provide a summary of the main demographic characteristics of the respondents. The majority of participants are younger, as indicated by the age variable's mean of 1.73 and standard deviation of 0.932. The gender variable shows a distribution that is nearly uniformly distributed but somewhat skewed, with a mean of 1.40 and a standard deviation of 0.494. The qualification variable's average of 3.38 and standard deviation of 0.652 indicate that most respondents had higher educational degrees. Lastly, with a mean of 1.36 and a standard deviation of 0.485, the occupation variable shows that the majority of participants belong to a specific job category.

Table 2. Statistics

Statstics		
N	Considered	55
	Error	0
M		1.73
Median		1.00
SD		.932

Table 3. Age

		F	%	Valid %	Cumulative %
Considered	18-24	29	52.7	52.7	52.7
	25-30	16	29.1	29.1	81.8
	31-35	6	10.9	10.9	92.7
	36 and higher	4	7.3	7.3	100.0
	Total	55	100.0	100.0	

Young adults predominate in the sample, as evidenced by the age distribution table, which reveals that the highest percentage of respondents (52.7%) are between the ages of 18 and 24. With 29.1% of all responders, the 25–30 age group is the second largest. Just 7.3% of respondents are 36 years of age or older, while 10.9% of respondents are between the ages of 31 and 35. According to the cumulative proportion, a noteworthy 81.8% of the sample is under 30 years old, indicating a young population that may have an impact on investing behaviour through peer pressure and social media use.

Table 4. Statistics

		Qualification
N	Considered	55
	Error	0
M		3.38
Median		3.00
SD		.652

Table 5. Qualification

		Qualification			
		F	%	Valid %	Cumulative %
Valid	PU / DIPLOMA	5	9.1	9.1	9.1
	UG	24	43.6	43.6	52.7
	PG	26	47.3	47.3	100.0
	Total	55	100.0	100.0	

According to the qualification statistics, the majority of respondents have higher educational levels, with a mean value of 3.38 and a standard deviation of 0.652. The majority of participants appear to be in the mid-to-high qualification range, based on the median qualification value of 3.00. A lower standard deviation suggests that there is little variation in the educational backgrounds of the respondents. According to this distribution, a sample with higher levels of education is probably more financially savvy, which could affect their choice of investments through peer pressure and social media. According to the occupation statistics, the majority of respondents fall into one of the following occupation categories: students or early-career professionals, with a mean value of 1.36 and a standard deviation of 0.485. The occupation variable's reduced standard deviation suggests that the sample's employment status is more uniform. This would suggest that the respondents' financial and investing interests are similar, which might have been influenced by their friends and social media contacts.

Table 6. Statistics

Statistics		
Have you anytime made an investment from the suggestion of your peer		
N	Considered	55
	Error	0
	M	1.89
	Median	2.00
	SD	.854

Table 7. Peer suggestion investments.

Have you anytime made an investment from the suggestion of your peer					
		F	%	Valid %	Cumulative %
Valid	YES	23	41.8	41.8	41.8
	NO	15	27.3	27.3	69.1
	MAY BE	17	30.9	30.9	100.0
	Total	55	100.0	100.0	

Peer Influence on Investment Decisions Interpretation

The data reveals that investment decisions influenced by peer recommendations have a mean of 1.89, a median of 2.00, and a standard deviation of 0.854. This shows a range of answers, representing people who have accepted, disregarded, or are still unsure of how peer advice may affect their investing decisions.

Frequency Distribution Interpretation

Social influence has a significant role in financial decisions, as evidenced by the frequency analysis, which shows that 41.8% of participants made investments based on peer recommendations. On the other hand, 27.3% of investors said that peers had no influence, suggesting that some investors prefer to make their own decisions.

Additionally, 30.9% of respondents chose "May Be," indicating that their investment decisions were influenced indirectly or with ambiguity. According to the cumulative percentage study, a sizable majority of respondents (69.1%) are either persuaded by or unsure of peer recommendations, underscoring the possible influence of social circles on investing behaviour.

Regression

Table 8. Variables Entered/Removed[a]

Model	Variables Entered	Variables Removed	Method
1	IV2, Peer Influence IV1_Social_Networkb	.	Enter

a. Dependent Variable: Investment Decisions
b. All requested variables entered.

Table 9. Summary

Summary				
Model	R	R Square	Adjusted R Square	Std. Error of the Estimate
1	.766[a]	.586	.570	.46221

a. Predictors: (Constant), IV2, Peer Influence, IV1_Social_Network

Regression Analysis Interpretation

Regression analysis is used to examine how peer influence and social media participation affect investing choices. The results demonstrate a strong correlation (R = 0.766) between the independent and dependent variables, suggesting that peer influence and social network membership significantly affect investing behaviour. The R Square value of 0.586 shows that these two factors explain 58.6% of the variation in investment decisions, which is a rather strong predictive power. The Adjusted R Square score (0.570), which indicates that the model remains robust even after adjusting for the number of predictors, lends more credence to this.

Additionally, the estimate's standard error (0.46221) indicates a moderate level of prediction accuracy, suggesting that while the model does a reasonable job of predicting investing behaviour, other factors may still influence decisions. Given that 41.4% of the variation in investment decisions cannot be accounted for, additional variables such as prevailing economic conditions, individual risk tolerance, or financial literacy may be at play. All things considered, the findings support the idea that people usually rely on external influences when making financial decisions by demonstrating the significance of peer discussions and social media connections in affecting investing decisions.

Table 10. ANOVA

ANOVA[a]						
Model		Sum of Squares	df	Mean Square	F	Sig.
1	Regression	15.724	2	7.862	36.802	.000[b]
	Residual	11.109	52	.214		
	Total	26.833	54			

The ANOVA (Analysis of Variance) table assesses the regression model's overall significance in clarifying investment choices. The very high F-value of 36.802 indicates that the dependent variable (investment decisions) is significantly impacted by the combination of two independent factors, peer influence and social network membership. With a significance value (Sig.) of 0.000, which is far lower than the traditional cut off of 0.05, the model is verified to be statistically significant.

The percentage of variation in investment decisions that can be accounted for by social media participation and peer influence is shown by the regression sum of squares (15.724). In the meantime, fluctuations that cannot be explained by additional components not included in the model are taken into account by the residual sum of squares (11.109). A significant amount of the diversity in investment behaviour appears to be explained by the model, as indicated by the total sum of squares of 26.833.

The regression model is very significant, according to the ANOVA results overall, indicating that social media involvement and peer pressure are important factors in determining investment choices. Other elements like financial literacy, risk tolerance, and prevailing economic conditions, however, might also influence investing decisions because there is still some unexplained variance.

Table 11.

Coefficients[a]		
Standardized Coefficients	t	Sig.
Beta		
	2.836	.006
.466	2.913	.005
.334	2.086	.042

a. Dependent Variable: DV Investment decisions

Regression Coefficients Interpretation

The regression results provide insight into how peer pressure and involvement in social networks impact investing decisions. Even when these independent variables are not present, a baseline impact still affects investment decisions, as indicated by the constant value of 2.836 ($p = 0.006$). Among the predictors, peer influence had the strongest positive impact on investment choices ($\beta = 0.466$, $t = 2.913$, $p = 0.005$), indicating that people take their peers' advice very seriously when making financial decisions. The low p-value (0.005) confirms that this impact is statistically significant.

Participation in social networks also has a positive effect on investment decisions ($\beta = 0.334$, $t = 2.086$, $p = 0.042$), though not as much as peer influence. The p-value of 0.042 shows that social media use has a significant effect on investing behaviour, albeit not as much as face-to-face peer interactions. Given that both variables have statistically significant p-values (less than 0.05), the results show that social factors—particularly peer recommendations—have a major influence on investing decisions. Peer pressure is more important than just seeing investment-related articles on social media, which highlights how important social connections are when making financial decisions.

LIMITATIONS OF THE STUDY

Understanding the study's scope requires acknowledging its limits. First off, there were only 75 participants in the study, most of them were young investors under 30, which restricts the findings' applicability to the larger retail investor population, particularly those who are older or more seasoned. Self-reported surveys provided the primary data, yet such instruments are notoriously vulnerable to biases like social desirability and memory distortion. Respondents may have inadvertently recalled past trades inaccurately or, more strategically, supplied replies that sound socially acceptable rather than offering a straightforward account of their behaviour. A cross-sectional snapshot was the only temporal lens available, freezing investor activity at a single point instead of tracing how peer pressure and market fads evolve. Longitudinal tracking would have illuminated those dynamics over time. Several psychological and cognitive variables—emotional stability, risk tolerance, and financial literacy, to name a few—remained unexamined, leaving a significant interpretive gap. Outside forces, such as shifting political climates or economic data releases, were briefly acknowledged but never formally controlled. Each of these limitations suggests fertile ground for follow-up research and urges caution in drawing sweeping conclusions from the present findings.

SUGGESTIONS

Follow-up studies could widen the net by recruiting middle-aged and retiree investors alongside younger cohorts, thereby enhancing the diversity—and generalisability—of the sample. A shift from a one-off snapshot to a longitudinal design would allow researchers to watch peer pressure unfold over quarters or years, yielding richer and more dynamic data. Adding qualitative methods—focus groups or one-on-one interviews—might surface hidden currents such as crowd herding, misplaced confidence, and the ever-looming fear of missing out.

Investigators may also treat online spaces as test beds by contrasting professional forums such as LinkedIn with loose networks on Facebook, then measuring differential impact on trading choices. Contextual variables—economic mood, market volatility, and baseline financial literacy—could be folded into the analysis for a multi-layered portrait of investor behaviour. Partnering with behavioural finance scholars to refine the conceptual framework would sharpen the focus on how emotion and cognition really drive decisions. Taken together, these refinements promise a fuller and more accurate picture of how social signals and psychological states steer capital allocation.

CONCLUSION

Empirical evidence emerging from the present inquiry points toward a striking conclusion: the weight of peer pressure on portfolio formation frequently usurps that of standard financial diagnostics. A joint regression on referral intensity, network footprint, and trading response yields an effect size of R = 0.766 and an explained variance of R2 = 0.586, numbers that situate social scaffolding squarely in the centre of contemporary decision theory. Absent such informal cues, models run lean and often miss the mark when forecasting investor moves.

Younger investors are more susceptible to peer pressure because they participate actively in online financial communities, particularly those under 30. The results demonstrate that direct peer recommendations have a greater impact on investing choices than broad exposure to financial discourse on social media. This demonstrates how crucial social approval is when making decisions. Peer influence is also increased on digital platforms where investors look for advice, approval, and behavioural imitation. Peer influence on investment behaviour is further reinforced by psychological factors including the third-person effect and sensitivity to social incentives.

Even if social networks have a big influence on investing choices, other elements including risk tolerance, financial literacy, and the state of the economy also matter. In order to provide a more thorough knowledge of investment decision-making, future study should incorporate broader behavioural and economic variables, as indicated by the unexplained variation (41.4%). The results have important ramifications for legislators, financial advisors, and investors. Investors must to be conscious of the possible prejudices brought about by peer pressure and work toward a well-rounded strategy that blends objective financial analysis with social understanding. Financial advisors can effectively engage customers by utilizing social networks to craft advice that speaks to their social and psychological motives. Programs for educating investors that encourage well-informed choices while taking social factors into account can be created by policymakers.

In conclusion, social media peer pressure is a major factor in determining how people behave while making investments. Understanding the dynamics of social influence will be essential to promoting logical and informed investing decisions as digital technologies continue to change the financial landscape. Future research ought to examine behavioural trends and the changing role of technology in financial decision-making in greater detail.

REFERENCES

Al Atoom, S. A., Alafi, K. K., & Al-Fedawi, M. M. (2021). The effect of social media on making investment decisions for investors in Amman Financial Market. International Journal of Innovation. *Creativity and Change*, *15*(6), 934–960.

Albert, D., Chein, J., & Steinberg, L. (2013). The teenage brain: Peer influences on adolescent decision making. *Current Directions in Psychological Science*, *22*(2), 114–120. DOI: 10.1177/0963721412471347 PMID: 25544805

Alwajud-Adewusi, M. B., Oduola, O. Z., & Ifabiyi, B. (2025). Social Media Usage and Peer Pressure as Predictors of Substance Abuse among In-School Adolescents in Kwara State, Nigeria. Jurnal Kajian Bimbingan dan Konseling, 10(1), 9-

Bursztyn, L., Ederer, F., Ferman, B., & Yuchtman, N. (2012). *Understanding peer effects in financial decisions: Evidence from a field experiment (No. w18241)*. National Bureau of Economic Research. DOI: 10.3386/w18241

Buzohera, M. I. (2025). The Dynamics of Tax Compliance: How Attitudes, Social Influence, and Peer Effects Shape SME's Compliance Behaviour in Tanzania. *Journal of Tax Reform*, *11*(1), 200–220. DOI: 10.15826/jtr.2025.11.1.198

Hasselgren, B., Chrysoulas, C., Pitropakis, N., & Buchanan, W. J. (2022). Using social media & sentiment analysis to make investment decisions. *Future Internet*, *15*(1), 5. DOI: 10.3390/fi15010005

Irfan, M. (2021, January). Do Shariah Indices converge? Evidence from Gulf Co-operation Council countries. *International Journal of Business Excellence*, *23*(2), 251–269. DOI: 10.1504/IJBEX.2021.113448

Irfan, M., Elhoseny, M., Kassim, S., & Metawa, N. (2023). *Advanced Machine Learning Algorithms for Complex Financial Applications*. IGI Global., DOI: 10.4018/978-1-6684-4483-2

Irfan, M., Elmogy, M., Gupta, S., Khalifa, F., & Dias, R. (2024). *AI-Driven Decentralized Finance and the Future of Finance*. IGI Global., DOI: 10.4018/979-8-3693-6321-8

Irfan, M., Elmogy, M., Majid, M. S., & El-Sappagh, S. (2023). *The Impact of AI Innovation on Financial Sectors in the Era of Industry 5.0*. IGI Global., DOI: 10.4018/979-8-3693-0082-4

Irfan, M., Hussainey, K., Chan Bukhari, S. A., & Nam, Y. (Eds.). (2024). *Issues of Sustainability in AI and New-Age Thematic Investing*. IGI Global Publisher., DOI: 10.4018/979-8-3693-3282-5

Irfan, M., Kadry, S., Sharif, M., & Ullah Khan, H. (2023). *Fintech Applications in Islamic Finance: AI, Machine Learning, and Blockchain Techniques*. IGI Global., DOI: 10.4018/979-8-3693-1038-0

Li, Y. (2020). *Decision Making with Peer Opinions on Social Media Platforms*. Drexel University.

Ling, L., & Peng, L. (2025). The complexity of ECF investors' peer-effect: A test of structural social influence theory by fsQCA approach. *Business Process Management Journal, 31*(1), 95–117. DOI: 10.1108/BPMJ-12-2023-0964

Luo, S. (2025). When Climate Risk Spreads: The Role of Social Network in Portfolio Sustainability Tilting. Available at *SSRN* 5132522. DOI: 10.2139/ssrn.5132522

Manap, A., Hawari, Y., Lubis, A., Sukandar, E., & Pujadi, A. (2023). The Effect of Return Expectation, Motivation, Perceived Value of Risk and Technological Progress on Investment Decision in Sharia Peer to Peer Lending. JEMSI (Jurnal Ekonomi, Manajemen, dan Akuntansi), 9(2), 232-237.

Qin, F., Mickiewicz, T., & Estrin, S. (2022). Homophily and peer influence in early-stage new venture informal investment. *Small Business Economics*, *59*(1), 93–116. DOI: 10.1007/s11187-021-00523-3

Riefel, D. (2024). Social media exposure and its influence on individual investment decisions (Master's thesis, University of Twente).

Subedi, D. P., & Bhandari, D. R. (2024). Assessing the Role of Digital Literacy in Investment Decisions among Graduate Business Students in Nepal: The Mediating Effects of Peer Group Influence. Multi-Disciplinary Explorations. *The Kasthamandap College Journal*, 2(2), 47–62.

Utami, R., & Soesetyo, H. (2023). The important role of education in moderating the impact of perceived security, social influence, and platform reputation on investment intention on SMEs with peer-to-peer lending platform. *International Journal of The Newest Social and Management Research*, *1*(1), 1–11.

Vasquez, H. E. (2023). The effects of social media on investment decisions within an online community (Doctoral dissertation, Northcentral University).

Wang, X., Yu, C., & Wei, Y. (2012). Social media peer communication and impacts on purchase intentions: A consumer socialization framework. *Journal of Interactive Marketing*, *26*(4), 198–208. DOI: 10.1016/j.intmar.2011.11.004

Xiao, R., Ma, C. A., Song, G. R., & Chang, H. Y. (2022). Does peer influence improve firms' innovative investment? Evidence from China. *Energy Reports*, *8*, 1143–1150. DOI: 10.1016/j.egyr.2021.12.029

Yanto, H., Ismail, N., Kiswanto, K., Rahim, N. M., & Baroroh, N. (2021). The roles of peers and social media in building financial literacy among the millennial generation: A case of indonesian economics and business students. *Cogent Social Sciences*, *7*(1), 1947579. DOI: 10.1080/23311886.2021.1947579

Zaighum, I., & Abd Karim, M. Z. (2019). Peer effects, financial decisions and industry concentration: A review. *SEISENSE Journal of Management*, *2*(2), 13–21. DOI: 10.33215/sjom.v2i2.116

Compilation of References

Aaker, D. A., Kumar, V., & Day, G. S. (2004). *MarketingResearch*. Wiley.

Abbas, K., & Hafeez, M. (2021). Wıll Artıfıcıal Intellıgence Rejuvenate Islamıc Fınance? A Versıon of World Academıa. *Hitit Theology Journal*, *20*(3), 311–324. DOI: 10.14395/hid.931401

Abdallah, W., Tfaily, F., & Harraf, A. (2024). The impact of digital financial literacy on financial behavior: Customers' perspective. *Competitiveness Review: An International Business Journal*, ahead-of-print. https://doi.org/DOI: 10.1108/CR-11-2023-0297

Abdallah, A., Maarof, M. A., & Zainal, A. (2016). Fraud detection system: A survey. *Journal of Network and Computer Applications*, *68*, 90–113. DOI: 10.1016/j.jnca.2016.04.007

Abdelhady, A. S. (2024) 'Green finance growth prediction model based on time-series conditional generative adversarial networks', *PLOS ONE*. Edited by M.I. Solihin, 19(7), p. e0306874. Available at: DOI: 10.1371/journal.pone.0306874

Abdellatif, A. A., Shaban, K., & Massoud, A. (2025). Blockchain-Enabled Distributed Learning for Enhanced Smart Grid Security and Efficiency. *Computers & Electrical Engineering*, *123*, 110012. Advance online publication. DOI: 10.1016/j.compeleceng.2024.110012

Abebe, E., Behl, D., Govindarajan, C., Hu, Y., Karunamoorthy, D., Novotny, P., Pandit, V., Ramakrishna, V., & Vecchiola, C. (2019). Enabling Enterprise Blockchain Interoperability with Trusted Data Transfer (industry track). *Middleware Industry 2019 - Proceedings of the 2019 20th International Middleware Conference Industrial Track, Part of Middleware 2019*, 29–35. DOI: 10.1145/3366626.3368129

Abey, J., Velmurugan, R., & Shaikh, Z. H. (2025). Analyzing the Performance of a Deep Learning-Based Model for Stock Market Trend Prediction. In Hamdan, R. K. (Ed.), *Sustainable Data Management. Studies in Big Data* (Vol. 170). Springer. DOI: 10.1007/978-3-031-83915-3_59

Abida, M. (2025). Blockchain Technology's Moderating Effect on the Relationships Between Corporate Governance, the Environment and Financial Performance. *International Journal of Business and Emerging Markets*, *1*(1), 10059108. Advance online publication. DOI: 10.1504/IJBEM.2025.10059108

Aboalsamh, H. M., Khrais, L. T., & Albahussain, S. A. (2023). Pioneering Perception of Green Fintech in Promoting Sustainable Digital Services Application within Smart Cities. *Sustainability (Basel)*, *15*(14), 11440. Advance online publication. DOI: 10.3390/su151411440

Abrol, A. (2024, July 18). *Solana vs Polygon vs Ethereum - blockchain Council.* Https://Www.Blockchain-Council.Org/https://www.blockchain-council.org/blockchain/solana-vs-polygon-vs-ethereum/

Abuamria, F., & Ajouz, M. (2025). Leveraging FinTech Innovations for Sustainable and Social Finance: A Comprehensive Analysis of Their Contributions to Social Impact Investment. In *From Digital Disruption to Dominance: Leveraging FinTech Applications for Sustainable Growth* (pp. 245–264). Emerald Group Publishing Ltd. DOI: 10.1108/978-1-83549-608-420251012

Abubakar, A. M., Elrehail, H., Alatailat, M. A., & Elçi, A. (2019). Knowledge management, decision-making style and organizational performance. *Journal of Innovation and Knowledge*, *4*(2), 104–114. DOI: 10.1016/j.jik.2017.07.003

Adhikari, P., Hamal, P., & Baidoo, F.Jnr. (2024). Artificial Intelligence in fraud detection: Revolutionizing financial security. *International Journal of Science and Research Archive*, *13*(1), 1457–1472. DOI: 10.30574/ijsra.2024.13.1.1860

Afiani, M. Z., Rahmawati, I. Y., Tubastuvi, N., & Utami, R. F. (2024). Analysis of factors that influence millennial and Generation Z investment decisions. *Formosa Journal of Multidisciplinary Research*, *3*(9), 3269–3286. DOI: 10.55927/fjmr.v3i9.10813

Aggarwal, S., & Kumar, N. (2021, January 1). *Chapter Ten - Core components of blockchain Introduction to blockchain.* (S. Aggarwal, N. Kumar, & P. Raj, Eds.). ScienceDirect;Elsevier.https://www.sciencedirect.com/science/article/abs/pii/S0065245820300656

Aggarwal, S., Budhiraja, M., & Kataria, I. (2023). A systematic literature review on "financial technology (fintech): Trends, challenges, and future directions".

Agnola, T., Ambrosini, L., Beretta, E., & Gremlich, G. (2025). Empowering Global Supply Chains Through Blockchain-Based Platforms: New Evidence from the Coffee Industry. *FinTech*, *4*(1), 3. DOI: 10.3390/fintech4010003

Ahmed, H., & Shafi, I. (2023). A Systematic Survey of AI Models in Financial Market Forecasting for Profitability Analysis. *IEEE Access : Practical Innovations, Open Solutions*, *11*, 125359–125380. DOI: 10.1109/ACCESS.2023.3330156

Ahmed, M., Al-Hussaini, A. I. S., & Ibrahim, A. A. (2025). Factors influencing the intention to use the Nigerian central bank digital currency (E-Naira) among Nigerian retailers. *Journal of Financial Services Marketing*, *30*(1), 1–16. DOI: 10.1057/s41264-024-00294-4

Aishwaryalaxmi, N. S., & Rathod, P. (2024). Artificial Intelligence (AI) as a Moderating Variable in the Relationship Between Financial Inclusion, Digital Adoption, and Financial Literacy in Developing Economies. In *ITM Web of Conferences* (Vol. 68, p. 01034). EDP Sciences.

Aketch, S., Mwambia, F., & Baimwera, B. (2021). Effects of blockchain technology on performance of financial markets in Kenya. *International Journal of Finance and Accounting*, *6*(1), 1–15. DOI: 10.47604/ijfa.1237

Akhavan, A., & Jalali, M. S. (2024). Generative AI and simulation modeling: How should you (not) use large language models like ChatGPT. *System Dynamics Review*, *40*(3), e1773. DOI: 10.1002/sdr.1773

Akkaya, K., Mercan, S., & Erdin, E. (2021). An evaluation of cryptocurrency payment channel networks and their privacy implications. *ITU Journal : ICT Discoveries*, *2*(1), 35–44. Advance online publication. DOI: 10.52953/CLBL7402

Akour, I., Alzyoud, M., Alquqa, E. K., Tariq, E., Alzboun, N., Al-Hawary, S. I. S., & Alshurideh, M. T. (2024). Artificial Intelligence and Financial Decisions: Empirical Evidence from Developing Economies. *International Journal of Data and Network Science*, *8*(1), 101–108. DOI: 10.5267/j.ijdns.2023.10.013

Akpobome, O. (2024). The Impact of Emerging Technologies on Legal Frameworks: A Model for Adaptive Regulation. *International Journal of Research Publication and Reviews Journal*, *5*(7), 5046–5060. Www.Ijrpr.Com. DOI: 10.55248/gengpi.5.1024.3012

Akram, T., Muhammad, N., & RamaKrishnan, S. (2025). How does financial inclusion act as a catalyst for reducing financial crime among women? *Journal of Financial Crime*, *32*(2), 279–287. DOI: 10.1108/JFC-02-2024-0058

Al Atoom, S. A., Alafi, K. K., & Al-Fedawi, M. M. (2021). The effect of social media on making investment decisions for investors in Amman Financial Market. International Journal of Innovation. *Creativity and Change*, *15*(6), 934–960.

Alamsyah, A., Kusuma, G. N. W., & Ramadhani, D. P. (2024). A Review on Decentralized Finance Ecosystems. *Future Internet*, *16*(3), 76. DOI: 10.3390/fi16030076

Al-Anezi, F. (2024). Interlinking FinTech and eHealth: A qualitative study. *Frontiers in Public Health*, *12*, 1398136. Advance online publication. DOI: 10.3389/fpubh.2024.1398136 PMID: 39157524

Alawi, A. B., & Bozkurt, F. (2024). A hybrid machine learning model for sentiment analysis and satisfaction assessment with Turkish universities using Twitter data. *Decision Analytics Journal*, *11*, 1–13. DOI: 10.1016/j.dajour.2024.100473

Albert, D., Chein, J., & Steinberg, L. (2013). The teenage brain: Peer influences on adolescent decision making. *Current Directions in Psychological Science*, *22*(2), 114–120. DOI: 10.1177/0963721412471347 PMID: 25544805

Aldalaien, B. A., & Awamleh, F. T. (2025). Integrating fintech into strategic management practices for achieving sustainable development goals. *International Journal of Innovative Research and Scientific Studies*, *8*(3), 3446–3454. DOI: 10.53894/ijirss.v8i3.7254

Alex Avelar, E., & Jordão, R. V. D. (2024). The role of artificial intelligence in the decision-making process: A study on the financial analysis and movement forecasting of the world's largest stock exchanges [Preprint]. *Management Decision*. Advance online publication. DOI: 10.1108/MD-09-2023-1625

Ali, A. (2024). Decentralized Finance (DeFi) and Its Impact on Traditional Banking Systems: Opportunities, Challenges, and Future Directions. *Challenges, and Future Directions (August 01, 2024)*.

Aliano, M., Cestari, G., & Madonna, S. (2024). Sustainable Finance for SMEs: The Role of Capital for Sustainable and Inclusive Growth. In *Sustainable Finance: Vol. Part F4266* (pp. 1–210). Springer Nature. DOI: 10.1007/978-3-031-74193-7

Ali, K., Shahzad, A., & Chaudhary, H. K. (2024). The Role of Decentralized Finance (DeFi) in Reshaping Global Financial Inclusion: Opportunities and Risks. *Social Science Review Archives*, *2*(2), 560–579.

Alkhateeb, A., Catal, C., Kar, G., & Mishra, A. (2022). Hybrid blockchain platforms for the internet of things (IoT): A systematic literature review. *Sensors (Basel)*, *22*(4), 1304. DOI: 10.3390/s22041304 PMID: 35214212

Allegrezza, S., & Bruzzese, G. (2025). Supervision and Enforcement of EU's Anti-Money-Laundering and Countering the Financing of Terrorism. In *EU Banking and Capital Markets Regulation: Open Issues of Vertical Interplay with National Law* (pp. 487–521). Springer Nature Switzerland. DOI: 10.1007/978-3-031-70529-8_14

Allen, F., Gu, X., & Jagtiani, J. (2022). Fintech, cryptocurrencies, and CBDC: Financial structural transformation in China. *Journal of International Money and Finance*, *124*, 102625. DOI: 10.1016/j.jimonfin.2022.102625

Ally, A. M. (2025). Artificial intelligence (AI) and financial technology (FinTech) in Tanzania; legal and regulatory issues. *International Journal of Law and Management*.

Almasria, N. A., Alhatabat, Z., Ershaid, D., Ibrahim, A., & Ahmed, S. (2024). The Mediating Impact of Organizational Innovation on the Relationship Between Fintech Innovations and Sustainability Performance. *Sustainability (Basel)*, *16*(22), 10044. Advance online publication. DOI: 10.3390/su162210044

Alonso-Robisco, A., & Carbó, J. M. (2023). Analysis of CBDC narrative by central banks using large language models. *Finance Research Letters*, *58*, 104643. DOI: 10.1016/j.frl.2023.104643

Alwajud-Adewusi, M. B., Oduola, O. Z., & Ifabiyi, B. (2025). Social Media Usage and Peer Pressure as Predictors of Substance Abuse among In-School Adolescents in Kwara State, Nigeria. Jurnal Kajian Bimbingan dan Konseling, 10(1), 9-

Alzoubi, Y. I., & Mishra, A. (2024). Green artificial intelligence initiatives: Potentials and challenges. *Journal of Cleaner Production*, *468*, 143090. DOI: 10.1016/j.jclepro.2024.143090

Amin, R., Gantassi, R., Ahmed, N., & Alshehri, A. H. (2024). A hybrid approach for adversarial attack detection based on sentiment analysis model using Machine learning. *Engineering Science and Technology, an International Journal*, *58*, 1–12. DOI: 10.1016/j.jestch.2024.101829

Amiri, M. (2024). Application of artificial intelligence in business management and financial market forecasting. *Power System Technology*, *48*(3), 781–808. DOI: 10.52783/pst.875

Andoni, M., Robu, V., Flynn, D., Abram, S., Geach, D., Jenkins, D., McCallum, P., & Peacock, A. (2019). Blockchain technology in the energy sector: A systematic review of challenges and opportunities. *Renewable & Sustainable Energy Reviews, 100*, 143–174. DOI: 10.1016/j.rser.2018.10.014

Anica-Popa, I., Anica-Popa, L., Rădulescu, C., & Vrîncianu, M. (2021). The Integration of Artificial Intelligence in Retail: Benefits, Challenges and a Dedicated Conceptual Framework. *Amfiteatru Economic*, *23*(56), 122–122. DOI: 10.24818/EA/2021/56/120

Anjorin, K. F., Raji, M. A., & Olodo, H. B.Kikelomo Fadilat AnjorinMustafa Ayobami RajiHameedat Bukola Olodo. (2024). A review of strategic decision-making in marketing through big data and analytics. *Computer Science & IT Research Journal*, *5*(5), 1126–1144. DOI: 10.51594/csitrj.v5i5.1139

Anker-Sørensen, L., & Zetzsche, D. A. (2021). From Centralized to Decentralized Finance: The Issue of'Fake-DeFi'. *Available at SSRN* 3978815. DOI: 10.2139/ssrn.3978815

Ante, L. (2021). Smart contracts on the blockchain–A bibliometric analysis and review. *Telematics and Informatics*, *57*, 101519. DOI: 10.1016/j.tele.2020.101519

Ante, L., Fiedler, I., Willruth, J. M., & Steinmetz, F. (2023). A Systematic Literature Review of Empirical Research on Stablecoins. *FinTech*, *2*(1), 34–47. Advance online publication. DOI: 10.3390/fintech2010003

Araci, D. (2019). FinBERT: Financial Sentiment Analysis with Pre-trained Language Models. ArXiv. 2019; abs/1908. 10063. Available from: https//api.semanticscholar.org/CorpusID:201646244

Aramonte, S., Huang, W., & Schrimpf, A. (2021). DeFi risks and the decentralization illusion. *BIS Quarterly Review, 6.*

Archana, K., & Kumar, M. (2025). Blockchain and Its Applications in Supply Chain Transparency. *Innovative Journal of Interdisciplinary Research and Technological Innovations*, 26-35.

Arnone, G. (2025). Legal Aspects of Smart Contracts and Application of Blockchain Technology in FinTech. *Fintech for ESG and the Circular Economy*, 173-191.

Arslanian, H., & Fischer, F. (2019). *The Future of Finance*. Springer International Publishing., DOI: 10.1007/978-3-030-14533-0

ARTIFICIAL INTELLIGENCE (AI) AND BUSINESS. (2024). https://books.google.co.in/books

Arya, A., Singh, J., Gupta, A., & Dwivedi, R. K. (2024, February). Developing an Effective Consensus Mechanism for a Secure Blockchain-Based Cross-Border Fund Transfer System. In *2024 IEEE International Conference on Computing, Power and Communication Technologies (IC2PCT)* (Vol. 5, pp. 636-642). IEEE. DOI: 10.1109/IC2PCT60090.2024.10486373

Ashrafi, D. M., & Akhter, M. (2025). The green Fintech paradox: Understanding the dynamics of green brand positioning and user decision-making in the digital financial landscape. *Journal of Modelling in Management, 20*(2), 348–389. DOI: 10.1108/JM2-12-2023-0294

Asif, R., Hassan, S. R., & Parr, G. (2023). Integrating a Blockchain-Based Governance Framework for Responsible AI. In *Future Internet* (Vol. 15, Issue 3). DOI: 10.3390/fi15030097

Asif, M., Khan, M. N., Tiwari, S., Wani, S. K., & Alam, F. (2023). The Impact of Fintech and Digital Financial Services on Financial Inclusion in India. *Journal of Risk and Financial Management, 16*(2), 122. Advance online publication. DOI: 10.3390/jrfm16020122

Asif, R., & Hassan, S. R. (2023). Shaping the future of Ethereum: Exploring energy consumption in Proof-of-Work and Proof-of-Stake consensus. *Frontiers in Blockchain, 6*, 1151724. DOI: 10.3389/fbloc.2023.1151724

Ata, B., Cong, L. W., Giesecke, K., Sun, P., & Teo, C. P. (2024). Call for Papers—*Management Science* Virtual Special Issue on AI for Finance and Business Decisions. *Management Science, 70*(10), xi–xii. DOI: 10.1287/mnsc.2024.Call.V70.n10

Atif, M., Hassan, M. K., Rabbani, M. R., & Khan, S. (2021). Islamic FinTech: The digital transformation bringing sustainability to islamic finance. In *COVID-19 and Islamic Social Finance* (pp. 91–103). Taylor and Francis. DOI: 10.4324/9781003121718-9

Atiyah, G. A., Ibrahim, A. I., & Jasim, A. A. (2024). Enforcement of smart contracts in cross-jurisdictional transactions. *International Journal of Law and Management, ahead-of-print* (ahead-of-print). https://doi.org/DOI: 10.1108/IJLMA-06-2024-0220/FULL/XML

Avci, G., & Erzurumlu, Y. O. (2023). Blockchain Tokenization of Real Estate Investment: A Security Token Offering Procedure and Legal Design Proposal. *Journal of Property Research, 40*(2), 188–207. DOI: 10.1080/09599916.2023.2167665

Awal, V. (2024). Riding high on the AI wave. *Voice & Data, June 2024*, 26–29.

Awoyemi, J. O., Adetunmbi, A. O., & Oluwadare, S. A. (2017). Credit card fraud detection using machine learning techniques: A comparative analysis. *2017 International Conference on Computing Networking and Informatics (ICCNI)*, 1–9. https://doi.org/DOI: 10.1109/ICCNI.2017.8123782

Ayyaswamy, K., Kathirvel, N., & Maheswaran, C. P. (2025). Ethical AI Entrepreneurial Strategies for Business Intelligence and Blockchain. In *Corporate Social Responsibility Approaches to Ethical AI in Business* (pp. 1–26). IGI Global Scientific Publishing.

Azar, P. D. (2009). *Sentiment Analysis in Financial News* [Thesis]. Harvard College., Retrieved from https://people.csail.mit.edu/azar/wp-content/uploads/2011/09/thesis.pdf

Azman, N. H. N., & Zabri, M. Z. (2020). The Utilisation Of Islamic Fintech (I-Fintech) In Promoting Sustainable Inclusive Growth: Evidence From Micro-Entrepreneurs In Malaysia. *Journal of Islamic Monetary Economics and Finance*, *6*(3), 555–576. DOI: 10.21098/jimf.v6i3.1180

Azman, N. H. N., & Zabri, M. Z. M. (2022). SHARI'AH-COMPLIANT FINTECH USAGE AMONG MICROENTREPRENEURS IN MALAYSIA: AN EXTENSION OF UTAUT MODEL. *Journal of Islamic Monetary Economics and Finance*, *8*(2), 305–324. DOI: 10.21098/jimf.v8i2.1417

Bai, X., Zhuang, S., Xie, H., & Guo, L. (2024). Leveraging Generative Artificial Intelligence for Financial Market Trading Data Management and Prediction. https://doi.org/DOI: 10.20944/preprints202407.0084.v1

Bajra, U. Q., Ermir Rogova, , & Avdiaj, S. (2024). Cryptocurrency blockchain and its carbon footprint: Anticipating future challenges. *Technology in Society*, *77*, 102571. DOI: 10.1016/j.techsoc.2024.102571

Bakare, F. A., Omojola, J., & Iwuh, A. C. (2024). Blockchain and decentralized finance (DEFI): Disrupting traditional banking and financial systems. Https://Wjarr.Com/Sites/Default/Files/WJARR-2024-2968.Pdf, *23*(3), 3075–3089. DOI: 10.30574/wjarr.2024.23.3.2968

Balasubramanian, M., & Sheykhmaleki, P. (2024). Comprehending the Consumer Behavior toward Sustainable Apparel. *Sustainability (Basel)*, *16*(18), 8026. DOI: 10.3390/su16188026

Baldissarro, G., Farinelli, E., Iazzolino, G., Maiolini, R., & Morea, D. (2025). The link between crowdfunding and sustainability: A literature review in the field of entrepreneurs and academic spinoffs. *Finance Research Letters*, *77*, 107097. Advance online publication. DOI: 10.1016/j.frl.2025.107097

Bandi, A., Mandal, K., Bindu, P., & Dwivedi, A. D. (2023). The power of Generative AI: A review of requirements, models, input–output formats, evaluation metrics, and challenges. *Future Internet*, *15*(8), 260. DOI: 10.3390/fi15080260

Banerjee, S., & Sinha, M. (2025). The policy endorsement of central bank digital currency-trend analysis and research scope using bibliometric review. *International Journal of Management Practice*, *18*(1), 64–91. DOI: 10.1504/IJMP.2025.143077

Banh, L., & Strobel, G. (2023). Generative artificial intelligence. *Electronic Markets*, *33*(1), 63. DOI: 10.1007/s12525-023-00680-1

BaniHani, I., Alawadi, S., & Elmrayyan, N.BaniHani. (2024). AI and the decision-making process: A literature review in healthcare, financial, and technology sectors. *Journal of Decision Systems*, *33*(sup1), 1–11. DOI: 10.1080/12460125.2024.2349425

Baninemeh, E., Farshidi, S., & Jansen, S. (2023). A decision model for decentralized autonomous organization platform selection: Three industry case studies. *Blockchain: Research and Applications*, *4*(2), 100127.

Bansal, A. (2023). Unified strategy for AI, RPA, and generative AI deployments. *IT Next, October–December 2023*, 15–16.

Bansal, U., S. Bharatwal, D. S. Bagiyam, and E. R. Kismawadi. 2024. "Fraud Detection in the Era of AI: Harnessing Technology for a Safer Digital Economy." Pp. 143–64 in *AI-Driven Decentralized Finance and the Future of Finance*.

Bansal, D., & Tandon, N. (2025). *Securing the Future: Addressing Risks and Vulnerabilities in Generative AI for Fintech*. Springer., DOI: 10.1007/978-3-031-76957-3_14

Barberis, N., & Huang, M. (2001). Mental accounting, loss aversion, and individual stock returns. *The Journal of Finance*, *56*(4), 1247–1292. DOI: 10.1111/0022-1082.00367

Barde, K., & Parth Atul Kulkarni. (2023). Applications of Generative AI in Fintech. https://doi.org/DOI: 10.1145/3639856.3639893

Barile, D., Secundo, G., & Bussoli, C. (2024). Exploring artificial intelligence robo-advisor in banking industry: A platform model [Preprint]. *Management Decision*. Advance online publication. DOI: 10.1108/MD-08-2023-1324

Barone, M., Bussoli, C., & Fattobene, L. (2024). Digital financial consumers' decision-making: A systematic literature review and integrative framework. *International Journal of Bank Marketing*, *42*(7), 1978–2022. DOI: 10.1108/IJBM-07-2023-0405

Basdekidou, V., & Papapanagos, H. (2024). Blockchain Technology Adoption for Disrupting FinTech Functionalities: A Systematic Literature Review for Corporate Management, Supply Chain, Banking Industry, and Stock Markets. *Digital*, *4*(3), 762–803. DOI: 10.3390/digital4030039

Basdekidou, V., & Papapanagos, H. (2025). Blockchain Technology Adoption for Agriculture, Manufacturing, Services, Knowledge, Culture, and Research: A Systematic Literature Review. *WSEAS Transactions on Systems*, *24*, 229–278. DOI: 10.37394/23202.2025.24.23

Basu, R., Lim, W. M., Kumar, A., & Kumar, S. (2023). Marketing analytics: The bridge between customer psychology and marketing decision-making. In Psychology and Marketing (Vol. 40, Issue 12, pp. 2588–2611). John Wiley and Sons Inc. https://doi.org/DOI: 10.1002/mar.21908

Basu, B., Mandal, S., & Kar, A. K. (2025). Beyond and beneath the Metaverse Dazzle: The Interplay of VR and Blockchain-Based Social Exchanges and Affordances in Determining NFT Trading User Experience. *Journal of Retailing and Consumer Services*, *84*, 104180. Advance online publication. DOI: 10.1016/j.jretconser.2024.104180

Baur, D. G., Karlsen, J. R., Smales, L. A., & Trench, A. (2024). Digging deeper - Is bitcoin digital gold? A mining perspective. *Journal of Commodity Markets*, *34*, 100406. DOI: 10.1016/j.jcomm.2024.100406

Bayram, O. (2020). Importance of Blockchain use in cross-border payments and evaluation of the progress in this area. *Doğuş Üniversitesi Dergisi*, *21*(1), 171–189. DOI: 10.31671/dogus.2020.444

Beck, T., Demirgüç-Kunt, A., & Martinez Peria, M. S. (2008). Bank financing for SMEs around the world: Drivers, obstacles, business models, and lending practices. *World Bank Policy Research Working Paper*, (4785).

Becker, F., Skirzyński, J., van Opheusden, B., & Lieder, F. (2022). Boosting Human Decision-making with AI-Generated Decision Aids. *Computational Brain & Behavior*, *5*(4), 467–490. DOI: 10.1007/s42113-022-00149-y

Bellagarda, J. S., & Abu-Mahfouz, A. M. (2022). An updated survey on the convergence of distributed ledger technology and artificial intelligence: Current state, major challenges and future direction. *IEEE Access : Practical Innovations, Open Solutions*, *10*, 50774–50793. DOI: 10.1109/ACCESS.2022.3173297

Bellavitis, C., Fisch, C., & Momtaz, P. P. (2023). The rise of decentralized autonomous organizations (DAOs): A first empirical glimpse. *Venture Capital*, *25*(2), 187–203. DOI: 10.1080/13691066.2022.2116797

Bello, O. A. Adebola Folorunso, Onwuchekwa, J., & Ejiofor, O. E. (2023). A Comprehensive Framework for Strengthening USA Financial Cybersecurity: Integrating Machine Learning and AI in Fraud Detection Systems. European Journal of Computer Science and Information Technology, 11(6). https://eajournals.org/ejcsit/vol11-issue-6-2023/a-comprehensive-framework-for-strengthening-usa-financial-cybersecurity-integrating-machine-learning-and-ai-in-fraud-detection-systems/

Benson, V., Saridakis, G., Adamyk, B., Mishra, T., & Adamyk, O. (2024). Unravelling Societal Risks of Decentralized Finance: A Systematic Review. *Available at SSRN* 4862893. DOI: 10.2139/ssrn.4862893

Bevilacqua, S., Ferraris, A., Kozel, R., & Vincurova, Z. (2025), "Exploring the artificial intelligence integration in top management team decision-making: an empirical analysis", *Business Process Management Journal*, Vol. ahead-of-print No. ahead-of-print. DOI: 10.1108/BPMJ-07-2024-0659

Bhattacharya, S., & Singla, B. (2024). Metaverse Banking 2.0: Future Trends and Challenges in Metaverse Banking Strategies. *Exploring the Use of Metaverse in Business and Education*, 166-192.

Bhattacharya, D. (2022). Digital Yuan (e-CNY): China's Official Digital Currency. *Strategic Analysis*, *46*(1), 93–99. Advance online publication. DOI: 10.1080/09700161.2022.2039582

Bhawnra, S. X., & Singh, K. B. (2024). Artificial Intelligence for Financial Inclusion in India. *Conversational Artificial Intelligence*, 589-606.

Bindu, H., & Muvvala, S. (2025). Secure Collaboration for Storing and Processing of Criminal Records Using Blockchain Technology. In *Advanced Cyber Security Techniques for Data, Blockchain, IoT, and Network Protection* (pp. 205-224). IGI Global Scientific Publishing.

Bittini, J. S., Rambaud, S. C., Pascual, J. L., & Moro-Visconti, R. (2022). Business Models and Sustainability Plans in the FinTech, InsurTech, and PropTech Industry: Evidence from Spain. *Sustainability (Basel), 14*(19), 12088. Advance online publication. DOI: 10.3390/su141912088

Blockchain-Based Distributed Trust and Reputation Management Systems. A Survey. (n.d.). Ieeexplore.ieee.org. https://ieeexplore.ieee.org/document/8970496

Bok, K. (2024). *Decentralizing Finance: How DeFi, Digital Assets, and Distributed Ledger Technology are Transforming Finance*. John Wiley & Sons.

Bond-Taylor, S., Leach, A., Long, Y., & Willcocks, C. G. (2022). Deep Generative Modelling: A Comparative Review of VAEs, GANs, Normalizing Flows, Energy-Based and Autoregressive Models. *IEEE Transactions on Pattern Analysis and Machine Intelligence, 44*(11), 7327–7347. DOI: 10.1109/TPAMI.2021.3116668 PMID: 34591756

Boufounou, P., Mavroudi, M., Toudas, K., & Georgakopoulos, G. (2022). Digital transformation of the Greek banking sector in the COVID era. *Sustainability (Basel), 14*(19), 11855. DOI: 10.3390/su141911855

Boulila, H., Metadjer, W., & Benbekhti, S. E. (2024). What if Banking was Green? An Essay to Quantify the Effect of Fintech on Financial Inclusion and Environmental Sustainability. In Ciasullo, M. V., Martin, J., & Brunetti, F. (Eds.), *Springer Proceedings in Business and Economics* (pp. 106–125). Springer Nature., DOI: 10.1007/978-3-031-65115-1_6

Boumaiza, A. (2025). Advancing Sustainable Investment Efficiency and Transparency Through Blockchain-Driven Optimization. *Sustainability (Basel), 17*(5), 2000. Advance online publication. DOI: 10.3390/su17052000

Brewer, J., Patel, D., Kim, D., & Murray, A. (2024). Navigating the challenges of generative technologies: Proposing the integration of artificial intelligence and blockchain. *Business Horizons, 67*(5), 525–535. DOI: 10.1016/j.bushor.2024.04.011

Brynjolfsson, E., & Mitchell, T. (2017). What can machine learning do? Workforce implications. *Science, 358*(6370), 1530–1534. DOI: 10.1126/science.aap8062 PMID: 29269459

Bubeck, S., Chandrasekaran, V., Eldan, R., Gehrke, J., Horvitz, E., Kamar, E., Lee, P., Lee, Y. T., Li, Y., Lundberg, S., Nori, H., Palangi, H., Ribeiro, M. T., & Zhang, Y. (2023). Sparks of Artificial General Intelligence: Early experiments with GPT-4. ArXiv:2303.12712 [Cs]. https://arxiv.org/abs/2303.12712

Burri, S. R., Kumar, A., Baliyan, A., & Kumar, T. A. (2023). Transforming Payment Processes: A Discussion of AI-Enabled Routing Optimization. *2023 2nd International Conference on Smart Technologies and Systems for Next Generation Computing, ICSTSN 2023*. DOI: 10.1109/ICSTSN57873.2023.10151455

Burström, T., Parida, V., Lahti, T., & Wincent, J. (2021). AI-enabled business-model innovation and transformation in industrial ecosystems: A framework, model and outline for further research. *Journal of Business Research*, *127*, 85–95. DOI: 10.1016/j.jbusres.2021.01.016

Bursztyn, L., Ederer, F., Ferman, B., & Yuchtman, N. (2012). *Understanding peer effects in financial decisions: Evidence from a field experiment (No. w18241)*. National Bureau of Economic Research. DOI: 10.3386/w18241

Busayatananphon, C., & Boonchieng, E. (2022, January). Financial technology DeFi protocol: A review. In *2022 Joint International Conference on Digital Arts, Media and Technology with ECTI Northern Section Conference on Electrical, Electronics, Computer and Telecommunications Engineering (ECTI DAMT & NCON)* (pp. 267-272). IEEE.

Buzohera, M. I. (2025). The Dynamics of Tax Compliance: How Attitudes, Social Influence, and Peer Effects Shape SME's Compliance Behaviour in Tanzania. *Journal of Tax Reform*, *11*(1), 200–220. DOI: 10.15826/jtr.2025.11.1.198

Cai, W., Wang, Z., Ernst, J. B., Hong, Z., Feng, C., & Leung, V. C. (2018). Decentralized applications: The blockchain-empowered software system. *IEEE Access : Practical Innovations, Open Solutions*, *6*, 53019–53033. DOI: 10.1109/ACCESS.2018.2870644

Cam, H., Cam, A. V., Demirel, U., & Ahmed, S. (2024). Sentiment analysis of financial Twitter posts on Twitter with the machine learning classifiers. *Heliyon*, *10*(1), 1–15. DOI: 10.1016/j.heliyon.2023.e23784 PMID: 38205287

Cao, H., Kong, X., & Tsang, A. (2024). Corporate Social Responsibility and Economic Stability: International Evidence. *Accounting Horizons*, •••, 1–23. DOI: 10.2308/HORIZONS-2022-196

Cao, L., Yang, Q., & Yu, P. S. (2021). Data science and AI in FinTech: An overview. *International Journal of Data Science and Analytics*, *12*(2), 81–99. DOI: 10.1007/s41060-021-00278-w

Cardoso-Silva, J., Sallai, D., & Barreto, M. (2024). Approach generative AI tools proactively or risk bypassing the learning process in higher education. SSRN *Electronic Journal*. https://doi.org/DOI: 10.2139/ssrn.4886015

Case Study Asset Management Firm Supercharged User Experience with a Gen AI Chatbot. (2024, January 30). Damco Solutions. https://www.damcogroup.com/client-success/asset-management-firm-delivered-elevated-user-experience-with-gen-ai

Caton, J. L.Jr, & Harwick, C. (2022). Cryptocurrency, Decentralized Finance, and the Evolution of Money: A Transaction Costs Approach. *Journal of New Finance*, *2*(4). Advance online publication. DOI: 10.46671/2521-2486.1027

Caudevilla, O., & Kim, H. M. (2023). The Digital Yuan and Cross-Border Payments: China's Rollout of Its Central Bank Digital Currency. SSRN *Electronic Journal*. DOI: 10.2139/ssrn.4371414

Cedra, A. (2024). Mitigating risks in decentralized finance: A Systematic review of challenges and solutions. *International journal of economic perspectives, 18*(1), 104-125.

Cermeño, J. S. (2016). *Blockchain in financial services: Regulatory landscape and future challenges for its commercial application*. BBVA Research.

Černevičienė, J., & Kabašinskas, A. (2024). Explainable artificial intelligence (XAI) in finance: A systematic literature review. *Artificial Intelligence Review*, *57*(8), 216. DOI: 10.1007/s10462-024-10854-8

Chadha, A., & Gupta, A. (2024). The Impact of Artificial Intelligence on Financial Inclusion. In *Utilizing Technology for Sustainable Resource Management Solutions* (pp. 180–193). IGI Global. DOI: 10.4018/979-8-3693-2346-5.ch012

Chan, Y. K. C., & Lee, W. K. K. (2023). The AI generation gap: Are Gen Z students more interested in adopting generative AI such as ChatGPT in teaching and learning than their Gen X and Millennial generation teachers? *arXiv Preprint*. https://doi.org//arxiv.2305.02878DOI: 10.48550

Chang, E., Luo, H. L., & Chen, Y. C. (2019). Blockchain-Enabled Trade Finance Innovation: A Potential Paradigm Shift on Using Letter of Credit. *Sustainability (Basel)*, *12*(1), 1–16. https://ideas.repec.org/a/gam/jsusta/v12y2019i1p188-d301819.html. DOI: 10.3390/su12010188

Chang, V., Baudier, P., Zhang, H., Xu, Q., Zhang, J., & Arami, M. (2020). How Blockchain can impact financial services–The overview, challenges and recommendations from expert interviewees. *Technological Forecasting and Social Change*, *158*, 120166. DOI: 10.1016/j.techfore.2020.120166 PMID: 32834134

Chang, Y., Wang, X., Wang, J., Wu, Y., Yang, L., Zhu, K., Chen, H., Yi, X., Wang, C., Wang, Y., Ye, W., Zhang, Y., Chang, Y., Yu, P. S., Yang, Q., & Xie, X. (2024). A survey on evaluation of large language models. *ACM Transactions on Intelligent Systems and Technology*, *15*(3), 1–45. DOI: 10.1145/3641289

Channi, H. K., & Kumar, P. (2025). Automating and Streamlining Drug Payments Through Smart Contracts. *Blockchain-Enabled Solutions for the Pharmaceutical Industry*, 153-173.

Chao, G., Cheung, J., Haller, K., & Lee, J. (2019). The coming AI revolution in retail and consumer products: Intelligent automation is transforming both industries in unexpected ways.

Chapagain, D., Kshetri, N., & Sihag, V. K. (2025). Cybersecurity and Cyber Ethics via Blockchain Technology–Need for Web Security, Software Practices, and End-User Cyber Education. *Blockchain Technology for Cyber Defense, Cybersecurity, and Countermeasures: Techniques, Solutions, and Applications*, 123.

Charles, D. (2024). A Blockchain Solution for Cross-Border Payments. In *Fintech, and Blockchains Trends in The Financial Sector* (pp. 23–41). Bentham Science Publishers. DOI: 10.2174/9789815256833124010004

Chatterjee, P., Das, D., & Rawat, D. B. (2024). A Generative AI Approach for Ensuring Data Integrity Security Resilience in Fintech Systems. *Proceedings - 2024 IEEE/ACM 24th International Symposium on Cluster, Cloud and Internet Computing Workshops, CCGridW 2024*, 168–173. DOI: 10.1109/CCGridW63211.2024.00027

Chauhan, A., Malviya, O. P., Verma, M., & Mor, T. S. (2018). Blockchain and Scalability. *Proceedings - 2018 IEEE 18th International Conference on Software Quality, Reliability, and Security Companion, QRS-C 2018*, 122–128. DOI: 10.1109/QRS-C.2018.00034

Cheah, S., Pattalachinti, S., & Ho, Y. P. (2018). Blockchain industries, regulations and policies in Singapore. *Asian Research Policy*, *9*(2), 83–98.

Chen, B., Wu, Z., & Zhao, R. (2023). Taylor and Francis. From fiction to fact: The growing role of generative AI in business and finance. *Journal of Chinese Economic and Business Studies*, *21*(4), 1–26. DOI: 10.1080/14765284.2023.2245279

Cheng, H. K., Hu, D., Puschmann, T., & Zhao, J. L. (2021). The landscape of Blockchain research: Impacts and opportunities. *Information Systems and e-Business Management*, *19*(3), 749–755. DOI: 10.1007/s10257-021-00544-1

Chen, J., & Nesterov, I. O. (2023). Central bank digital currencies: Digital Yuan and its role in Chinese digital economy development. *RUDN Journal of Economics*, *31*(1), 120–133. DOI: 10.22363/2313-2329-2023-31-1-120-133

Chen, Y., & Bellavitis, C. (2020). Blockchain disruption and decentralized finance: The rise of decentralized business models. *Journal of Business Venturing Insights*, *13*, e00151. DOI: 10.1016/j.jbvi.2019.e00151

Chen, Y., & Volz, U. (2022). Scaling up sustainable investment through blockchain-based project bonds. *Development Policy Review*, *40*(3), e12582. Advance online publication. DOI: 10.1111/dpr.12582

Chin, W. W. (1998). The Partial Least Squares Approach to Structural Equation Modeling. Lawrence Erlbaum Associates. https://www.researchgate.net/publication/311766005

Choudhary, P., Ghosh, C., & Thenmozhi, M. (2025). Impact of fintech and financial inclusion on sustainable development goals: Evidence from cross country analysis. *Finance Research Letters*, *72*, 106573. DOI: 10.1016/j.frl.2024.106573

Christidis, K., & Devetsikiotis, M. (2016). Blockchains and Smart Contracts for the Internet of Things. In *IEEE Access* (Vol. 4). DOI: 10.1109/ACCESS.2016.2566339

Christodoulou, I., Rizomyliotis, I., Konstantoulaki, K., Nazarian, A., & Binh, D. (2024). Transforming the remittance industry: Harnessing the power of blockchain technology. *Journal of Enterprise Information Management*, *37*(5), 1551–1577. DOI: 10.1108/JEIM-03-2023-0112

Chromjakova, F., Trentesaux, D., & Kwarteng, M. A. (2021). Human and cobot cooperation ethics: The process management concept of the production workplace. *Journal of Competitiveness*, *13*(3), 21–38. DOI: 10.7441/joc.2021.03.02

Chuma, A., & de Oliveira, B. (2023). Behavioral biases and Gen Z: The role of information overload and digital fatigue. *Dinasti International Journal of Economics, Finance, and Accounting*, *4*(2), 65–74. DOI: 10.12345/dinasti.2023.421

Chung, S., Kim, K., Lee, C. H., & Oh, W. (2023). Interdependence between online peer-to-peer lending and cryptocurrency markets and its effects on financial inclusion. *Production and Operations Management*, *32*(6), 1939–1957. DOI: 10.1111/poms.13950

Ciaian, P., Kancs, D. A., & Rajcaniova, M. (2021). Interdependencies between mining costs, mining rewards and blockchain security. *arXiv preprint arXiv:2102.08107*.

Claessens, S., Cong, L. W., Moshirian, F., & Park, C. Y. (2024). Opportunities and challenges associated with the development of FinTech and Central Bank Digital Currency. *Journal of Financial Stability, 73*, 101280. DOI: 10.1016/j.jfs.2024.101280

Collins, C., Dennehy, D., Conboy, K., & Mikalef, P. (2021). Artificial intelligence in information systems research: A systematic literature review and research agenda. *International Journal of Information Management, 60*, 102383. Advance online publication. DOI: 10.1016/j.ijinfomgt.2021.102383

Consoli, S., Barbaglia, L., & Manzan, S. (2022). Fine-grained, aspect-based sentiment analysis on economic and financial lexicon. *Knowledge-Based Systems, 247*, 1–15. DOI: 10.1016/j.knosys.2022.108781

Conti, M., Hassan, M., & Lal, C. (2019). BlockAuth: BlockChain based distributed producer authentication in ICN. *Computer Networks, 164*, 106888. DOI: 10.1016/j.comnet.2019.106888

Cornelius, K. (2021). Betraying blockchain: Accountability, transparency and document standards for non-fungible tokens (NFTs). *Information (Basel), 12*(9), 358. DOI: 10.3390/info12090358

Corrigan, C. C. (2017). The effects of increased revenue transparency in the extractives sector: The case of the Extractive Industries Transparency Initiative. *The Extractive Industries and Society, 4*(4), 779–787. DOI: 10.1016/j.exis.2017.03.004

Cosahan, S. R., Hayat, A., & Juniar, A. (2024). The Role of Decentralized Financial Ecosystems in Exchange Transformation in the Digital Era. *Asian Journal of Management. Entrepreneurship and Social Science, 4*(03), 1327–1332.

Croman, K., Decker, C., Eyal, I., Gencer, A. E., Juels, A., Kosba, A., . . . Wattenhofer, R. (2016, February). On Scaling Decentralized Blockchains: (A Position Paper). In *International conference on financial cryptography and data security* (pp. 106-125). Berlin, Heidelberg: Springer Berlin Heidelberg. DOI: 10.1007/978-3-662-53357-4_8

Cruz Rambaud, S., & Expósito Gázquez, A. (2022). A RegTech Approach to Fintech Sustainability: The Case of Spain. *European Journal of Risk Regulation, 13*(2), 333–349. DOI: 10.1017/err.2021.62

d'Aquin, M. (2018) 'Towards an "Ethics by Design" Methodology for AI Research Projects', in *Proceedings of the 2018 AAAI/ACM Conference on AI, Ethics, and Society. AIES '18: AAAI/ACM Conference on AI, Ethics, and Society*, New Orleans LA USA: ACM, pp. 54–59. Available at: DOI: 10.1145/3278721.3278765

Dadabada, P. K. (2024). Analyzing the Impact of ESG Integration and FinTech Innovations on Green Finance: A Comparative Case Studies Approach. *Journal of the Knowledge Economy*. Advance online publication. DOI: 10.1007/s13132-024-02197-0

Dahal, S. B. (2023). Utilizing Generative AI for Real-Time Financial Market Analysis Opportunities and Challenges. Advances in Intelligent Information Systems,8(4),1–11. https://questsquare.org/index.php/JOURNALAIIS/article/view/29

Dahal, R. (2023). Artificial intelligence and investment behavior during market volatility: Evidence from the COVID-19 crisis. *Journal of Financial Innovation and Technology*, *5*(1), 41–59.

Dalal, A., & Samal, B. (2022). Transforming Financial Landscapes: Case Studies on the Positive Disruption of Cross-Border Payments through Ripple. *International Journal of Research Radicals in Multidisciplinary Fields, ISSN: 2960-043X, 1*(2), 77-82.

Das, B. C., Amini, M. H., & Wu, Y. (2025). Security and privacy challenges of large language models: A survey. *ACM Computing Surveys*, *57*(6), 1–39. DOI: 10.1145/3712001

Daudert, T. (2021). Exploiting textual and relationship information for fine-grained financial sentiment analysis. *Knowledge-Based Systems*, *230*, 1–12. DOI: 10.1016/j.knosys.2021.107389

Davenport, T. H. (2014). How strategists use "big data" to support internal business decisions, discovery and production. *Strategy and Leadership*, *42*(4), 45–50. DOI: 10.1108/SL-05-2014-0034

Davenport, T. H., & Prusak, L. (1998). *Working Knowledge: How Organizations Manage What They Know*. Harvard Business School Press., DOI: 10.1145/348772.348775

David, P. S., Dheenadhayalan, K., Suson, W. P., Devapitchai, J. J., & Manickam, T. (2025). AI-Powered Financial Inclusion: Bridging the Gap for the Unbanked. In *Utilizing AI and Machine Learning in Financial Analysis* (pp. 449–480). IGI Global Scientific Publishing.

Dawod, A., Georgakopoulos, D., Jayaraman, P. P., Nirmalathas, A., & Parampalli, U. (2022). IoT Device Integration and Payment via an Autonomic Blockchain-Based Service for IoT Device Sharing. *Sensors (Basel)*, *22*(4), 1344. Advance online publication. DOI: 10.3390/s22041344 PMID: 35214244

Daza, A., N'estor, D. G. R., Mirelly, S. A. S., Wilmer, F. R. E., & María, E. C. Q. (2024). Sentiment Analysis on E-Commerce Product Reviews Using Machine Learning and Deep Learning Algorithms: A Bibliometric Analysis, Systematic Literature Review, Challenges and Future Works. *International Journal of Information Management Data Insights*, *4*(100267), 1–20. DOI: 10.1016/j.jjimei.2024.100267

De Rynck, S. (2016). Banking on a union: The politics of changing eurozone banking supervision. *Journal of European Public Policy*, *23*(1), 119–135. DOI: 10.1080/13501763.2015.1019551

Debe, M., Salah, K., Rehman, M. H. U., & Svetinovic, D. (2019). IoT public fog nodes reputation system: A decentralized solution using Ethereum blockchain. *IEEE Access : Practical Innovations, Open Solutions*, *7*, 178082–178093. DOI: 10.1109/ACCESS.2019.2958355

Decardi-Nelson, B., Alshehri, A. S., Ajagekar, A., & You, F. (2024). Generative AI and process systems engineering: The next frontier. *Computers & Chemical Engineering*, *187*, 108723. DOI: 10.1016/j.compchemeng.2024.108723

Dekimpe, M. G. (2020). Retailing and retailing research in the age of big data analytics. *International Journal of Research in Marketing*, *37*(1), 3–14. DOI: 10.1016/j.ijresmar.2019.09.001

Demirguc-Kunt, A., Klapper, L., Singer, D., Ansar, S., & Hess, J. (2018a). Global Findex Database 2017: Measuring Financial Inclusion and the Fintech Revolution. *The Global Findex Database 2017: Measuring Financial Inclusion and the Fintech Revolution*. DOI: 10.1596/978-1-4648-1259-0

Deng, Y., Cao, Z., & Yang, N. (2024). Understanding the nexus between fintech, natural resources, green investment, and environmental sustainability in China: A DYNARDL approach. *Resources Policy*, *91*, 104900. Advance online publication. DOI: 10.1016/j.resourpol.2024.104900

DeSola, V., Hanna, K., & Nonis, P. (2019). Finbert: pre-trained model on sec filings for financial natural language tasks. *University of California*. DOI:DOI: 10.13140/RG.2.2.19153.89442

Devlin, J., Chang, M. W., Lee, K., & Toutanova, K. (2019). Bert: Pre-training of deep bidirectional transformers for language understanding, *Proceedings of the 2019 Conference of the North American Chapter of the Association for Computational Linguistics: Human Language Technologies*, Volume 1, 4171–4186. DOI:DOI: 10.18653/v1/N19-1423

Dhali, M., Hassan, S., Mehar, S. M., Shahzad, K., & Zaman, F. (2023). Cryptocurrency in the Darknet: Sustainability of the current national legislation. *International Journal of Law and Management*, *65*(3), 261–282. DOI: 10.1108/IJLMA-09-2022-0206

Diener, F., & Špaček, M. (2021). Digital transformation in banking: A managerial perspective on barriers to change. *Sustainability (Basel)*, *13*(4), 2032. DOI: 10.3390/su13042032

Dinesha, D. L., & Patil, B. (2023). A Conceptual Insight Into Achieving Interoperability Between Heterogeneous Blockchain Enabled Interconnected Smart Microgrids. *2023 IEEE PES Innovative Smart Grid Technologies - Asia. ISGT Asia*, *2023*, 1–5. Advance online publication. DOI: 10.1109/ISGTAsia54891.2023.10372801

Ding, N., Qin, Y., Yang, G., Wei, F., Yang, Z., Su, Y., Hu, S., Chen, Y., Chan, C. M., Chen, W., Yi, J., Zhao, W., Wang, X., Liu, Z., Zheng, H.-T., Chen, J., Liu, Y., Tang, J., Li, J., & Sun, M. (2023). Parameter-efficient fine-tuning of large-scale pre-trained language models. *Nature Machine Intelligence*, *5*(3), 220–235. DOI: 10.1038/s42256-023-00626-4

Ding, W., Tan, H., Zhou, H., Li, Z., & Fan, C. (2024). Immediate traffic flow monitoring and management based on multimodal data in cloud computing. *Applied and Computational Engineering*, *71*(1), 1–6. DOI: 10.54254/2755-2721/71/2024MA0052

Dominic Ochigbo, A., Tuboalabo, A., Temitope Labake, T., Buinwi, U., Layode, O., Adama Buinwi, J., & Author, C. (2024). Legal frameworks for digital transactions: Analyzing the impact of Blockchain technology. *Finance & Accounting Research Journal*, *6*(7), 1205–1223. DOI: 10.51594/farj.v6i7.1313

Dorfleitner, G., Hornuf, L., & Kreppmeier, J. (2023). Promise not fulfilled: FinTech, data privacy, and the GDPR. *Electronic Markets*, *33*(1), 33. Advance online publication. DOI: 10.1007/s12525-023-00622-x

Dorminey, J., Fleming, A. S., Kranacher, M.-J., & Riley, R. A.Jr. (2012). The evolution of fraud theory. *Issues in Accounting Education*, *27*(2), 555–579. DOI: 10.2308/iace-50131

Doshi, A. R. (2024) 'Generative artificial intelligence and evaluating strategic decisions', *Strategic Management Journal*, p. smj.3677. Available at: DOI: 10.2139/ssrn.4714776

Doshi, S., & Kapadia, K. (2025, January 5). Strengthening compliance. *Business Today (Norwich)*, •••, 72–74.

Dote-Pardo, J.S., Cordero-Díaz, M.C., Espinosa Jaramillo, M.T. and Parra-Domínguez, J. (2025), "Leveraging artificial intelligence for enhanced decision-making in finance: trends and future directions", *Journal of Accounting Literature*, Vol. ahead-of-print No. ahead-of-print. .DOI: 10.1108/JAL-02-2025-0100

Drăgan, G. B., Ben Arfi, W., Tiberius, V., Ammari, A., & Khvatova, T. (2025). Navigating the green wave: Understanding behavioral antecedents of sustainable cryptocurrency investment. *Technological Forecasting and Social Change*, *210*, 123909. Advance online publication. DOI: 10.1016/j.techfore.2024.123909

Du, S., & Xie, C. (2021). Paradoxes of artificial intelligence in consumer markets: Ethical challenges and opportunities. Journal of Business Research, 129, 961 974. https://doi.org/DOI: 10.1016/j.jbusres.2020.08.024

Duan, H., Li, J., Fan, S., Lin, Z., Wu, X., & Cai, W. (2021, October). Metaverse for social good: A university campus prototype. In *Proceedings of the 29th ACM international conference on multimedia* (pp. 153-161). DOI: 10.1145/3474085.3479238

Duan, K., & Urquhart, A. (2023). The instability of stablecoins. *Finance Research Letters*, *52*, 103573. DOI: 10.1016/j.frl.2022.103573

Duan, Y., Edwards, J. S., & Dwivedi, Y. K. (2019). Artificial intelligence for decision making in the era of Big Data – evolution, challenges and research agenda. *International Journal of Information Management*, *48*, 63–71. DOI: 10.1016/j.ijinfomgt.2019.01.021

Dubey, C., Kumar, D., Singh, A. K., & Dwivedi, V. K. (2022). Confluence of Artificial Intelligence and Blockchain Powered Smart Contract in Finance System. *3rd IEEE 2022 International Conference on Computing, Communication, and Intelligent Systems, ICCCIS 2022*. DOI: 10.1109/ICCCIS56430.2022.10037701

Dubey, R., Gunasekaran, A., Childe, S. J., Blome, C., & Papadopoulos, T. (2019). Big Data and Predictive Analytics and Manufacturing Performance: Integrating Institutional Theory, Resource-Based View and Big Data Culture. *British Journal of Management*, *30*(2), 341–361. DOI: 10.1111/1467-8551.12355

Dunbar, K., Sarkis, J., & Treku, D. N. (2024). FinTech for environmental sustainability: Promises and pitfalls. *One Earth*, *7*(1), 23–30. DOI: 10.1016/j.oneear.2023.12.012

Dunis, C. L., Middleton, P. W., Karathanasopolous, A., & Theofilatos, K. (Eds.). (2016). *Artificial Intelligence in Financial Markets*., DOI: 10.1057/978-1-137-48880-0

Du, W., Pan, S. L., Leidner, D. E., & Ying, W. (2019). Affordances, experimentation and actualization of FinTech: A blockchain implementation study. *The Journal of Strategic Information Systems*, *28*(1), 50–65. DOI: 10.1016/j.jsis.2018.10.002

Dwivedi, Y. K., Kshetri, N., Hughes, L., Slade, E. L., Jeyaraj, A., Kar, A. K., Baabdullah, A. M., Koohang, A., Raghavan, V., Ahuja, M., Albanna, H., Albashrawi, M. A., Al-Busaidi, A. S., Balakrishnan, J., Barlette, Y., Basu, S., Bose, I., Brooks, L., Buhalis, D., & Carter, L. (2023). "So what if ChatGPT wrote it?" Multidisciplinary perspectives on opportunities, challenges and implications of generative conversational AI for research, practice and policy. International Journal of Information Management, 71(0268-4012), 102642. https://doi.org/DOI: 10.1016/j.ijinfomgt.2023.102642

E R Kismawadi, Irfan, M., Al Muddatstsir, U. D., & Abdulkarim, F. M. 2023. "Fintech Innovations: Risk Mitigation Strategies in Islamic Finance." Pp. 35–58 in *Fintech Applications in Islamic Finance: AI, Machine Learning, and Blockchain Techniques*.

Ebirim, G. U., & Odonkor, B. (2024). Enhancing Global Economic Inclusion With Fintech Innovations And Accessibility. *Finance & Accounting Research Journal*, *6*(4), 648–673. DOI: 10.51594/farj.v6i4.1067

Efanov, D., & Roschin, P. (2018). The all-pervasiveness of the blockchain technology. *Procedia Computer Science*, *123*, 116–121. DOI: 10.1016/j.procs.2018.01.019

El Faqir, Y., Arroyo, J., & Hassan, S. (2020, August). An overview of decentralized autonomous organizations on the blockchain. In *Proceedings of the 16th international symposium on open collaboration* (pp. 1-8). DOI: 10.1145/3412569.3412579

Ellili, N. O. D. (2023). Is there any association between FinTech and sustainability? Evidence from bibliometric review and content analysis. *Journal of Financial Services Marketing*, *28*(4), 748–762. DOI: 10.1057/s41264-022-00200-w

Elsafty, A., & Yehia, A. (2023). Digital transformation challenges for government sector. *Business and Management Studies*, *9*(1), 6160. DOI: 10.11114/bms.v9i1.6160

Emami, A., Afshar, M., & Aliyari, M. (2025). Financial Innovations in the Era of Industry 5.0: Opportunities and Challenges. In *Dynamic and Safe Economy in the Age of Smart Technologies* (pp. 209–222). IGI Global. DOI: 10.4018/979-8-3693-4369-2.ch013

Erdin, E., Cebe, M., Akkaya, K., Solak, S., Bulut, E., & Uluagac, S. (2020). A Bitcoin payment network with reduced transaction fees and confirmation times. *Computer Networks*, *172*, 107098. Advance online publication. DOI: 10.1016/j.comnet.2020.107098

Esmat, A., de Vos, M., Ghiassi-Farrokhfal, Y., Palensky, P., & Epema, D. (2021). A novel decentralized platform for peer-to-peer energy trading market with blockchain technology. *Applied Energy*, *282*, 116123. DOI: 10.1016/j.apenergy.2020.116123

Ezzat, S. K., Saleh, Y. N., & Abdel-Hamid, A. A. (2022). Blockchain oracles: State-of-the-art and research directions. *IEEE Access : Practical Innovations, Open Solutions*, *10*, 67551–67572. DOI: 10.1109/ACCESS.2022.3184726

Fahlin, J., & Gustafsson, L. (2024). Algorithmic finance and sentiment-based trading in the age of AI: An empirical study. *European Review of Financial Studies*, *31*(2), 134–152.

Fanea-Ivanovici, M., & Baber, H. (2024). Alternative Finance: A Framework for Innovative and Sustainable Business Models. In *Alternative Finance: A Framework for Innovative and Sustainable Business Models*. Taylor and Francis., DOI: 10.4324/9781032713533

Fatouros, G., Soldatos, J., Kouroumali, K., Makridis, G., & Kyriazis, D. (2023). Transforming sentiment analysis in the financial domain with ChatGPT. *Machine Learning with Applications*, *14*, 1–13. DOI: 10.1016/j.mlwa.2023.100508

Fazal, A., Ahmed, A., & Abbas, S. (2025). Importance of artificial intelligence in achieving sustainable development goals through financial inclusion. *Qualitative Research in Financial Markets*, *17*(2), 432–452. DOI: 10.1108/QRFM-04-2023-0098

Ferdous, M. S., Chowdhury, M. J. M., & Hoque, M. A. (2021). A survey of consensus algorithms in public blockchain systems for crypto-currencies. *Journal of Network and Computer Applications*, *182*, 103035. DOI: 10.1016/j.jnca.2021.103035

Fernández, F. J. J., Fernández, M. Á. E., & Alonso, S. L. N. (2024). The asset-backing risk of stablecoin trading: The case of Tether. *Economics and Business Review*, *10*(1), 57–80. DOI: 10.18559/ebr.2024.1.1211

Fernández, S. S. (2021). Islamic fintech. In *Islamic Fintech*. Taylor and Francis., DOI: 10.4324/9781003014614

Fernandez-Vazquez, S., Rosillo, R., De La Fuente, D., & Priore, P. (2019). Blockchain in FinTech: A mapping study. *Sustainability (Basel)*, *11*(22), 6366. Advance online publication. DOI: 10.3390/su11226366

Ferrari, M. V. (2022). The platformisation of digital payments: The fabrication of consumer interest in the EU FinTech agenda. *Computer Law & Security Review*, *45*, 105687. DOI: 10.1016/j.clsr.2022.105687

Ferreira, A. (2024). Decentralized finance (DeFi): The ultimate regulatory frontier? *Capital Markets Law Journal*, *19*(3), 242–259. DOI: 10.1093/cmlj/kmae007

Fersini, E., Messina, E., & Pozzi, F. A. (2016). Expressive Signals in Social Media Languages to Improve Polarity Detection. *Information Processing & Management*, *52*(1), 20–35. DOI: 10.1016/j.ipm.2015.04.004

Feuerriegel, S., Hartmann, J., Janiesch, C., & Zschech, P. (2023). Generative AI. *Business & Information Systems Engineering*, *66*(1), 111–126. DOI: 10.1007/s12599-023-00834-7

Fich, E. M., & Shivdasani, A. (2007). Financial fraud, director reputation, and shareholder wealth. *Journal of Financial Economics*, *86*(2), 306–336. DOI: 10.1016/j.jfineco.2006.05.012

Foroozan, S., Murad, M. A. A., Sharef, N. M., & Latiff, R. A. (2015). Improving Sentiment Classification Accuracy of Financial News using N-Gram Approach and Feature Weighting Methods. In *2015 2nd International Conference on Information Science and Security (ICISS 2015)* (pp. 296-304). IEEE. DOI: 10.1109/ICISSEC.2015.7371008

Fowowe, B. (2025). Financial inclusion, gender gaps and agricultural productivity in Mali. *Review of Development Economics*, *29*(1), 3–42. DOI: 10.1111/rode.13034

Fraisse, H., & Laporte, M. (2022). Return on investment on artificial intelligence: The case of bank capital requirement. *Journal of Banking & Finance*, *138*, 106401. DOI: 10.1016/j.jbankfin.2022.106401

Freitas, L. P., Cerdeira, J., & Lourenço, D. (2025). Hayekian Hurdles: Challenges to Cryptocurrency as a Viable Basis for a New Monetary Order. *Economies*, *13*(1), 12. DOI: 10.3390/economies13010012

Friesendorf, C., & Blütener, A. (2023). Decentralized Finance: How dApps Disrupt Banking. In *Decentralized Finance (DeFi) How Decentralized Applications (dApps) Disrupt Banking* (pp. 1–9). Springer Nature Switzerland. DOI: 10.1007/978-3-031-37488-3_1

Frost, J., Gambacorta, L., & Shin, H. S. (2021). From financial innovation to inclusion. *Finance & Development*, •••, 14–17.

Future-Forward Blockchain Alliances. (2024). Deloitte United States. https://www2.deloitte.com/us/en/pages/about-deloitte/solutions/future-forward-blockchain-alliances.html

Gai, K., Qiu, M., Sun, X., & Zhao, H. (2017). Security and Privacy Issues: A Survey on FinTech. *Lecture Notes in Computer Science, 10135*, 236–247. DOI: 10.1007/978-3-319-52015-5_24

Ganesh, U. (2025) "Gen AI is the new CFO weapon", *Financial Express*, 15th May 2025 p.9.

Gangi, F., Meles, A., Daniele, L. M., Varrone, N., & Salerno, D. (2021). The evolution of sustainable investments and finance: Theoretical perspectives and new challenges. In *The Evolution of Sustainable Investments and Finance: Theoretical Perspectives and New Challenges*. Springer International Publishing., DOI: 10.1007/978-3-030-70350-9

Gao, T. (2021). Study on the Intention of Foreign Trade Driven by Cross-Border E-Commerce Based on Blockchain Technology. *Security and Communication Networks, 2021*, 1–10. Advance online publication. DOI: 10.1155/2021/9623672

Garry, M., Chan, W. M., Foster, J., & Henkel, L. A. (2024). Large language models (LLMs) and the institutionalization of misinformation. *Trends in Cognitive Sciences, 28*(12), 1078–1088. DOI: 10.1016/j.tics.2024.08.007 PMID: 39393958

Gąsiorkiewicz, L., & Monkiewicz, J. (2021). Innovation in Financial Services. *Balancing Public and Private Interests. London and New York: Routledge. Gąsiorkiewicz L. Monkiewicz J.(eds).*

Gatauwa, J. M., Aluoch, M. O., & Adhing'a, D. C. (2024). Fintech Services and Corporate Sustainability in Commercial Banks in Kenya. In *The Adoption of Fintech Using Technology for Better Security, Speed, and Customer Experience in Finance* (pp. 114–126). Taylor and Francis. DOI: 10.4324/9781032644165-8

Geetha, S., & Biju, A. V. N. (2024). Is green FinTech reshaping the finance sphere? Unravelling through a systematic literature review. *Environmental Science and Pollution Research International, 31*(2), 1790–1810. DOI: 10.1007/s11356-023-31382-y PMID: 38057679

Ghaemi Asl, M., Ben Jabeur, S., Hosseini, S. S., & Tajmir Riahi, H. (2024). Fintech's impact on conventional and Islamic sustainable equities: Short- and long-term contributions of the digital financial ecosystem. *Global Finance Journal, 62*, 101022. Advance online publication. DOI: 10.1016/j.gfj.2024.101022

Ghatak, A. (2024). The rise of generative AI in intra. *Dataquest, May 2024*, 16–20.

Ghorbian, M., & Ghorbian, S. (2025). Empowering Clinical Decision-Making with Generative AI in Intelligent Decision Support Systems. In *Generative Artificial Intelligence (AI) Approaches for Industrial Applications* (pp. 241–259). Springer Nature Switzerland. DOI: 10.1007/978-3-031-76710-4_12

Ghosh, B., Kazouz, H., & Umar, Z. (2023). Do Automated Market Makers in DeFi Ecosystem Exhibit Time-Varying Connectedness during Stressed Events? *Journal of Risk and Financial Management*, *16*(5), 259. Advance online publication. DOI: 10.3390/jrfm16050259

Gilad, Y., Hemo, R., Micali, S., Vlachos, G., & Zeldovich, N. (2017). Algorand: Scaling Byzantine Agreements for Cryptocurrencies. *SOSP 2017 - Proceedings of the 26th ACM Symposium on Operating Systems Principles*. DOI: 10.1145/3132747.3132757

Goel, A., Garg, P., & Kumar, M. (2024). Decentralized finance: A catalyst for smart global value chains in future financial ecosystems. In *Smart Global Value Chain* (pp. 198–211). CRC Press. DOI: 10.1201/9781003461432-13

Golosova, J., & Romanovs, A. (2018, November). The advantages and disadvantages of the blockchain technology. In *2018 IEEE 6th workshop on advances in information, electronic and electrical engineering (AIEEE)* (pp. 1-6). IEEE. DOI: 10.1109/AIEEE.2018.8592253

Gomber, P., Kauffman, R. J., Parker, C., & Weber, B. W. (2018). On the fintech revolution: Interpreting the forces of innovation, disruption, and transformation in financial services. *Journal of Management Information Systems*, *35*(1), 220–265. DOI: 10.1080/07421222.2018.1440766

González-Sendino, R., Serrano, E., & Bajo, J. (2024). Mitigating bias in artificial intelligence: Fair data generation via causal models for transparent and explainable decision-making. *Future Generation Computer Systems*, *155*, 384–401. DOI: 10.1016/j.future.2024.02.023

Goodfellow, I., Pouget-Abadie, J., Mirza, M., Xu, B., Warde-Farley, D., Ozair, S., Courville, A., & Bengio, Y. (2020). Generative adversarial networks. *Communications of the ACM*, *63*(11), 139–144. DOI: 10.1145/3422622

Guo, Y., & Liang, C. (2016). Blockchain application and outlook in the banking industry. In *Financial Innovation* (Vol. 2, Issue 1). DOI: 10.1186/s40854-016-0034-9

Gupta, P. (2024). A new dawn for crypto. *Entrepreneur, December 2024–January 2025*, 40–41.

Gupta, B., Iyer, L. S., & Aronson, J. E. (2000). Knowledge management: Practices and challenges. *Industrial Management & Data Systems, 100*(1), 17–21. DOI: 10.1108/02635570010273018

Gupta, M., Jain, R., Arora, S., Gupta, A., Javed Awan, M. J., Chaudhary, G., & Nobanee, H. (2021). AI-enabled COVID-19 outbreak analysis and prediction: Indian states vs. union territories. *Computers, Materials & Continua, 67*(1), 933–950. DOI: 10.32604/cmc.2021.014221

Gupta, S., Justy, T., Kamboj, S., Kumar, A., & Kristoffersen, E. (2021). Big data and firm marketing performance: Findings from knowledge-based view. *Technological Forecasting and Social Change, 171*, 171. DOI: 10.1016/j.techfore.2021.120986

Gupta, S., Srivastava, R., Shaikh, Z. H., & Irfan, M. (2024). Revolutionizing Rural Finance: Exploring the Impact of FinTech on Financial Inclusion in India. In Irfan, M., Muhammad, K., Naifar, N., & Khan, M. A. (Eds.), *Applications of Block Chain technology and Artificial Intelligence. Financial Mathematics and Fintech.* Springer., DOI: 10.1007/978-3-031-47324-1_3

Habernal, I., Pracek, T., & Steinberger, J. (2014). Supervised Sentiment Analysis in Czech Social Media. *Information Processing & Management, 50*(5), 693–707. DOI: 10.1016/j.ipm.2014.05.001

Hajian, S., Bonchi, F., & Castillo, C. (2016) 'Algorithmic Bias: From Discrimination Discovery to Fairness-aware Data Mining', in *Proceedings of the 22nd ACM SIGKDD International Conference on Knowledge Discovery and Data Mining. KDD '16: The 22nd ACM SIGKDD International Conference on Knowledge Discovery and Data Mining*, San Francisco California USA: ACM, pp. 2125–2126. Available at: DOI: 10.1145/2939672.2945386

Haldane, A. G., Millard, S., & Saporta, V. (Eds.). (2008). *The future of payment systems* (p. 31). Routledge.

Halliday, M.A.K., & Ruqaiya Hasan. (1976). *Cohesion in English.* Longman. https://doi.org/DOI: 10.4324/9781315836010

Hallipelto, A., & Küçüközmen, C. C. (2025). Central Bank Digital Currency: Redefining the Concept of Money in a Digital Context. *Central Banking and Monetary Policy in the G20: Paradigms and Challenges*, 219.

Harrison, M. (2024). The role of FinTech in driving sustainability and inclusive practices in banking. In *International Banking in Global Perspective* (pp. 158–176). Taylor and Francis., DOI: 10.4324/9781003307846-9

Harrison, R., Parker, A., Brosas, G., Chiong, R., & Tian, X. (2015). The role of technology in the management and exploitation of internal business intelligence. *Journal of Systems and Information Technology*, *17*(3), 247–262. DOI: 10.1108/JSIT-04-2015-0030

Hartmann, M. E. (2006). *E-payments evolution*. Physica-Verlag HD. DOI: 10.1007/3-7908-1652-3_2

Harvey, C. R., Ramachandran, A., & Santoro, J. (2021). *DeFi and the Future of Finance*. John Wiley & Sons.

Hasanbeig, H., Sharma, H., Betthauser, L., Frujeri, F. V., & Momennejad, I. (2023). Allure: A systematic protocol for auditing and improving llm-based evaluation of text using iterative in-context-learning. *arXiv preprint arXiv:2309.13701*.

Hashemi Joo, M., Nishikawa, Y., & Dandapani, K. (2020). Cryptocurrency, a successful application of blockchain technology. *Managerial Finance*, *46*(6), 715–733. DOI: 10.1108/MF-09-2018-0451

Hasselgren, B., Chrysoulas, C., Pitropakis, N., & Buchanan, W. J. (2022). Using social media & sentiment analysis to make investment decisions. *Future Internet*, *15*(1), 5. DOI: 10.3390/fi15010005

Hassouba, T. A. (2025). Financial inclusion in Egypt: The road ahead. *Review of Economics and Political Science*, *10*(2), 90–111. DOI: 10.1108/REPS-06-2022-0034

Hayes, A. (2024, September 16). Blockchain Facts: What Is It, How It Works, and How It Can Be Used. Investopedia. https://www.investopedia.com/terms/b/blockchain.asp

Hazarika, C. A. I., Khalfan, J., Ahmed, M., Yousif, A., & Hussain, J. (2024). Role of Fintech as an Enabler to Fulfill HR Requirements and Attain Sustainability. In *Studies in Systems, Decision and Control* (Vol. 537, pp. 59–67). Springer Science and Business Media Deutschland GmbH. DOI: 10.1007/978-3-031-62106-2_5

He, D. (2021). Digitalization of cross-border payments. *China Economic Journal*, *14*(1), 26–38. Advance online publication. DOI: 10.1080/17538963.2020.1870272

Helina, S. T., & Rathiha, R. (2018). Transformation in banks through e-banking services: Employee's perception. *International Journal of Management Studies*, *5*(3[6]), 80–88. DOI: 10.18843/ijms/v5i3(6)/10

Henshall, B. (2019). Open banking: A strategic approach to win digital consumers. *The Banking & Finance Post, January–February 2019*, 20–21.

He, S., Xing, X., Wang, G., & Sun, Z. (2023). A Data Integrity Verification Scheme for Centralized Database Using Smart Contract and Game Theory. *IEEE Access : Practical Innovations, Open Solutions*, *11*, 59675–59687. Advance online publication. DOI: 10.1109/ACCESS.2023.3284850

Hirst, G., & St-Onge, D. (1998). Lexical chains as representations of context for the detection and correction of malapropisms. In Fellbaum, C., & Miller, G. (Eds.), *WordNet: An electronic lexical database* (pp. 305–322). The MIT Press., DOI: 10.1111/1911-3846.12832

HMADOUCH, Y. A. (2025). Decentralized Finance: A Future Research Agenda. *RMd• Economics, Management &. Social Sciences*, *2*(1), e202504–e202504.

Hmimnat, C., & El Bakouchi, M. (2023). Blockchain, Cryptocurrency, and the Quest for Financial Stability in Morocco. *International Journal of Accounting, Finance, Auditing, Management and Economics, 4*(6-1), 21-40.

Holotiuk, F., Moormann, J., & Pisani, F. (2019b). Blockchain in the payments industry: developing a discussion agenda based on pain points and opportunities. *Business Transformation through Blockchain: Volume I*, 197-231.

Holotiuk, F., Pisani, F., & Moormann, J. (2019a). Radicalness of blockchain: An assessment based on its impact on the payments industry. *Technology Analysis and Strategic Management*, *31*(8), 915–928. DOI: 10.1080/09537325.2019.1574341

Hongmei, Z. (2021). A Cross-Border E-Commerce Approach Based on Blockchain Technology. *Mobile Information Systems*, *2021*(1), 2006082. DOI: 10.1155/2021/2006082

Hu, K. (2023, February 2). ChatGPT sets record for fastest-growing user base. Reuters. https://www.reuters.com/technology/chatgpt-sets-record-fastest-growing-user-base-analyst-note-2023-02-01/

Hu, M., & Liu, B. (2004). Mining and summarizing customer reviews. In *Proceedings: Tenth ACM SIGKDD international conference on Knowledge discovery and data mining (KDD 2004)* (pp. 168-177). New York: ACM. DOI: 10.1145/1014052.1014073

Huang, J., Gu, S. S., Hou, L., Wu, Y., Wang, X., Yu, H., & Han, J. (2022). Large language models can self-improve. *arXiv preprint arXiv:2210.11610.*

Huang, A. H., Zang, A. Y., & Zheng, R. (2014). Evidence on the information content of text in analyst reports. *The Accounting Review*, *89*(6), 2151–2180. DOI: 10.2308/accr-50833

Huang, M., Singh, D., & Patel, A. (2024). Behavioral nudges in AI-driven investment platforms: A machine learning approach. *Finance and AI Review*, *2*(1), 77–93.

Huang, Z., Zhang, Z., Hua, C., Liao, B., & Li, S. (2024). Leveraging enhanced egret swarm optimization algorithm and artificial intelligence-driven prompt strategies for portfolio selection. *Scientific Reports*, *14*(1), 26681. DOI: 10.1038/s41598-024-77925-2 PMID: 39496781

Huberman, G., Leshno, J. D., & Moallemi, C. (2021). Monopoly without a Monopolist: An Economic Analysis of the Bitcoin Payment System. *The Review of Economic Studies*, *88*(6), 3011–3040. Advance online publication. DOI: 10.1093/restud/rdab014

Hughes, H. (2021). The Complex Implications Of Fintech For Financial Inclusion. *Law and Contemporary Problems*, *84*(1), 115–128. https://www.scopus.com/inward/record.uri?eid=2-s2.0-85104780101&partnerID=40&md5=fa86df16b7cbfe7c0e87aebe79ad2b8d

Hu, M., Pang, Y., & Gao, L. (2023). Advances in Silicon-Based Integrated Lidar. *Sensors (Basel)*, *23*(13), 5920. DOI: 10.3390/s23135920 PMID: 37447770

Ibeh, C. V., Asuzu, O. F., Olorunsogo, T., Elufioye, O. A., Nduubuisi, N. L., & Daraojimba, A. I. (2024). Business analytics and decision science: A review of techniques in strategic business decision making. *World Journal of Advanced Research and Reviews*, *21*(2), 1761–1769. DOI: 10.30574/wjarr.2024.21.2.0247

Im, T. L., San, P. W., Anthony, P., & On, C. K. (2018). Improving Polarity Classification for Financial News Using Semantic Similarity Techniques. *International Journal of Intelligent Information Technologies*, *14*(4), 39–54. DOI: 10.4018/IJIIT.2018100103

Ionescu, S. A., & Diaconita, V. (2023). Transforming Financial Decision-Making: The Interplay of AI, Cloud Computing and Advanced Data Management Technologies. *International Journal of Computers, Communications & Control*, *18*(6), 1–19. DOI: 10.15837/ijccc.2023.6.5735

Irfan, M., Elmogy, M., Majid, M. S. A., & El-Sappagh, S. (2023). The impact of AI innovation on financial sectors in the era of industry 5.0. In *The Impact of AI Innovation on Financial Sectors in the Era of Industry 5.0*. https://doi.org/DOI: 10.4018/9798369300824

Irfan, M. (2021, January). Do Shariah Indices converge? Evidence from Gulf Cooperation Council countries. *International Journal of Business Excellence*, *23*(2), 251–269. DOI: 10.1504/IJBEX.2021.113448

Irfan, M., Elhoseny, M., Kassim, S., & Metawa, N. (2023). *Advanced Machine Learning Algorithms for Complex Financial Applications*. IGI Global., DOI: 10.4018/978-1-6684-4483-2

Irfan, M., Elmogy, M., Gupta, S., Khalifa, F., & Dias, R. (2024). *AI-Driven Decentralized Finance and the Future of Finance*. IGI Global., DOI: 10.4018/979-8-3693-6321-8

Irfan, M., Elmogy, M., Majid, M. S., & El-Sappagh, S. (2023). *The Impact of AI Innovation on Financial Sectors in the Era of Industry 5.0*. IGI Global., DOI: 10.4018/979-8-3693-0082-4

Irfan, M., Hussainey, K., Chan Bukhari, S. A., & Nam, Y. (Eds.). (2024). *Issues of Sustainability in AI and New-Age Thematic Investing*. IGI Global Publisher., DOI: 10.4018/979-8-3693-3282-5

Irfan, M., Kadry, S., Sharif, M., & Ullah Khan, H. (2023). *Fintech Applications in Islamic Finance: AI, Machine Learning, and Blockchain Techniques*. IGI Global., DOI: 10.4018/979-8-3693-1038-0

Islam, M. R., & Rashid, M. M.Mohammed Ataur RahmanMuslin Har Sani Bin MohamadAbd Halim Bin Embang. (2022). Analysis of Blockchain-Based Ripple and Swift. *Asian Journal of Electrical and Electronic Engineering*, *2*(1), 1–8. DOI: 10.69955/ajoeee.2022.v2i1.26

Issa, H., Jabbouri, R., & Mehanna, R.-A. (2023). AI micro-decisions in FinTechs: A mixed method research design. *Management Decision*, *61*(11), 3316–3342. DOI: 10.1108/MD-10-2022-1336

Ivanov, N., Li, C., Yan, Q., Sun, Z., Cao, Z., & Luo, X. (2023). Security threat mitigation for smart contracts: A comprehensive survey. *ACM Computing Surveys*, *55*(14s), 1–37. DOI: 10.1145/3593293

Iyer, R., & Maralapalle, V. C. (2025), "Integrating AI and ML Technologies Into Indigenous Financial Systems: Applications of AI and ML in Indigenous Financial Management", Ghosal, I., Gupta, S., Rana, S. and Saha, D. (Ed.) Indigenous Empowerment through Human-Machine Interactions, Emerald Publishing Limited, Leeds, pp. 237-251. DOI: 10.1108/978-1-83608-068-820251014

Jain, A. (2023). Trend: Generative AI++. *IT Next, October–December 2023*, 8–9.

Jain, A., & Jhajharia, K. (2025). Blockchain Interoperability: Protocols, Frameworks, and Practical Implications. In *Blockchain Technology Applications in Knowledge Management* (pp. 115-152). IGI Global Scientific Publishing.

Jain, A. K., Gupta, N., & Gupta, B. B. (2025). A survey on scalable consensus algorithms for blockchain technology. *Cyber Security and Applications*, *3*, 100065. DOI: 10.1016/j.csa.2024.100065

Jameel, K., & Janjua, L. R.Dr. Kiran JameelDr Laeeq Razzak Janjua. (2024). Harnessing Artificial Intelligence for Digital Financial Inclusion: Transforming Economies in the Era of Industry 4.0. *The Critical Review of Social Sciences Studies*, *2*(2), 1436–1457. DOI: 10.59075/c00w3s24

Janczuk-Gorywoda, A. (2019). Blockchain and Payment Systems: A Tale about Re-Intermediation. *Regulating Blockchain*, 259–274. DOI: 10.1093/oso/9780198842187.003.0015

Jarrahi, M. H., Askay, D., Eshraghi, A., & Smith, P. (2023). Artificial intelligence and knowledge management: A partnership between human and AI. *Business Horizons*, *66*(1), 87–99. DOI: 10.1016/j.bushor.2022.03.002

Javaid, M., Haleem, A., Singh, R. P., Khan, S., & Suman, R. (2021). Blockchain technology applications for Industry 4.0: A literature-based review. *Blockchain: Research and Applications*, *2*(4), 100027.

Javaid, M., Haleem, A., Singh, R. P., Suman, R., & Khan, S. (2022). *A review of Blockchain Technology applications for financial services. BenchCouncil Transactions on Benchmarks, Standards and Evaluations, 2(3), 100073*. Sciencedirect., DOI: 10.1016/j.tbench.2022.100073

Javaid, M., Haleem, A., Singh, R. P., Suman, R., & Khan, S. (2022). A review of Blockchain Technology applications for financial services. *BenchCouncil Transactions on Benchmarks. Standards and Evaluations*, *2*(3), 100073.

Jensen, J. R., von Wachter, V., & Ross, O. (2021). An introduction to decentralized finance (defi). *Complex Systems Informatics and Modeling Quarterly*, (26), 46–54. DOI: 10.7250/csimq.2021-26.03

Jessel, B., & DiCaprio, A. (2018). Can blockchain make trade finance more inclusive? *Journal of Financial Transformation*, *47*, 35–50. https://ideas.repec.org/a/ris/jofitr/1608.html

Jha, B., Giri, P., Jha, D., & Badhera, U. (2022). Unlocking IoT: AI-enabled green fintech innovations. In *AI-Enabled Agile Internet of Things for Sustainable FinTech Ecosystems* (pp. 1–22). IGI Global. DOI: 10.4018/978-1-6684-4176-3.ch001

Jhansi Rani, T. (2025). Blockchain Based Analytical Bug Tracking in Software Engineering. *Communications on Applied Nonlinear Analysis*, *32*(1), 127–147. DOI: 10.52783/cana.v32.1626

Jiang, J., & Conrath, D. W. (1997). Semantic similarity based on corpus statistics and lexical taxonomy. In *Proceedings: 10th International Conference on Research in Computational Linguistics* (pp. 19-33).

Jiang, X. J., & Liu, X. F. (2021). CryptoKitties Transaction Network Analysis: The Rise and Fall of the First Blockchain Game Mania. *Frontiers in Physics (Lausanne)*, *9*, 631665. Advance online publication. DOI: 10.3389/fphy.2021.631665

Jiang, Y., Wang, X., & Zheng, H. (2014). A Semantic Similarity Measure Based on Information Distance for Ontology Alignment. *Information Sciences*, *278*, 76–87. DOI: 10.1016/j.ins.2014.03.021

Jiang, Z., Xu, F. F., Araki, J., & Neubig, G. (2020). How can we know what language models know? *Transactions of the Association for Computational Linguistics*, *8*, 423–438. DOI: 10.1162/tacl_a_00324

Jibo, A. U. (2025). Green Fintech Innovations in Islamic Banking: Opportunities and Challenges. In *Islamic Finance and Sustainability: A Research Companion* (pp. 53–74). Taylor and Francis. DOI: 10.4324/9781003518617-4

Ji, F., & Tia, A. (2022). The effect of blockchain on business intelligence efficiency of banks. *Kybernetes*, *51*(8), 2652–2668. DOI: 10.1108/K-10-2020-0668

Joachim, N. (2023). Economic Impacts And Innovations In Materials Science: A Holistic Exploration Of Nanotechnology And Advanced Materials. *Engineering Science & Tecnology Journal*, *4*(3), 84–100. DOI: 10.51594/estj.v4i3.553

Johnsen, M. (2020). *Blockchain in digital marketing: a new paradigm of trust.* Maria Johnsen.

Johnson, C. (2024). Decentralized finance (DeFi): Opportunities and risks in the global financial ecosystem. *Business, Marketing, and Finance Open*, *1*(2), 53–64.

Johnson, K. N. (2020). Decentralized finance: Regulating cryptocurrency exchanges. *Wm. & Mary L. Rev.*, *62*, 1911.

Joia, L. A., & Cordeiro, J. P. V. (2021). Unlocking the potential of fintechs for financial inclusion: A delphi-based approach. *Sustainability (Basel)*, *13*(21), 11675. Advance online publication. DOI: 10.3390/su132111675

Jovanić, T. (2021). *An Overview of Regulatory Strategies on Crypto-Asset Regulation - Challenges for Financial Regulators in the Western Balkans.*

Judmayer, A., Stifter, N., Krombholz, K., & Weippl, E. (2022). *Blocks and chains: introduction to bitcoin, cryptocurrencies, and their consensus mechanisms.* Springer Nature.

Kadur, M. P., & Supriya, D. R. (2022). Digital transformation and banking sector workforce: An evaluation study. *International Journal of Scientific Research and Management, 10*(5), 238–246. DOI: 10.18535/ijsrm/v10i5.em11

Kahneman, D., & Tversky, A. (1979). Prospect theory: An analysis of decision under risk. *Econometrica, 47*(2), 263–291. DOI: 10.2307/1914185

Kakar, S. K., Ali, J., Wang, J., Wu, X., Arshed, N., Le Hien, T. T., & Yadav, R. S. (2024). Exploring the impact of industrialization and electricity use on carbon emissions: The role of green FinTech in Asian countries using an asymmetric panel quantile ARDL approach. *Journal of Environmental Management, 370*, 122970. Advance online publication. DOI: 10.1016/j.jenvman.2024.122970 PMID: 39426172

Kakar, S. K., Wang, J., Arshed, N., Le Hien, T. T., Akhter, S., & Abdullahi, N. M. (2025). The impact of circular economy, sustainable infrastructure, and green FinTech on biodiversity in Europe: A holistic approach. *Technology in Society, 81*, 102841. Advance online publication. DOI: 10.1016/j.techsoc.2025.102841

Kandpal, V., Ozili, P. K., Jeyanthi, P. M., Ranjan, D., & Chandra, D. (2025), "Creative Artificial Intelligence Supports to FinOps", Digital Finance and Metaverse in Banking, Emerald Publishing Limited, Leeds, pp. 87-113. DOI: 10.1108/978-1-83662-088-420251004

Kanojia, S., Kaur, S., & Bhavya, . (2024). Business sustainability in the era of Fintech and Regtech: A systematic literature review. *Discover Sustainability, 5*(1), 525. Advance online publication. DOI: 10.1007/s43621-024-00767-5

Kaplan, A., & Haenlein, M. (2019). Siri, Siri, in my hand: Who's the fairest in the land? On the interpretations, illustrations, and implications of artificial intelligence. In Business Horizons (Vol. 62, Issue 1, pp. 15–25). Elsevier Ltd. https://doi.org/ DOI: 10.1016/j.bushor.2018.08.004

Kartik, A. (2025). The innovation leap. *Outlook Business, January 2025*, 52–53.

Karulkar, Y., Shah, A., & Naik, R. (2024). AI-Powered Business Evolution. *Advances in Business Information Systems and Analytics Book Series*, 39–72. https://doi.org/ DOI: 10.4018/979-8-3693-4187-2.ch003

Katib, I., Albassam, E., Sharaf, S. A., & Ragab, M. (2024). Harnessing probabilistic neural network with triple tree seed algorithm-based smart enterprise quantitative risk management framework. *Scientific Reports, 14*(1), 22293. DOI: 10.1038/s41598-024-73876-w PMID: 39333638

Kaur, G., Habibi Lashkari, A., Sharafaldin, I., & Habibi Lashkari, Z. (2023). The Origin of Modern Decentralized Finance. In *Understanding Cybersecurity Management in Decentralized Finance: Challenges, Strategies, and Trends* (pp. 1–28). Springer International Publishing. DOI: 10.1007/978-3-031-23340-1_1

Kaur, J., & Pathak, N. (2023). The financial and sustainability impact of fintech on Indian deposit money institutions: A study of the last decade. In Chate, V. R. (Ed.), *E3S Web of Conferences* (Vol. 455). EDP Sciences., DOI: 10.1051/e3sconf/202345502019

Kauter, M. V., Breesch, D., & Hoste, V. (2015). Fine-grained analysis of explicit and implicit sentiment in financial news articles. *Expert Systems with Applications*, *42*(11), 4999–5010. DOI: 10.1016/j.eswa.2015.02.007

Kayani, U., & Hasan, F. (2024). Unveiling Cryptocurrency Impact on Financial Markets and Traditional Banking Systems: Lessons for Sustainable Blockchain and Interdisciplinary Collaborations. *Journal of Risk and Financial Management*, *17*(2), 58. DOI: 10.3390/jrfm17020058

Ken's Korner Newsletter Blockchains. (2024). Ken's Korner. https://myemail.constantcontact.com/Ken-s-Korner-Newsletter-Blockchains--.html?soid=1119929876329&aid=fm5enP1tKko

Kennedy, A., & Inkpen, D. (2006). Sentiment classification of movie reviews using contextual valence shifters. *Computational Intelligence*, *22*(2), 110–125. DOI: 10.1111/j.1467-8640.2006.00277.x

Kethepalli, Y., Joseph, R., Raja Vajrala, S., Vemula, J., Srinivas Naik, N., & Naya Raipur, I. (2023). *Reinforcing Security and Usability of Crypto-Wallet with Post-Quantum Cryptography and Zero-Knowledge Proof*. https://arxiv.org/abs/2308.07309v2

Khan, D., Jung, L. T., & Hashmani, M. A. (2021). Systematic Literature Review of Challenges in Blockchain Scalability. *Applied Sciences 2021, Vol. 11, Page 9372*, *11*(20), 9372. DOI: 10.3390/app11209372

Khan, A. A., Hidthir, M. H. B., Mansur, M., & Ahmad, Z. (2025). Role of financial inclusion in enhancing the effect of remittance on economic growth in developing countries. *Cogent Economics & Finance*, *13*(1), 2476093. DOI: 10.1080/23322039.2025.2476093

Khan, B. U. I., Goh, K. W., Khan, A. R., Zuhairi, M. F., & Chaimanee, M. (2025). Resource Management and Secure Data Exchange for Mobile Sensors Using Ethereum Blockchain. *Symmetry*, *17*(1), 61. DOI: 10.3390/sym17010061

Khan, M. S., & Umer, H. (2024). ChatGPT in finance: Applications, challenges, and solutions. *Heliyon, 10*(2), e24890. DOI: 10.1016/j.heliyon.2024.e24890 PMID: 38304767

Khan, N., Ahmad, T., & State, R. (2019, October). Feasibility of stellar as a blockchain-based micropayment system. In *International Conference on Smart Blockchain* (pp. 53-65). Cham: Springer International Publishing. DOI: 10.1007/978-3-030-34083-4_6

Kismawadi, E. R. (2024a). "Blockchain Technology and Islamic Finance: Empowering Small Businesses for Financial Sustainability." Pp. 50–77 in Technopreneurship in Small Businesses for Sustainability.

Kismawadi, E. R. (2024b). "Sustainable Islamic Financial Inclusion: The Ethical Challenges of Generative AI in Product and Service Development." Pp. 237–58 in Exploring the Ethical Implications of Generative AI.

Kitsios, F., Giatsidis, I., & Kamariotou, M. (2021). Digital transformation and strategy in the banking sector: Evaluating the acceptance rate of e-services. *Journal of Open Innovation*, *7*(3), 204. DOI: 10.3390/joitmc7030204

Klenner, M., Petrakis, S., & Fahrni, A. (2009). Robust Compositional Polarity Classification. In *Proceedings held in conjunction with the International Conference RANLP - 2009, September 14 - 16, Borovets, Bulgaria* (pp. 180-184). Shoumen: INCOMA.

Koemtzopoulos, D., Zournatzidou, G., & Sariannidis, N. (2025). Can Cryptocurrencies Be Green? The Role of Stablecoins Toward a Carbon Footprint and Sustainable Ecosystem. *Sustainability (Basel)*, *17*(2), 483. DOI: 10.3390/su17020483

Komalavalli, C., Saxena, D., & Laroiya, C. (2020). Overview of blockchain technology concepts. In *Handbook of research on blockchain technology* (pp. 349–371). Academic Press. DOI: 10.1016/B978-0-12-819816-2.00014-9

Kong, L., & Smith, N. A. (1994). An Empirical Comparison of Parsing Methods for Stanford Dependencies. Retrieved from http://arxiv.org/pef/1404.4314v1.pdf

Kowsick, N. P., & Ramasamy, K. (2025). Blockchain Technology Transforming Libraries and Financial Services Towards Inclusive Development. In *Leveraging Blockchain for Future-Ready Libraries* (pp. 93–104). IGI Global Scientific Publishing.

Krasonikolakis, I., Tsarbopoulos, M., & Eng, T. (2020). Are incumbent banks bygones in the face of digital transformation? *Journal of General Management*, *46*(1), 60–69. DOI: 10.1177/0306307020937883

Krause, D. (2024). Finfluencers and market distortions: An analysis of herding behavior on social media platforms. *Social Finance Quarterly*, *29*(2), 90–107.

Krause, D. (2024). Generative AI in FinTech: Transforming Financial Activities through Advanced Technologies. https://doi.org/DOI: 10.2139/ssrn.4923224

Kukman, T., & Gričar, S. (2025). Blockchain for Quality: Advancing Security, Efficiency, and Transparency in Financial Systems. *FinTech*, *4*(1), 7. DOI: 10.3390/fintech4010007

Kulkarni, R., Schintler, L., Koizumi, N., & Stough, R. R. (2020). Cryptocurrency, Stablecoins and Blockchain: Exploring Digital Money Solutions for Remittances and Inclusive Economies. SSRN *Electronic Journal*. DOI: 10.2139/ssrn.3511139

Ku-Mahamud, K. R., Bakar, N. A. A., & Omar, M. (2018). Blockchain, cryptocurrency and Fintech market growth in Malaysia. *Journal of Advanced Research in Dynamical and Control Systems*, *10*(14), 2074–2082. https://www.scopus.com/inward/record.uri?eid=2-s2.0-85062364401&partnerID=40&md5=069874992ec5f5139bba69d5a95a10cb

Kumar, S. (2023). What is the future of fintech funding in 2023? *Asian Banking & Finance*, *Q3*, 8.

Kwong, R., Kwok, M. L. J., & Wong, H. S. M. (2023). Green FinTech Innovation as a Future Research Direction: A Bibliometric Analysis on Green Finance and FinTech. *Sustainability (Basel)*, *15*(20), 14683. Advance online publication. DOI: 10.3390/su152014683

Kwon, S. (2022). Regulation of DeFi Lending: Agency Supervision on Decentralization. *The Columbia Science and Technology Law Review*, *24*(2), 379–413. DOI: 10.52214/stlr.v24i2.11629

Lanzolla, G., Pesce, D., & Tucci, C. L. (2021). The Digital Transformation of Search and Recombination in the Innovation Function: Tensions and an Integrative Framework*. *Journal of Product Innovation Management*, *38*(1), 90–113. DOI: 10.1111/jpim.12546

Lasla, N., Al-Sahan, L., Abdallah, M., & Younis, M. (2022). Green-PoW: An energy-efficient blockchain Proof-of-Work consensus algorithm. *Computer Networks*, *214*, 109118. DOI: 10.1016/j.comnet.2022.109118

Le, D., Kumar, R., Mishra, B. K., Khari, M., & Chatterjee, J. M. (Eds.). (2019). *Cyber Security in Parallel and Distributed Computing*. Wiley., DOI: 10.1002/9781119488330

Lee, D. K. C., Guan, C., Yu, Y., & Ding, Q. (2024). A Comprehensive Review of Generative AI in Finance. *FinTech*, *3*(3), 460–478. DOI: 10.3390/fintech3030025

Lee, J., & Khan, V. M. (2022). Blockchain and energy commodity markets: Legal issues and impact on sustainability. *Journal of World Energy Law and Business*, *15*(6), 462–484. DOI: 10.1093/jwelb/jwac030

Lee, J., & Lee, J.-A. (2025). Web3 Governance: Law and Policy. In *Web3 Governance: Law and Policy*. Taylor and Francis., DOI: 10.4324/9781032618975

Lee, J., Serafin, A. M., & Courteau, C. (2023). Corporate disclosure, ESG and green fintech in the energy industry. *Journal of World Energy Law and Business*, *16*(6), 473–491. DOI: 10.1093/jwelb/jwad018

Lee, M. C., Chang, J. W., & Hsieh, T. C. (2014). A Grammar-Based Semantic Similarity Algorithm for Natural Language Sentences. *TheScientificWorldJournal*, *24*, 1–17. DOI: 10.1155/2014/437162 PMID: 24982952

Lee, S. (2024). *Strategic corporate social responsibility in the tourism and hospitality industry: Conceptual proposal*. Tourism Economics., DOI: 10.1177/13548166241299140

Lengkeek, M., van der Knaap, F., & Frasincar, F. (2023). Leveraging hierarchical language models for aspect-based sentiment analysis on financial data. *Information Processing & Management*, *60*(5), 1–18. DOI: 10.1016/j.ipm.2023.103435

Lepore, C., Ceria, M., Visconti, A., Rao, U. P., Shah, K. A., & Zanolini, L. (2020). A survey on blockchain consensus with a performance comparison of PoW, PoS and pure PoS. *Mathematics*, *8*(10), 1782. DOI: 10.3390/math8101782

Lesk, M. (1986). Automatic sense disambiguation using machine readable dictionaries: how to tell a pine cone from an ice cream cone. In *Proceedings: ACM SIGDOC 86, the Fifth International Conference on Systems Documentation, June 8-11, University of Toronto* (pp. 24-26). New York, NY: ACM Press. DOI: 10.1145/318723.318728

Letts, A. (2017). What do consumers want from next generation banking, and how will challenger and established banks provide it? *Journal of Digital Banking*, *1*(4), 329. Advance online publication. DOI: 10.69554/BRFD2666

Li, X., Wang, X., Kong, T., Zheng, J., & Luo, M. (2022). From Bitcoin to Solana – Innovating Blockchain Towards Enterprise Applications. *Lecture Notes in Computer Science (Including Subseries Lecture Notes in Artificial Intelligence and Lecture Notes in Bioinformatics), 12991 LNCS*. DOI: 10.1007/978-3-030-96527-3_6

Liebau, D. (2024). Decentralized Finance: Impact on Financial Services and required DeFi Literacy in 2034. *arXiv preprint arXiv:2410.14173*. DOI: 10.2139/ssrn.4987462

Li, J., Fong, S., Zhuang, Y., & Khoury, R. (2015). Hierarchical Classification in Text Mining for Sentiment Analysis of Online News. *Soft Computing*, *20*(9), 3411–3420. DOI: 10.1007/s00500-015-1812-4

Lilge, M. (2001, May). Evolution of PrePaid Service towards a real-time payment system. In *IEEE Intelligent Network 2001 Workshop. IN 2001 Conference Record (Cat. No. 01TH8566)* (pp. 195-198). IEEE. DOI: 10.1109/INW.2001.915313

Lin, D. (1998). An Information Theoretic Definition of Similarity. In *Proceedings: Fifteenth International Conference on Machine Learning (ICML '98)* (pp. 296-304). Morgan Kaufmann

Lindawati, M., & Parwoto, P. (2021). The impact of transformational leadership and motivation on employee performance during digital transformation. *Journal of Industrial Engineering Management and Research*, *2*(4), 51–66. DOI: 10.7777/jiemar.v2i4.162

Ling, L., & Peng, L. (2025). The complexity of ECF investors' peer-effect: A test of structural social influence theory by fsQCA approach. *Business Process Management Journal*, *31*(1), 95–117. DOI: 10.1108/BPMJ-12-2023-0964

Lin, W., & Liao, L.-C. (2024). Lexicon-based prompt for financial dimensional sentiment analysis. *Expert Systems with Applications*, *244*, 1–7. DOI: 10.1016/j.eswa.2023.122936

Liu, Y., Ott, M., Goyal, N., Du, J., Joshi, M., Chen, D., ... & Stoyanov, V. (2019). Roberta: A robustly optimized bert pretraining approach. arXiv preprint arXiv:1907.11692.

Liu, A., Urquía-Grande, E., López-Sánchez, P., & Rodríguez-López, Á. (2023). Research into microfinance and ICTs: A bibliometric analysis. *Evaluation and Program Planning*, *97*, 102215. Advance online publication. DOI: 10.1016/j.evalprogplan.2022.102215 PMID: 36571966

Liu, G., Wang, R., Buckley, J., & Zhou, H. M. (2011). A WordNet-base Semantic Similarity Measure Enhanced by Internet-based Knowledge. In *Proceedings: 23rd International Conference on Software Engineering and Knowledge Engineering (SEKE2011)* (pp. 175-178).

Liu, X., Li, L., Sun, R., Li, W., & Liu, T. (2023). Lightweight multi-departmental data sharing scheme based on consortium blockchain. *Peer-to-Peer Networking and Applications*, *16*(5), 2399–2414. DOI: 10.1007/s12083-023-01523-8

Liu, X., Salem, S., Bian, L., Seong, J.-T., & Alshanbari, H. M. (2024). Application of machine learning algorithms in the domain of financial engineering. *Alexandria Engineering Journal*, *95*, 94–100. DOI: 10.1016/j.aej.2024.03.058

Liu, Y., Zhang, S., Chen, M., Wu, Y., & Chen, Z. (2021). The sustainable development of financial topic detection and trend prediction by data mining. *Sustainability (Basel)*, *13*(14), 7585. Advance online publication. DOI: 10.3390/su13147585

Liu, Z., Qian, P., Wang, X., Zhuang, Y., Qiu, L., & Wang, X. (2021).. . *IEEE Transactions on Knowledge and Data Engineering*, *35*, 1296–1310.

Li, X., Xie, H., Chen, L., Wang, J., & Deng, X. (2014). News Impact on Stock Price Return via Sentiment Analysis. *Knowledge-Based Systems*, *69*, 14–23. DOI: 10.1016/j.knosys.2014.04.022

Li, Y. (2020). *Decision Making with Peer Opinions on Social Media Platforms*. Drexel University.

Li, Y., Zhong, H., & Tong, Q. (2024). Artificial Intelligence, Dynamic Capabilities, and Corporate Financial Asset Allocation. *International Review of Financial Analysis*, *96*, 103773. Advance online publication. DOI: 10.1016/j.irfa.2024.103773

Li, Z., Lunku, H. S., & Yang, S. (2025). Financial inclusion in the digital era: A key driver for reducing income inequality. *Technological and Economic Development of Economy*, *31*(3), 1–26. DOI: 10.3846/tede.2025.23068

Long, L., Wang, R., Xiao, R., Zhao, J., Ding, X., Chen, G., & Wang, H. (2024). On llms-driven synthetic data generation, curation, and evaluation: A survey. *arXiv preprint arXiv:2406.15126*. DOI: 10.18653/v1/2024.findings-acl.658

Looman, J. (2024). *Credit Unions & Cryptocurrencies: A Quantitative Study of the Applicability and Sustainability in the Age of Decentralized Finance* (Doctoral dissertation, Wilmington University (Delaware).

Lopez, P. G., Montresor, A., & Datta, A. (2019, July). Please, do not decentralize the Internet with (permissionless) blockchains! In *2019 IEEE 39th International Conference on Distributed Computing Systems (ICDCS)* (pp. 1901-1911). IEEE.

Lucarelli, C., Mazzocchini, F. J., & Severini, S. (2024). Green FinTech: State of the art of the literature and future perspectives. *International Journal of Green Economics*, *18*(3), 295–317. DOI: 10.1504/IJGE.2024.141407

Lundqvist, T., De Blanche, A., & Andersson, H. R. H. (2017). *Thing-to-thing electricity micro payments using blockchain technology. GIoTS 2017 - Global Internet of Things Summit*. Proceedings., DOI: 10.1109/GIOTS.2017.8016254

Luo, S. (2025). When Climate Risk Spreads: The Role of Social Network in Portfolio Sustainability Tilting. Available at *SSRN* 5132522. DOI: 10.2139/ssrn.5132522

Lu, S., Liang, S., Xue, Q., & Bian, H. (2024). Enhancing cross-border payments: The convergence of AI and blockchain for currency exchange optimization. *Applied and Computational Engineering*, *75*(1), 160–165. DOI: 10.54254/2755-2721/75/20240531

Luthra, V., & Trott, A. (2024). Generative AI's role in the evolution of banking. *Asian Banking & Finance*, *Q3*, 32.

Lyons, R. K., & Viswanath-Natraj, G. (2023). What keeps stablecoins stable? *Journal of International Money and Finance*, *131*, 102777. DOI: 10.1016/j.jimonfin.2022.102777

Macchiavello, E., & Siri, M. (2022). Sustainable Finance and Fintech: Can Technology Contribute to Achieving Environmental Goals? A Preliminary Assessment of "Green Fintech" and "Sustainable Digital Finance.". *European Company and Financial Law Review*, *19*(1), 128–174. DOI: 10.1515/ecfr-2022-0005

Madanchian, M. (2024). Generative AI for Consumer Behavior Prediction: Techniques and Applications. *Sustainability (Basel)*, *16*(22), 9963. DOI: 10.3390/su16229963

Madir, J. (2018). Smart Contracts: (How) Do They Fit Under Existing Legal Frameworks? SSRN *Electronic Journal*. DOI: 10.2139/ssrn.3301463

Mahadi, N. F., Yusuf, M. B. O., Kassim, S., & Yusoff, S. S. B. M. (2024). FINANCIAL RESILIENCE AMONG WOMEN SMALL AND MEDIUM ENTERPRISE IN MALAYSIA DURING AND AFTER COVID-19: THE ROLE OF ISLAMIC SOCIAL FINANCE. *Journal of Islamic Monetary Economics and Finance*, *10*(4), 631–656. DOI: 10.21098/jimf.v10i4.2009

Maheshwari, H., Samantaray, A.K., Sandhu, K. and Panigrahi, R.R. (2025), "Insight over instinct: AI's role in rationalizing investment decisions", *International Journal of Accounting & Information Management,* Vol. ahead-of-print No. ahead-of-print. .DOI: 10.1108/IJAIM-12-2024-0455

Maiti, M. (2023). The pocket aide to sort your finances. *Outlook Money, February 2023*, 8–18.

Makhdomi, A. A., & Gillani, I. A. (2025, January). Decentralized Ridesharing: Overcoming Scalability Issues with Layer 2 Solution. In *Proceedings of the 26th International Conference on Distributed Computing and Networking* (pp. 319-324). DOI: 10.1145/3700838.3703682

Makhdoom, I., Zhou, I., Abolhasan, M., Lipman, J., & Ni, W. (2020). PrivySharing: A blockchain-based framework for privacy-preserving and secure data sharing in smart cities. *Computers & Security*, *88*, 101653. DOI: 10.1016/j.cose.2019.101653

Maleh, Y., Zhang, J., & Hansali, A. (2024). Advances in Emerging Financial Technology and Digital Money. In *Advances in Emerging Financial Technology and Digital Money*. CRC Press., DOI: 10.1201/9781032667478

Malo, P., Sinha, A., Korhonen, P., Wallenius, J., & Takala, P. (2014). Good debt or bad debt: Detecting semantic orientations in economic texts. *Journal of the Association for Information Science and Technology*, *65*(4), 782–796. DOI: 10.1002/asi.23062

Manap, A., Hawari, Y., Lubis, A., Sukandar, E., & Pujadi, A. (2023). The Effect of Return Expectation, Motivation, Perceived Value of Risk and Technological Progress on Investment Decision in Sharia Peer to Peer Lending. JEMSI (Jurnal Ekonomi, Manajemen, dan Akuntansi), 9(2), 232-237.

Manda, J. K. (2024). Blockchain-based Identity Management in Telecom: Implementing Blockchain for Secure and Decentralized Identity Management Solutions in. *Available at SSRN* 5136783.

Manoharan, G., & Darwish, D. (2025). Revolutionize the Financial Services: Artificial Intelligence in the Finance Sector. In *Utilizing AI and Machine Learning in Financial Analysis* (pp. 381-402). IGI Global Scientific Publishing, Pennsylvania, USA.

Manu, M. R., & Namya Musthafa, B. (2020). *Balamurugan, & Chauhan, R.* Blockchain Components and Concept., DOI: 10.1201/9781003081487-2

Maqbool, J., Aggarwal, P., Kaur, R., Mittal, A., & Ganaie, I. A. (2023). Stock Prediction by Integrating Sentiment Scores of Financial News and MLP-Regressor: A Machine Learning Approach. *Procedia Computer Science*, *218*, 1067–1078. DOI: 10.1016/j.procs.2023.01.086

Maramganti, K., & Rajyalakshmi, N. C. (2019). Role of artificial intelligence in business transformation. In International Journal on Recent Trends in Business and Tourism | (Vol. 3, Issue 3).

Margaret Sangeetha, J., & Joy Alfia, K. (2024). Financial stock market forecast using evaluated linear regression based machine learning technique. *Measurement. Sensors*, *31*, 1–7. DOI: 10.1016/j.measen.2023.100950

Marian, O. (2020). Blockchain Havens and the Need for Their Internationally-coordinated Regulation. *Florida Tax Review*, *23*(2). Advance online publication. DOI: 10.5744/ftr.2020.2011

Martinez, D., Magdalena, L., & Savitri, A. N. (2024). AI and Blockchain Integration: Enhancing Security and Transparency in Financial Transactions. *International Transactions on Artificial Intelligence*, *3*(1), 11–20. DOI: 10.33050/italic.v3i1.651

Mathew, J. C. (2024). India's deep tech disruption. *Fortune, June 2024*, 28–38.

Matta, P. (2020). Leveraging AI for Predictive Market Insights: Practical Applications and Implementation. *International Journal on Science and Technology (IJSAT) IJSAT20041131, 11*(4). https://www.ijsat.org/papers/2020/4/1131.pdf

Mbaidin, H. O., Sbaee, N. Q., Almubydeen, I. O., & Alomari, K. M. (2024). Key Success Drivers for Implementation Blockchain Technology in UAE Islamic Banking. *Uncertain Supply Chain Management*, *12*(2), 1175–1188. DOI: 10.5267/j.uscm.2023.11.016

McKinsey & Company. (2023, June 14). Economic potential of generative AI | McKinsey. https://www.mckinsey.com/capabilities/mckinsey-digital/our-insights/the-economic-potential-of-generative-ai-the-next-productivity-frontier

McMenamin, C., Daza, V., Fitzi, M., & O'Donoghue, P. (2022, November). Fairtradex: A decentralised exchange preventing value extraction. In *Proceedings of the 2022 ACM CCS Workshop on Decentralized Finance and Security* (pp. 39-46). DOI: 10.1145/3560832.3563439

Mer, A., Singhal, K., & Virdi, A. S. (2024), "A Review of the Role of Artificial Intelligence in Banking and Stock Market Trading", Taneja, S., Kumar, P., Sood, K., Özen, E. and Grima, S. (Ed.) Finance Analytics in Business (Emerald Studies in Finance, Insurance, and Risk Management), Emerald Publishing Limited, Leeds, pp. 175-198. DOI: 10.1108/978-1-83753-572-920241009

Merello, P., Barbera, A., & De la Poza, E. (2023). Analysing the determinant factors of the sustainability profile of Fintech and Insurtech companies. *Journal of Cleaner Production*, *421*, 138437. Advance online publication. DOI: 10.1016/j.jclepro.2023.138437

Met, I., Kabukçu, D., Uzunoğulları, G., Soyalp, Ü., & Dakdevir, T. (2019). Transformation of business model in finance sector with artificial intelligence and robotic process automation. In Contributions to management science. https://doi.org/DOI: 10.1007/978-3-030-29739-8_1

Meyer, D., & Shera, A. (2017). The impact of remittances on economic growth: An econometric model. *Economía*, *18*(2), 147–155. Advance online publication. DOI: 10.1016/j.econ.2016.06.001

Mhlanga, D. (2023). Block chain technology for digital financial inclusion in the industry 4.0, towards sustainable development? In *Frontiers in Blockchain* (Vol. 6). DOI: 10.3389/fbloc.2023.1035405

Mhlanga, D. (2025). 9 The Critical Developmental Importance of Blockchain Technology in Africa. *Financial Inclusion and Sustainable Development in Sub-Saharan Africa*, 136.

Mhlongo, A. F. (2025). The Impact of Financial Inclusion on Women Entrepreneurship in South Africa. In Moloi, T. (Ed.), *Impacting Society Positively Through Technology in Accounting and Business Processes. ICAB 2024. Springer Proceedings in Business and Economics*. Springer., DOI: 10.1007/978-3-031-84885-8_39

Minz, N. K., Mushir, N., Tanwar, S., & Chaffai, M. (2023). Islamic Finance and Fintech: A scoping review. In *Fintech Applications in Islamic Finance: AI, Machine Learning, and Blockchain Techniques* (pp. 150–170). IGI Global. DOI: 10.4018/979-8-3693-1038-0.ch010

Mirdala, R. (2024). Revolutionizing Finance: Decentralized Finance as a Disruptive Challenge to Traditional Finance. *Theoretical and Practical Research in Economic Fields, 15*(3), 517–538. DOI: 10.14505/tpref.v15.3(31).02

Miron, R., Hulea, M., Muresan, V., Clitan, I., & Rusu, A. (2025). Integrating Blockchain Technology into Mobility-as-a-Service Platforms for Smart Cities. *Smart Cities, 8*(1), 9. DOI: 10.3390/smartcities8010009

Mishion, N. (2024, December). Ethics in AI: Navigating the future responsibly. *Banking & Finance, XXXVII*(12), 37–38.

Misra, A. (2024). Tax Policy Handbook for Crypto Assets. *arXiv preprint arXiv:2403.15074*.

Misra, N., Gupta, S., & Rao, T. J. (2024). Fintech's Role in Green Finance: Procuring Funds for Sustainable Energy. *International Research Journal of Multidisciplinary Scope, 5*(2), 290–312. DOI: 10.47857/irjms.2024.v05i02.0455

Mittal, U., Sai, S., Chamola, V., & Sangwan, D. (2024). A Comprehensive Review on Generative AI for Education. *IEEE Access : Practical Innovations, Open Solutions, 12*, 142733–142759. DOI: 10.1109/ACCESS.2024.3468368

Mohamed, H., and H. Ali. 2022. Blockchain, Fintech, and Islamic Finance: Building the Future in the New Islamic Digital Economy.

Mohamed, K. A. M. (2022). The effect of digital transformation on the strategic flexibility applied to the bank sector. *The Scientific Journal of Commercial and Environmental Studies, 3*(1), 267365. DOI: 10.21608/jces.2022.267365

Mohammad, S. M., Zhu, X., Kiritchenko, S., & Martin, J. (2015). Sentiment, Emotion, Purpose, and Style in Electoral Tweets. *Information Processing & Management, 51*(4), 480–499. DOI: 10.1016/j.ipm.2014.09.003

Mohanty, B., & Mishra, S. (2023). Role of Artificial Intelligence in Financial Fraud Detection. *Academy of Marketing Studies Journal, 27*, •••. https://www.abacademies.org/articles/role-of-artificial-intelligence-in-financial-fraud-detection.pdf

Molavi, H., Zhang, L., & Khanbabaei, M. (2025). Sustainable financial infrastructure and governance: A fuzzy multi-criteria decision-making analysis of open service innovation in unstable economies. *Sustainable Futures : An Applied Journal of Technology, Environment and Society, 9*, 100485. Advance online publication. DOI: 10.1016/j.sftr.2025.100485

Molina-Gonzalez, M. D., Martinez-Camara, E., Martin-Valdivia, M. T., & Urena-Lopez, L. A. (2015). A Spanish Semantic Orientation Approach to Domain Adaptation for Polarity Classification. *Information Processing & Management, 51*(4), 520–531. DOI: 10.1016/j.ipm.2014.10.002

Monisha, J., Anitha, K., & Selvam, P. P. (2025). Charting the Fintech Frontier: Transformative Technologies for Sustainable Industries. In *FinTech and Financial Inclusion: Leveraging Digital Finance for Economic Empowerment and Sustainable Growth* (pp. 179–197). Taylor and Francis. DOI: 10.4324/9781003514114-13

Moro-Visconti, R., Rambaud, S. C., & Pascual, J. L. (2020). Sustainability in FinTechs: An explanation through business model scalability and market valuation. *Sustainability (Basel), 12*(24), 1–24. DOI: 10.3390/su122410316

Motley Fool. (2023). Gen Z's investing habits: Trends and expectations. *The Motley Fool Research Briefs*. https://www.fool.com/research/gen-z-investing-trends/

Moura de Carvalho, R., Inácio, H. C., & Marques, R. P. (2025). Stablecoin: A Story of (In) Stabilities and Co-Movements Written Through Wavelet. *Journal of Risk and Financial Management, 18*(1), 20. DOI: 10.3390/jrfm18010020

Moussawi, S., Koufaris, M., & Benbunan-Fich, R. (2020). How perceptions of intelligence and anthropomorphism affect adoption of personal intelligent agents. *Electronic Markets, 31*(2), 343–364. Advance online publication. DOI: 10.1007/s12525-020-00411-w

Murray, A., Kim, D., & Combs, J. (2023). The promise of a decentralized internet: What is Web3 and how can firms prepare? *Business Horizons*, *66*(2), 191–202. DOI: 10.1016/j.bushor.2022.06.002

Murugan, R., Yenduri, G., Maran, P., & Reddy Gadekallu, T. (2025). The Synergy of Artificial Intelligence and Blockchain in 6G Spectrum Management. *Intelligent Spectrum Management: Towards, 6G*, 237–262. DOI: 10.1002/9781394201235.ch10

Musungwini, S., & Furusa, S. S. (2024). A Framework for Implementation of Decentralized Finance for Financial Inclusion of Unbanked Populations in a Developing Context. A Case of Zimbabwe. In *Decentralized Finance: The Impact of Blockchain-Based Financial Innovations on Entrepreneurship* (pp. 51–76). Springer International Publishing. DOI: 10.1007/978-3-031-49515-1_4

Naderi, N. (2021). Utilizing blockchain technology in international remittances for poverty reduction and inclusive growth. *Poverty Reduction for Inclusive Sustainable Growth in Developing Asia*, 149-163.

Nair, V. (2024). AI-augmented investor behavior: A study on cognitive load and digital finance. *International Journal of Financial Management and Research*, *6*(1), 12–24.

Nakamoto, S. (2008). Bitcoin: A Peer-to-Peer Electronic Cash System | Satoshi Nakamoto Institute. *Bitcoin.Org*.

Nakamoto, S. (2008). Bitcoin: A Peer-to-Peer Electronic Cash System. 31611263538139.pdf

Nakonechnyi, V., Toliupa, S., Saiko, V., Lutsenko, V., Ghno, G. S. N., & Hussain, A. K. (2024, April). Blockchain Implementation in the Protection System of Banking System During Online Banking Operations. In *2024 35th Conference of Open Innovations Association (FRUCT)* (pp. 492-500). IEEE. DOI: 10.23919/FRUCT61870.2024.10516404

Namasudra, S., & Akkaya, K. (2023). Introduction to Blockchain Technology. *Studies in Big Data*, 1–28. https://doi.org/DOI: 10.1007/978-981-19-8730-4_1

Nartey, J. N. (2024). The Convergence of Decentralized Finance (DeFi) and Artificial Intelligence (AI): Synergies, Opportunities, and Challenges. *International Journal of Blockchain Technologies and Applications*, *2*(2). Advance online publication. DOI: 10.18178/IJBTA.2024.2.2.78-89

Nasir, N. M., Hassan, S., & Zaini, K. M. (2024). Securing Permissioned Blockchain-based Systems: An Analysis on the Significance of Consensus Mechanisms. *IEEE Access : Practical Innovations, Open Solutions*, *12*, 138211–138238. DOI: 10.1109/ACCESS.2024.3465869

Navigli, R., Conia, S., & Ross, B. (2023). Biases in large language models: Origins, inventory, and discussion. *ACM Journal of Data and Information Quality*, *15*(2), 1–21. DOI: 10.1145/3597307

Needhi, J. (2024, July 8). How AI Transformed Financial Fraud Detection: A Case Study of JP Morgan Chase. Medium; Medium. https://medium.com/@jeyadev_needhi/how-ai-transformed-financial-fraud-detection-a-case-study-of-jp-morgan-chase-f92bbb0707bb

Neekhara, P., Hussain, S., Ghosh, S., Li, J., Valle, R., Badlani, R., & Ginsburg, B. (2024). Improving robustness of llm-based speech synthesis by learning monotonic alignment. *arXiv preprint arXiv:2406.17957*. DOI: 10.21437/Interspeech.2024-335

Nefla, D., & Jellouli, S. (2025). Emerging technologies in finance: Challenges for a sustainable finance. *Cogent Business & Management*, *12*(1), 2495191. Advance online publication. DOI: 10.1080/23311975.2025.2495191

Ng, P. S. J., Zhang, X., Fu, L., Ye, L., & Phan, K. Y. (2025). The Inclusive Innovation of Blockchain in Securities Issuance: Reduced Inequalities of Investors. *Journal of Advanced Research in Applied Sciences and Engineering Technology*, *46*(2), 188–212. DOI: 10.37934/araset.46.2.188212

Nguyen, C. T., Hoang, D. T., Nguyen, D. N., Niyato, D., Nguyen, H. T., & Dutkiewicz, E. (2019). Proof-of-stake consensus mechanisms for future blockchain networks: Fundamentals, applications and opportunities. *IEEE Access : Practical Innovations, Open Solutions*, *7*, 85727–85745. DOI: 10.1109/ACCESS.2019.2925010

Nguyen, T., Tran, M., & Le, H. T. (2020). Behavioral biases and investment decisions: Evidence from emerging markets. *Journal of Behavioral Finance and Economics*, *12*(3), 150–163.

Nguyen-Thi-Huong, L., Nguyen-Viet, H., Nguyen-Phuong, A., & Van Nguyen, D. (2023). How does digital transformation impact bank performance? *Cogent Economics & Finance*, *11*(1), 2217582. DOI: 10.1080/23322039.2023.2217582

Nicoletti, B. (2017). *The Future of FinTech*. Springer International Publishing., DOI: 10.1007/978-3-319-51415-4

Nurminen, J., Räsänen, T., & Määttä, I. (2024). Instability in crypto-asset markets is a reminder of the risks and underlines the need for regulation.

Olanrewaju, A. (2024). Assessing the environmental health and safety risks of solar energy production. *World Journal of Biology Pharmacy and Health Sciences*, *17*(2), 225–231. DOI: 10.30574/wjbphs.2024.17.2.0080

Onyekwere, E., Ogwueleka, F. N., & Irhebhude, M. E. (2023). Adoption and sustainability of bitcoin and the blockchain technology in Nigeria. *International Journal of Information Technology : an Official Journal of Bharati Vidyapeeth's Institute of Computer Applications and Management*, *15*(5), 2793–2804. DOI: 10.1007/s41870-023-01336-1 PMID: 37360314

Ooi, K. (2023). (Taylor and Francis)The Potential of Generative Artificial Intelligence Across Disciplines: Perspectives and Future Directions. *Journal of Computer Information Systems*, *1*(1), 1–32. DOI: 10.1080/08874417.2023.2261010

Oriekhoe, O. I., Oyeyemi, O. P., Bello, B. G., Omotoye, G. B., Daraojimba, A. I., & Adefemi, A. (2024). Blockchain in SCM: A review of efficiency, transparency, and innovation. *International Journal of Science and Research Archive*, *11*(1), 173–181. DOI: 10.30574/ijsra.2024.11.1.0028

Oseremi Onesi-Ozigagun, Yinka James Ololade, Nsisong Louis Eyo-Udo, & Damilola Oluwaseun Ogundipe. (2024). AI-driven biometrics for secure fintech: Pioneering safety and trust. International Journal of Engineering Research Updates, 6(2), 001-012. https://doi.org/DOI: 10.53430/ijeru.2024.6.2.0023

Overgoor, G., Chica, M., Rand, W., & Weishampel, A. (2019). Letting the computers take over: Using Ai to solve marketing problems. *California Management Review*, *61*(4), 156–185. DOI: 10.1177/0008125619859318

Ozelli, S. (2024). Sustainably Investing in Digital Assets Globally. In *Sustainably Investing in Digital Assets Globally*. wiley. https://www.scopus.com/inward/record.uri?eid=2-s2.0-85185359366&partnerID=40&md5=b0146b6804fb8f69102861ee485b0234

Ozili, P. K. (2025b). Financial inclusion, religiosity and economic welfare in majority Christian, Hindu and Muslim countries. *foresight*.

Ozili, P. K. (2023). Assessing global interest in decentralized finance, embedded finance, open finance, ocean finance and sustainable finance. *Asian Journal of Economics and Banking*, *7*(2), 197–216. DOI: 10.1108/AJEB-03-2022-0029

Ozili, P. K. (2025a). Effect of CO2 emissions on financial inclusion through physical financial access points. *Management of Environmental Quality*. Advance online publication. DOI: 10.1108/MEQ-11-2024-0518

Ozili, P. K. (2025c). Artificial Intelligence and Digital Financial Inclusion. In Al-Sartawi, A., & Ghura, H. (Eds.), *Artificial Intelligence, Sustainable Technologies, and Business Innovation: Opportunities and Challenges of Digital Transformation. Studies in Computational Intelligence* (Vol. 1171). Springer., DOI: 10.1007/978-3-031-77925-1_23

Paladini, S., Yerushalmi, E., & Castellucci, I. (2021). Public governance of the blockchain revolution and its implications for social finance: A comparative analysis. In *Innovations in Social Finance: Transitioning Beyond Economic Value* (pp. 293–318). Springer International Publishing. DOI: 10.1007/978-3-030-72535-8_14

Panda, S. S., & Jena, D. (2021). *Decentralizing AI Using Blockchain Technology for Secure Decision Making*. DOI: 10.1007/978-981-15-5243-4_65

Panda, S. K., Sathya, A. R., & Das, S. (2023). Bitcoin: Beginning of the cryptocurrency era. In *Recent Advances in Blockchain Technology: Real-World Applications* (pp. 25–58). Springer International Publishing. DOI: 10.1007/978-3-031-22835-3_2

Pan, X., Zhang, M., Ji, S., & Yang, M. (2020). Privacy risks of general-purpose language models. In *2020 IEEE Symposium on Security and Privacy (SP)* (pp. 1314-1331). IEEE. DOI: 10.1109/SP40000.2020.00095

Papadis, N., & Tassiulas, L. (2020). Blockchain-based payment channel networks: Challenges and recent advances. *IEEE Access : Practical Innovations, Open Solutions*, *8*, 227596–227609. DOI: 10.1109/ACCESS.2020.3046020

Parisi, C., & Budorin, D. (2023). Smart Contract Security. In *A Comprehensive Guide for Web3 Security: From Technology, Economic and Legal Aspects* (pp. 81–102). Springer Nature Switzerland. DOI: 10.1007/978-3-031-39288-7_4

Patcha, A., & Park, J.-M. (2007). An overview of anomaly detection techniques: Existing solutions and latest technological trends. *Computer Networks*, *51*(12), 3448–3470. DOI: 10.1016/j.comnet.2007.02.001

Patil, D. (2024, November 8). Artificial intelligence in financial risk assessment and fraud detection: Opportunities and ethical concerns. https://www.researchgate.net/publication/385746635_Artificial_intelligence_in_financial_risk_assessment_and_fraud_detection_Opportunities_and_ethical_concerns

Patil, D. (2025). *Artificial Intelligence In Financial Risk Assessment And Fraud Detection: Opportunities And Ethical Concerns*. https://doi.org/DOI: 10.2139/ssrn.5057434

Pattnaik, D. (2024). The Fintech Landscape: A Bibliometric Analysis. In *The Emerald Handbook of Fintech* (pp. 17-42). Emerald Publishing Limited. DOI: 10.1108/978-1-83753-608-520241003

Peng, B., Chen, K., Li, M., Feng, P., Bi, Z., Liu, J., & Niu, Q. (2024). Securing large language models: Addressing bias, misinformation, and prompt attacks. *arXiv preprint arXiv:2409.08087.*

Peng, B., Chersoni, E., Hsu, Y., Qiu, L., & Huang, C. (2024). Supervised Cross-Momentum Contrast: Aligning representations with prototypical examples to enhance financial sentiment analysis. *Knowledge-Based Systems*, *295*, 1–13. DOI: 10.1016/j.knosys.2024.111683

Peng, Y., Ahmad, S. F., Ahmad, A. Y. A. B., Al Shaikh, M. S., Daoud, M. K., & Alhamdi, F. M. H. (2023). Riding the Waves of Artificial Intelligence in Advancing Accounting and Its Implications for Sustainable Development Goals. *Sustainability (Basel)*, *15*(19), 14165. DOI: 10.3390/su151914165

Pennino, D., Pizzonia, M., Vitaletti, A., & Zecchini, M. (2022). Blockchain as IoT Economy Enabler: A Review of Architectural Aspects. In *Journal of Sensor and Actuator Networks* (Vol. 11, Issue 2). DOI: 10.3390/jsan11020020

Peters, G. W., Panayi, E., & Chapelle, A. (2015). Trends in Crypto-Currencies and Blockchain Technologies: A Monetary Theory and Regulation Perspective. SSRN *Electronic Journal*. DOI: 10.2139/ssrn.2646618

Piotrowska, A. I., & Piotrowski, D. (2025). Green FinTech: A Consumer Awareness Study. *Sustainability (Basel)*, *17*(8), 3701. Advance online publication. DOI: 10.3390/su17083701

Platt, M., Pierangeli, F., Livan, G., & Righi, S. (2020, September). Facilitating the decentralised exchange of cryptocurrencies in an order-driven market. In *2020 2nd Conference on Blockchain Research & Applications for Innovative Networks and Services (BRAINS)* (pp. 30-34). IEEE. DOI: 10.1109/BRAINS49436.2020.9223286

Politou, E., Casino, F., Alepis, E., & Patsakis, C. (2019). Blockchain mutability: Challenges and proposed solutions. *IEEE Transactions on Emerging Topics in Computing*, *9*(4), 1972–1986. DOI: 10.1109/TETC.2019.2949510

Pólvora, A., Nascimento, S., Lourenço, J. S., & Scapolo, F. (2020). Blockchain for industrial transformations: A forward-looking approach with multi-stakeholder engagement for policy advice. *Technological Forecasting and Social Change*, *157*, 120091. DOI: 10.1016/j.techfore.2020.120091

Poonam, P. (2025). Application of Blockchain Technology in Secure DataTransmission for Autonomous Vehicle Systems. *Shodh Prakashan: Journal of Engineering & Scientific Research, 1*(1), 99–114.

Prakash, N., & Roy, L. K. W. (2024). Interpreting Bias in Large Language Models: A Feature-Based Approach. *arXiv preprint arXiv:2406.12347.*

Pramanik, S., Bag, S., & Roy, A. (2025). Grading the Blockchain Using Sharding. In *Blockchain Technology Applications in Knowledge Management* (pp. 269–292). IGI Global Scientific Publishing. DOI: 10.4018/979-8-3693-3956-5.ch009

Pratiwi, E. N. (2024). The Impact Of Central Bank Digital Currency (Cbdc) Volatility On Monetary Policy Efficiency In Financial Inclusion And Investment. *Journal of Social and Economics Research, 6*(2), 195–222. DOI: 10.54783/jser.v6i2.659

Priyadarshana, D., Ramachandra Rao, T., & Sambasiva Rao, M. (2024). AI and blockchain technology for secure and transparent financial transactions. *International Journal of Science and Research Archive, 2024*(01), 2013–2019. DOI: 10.30574/ijsra.2024.13.1.1845

Prodan, S., Konhäusner, P., Dabija, D. C., Lazaroiu, G., & Marincean, L. (2024). The rise in popularity of central bank digital currencies. A systematic review. *Heliyon, 10*(9), e30561. DOI: 10.1016/j.heliyon.2024.e30561 PMID: 38756603

Purwatiningsih, A., Purnamasari, S., Setyawati, H., Indriani, A., Prawitasari, D., & Fitria, S. (2024). Bibliometric Analysis of Islamic Crowdfunding: A Literature Review of Its Journey. *F1000Research, 13.* DOI: 10.12688/f1000research.146797.2

Puschmann, T., Hoffmann, C. H., & Khmarskyi, V. (2020). How green fintech can alleviate the impact of climate change—The case of Switzerland. *Sustainability (Basel), 12*(24), 1–28. DOI: 10.3390/su122410691

Puschmann, T., & Khmarskyi, V. (2024). Green fintech: Developing a research agenda. *Corporate Social Responsibility and Environmental Management, 31*(4), 2823–2837. DOI: 10.1002/csr.2675

Puthal, D., & Mohanty, S. P. (2019). Proof of Authentication: IoT-Friendly Blockchains. *IEEE Potentials, 38*(1), 26–29. DOI: 10.1109/MPOT.2018.2850541

Qatawneh, A. M., Lutfi, A., & Al Barrak, T. (2024). Effect of Artificial Intelligence (AI) on Financial Decision-Making: Mediating Role of Financial Technologies (Fin-Tech). *HighTech and Innovation Journal, 5*(3), 759–773. DOI: 10.28991/HIJ-2024-05-03-015

Qiang, Ye., & Zhang, Z. (2009). Sentiment classification of online reviews to travel destinations by supervised machine learning approaches. *Expert Systems with Applications*, *35*(3), 6527–6535. DOI: 10.1016/j.eswa.2008.07.035

Qin, K., Zhou, L., Afonin, Y., Lazzaretti, L., & Gervais, A. (2021). CeFi vs. DeFi—Comparing Centralized to Decentralized Finance. *arXiv preprint arXiv:2106.08157*.

Qin, F., Mickiewicz, T., & Estrin, S. (2022). Homophily and peer influence in early-stage new venture informal investment. *Small Business Economics*, *59*(1), 93–116. DOI: 10.1007/s11187-021-00523-3

Qiu, T., Zhang, R., & Gao, Y. (2019). Ripple vs. SWIFT: Transforming Cross Border Remittance Using Blockchain Technology. *Procedia Computer Science*, *147*, 428–434. Advance online publication. DOI: 10.1016/j.procs.2019.01.260

Qu, L., Wen, F., Huang, H., & Wang, Z. (2025). Aggregation-Chain: A Consortium Blockchain Based Multi-Chain Data Sharing Framework with Efficient Query. *Cluster Computing*, *28*(1), 46. Advance online publication. DOI: 10.1007/s10586-024-04777-w

Qu, Y., & Wang, J. (2024). Performance and biases of Large Language Models in public opinion simulation. *Humanities & Social Sciences Communications*, *11*(1), 1–13. DOI: 10.1057/s41599-024-03609-x

Rabbani, M. R., Alshaikh, A., Jreisat, A., Bashar, A., & Moh'd Ali, M. A. (2021, December). *Whether Cryptocurrency is a threat or a revolution? An analysis from ESG perspective. In 2021 international conference on sustainable Islamic business and finance*. IEEE.

Raddatz, N., Coyne, J., Menard, P., & Crossler, R. E. (2023). Becoming a blockchain user: Understanding consumers' benefits realisation to use blockchain-based applications. *European Journal of Information Systems*, *32*(2), 287–314. DOI: 10.1080/0960085X.2021.1944823

Radev, D. (2024). FINTECH AND THE FORESTRY INDUSTRY. In D. V Georgieva & A. P. Barcic (Eds.), *WoodEMA 2024 - Green Deal Initiatives, Sustainable Management, Market Demands, and New Production Perspectives in the Forestry-Based Sector - Proceedings of Scientific Papers* (pp. 119–124). WoodEMA, i.a. https://www.scopus.com/inward/record.uri?eid=2-s2.0-85196739914&partnerID=40&md5=ed203fa6349c7055f6c820e05b7d5b27

Rahayu, N., Widodo, A., & Hartono, M. (2021). The influence of herding behavior on investment decisions in the digital era. *International Journal of Financial Research*, *12*(2), 88–96. DOI: 10.5430/ijfr.v12n2p88

Rahman, J. A., Ooi, H. L., & Lee, C. K. (2025). Blockchain Architecture Adoption in Supply Chain Management: A DEMATEL-Based Analysis of Critical Factors. *Journal of Future Sustainability*, *5*(1), 41–58. Advance online publication. DOI: 10.5267/j.jfs.2025.2.004

Raimi, L., Adekunle, S. M., & Shabbir, M. S. (2023). Contemporary Discourse of Halal and Islamic Entrepreneurship: Trends and Future Opportunities. In *Contemporary Discourse of Halal and Islamic Entrepreneurship: Trends and Future Opportunities*. Springer Nature. DOI: 10.1007/978-981-99-6427-7

Rajasekaran, A. S., Azees, M., & Al-Turjman, F. (2022). A comprehensive survey on blockchain technology. *Sustainable Energy Technologies and Assessments, 52*, 102039. DOI: 10.1016/j.seta.2022.102039

Raju, A. B. A., & Raju, A. B. A. (2021). Digital Currency Issuance by Central Banks: CBDCs and Monetary Policy. [IJSR]. *International Journal of Science and Research (Raipur, India)*, *10*(11), 1587–1589. DOI: 10.21275/SR24914160743

Ram, P. (2024). Gen AI: Powering enterprise transformation through trust. *Dataquest, May 2024*, 52–54.

Raman, R., Ray, S., Das, D., & Nedungadi, P. (2024). Innovations and barriers in sustainable and green finance for advancing sustainable development goals. *Frontiers in Environmental Science*, *12*, 1513204. Advance online publication. DOI: 10.3389/fenvs.2024.1513204

Ranchordás, S., & Meoli, R. (2024). REGULATORY SANDBOXES FOR SUSTAINABLE FINANCE. *Law and Economics Yearly Review, 13*, 243–280. https://www.scopus.com/inward/record.uri?eid=2-s2.0-105005535965&partnerID=40&md5=95ce53d85952da0d7c821b0db90259e5

Rani, S., Kumar, N., Srivastva, A., & Sharma, A. (2024). Leveraging Artificial Intelligence and Machine Learning for Enhanced Privacy and Security. *2024 IEEE International Conference on Blockchain and Distributed Systems Security (ICBDS)*, 1–6. DOI: 10.1109/ICBDS61829.2024.10837569

Ranjithamani, D. A., Subbulakshmi, M. K., Harshini, T., Ramya, V., Aaron, T. S., & Srithar, T. B. (2025). Product Integrity Assurance on E-Marketplace Using Quantum Blockchain. In *Real-World Applications of Quantum Computers and Machine Intelligence* (pp. 155–164). IGI Global Scientific Publishing.

Rathod, V., Nabavirazavi, S., Zad, S., & Iyengar, S. S. (2025, January). Privacy and security challenges in large language models. In *2025 IEEE 15th Annual Computing and Communication Workshop and Conference (CCWC)* (pp. 00746-00752). IEEE. DOI: 10.1109/CCWC62904.2025.10903912

Rawat, A., & Ur Rahman, H. (2023). Implementation of algorithms for fixed deposit using smart contract. Journal of Emerging Technologies and Innovative Research (JETIR) JETIR, 10(6).

Rawat, A., & Verma, R. Enhancing the Security of Resource Constraints Devices Using Blockchain. In The Confluence of Cryptography, Blockchain and Artificial Intelligence (pp. 76-99). CRC Press. DOI: 10.1201/9781032711515-4

Rawat, A., Suryavanshi, R. S., Nagar, V., & Yadav, D. (2023, March). Blockchain Integration in Emergency Medical Transportation: Advancing Security and Coordination for Critical Care Scenarios. In Doctoral Symposium on Computational Intelligence (pp. 393-402). Singapore: Springer Nature Singapore.

Rawat, A., Suryavanshi, R. S., Nagar, V., & Yadav, D. (2023, November). Development of blockchain-enabled e-healthcare appointment system. In International Conference on Trends in Computational and Cognitive Engineering (pp. 359-369). Singapore: Springer Nature Singapore.

Rawat, A., Verma, R., & Suryavanshi, R. S. (2023, March). Blockchain Approach for Analyzing the Issues of IoT Systems. In Doctoral Symposium on Computational Intelligence (pp. 227-235). Singapore: Springer Nature Singapore.

Rawat, A., Verma, R., & Suryavanshi, R. S. (2025). The Introduction of Cryptography, Blockchain, and Artificial Intelligence in the Modern World of Computing. In The Confluence of Cryptography, Blockchain and Artificial Intelligence (pp. 1-19). CRC Press.

Rawat, A., & Rahman, D. H. U. (2023). Smart contract based approach for fixed deposit in blockchain networks with remix IDE. [IJCRT]. *International Journal of Creative Research Thoughts*, *11*(5).

Redzuan, N. H., Kassim, S., & Shaharuddin, S. S. (2024). Literature Review on Islamic Crowdfunding. In *Islamic Sustainable Finance: Policy, Risk and Regulation* (pp. 170–184). Taylor and Francis. DOI: 10.4324/9781003395447-20

Rehman, K. U., & Chen, R. (2025). The nexus between financial inclusion and energy efficiency in developed countries. *Quality & Quantity*, •••, 1–32. DOI: 10.1007/s11135-025-02139-1

Rejeb, A., Rejeb, K., Appolloni, A., & Treiblmaier, H. (2023). Navigating the crowdfunding landscape: A study of knowledge trajectories based on main path analysis. *European Journal of Innovation Management, 26*(7), 415–448. DOI: 10.1108/EJIM-03-2023-0201

Remolina, N. (2023). Generative AI in Finance: Risks and Potential Solutions. Social Science Research Network. https://doi.org/DOI: 10.2139/ssrn.4628235

Rey, W. P., & Rey, K. W. J. D. (2024, February). The Role of Mobile Wallets in Promoting Cashless Transactions: A Case Study of the Philippines. In *International Conference on E-Business and Applications* (pp. 155-170). Singapore: Springer Nature Singapore. DOI: 10.1007/978-981-97-3409-2_14

Ridho Kismawadi, E., M. Irfan, and S. M. A. R. Shah. (2023). "Revolutionizing Islamic Finance: Artificial Intelligence's Role in the Future of Industry." Pp. 184–207 in The Impact of AI Innovation on Financial Sectors in the Era of Industry 5.0.

Riefel, D. (2024). Social media exposure and its influence on individual investment decisions (Master's thesis, University of Twente).

Riva, G. M. (2020). What Happens in Blockchain Stays in Blockchain. A Legal Solution to Conflicts Between Digital Ledgers and Privacy Rights. *Frontiers in Blockchain, 3*, 36. Advance online publication. DOI: 10.3389/fbloc.2020.00036

Rizinski, M., Peshov, H., Mishev, K., Chitkushev, L. T., Vodenska, I., & Trajanov, D. (2022). Ethically Responsible Machine Learning in Fintech. *IEEE Access : Practical Innovations, Open Solutions, 10*, 97531–97554. DOI: 10.1109/ACCESS.2022.3202889

Rizwan, A., Naveed, S., Mustafa, F., Hanif, M. S., Khurshid, A., & Khan, T. Z. A. (2024). Prospects for institutionalization of crowdfunding: A developing country perspective. *Journal of Entrepreneurship and Public Policy, 13*(4), 566–598. DOI: 10.1108/JEPP-09-2023-0086

Roopalatha, H. (2024). Microsoft AI CEO is building AI companions for India. *CEO Insights, December 2024*, 16–17.

Roshanaei, M., Khan, M. R., & Sylvester, N. N. (2024). Navigating AI Cybersecurity: Evolving Landscape and Challenges. *Journal of Intelligent Learning Systems and Applications, 16*(03), 155–174. DOI: 10.4236/jilsa.2024.163010

Roth, J., Schär, F., & Schöpfer, A. (2019). The Tokenization of Assets: Using Blockchains for Equity Crowdfunding. SSRN *Electronic Journal*. DOI: 10.2139/ssrn.3443382

Rouhani, S., & Deters, R. (2021). Data trust framework using blockchain technology and adaptive transaction validation. *IEEE Access : Practical Innovations, Open Solutions*, *9*, 90379–90391. DOI: 10.1109/ACCESS.2021.3091327

Roy, J. K., & Vasa, L. (2025). Financial technology and environmental, social and governance in sustainable finance: A bibliometric and thematic content analysis. *Discover Sustainability*, *6*(1), 148. Advance online publication. DOI: 10.1007/s43621-025-00934-2

Roy, P. K. (2023). Enriching the green economy through sustainable investments: An ESG-based credit rating model for green financing. *Journal of Cleaner Production*, *420*, 138315. DOI: 10.1016/j.jclepro.2023.138315

Ryabov, O., Bobryshev, A., Lebedev, K., & Ryabov, D. (2021). Decentralized finance (DeFi) as the basis for the transformation of the financial sector of the future. *14 Oct. 2021*. https://doi.org/DOI: 10.1145/3527049.3527080

Ryll, L., Barton, M. E., Zhang, B. Z., McWaters, R. J., Schizas, E., Hao, R., Bear, K., Preziuso, M., Seger, E., Wardrop, R., Rau, P. R., Debata, P., Rowan, P., Adams, N., Gray, M., & Yerolemou, N. (2020, February 4). Transforming Paradigms: A Global AI in Financial Services Survey. Papers.*ssrn*.com. https://papers.ssrn.com/sol3/papers.cfm?abstract_id=3532038 DOI: 10.2139/ssrn.3532038

Sabharwal, C. L., & Anjum, B. (2018) 'Robo-Revolution in the Financial Sector', in *2018 International Conference on Computational Science and Computational Intelligence (CSCI). 2018 International Conference on Computational Science and Computational Intelligence (CSCI)*, Las Vegas, NV, USA: IEEE, pp. 1289–1292. Available at: DOI: 10.1109/CSCI46756.2018.00249

Sachan, S., Almaghrabi, F., Yang, J.-B., & Xu, D.-L. (2024). Human-AI collaboration to mitigate decision noise in financial underwriting: A study on FinTech innovation in a lending firm. *International Review of Financial Analysis*, *93*, 103149. DOI: 10.1016/j.irfa.2024.103149

Sachdeva, P., Rawal, R., & Sharma, V. (2025). *The Significance of Generative AI in Enhancing Fraud Detection and Prevention Within the Banking Industry*. Wiley., DOI: 10.1002/9781394271078.ch9

Sagala, Y. P., Juniawan, M. A., Effendy, V. A., Putrianasari, R., Nuraini, W., Rahmatika, V. A., Shihab, M. R., & Ranti, B. (2022). Digital transformation impact analysis towards transition in the role of information technology for organization in new digital bank. In *Proceedings of the 7th International Conference on Informatics and Computing (ICIC)* (pp. 1–6). https://doi.org/DOI: 10.1109/ICIC56845.2022.10007003

Said, A., & Angelita, M. (2020). Determining factors for the success of banking digital transformation. In *Proceedings of the 8th International Conference on Advanced Research in Business* (pp. 238–241). https://doi.org/DOI: 10.2991/aebmr.k.200812.041

Saif, M. Bin, Migliorini, S., & Spoto, F. (2024). A Survey on Data Availability in Layer 2 Blockchain Rollups: Open Challenges and Future Improvements. *Future Internet 2024, Vol. 16, Page 315, 16*(9), 315. DOI: 10.3390/fi16090315

Sakho, S., Jianbiao, Z., Essaf, F., & Badiss, K. (2019). Improving Banking Transactions Using Blockchain Technology. *2019 IEEE 5th International Conference on Computer and Communications, ICCC 2019*. DOI: 10.1109/ICCC47050.2019.9064344

Sakib, S. K., Das, A. B., & Ahmed, S. (2025). Battling misinformation: An empirical study on adversarial factuality in open-source large language models. *arXiv preprint arXiv:2503.10690*. DOI: 10.18653/v1/2025.trustnlp-main.28

Sakiz, B. (2019). New financial technologies, cryptocurrencies, blockchain, and challenges. In *Handbook of Research on Creating Sustainable Value in the Global Economy* (pp. 85–102). IGI Global., DOI: 10.4018/978-1-7998-1196-1.ch006

Saleem, M., & Chawla, C. (2023, December). Blockchain-Powered Decentralized Finance (DeFi): Transforming Financial Inclusion & Investment Landscapes. In *2023 12th International Conference on System Modeling & Advancement in Research Trends (SMART)* (pp. 342-346). IEEE.

Salerno, D., Gatto, A., & Russo, S. (2024). New data and descriptor for crowdfunding and renewable energy. *Quality & Quantity, 58*(5), 4703–4713. DOI: 10.1007/s11135-024-01850-9

Samuel-Okon, A. D., & Abejide, O. O. (2024). Bridging the Digital Divide: Exploring the Role of Artificial Intelligence and Automation in Enhancing Connectivity in Developing Nations. *Journal of Engineering Research and Reports, 26*(6), 165–177. DOI: 10.9734/jerr/2024/v26i61170

Santibanez Gonzalez, E. D. R., Kandpal, V., Ozili, P. K., & Chatterjee, P. (2024). Fintech for ESG and the Circular Economy. In *Fintech for Esg and the Circular Economy*. wiley. DOI: 10.1002/9781394234035

Saravanakrishnan, V., Nandhini, M., & Palanivelu, P. (2024). DeFi's Transformative Influence on the Global Financial Landscape. In *Digital Technologies, Ethics, and Decentralization in the Digital Era* (pp. 99-120). IGI Global. DOI: 10.4018/979-8-3693-1762-4.ch006

Sarea, A., Subramanian, S., Alareeni, B., Shaikh, Z. H., Hawaldar, I. T., & Elshaker, A. H. (2021). Financial Disclosures by Using Machine Learning Analysis. In Alareeni, B., Hamdan, A., & Elgedawy, I. (Eds.), *The Importance of New Technologies and Entrepreneurship in Business Development: In The Context of Economic Diversity in Developing Countries. ICBT 2020. Lecture Notes in Networks and Systems* (Vol. 194). Springer., DOI: 10.1007/978-3-030-69221-6_5

Sarma, M., & Pais, J. (2011). Financial inclusion and development. *Journal of International Development*, *23*(5), 613–628. DOI: 10.1002/jid.1698

Savelyev, A. (2017). Contract law 2.0: 'Smart' contracts as the beginning of the end of classic contract law. *Information & Communications Technology Law*, *26*(2), 116–134. Advance online publication. DOI: 10.1080/13600834.2017.1301036

Saxena, A., & Rishi, B. (2025). Designing an artificial intelligence-enabled large language model for financial decisions. *Management Decision*. Advance online publication. DOI: 10.1108/MD-02-2024-0305

Scardovi, C. (2017). *Digital transformation in financial services* (Vol. 236). Springer International Publishing. DOI: 10.1007/978-3-319-66945-8

Schär, F. (2021). Decentralized finance: On blockchain-and smart contract-based financial markets. *FRB of St. Louis Review*.

Schueffel, P. (2021). Defi: Decentralized finance-an introduction and overview. *Journal of Innovation Management*, *9*(3), I–XI. DOI: 10.24840/2183-0606_009.003_0001

Sebai, M., Talbi, O., & Guerchi-Mehri, H. (2025). Optimal financial inclusion for financial stability: Empirical insight from developing countries. *Finance Research Letters*, *71*, 106467. DOI: 10.1016/j.frl.2024.106467

Sengar, S. S., Hasan, A. B., Kumar, S., & Carroll, F. (2024). Generative artificial intelligence: A systematic review and applications [Preprint]. *Multimedia Tools and Applications*. Advance online publication. DOI: 10.1007/s11042-024-20016-1

Sethi, M., Bohra, N. S., Johri, A., & Asif, M. (2025). Emerging dimensions in Fintech: Insights from bibliometric analysis. *Digital Business*, *5*(1), 100113. Advance online publication. DOI: 10.1016/j.digbus.2025.100113

Sevin, A., & Osman Mohammed, A. A. (2024). Comparative Study of Blockchain Hashing Algorithms with a Proposal for HashLEA. *Applied Sciences (Basel, Switzerland)*, *14*(24), 11967. DOI: 10.3390/app142411967

Shah, D. (2024). AI in FinTech: Revolutionizing the customer experience and driving innovation. *Silicon India, June 2024*, 36–37.

Shah, K., Lathiya, D., Lukhi, N., Parmar, K., & Sanghvi, H. (2023). A systematic review of decentralized finance protocols. *International Journal of Intelligent Networks*, *4*, 171–181. DOI: 10.1016/j.ijin.2023.07.002

Shaikh, Z. H., Sarea, A., & Irfan, M. (2022). *Islamic Banking Strategies in the World of Fintech: Success Story of Bahrain* (Vol. 423). Springer., DOI: 10.1007/978-3-030-93464-4_10

Shaikh, Z., Irfan, M., Sarea, A., & Panigrahi, R. R. (2024). *The Emergence of Islamic Fintech and Bahrain: Prospect for Global Financial Sectors* (Vol. 503). Springer., DOI: 10.1007/978-3-031-43490-7_52

Shamugasamy, K. (2024). Enhancing Payment Settlement Processes Through Generative AI. *International Journal for Multidisciplinary Research (IJFMR)*. www.ijfmr.com

Shang, S., Du, X., Wang, X., & Liu, A. (2025). Private Approximate Nearest Neighbor Search for On-Chain Data Based on Locality-Sensitive Hashing. *Future Generation Computer Systems*, *164*, 107586. Advance online publication. DOI: 10.1016/j.future.2024.107586

Shankar, V. (2018). How Artificial Intelligence (AI) is Reshaping Retailing. *Journal of Retailing*, *94*(4), vi–xi. DOI: 10.1016/S0022-4359(18)30076-9

Shao, Q. F., Jin, C. Q., Zhang, Z., Qian, W. N., & Zhou, A. Y. (2018). Blockchain: Architecture and Research Progress. In *Jisuanji Xuebao/Chinese Journal of Computers* (Vol. 41, Issue 5). DOI: 10.11897/SP.J.1016.2018.00969

Sharma, R., Vasishta, P., & Singla, A. (2025). Impact of green banking awareness on green FinTech adoption: A way towards profitable and sustainable practices. *Managerial Finance*, *51*(3), 377–394. DOI: 10.1108/MF-04-2024-0272

Sharma, V., Gupta, M., Arora, N., & Shaikh, A. A. (2025). FinTech and Financial Inclusion: Leveraging Digital Finance for Economic Empowerment and Sustainable Growth. In *FinTech and Financial Inclusion: Leveraging Digital Finance for Economic Empowerment and Sustainable Growth*. Taylor and Francis., DOI: 10.4324/9781003514114

Shefrin, H. (2000). *Beyond greed and fear: Understanding behavioral finance and the psychology of investing*. Harvard Business School Press.

Shi, Y., & Yang, B. (2025). China's energy system building toward an era of resilience: How green fintech can empower? *International Review of Economics & Finance*, *98*, 103876. Advance online publication. DOI: 10.1016/j.iref.2025.103876

Shkodina, I., Derid, I., & Zelenko, O. (2019). Digital transformation of global banking: Challenges and prospects. *Financial and Credit Activity: Problems of Theory and Practice, 3*(30). Advance online publication. DOI: 10.18371/fcaptp.v3i30.179680

Shukla, R., & Sawai, C. (2023). Policy implication of green finance. In *The Sustainable Fintech Revolution: Building a Greener Future for Finance* (pp. 114–144). IGI Global., DOI: 10.4018/979-8-3693-0008-4.ch007

Si Mohammed, K., Serret, V., Ben Jabeur, S., & Nobanee, H. (2024). The role of artificial intelligence and fintech in promoting eco-friendly investments and non-greenwashing practices in the US market. *Journal of Environmental Management, 359*, 120977. DOI: 10.1016/j.jenvman.2024.120977 PMID: 38678903

Sibindi, A. B. (2025). Final Synthesis and Future Directions. In *Advances in African Economic, Social and Political Development: Vol. Part F326* (pp. 183–185). Springer Nature. DOI: 10.1007/978-3-031-86516-9_10

Silber, D., Hoffmann, A. and Belli, A. (2025), "Embracing AI advisors for making (complex) financial decisions: an experimental investigation of the role of a maximizing decision-making style", *International Journal of Bank Marketing*, Vol. ahead-of-print No. ahead-of-print. https://doi.org/.DOI: 10.1108/IJBM-10-2024-0647

Singh, P. (2025, April 11). *AI and Financial Risk Management Revolutionizing Risk Assessment and Mitigation*. https://doi.org/DOI: 10.4018/979-8-3373-1200-2.ch019

Singh, R. P., Rawat, A., & Verma, R. (2025). Application of Cryptography and Deep Learning for Smart Environments. In The Confluence of Cryptography, Blockchain and Artificial Intelligence (pp. 244-263). CRC Press. DOI: 10.1201/9781032711515-12

Singh, C. (2025). Is generative AI (artificial intelligence) the next advent in the evolution of finance and navigating financial crime and regulation? *Journal of Financial Crime, 32*(3), 751–759. DOI: 10.1108/JFC-07-2024-0232

Singh, R., Singh, A., & Singh, R. P. (2025). Constructing a Hierarchical Model Based on the Blockchain in Health Care. In *International Conference on Cognitive Computing and Cyber Physical Systems* (pp. 567-577). Springer, Singapore. DOI: 10.1007/978-981-97-7371-8_44

Soavi, M. (2022). From legal contracts to formal specifications.

Sohail, M., Khan, S., Akbar, A., & Svobodova, L. (2024). Empowering sustainable development: The crucial nexus of green fintech and green finance in Luxembourg's banking sector. *Journal of Infrastructure. Policy and Development, 8*(7), 4979. Advance online publication. DOI: 10.24294/jipd.v8i7.4979

Som, A., & Kayal, P. (2022). Ai, blockchain, and iot. In *Digitalization and the Future of Financial Services: Innovation and Impact of Digital Finance* (pp. 141–161). Springer International Publishing. DOI: 10.1007/978-3-031-11545-5_8

Somda, M. M. Y. G., Ouya, S., & Mendy, G. (2025, January). Central bank digital currency design architecture: a systematic review using text mining. In *Third International Conference on Communications, Information System, and Data Science (CISDS 2024)* (Vol. 13519, pp. 144-151). SPIE. DOI: 10.1117/12.3057590

Song, Y., Sun, C., Peng, Y., Zeng, Y., & Sun, B. (2022). Research on Multidimensional Trust Evaluation Mechanism of FinTech Based on Blockchain. *IEEE Access : Practical Innovations, Open Solutions*, *10*, 57025–57036. DOI: 10.1109/ACCESS.2022.3177275

Soni, A., Shaikh, Z. H., Irfan, M., & Bijja, V. (2025). Indigenous Empowerment as a Catalyst for Sustainable Development. In Irfan, M., Majeed, M., Kassim, S., & Ofori, K. (Eds.), *The Future of Indigenous Inclusivity: Unlocking Finance for Economic Development* (pp. 253–274). IGI Global Scientific Publishing., DOI: 10.4018/979-8-3693-7924-0.ch012

Sood, K., Sharma, V., & Kumar, R. (2024, October). Unveiling Risks in Decentralized Finance: A Systematic Literature Review. In *2nd International Conference on Emerging Technologies and Sustainable Business Practices-2024 (ICETSBP 2024)* (pp. 320-340). Atlantis Press. DOI: 10.2991/978-94-6463-544-7_21

Soualhi, Y., & Hasan Saleh, A. O. (2024). SMART CONTRACTS AND THEIR APPLICATION PROSPECTS IN SOCIAL BANKING: A MAQASID JURISPRUDENTIAL PERSPECTIVE. *Malaysian Journal of Syariah and Law*, *12*(2), 490–510. DOI: 10.33102/mjsl.vol12no2.599

Soundararajan, R., & Shenbagaraman, V. M. (2024). Enhancing financial decision-making through explainable AI and Blockchain integration: Improving transparency and trust in predictive models. *Educational Administration: Theory and Practice*, *30*(4), 9341–9351.

Springler, E. (2024). A neoliberal agenda: decentralized financial innovation to enhance sustainable finance. In *Understanding Green Finance* (pp. 134–145). Edward Elgar Publishing. DOI: 10.4337/9781803927558.00018

Spytska, A. (2024). Overconfidence bias in Gen Z investors and the role of AI-enhanced education. *Journal of Youth Finance and Technology*, *3*(1), 22–35.

Stark, J. (2020). Digital transformation at a bank. In Stark, J. (Ed.), *Management science* (Vol. 3, pp. 67–72). Springer., DOI: 10.1007/978-3-030-41001-8_11

Statman, M. (1995). Behavioral finance: Past battles and future engagements. *Financial Analysts Journal*, *51*(6), 18–27. DOI: 10.2469/faj.v55.n6.2311

Stewart, H., & Jürjens, J. (2018). Data security and consumer trust in FinTech innovation in Germany. *Information and Computer Security*, *26*(1), 109–128. DOI: 10.1108/ICS-06-2017-0039

Stone, M., Aravopoulou, E., Ekinci, Y., Evans, G., Hobbs, M., Labib, A., Laughlin, P., Machtynger, J., & Machtynger, L. (2020). Artificial intelligence (AI) in strategic marketing decision-making: A research agenda. *The Bottom Line (New York, N.Y.)*, *33*(2), 183–200. DOI: 10.1108/BL-03-2020-0022

Stone, P. J., Dunphy, D. C., Smith, M. S., & Ogilvie, D. M. (1967). *The General Inquirer: A Computer Approach to Content Analysis*. MIT Press.

Subedi, D. P., & Bhandari, D. R. (2024). Assessing the Role of Digital Literacy in Investment Decisions among Graduate Business Students in Nepal: The Mediating Effects of Peer Group Influence. Multi-Disciplinary Explorations. *The Kasthamandap College Journal*, *2*(2), 47–62.

Subramaniam, Y., Loganathan, N., Khan, F. N. H. T., & Subramaniam, T. (2024). Exploring the Impact of Artificial Intelligence on Financial Inclusion: Cross-Country Analysis. *Social Indicators Research*, •••, 1–18. DOI: 10.1007/s11205-024-03380-1

Sulastri, L. (2023). The Role of Artificial Intelligence in Enhancing Customer Experience: A Case Study of Global E-commerce Platforms. *The International Journal of Science in Society*, *5*(3), 451–469. DOI: 10.54783/ijsoc.v5i3.1257

Sulhia, B. A., Handajani, L., & Surasni, N. K. (2022). The effect of financial literacy, herding behaviour, and overconfidence on investment decisions in the millennial generation. *Traektoriâ Nauki = Path of Science, 8*(7), 1030–1034.

Sundharesalingam, P., Somasundaram, R., Sushmitha, S. S. S., Rithanya, R., & Archana, M. (2025). AI Enhanced FinTech Strategies for Driving ESG Investments in Sustainable Finance. In A. Bajaj, A. Abraham, K. R. Madhavi, & O. Castillo (Eds.), *Lecture Notes in Networks and Systems: Vol. 1247 LNNS* (pp. 221–228). Springer Science and Business Media Deutschland GmbH. DOI: 10.1007/978-3-031-81086-2_24

Surve, T., Tyagi, A., & Kaur, G. (2023). The Governance Layer of The Leading Defi Protocols: A Review of The Literature. *International Journal of Advanced Research in Engineering and Technology*, *14*(7), 48–73.

Svoboda, A. (2024). *Scholars Journal of Economics, Business and Management Central Bank Digital Currencies (CBDCs) and Financial Inclusion: Explore How CBDCs Can Promote Financial Inclusion for Unbanked or Underbanked Populations, Considering both Benefits and Challenges*. DOI: 10.36347/sjebm.2024.v11i05.002

Syarif, M. F., & Aysan, A. F. (2024). Sharia crowdfunding in Indonesia: a regulatory environment perspective. *Journal of Science and Technology Policy Management*. DOI: 10.1108/JSTPM-07-2023-0108

Taboada, M., Brooke, J., Tofiloski, M., Voll, K., & Stede, M. (2011). Lexicon-based methods for sentiment analysis. *Computational Linguistics*, *37*(2), 267–307. DOI: 10.1162/COLI_a_00049

Taghizadeh-Hesary, F. (2025). The impact of artificial intelligence adoption and financial accessibility on energy sustainability. *Energy Strategy Reviews*, *59*, 101744. Advance online publication. DOI: 10.1016/j.esr.2025.101744

Tajudin, M., Omar, R., Smedlund, A., & Aziz, R. P. (2020). Financing with heart and intelligence: augmenting intimacy and sustainability through islamic fintech. *International Journal of Advanced Science and Technology, 29*(9 Special Issue), 1638–1664. https://www.scopus.com/inward/record.uri?eid=2-s2.0-85084368157&partnerID=40&md5=c195213f22e8b1fa570194ac7037a627

Tamasiga, P., Onyeaka, H., & Ouassou, E. H. (2022). Unlocking the Green Economy in African Countries: An Integrated Framework of FinTech as an Enabler of the Transition to Sustainability. *Energies*, *15*(22), 8658. Advance online publication. DOI: 10.3390/en15228658

Taneja, S., Bansal, N., & Kumar, P. (2023). Tech-driven sustainability: Fintech innovations revolutionizing green banking. In *Green Management - A New Paradigm in the World of Business* (pp. 185–203). Nova Science Publishers, Inc., https://www.scopus.com/inward/record.uri?eid=2-s2.0-85183523311&partnerID=40&md5=1184f038fcfdd472ca2c523f6294b7c2

Tang, Y., Xiong, J., Becerril-Arreola, R., & Iyer, L. (2020). Ethics of blockchain: A framework of technology, applications, impacts, and research directions. *Information Technology & People*, *33*(2), 602–632. DOI: 10.1108/ITP-10-2018-0491

Taufiq, R., Hidayanto, A. N., & Prabowo, H. (2018, September). The affecting factors of blockchain technology adoption of payments systems in Indonesia banking industry. In *2018 International Conference on Information Management and Technology (ICIMTech)* (pp. 506-510). IEEE. DOI: 10.1109/ICIMTech.2018.8528104

Tepe, G., Geyikci, U. B., & Sancak, F. M. (2022). FinTech Companies: A Bibliometric Analysis. *International Journal of Financial Studies*, *10*(1), 2. Advance online publication. DOI: 10.3390/ijfs10010002

Teubner, T., Flath, C. M., Weinhardt, C., van der Aalst, W., & Hinz, O. (2023). Welcome to the Era of ChatGPT et al. *Business & Information Systems Engineering*, *65*(2), 95–101. https://doi.org/. DOI: 10.1007/s12599-023-00795-x

Therry, A. C. D., Ardiansyah, R., Pusadan, M. Y., Joefrie, Y. Y., & Kasim, A. A. (2024). The Implementation and Analysis of The Proof of Work Consensus in Blockchain. *Advance Sustainable Science, Engineering and Technology*, *6*(1), 02401018. Advance online publication. DOI: 10.26877/asset.v6i1.17878

Thommandru, A., & Chakka, D. B. (2023). Recalibrating the Banking Sector with Blockchain Technology for Effective Anti-Money Laundering Compliances by Banks. *Sustainable Futures : An Applied Journal of Technology, Environment and Society*, *5*, 100107. DOI: 10.1016/j.sftr.2023.100107

Thong, M. S. (2025). Blockchain Drive for Financial Inclusion. In *Blockchain for Financial Governance in Malaysia and Singapore: Transforming Regulatory and Shariah Compliance to Drive Financial Inclusion* (pp. 139–176). Springer Nature Singapore. DOI: 10.1007/978-981-96-1281-9_4

Thuraisamy, K. S., Baig, Z., & Zeadally, S. (2025). Generative Artificial Intelligence in Financial Services: Opportunities, Challenges, and Cyberthreats. *IT Professional*, *27*(2), 35–41. DOI: 10.1109/MITP.2025.3534270

Tikhomirov, S. (2018). Ethereum: State of knowledge and research perspectives. *Lecture Notes in Computer Science (Including Subseries Lecture Notes in Artificial Intelligence and Lecture Notes in Bioinformatics), 10723 LNCS*. DOI: 10.1007/978-3-319-75650-9_14

Tiku, N. (2022, June 11). The Google engineer who thinks the company's AI has come to life. Washington Post; The Washington Post. https://www.washingtonpost.com/technology/2022/06/11/google-ai-lamda-blake-lemoine/

Tiwari, S., Agarwal, P., & Singh, R. (2023). The impact of digital transformation on workforce engagement in Indian banking sector. *Journal of Information & Optimization Sciences*, *44*(2), 15–28. DOI: 10.47974/JIOS-1305

Toshniwal, R., Sethi, A., & Jangir, K. (2025). Applications of Generative AI in Fintech. IGI Global. https://www.igi-global.com/chapter/applications-of-generative-ai-in-fintech/368343

Trautman, L. J. (2016). Is disruptive blockchain technology the future of financial services?.

Treleaven, P., Gendal Brown, R., & Yang, D. (2017). Blockchain Technology in Finance. *Computer*, *50*(9), 14–17. DOI: 10.1109/MC.2017.3571047

Trestioreanu, L., Shbair, W. M., De Cristo, F. S., & State, R. (2023). XRP-NDN overlay: Improving the Communication Efficiency of Consensus-Validation based Blockchains with an NDN Overlay. *Proceedings of IEEE/IFIP Network Operations and Management Symposium 2023, NOMS 2023*. DOI: 10.1109/NOMS56928.2023.10154402

Tripathi, G., Ahad, M. A., & Casalino, G. (2023). A comprehensive review of blockchain technology: Underlying principles and historical background with future challenges. *Decision Analytics Journal*, *9*, 100344. DOI: 10.1016/j.dajour.2023.100344

Truong, Y., & McColl, R. (2011). Intrinsic motivations, self-esteem, and luxury goods consumption. *Journal of Retailing and Consumer Services*, *18*(6), 555–561. DOI: 10.1016/j.jretconser.2011.08.004

Tseng, M.-L., Bui, T.-D., Lim, M. K., Tsai, F. M., & Tan, R. R. (2021). Comparing world regional sustainable supply chain finance using big data analytics: A bibliometric analysis. *Industrial Management & Data Systems*, *121*(3), 657–700. DOI: 10.1108/IMDS-09-2020-0521

Turi, A. N. (Ed.). (2023). *Financial technologies and DeFi: A revisit to the digital finance revolution*. Springer Nature. DOI: 10.1007/978-3-031-17998-3

Turney, P. D., & Littman, M. L. (2002). Unsupervised learning of semantic orientation from a hundred-billion-word corpus, *Technical Report EGB-1094, National Research Council Canada*. https://doi.org/DOI: 10.48550/arXiv.cs/0212012

Turney, P. D. (2002). Thumbs up or thumbs down? Semantic orientation applied to unsupervised classification of reviews. In *Proceedings: 40*th *Annual Meeting of Association for Computational Linguistics (ACL '02)* (pp. 417-424). DOI: 10.3115/1073083.1073153

Tyagi, R. (2019). Un-chaining the telecom with blockchain. *Enterprise IT World, June 2019*, 30–32.

Udvaros, J., Forman, N., & Avornicului, S. M. (2023). Agile Storyboard and Software Development Leveraging Smart Contract Technology in Order to Increase Stakeholder Confidence. *Electronics (Basel)*, *12*(2), 426. Advance online publication. DOI: 10.3390/electronics12020426

Ukanwa, K. (2024). Algorithmic bias: Social science research integration through the 3-D Dependable AI Framework. *Current Opinion in Psychology*, *58*, 101836. DOI: 10.1016/j.copsyc.2024.101836 PMID: 38981371

Utami, R., & Soesetyo, H. (2023). The important role of education in moderating the impact of perceived security, social influence, and platform reputation on investment intention on SMEs with peer-to-peer lending platform. *International Journal of The Newest Social and Management Research*, *1*(1), 1–11.

Uzougbo, N. S., Ikegwu, C. G., & Adewusi, A. O.Ngozi Samuel UzougboChinonso Gladys IkegwuAdefolake Olachi Adewusi. (2024). Regulatory frameworks for decentralized finance (DEFI): Challenges and opportunities. *GSC Advanced Research and Reviews*, *19*(2), 116–129. DOI: 10.30574/gscarr.2024.19.2.0170

Vaigandla, K. K., Siluveru, M., Kesoju, M., & Karne, R. (2023). Review on Blockchain Technology: Architecture, Characteristics, Benefits, Algorithms, Challenges and Applications. In *Mesopotamian Journal of CyberSecurity* (Vol. 2023). DOI: 10.58496/MJCS/2023/012

Vaquero, R. (2023). Literature review of credit card fraud detection with machine learning. *Tuni.fi.* https://trepo.tuni.fi/handle/10024/152542

Vasquez, H. E. (2023). The effects of social media on investment decisions within an online community (Doctoral dissertation, Northcentral University).

Vaswani, A., Shazeer, N., Parmar, N., Uszkoreit, J., Jones, L., Gomez, A. N., & Kaiser, L. (2017). Attention is all you need. *Proceedings of the 31st Conference on Neural Information Processing Systems (NIPS 2017),* Long Beach, CA, USA.,6000-6010

Velikonja, U. (2012). The cost of securities fraud. *William and Mary Law Review*, *54*, 1887.

Velmurugadass, P., Dhanasekaran, S., Anand, S. S., & Vasudevan, V. (2021). Enhancing Blockchain security in cloud computing with IoT environment using ECIES and cryptography hash algorithm. *Materials Today: Proceedings*, *37*, 2653–2659. DOI: 10.1016/j.matpr.2020.08.519

Verma, P., Srivastava, R., & Kumar, S. (2025). Blockchain Technology: Applications and Challenges. *Blockchain for IoT Systems*, 1-12.

View of Enhancing Market Trend Analysis Through AI Forecasting Models. (2025). IaicPublisher.org.https://iiast.iaicpublisher.org/ijcitsm/index.php/IJCITSM/article/view/162/94

View of Review on Blockchain Technology: Architecture, Characteristics, Benefits, Algorithms, Challenges and Applications. (2024). Mesopotamian.press. https://journals.mesopotamian.press/index.php/CyberSecurity/article/view/68/86

Vikas, N., Venegas, P., & Aiyer, S. (2022). Role of Banks and Other Financial Institutions in Enhancing Green Digital Finance. In *Economics, Law, and Institutions in Asia Pacific* (pp. 329–352). Springer. DOI: 10.1007/978-981-19-2662-4_16

Von Arx, T., Tran, M., & Vanbever, L. (2023). Revelio: A Network-Level Privacy Attack in the Lightning Network. *Proceedings - 8th IEEE European Symposium on Security and Privacy, Euro S and P 2023*, 942–957. DOI: 10.1109/EuroSP57164.2023.00060

Vovchenko, N. G., Zenin, K. A., Spiridonov, S. P., & Kuznetsov, V. P. (2023). Managing the Development of Climate-Responsible Entrepreneurship in the Digital Economy Markets in Fintech. In *Environmental Footprints and Eco-Design of Products and Processes* (pp. 219–227). Springer., DOI: 10.1007/978-3-031-28457-1_23

Vuletić, M., Prenzel, F., & Cucuringu, M. (2024). Fin-GAN: Forecasting and classifying financial time series via generative adversarial networks. *Quantitative Finance*, *24*(2), 175–199. DOI: 10.1080/14697688.2023.2299466

Walunj, V., Rajaraman, V., Dutta, J., & Sharma, A. (2025). Integrating Crypto-Based Payment Systems for Data Marketplaces: Enhancing Efficiency, Security, and User Autonomy. In *International Conference on Information Systems Security* (pp. 443-452). Springer, Cham. DOI: 10.1007/978-3-031-80020-7_25

Wamba, S. F., Gunasekaran, A., Akter, S., Ren, S. J., Dubey, R., & Childe, S. J. (2017). Big data analytics and firm performance: Effects of dynamic capabilities. *Journal of Business Research*, *70*, 356–365. DOI: 10.1016/j.jbusres.2016.08.009

Wang, X., Yu, C., & Wei, Y. (2012). Social media peer communication and impacts on purchase intentions: A consumer socialization framework. *Journal of Interactive Marketing*, *26*(4), 198–208. DOI: 10.1016/j.intmar.2011.11.004

We.trade. (n.d.). Www.ibm.com. https://www.ibm.com/case-studies/wetrade-blockchain-fintech-trade-finance

Weber, P., Carl, K. V., & Hinz, O. (2024). Applications of Explainable Artificial Intelligence in Finance—A systematic review of Finance, Information Systems, and Computer Science literature. *Management Review Quarterly*, *74*(2), 867–907. DOI: 10.1007/s11301-023-00320-0

Wei, F., Xie, B., & Chen, M. (2025). Digital financial inclusion, e-commerce development and entrepreneurial activity. *International Review of Financial Analysis, 97*, 103806. DOI: 10.1016/j.irfa.2024.103806

Weingärtner, T., Fasser, F., Reis Sá da Costa, P., & Farkas, W. (2023). Deciphering DeFi: A Comprehensive Analysis and Visualization of Risks in Decentralized Finance. *Journal of Risk and Financial Management, 16*(10), 454. DOI: 10.3390/jrfm16100454

Werth, O., Schwarzbach, C., Rodríguez Cardona, D., Breitner, M., & Graf von der Schulenburg, J. (2020). Influencing factors for the digital transformation in the financial services sector. *Zeitschrift für die gesamte Versicherungswissenschaft, 109*(1), 155–179. https://doi.org/DOI: 10.1007/s12297-020-00486-6

Wessel, M., Adam, M., Benlian, A., & Majchrzak, A. (n.d.). Journal of Management Information Systems Generative AI and its Transformative Value for Digital Platforms Guest Editors. https://www.jmis-web.org/cfps/JMIS_SI_CfP_Generative_AI.pdf

Wessel, M., Gleasure, R., & Kauffman, R. J. (2021). Sustainability of Rewards-Based Crowdfunding: A Quasi-Experimental Analysis of Funding Targets and Backer Satisfaction. *Journal of Management Information Systems, 38*(3), 612–646. DOI: 10.1080/07421222.2021.1987622

Westermeier, C. (2024). The digital euro: A materialization of (in)security. *Review of International Political Economy, 31*(5), 1569–1592. Advance online publication. DOI: 10.1080/09692290.2024.2345613

West, J., & Bhattacharya, M. (2016). Intelligent financial fraud detection: A comprehensive review. *Computers & Security, 57*, 47–66. DOI: 10.1016/j.cose.2015.09.005

Whitford, A. B., & Anderson, D. (2021). Governance landscapes for emerging technologies: The case of cryptocurrencies. *Regulation & Governance, 15*(4), 1053–1070. DOI: 10.1111/rego.12366

Wieandt, A., & Heppding, L. (2023). Centralized and decentralized finance: Coexistence or convergence? In *The Fintech Disruption: How Financial Innovation Is Transforming the Banking Industry* (pp. 11–51). Springer International Publishing. DOI: 10.1007/978-3-031-23069-1_2

Wilson, H., & Daugherty, P. (2019). Collaborative intelligence: Humans and AI are joining forces. In Artificial Intelligence, Data Analytics, and the New Machine Age (pp. 161–180). Harvard Business Review Press.

Wilson, T., Wiebe, J., & Hoffmann, P. (2005). Recognising contextual polarity in phrase-level sentiment analysis. In Proceedings: Conf. on Human Language Technology and Empirical Methods in Natural Language Processing (HLT'05) (pp. 347-354). DOI: 10.3115/1220575.1220619

Winasis, S., Djumarno, D., Riyanto, S., & Ariyanto, E. (2021). The effect of transformational leadership climate on employee engagement during digital transformation. *International Journal of Data and Network Science*, *5*(3), 475–482. DOI: 10.5267/j.ijdns.2021.3.001

Wiwoho, J., Trinugroho, I., Kharisma, D. B., & Suwadi, P. (2024). Islamic Crypto Assets and Regulatory Framework: Evidence from Indonesia and Global Approaches. *International Journal of Law and Management*, *66*(2), 155–171. DOI: 10.1108/IJLMA-03-2023-0051

Wong, M. C. S., Chan, E. K. H., & Yousaf, I. (2025). CBDCs, regulated stablecoins and tokenized traditional assets under the Basel Committee rules on cryptoassets. *Journal of Financial Regulation and Compliance*, *33*(1), 31–47. DOI: 10.1108/JFRC-03-2024-0050

World Bank. (2021). *Trends in the global cost of sending $200 in remittances*. World Bank. https://remittanceprices.worldbank.org/sites/default/files/rpw_main_report_and_annex_q221.pdf

Worldbank. (2024, June 26). *Remittances Slowed in 2023, Expected to Grow Faster in 2024*. https://www.worldbank.org/en/news/press-release/2024/06/26/remittances-slowed-in-2023-expected-to-grow-faster-in-2024

Wu, A.-C., & Kao, D.-D. (2022). Mapping the Sustainable Human-Resource Challenges in Southeast Asia's FinTech Sector. *Journal of Risk and Financial Management*, *15*(7), 307. Advance online publication. DOI: 10.3390/jrfm15070307

Wu, H., Yao, Q., Liu, Z., Huang, B., Zhuang, Y., Tang, H., & Liu, E. (2024). Blockchain for finance: A survey. *IET Blockchain*, *4*(2), 101–123. Advance online publication. DOI: 10.1049/blc2.12067

Wu, L., Zheng, Z., Qiu, Z., Wang, H., Gu, H., Shen, T., Qin, C., Zhu, C., Zhu, H., Liu, Q., Xiong, H., & Chen, E. (2024). A survey on large language models for recommendation. *World Wide Web (Bussum)*, *27*(5), 60. DOI: 10.1007/s11280-024-01291-2

Wu, X., & Liang, J. (2021). A blockchain-based trust management method for Internet of Things. *Pervasive and Mobile Computing*, *72*, 101330. DOI: 10.1016/j.pmcj.2021.101330

Wu, Y., Song, P., & Wang, F. (2020). Hybrid Consensus Algorithm Optimization: A Mathematical Method Based on POS and PBFT and Its Application in Blockchain. *Mathematical Problems in Engineering, 2020*, 1–13. Advance online publication. DOI: 10.1155/2020/7270624

Xiang, S., Deng, L., Zhou, Z., & Zhang, Z. (2024). Digital Finance, ESG Performance, and Financial Performance in Chinese Firm Levels: The Pathway to Sustainability. *Sustainability (Basel), 16*(18), 7976. DOI: 10.3390/su16187976

Xiao, R., Ma, C. A., Song, G. R., & Chang, H. Y. (2022). Does peer influence improve firms' innovative investment? Evidence from China. *Energy Reports, 8*, 1143–1150. DOI: 10.1016/j.egyr.2021.12.029

Xiao, Y., Zhang, N., Lou, W., & Hou, Y. T. (2020). A survey of distributed consensus protocols for blockchain networks. *IEEE Communications Surveys and Tutorials, 22*(2), 1432–1465. DOI: 10.1109/COMST.2020.2969706

Xia, R., Xu, F., Yu, J., Qi, Y., & Cambria, E. (2016). Polarity Shift Detection, Elimination and Ensemble: A Three-Stage Model for Document-Level Sentiment Analysis. *Information Processing & Management, 52*(1), 36–45. DOI: 10.1016/j.ipm.2015.04.003

Xu, J., & Vadgama, N. (2022). From banks to defi: the evolution of the lending market. *Enabling the Internet of Value: How Blockchain Connects Global Businesses*, 53-66.

Xue, Y., Fan, D., Su, S., Fu, J., Hu, N., Liu, W., & Tian, Z. (2024). A Review on the Security of the Ethereum-Based DeFi Ecosystem. *CMES-Computer Modeling in Engineering & Sciences, 139*(1).

Xu, J., Yang, T., Zhuang, S., Li, H., & Lu, W. (2024). AI-based financial transaction monitoring and fraud prevention with behaviour prediction. *Applied and Computational Engineering, 77*(1), 218–224. DOI: 10.54254/2755-2721/67/2024MA0068

Yadav, O. P., Teotia, R., & Baliyan, R. (2024). Fintech and Data Science: Shaping the Future of the Digital Economy. In *Synergy of AI and Fintech in the Digital Gig Economy* (pp. 332–349). CRC Press. DOI: 10.1201/9781032720104-21

Yadav, O. P., Teotia, R., & Baliyan, R. (2025). Fintech and Data Science: Shaping the Future of the Digital Economy. In *Synergy of AI and Fintech in the Digital Gig Economy* (pp. 316–333). CRC Press. DOI: 10.1201/9781003621454-20

Yadava, A. (2020). Sentiment analysis of financial news using unsupervised approach. *Procedia Computer Science, 167*, 589–598. DOI: 10.1016/j.procs.2020.03.325

Yan, B., Li, K., Xu, M., Dong, Y., Zhang, Y., Ren, Z., & Cheng, X. (2024). On protecting the data privacy of large language models (llms): A survey. *arXiv preprint arXiv:2403.05156*.

Yang, F., & Chen, J. (2024). Research on the Application of Intelligent Technology in Promoting Digital Finance and High-Quality Economic Development. *Applied Mathematics and Nonlinear Sciences*, *9*(1), 20243271. DOI: 10.2478/amns-2024-3271

Yang, L., Li, Y., Wang, J., & Sherratt, R. S. (2020). Sentiment Analysis for E-Commerce Product Reviews in Chinese Based on Sentiment Lexicon and Deep Learning. *IEEE Access : Practical Innovations, Open Solutions*, *8*, 3522–3530. DOI: 10.1109/ACCESS.2020.2969854

Yang, Q., & Lee, Y. C. (2024). Ethical AI in financial inclusion: The role of algorithmic fairness on user satisfaction and recommendation. *Big Data and Cognitive Computing*, *8*(9), 105. DOI: 10.3390/bdcc8090105

Yang, Q., Zhao, Y., Huang, H., Xiong, Z., Kang, J., & Zheng, Z. (2022). Fusing blockchain and AI with metaverse: A survey. *IEEE Open Journal of the Computer Society*, *3*, 122–136. DOI: 10.1109/OJCS.2022.3188249

Yanto, H., Ismail, N., Kiswanto, K., Rahim, N. M., & Baroroh, N. (2021). The roles of peers and social media in building financial literacy among the millennial generation: A case of indonesian economics and business students. *Cogent Social Sciences*, *7*(1), 1947579. DOI: 10.1080/23311886.2021.1947579

Yao, X. (2025). The green premium in sustainable fintech: Cross-country evidence from crowdfunding. *Finance Research Letters*, *77*, 107131. Advance online publication. DOI: 10.1016/j.frl.2025.107131

Yao, Y., Duan, J., Xu, K., Cai, Y., Sun, Z., & Zhang, Y. (2024). A survey on large language model (llm) security and privacy: The good, the bad, and the ugly. *High-Confidence Computing*, *4*(2), 100211. DOI: 10.1016/j.hcc.2024.100211

Yi, T. Z., Rom, N. A. M., Hassan, N. M., Samsurijan, M. S., & Ebekozien, A. (2023). The Adoption of Robo-Advisory among Millennials in the 21st Century: Trust, Usability and Knowledge Perception. *Sustainability (Basel)*, *15*(7), 6016. Advance online publication. DOI: 10.3390/su15076016

Yoo, K. M., Park, D., Kang, J., Lee, S. W., & Park, W. (2021). Gpt3mix: Leveraging large-scale language models for text augmentation. *arXiv preprint arXiv:2104.08826*. DOI: 10.18653/v1/2021.findings-emnlp.192

Yousaf, I., Abrar, A., & Yarovaya, L. (2023). Decentralized and centralized exchanges: Which digital tokens pose a greater contagion risk? *Journal of International Financial Markets, Institutions and Money*, *89*, 101881. DOI: 10.1016/j.intfin.2023.101881

Yulian, C., Irwanto, R., Angtonius, F., Young Siahaan, P., Ng, J., Thamrin Nomor, J., Sei Rengas, K. I., Medan Area, K., & Utara, S. (2024). Analisis Implementasi Teknologi Blockchain dalam Meningkatkan Transparansi dan Kepercayaan di Sektor Keuangan di Indonesia. *Jurnal Sistem Informasi Dan Ilmu Komputer, 2*(4), 09–31. DOI: 10.59581/jusiik-widyakarya.v2i4.4158

Yuspin, W., Wardiono, K., Budiono, A., & Gulyamov, S. (2022). "The Law Alteration on Artificial Intelligence in Reducing Islamic Bank's Profit and Loss Sharing Risk." Legality. *Jurnal Ilmiah Hukum*, *30*(2), 267–282. DOI: 10.22219/ljih.v30i2.23051

Zachariadis, M., Hileman, G., & Scott, S. V. (2019). Governance and control in distributed ledgers: Understanding the challenges facing blockchain technology in financial services. *Information and Organization*, *29*(2), 105–117. DOI: 10.1016/j.infoandorg.2019.03.001

Zaighum, I., & Abd Karim, M. Z. (2019). Peer effects, financial decisions and industry concentration: A review. *SEISENSE Journal of Management*, *2*(2), 13–21. DOI: 10.33215/sjom.v2i2.116

Zetzsche, D. A., & Anker-Sørensen, L. (2022). Towards a Smart Regulation of Sustainable Finance. In *The Palgrave Handbook of ESG and Corporate Governance* (pp. 87–113). Springer International Publishing., DOI: 10.1007/978-3-030-99468-6_4

Zetzsche, D. A., Arner, D. W., & Buckley, R. P. (2020). Decentralized finance. *Journal of Financial Regulation*, *6*(2), 172–203. DOI: 10.1093/jfr/fjaa010

Zha, D., Bhat, Z. P., Lai, K.-H., Yang, F., Jiang, Z., Zhong, S., & Hu, X. (2023). Data centric Artificial Intelligence: A Survey. http://arxiv.org/abs/2303.10158

Zhang, H., Zhang, J., & Pai, C.-H. (2024). Promoting carbon neutrality and green growth through cultural industry financing. *Humanities & Social Sciences Communications*, *11*(1), 71. Advance online publication. DOI: 10.1057/s41599-023-02554-5

Zhang, L., Xie, Y., Zheng, Y., Xue, W., Zheng, X., & Xu, X. (2020). The challenges and countermeasures of blockchain in finance and economics. *Systems Research and Behavioral Science*, *37*(4), 691–698. DOI: 10.1002/sres.2710

Zhang, Q., Lu, J., & Jin, Y. (2021). Artificial intelligence in recommender systems. *Complex & Intelligent Systems*, *7*(1), 439–457. DOI: 10.1007/s40747-020-00212-w

Zhang, R., Xue, R., & Liu, L. (2019). Security and privacy on blockchain. *ACM Computing Surveys, 52*(3), 1–34. DOI: 10.1145/3316481

Zhang, Y., Sun, Z., Qin, R., & Xiong, H. (2021). Idle Duration Prediction for Manufacturing System Using a Gaussian Mixture Model Integrated Neural Network for Energy Efficiency Improvement. *IEEE Transactions on Automation Science and Engineering, 18*(1), 47–55. DOI: 10.1109/TASE.2019.2938662

Zhan, Y., Tan, K. H., Li, Y., & Tse, Y. K. (2018). Unlocking the power of big data in new product development. *Annals of Operations Research, 270*(1–2), 577–595. DOI: 10.1007/s10479-016-2379-x

Zhao, L., Hussam, E., Seong, J.-T., Elshenawy, A., Kamal, M., & Alshawarbeh, E. (2024). Revolutionizing art education: Integrating AI and multimedia for enhanced appreciation teaching. *Alexandria Engineering Journal, 93*, 33–43. DOI: 10.1016/j.aej.2024.03.011

Zheng, Z., Xie, S., Dai, H., Chen, X., & Wang, H. (2017, June). *An overview of blockchain technology: Architecture, consensus, and future trends. In 2017 IEEE international congress on big data (BigData congress)*. Ieee.

Zhihan, L. (2023). Generative Artificial Intelligence in the Metaverse Era. *Cognitive Robotics, 3*(1), 208–217. Advance online publication. DOI: 10.1016/j.cogr.2023.06.001

Zhu, A. Y. F. (2024). Optimizing Financial Decision-Making for Emerging Adults: A Compact Python-Based Personalized Financial Projection Approach. *Technology in Society, 77*, 102599. Advance online publication. DOI: 10.1016/j.techsoc.2024.102599

Zhuk, A. (2025). From Cypherpunks to Decentralized Finance: How Crypto-Anarchy is Redefining Legal and Economic Systems. *Markets, Globalization &. Developmental Review, 9*(3).

Zhu, P., Hu, J., Li, X., & Zhu, Q. (2021). Using blockchain technology to enhance the traceability of original achievements. *IEEE Transactions on Engineering Management, 70*(5), 1693–1707. DOI: 10.1109/TEM.2021.3066090

About the Contributors

Mohammad Irfan is presently working as a Professor at School of Business and Commerce, Chandigarh University, Lucknow, Unnao, India. Dr. Irfan has done his Ph.D. from the Central University of Haryana. He has MBA (Finance), M.Com (Account and Law), and MA (Economics). He has qualified UGC-JRF/SRF/NET in Management and Commerce. Dr. Irfan certified NSEs (NCFM) and BSEs certification. He has experience of more than eighteen years in the area of SAPM, Integration of AI/ML in Finance, Blockchain, Cryptocurrency, Financial Engineering, Fintech, Green Finance, and Alternative Finance. He has to his credit more than 87+ Scopus-indexed articles, including The Journal of Economic Cooperation and Development (Q2), International Journal of Business Excellence (IJBEX), International Journal of Economics and Management (IJEM), Montenegrin Journal of Economics (Q2), Cogent Business & Management (Taylor & Francis) (Q2), Indian Journal of Finance (IJF), and Journal of Islamic Monetary Economics and Finance (JIMF). His citations reached 619+ along with 13 H-index. Dr. Irfan has published 11 books in Springer, Bentham Sciences, Apple Academic Press (CRC Press, Taylor & Francis, and IGI Global Publication (Scopus indexed).

***

Sina Ahmadi is a Lead Engineer at Block Inc., where he oversees global platform and networking infrastructure, focusing on cloud architecture and security. He is also a researcher with the National Coalition of Independent Scholars (NCIS), contributing to studies on AI, cybersecurity, and financial technologies. With extensive experience in infrastructure engineering and security optimization, Sina has authored multiple peer-reviewed publications in Cybersecurity, AI and networking. His expertise spans advanced fraud prevention, cloud security, and scalable infrastructure solutions, blending technical innovation with academic rigor to drive impactful outcomes.

Shilpi Bagga is an Associate Professor at School of Business &Management at Jaipur National University, with more than 17 years of Experience, she has conducted number of faculty Development Programs. Her area of interest is Marketing. She has published several research articles in leading National and International Journals.

Samuel Mores Geddam is an academic with over 14 years of experience in higher education, specializing in Human Resources, Business Analytics, and General Management. Currently an Assistant Professor at St. Joseph's University, Bengaluru, he also serves on the ORCID Researcher Advisory Council. Dr. Samuel earned his Ph.D. from Presidency University, where his research focused on Smart Human Augmentation through AI using the Technology Acceptance Model. His work on AI adoption, sustainable development, and organizational behavior is widely published and recognized in Scopus and Web of Science. A frequent speaker at international conferences and workshops, he excels in training researchers in advanced methods and tools such as SPSS, AMOS, R, and Tableau. Passionate about innovation and mentoring, Dr. Samuel is committed to fostering critical thinking and impactful academic initiatives that bridge technology and management.

Ramratan Guru is an Assistant Professor Level III with the School of Design (SOD) at Mody University, India. His research interests include new materialism, sustainability in fashion and textiles; circular fashion; waste management; technical textile, green composite materials and ethical fashion. Dr. Ramratan has authored six books, published over 170 high-impact journal and conference papers, and contributed to more than 15 book chapters. He holds five granted patents and has filed more than 25 patent National and International applications. Dr. Ramratan has developed over eight innovative cellulosic fibers, earning recognition for his research in various countries, including Canada, the USA, Europe, the UK, and Brazil. He actively collaborates with universities across Brazil, Europe, Canada, the USA, and Asia. Currently, he is pursuing postdoctoral research at the School of Engineering, Department of Textile Engineering, University of Minho, Portugal. He has extensive publications in high impact journals as well as books and book chapters.

S. Ida Evangeline is an Assistant Professor in the Department of Electrical and Electronics Engineering at Government College of Engineering, Tirunelveli, Tamil Nadu, India. She holds a Bachelor's degree in Electrical and Electronics Engineering from Manonmaniam Sundaranar University (2003) and a Master's degree in Power Systems Engineering from Anna University, Chennai (2005). She earned her Ph.D. from Anna University, Chennai, in 2023. She has published six research papers in international journals. Her areas of interest include optimal power flow, renewable energy, soft computing, artificial intelligence, machine learning, and deep learning.

Yashodhan Karulkar is a seasoned marketing professional with a robust career spanning over two decades in both the academic and corporate sectors. Since September 2016, he has been serving as a full-time faculty member at NMIMS University, where he plays a pivotal role in shaping the future of MBA Tech students. As the Area Chair for Marketing, Dr. Karulkar also mentors the Marketing Club, named 4C, actively engaging students in real-world marketing challenges. His corporate experience includes nearly 20 years in leadership roles with some of the most prominent companies in India, such as Birla Sun Life,Max New York Life,Standard Chartered Bank,Airtel and Wipro. Dr. Karulkar's expertise spans the entire marketing spectrum, including Product Management, Sales and Distribution, Relationship Management, Customer Service, and Business Development. He has managed large Pan-India sales teams, leading over 300 employees to successfully achieve critical business and profitability goals.

Early Ridho Kismawadi, S.E.I, MA is a lecturer at the Department of Islamic Banking, Faculty of Islamic Economics and Business IAIN Langsa, Aceh, Indonesia, he has been a lecturer since 2013, he has completed a doctoral program in 2018 majoring in Sharia economics at the State Islamic University of North Sumatra. He was appointed head of the Islamic economics Law study program (2023) Islamic banking study program (2020) and Islamic financial management study program (2019) at Langsa State Islamic Institute (IAIN Langsa), Aceh, Indonesia. His research interests include financial economics, applied econometrics, Islamic economics, banking, and finance. He has published articles in national and international journals. In addition, he is also a reviewer of several reputable international journals such as Finance Research Letters, Financial Innovation, Cogent Business &; Management, Journal of Islamic Accounting and Business Research. He has also presented his papers at various local and international seminars.

M. Murali is currently working in Department of Computing Technologies, SRM Institute of science and technology, Kattankulathur 603203, India. He completed his M.Tech Degree from Manonmaniam Sundaranar University in 2004. Further, he completed his Ph.D degree from SRM University in December, 2013. Currently he is guiding four research scholars. His area of research interests are NLP, Image Processing, Machine Learning.

Maral Mazjini holds a Ph.D. in Statistics and works as a Senior Scientist. Her research focuses on data modeling using dynamic mixture models, heavy-tailed distributions, AI and time-varying volatility structures. Her research combines theoretical development with real-world applications. Building on this foundation, her current work applies statistical and data science methodologies to support data-informed decision-making through trend analysis and AI. Her interests lie at the intersection of statistical theory and the applied use of data science and AI in studying complex, real-world data.

Mir Satar is Associate Professor in the Department of Business Administration at Saudi Electronic University (SEU), Saudi Arabia. Before joining SEU, he served as an Assistant Professor at the University of Kashmir and worked with the Government of India as an Assistant Training Instructor. Additionally, he had a short stint in the corporate sector before transitioning into academics. Dr. Satar holds a Ph.D. in Management Studies from Jamia Hamdard University India. His research primarily focuses on social entrepreneurship and sustainable development. His work often explores innovation and entrepreneurship management in social enterprises, entrepreneurial psychology, and small business management. Dr. Satar's research has been published in esteemed scholarly journals (Scopus/ABDC/ESCI/SSCI) such as Entrepreneurship & Regional Development, Management Decision, The International Journal of Management Education, Sustainability, Entrepreneurship Research Journal, and International Journal of Innovation Science. He is affiliated with numerous international professional organizations and serves on the editorial boards of several international journals. He is also a reviewer for various academic publications. In addition to his academic contributions, Dr. Satar has presented at numerous conferences and has chaired and organized national and international conferences and workshops on contemporary themes. He is skilled in leading training sessions on critical topics such as motivation, corporate life, leadership development, research acumen, communication skills, and entrepreneurship development. His most recent workshop was held at the SEU Jeddah branch.

Bhabani Shankar Mohanty is currently working as an Assistant Professor in the Department of Statistics and Applied Mathematics, School of Mathematics and Computer Sciences, Central University of Tamil Nadu, Tamil Nadu. He has an M.Phil and a Doctorate (Ph.D.) in Statistics from the P.G. Department of Statistics, Utkal University, Bhubaneswar. He has completed a Master's Degree in Statistics from Utkal University and worked for one year as a Project-JRF at IIT-Bhubaneswar. He has presented research papers at National/ International conferences in India and has published papers in indexed international journals of repute. He has over 10 years of teaching and research experience. His research interests are inventory control, fuzzy logic, optimization techniques, and sustainable supply chains. He also has command over analyzing high-dimension data generated from different real-life phenomena.

Rishab Naik is a dedicated professional currently pursuing an MBA Tech program at SVKM NMIMS Mukesh Patel School of Technology Management and Engineering, Mumbai. He specializes in Mechanical Engineering, with a focus on Finance and Business Intelligence & Analytics for his MBA Tech. Additionally, he has earned Honours in Data Analytics and Machine Learning. With a strong foundation in both technology and business, Rishab brings a unique blend of expertise to the fields of finance and technology. He has a keen interest in financial markets and technological advancements.

Arshi Shah is a dedicated professional who is pursuing her MBA Tech program at SVKM's NMIMS Mukesh Patel School of Technology Management and Engineering, Mumbai, specializing in Electronics and Telecommunication for her B.Tech as well as Finance and Business Intelligence and Analytics for her MBA Tech. With a strong foundation in both technology and business, she brings a unique blend of expertise to the fields of finance and technology. Arshi has a keen interest in research and analytics, demonstrated through her work on research projects.

Bruno Barbosa Sousa is Adjunct Professor of Marketing at Polytechnic Institute of Cávado and Ave (IPCA), Portugal and PhD in Marketing and Strategy in Universidade do Minho, Portugal. Head of Masters Program - Tourism Management and Marketing Tourism (IPCA); CiTUR – Center for Tourism Research, Development and Innovation and UNIAG research member. He has published in the Journal of Enterprising Communities, Tourism Management Perspectives, Current Issues in Tourism, Journal of Organizational Change Management, World Review of Entrepreneurship, Management and Sust. Development, among others.

Index

A

B

C

D

E

F

G

H

I

L

M

O

P

R

S

T

www.ingramcontent.com/pod-product-compliance
Lightning Source LLC
LaVergne TN
LVHW080350011026
849161LV00009B/2249

* 9 7 9 8 3 3 7 3 1 2 5 0 7 *